The Korean War

MILITARY HISTORY OF THE UNITED STATES (VOL. 4)

GARLAND REFERENCE LIBRARY OF THE HUMANITIES (VOL. 872)

The Korean War
An Encyclopedia

Edited by
Stanley Sandler

GARLAND PUBLISHING, INC.
New York & London
1995

Library of Congress Cataloging-in-Publication Data

The Korean War : an encyclopedia / editor, Stanley Sandler.
            p.   cm. — (Garland reference library of the humanities ;
    vol. 872) (Military history of the United States ; v. 4)
        Includes bibliographical references and index.
        ISBN 0-8240-4445-2
        1. Korean War, 1950–1953.   I. Sandler, Stanley, 1937–
II. Series.   III. Series: Garland reference library of the humanities.
Military history of the United States ; v. 4.
DS918.K5645   1995
951.904'2—dc20   95–1932
                                                                   CIP

Cover design by Larry Wolfson Design, New York. Cover photograph courtesy of
FPG International Corp.

Printed on acid-free, 250-year-life paper
Manufactured in the United States of America

Contents

Introduction

The Korean War, 25 June 1950–27 July 1953, was America's first "ideological war." As such, both sides made concerted efforts to convert or influence their adversaries' troops and home front. The United Nations command prolonged the war for a full two years over the ideological question as to whether prisoners of war should be repatriated regardless of their preferences. It is significant that the Communist negotiators, supposedly far more keenly attuned to propaganda nuances than the "naive" Americans, professed complete unfamiliarity with this point and thereby lost a propaganda victory. (It is not apparent that America's allies had any particular interest in this question.)

Contrary to contemporary popular opinion, this conflict was not the first American war that had not been fought through to victory. Certainly the War of 1812 was a draw. Yet twentieth-century Americans had become habituated to victory. For those who remembered the wild celebrations of 11 November 1918, or V-E and V-J Days, the armistice of 27 July 1953 was a "poor substitute for victory" and was generally greeted with sullen indifference. Indeed, how many Americans can, within a year, correctly date the end of the Korean War? It was difficult for Americans to become excited over an armistice that ended a three-year war with the status quo.

This war opened with a World War II blitzkrieg-style campaign that almost achieved victory for the enemy. And for the remainder of 1950, the war was characterized by sweeping movements of armies, divisions, and regiments. Cities fell several times over as opposing forces advanced, retreated, or dug in. The World War II analogy was strengthened by the fact that almost all of the military equipment employed by both sides dated from that war; even the uniforms (of the U.N. forces, at least) were identical to those of 1942–1945. But from the spring of 1951 to the armistice of 1953, the Korean War seemed to harken even further back in time, to the dreary trench warfare of World War I's western front. As in 1914–1918, the battle lines of the Korean War changed remarkably little. Unmoved trench lines, massive bombardments, raids, patrols, strongpoints, salients, limited offensives, and a blasted landscape combined to give a sense of déja vu. Fortunately, neither side saw fit to mount the massive and futile offensives that had wasted an earlier generation. But whether the blitzkrieg of 1950 or the wearying trench warfare of 1951–1953, the form and course of the Korean War came as an almost total refutation of those Sunday Supplement pundits—and even those more serious military civilian prognosticators—who had consistently predicted "The Next War" as one of push-buttons, air power, and nuclear devastation.

This war made few real demands on Americans at home. The draft interrupted only the lives of the young. There was no rationing, and material shortages seemed to have mostly affected the quality of chromium on 1952–1953 automobiles (to the dismay of later collectors). The fierce inflation of the first year of war was more than countered by the wartime industrial and employment boom that delayed the recession "due" in 1950 until 1954, after the armistice.

But for many of America's political and governmental elite, the Korean War was an apocalyptic challenge, testing the nation's "resolve" against Soviet aggression. For those who concerned themselves about such matters, the Korean War was a feint designed to draw attention away from the real focus of the Cold War, Western Europe was practically defenseless against the Red Army. The Truman administration had little doubt that Joseph Stalin had encouraged, probably even ordered, the North Korean attack. Yet these fears actually predated the Korean War. National Security Council document NSC-68, drawn up two months before the North Korean invasion, called for no less than a tripling of the U.S. defense budget in the wake of a conviction that as a result of growing Soviet power, evidenced by their explosion of a nuclear device in September of 1949, the United States was "in greater jeopardy than ever before in our history." (This statement was certainly a precursor of the perfervid imaginings that would come with the Korean War.)

President Harry S. Truman signed NSC-68 in September 1950 and proceeded to implement most of its recommendations, particularly the tripling of the defense budget. By 1952, the U.S. defense establishment was slightly larger than it had been on the eve of Pearl Harbor, when the nation very obviously faced a global threat. In Korea itself no less than seven divisions were in combat. This was a long way, indeed, from that "arrogant display of force," Task Force Smith, that had so disastrously opened American ground combat in Korea.

It can be fairly conclusively argued, albeit with the admitted benefit of hindsight, that the United States overreacted to the Korean War, imposing costs on the nation that were felt for at least three decades in taxes, government regulations, outdated subsidies, and in a coarsening of public discourse.

This exaggeration of Communist power produced an intensification of the "Red Scare II" in Hollywood films and magazine articles. *Colliers* ran a series of frightening articles on a near-future U.S.–Soviet war which saw Washington, D.C., devastated by one-way Soviet nuclear bombers. Existing loyalty oaths required of federal employees were extended to many state workers, including college professors. Senator Joseph McCarthy enjoyed renewed impetus from the war in his anti-Communist crusade as well as from the fortuitous exposure of an exasperating number of "atom bomb spies." Recent archival openings in the former Soviet Union seem to indicate an ailing Stalin fearful of the United States (and even of Great Britain) but at the same time convinced that the Soviet Union could survive a nuclear exchange quite well.

The Korean War was supposedly the first war that the United States had to fight with "one hand tied behind its back," as so many military commanders bitterly put it. Yet it could be pointed out that the other side also did not throw itself fully into the struggle. North Korea and Chinese air power, for example, meticulously refrained from attacking U.N. logistical lines, either in Korea or on the sea routes to that peninsula. (A restriction that Soviet pilots on the scene complained about, in roughly the same language as that employed by frustrated USAF airmen.) Throughout the war, allied trucks and ships, lights blazing, could proceed along their routes with no fear of enemy interference. The vital port of Pusan was never bombed, even though the North Korean capital, Pyongyang, was blitzed to the ground, its remaining inhabitants reduced to a troglodyte existence. The U.N. forces in Korea, in truth, for whatever reasons, enjoyed their own "privileged sanctuaries."

But as in Vietnam a decade or so later, Americans in Korea did fight under one indisputable disadvantage, one that their enemies were well aware of: Americans were fighting a "limited" war for limited geopolitical ends that even most participants found sometimes difficult to grasp. Their enemy fought a more or less total war simply for the unification of Korea under communism. That U.N. forces did not perform even worse in the early days of this war was undoubtedly a result of their air power and superior mobility, logistics, firepower, and individual courage. Later in the war, improved training and accumulated combat experience made a Communist victory literally impossible. But in the first few months of the war, as the Duke of Wellington had remarked about Waterloo, it indeed had been a "damned nice [i.e., 'close'] thing."

This was the first war that Americans fought under the banner of the United Nations. The Truman administration was well aware of the awful "lesson" of Munich, of the failure of collective security by the League of Nations. The "lesson" went something like this: Had the democracies of Europe and North America banded together to stop the dictators, World War II might well have been averted. The cost would probably have been a small war, but better that than the alternative of a global conflict that came close to being lost to the forces of darkness. And was Korea (in Neville Chamberlain's words) "a small, far-away nation" that the democracies were too irresolute to defend? The analogy was simple: the Republic of Korea was Czechoslovakia (or Spain or China or Ethiopia), North Korea was Nazi Germany, and the United Nations here had the opportunity to not be the League of Nations. The analogy is not entirely unconvincing. But the immediate problem was that the "patron" of the aggressor state was a member in good standing of the United Nations. The only international security organization that could "stand up to Communist aggression" was the North Atlantic Treaty Organization (NATO), founded just the year previous to "contain" Soviet expansion, and dominated by the economic and military power of the United States.

As a result of U.S. prompting, every NATO nation but prickly Iceland contributed land, sea, and air forces to the U.N. command in Korea. (Turkey, although not a NATO member, sent a well-regarded infantry brigade.) Nearly 3,000 soldiers from NATO nations were killed in action and another 10,000 wounded. Still, the main focus of U.N./U.S. "containment" of Soviet expansion remained Western Europe, and more U.S. troops were actually sent to that Cold War arena than to the "hot" war in Korea.

Both the U.S. and the Communists employed a rotation system in Korea. The American military's was the best known. It codified a point system after the start of truce talks: the closer the soldier was to combat the more his points toward rotation home. A combat infantryman (if he survived) could expect to rotate home after one year. The Communist authorities did not bother about any point system and held their troops in the line until death, wounds, capture, or defections removed them. Those who survived were combat-fit veterans. But the U.S. military removed experienced soldiers just as they were putting that experience to good use. The U.S. system was vastly popular with its troops; the opinions of Communist soldiers have not been revealed.

The Korean War has been termed "The Unknown War," "The Forgotten War," or "The War Before Vietnam." Certainly the American public knows little more about this conflict than as the setting for the movie and television series M.A.S.H. (which was, in reality of course, more of a Vietnam War–era "statement"). Yet it can be seriously argued that this war "had as much to do with shaping the world of the second half of the twentieth century as did World War II." (*History of the Office of the Secretary of Defense*, II, *The Test of War, 1950–1953*, Historical Office, Office of the Secretary of Defense, Washington: 1988.)

Certainly Korea polarized much of the world far more than had the loss of Eastern Europe and China, the Berlin Airlift, or the explosion of the first Soviet atomic bomb. The aggressor had taken arms and invaded a part of the "Free World." Although Senator Joseph McCarthy had made his first sensational charge of Communists in government several months before the start of the Korean War, that conflict seemed to validate even his most lurid assertions. Apart from treason, how indeed could one account for the fact that U.S.-backed South Korea seemed almost defenseless against the army of a third-rate country, and that the United States, at least in the first weeks of the war, could do little better?

No American soldiers in this century, including those in Vietnam, faced such questioning of their fighting abilities, even their courage, than did those who fought the early battles in Korea. In the first month, as they fell back, there was surprisingly little criticism. Later, as stories of "brainwashing" and "giveupitis" in the prison camps gained wide publicity, "experts" began to expatiate on a "soft generation" that supposedly lacked the moral fiber of their fathers in World War II. The fact that most of these allegations proved baseless or greatly exaggerated did little to change public perceptions in the following decades.

Many Americans remembered the "bugouts" at Osan and Taejon and the Chosin Reservoir, forgetting Bataan and the Bulge. To run from the enemy was simply un-American.

Yet no soldiers were so cared for by their government, at least after the battle lines had stabilized in 1951. Rapid medical evacuation and medical care; generous "rest and recreation" leave in Seoul or Tokyo, where their dollars could seemingly buy out bars and brothels; body armor; and comparatively good chow, which included the great American staple of ice cream, eased the lot of U.S. troops caught up in the Korean War. But most important, the rotation system ensuring that no American soldier involuntarily remained in combat for more than nine months maintained morale within a primarily draftee army, whatever the cost in personnel churning, loss of unit cohesion, and individual battle cautiousness near the end of a combat tour.

The U.S. armed forces amassed detailed "lessons learned" from the Korean War, dealing with training, equipment, mobilization, logistics, discipline, and code of conduct for prisoners of war. As a result, the military that entered Vietnam a decade and more later was far better prepared than that of 1950. There were no "Task Force Smiths" in Vietnam. But these lessons learned were on the operational and tactical level. On the governmental and strategic levels, Korea was looked on as an aberration, a very unwelcome interruption of America's "Europe first" and "no Asian land wars" beliefs. With the advent of the Republican administration of Dwight Eisenhower six months before the signing of the armistice, a "new look" was formulated that drastically scaled down the importance of ground combat, although the draft was retained, and built its "new look" defense policy primarily on deterrence of the Soviet Union through nuclear threat.

Of course North and South Korea suffered the most in the Korean War. Possibly three million Koreans died from one cause or another in the three years of combat. (The exact numbers remain elusive.) The nation remained divided, roughly as it had been since 1945. And the bitterness between both sides festered unabated, although they continued through the decades to talk at Panmunjom.

In fact, it would be hard to imagine a nation less suited to division than Korea. The Korean language, Hangul, and Korean culture have prevailed throughout the peninsula for centuries. The land harbors no disaffected ethnic or racial minorities, no "lost territories" to spark irredentists' dreams. (There was no question as to where China or the former Soviet Union ended and Korea began.) Thus the continuing division of Korea is a continuing burden for the people of Korea.

Although large numbers of U.S. troops remained along the Demilitarized Zone, the Korean War faded from America's general interest in the decades following the conflict. Aggression had been stopped, true, but South Korea remained a somewhat chaotic dictatorship punctuated by violent demonstrations and equally violent repression. The nation continued poor and underdeveloped. But in the mid-1970s, the Republic of Korea was poised for economic "takeoff" and by the mid-1980s had developed into one of the economic powerhouses known as the "Asian Tigers." Democracy was an unconscionable time in coming, but by the end of the 1980s even that goal of countless fierce demonstrations had been substantially achieved.

In contrast, the Democratic People's Republic of Korea (North Korea) seemed to retrogress. At one time North Korea could be held up by "progressive" opinion as at least one area of the world in which a Communist state might well offer its citizens a higher standard of living than its anti-Communist neighbor, thanks in large measure to its vast Japanese-developed hydroelectric resources and its disciplined citizens. But the Republic of Korea accelerated economically far past any claims that North Korea could believably make. As of this writing, North Koreans face poverty and shortages in addition to pressures for total conformity. The regime more than ever clings to a bizarre cult of personality that, incredibly, goes even beyond those accorded Stalin or Mao. Any Western apologias for the regime now bear an unpleasant resemblance to those made in the past for Eastern Europe or the former Soviet Union. (Citizens seem reasonably content; no great differences separate classes, unlike in the West; one is safer on the streets of Moscow or Pyongyang than on those of New York, etc.) The fiercest criticism that could be summoned by two recent "enlightened" Western authorities on Korea was that the regime, admittedly, did have its "tacky" moments. (No such latitude was to be granted to the sins of the South Korean government.) Today, the Democratic Republic of Korea shares with the Republic of Cuba the lonely distinction of being the only nations on earth whose leaders still seem to believe completely in the economic and the political promises of communism. History has passed by both.

Chronology

c. 2000 B.C.	Minuscule kingdom of Chosun ("land of the morning calm") established.
July 1844.	Treaty establishing commercial relations between Kingdom of Korea and the United States signed.
August 1866.	Crew of U.S. schooner *General Sherman* massacred by Korean soldiers.
June 1870.	U.S. punitive attacks on Korean fortresses along the Yom-ha River. More than 250 Koreans killed.
1876.	Treaty of Kanghwa between Korea and Japan.
May 1882.	Treaty of Chemulpo between Korea and U.S.A.
1904–1905.	Russo-Japanese War. U.S. President Theodore Roosevelt brokers the Treaty of Portsmouth (September 1905) ending that war. Russia agrees to Japan's exercising a free hand in Korea.
November 1905.	The Japanese coerce the Korean king to allow his nation to become a protectorate of Japan.
1908.	Root-Takahira agreement recognizes Japan's primacy in Korea and southern Manchuria.
1910.	Japan annexes Korea.
December 1918.	Korean residents in the United States petition President Wilson "to aid the Koreans in their aspirations for self-determination" as a moral obligation resulting from the unabrogated Treaty of Chemulpo.
April 1919.	Provisional government-in-exile established in Shanghai.
March–April 1919.	"Mansei Revolution." Korean patriotic demonstrations put down by Japanese occupation forces.
15 August 1943.	Premier Stalin approves President Harry Truman's General Order Number One, providing for the temporary division of Korea at the Thirty-Eighth Parallel of latitude into two temporary zones of military occupation, Soviet and United States.
1 December	Cairo Conference Declaration declares that "in due course Korea shall become free and independent." Korean nationalists object to "in due course" qualifying phrase.
2 September 1945.	Instrument of Japanese unconditional surrender signed in Tokyo Bay.

First week in September.	U.S. occupation troops land at Inchon.
December.	U.S. and Soviet Union draw up agreement providing for five-year trusteeship for Korea. Large-scale demonstrations by resentful Korean patriots.
1946.	Activation of "Peace Preservation Officers' Training Schools," nucleus of North Korean Army.
September.	U.S. State Department agrees that South Korea should be left to its fate.
17 September 1947.	U.S. refers issue of reunification and independence of Korea to the U.N.
29 September.	U.S. Joint Chiefs of Staff agree that South Korea is of too little strategic value to justify the stationing of 45,000 U.S. occupational troops.
14 November.	General Assembly of the U.N., over Soviet objections, approves American-sponsored resolution calling for one government for all of Korea, and providing for a U.N. Temporary Commission (UNTCOK) to supervise national elections to lead to independence and unification.
24 January 1948.	Refusal of Soviet occupation commander in North Korea to permit entry of UNTCOK into his jurisdiction prevents Korea-wide elections.
February.	Joint Chiefs of Staff recommend pulling out of all American troops, even though this move will probably result in the "eventual domination of Korea by the USSR. . . ."
February.	[North] Korean People's Army formally activated.
April.	Opening of Chedu-do rebellion, lasting until at least autumn of 1949.
2 April.	U.S. National Security Council paper NSC-8 agrees that the U.S. should help build up the Korean economy and armed forces, but beyond that, the South Koreans would have to maintain their own security against the Communist north. Paper approved by President Truman as basis for U.S. Korea policy.
10 May.	With the Soviets refusing to admit United Nations commissioners to North Korea, U.N.-sponsored elections in southern Korea return representatives to a National Assembly, which elects Syngman Rhee the first President of a new republic.
15 August.	Republic of Korea (ROK) formally inaugurated.
9 September.	Establishment of the Democratic People's Republic of Korea (DPRK).
October.	Yosu-Sunchon communist-led uprising brutally suppressed by ROK forces.
December.	Arrival of small but high-level Soviet military mission in Pyongyang.
31 December.	Soviets announce that their forces have been withdrawn from North Korea.
January 1949.	General MacArthur informs the Joint Chiefs of Staff that ROK armed forces could not turn back an invasion from the North, that the U.S. should not commit troops in case of such an invasion, and that the U.S. should remove all of its combat forces as soon as possible.

	U.S.-Korean Military Advisory Group (KMAG) activated.
	U.S. State Department concludes that U.S. should respond to an invasion from the North by submitting the matter to the U.N.
	Last U.S. combat troops leave ROK.
	Activation of South Korean Air Force.
1950.	U.S. Secretary of State Dean Acheson, in a speech before the National Press Club in Washington, omits South Korea from America's defense perimeter in Asia. Those omitted states would have to rely upon their own resources until the U.N. could mobilize against an aggressor.
19 January.	U.S. House of Representatives defeats Korean aid bill for 1949–1950.
January–March.	MacArthur's Intelligence Section evaluates reports of impending invasion of the ROK from the North (including one that pinpoints the month of June 1950), but does not believe that an invasion is imminent.
14 February.	Sino-Soviet Treaty of Friendship and Alliance signed.
15 March.	The Commanding Officer of Korean Military Advisory Group concedes that the DPRK would give the ROK "a bloody nose," that the southern civil population would accede to the new regime and that the ROK "would be gobbled up to be added to the rest of Red Asia."
2 May.	The Chairman of the Senate Foreign Relations Committee (Senator Tom Connally of Texas), in an interview with *U.S. News and World Report*, concedes that the Republic of Korea would be abandoned in case of enemy aggression and that the security of that nation was not essential to America's defensive Asian strategy.
30 May.	ROK-wide elections produce a majority of National Assembly representatives opposed to the Rhee government.
1 June.	The Intelligence Section of the USAF Far East Air Force (FEAF) concludes that "South Korea will fall before a North Korean invasion. . . ."
19 June.	The Central Intelligence Agency (CIA) determines that North Korea could seize and hold at least the upper reaches of South Korea, including Seoul, without Chinese or Soviet military units.
25 June.	Military forces of the Democratic Republic of (North) Korea invade the Republic of (South) Korea, opening the Korean War.
27 June.	USAF provides evacuation and cover for evacuation of U.S. nationals from Seoul and Inchon; first use of U.S. military forces in Korean War.
28 June.	Seoul falls to invading North Korean military forces.
29 June.	President Truman agrees with reporter's characterization of the conflict as a "police action."
30 June.	President Truman commits ground forces to the Korean conflict.
3 July.	First U.N. naval operations against North Koreans. Aircraft carriers USS *Valley Forge* and HMS *Triumph* launch air strikes against enemy airfields and the North Korean capital of Pyongyang.

2 July.	U.N. naval forces destroy North Korean torpedo and motor gunboats in the only naval engagement of the Korean War.
5 July.	Task Force Smith, the U.S. Army's first attempt to blunt North Korean advance, destroyed, three miles north of Osan.
8 July.	General Douglas MacArthur appointed United Nations Commander in Chief to repel North Korean aggression against South Korea.
14–20 July.	U.S. ground forces defeated at Taejon-Kum River. The commander of the U.S. 24th Infantry Division captured, but some time is won to form perimeter along Naktong River farther south.
25 July.	U.S. Naval aircraft make first emergency close support air strikes against North Korean forces.
4 August.	U.N. troops take up defensive positions around the Pusan perimeter.
15 August.	Eighth Army directed to employ recruits in U.S. Army divisions, beginning the Korean Augmentation to the U.S. Army (KATUSA).
18 August.	First tank-to-tank battle of the war.
12 September.	George C. Marshall succeeded Louis Johnson as U.S. Secretary of Defense.
15 September.	MacArthur's Inchon landings far behind the enemy's lines open a temporary turn-of-the-war in favor of U.N. forces.
16–22 September.	U.N. forces break out from the Pusan perimeter in the wake of the Inchon landings to their enemy's rear.
27 September.	Seoul falls to U.N. forces, three months to the day after it was occupied by North Korean military.
October.	Arrival of first Greek Army forces in Korea.
24 October.	Arrival of first Netherlands forces in Korea.
1 November.	First jet-to-jet air combat in history.
20 November.	Arrival of Indian 60th Field Ambulance and Surgical Unit, India's sole contribution to the U.N. Korean effort.
23 November.	Full battalion of the Netherlands forces reaches Korea.
25 November.	Chinese forces enter combat in Korea.
29 November.	Arrival of first French forces in Korea.
9 December.	Arrival of Greek Battalion at Pusan.
16 December.	President Truman declares State of National Emergency.
23 December.	Lt. Gen. Walton Walker, 8th U.S. Army Commander, killed in motor accident. Walker is immediately replaced by General Matthew B. Ridgway.
21 December.	UNC imposes full military censorship.
31 December.	New Chinese offensive begins. U.N. forces retreat eventually to as far as seventy miles south of the 38th parallel. Arrival of first New Zealand forces.
4 January 1951.	Seoul falls again to Communist forces.
25 January.	First U.N. counteroffensives since entry of Chinese Communist forces, ending talk of evacuating U.N. forces from Korea. Series of such offensives, lasting through the spring of 1951, eventually drives Communist forces to positions substantially north of the 38th parallel by the end of March.
13 February.	General MacArthur issues statement critical of U.N./U.S. military policy. Makes similar statement on 7 March.
14 March.	Seoul retaken by U.N. forces.

24 March.	General MacArthur issues demand for Communist surrender.
5 April.	House Republican Minority Leader Joseph W. Martin, releases letter from General MacArthur calling for victory in the Korean War.
10 April.	General MacArthur relieved by President Harry Truman. General Ridgway succeeds MacArthur as U.N. commander.
14 April.	Lt. Gen. James A. Van Fleet arrives in Korea to succeed General Ridgway as 8th Army commander.
19 April.	General MacArthur delivers "No Substitute for Victory"/ "Old Soldiers Never Die" speech before joint session of Congress.
22 April.	Chinese Communist forces open first stage of their fifth offensive, drive almost to outskirts of Seoul before being stopped by the end of May. Chinese suffer extremely heavy casualties.
3 May.	U.S. Senate opens committee hearings on the dismissal of General MacArthur and U.S. strategy in Korea.
2 June.	U.N. command initiates Operation Strangle, an attempt to interdict Communist supply lines through air action, with only problematic success.
1 June.	U.S. Secretary of State, Dean Acheson, indicates that the U.S. prepared to accept truce line in vicinity of the 38th parallel.
23 June.	Soviet U.N. Ambassador, J. Malik, calls for negotiations for a cease-fire.
2 July.	Communist authorities agree to cease-fire negotiations at Kaesong.
10 July.	First meeting of complete delegations from opposing sides in the Korean War.
28 July.	Commonwealth Division activated from smaller British Commonwealth units in Korea.
8 September.	Japanese Peace Treaty signed at San Francisco.
13 September.	Opening of battle of Heartbreak Ridge.
25 October.	Truce talks transferred to Panmunjom.
12 November.	General Ridgway orders end of U.N. ground offensive military action and implements "active defense" strategy.
27 November.	Agreement reached at Panmunjom on line of military demarcation and Demilitarized Zone. Agreement subsequently invalidated on 27 December.
2 January 1952.	U.N. command proposes voluntary repatriation of all POWs at Panmunjom negotiations.
18 February.	Major clash between U.N. guards and POWs at Koje-do prison camp. Also, opening of Communist campaign claiming that U.S. was waging biological warfare in the Korean War.
8 April.	President Truman seizes control of strike-bound steel mills.
7 May.	Kidnapping of commander of Koje-do prisoner camp and subsequent negotiations with kidnappers leads to humiliation of U.N. command, but in a military operation the command takes back control of the camp compounds and vastly improves security and living conditions.
7 May.	Truce negotiations stall over question of repatriation of Chinese and North Korean prisoners.

12 May.	General Mark Clark replaces General Ridgway as U.N. Commander.
2 June.	U.S. Supreme Court declares unconstitutional President Truman's seizure of steel mills.
23–24 June.	U.N. air attacks on North Korean Suiho power generation complex to hasten armistice negotiations.
July–August.	Heavy U.N. air strikes on Pyongyang practically destroy city.
November.	Dogfight between U.S. Naval aircraft and Soviet MIG-15s near carrier *Oriskany*; only known direct attempt by Soviet airpower to attack U.N. sea forces.
4 November.	Dwight Eisenhower elected President of the U.S.
2–5 December.	President-Elect Eisenhower tours Korea to fulfill his election pledge, "I Will Go to Korea."
23 March–7 July 1953.	Battle of Pork Chop Hill.
20 April–3 May.	Operation Little Switch exchanges sick and wounded POWs.
June.	Series of Chinese offensives against ROK forces demonstrate that South Korea could not survive on its own militarily, despite President Rhee's bluster of "on to the North."
July.	USN Task Force 77 equipped with nuclear weapons.
27 July.	Signing of the Korean armistice agreements.
28 July.	First meeting of the Military Armistice Commission. The armistice holds through the decades, and these meetings continue to the present time.
August–23 December.	Operation Big Switch exchanges all POWs willing to be repatriated.
26 April 1954.	Opening of fifth Geneva Conference on the reunification of Korea and other Asian matters.

Maps

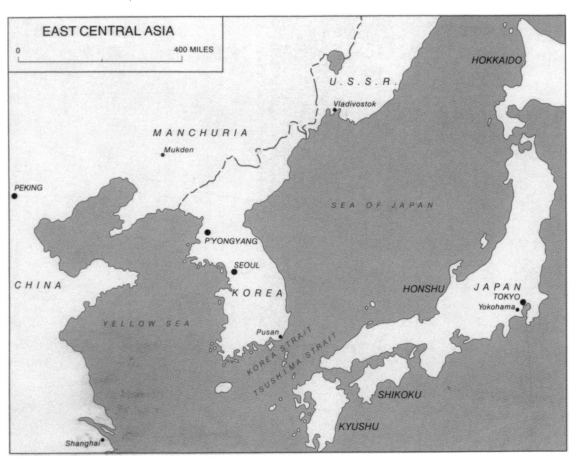

EAST CENTRAL ASIA

0   400 MILES

HOKKAIDO

U.S.S.R.

Vladivostok

MANCHURIA

Mukden

SEA OF JAPAN

PEKING

P'YONGYANG

SEOUL

CHINA

KOREA

HONSHU

JAPAN

TOKYO

Yokohama

YELLOW SEA

Pusan

KOREA STRAIT

TSUSHIMA STRAIT

SHIKOKU

KYUSHU

Shanghai

Billy C. Mossman. Ebb & Flow, November 1950–July 1951. United States Army in the Korean War. Center of Military History. Washington: 1990.

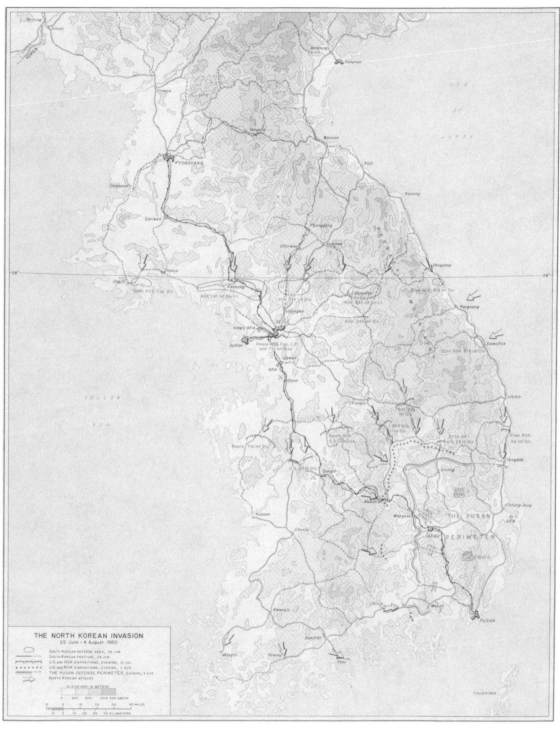

James F. Schnabel. Policy & Direction: The First Year. United States Army in the Korean War. Office of the Chief of Military History. Washington: 1972.

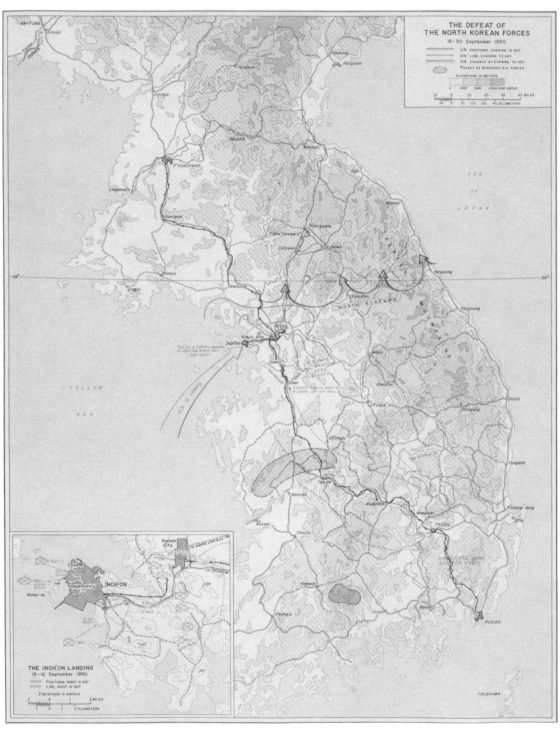

James F. Schnabel. Policy & Direction: The First Year. United States Army in the Korean War.
Office of the Chief of Military History. Washington: 1972.

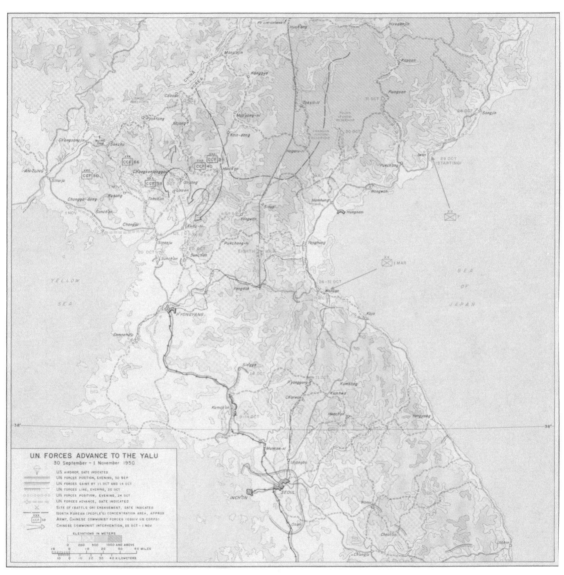

James F. Schnabel. Policy & Direction: The First Year. United States Army in the Korean War.
Office of the Chief of Military History. Washington: 1972.

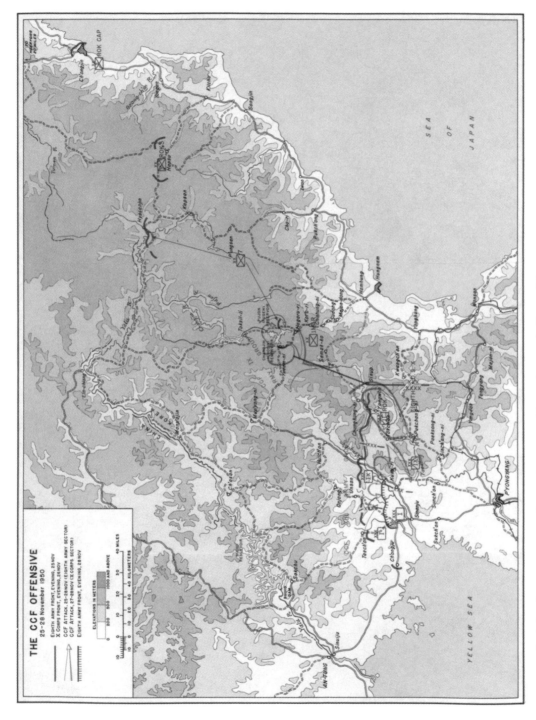

James F. Schnabel. Policy & Direction: The First Year. United States Army in the Korean War.
Office of the Chief of Military History. Washington: 1972.

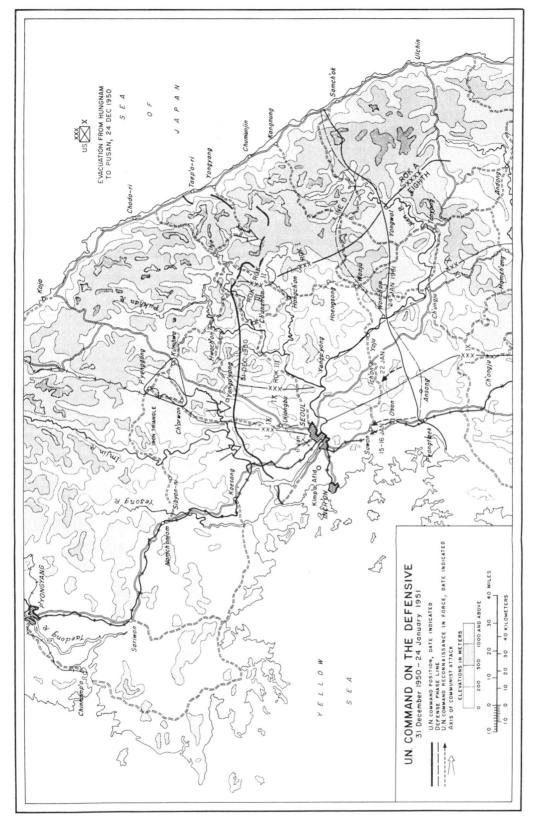

James F. Schnabel. *Policy & Direction: The First Year. United States Army in the Korean War.*
Office of the Chief of Military History. Washington: 1972.

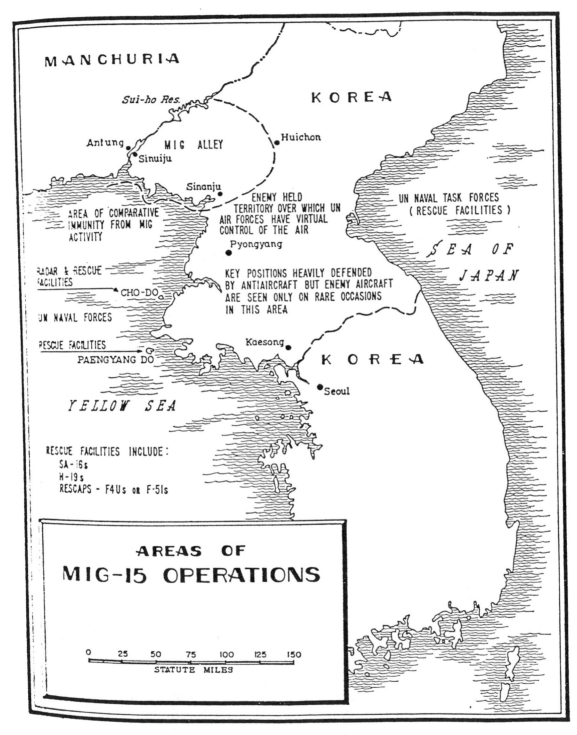

R.F. Futrell. *United States Air Force in Korea. 1950–1957. New York: 1961.*

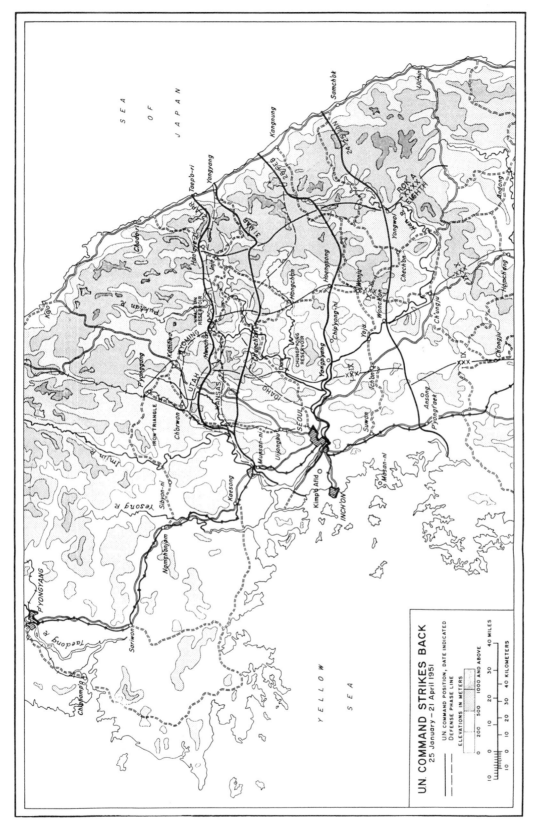

James F. Schnabel. Policy & Direction: The First Year. United States Army in the Korean War. Office of the Chief of Military History. Washington: 1972.

U.N. COMMAND STRIKES BACK
25 January – 21 April 1951

    ━━━━ UN COMMAND POSITION, DATE INDICATED

    ━━━━ DEFENSE PHASE LINE

ELEVATIONS IN METERS

| 200 | 500 | 1000 AND ABOVE |

0   10   20   30   40 MILES

0   10   20   30   40 KILOMETERS

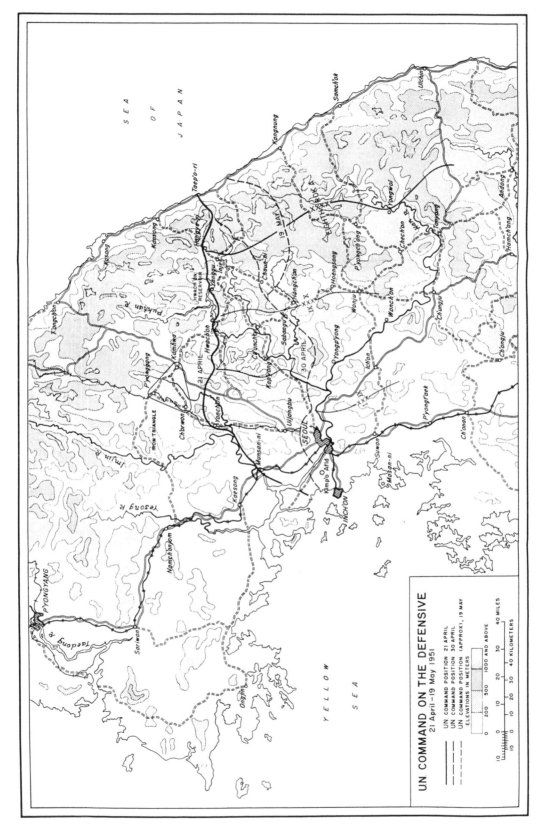

UN COMMAND ON THE DEFENSIVE
21 April–19 May 1951

UN COMMAND POSITION 21 APRIL
UN COMMAND POSITION 30 APRIL
UN COMMAND POSITION (APPROX), 19 MAY
ELEVATIONS IN METERS

200   500   1000 AND ABOVE

0   10   20   30   40 MILES
0   10   20   30   40 KILOMETERS

James F. Schnabel. Policy & Direction: The First Year. United States Army in the Korean War. Office of the Chief of Military History. Washington: 1972.

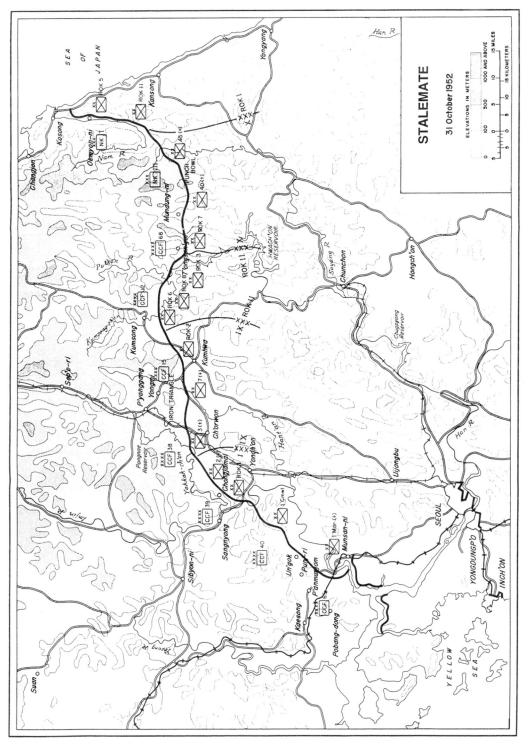

Walter G. Hermes. *Truce Tent and Fighting Front. United States Army in the Korean War.*
Office of the Chief of Military History. Washington: 1966.

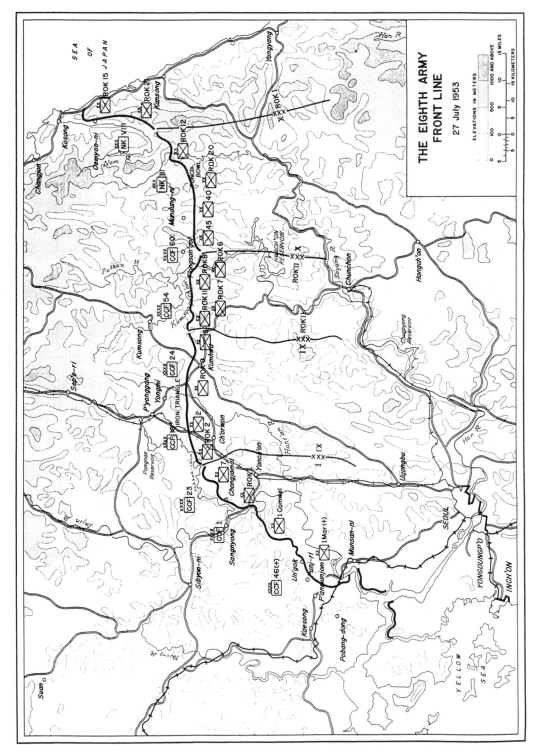

THE EIGHTH ARMY
FRONT LINE

27 July 1953

ELEVATIONS IN METERS

100   500   1000 AND ABOVE

0   5   10   15 MILES

0   5   10   15 KILOMETERS

Walter G. Hermes. *Truce Tent and Fighting Front. United States Army in the Korean War.*
Office of the Chief of Military History. Washington: 1966.

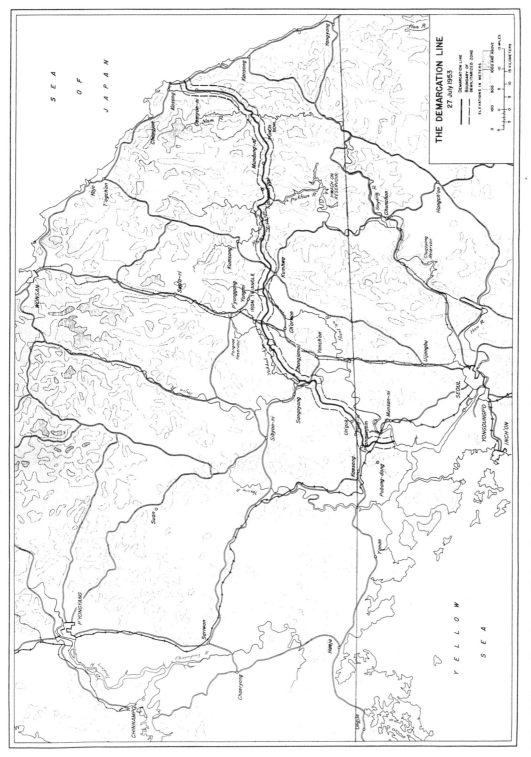

Walter G. Hermes. *Truce Tent and Fighting Front. United States Army in the Korean War.*
Office of the Chief of Military History. Washington: 1966.

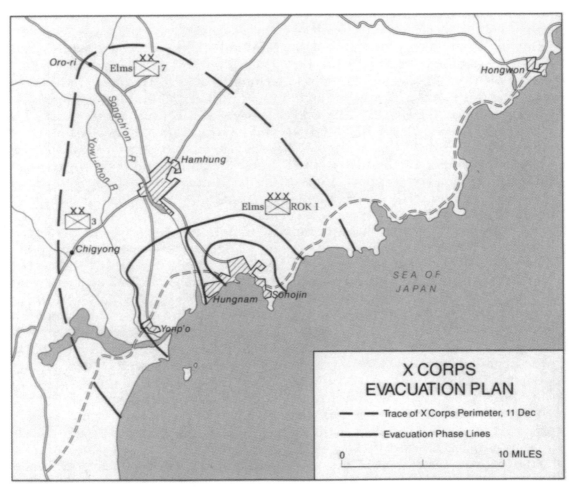

Oro-ri
Elms [XX] 7
Songch'on R.
Yonu-chon R.
Hamhung
[XX] 3
Elms [XXX] ROK I
Chigyong
Hungnam
Sohojin
Yonp'o

SEA OF JAPAN

Hongwon

X CORPS
EVACUATION PLAN

‒ ‒ ‒ Trace of X Corps Perimeter, 11 Dec

───── Evacuation Phase Lines

0   10 MILES

Billy C. Mossman. Ebb & Flow, November 1950–July 1951. United States Army in the Korean War. Center of Military History. Washington: 1990.

Photograph Credits

MacArthur (in non-regulation boots and scarf) inspects U.S. troops. Courtesy National Archives.

U.S. naval air power in Korea. WW II–vintage Corsair Navy fighter-bombers over WW II–era Essex-class carrier. Courtesy National Archives.

The "workhorse" of two wars: The immortal C-47 transport. Courtesy Air and Space Museum, Smithsonian Institutiton.

F9F Grumman U.S. Navy jet fighters making a carrier landing. Courtesy U.S. Naval Institute.

Boeing B-29 bombers over North Korea early in the Korean War. (By 1951, their undersides were painted black, a reflection of the potency of enemy antiaircraft guns). Courtesy Air and Space Museum, Smithsonian Institution.

Commonwealth troops disembarking from USAF Douglas C-54 (DC-4) transport. Courtesy Air and Space Museum, Smithsonian Institution.

ROK civilians being armed for defense of Taejon, July 1950. Courtesy National Archives.

USAF North American F-86 fighter aircraft. Courtesy Air and Space Museum, Smithsonian Institution.

As usual, the American Army did not stint on equipment. Every U.S. soldier in Korea could easily have ridden into battle. Courtesy National Archives.

The most reliable — often the only means of supply in Korea's hills — native manpower and the "A" Frame. Courtesy National Archives.

U.S. troops manhandle artillery piece up Korean hill. Courtesy National Archives.

Shovelling out" leaflets from a Douglas C-47 (DC-3) transport. Courtesy Air and Space Museum, Smithsonian Institution.

ROK troops on the march. Courtesy National Archives.

Massacred U.S. troops from early retreat, summer, 1950. Courtesy National Archives.

Burned-out terminal of Kimpo airfield, Seoul, shortly after capture by U.S. forces September, 1950; floodlights and antennas erected. Courtesy National Archives.

U.S. Marines go over the seawall at Inchon, September 1950. Courtesy National Archives.

Human crush of citizens of Pyongyang pick their way across wrecked bridge over the icy Taedong River, fleeing the advancing North Korean and Chinese communists, early December 1950. Courtesy National Archives.

HST signs state of national emergency, 16 December 1950. Courtesy National Archives.

Wary replacements learn how to stay alive as they enter the line. Courtesy National Archives.

Exploit of the U.S. Army Engineers. Courtesy National Archives.

Troop entertainment for a division. Photo gives good indication of the size of a U.S. Army infantry division. Courtesy National Archives.

U.N. partisans and their U.S. advisors on an island off the west coast of North Korea. Courtesy R. Paschall collection.

Ambush site of U.N. convoy; work of communist guerrillas. Courtesy National Archives.

South African Air Force North American P-51 Mustang fighter. Courtesy Air and Space Museum, Smithsonian Institution.

USAF Lockheed F-84 fighter and ground attack aircraft. Courtesy Air and Space Museum, Smithsonian Institution.

Belgian troops in Korea write notes. Courtesy National Archives.

The blasted terrain around "Old Baldy." Courtesy National Archives.

Korean civilians packing U.S. Army psychological warfare leaflet bombs. Courtesy Air and Space Museum, Smithsonian Institution.

The Korean War saw the complete racial integration of the U.S. armed forces, fully a decade before civilian society took the step. Courtesy National Archives.

Jubilant ROK troops roll into North Korea. Courtesy National Archives.

Haggard American prisoners of war, forced to parade through Pyongyang, summer 1950. Courtesy Air and Space Museum, Smithsonian Institution.

U.S. Army "psywar" leaflet bundles dropped over enemy lines. Courtesy Air and Space Museum, Smithsonian Institution.

Captured MIG-15 taking off for flight testing, closely followed by a North American F-86, the two main combatants of "Mig Alley" along the Yalu River. Courtesy Air and Space Museum, Smithsonian Institution.

Battle lines during period of near-total stalemate, 1951–1953. "Here we were and there they were." Courtesy National Archives.

Demarcating the armistice line, Panmunjom. Courtesy National Archives.

A

Acheson, Dean (1893–1971)

Dean Gooderham Acheson served as U.S. secretary of state from 1949–1953 and spearheaded the Cold War policies of containment of communism following World War II. He served as advisor on foreign policy to four presidents, and his book, *Present at the Creation*, which won the Pulitzer Prize in history in 1970, was dedicated to Harry S. Truman—"The Captain with the mighty heart." A graduate of Yale and Harvard Law School, he served Supreme Court Justice Louis Brandeis as his private secretary, worked for President Franklin D. Roosevelt as undersecretary of the treasury in 1933, then entered the State Department in 1941 as assistant secretary and later undersecretary from 1945–47. Acheson gathered Senate approval of U.S. entry into the United Nations (U.N.). After the refusal of the Soviets to evacuate Eastern Europe, and because of perceived threats to the Middle East, Acheson designed what became known as the Truman Doctrine in 1947, securing aid to defend Greece and Turkey when Britain could no longer shoulder the burden in that region. Acheson was also present at the creation of the Marshall Plan for Western Europe as a bulwark against Communism. During the Berlin Blockade, he initiated the formation of the North Atlantic Treaty Organization (NATO), the Western alliance against the Soviet Union and its Communist satellites.

As secretary of state, he first received word of the North Korean invasion across the 38th parallel into South Korea on June 24, 1950, while he was at his "Harewood Farm" estate outside Washington, D.C. A cable had been sent to the White House from John Muccio, American ambassador in Seoul, and relayed to Acheson. An emergency session of the U.N. Security Council was called after consultation with General Omar N. Bradley, chairman of the Joint Chiefs of Staff; Louis Johnson, secretary of defense; Frank Pace, secretary of the army, and former Senator Warren Austin, U.S. ambassador at the U.N. Acheson endorsed this call, Trygve Lie, U.N. secretary general, responded, and the Security Council adopted the resolution that an armed attack on the Republic of Korea (ROK) by forces from North Korea constituted a breach of the peace. Soviet representative Jacob Malik was not present; he was boycotting the council over the issue of a Nationalist Chinese rather than a People's Republic of China representative being seated. This resolution was adopted 9–0 (Yugoslavia abstained, USSR absent) on Sunday, June 25, 1950. Acheson's goal was not victory but to see that the North Korean attack failed.

Acheson authorized General Douglas MacArthur to supply Korea with arms and other equipment over and above that already allocated under the military assistance program; the U.S. Air Force was directed to protect Kimpo Airfield during the evacuation of U.S. dependents; the Seventh Fleet was ordered to proceed from the Philippines north to prevent any attack from China on Formosa, or vice versa. Secretary Acheson urged additional aid to Indochina and sent a survey team to Korea to appraise the military situation. Acheson supported the South Korean ambassador's pleas for U.S. military protection and accompanied the ambassador to a White House session with President Truman. Acheson manfully took partial responsibility for the war's outbreak, as he explained that his January 12, 1950 speech to the National Press Club in Washington, D.C. had appeared to be an invitation to attack when he had wrongly implied that South Korea was outside the defensive perimeter of the U.S.

However, Acheson took swift and sure action to halt aggression and defend South Korea once the war had broken out. He spoke against the challenges raised by Senator Robert A. Taft, who complained of Truman's use of "executive actions" to aid South Korea. Acheson from the beginning felt that the Chinese might intervene to aid North Korea in its invasion of the South, but that the Russians would not, and he was proved correct. Acheson would not accept an offer from General Chiang Kai-shek to contribute 33,000 troops to the Korean action, desiring to keep these forces where they were needed—to defend Formosa (Taiwan). This was in contrast to the friendliness shown by General MacArthur, who visited Chiang on Formosa, and his order that three squadrons of jet fighters be sent to Chiang without Pentagon approval. As a result, Acheson would be supportive of President Truman in Truman's later differences with MacArthur.

Acheson advised the president, in preparations to aid South Korea, not to ask for a resolution of approval from Congress, but to rest on his constitutional authority as commander in chief of the armed forces. He was instrumental in securing support from the British (as was Omar N. Bradley) to place their warships in Japanese waters at General MacArthur's disposal, to aid South Korea. Acheson convinced the president not to agree on a forced trade of Formosa to the Communists for their withdrawal from Korea. Acheson's policy aimed at ending the Korean problem swiftly without concessions that would encourage Communist aggressions elsewhere. He aimed at a peaceful solution to the Formosa question, possibly through the U.N. On the question of which nation should represent China, the Nationalist government on Formosa or the People's Republic of China (PRC), he felt the resolution should come through peaceful negotiation and not under blackmail or the duress of the Korean invasion. Acheson skillfully maneuvered to bring the Soviet Union's delegate back into the Security Council's meetings, not giving in to pressure from Indian Prime Minister Jawaharlal Nehru, who demanded that the PRC be admitted instead of Taiwan as a price for negotiating the end of the Korean War.

In addition to defending South Korea, Acheson also took the point position in drafting the peace treaty with Japan in 1950. Acheson oversaw the end of military control over Japan, the conclusion of the treaty of peace, and the transformation of Japan into a bastion of democracy in the Pacific friendly to and allied with the U.S. He suggested that John Foster Dulles prepare the draft of the peace treaty with Japan, and later claimed that he, in doing so, had elevated Dulles to become the future secretary of state, saying Dulles was ambitious to succeed him. Simultaneously, Secretary Acheson oversaw the transformation of the other former enemy, Germany, into an anti-Communist power, and shepherded West Germany into NATO and the integrated defense system of Europe. On the homefront, Acheson did not bow to the McCarthyites; he did not fire any of his employees in the State Department, even refusing to "turn his back" on Alger Hiss, a former high-ranking State Department officer later convicted of perjury in lying about his former Communist connections.

The People's Republic of China entered the Korean War in late 1950, and Acheson spearheaded the American nonrecognition policy, stepping up aid to the Nationalists on Formosa. Truman and Acheson, responding to the Communist threat, also gradually increased American commitments to sustaining the French attempts to rebuild the wreck of their colonial regime in Indochina (Vietnam).

After the elections of 1952 brought Dwight D. Eisenhower and the Republicans to power, Acheson, paradoxically pilloried as an "appeaser" of the communists, returned to private law practice and to additional writing, producing *Power and Diplomacy* in 1958, *Morning and Noon* in 1965, and *The Korean War* in 1971. His *Grapes from Thorns* was published after his death October 12, 1971.

Barbara Peterson

Bibliography

Acheson, Dean. *Present at the Creation: My Years in the State Department* (1969).

Ridgway, Matthew B. *The Korean War* (1967).

Senate Committees on Armed Services and Foreign Relations, 82nd Congress, 1st Session. *Hearings to Conduct an Inquiry into the Military Situation in the Far East and the Facts Surrounding the Relief of General of the Army Douglas MacArthur from His Assignments in that Area.*

Truman, Harry S. *Years of Trial and Hope,* Vol. II, *Memoirs* (1956) *Department of State Bulletin*, Vol. XXIII, July 3, 1950, October 9, 1950, November 27, 1951.

See also STATE DEPARTMENT, U.S.

ADCOM: GHQ Advance Command, Korea

When North Korea invaded South Korea on June 25, 1950, General of the Army Douglas MacArthur, commander in chief, Far East, was responsible for the support of KMAG (U.S. Military Advisory Group to the Republic of Korea) and the American embassy in Korea. The next day President Harry S. Truman authorized the dispatch of a survey team to Korea to determine the facts and to arrange for support of the Republic of Korea Army (ROKA).

MacArthur formed a survey team of thirteen officers and two enlisted men. Brigadier General John H. Church, a section chief of GHQ (general headquarters) Tokyo, was placed in command. On June 27, at 0400, the group departed Haneda Airfield bound for Seoul. They arrived at Itazuke Air Base in southern Japan two hours later and while awaiting further orders their destination was changed to Suwon, as Seoul was in imminent danger of falling.

Meanwhile MacArthur had received the Joint Chiefs of Staff directive giving him control of U.S. military activities in Korea. General MacArthur then renamed the survey team as the GHQ Advance Command and Liaison Group in Korea (ADCOM). Its duties were expanded to assuming control of KMAG and to providing as much help as possible to the Republic of Korea Army.

General Church and his ADCOM group arrived at Suwon at 1900 on June 27 and set up shop in the experimental agriculture building. The next morning Major General Chae Byung Duk, ROKA chief of staff, arrived at ADCOM and established ROKA headquarters there. The first task for ADCOM was to assist the ROKA in bringing order from chaos, and to stop the crumbling of the South Korean forces. Roadblocks were established south of Seoul to collect fleeing ROKA soldiers and to reorganize them into units to be returned to the Han River line. The first day some 9,000 troops were returned.

That following day, June 28, 1950, General Church radioed MacArthur his momentous assessment that it would be necessary to commit United States troops to restore the preinvasion boundaries. Two days later General Church traveled to Osan, twelve miles south of Suwon (the site a little over a week later of the first clash between U.S. and North Korean ground forces) to telephone GHQ Tokyo and report the near-collapse of the Han River defense. At GHQ, Major General Edward M. Almond, chief of staff, indicated that MacArthur had received the authority to commit U.S. ground troops to Korea and that they would start to arrive the next day.

While General Church was making his call to Tokyo the situation at ADCOM briefly turned to panic. Fearing that the enemy was about to overrun Suwon, the headquarters staff destroyed signal equipment with Thermit grenades and abandoned the headquarters. They fled to Suwon Airfield, planning to establish a defense perimeter but on arrival decided to move south instead. General Church returned from Osan as his staff was withdrawing south to Taejon. An angry Church halted the withdrawal but after a review realistically ordered the move continued.

Enroute to Taejon, Church stopped at Osan for another call to General Almond. Church informed the chief of staff of the move and changed the destination of incoming troops from Suwon to Pusan. ADCOM was reestablished at Taejon during the morning of July 1. That same day American ground troops arrived to delay the North Koreans and to improve South Korean morale.

The U.S. contingent, named Task Force Smith, pulled into the Taejon railroad station at 0800, July 2. Its commander, Colonel Charles B. Smith, met with General Church for instructions. Task Force Smith was to stop the North Koreans just north of Osan. But the force, as it turned out, lacked the firepower to halt the enemy armor column.

The next day United States Forces in Korea (USAFIK) was activated with General William F. Dean as commander and General Church deputy commander. The ADCOM and KMAG staffs were assigned to USAFIK. On July 13, Eighth U.S. Army assumed command of ground operations and General Church and the ADCOM group were ordered back to Tokyo. ADCOM, on the ground and often on the run, had made recommendations that led the U.S. into its fourth-bloodiest war.

D. Colt Denfield

Bibliography

Appleman, Roy. *South to the Naktong, North to the Yalu: June–November, 1950.* (Office of the Chief of Military History, Washington: 1961).

Blair, Clay. *The Forgotten War: America in Korea, 1950–1953* (New York: 1987).

Republic of Korea. *History of U.N. Forces in the Korean War*, Vol. IV (Ministry of National Defense, Seoul: 1975).

U.S. Army Second Infantry Division (Historical Center, Camp Casey, Korea: n.d.)

Air Attacks on Power Plants
See POWER PLANTS, U.N. AIR ATTACKS ON

Airborne Operations
Airborne assaults during the Korean War were limited to two operations. The first was conducted by the 187th Airborne Regimental Combat Team (RCT) at drop zones near Sukchon and Sunchon, North Korea. The second involved both the 187th and the 2nd and 4th Ranger Infantry Companies (Airborne) at Musan. Both operations were on a fairly small scale.

Early in his planning for the Inchon operation, General Douglas MacArthur identified the need for an airborne regimental combat team. Airborne troops during World War II had proven themselves fully capable of dropping behind enemy positions, severing lines of communication, and disrupting rear areas. The North Koreans might be vulnerable to such an assault, especially if conducted in conjunction with an amphibious operation.

Unfortunately, MacArthur did not have any airborne units at his disposal. He requested an RCT from the 82nd Airborne Division, but since that unit constituted the country's only combat-ready strategic reserve, the Joint Chiefs of Staff (JCS) denied his request. Instead, they offered an RCT from the less-ready 11th Airborne Division which had returned to the United States from occupation duty more than a year earlier. The 11th Airborne, however, was in a much depleted condition, as many of its personnel had been stripped in order to keep the 82nd manned. Without relying on replacements from the 82nd, the 11th could not field even one full-strength RCT until well into September 1950. MacArthur protested that such a delay would disrupt his Inchon timetable, but he was unable to convince the joint chiefs of a sufficient need for an earlier deployment of the RCT. He would have to adjust his plan to exclude an airborne operation in the initial stages of the offensive. In the meantime, however, the 187th Airborne RCT left Camp Stoneman, California, on 6 September and arrived in Japan on 20 September with a strength of 4,400 paratroopers. Its date for operational readiness in the Far East command was set for 21 October.

Even without the airborne RCT, MacArthur's Inchon landing was brilliantly successful. By the later part of September, he was prepared to continue his attack across the 38th parallel into North Korea. At this point he found an opportunity to make use of his new paratrooper asset.

As the Eighth Army advanced, MacArthur held the RCT in GHQ reserve around Kimpo Airfield near Seoul. He directed its commander to prepare to conduct an airborne drop north of the enemy capital of Pyongyang in an effort to cut off enemy withdrawal routes, disrupt communications, and rescue POWs. The original date of the operation coincided with the 187th's operational readiness date, 21 October. However, MacArthur later moved the date to 20 October.

The plan called for two drop zones (DZs) some thirty miles north of Pyongyang. The main one was DZ William at Sukchon, and the other one was DZ Easy at Sunchon. Both drop zones would cut highways which ran north from Pyongyang.

The regiment boarded 133 C-119s and C-47s of the 314th and 21st Troop Carrier Squadrons, and by noon on 20 October the first plane was airborne. This was the first time that C-119 "Flying Boxcars" had been used in a combat jump. A typical C-119 carried forty-six men divided into two even "sticks," fifteen monorail bundles, and four door bundles. Each paratrooper carried his main parachute, a .45 caliber pistol, and a carbine or M1 rifle.

The transport planes were preceded by fighters which strafed and rocketed the drop zones. Paratroopers from the lead plane began jumping into Sukchon at about 1400. There was no enemy antiaircraft and only sporadic sniper fire.

The first drop landed 1,470 men of the 1st Battalion, the regimental headquarters and headquarters company, and supporting engineer, medical, and service troops. Some seventy-four tons of equipment accompanied the personnel. At least one man was killed by enemy fire while still in his parachute, and twenty-five paratroopers were injured.

Heavy equipment, including seven 105mm howitzers of the 674th Field Artillery Battalion and 1,125 rounds of ammunition, followed. Six howitzers were recovered in usable condition, and about 90 percent of the shells were undamaged. This was the first time heavy equipment had been dropped in a combat operation.

Once the unit was on the ground, the 1st Battalion seized Hill 97 east of Sukchon and

Hill 104 to the north. Resistance was light, and the battalion quickly cleared the town and established a roadblock to the north. Colonel Bowen set up his command post on Hill 97.

The 3rd Battalion followed the 1st into DZ William and took up defensive positions, which included roadblocks, on the low hills two miles south of Sukchon. By 1700, the battalion had seized its objectives, killed five enemy soldiers and captured forty-two, and suffered no friendly casualties.

In the meantime, the 2nd Battalion had begun jumping into DZ Easy at 1420. Again resistance was light, but twenty paratroopers were injured during the jump. By nightfall, two companies had established roadblocks to the south and west of Sunchon, and a third had established contact in the town with elements of the ROK 6th Infantry Division, which had advanced from the southeast.

The next morning, the 1st Battalion captured the high ground north of Sukchon needed to cut the highway running north. That afternoon, contact between the 1st and 2nd Battalions was established at Sunchon. In the meantime, the 3rd Battalion had started south toward Pyongyang with I Company moving along the railroad and K Company along the highway. At 1300, I Company reached Opa-ri, where it was vigorously attacked by a North Korean battalion. After two-and-a-half hours of fighting, the enemy forced I Company to withdraw with ninety men missing. The North Koreans did not pursue, instead opting to withdraw to their defenses around Opa-ri.

While this battle was going on, K Company encountered another approximately battalion-sized enemy force a mile north of Yongyu. This time the paratroopers overcame the enemy, who withdrew to defensive positions to the south and the east. K Company continued into Yongyu and to Hill 163 to its north. Yongyu and Opa-ri were almost opposite each other and separated by a three-mile gap.

The 239th North Korean Regiment of some 2,500 men had been defending the high ground in this gap in order to fight a delaying action against U.N. troops expected to advance north from Pyongyang. The regiment was now being hit from the rear by two separate forces and was in danger of being surrounded.

At midnight, the 239th attempted a breakout to the north. The North Koreans launched a total of five attacks which seriously dented but did not break the paratroopers' line. The 187th could not hold out much longer, but as things developed, they did not have to. With Pyongyang secured on 20 October, the U.S. I Corps was continuing its attack to the north. The 27th British Commonwealth Brigade led the way, and at first light on 22 October their lead elements reached Yongyu. The North Koreans were trapped between the 187th and the British brigade and in fierce fighting the enemy was practically destroyed. The 3rd Battalion reported it had killed 805 enemy and captured 681 at Yongyu—that after the 3rd Battalion returned to Sukchon. The British followed and relieved the 187th in their positions. During the battle at Yongyu, the 2nd Battalion had remained relatively idle at Sunchon.

On 23 October, the 187th returned to Pyongyang by way of the secondary road through Sunchon. Throughout the operation, the 187th had suffered forty-six jump casualties and sixty-five battle casualties. A total of 4,000 troops and more than 600 tons of equipment had been dropped. The regiment had captured 3,818 North Korean prisoners, but none of these were the high-ranking military or government officials the operation's planners had hoped to snare. In fact, the mission had not lived up to its expectations of cutting off any sizable part of the North Korean Army. The enemy's main body had already withdrawn north of Sukchon and Sunchon and was either north of the Chongchon River or in the process of crossing it. Unfortunately, most of the American and South Korean POWs had likewise been removed to the north. However these shortcomings were not the fault of the 187th. The regiment had conducted itself very well in its initial combat action in Korea.

Musan

The 187th participated in a second airborne assault during a limited U.N. counteroffensive in March 1951. This time the regiment was joined by the 2nd and 4th Infantry Ranger Companies (Airborne). The paratroopers jumped into drop zones ahead of an armored advance toward Musan, South Korea. They succeeded in harassing the enemy and established contact with the ground forces before nightfall. However, this action was limited in scope and not essential to the overall operation's success.

Kevin Dougherty

A

Bibliography

Tugwell, Maurice. *Airborne to Battle: A History of Airborne Warfare, 1918–1971* (London: 1971).

Ranger Unit Operations. Department of the Army (Washington: 1987).

Aircraft

The aircraft of the Korean War ranged from the most technologically advanced to old and proven designs. The war also saw the introduction of tactics and new aviation technologies into combat and combat support areas.

North Korea supported its initial invasion of South Korea in 1950 with World War II–era Russian designed and built propeller-driven Yak-3, -7, and -9, and Ilyshin IL-10 Stormovik fighters and bombers. The Yaks were single-seat, single-engine fighters whose performance approached that of the P-51 Mustang. The IL-10 was a rugged, low-wing, single-engine ground attack plane with a top speed of about 335 mph. Armed with two 23mm cannons and two 7.62mm machine guns, it had a bomb capacity of 2,000 lbs. For night intrusion and harassment behind U.N. lines, the enemy flew the Polikarpov PO-2, a slow, wire-and-fabric biplane trainer.

The South Korean Air Force was equipped only with a few U.S.-supplied Piper L-4 Cubs, Stinson (later Vultee) L-5 Sentinels, and North American T-6 Texans, usually used for liaison, gunfire spotting, and training. The Cubs were light, high-wing two-seaters that made all of 85 mph on their tiny 65 hp Continental O-170 engines. The Stinsons did a little better with a top speed of 120 mph from their Lycoming 0-435s of 190 hp. Powered by a Pratt and Whitney 1340 piston engine of 600 hp, the unarmed, unarmored, steady T-6 made 215 mph. Developed as an advanced trainer for the U.S. Air Force in World War II, it did not present any threat to enemy air power.

The U.S. responded to the North Korean threat with a mixture of piston-engine planes, some of them of World War II and postwar vintage, and early model jets, with which they drove strafing enemy planes from retreating U.S. and ROK ground forces, and bombed enemy front lines. A fast, maneuverable, single-seat fighter, the U.S. Air Force's F-51D Mustang, had earned its classic reputation as a long-range bomber escort over Europe during World War II. Powered by a U.S.-built Rolls-Royce–Packard Merlin V-1650-7 liquid-cooled piston engine developing 1,495 hp for takeoff, the Mustang averaged 350–450 mph and was well armed with six .50 caliber machine guns.

The F-80 Shooting Star was among the earliest operational jet fighters in the USAF inventory. Although its 5,200-pound thrust General Electric J-33 jet engine drove it at 600 mph to easily outpace Communist piston-driven planes, it had the straight wings and tail of older designs. The straight-winged F-84 Thunderjet was powered by an Allison J-35 axial-flow engine of 5,600 pounds thrust that drove it at 622 mph top speed. Based in Japan before the Inchon landings, the Thunderjets flew ground support missions in Korea that normally would have been outside their range. In a precedent for modern warfare, the F-84s extended their range through in-flight refueling provided by the KB-29, a tanker version of the B-29 Superfortress four-engine heavy bomber of World War II. A technology demonstrated in the 1920s, aerial refueling had since become dependable enough for support of planes flying combat missions. The F-84s and RF-80s (Shooting Stars equipped with cameras for reconnaissance) linked up to a hose with a basket-like probe trailing the KB-29, through which fuel was then passed to the thirsty fighters. North American piston-engine F-82 Twin Mustangs, normally employed in air defense duties over Japan, saw fighter-bomber and nightfighter action during the emergency of the initial retreats and evacuations, later returning to Japan and the U.S. West Coast. The F-82 gained brief glory by shooting down several enemy piston-engine fighters in the earliest days of the war in the first armed clash between U.S. and North Korean forces. Essentially two Mustangs sharing a common center wing section, the F-82 retained the cockpits of both aircraft, with one pilot relieving the other on long flights.

By the time the Pusan perimeter had stabilized in the summer of 1950, the U.S. Air Force had decimated the North Korean Air Force in combat, attaining total air superiority.

The U.S. Air Force attacked targets in North Korea with two piston-engine World War II bombers, the B-26 Invader and the B-29 Superfortress. Formerly known as the A-26, but redesignated in 1948 with the scrapping of the older Martin Marauder, the B-26 was particularly deadly. A mid-wing, light bomber powered by two Pratt and Whitney R-2800 engines of 2,000 hp each, the Invader had a top speed of 330 mph. A later development of 1942 gunship experiments, it pitted an astounding eighteen .50 caliber machine guns against enemy ground forces, ripping them apart in what was almost a continuous explosion of fire. The B-26 carried out day and night interdiction of enemy front lines through bombardment of convoys, trains, and supply lines. In this role many were equipped with Plexiglas noses for better visibility after dark.

With an F-80 escort against Yaks, the B-29 Superfortress, the heavily armed, long-range, mid-wing heavy bomber that had turned Japanese cities into cinders during World War II, systematically bombed North Korean military and industrial targets in a strategic effort to cripple the enemy's ability and will to fight. Powered by four double-row Wright R-2800 Cyclone piston engines of 2,200 hp each, the B-29 had a top speed of 358 mph, a wingspan of 141 feet, a length of 99 feet, and a bomb capacity of approximately ten tons. The B-29 was the only four-engine piston bomber used in the Korean War.

The U.S. Navy and Marines flew a variety of propeller-driven fighter-bombers in Korea. The F4U Corsair and the F7F Tigercat dated to World War II. The Vought F4U-4, an inverted gull-wing, piston-engine fighter-bomber, was armed with four 20mm cannons, bombs, and rockets. Powered by a Pratt and Whitney 2-2800-18W 2,000 hp engine, it flew at almost 425 mph. The Marines acquired a heavily armored attack model of the Corsair for ground support, known as the AU-1. The Grumman F7F-3 Tigercat, deployed just a little too late for World War II combat, was a swift, mid-wing, single-seat fighter-bomber armed with four .50 caliber machine guns, four 20mm cannons, and two 2,000-pound bombs. Powered by two Pratt and Whitney R-2800-34W engines of 2,100 hp each, it had a top speed of about 425 mph. These aircraft supported ground troops and joined F-82s and B-26s in night intruder missions against enemy truck convoys and trains, hindering resupply of front-line troops. The postwar Douglas AD Skyraider, an enormous low-wing, piston-engine, single-seat, carrier-based bomber with a tremendous load-carrying capacity, would serve through the Vietnam era although its design dated from World War II. Powered by a Wright R-3350-26W engine of 2,700 hp, it made 365 mph. The Skyraider, possibly the largest single-seat war-plane ever built, was used for ground support, night interdiction, radar picket, and even electronic countermeasures duties.

Two other Marine aircraft of the Korean War, the Avenger and the Savage, were used in small numbers. The Marines borrowed two TBM-3N Avengers from the Navy to serve as air ambulances during the Chosin Reservoir breakout. A mid-wing, single-engine World War II torpedo bomber, the TBM was a bulky design with a capacious fuselage. Its R-2600-8 engine of 1,500 hp gave the Avenger a top speed of about 250 mph. During the breakout, the Avengers flew out 103 seriously wounded Marines who probably would have died without immediate evacuation. Later in the war Avengers continued in the ambulance role, flying seriously wounded men to hospitals in Japan. The Marines also kept a squadron of North American AJ-1 Savage attack bombers, armed with nuclear warheads, on readiness from 1952 on in case they were needed for a strike against China. Despite two powerful Wright R-2800-44W piston engines of 2,300 hp each and a single J-33-A10 jet of 4,600-pound thrust, the monstrous Savage, 63 feet long, with a wingspan of 71 feet, had a top speed of only 392 mph. Even the F6F Hellcat, an early World War II carrier fighter of sterling reputation which had bloodied the Japanese Zero, saw service as a pilotless drone guided weapon armed with a 2,000-pound bomb and flown into the target by radio control.

Of course, jets as well as piston-engine aircraft equipped U.S. Navy and Marine units. Among them was the Grumman F9F Panther, a single-seat, straight-wing fighter-bomber powered by a Pratt and Whitney J42 jet of 5,000 pounds thrust. Achieving 625 mph, the Panther was armed with four 20mm cannons in the nose, and bombs. The later improved performance F9F-5 model incorporated airframe modifications and a 6,250-pound thrust engine. Of similar layout was the McDonnell F2H-2 Banshee, equipped with two Westinghouse J-34-WE-34 jets of 3,150 pounds thrust each, which drove it at 586 mph. Armed with four 20mm cannons, the Banshee saw service as a fighter-bomber, and with cameras, as a reconnaissance plane.

The Royal Navy flew Supermarine Seafire 47s, Hawker Sea Furies, and Fairy Fireflies from their aircraft carriers. The liquid-cooled Seafire and the air-cooled Sea Fury were fast, maneuverable piston-engine aircraft with performance comparable to the Mustang. The two-seat, liquid-cooled Firefly had a top speed of around 300 mph. All flew ground support missions and all were of World War II design. Australia's No. 77 Squadron brought to Korea in 1951 one of the earliest jet designs, the Gloster Meteor. A mid-wing fighter with one engine mounted in each wing, the Meteor was badly outclassed by the MIG-15 in air combat, indicating the rapid advance of jet technology in just the six years since V-J day. Soon withdrawn from air combat, the Meteor was confined to fighter-bomber duties, at which it excelled. With the North Korean Air Force destroyed, U.N. air forces enjoyed free run of North Korean airspace by the fall of 1950, with even Superfortresses strafing trains and the occasional single enemy soldier.

By the end of 1950 the struggle for air superiority forced a rapid upgrade of the contending air forces' fighters from World War II–vintage piston-engine aircraft and early jets to higher-performance, swept-wing jets, reflecting aviation technology's rapid post–World War II advance. The gradual phase-out of Mustangs, as pilots rotated through F-80 training during the summer of 1950, was only a clue to the future. In November 1950 the enemy reinvigorated its fighter units with one of the world's most advanced production aircraft, the MIG-15 jet fighter. With swept wings and tail and a British-derived VK-1 engine of 6,000 pounds thrust, the MIG-15 was fast, with a maximum speed of 670 mph, and heavily armed with two 23mm and one 37mm cannons. The MIG-15's ability to outfly and outfight the F-80, not to mention the U.N. piston-engine fighters and fighter-bombers, not only ended the freedom of North Korean skies enjoyed by U.N. air forces, but also endangered the B-29. The designers of the Superfortress never expected that its gunsights would have to track aircraft almost twice as fast as the 300 mph Japanese interceptors of World War II. The Communists also brought in some examples of the Yak-15, a Yak-3 equipped with a single RD-10 jet of 1,980 pounds thrust. Armed with two 23mm cannons, the Yak's top speed of 488 mph was well under that of the MIG.

The U.S. Air Force responded to the MIG-15 with its most advanced fighter, the North American F-86 Sabre, a swept-wing, 500–600 mph fighter powered by a J47-GE engine providing 5,200 pounds of thrust. Arriving in Korea with the 4th FIG (Fighter-Interceptor Group) in December 1950, and later equipping the 51st Fighter Wing, the F-86 regained and held air superiority over the MIG's. Much more skilled and aggressive than the enemy, U.S. fighter pilots had scored a 10 to 1 kill ratio over the MIGs by July 1953.

Sabre air superiority enabled U.N. fighter-bombers to continue operating, but did not halt by any means the chess game of technological and tactical advance. Despite Sabre escorts, Superfortresses and piston-engine fighter-bombers did not fare well when within MIG range. In reply, the Air Force moved the B-29s to night bombing to avoid MIGs, and replaced most of the fighter-bomber force's F-51s and F-80s with the F-84. Although no match for the MIG in a dogfight, the F-84 was quick enough to avoid situations that doomed such slower planes as the F-51 and F-80. In 1953 the enemy added more MIGs along the Yalu, threatening to overtax the capacity of the two existing F-86 wings. The Air Force countered by converting the last two F-51 and F-80 wings to F-86F fighter-bombers. As a result of the success of F-86s that strafed on the way home from fighter missions to the North, the F-86F had added two additional underwing shackles for bombs. Late in the war, MIGs once again challenged the Superfortresses with night-flying capability of their own, putting the B-29s back where they started. The Air Force responded with an all-weather night fighter developed from the F-90, the Lockheed F-94 Starfire. In November 1952 the Marines acquired Douglas F35-2N Skyknights, each equipped with two Westinghouse J46 jets, for nighttime base defense and bomber escort duties. These aircraft reduced the MIG threat to the B-29, with Skyknight crews credited with six kills by the war's end.

In a curious turn, the high-performance aircraft with which the United Nations responded to the Communist threat could not end the problem of enemy PO-2 night intrusions. Soon known as "Bedcheck Charlie," the PO-2 raids were a negligible military threat, causing minimal physical damage; their chief effect was the disruption of sleep and routine at Allied air bases. Almost every type of aircraft was tried against them, even Avenger ambulances with radar under the wings. However, the PO-2 was so slow that high-speed night fighters had little luck against it. Radar beams went right through its fabric fuselage. An F-94 even flew through one, causing the loss of both aircraft. Marine Tigercats bagged a few. Navy Lieutenant Guy Bordelon, of Navy night fighter squadron VC-3, had the most luck, downing five PO-2s in an F4U-5N during the summer of 1953, ironically to become the U.S. Navy's only ace of the war. Despite all efforts, nocturnal "Bedcheck Charlie" blithely putted on throughout the war, showing that, even in military aviation, technology could not solve every problem.

The large scale use of the helicopter marked another facet of the war's use of technological advances. Korea marked the first time in warfare that battlefield casualties could rapidly be evacuated, cutting the overall loss rate. A key factor in this was the Bell H-13 helicopter, which had room for three, including the pilot. A utilitarian design, it consisted of a cockpit covered by a Plexiglas bubble from which extended the engine and a tail boom of uncovered struts. The H-13 carried two wounded men in litters mounted on either side of the cockpit. It took over rescue duties in mid-1951 from the Sikorsky H-5, known in the Navy and Marines as the H03S-1, and later H05S-1. The narrow fuselage H-5, powered by a Pratt and Whitney 985 engine of 450 hp, had a capacity of one passenger inside the fuselage and two external litter baskets, and a range of 85 miles. It did yeoman duty early in the war, rescuing many wounded soldiers and Marines from the rough Korean terrain. H-5s and H03S-1s were also used for aerial resupply and observation, and plane guard duties off aircraft carriers.

The 120-mile range, 115 mph H-19 (U.S. Navy HRS-1, 2) powered by a Pratt and Whitney R-1340 engine of 600 hp (Navy HRS-1, 2), arrived in Korea in March 1951. Its capacity for up to ten people inside its fuselage, besides adding effectiveness to the rescue mission, encouraged the advent of the first helicopter assaults, an innovation that would become a major tactic fifteen years later. Working in concert with VB-17Gs, World War II B-17 Flying Fortress bombers modified for intelligence work, the H-19 infiltrated and recovered CIA agents in North Korea.

The U.S. Air Force at first met the war's tremendous air cargo and air lift needs with venerable World War II transports, later adding aircraft that hauled much higher volumes of troops and material per flight. Both airliners converted to cargo use for World War II, the C-47 Skytrain and C-54 Loadmaster had carried the burden of World War II air transport duties. Originally developed from the Douglas DC-3 airliner to serve as the major U.S. air cargo transport during World War II, the C-47, powered by two Pratt and Whitney R-1830-92 piston engines of 1,200 hp each, flew at a top speed of 250 mph. The C-54 had originated as the DC-4 airliner. Four Pratt and Whitney R-2000 engines of 1,350 hp each drove it at 275 mph maximum. Both aircraft had lately distinguished themselves in the Berlin Airlift with their lifting capacity and reliability, flying food and coal into the city to foil Soviet attempts to starve out Allied forces. In Korea they supplied the Pusan perimeter, then went on to feed the combat units as they moved up and down the peninsula. With the Navy and Marines the C-47 was known as the R4D. United Nations air forces such as Greece and Thailand also flew the C-47. Critical transport needs accompanying the rapid buildup of U.N. forces in the summer of 1950 soon overrode the abilities of available air cargo aircraft, spurring a hunt for more capacity.

By summer 1950, two aircraft designed and mass-produced specifically for military cargo transport needs, the Fairchild C-119 Flying Boxcar and the Douglas C-124 Globemaster, arrived in Korea. The C-119 consisted of a short, roomy rectangular fuselage mounted between twin tail booms on a high wing. Powered at a maximum of 250 mph by two Wright R-3350-85 engines of 3,500 hp each, the C-119 could carry almost seventy troops, compared to the C-47's twenty-four. Developed just in time for the war, it was easily and quickly loaded and unloaded, on the ground or in flight. In Korea, C-119s were famed for parachuting a Bailey Bridge to enable U.S. Marines to safely continue their evacuation to the coast from the Chosin Reservoir in December 1950. Paratroopers also dropped from both C-47s and C-119s. The newer C-124, powered by four Pratt and Whitney R-4360 piston engines of 3,800 hp each, had the oversized, bulbous fuselage of a true transport. The C-124 revolutionized cargo transport and evacuation of wounded on its arrival in September 1951, carrying almost 200 troops, or five times as much cargo as its counterparts.

A few other cargo aircraft helped fill U.N. transport needs. Before the larger cargo planes arrived, a search all over the Far East garnered some World War II vintage Curtiss C-46 Commandos to help fill immediate air transport needs in the summer of 1950. A low-wing transport similar, but not identical, in layout to the C-47, the Commando was larger, carrying about 15,000 pounds of cargo compared to the C-47's 5,500, and was powered by two Pratt and Whitney R-2800-51 engines of 2,000 hp each. A few C-69As, a military version of the elegantly designed and fast Lockheed Constellation airliner, also served with Military Air Transport Command. A combination of cargo aircraft technology, superb organization, and dedicated soldiers helped the U.N. command meet its supply goals by war's end.

A variety of light, low-powered, unarmed aircraft accomplished forward air control for fighter-bombers in the Korean War. Besides the Cub and L-5, which dated to World War II and served with both the Korean and U.S. Air Forces, was the Cessna L-19, developed in 1950. Similar in layout to its World War II sisters, its 213 hp Continental O-470 piston engine drove it at 130 mph. The Marines referred to various models of the L-5 as OY-1 and OY-2, and the L-19 as the OE-1 Bird Dog when it reached combat units in 1951. A slightly heavier, more powerful forward air control aircraft, the T-6 Texan, known as the "Mosquito," patrolled the front lines, calling in fighter-bombers when necessary. The L-17 Navion, a low-wing, unarmed light plane powered by a Continental O-470 piston engine of 250 hp, was used primarily to move division-level ground force commanders about. A more powerful liaison aircraft was the T-33, a trainer evolved from the F-80, which it closely resembled, and used as a headquarters liaison, commanders' observation craft, and jet trainer.

Variants of combat-proven aircraft performed most photographic reconnaissance of enemy troops, supply lines, ports, air bases, and factories in Korea. With an "R" for "Reconnaissance" added to the aircraft prefix, F-51s, F-80s, and B-26s, equipped with cameras and known as RF-51s, RF-80s, and RB-26s, respectively, handled most tactical reconnaissance duties early in the war. Later in the war F-86s were modified to take photos, eliminating the threat of MIGs to reconnaissance planes. Such modifications of the B-29 as the RB-29 and RB-50 procured photos of air bases and industries deep in North Korea, while the photo variant of the Air Force's giant piston and jet-engine strategic bomber, the RB-36, made secret reconnaissance flights over Manchuria and the USSR itself.

U.N. forces maintained an extensive air-sea rescue capability to recover airmen downed over enemy territory or at sea. The twin-engine Grumman SA-16 Albatross and the Martin PBM-5 Mariner picked up pilots downed over water. The Albatross, designed after World War II, was a high-wing, boat-hulled amphibian powered by two Wright R-1820-76 engines of 1,425 hp each, with a speed of 255 mph. Its spacious hull could carry sixteen stretchers or fourteen passengers. The Mariner, which dated to World War II, similarly was a twin-engine,

high gull-wing flying boat. The SB-17, a modification of the B-17 Flying Fortress, was equipped with a droppable life boat. The SB-29 was a similarly equipped B-29 which accompanied Superfortresses to Korea and back.

Long-range maritime patrols by aircraft ensured control of the seas around Korea. Mariners, Consolidated P4Y-2 Privateers, a development of the four-engine, high-wing B-24 Liberator bomber of World War II, and the Lockheed P2V Neptune, a postwar twin-engine, mid-wing aircraft, flew these missions, photographing shipping to ensure that enemy forces did not infiltrate by sea. Powered by two Wright R-3350-26W engines of 2,600 hp each, the Neptune had a top speed of 338 mph. The P2V's heavy offensive armament of six 20mm cannons in the nose also admirably suited it for ground support missions, which it flew early in the war. A few British Short Sunderlands, four-engine, high-wing flying boats dating to World War II, also flew long-range search and rescue and patrol missions.

Combat exigencies brought about the use of many different kinds of aircraft of varying design and performance in the Korean War, some representing the great ferment in aviation technology and design of the 1950s, others older but proven ideas. Swept-wing F-86 fighter jets preserved air superiority against MIG 15s. Slower piston aircraft designs and technologies dating to World War II successfully played a valuable role in such missions as ground support, forward air control, air-sea rescue, and maritime patrol, as well as night harassment. The jet night fighter and the high-capacity cargo aircraft, as well as technologies new to combat and combat support such as helicopters and in-flight refueling, made United Nations air power supreme throughout the Korean War.

Steven Agoratus

Bibliography

Angelucci, Enzo. *The Rand McNally Encyclopedia of Military Aircraft, 1914–1980* (1980).

Brown, David. *The United States Air Force in Korea, 1950–1953* (GPO, Washington, 1983).

Higham, Robin, and Abigail Siddal, eds. *Flying Combat Aircraft of the USAAF-USAF* (1975).

Air Force, North Korean People's

See KOREAN PEOPLE'S AIR FORCE

Air Force, U.S.

In 1950, the United States Air Force (USAF), barely three years old as a separate service, found itself in a war on the peninsula of Korea. By the end of that war three years later, the USAF would have in the Korean theater 1,800 aircrews and more than 1,240 aircraft. Also, they would have flown nearly 217,000 interdiction and armed reconnaissance sorties during the thirty-seven-month conflict. The aircraft and crews who flew these sorties were assigned to the Far East Air Forces (FEAF).

FEAF was the air force component of General Douglas MacArthur's U.S. Far East command which had the responsibility to defend the geographical region that included Japan, the Ryukyus, the Marianas, and the American bases in the Philippines. The Republic of Korea (South Korea) was outside the U.S. defense perimeter. The United States air forces assigned to FEAF included the Fifth Air Force, which was the largest subordinate command; the Twentieth Air Force and the Thirteenth Air Force—with their subordinate tactical air wings, a medium bombardment group and wing, and troop carrier groups and wings; and tactical support wings. The FEAF bomber command (provisional) was organized after the war began, and the Far East Air Logistical Command, which was responsible for all the logistical support for the USAF in the U.S. Far East Command. Additionally, there were several attached units that completed the Far East Air Force's organization.

FEAF's primary mission was principally defensive, but it was also charged to maintain an appropriate mobile strike force and to provide air support for operations as arranged with the appropriate Army and Navy commanders. The duties of FEAF were as explicitly required and specified by General MacArthur, commander in chief of the U.S. Far East command (CINCFE). (Additionally, General MacArthur would become commander in chief of the United Nations command when the Allied command in Korea was organized to include the United States Far East command.) The overriding mission of FEAF was to provide air defense, including air warning service, for the Japanese Islands, the Ryukyu Islands, the Marianas, Volcano, and Bonin Islands, and the American bases in the Philippines. Beyond a directive by CINCFE to be prepared to evacuate Americans from the Republic of Korea, FEAF had no responsibilities in Korea prior to the war. In preparation for war, if it were to come, the commanding general of the Fifth Air Force, Lieutenant General Earle E. Partridge, designated the commander of the 8th Fighter-Bomber Wing to be the task force commander in Korea. Except for the operations listed above, the FEAF had no other military requirements in Korea; however, after 25 June 1950, all that changed.

At four A.M. on 25 June 1950, the armed forces of North Korea attacked across the 38th parallel into South Korea to begin the Korean War. The following day, the American ambassador ordered the evacuation of all American nationals from Seoul and Inchon, and General MacArthur directed FEAF to provide fighter cover for the evacuation. The 8th Fighter-Bomber Wing provided combat air patrol for the evacuation, and on the 27th of June began air evacuation using transport aircraft, with fighters providing protection. All of this was possible only because of the proximity of U.S. air bases in Japan. On the 27th the USAF scored its first victories over the North Korean Air Force, which had until then dominated the skies with its Soviet-built World War II-vintage propeller-driven Yak fighters. On that day, FEAF F-82 propeller-driven "Twin Mustangs" shot down three out of three Yaks over Inchon which had the temerity to interfere with the evacuation; later in the day, four more Yaks were destroyed by these USAF fighters. For the remainder of the war, the Korean People's Air Force remained conspicuous by its absence. (The F-82s were soon withdrawn from the war, however, because of replacement parts shortages.)

This would be the first war in which U.S. air power would not be charged with the mission of winning a war. The USAF had been founded on the slogan "Victory Through Air Power." Its commanders were indoctrinated to the unlimited offensive, had calmly planned and executed the incineration of enemy cities and their inhabitants in World War II, and held no apparent qualms over dropping the atomic bomb to "end the war." Thus they found the unprecedented restrictions on their actions incomprehensible. They could not, of course, use their "ultimate weapon," the atomic bomb, and they could not go after the enemy's airpower or economic and military vitals in China. But even with these limitations the FEAF retained the initiative and fulfilled its mission. The basic missions carried out by FEAF during the Korean War included close air support, air defense, air superiority, interdiction, reconnaissance, transport, and rescue operations.

A

Close Air Support

Victory in World War II was due in large part to the cooperation between air and ground forces, and this was, if anything, even more true in Korea. Units of the Fifth Air Force provided tactical air support to the Eighth Army. For example, on 7 March 1951, units of the Fifth flew 575 sorties in support of the U.S. 25th Division, which had the mission of establishing a bridgehead across the Han River. Of those 575 sorties, some 200 directly supported the advancing ground troops, while the remaining sorties attacked enemy positions in the immediate rear in indirect support of the operation. Overall, no ground forces ever received so much close air support as did U.N. forces from FEAF.

But FEAF nevertheless had much to relearn about close air support, particularly in the war's earliest days when careless air attacks inflicted heavy casualties on ROK troops. Task Force Smith, the first American ground unit engaged in the Korean War, had no air support; all U.N. air assets had been earlier confined to the Seoul area to avoid further air fratricide. The failing was not confined to the FEAF; Australian Mustangs shot up several ROK convoys in those early days. At that time a bitter dispute developed between the Army and USAF commanders which was never resolved to the end of the war. Many Army commanders, including X Corps commander Lieutenant General Edward Almond, felt strongly that close air support was a poor relation indeed compared to strategic bombing as far as the USAF was concerned. In 1951, for example, the USAF blocked the assignment of a fighter-bomber squadron to each of the Eighth Army's corps commanders, arguing that this move would divert resources from more important missions. Those on the ground wondered what could be a "more important mission" than close air support when the enemy was close at hand and perhaps making a breakthrough. The Eighth Army continued to believe that FEAF would much rather flatten Pyongyang than knock out a roadblock. There is certainly no doubt that U.N. ground troops preferred Marine or naval air for truly close air support. (In all fairness, it should be pointed out that Marine air forces had no strategic bombing mission, and the Navy's primary interest was on tactical missions; both could thus concentrate their training on close air support.) Nonetheless, without FEAF close air support, Air Force, Navy, or Marine, there can be little doubt that the North Koreans could

have driven through to Pusan and victory sometime in the summer of 1950.

Air Defense and Air Superiority

Charged with the air defense of the entire U.S. Far East command, FEAF struggled to establish air superiority in Korea, especially from 1951 to the end of the war, as the Communists vastly increased their MIG buildup in Manchuria, just across the Yalu River dividing Korea from China. The Fifth Air Force and FEAF Bomber Command had held Communist air power at bay by implied threats of reprisal against the air bases and forces in Manchuria. However, as the war progressed, it became apparent that a formal air defense system would be required. By establishing radar surveillance units and ground control intercept radars, FEAF expanded its air defense coverage of Korea. The introduction of tactical control units and expansion of the surveillance radars (e.g., the 502nd Tactical Control Group and the 6132d Aircraft Control and Warning Squadron), and the integration of fighter aircraft into the air defense net completed FEAF's Korean air defense system. By November 1951, FEAF could divert its tactical fighters from an offensive to a defensive mission, and had the command and control network to effectively employ air power to maintain air superiority in Korea. In addition to USAF radars and fighters, the air defense team was composed of U.S. Marine aircraft and tactical control units and U.S. Army antiaircraft artillery.

The first task of tactical air power is to establish air superiority and to destroy enemy air power. Initially, orders from the U.S. Far East command did not permit the FEAF to effectively deal with the North Korean Air Force threat. That threat was increasing, and Lieutenant General George E. Stratemeyer, commanding general of FEAF until May 1951, took his case to General MacArthur to lift the restrictions so the FEAF could employ tactical air power in a wider air superiority and air defense role. General MacArthur, who was attending a conference at Suwon next to the airfield, saw the impact of tactical air power firsthand when the North Koreans launched an attack on the Suwon Airfield. The FEAF fighters shot down four of the attacking Yak fighter aircraft. Stratemeyer pressed General MacArthur to remove the restrictions, and MacArthur, sensing that the situation was grave enough to justify his action, verbally authorized Stratemeyer to commence air attacks against airfields north of the 38th parallel. On 29 June 1950, reconnaissance units flew photo cover of known North Korean airfields, and shortly thereafter the FEAF commenced tactical air attacks against targets in North Korea.

The U.N. command enjoyed air superiority except for brief periods in northwest North Korea. When the Chinese Air Force entered the war it possessed air superiority in this key area. A decision was made to attack interdiction targets in northwestern North Korea on 1 March 1951. The decision was to save the Superfortresses for use in the area known as "MIG Alley" (that area over the Yalu River border with China where MIGs from Manchuria and U.N. aircraft clashed throughout the war) with F-86 Sabres as escorts. "MIG Alley" was the first "jet-to-jet" air combat arena. On 8 November 1950, MIG-15s came up from Antung to engage the F-80C top-cover flights. "In history's first all jet battle, the swept-wing MIGs proved clearly superior to the older F-80Cs," wrote Robert F. Futrell, . . . "but the MIG pilots showed their lack of combat experience." Once the F-86s were pressed into service, the scale tipped in favor of the U.N. air forces. The F-86 Sabres tangled with the MIG-15s and between 1951 and 1953 the Sabres downed 850 MIGs, with a loss of only fifty-eight F-86s.

Rushed into combat, the F-86 Sabre proved able to overcome the Soviet-built MIG-15 in air-to-air combat. As was the case with most other air action against North Korea, the success or failure of the FEAF campaign in the Yalu/Chongchon River area would depend on the success of the Sabres in maintaining air superiority.

The F-86 Sabre was built by North American Aviation Company. The original F-86 was a straight-wing design, but North American added a version of the Luftwaffe's Messerschmitt M-262's fully-swept-wing to the F-86. The Sabre had a General Electric J-47-GE-13, 5,200-pound thrust engine that produced speeds around 650 mph. It carried six M-3 .50 caliber machine guns. Its combat range was only 490 nautical miles—one of its chief limitations. To achieve even this range, the F-86 had to carry two 120-gallon wing-tip fuel tanks.

The MIG-15 Fagot was a Soviet-built aircraft designed by the team of Artem Mikoyan and Michael I. Gurevich. The Fagot's swept-wing design also came from the German design; and the first models were powered by a Russian copy of the British Rolls-Royce Nene engine which produced 5,000 pounds of thrust with a speed of about 660 mph. The MIGs carried mixed caliber, low cyclic twin 23mm and single 37mm automatic forward-firing weapons.

Comparing performance of the two swept-wing jets, they were fairly matched in speed. At higher altitudes the MIG had better climb and zoom characteristics, but in level flight the F-86 enjoyed a slight advantage. In other flight characteristics, the Sabre appeared to be slightly better than the MIG. However, the Sabre's edge was due to its aircrews' flying abilities.

The Communist Chinese Air Force was very young and its pilots were not very skilled. For the most part, the MIG pilots hugged the Yalu River and made most attacks high and to the rear of the Sabres. While the Communists did not make maximum use of their MIGs, their garrison at Antung Airfield hampered U.N. air attacks along the Yalu River and MIG Alley.

MIG Alley posed not only a problem for the USAF in an air superiority role, but also in the interdiction role. In the month prior to November 1950, the U.N. forces observed a buildup of forces in the Yalu River area—particularly north into China and Manchuria, but also in the cities of Sinuiju, Chongsongjin, and Manpojin. The bridges across the Yalu River at the cities of Sinuiju, Chongsongjin, Namsan-ni, and Manpojin posed particular problems for the U.N. command.

On 7 November 1950, General MacArthur's air campaign directive was carried out. This directive was an all-out attack on the city of Sinuiju. It lay on the southern shore of the Yalu and directly across from the Manchurian city of Antung. The city had three bridges across the Yalu and was the seat of the fugitive Korean government. Plus it housed Communist troops and supplies. Weather prevented the 7 November attack, but on the 8th, F-80s and F-51 fighters softened up the Communist ground positions before the B-29s arrived. The MIGs came up to challenge the U.N. air forces and the result was the first air-to-air jet battle.

Interdiction Operations

General Hoyt S. Vandenberg, chief of staff of the Air Force, told General Stratemeyer that it was "axiomatic that tactical operations on the battlefield cannot be effective unless there is a simultaneous interdiction and destruction of sources behind the battlefield." Vandenberg restated this to the U.S. Congress and added that, "the proper way to use airpower is initially to stop the flow of supplies and ammunition, guns, and equipment of all kinds, at its source."

Operations were hampered from the very beginning of the Korean conflict by political considerations, and in 1951 when truce talks were beginning, the Joint Chiefs of Staff had instructed FEAF that "if Armistice discussions fail, it is of greatest importance that clear responsibility for failure rest upon the Communists." Under this rule, United Nations forces were denied any effective employment which could bring pressure upon the Communists. Unable to exercise a decisive role to speed armistice negotiations, air power, in August 1951, was once again cast into supporting the Eighth Army—which itself was limited to maintaining a stalemate along the 38th parallel. However, limited air interdiction operations were permitted to blunt the Communist attacks and counteroffensive.

For example, although the city of Rashin on the rail line to Siberia had been put off-limits to air attacks on 1 September 1950, the Joint Chiefs of Staff authorized interdiction operations against Pyongyang and Rashin on 1 August 1951. This authorization was due to aerial reconnaissance indications that the Communists were stockpiling supplies in the two cities. Two weeks after receiving authority to bomb the enemy supply and troop buildup areas in the capital city of Pyongyang, and military stockpiles in the port city of Rashin (which was only seventeen miles south of the Siberian border), units of FEAF's bomber command attacked military targets at Rashin on 26 August. (Of the more than 600,000 pounds of bombs dropped, 97 percent hit the target, the marshaling yards.) This action began a ten-month long, comprehensive railway interdiction campaign in the North.

Even with restraints, FEAF's bomber command and Fifth Air Force conducted intense interdiction missions against the North Korean railway system. By all accounts, the railway interdiction campaign was not too successful in denying supply buildups over time, but Far East command analysis indicated that the United Nations railway interdiction campaign brought some degree of pressure to bear on the Communists and markedly slowed their war effort. By laboriously bringing supplies forward, the Communists proved able to mount short, intense ground attacks, but each such attack rapidly used up stockpiles and the attacks faltered.

Other examples of interdiction missions included the bombings of the cities and bridges along the Yalu River. In November 1950, seventy B-29s came over the city of Sinuiju, on the

south shore of the Yalu, a key line of communication for the Communists, and dropped more than 584 tons of incendiary bombs. Also, nine other B-29s dropped 1,000-pound bombs on the two bridges linking Korea and China. For some reason, the MIGs from the Antung Airfield in Manchuria did not come up to challenge the U.N. air forces. Due to the altitude of the B-29s (18,000 feet), the antiaircraft flak did no damage to the bomber force and the interdiction mission was successful; 60 percent of the two-square-mile target area of Sinuiju was burned out, plus some damage was done to the approaches to the bridges.

The FEAF bomber command was also ordered to destroy the eleven international bridges at Sinuiju, Chongsongjin, Mansan-ni, Manpojin, Ongdmdong, Linchiang, Hyesanjin, Samankso, and Hoeryong and to destroy ten cities along the Yalu River and along major lines of communication. By the end of November, the bombing campaign exacted heavy damage on the ten key cities. Damage ranged from 95 percent destruction on Manpojin to 20 percent damage to Uiju. Although the destruction handed out by the medium bombers on the North Korean communication and supply centers can be assessed with little difficulty, the effect of the destruction on the Communist cities is more difficult to measure. The all-out air campaign ordered by MacArthur against the Yalu River bridges and cities was well executed but hardly accomplished the objective of stopping the movement of Chinese Communist troops into Korea.

But the lumbering World War II–vintage piston-engine B-29s, unable to track the enemy jets even with their electronic gunsights, would pay a heavy price when unescorted by the Sabres. In April 1951, three B-29s were destroyed and ten others badly damaged on daylight raids in MIG Alley. Large-scale B-29 raids against North Korean airfields in October of that same year saw no less than 150 MIGs break through escorting obsolete F-84s and shoot down five bombers while seriously damaging another eight, thus almost doubling total USAF bomber losses since the beginning of the war. A second wing of the scarce Sabres was rushed to Korea and bomber losses once again fell to "acceptable" levels.

But the USAF did not savor its triumphs much, always complaining that its jets had to wait until the MIGs had crossed the Yalu before they could engage. In fact, the Sabre pilots could often see the dust clouds kicked up by taxiing

MIGs at the Manchurian airfields but could not attack at this most vulnerable moment for their enemy.

There is no longer any question that the Soviet Air Force dominated Communist air combat over MIG Alley, although U.S. authorities were reluctant to release any proof. No less than twelve air divisions entered the war directly, deploying a maximum number of 200 aircraft and 26,000 personnel at any one time. All were based in China and no landings or take-offs were permitted in Korea, although Soviet mobile antiaircraft batteries operated as far south as Pyongyang. No radio transmissions were permitted in Russian.

A startling parallel existed between the opposing air forces in Korea. Both rotated their pilots in and out of the area of operations. More important, both were irked by restrictions imposed by their governments, and both were controlled by governments who wished no wider war. Both remained convinced that they were acting defensively and resented it. Apparently in this air war there were no aggressors. Stalin was intent on rear defense only, that is of the Yalu bridges, the Chinese and North Korean airfields, and the North Korean dams. Yet no MIG interfered with the USAF attacks on key hydroelectric facilities, or with the destruction of the even more vital rice irrigation dams. These restrictions, plus those already noted on Communist air operations over South Korea, make it obvious that the Communist air forces operated under even more strict constraints than did the USAF, and the USAF, unlike the Red Air Force, needed to make no secret of its participation. These restrictions are the more startling when it is realized that a small sliver of Soviet territory actually abuts North Korea and that on one occasion two USAF fighters rather leisurely shot up a bordering Soviet airfield without opposition. (The U.S. apologized for what was obviously the result of a serious navigational error.)

The only known case of any Communist violation of these tacit air restrictions came in November of 1952, when unmarked MIGs attacked U.N. naval Task Force 77 off the northeast coast of Korea, shooting down seven surprised U.S. Navy aircraft. The mysterious event remains unexplained to this day.

Air Reconnaissance, Transport, and Rescue Support

The combat support functions of air reconnaissance, air transport, and air rescue played a major role in the Korean War. Aerial reconnaissance was the most valuable means of obtaining intelligence of enemy activities. Of course, air reconnaissance was not only important to air forces in the planning of interdiction and close air support operations; it was of equal value to ground forces in the conduct of the operations. For example, in one month in 1953, the air reconnaissance units of FEAF furnished the Eighth Army with more than 64,000 photographic negatives which represented coverage of almost 130,000 square miles of Korean soil. (Yet the Eighth Army estimated this represented only 75 percent of their total requirement.)

The Military Air Transport Service sustained combat in Korea. Under the U.S. Far East command, the air transport control and priorities system, established in 1950, allocated airlift capacity to the combatant commands.

Neglect of airlift capability after World War II was almost disastrous, leaving the Military Air Transport Service unprepared for the Korean conflict. As a consequence, it took two months to get the first stateside reinforcement units to Korea—by boat, of course. The limitations of the existing transport fleet, consisting of military versions of commercial aircraft, spawned the requirement for uniquely military transport aircraft with global reach. However, it did not take long for the service to rally and provide support for the war effort.

The 315th Air Division (which replaced the Combat Cargo Command) provided centralized scheduling and control of FEAF airlift assets. During the Korean War, the 315th Air Division flew 210,343 sorties and employed an average of 210 air transport aircraft. The FEAF Combat Cargo Command and its successor, the 315th Air Division, flew 128,336,700 passenger miles and 15,836,400 ton-miles of cargo.

In addition to providing global air transportation for the military services, the Military Air Transport Service was also responsible for providing an air weather service and an airways and air communication service for the USAF. Under FEAF control, units of the service performed their assigned missions for the Far East command. They were attached to FEAF at the onset of the conflict.

Members of the air weather wing provided weather information not only for FEAF but also for the ground forces, as they assigned members of the wing to the two U.S. Army corps. Also, the 512th Reconnaissance Squadron Weather flew its first WB-29 "Buzzard Special" weather reconnaissance sortie over Korea on 27 June

1950. Units of the 20th Weather Squadron provided weather detachments at the airfields in South Korea. During the duration of the conflict, members of the weather wing provided air weather service and aerial weather support with flights over the North and South.

The Airways and Air Communications Service was a global command that provided airways communication facilities, navigational aids, and flight services for the USAF. A secondary mission of the Airways and Air Communications Service was to provide communication support for the Air Weather Service. These services included the operating of control towers, direction finders, radio ranges, ground-controlled approach control, instrument landing systems, radar beacons, message centers, and cryptocenters.

Units of the Airways and Air Communications Service were assigned to the FEAF to provide these services in support of the air operations in Korea. Men and equipment of the 1809th Airways and Air Communications Service Group began operations at Pusan, Taegu, and Pohang early in July 1950.

The first test of a search and rescue organization came during the Korean War. Evacuation of front-line Army casualties was the prime responsibility of the Air Rescue Service, a subordinate unit of the Military Air Transport Service. (Their operations were, however, controlled by FEAF.) In addition to air evacuation efforts, the rescue of downed aircrew members was carried out by units of the service. During the Korean War, the Air Rescue Service rescued 996 men from enemy territory and evacuated more than 8,600 men—most of whom were front-line casualties. At the beginning of the conflict air evacuation was thought of as an emergency method of transporting the sick and wounded when other methods could not be used (e.g., hospital ships and trains). However, the Korean War was a proving ground for the medical evacuation of the wounded. The rapid evacuation of the wounded to medical facilities saved many lives, and thus the use of medical air evacuation increased. At the outbreak of the war, the Military Air Transport Service was providing medical evacuation for about 350 patients a month. From the start of the war until its end in 1953, the Military Air Transport Service carried 43,196 war casualties to the U.S. for special medical treatment or further hospitalization.

Summary

The Korean War was the first conflict to test the unified military forces of the U.S. The Joint Chiefs of Staff had directed General MacArthur to establish a joint command staff to conduct the Korean War, yet for the first two and one-half years of the conflict, the U.S. Far East command operated without a joint headquarters. "The absence of this joint headquarters meant that the full force of United Nations air power was seldom effectively applied."

United Nations ground forces required the assistance of air forces to prevent the enemy from massing the full potential of its supplies, equipment, and men. In this context air interdiction assumed a new meaning. Airmen had no doubt that air interdiction was extremely important in Korea; however, many soldiers did not fully appreciate that fact. Some failed to appreciate that FEAF air attacks against the North Korean rear enabled the relatively weak U.N. ground forces to advance to the 38th parallel. Air interdiction attacks in the rear of the Communist armies were a decisive factor which allowed the Eighth Army to hold its position against enemy assaults and finally forced the enemy back across the 38th parallel. Of the three missions of tactical air power—air superiority, interdiction, and close air support—the close support of friendly forces is perhaps the most challenging and difficult. Close air support requires the cooperation of ground and air forces. Converting from an air defensive posture to tactical air support of ground forces proved to be a difficult task for the USAF from the beginning of the Korean conflict. This was due in part to the fact that the primary mission of the USAF in Korea prior to the outbreak of hostilities was to provide air defense operations. Now the tactical air forces would be required to provide another mission—one of close air support to ground forces.

The Korean War proved the validity of the USAF-U.S. Army joint air/ground operations system in the jet age. General MacArthur remarked in the spring of 1951 that "I would say the support that our tactical air has given to our ground troops in Korea has perhaps never been equaled in the history of modern war." The USAF continued throughout the war to perfect the system whereby joint Air Force and naval (Navy and Marine) air units would be responsive to the ground force requirement for tactical air support. A smoothly working joint operations center became the agency that jointly planned, coordinated, and implemented the ground and air operations.

The Korean War had an impact on the USAF in many ways. The end of the Korean War caused President Dwight D. Eisenhower to take a "new look" at the military forces and strategy requirements. The president wanted an increase in armed-force mobility, a larger ready reserve, an ever-ready professional corps, and finally, an industrial base capable of swift mobilization with an increased emphasis on continental defense. The national defense budget he submitted to Congress accounted for the increase in air power for the Air Force and Navy and the continued modernization of land and sea forces, but at a reduced level.

The combat record of the USAF in Korea was impressive. Of the more than 1 million sorties flown, the FEAF flew well over half—or 720,980—with the remainder flown by the U.S. Navy (167,552), U.S/ Marine Corps (107,303), and Allied air forces (44,873). Approximately 10 percent of all sorties flown by the USAF in Korea were close air support, 20 percent were air interdiction, 10 percent were cargo missions, 30 percent were counter-air, and 30 percent were miscellaneous sorties. The USAF expended more than 467,000 tons of bombs, napalm, rockets, and ammunition. And finally, the USAF suffered operational losses due to enemy action of approximately 800 aircraft. (The U.S. Navy and the U.S. Marine Corps lost approximately 600 aircraft due to enemy action.) In the course of its air operations, FEAF destroyed 976 enemy aircraft, 1,327 enemy tanks, 82,920 vehicles, 963 locomotives, 10,407 railway cars, 1,163 bridges, 118,231 buildings, 65 tunnels, 8,663 gun positions, 8,839 bunkers, sixteen oil storage tanks, and 539 boats and barges. Additionally, the FEAF aircrews claimed to have killed 184,808 enemy troops and made 28,671 enemy railroad cuts. (These claims are for all United Nations air forces—USAF, USMC, USN, and allied air forces.) However, by global standards the FEAF was never a large air force. In fact it was the smallest air force of any of the past conflicts. During the war FEAF averaged 840 combat-ready aircraft out of a total of 1240 aircraft.

Thomas A. Cardwell

Bibliography
Baer, Bud. "Three Years of Air War in Korea," *American Aviation* (6 July 1963).
Cardwell, Thomas A., III. *Command Structure for Theater Warfare* (Air University Press, Maxwell AFB: 1984, reprinted 1992).
Futrell, Robert F. *The United States Air Force in Korea 1950–1953* (Office of Air Force History, Washington: 1982, revised edition).
Goldberg, Alfred, ed. *A History of the United States Air Force, 1907–1957* (1957).
Momyer, William W. *Air Power in Three Wars* (GPO, Washington: 1978).
Stewart, James T. *Air Power: The Decisive Force in Korea* (1967).
Weyland, Otto P. "The Air Campaign in Korea," *Air University Quarterly Review* 6, no. 3 (Fall 1963).

See also POWER PLANTS, U.N. AIR ATTACKS ON

Air Force, U.S., Combat Cargo Command
See COMBAT CARGO COMMAND, U.S. AIR FORCE

Antiguerrilla Operations
When United Nations forces landed in Korea in mid-1950, they inherited a guerrilla problem that would demand the commitment of 30 percent of total troop strength for the next three years. Stemming from a popular but brutally repressed uprising on Cheju Island in April 1948 Communist guerrilla activities in the Republic of Korea (ROK) achieved varying degrees of success until the armistice was signed on 27 July 1953. Responsibility for conducting antiguerrilla operations fell to the Republic of Korea constabulary force, the U.S. IX Corps, and the ROK national police and security battalions.

Expressing opposition to mainland elections and other government policies, residents of Cheju-do staged a popular uprising on 3 April 1948. In response, the ROK government mobilized its constabulary force to quell the rebellion and to restore order. This year-long effort was punctuated in October by the Yosu Rebellion in which members of the Fourteenth Regiment mutinied in protest of government actions on the island. The rebels sought to obtain large supplies of weapons and to establish a guerrilla base in the Chiri Massif located in the southwest corner of the mainland. Seeking to exploit this indigenous opposition, North Korean Communists increased their efforts to reunify the peninsula, but the revolts were savagely suppressed by the authoritarian Rhee government.

Provoked by the U.S.-sponsored U.N. resolution to recognize the ROK as the only legitimate government on the Korean peninsula, the Communists renewed their emphasis on armed guerrilla struggle. Subsidized by the North Korean government and trained at the Kangdong Political Institute near Pyongyang, Communist-backed insurgents opened a major offensive in the South during the spring and summer of 1949. Numerous incursions along both sides of the 38th parallel coincided with this renewed guerrilla push. By September, guerrilla strength peaked at 3,000; an additional 10,000 to 15,000 supporters remained in base areas. Although independent guerrilla groups maintained radio contact with the North, geographic isolation prevented a coordinated effort. Little or no support arrived from the North, and many guerrillas abandoned their imminent hopes for a unified Korea. With the commencement of an ROK counterguerrilla offensive in October 1949, Communist insurgents concentrated in the Chiri Mountains, and in the eastern areas of Andong, the Odae Mountains, and the Taebaek Mountains.

Antiguerrilla operations followed a methodical process of isolating and reducing Communist strongholds. Initially, ROK forces blockaded key routes around known base areas. Furthermore, the rural population was relocated to government-controlled villages, thus creating "free fire zones" and forcing the guerrillas to forage for supplies. Finally, government forces conducted sweeps through isolated base areas, killing or capturing the bulk of the insurgents. Amnesty programs netted 40,000 defectors in a five-week period, and from September 1949 to April 1950, ROK forces reported 5,000 guerrillas killed. Consequently, many disheartened guerrilla leaders returned to the North where they made preparations for the forceful "liberation" of Korea south of the 38th parallel. In the spring of 1950, North Korean military forces attempted a final guerrilla-based coup d'etat in the South, which failed. By June, northern guerrilla efforts in the South were virtually nonexistent. Thus, the failure of insurrection opened the way for a new phase of conflict—conventional military attack.

In spite of the successful antiguerrilla operations, not all of the estimated 27,000 remaining Communist guerrillas left the South. The North Korean attack of 25 June 1950 and the ensuing Allied retreat provided ample opportunity for once-dormant guerrillas to rejoin the Communist cause. With the successful U.N. landing at Inchon and the subsequent advance north of the 38th parallel, guerrilla warfare intensified behind U.N. lines. In November 1950, U.S. X Corps, operating on the eastern side of the peninsula, identified sixty-two different organizations, and guerrilla activity gradually moved northward to the mountains west of Hungnam. The X Corps intelligence office recorded 109 separate guerrilla attacks during the month of November. Farther west, in Eighth Army's sector, 4,000 guerrillas operated in the vicinity of the Iron Triangle—a flat area bounded by the cities of Chorwon in the west, Kumhwa in the east, and Pyongyang in the north. This vital road and rail center linked the east and west coasts and served as the hub of the Communist communications nets to the South.

Northern guerrillas continued throughout the South, with an estimated 5,400 armed insurgents operating in the southwest region of Chiri-san. These insurgents harassed isolated villages, ambushed patrols, fired on trains, cut telephone lines, and attacked South Korean police stations. But U.N. counterguerrilla operations, coordinated by the U.S. IX Corps, achieved considerable success. Centered on Taejon, the U.S. 2nd Division operated to the west and southwest while the 25th Division directed its efforts to the south and east. Several smaller elements patrolled to the north, but guerrilla efforts increased through November 1951. Finally, on 1 December, ROK President Syngman Rhee declared martial law in southwestern Korea. The ROK government restricted the movement of civilians, established a curfew, and severed telephone connections between villages.

Immediately thereafter, the ROK Army initiated a concerted antiguerrilla campaign sardonically dubbed Operation Ratkiller. Led by Lieutenant General Paik Sun Yup, the ROK 8th Division pushed southward through Chiri-san while the Capital Division moved north. The national police, youth regiments, and local security units served as blocking forces along projected guerrilla escape routes. Flushing the Communist insurgents from their bases, ROK forces terminated Phase I of Ratkiller on 14 December, reporting 1,612 guerrillas killed and 1,842 prisoners. Phase II continued until 31 December when general headquarters of the Far East command (GHQ FEC) determined that Communist guerrillas no longer presented a threat to U.N. operations. Nevertheless, Phase

III extended from 6 January 1952 through the end of the month. Counterguerrilla units continued to encounter scattered resistance until the termination of Operation Ratkiller on 15 March. United Nations forces reported 9,789 guerrillas killed and 9,383 captured before relinquishing responsibility to local authorities.

After Ratkiller, guerrillas continued to harass U.N. lines of communication, but these operations constituted more of a nuisance than a serious threat. The ROK 1st Division, national police, and security battalions established four security command sectors in South Korea. By guarding key installations and transportation routes, these elements effectively identified and isolated remaining guerrilla bands. Surrounding the insurgents, ROK forces pounded them with a combination of mortar and artillery fire, armored forces, air strikes, and propaganda. Ultimately, the armistice and its political repercussions changed the nature of warfare in Korea and closed this phase of antiguerrilla operations.

Guerrilla operations in South Korea never posed a serious threat to the security of the Seoul government. The guerrillas operated in areas that lacked natural cover and were cut off from outside support. Finally, the U.N. command did not hesitate to use extensive and ruthless methods of suppression.

James Sanders Day

Bibliography

Appleman, Roy Edgar. *South to the Naktong, North to the Yalu* (Office of the Chief of Military History, Washington: 1961).

Cumings, Bruce, ed. *Child of Conflict* (1983).

Hermes, Walter. *Truce Tent and Fighting Front* (Office of the Chief of Military History, Washington: 1966).

Schnabel, James F. *Policy and Direction: The First Year* (Office of the Chief of Military History, Washington: 1972).

Schuetta, Lawrence V. "Guerrilla Warfare and Airpower in Korea, 1950–1953," photocopy of typescript (Aerospace Studies Institute, Maxwell AFB, AL: January 1964).

Antiwar Sentiment in the Korean War, 1950–1953

Antiwar sentiment during the Korean War presents some interesting paradoxes. At the outset, the American people gave their president immediate and widespread support, but as the prospect of quick victory faded and the war turned into a stalemate, the people became war-weary and frustrated. In contrast, among the soldiers fighting the war, morale was generally low at the beginning and improved noticeably later. Even when the war grew unpopular, American public opinion remained strongly anti-Communist, and those who sympathized with the enemy received short shrift. Opposition to the war involved more questions of method and expediency than of morality or pacifism. Yet it seems certain that the Korean War became, in the end, the most unpopular war the United States had engaged in up to that time.

When President Harry S. Truman on 30 June 1950 announced that United States forces would be sent to Korea, public reaction strongly supported his decision. A few Republicans in the Senate asked whether the president was taking on himself the power to declare war—a question reminiscent of the Mexican War controversy a century before. There were small leftist protests, mainly in New York City, but the voices of protest were drowned in the rising tide of public acclaim; White House mail ran 10 to 1 in favor of Truman's stand. The honeymoon lasted until Chinese Communist troops entered the conflict in November and what had promised to be an easy victory turned into a war of attrition. After the spring of 1951, a feeling of frustration, based on emotional rather than rational grounds, developed. But the opposition to the war never solidified in support of any well-defined alternative. Americans did not seem to know what they wanted—the bombing of Red China, the withdrawal of troops from Korea, an all-out war with the USSR, or a negotiated settlement. All they knew by 1951 was that they were sick and tired of the seemingly endless war. Those with relatives fighting in Korea were, of course, the most emotional in their attitude toward the conflict, but anger, resentment, and bewilderment became well-nigh universal.

The Korean War was a new and unfamiliar kind of conflict for the American people. In the two world wars of the twentieth century, the United States had waged "total war for total victory." To a generation reared in this tradition, the Korean "police action," with its political limitations on the scale of military action, was incomprehensible. People who at first supported the war in the same crusading spirit they had displayed in World War II grew unwilling to accept the human losses and the material cost when the ultimate goal became simply a stalemate. In some cases, anger and confusion gave way to apathy; the so-called police action went on and on, monotonous and interminable. Some ignored it completely; others hardly knew it was being fought.

Public opinion polls, conducted at intervals during the war, are useful in tracing the changing mood of the American people from optimism to disillusionment. An Elmo Roper survey made just after the outbreak of hostilities revealed that 75 percent of the people supported Truman's decision to commit United States forces in Korea. A Gallup poll in October 1950 showed 65 percent in favor of the decision to defend South Korea. But by early 1951 public opinion had altered drastically with the changing military situation in the Far East. In January, 66 percent believed the United States should pull out of Korea; 49 percent thought the United States had made a mistake in going to war, although 55 percent still believed that Truman was right in his original decision to intervene with American troops.

By 1952 public opinion was even more confused. A new Elmo Roper survey asked whether the United States should fight the USSR, work out an agreement even though it would involve important concessions to the Communists, or build up United States strength to such a point that the USSR would not dare to start a war. About 10 percent wanted all-out war, slightly over 10 percent wanted a settlement, and 63 percent voted for "peace through strength." But a further check of the 63 percent revealed important divisions. Only 26 percent were willing to endure a thirty-year Cold War with periodic flare-ups like the Korean conflict. A clear majority of the American people were not inclined to bear the brunt of future "police actions," but there was no agreement on an alternative policy.

A very small and relatively ineffective Communist and leftist group did attack the war as a rampant case of U.S. imperialism, an example of American support for antidemocratic regimes. One of its principal targets was the black American. The *Daily Worker* and other Communist publications began to emphasize race. Korea was called a war of color. Negroes who supported the war were helping American imperialism against the colored peoples of Asia, stated the party line. *Daily Worker* columnist John Pittman, writing in *Masses and Mainstream* in 1950, declared that Negroes saw the conflict as a white man's war and that they believed that America was replacing Europe in the enslavement of Asia and Africa. William Z. Foster spoke of the Korean War as "hated and reactionary" and avowed that the Negro people of the United States would not support it. Paul Robeson made his famous declaration that Negroes would never fight against the USSR.

Many blacks did, indeed, urge that the United States put its own house in order before attempting to deal with the problems of Asia. Their main concern, however, was with the civil rights movement. Almost all black publications rejected the Communist "race war" charges. *Ebony* magazine denounced the Communists for following the same technique the Japanese had utilized in World War II—a technique which the Communists themselves had loudly condemned at the time. Color was not involved in the Korean War, *Ebony* stated. Negroes were ready to fight for the American way of life while still trying to change it for the better.

Ebony and other black publications gave one answer to the Communist race war charges; another was provided by blacks fighting in Korea. Some headway had been made in the integration of the armed forces prior to 1950, but the war accelerated the process considerably. As the Army discovered that blacks performed far more effectively in integrated than in segregated units, the resulting process in eliminating segregation did much to counter the Communist "race war" propaganda. Though the process was far from complete in 1953, the impetus which the Korean War gave to armed forces integration was an immense step forward in the civil rights movement.

With all the confusion, disillusion, and resentment on the home front, the organized pacifist movement should have been in the vanguard of the opposition. But this was not the case; in fact, the initial public support for the Korean War virtually destroyed the post–World War II peace movement in the United States. Many pacifist groups approved the concept of police action under United Nations auspices; the United World Federalists, the socialists, and the Wallace progressives all supported the war, thus giving the lie to the old charges that such groups were somehow pro-Communist. The only vocal opposition came from die-hard pacifists, a few extreme isolationists, and members of the American Communist party. Those radical pacifists who were critical of United States foreign policy continued their activities in a small way; a favorite technique of protest was to refuse to register for the draft. The pacifist-anarchist periodical *Alternative* was banned from the mails by the New York postmaster because it urged readers to refuse to be drafted.

Individual socialists and pacifists took divergent and often contradictory views of the Korean War. The "independent socialist publication," *The Monthly Review*, portrayed the conflict as a civil war in which the United States had no business intervening. It also sponsored I. F. Stone's *Hidden History of the Korean War*, published in April 1952. Stone advanced the theory that Syngman Rhee's government had deliberately provoked the North Korean attack in the hope of securing United Nations intervention and the eventual unification of the country under Western auspices. According to Stone, the United States and the United Nations were the dupes of a cynical plot on the part of the corrupt South Korean government. (The biggest logical flaw in Stone's argument was the lack of any explanation as to how such a devious plot still almost lost Rhee his country.) A. J. Muste, a radical pacifist, took a similar but more balanced view of the conflict. He also believed that the "far from ideal" Rhee government had probably invited aggression, and he pointed out that from the point of view of Asians the United States looked like an aggressor and a warmonger. Muste argued that in the long run the Korean War would work to the advantage of the Communist ideology by providing conditions under which Communism could flourish. He urged widespread adoption of the principles of pacifism and conscientious objection and advocated a negotiated settlement to end the war.

Norman Thomas, the grand old man of American socialism, took a more conservative stand and one fairly typical of the majority of American socialists and liberals. A group of them, including Thomas, sponsored a manifesto sent in 1951 to their friends in Europe and Asia, declaring that the United States was not acting in the interests of American capitalism in supporting the United Nations in Korea, but was taking part in a worldwide struggle between democracy and totalitarianism. Thomas clung to his belief that universal and total disarmament was the world's one hope for peace, but insisted this goal could not be achieved as long as the Soviet Union and Red China supported aggressive war in Korea.

Aside from pacifists and Communists, a group of neo-isolationists opposed the war in Korea, charging that it was the unnecessary consequence of faulty policy. This group's solution to the dilemma was a unilateral policy; the United States should withdraw from all international alliances and if necessary fight the USSR alone. The neo-isolationists believed the chief Communist threat would come in Asia rather than in Europe, and they repeatedly criticized President Truman's preoccupation with the European situation.

The isolationists found their spokesman in Senator Robert A. Taft of Ohio, who early accused Truman of violating the Constitution in sending troops to Korea without congressional approval. Taft advocated pulling out of Korea entirely and setting up a new Pacific defense line based on Taiwan and Japan. The senator called Korea an "unnecessary conflict" that could have been prevented by common sense and a planned program against Communism. Truman and Secretary of State Dean Acheson had invited the North Korean attack, he charged, by publicly placing Korea outside the perimeter of American defense.

The whole mass sense of frustration at the course of the war found a natural outlet in the uproar over President Truman's dismissal of General Douglas MacArthur in April 1951. The reception given MacArthur obviously did not reflect antiwar sentiment, and his aggressive program to carry the war to China was anathema both to the leftist antiwar groups and the liberals who supported Truman's policies. But all the confusion and resentment of a bewildered people went into the ovation given MacArthur.

President Truman won a grudging approval from the American public in his contest with the general, but the growing unpopularity of the war became a burden he had to carry for the rest of his political life. The neo-isolationists seized on the MacArthur program. As Selig Adler wrote, men who had "been hysterically calling for a halt to the bloodshed in Korea now deified the man who wanted to carry the war into Manchuria." It was a commentary on the extent of confusion in the minds of the public over the Korean issue.

Amid the general confusion and disillusionment, it was inevitable that partisan politics should enter the picture. Korean reverses broke the post–World War II bipartisanship in foreign affairs. Political overtones were obvious as early as November of 1950, when the Democrats lost heavily in the midterm elections. Public dissatisfaction with the Korean War was a major factor in every area where the Republicans gained ground. But the major political confrontation came in the 1952 presidential election.

Korea was a ready-made issue for the Republicans to exploit; people were already referring derisively to "Mr. Truman's War," as they had referred to "Mr. Madison's War" a century and a half before. And the opposition party made the most of its opportunities.

By the opening of the 1952 campaign, antiwar sentiment had reached a new high. The Republican platform of that year charged that Truman had invited the Korean aggression, and that the war had been conducted without the will to victory. Eisenhower and his strategists saw the anomaly of a populace which hated communism but wanted relief from the war. They formulated a strategy which won the election, charging that the war was the avoidable blunder of a corrupt administration. The Korean affair had been so badly botched that the only alternative was to settle it quickly and honorably. The new Republican foreign policy would be to wage the Cold War with such pressure that the Communists would fear to start hot wars. Only a new administration could achieve this; the Democrats were too committed to their bankrupt policy.

Early in the campaign, Eisenhower began to reap political capital from the conflict. As he became increasingly conscious of popular dislike for the war, the general sharpened his attack, and by the end of the campaign was emphasizing this issue almost exclusively. He won a landslide victory. Selig Adler, in analyzing the result, contends that "Korea was the ultimate argument that convinced the masses that it was time for a change." It was the Achilles' heel of the Democratic campaign—one issue on which any Democratic answer had little chance. The Army had been denied air support and a naval blockade, and the commanding general had been removed in the middle of the campaign. When the war had been won despite all obstacles, the critics charged, Truman gave away the victory.

Antiwar dissent during the Korean War found its ultimate expression then in the repudiation of a Democratic administration and the election of Eisenhower. This dissent was neither an expression of antimilitarism nor a rejection of the basic philosophy of opposition to Communist aggression that had led to the decision for war in the first place. Indeed, many high-ranking military men, notably General James A. Van Fleet, supported the opposition to Truman's policies. It was not the kind of dissent that could be dealt with by any of the methods used in the Civil War or World Wars I and II,

particularly since the Korean conflict was not a formally declared war. Actual and suspected Communist sympathizers in all walks of life were dealt with roughly during the war—it was the era of Senator Joseph R. McCarthy's intensive search for subversives in government. But the anti-Communist drive could in no way be equated with support for "Mr. Truman's War," for much of its purpose appeared to be to prove that the Democratic administration had brought on the war because it was "soft on communism."

The confusion and resentment that marked American public opinion found some reflection in the armed forces themselves. The military services had been obliged to rebuild their strength hastily from the low post–World War II levels. The Army grew from 593,000 men in June 1950 to more than 1,500,000 a year later. While the war in Korea gave the main impetus to rearmament, the administration's eye was on Europe and the danger of a major Soviet move in that area. In order to preserve organized units for an emergency that might arise in Europe or elsewhere, the Army had to rely heavily on volunteer and inactive reservists to fight in Korea in the early stages of the war. Many of these men were World War II veterans, reluctant to put themselves in "double jeopardy" in a partial mobilization. There was extensive criticism of this policy from the public, Congress, and the press, and the Army had difficulty in defending it.

The fact was that the Army had no quick remedies for an inadequate reserve structure. More organized reserve units were called to active duty as the war wore on (six National Guard divisions were called up and four sent to the Far East), and as fast as selectees could be trained the World War II veterans were released. But the operation of the draft also involved a delicate question of who should serve in a limited war that did not require the all-out manpower mobilization of World War II. The vagaries and inequities of service in Korea contributed to the general discontent with the Korean War, affecting particularly the families of those engaged in the fighting.

Despite the unpopularity of the draft, there was no organized draft resistance movement during the Korean War. Evasion seems to have been of no greater proportion than in World War II. Between 1948 and 1953, the names of only 36,933 men failing to report for induction were forwarded to the Justice Department out of a total of 1.5 million inductees. About two-thirds of these cases occurred during the Korean War. One reason for the lack of an organized antiwar or antidraft movement may have been the preferential treatment given college students. The Universal Military Training and Service Act of 1951 set up a twofold criterion for student deferment—class standing and score on a college qualifying test. Under this system, any student who was relatively proficient in his studies could be eligible for a student deferment. The final decision was left to local draft boards, but they in practice normally awarded student deferments. Undoubtedly some college students were drafted during the Korean War, but the number appears to have been proportionately much smaller than that for eligible males in general.

The problem of conscientious objection seems also to have been about on the scale of that of World War II and to have been handled in much the same way. Objectors were classified 1-O if opposed to all military service, 1-A-O if opposed only to combat service. No figures are available as to the number of men classified 1-A-O, since they were considered an integral part of class 1-A, but the number was small and the men served creditably in noncombat positions. The class 1-O men were the ones who posed the problem.

In June 1951, amendments to the Selective Service Act provided that all 1-O registrants would be required to serve twenty-four consecutive months in civilian work contributing to the national health, safety, or interest. Responsibility for initiating such civilian work programs, as well as for ruling on claims of conscientious objectors, again was vested in the local draft boards. Religious training and belief remained the only criterion; "rational, political, and philosophical" objections were not recognized.

By June of 1951, 8,609 men had been classified as conscientious objectors, representing 0.1 percent of a total of more than 10 million men classified by selective service. By June 1952 the number had decreased to 7,601. Numerous problems, mainly lack of funds, delayed initiation of the work program until 1953. In June of that year, the total number of conscientious objector registrants had fallen to 6,552, of which 2,763 were at work. Many of the objectors, as in World Wars I and II, refused to accept any work assignment.

What the state of troop morale was during the Korean conflict is one of the more baffling questions of the war. Individual evaluations vary widely, but in general, morale seemed to have fluctuated with the fortunes of the United Nations forces. Initial overconfidence gave way in many cases to bitterness and disillusion during the early Communist drive south. Spirits revived with the Inchon landings and the drive to the Yalu, then plummeted as the United Nations forces were pushed south by the Chinese. This was the low point, the period of the "bugout." And it was this dispirited army which General Matthew B. Ridgway discovered when he took command of the troops in Korea in December of 1950. But in three months Ridgway had more than restored the fighting spirit of his men.

As the war settled into stalemate, troop morale found its own level—neither extremely high nor disastrously low. The men still disliked the war, Korea, and the life they led, and they continued to be baffled by the political objectives involved. It could in fact be argued that the soldiers, even more than the civilians, were unable to understand and accept the concept of limited war. But there were no more of the drastic swings of morale which had marked the first six months of the struggle. Many of the troops seemed almost indifferent to political events at home and even to changes in military strategy. A spirit of fatalism was in evidence, an attitude summed up in the popular expression, "That's the way the ball bounces."

One important morale factor was rotation, or the "big R." Combat troops were sent home at the end of a year's service, or whenever replacements became available. The turnover caused many headaches at the staff level and was wasteful of manpower, but it was unquestionably a morale booster. The necessity for a generous rotation policy, nevertheless, was indicative of the relative unpopularity of service in Korea.

Desertion, as usual in wartime, was a substantial problem. According to personnel records, no less than 57,776 enlisted men dropped from the rolls as deserters during the period 1 July 1951 to 31 May 1953—an average of 2,512 per month. Of these, a mere 6,659 were later apprehended and convicted. But in all three areas of overt antiwar action—draft evasion, conscientious objection, and desertion—offenders represented a very small minority of the total number of men registered and inducted into service. Their resistance was thus reduced to a token gesture in the eyes of the general public and had very little if any adverse effect on the overall war effort.

A

The most serious problem faced by the Army—and the most publicized—grew out of the real or apparent defections of American troops who had fallen into Chinese and North Korean hands. The prisoner of war story burst upon the nation, adding the word "brainwashing" to the language. A large proportion of U.S. soldiers in the Korean War, though they fought well, were seemingly too uncertain about the cause they were fighting for to withstand Communist pressures in prison. For the bulk of the prisoners, the story ended with repatriation, but the more notorious collaborators returned home to face court-martial charges that dragged on for years. The public furor eventually died down, but the experience forced the Army to reevaluate its whole concept of troop indoctrination and to develop a sterner code of conduct for military personnel.

The armistice signed on 27 July 1953 ending the Korean War left Korea divided, but the South Korean republic was far stronger than it had been in June 1950. The end of the war saw no massive demobilization such as that following World War I or World War II, but it did bring a change in American military policy. In the 1952 election the people had demonstrated that they would not stand for a prolonged limited war under conditions of stalemate (which, of course, is exactly what they got a decade or so later in Vietnam). In the ensuing years the Korean War would be looked on as an aberration, much as American entry into World War I had been regarded in the 1930s. The new administration accepted the need for a strong American defense posture but its policy of massive retaliation—stressing nuclear air power— seemed to promise "no more Koreas."

R. W. Coakley
P.J. Scheips
E.J. Wright with G. Horne

Bibliography

Adler, Selig. *The Isolationist Impulse* (1957).
Banks, Samuel. "The Korean Conflict," *Negro History Bulletin* 36, no. 6 (1973).
Coakley, Robert W., et al. *Antiwar Sentiment* (Office of the Chief of Military History, Washington: 11 March 1970).
Daily Worker. 1950–1951.
Griffith, Robert. "The Chilling Effect," *Wilson Quarterly*, 2, no. 3 (1978).
Harris, Louis. "Is There a Republican Majority?" *Political Trends, 1952–1956* (1954).
Horne, Gerald. *Communist Front? The Civil Rights Congress, 1946–1956* (London: 1988).
Masses and Mainstream. 1950.
Suchman, E.A. "Attitudes Toward the Korean War," *Public Opinion Quarterly*, 18 (Summer 1953).

Armistice Negotiations

After the Communist offensives in the spring of 1951, combat action subsided and the battle lines stabilized in the general vicinity of the 38th parallel, where the fighting had begun. With the status quo restored in the main, each side could claim some measure of success. Prospects for a military decision, however, dissipated as the opponents dug in and fortified their positions in depth. Under these conditions, continued stalemate or a negotiated agreement became the main alternatives since major offensives would require a high cost in casualties to breech the new defensive lines.

The Communists had spurned or ignored earlier attempts to initiate negotiations, but on 23 June Jacob Malik, the Soviet delegate to the United Nations, suggested that the belligerents discuss the possibilities of a cease-fire. The United States and its allies quickly instructed General Matthew B. Ridgway, the United Nations commander, to arrange a military settlement that would bring the fighting to a halt and reduce the heavy drain in manpower and funds. Since the Communists might not be ready to seek a permanent political settlement in Korea, the United States sought an agreement that would endure over an extended period of time. At the same time, General Ridgway was told to avoid any discussions of political matters, such as a return to the 38th parallel as a boundary, the seating of Communist China in the United Nations, or the future disposition of Taiwan.

The first contact with the Communists across the conference table came on 8 July when liaison officers met at Kaesong, the old capital of Korea, located just below the 38th parallel and thirty-five miles northwest of Seoul. Two days later the plenary sessions began amid high hopes that the conflict would soon be brought to an end; there was no indication that it would take more than two years to reach an agreement on an armistice. But it was obvious even at the time that when the Chinese delegates sat down as equals before the U.N. command representatives, the world power balance, at least in Asia, was for the foreseeable future profoundly changed. Certainly in this case, power for the Chinese had indeed "grown out of the barrel of a gun."

To head the United Nations command (UNC) truce team, Ridgway selected his capable naval commander, Vice Admiral C. Turner Joy. Together, they chose the other four members of the delegation: Major General Henry I. Hodes of the Army, Major General Laurence C. Craigie of the Air Force, Rear Admiral Arleigh A. Burke of the Navy, and Major General Paik Sun Yup of the Republic of Korea (ROK) Army. All five men were military professionals and had little or no political or diplomatic experience.

Across the table, the Communists had assembled a formidable group of negotiators. Chief delegate and nominal leader was General Nam Il, chief of staff of the North Korean Army and vice premier of the Communist regime. Assisting him were four other officers with both political and military experience, including Major General Lee Sang Cho, chief of the Reconnaissance Bureau of the North Korean Army and a former vice minister of commerce, and Major General Hsieh Fang, chief of propaganda of the Northeast Military District of China. According to many UNC observers, General Hsieh directed the Communist truce operations at Kaesong.

It took two weeks just to hammer out an agenda, as the Communists tried unsuccessfully to incorporate the restoration of the 38th parallel and the withdrawal of all foreign troops from Korea. When they met firm resistance from the UNC delegation, they finally settled for consideration of four major topics: establishment of a military demarcation line and a demilitarized zone; arrangements for the setting up of a supervisory organization to make sure that the terms of the armistice were carried out; disposition of prisoners of war (POWs); and recommendations to the concerned governments regarding follow-up actions after the truce was in operation. Each of these topics was assigned to a subcommittee so that negotiations could proceed concurrently rather than serially.

The UNC team discovered at the outset that the Communists were hard bargainers, yet highly sensitive to matters of tradition, protocol, and equality. Any effort or seeming effort by the UNC delegation to demonstrate superiority of any kind was swiftly countered by the Communists, since the matter of preserving "face" was of major importance in the Orient. When the UNC members brought in a small

UNC flag and stand to the meetings, the Communists responded with a larger flag and stand. The construction of modest sanitation facilities at the truce site for the UNC staff was quickly followed by the erection of a larger facility for the Communists that was brightly painted and landscaped as well. Admiral Joy, the senior UNC delegate, had a sedan to transport him to the conference building, the Communists imported a vehicle from the Soviet Union so that General Nam could arrive in similar style.

As the meetings that followed the settlement of the agenda got underway, the UNC delegation also found out that the Communists would use any tactic that would gain them an advantage. Bluster, rudeness, and profanity were a familiar part of the Communists arsenal when they wished to hector the opposition and secure concessions. Since few of the UNC staff members understood either Korean or Chinese, the rough words and insults lost much of their impact when they were later translated into English. On the other hand, the Communists could shift overnight from harsh, browbeating, name-calling attacks to quiet, reasonable, and businesslike approaches when they had determined that they could secure no more concessions on an issue and were ready to settle the matter.

The UNC team also discovered that the Communists were experienced and strong on substantive issues, but less rigid about procedural matters. In the latter area, the UNC staff members found that the Communists would never accept any of their proposals in toto; they deliberately would insert an error into a proposed agreement for the Communists to find, confident that their counterparts would probably leave the rest of the text alone. The enemy staff members, on the other hand, were tough negotiators throughout the lengthy discussions and regarded any effort on the part of the UNC team to reach quick compromises with suspicion. Every concession had to be matched by a demand for a similar Communist concession. The Communists understood and respected the principles of horse trading; gift horses were always looked in the mouth.

One favorite Communist technique was to let the UNC make the first proposals. By outwaiting their opponents, the Communists could accept the portions favorable to their position and haggle for more. Eventually, when they saw that the UNC would not yield further, they would bring forth their counter offer. In the debates that ensued, the Communists revealed

A

a consistent pattern of response; as long as they continued to argue a point, the door was still open to trading, but when they refused to discuss the matter any further, they had arrived at their final position. The key attributes in dealing with the Communists, the UNC delegation soon came to realize, were calmness, firmness, and patience.

Shortly after the truce discussions began, charges of violations of the Kaesong conference area surfaced and continued to hamper efforts to reach substantive agreements throughout the next two years. The first serious occurrence took place on 4 August when a company of fully armed Communist troops marched through the conference site and the UNC delegation promptly suspended the negotiations for five days until assurances were received that there would be no further recurrence of such blatant violations. Shocked by the strong UNC action and the attendant unfavorable publicity that it garnered in the world press, the Communists launched a flood of protests in the succeeding days and culminated their counteroffensive on 23 August. Claiming that a UNC plane had bombed the conference site, they rejected the UNC refutation of the charge and declared an indefinite suspension of the talks. Although the liaison officers continued to meet in the interim to discuss changing the site of the talks from Kaesong to Panmunjom, a village about five miles west of Kaesong, and rules and regulations that would reduce violations in the future, the plenary sessions did not resume until October.

In the meantime, the Communists had strengthened their forces and built up their military supplies in North Korea. With the possibility of an armistice in the near future, there appeared to be little reason for the UNC to mount offensives for objectives that might later have to be surrendered when a settlement was reached. But General James Van Fleet, the Eighth Army commander, became concerned that his troops had lost their edge during the early summer period of inactivity at the front and decided to carry out limited attacks to straighten out sags in the UNC's defensive lines, maintain pressure on the enemy, and keep his troops in combat condition.

In late July, Van Fleet mounted the first offensive action since the truce talks had started in the area known as the Punchbowl located about twenty miles northeast of the Hwachon Reservoir. Using the U.S. 2nd Infantry Division as the main attack force, the UNC won a foot-

hold in the area in July and then, in August, broadened the attack to include Bloody and Heartbreak Ridges, located about four miles west of the Punchbowl. The U.S. 1st Marine Division and elements of the ROK 7th, 8th, 11th and Capital Divisions joined the assault to wrest the fiercely defended terrain from the Communists during the ensuing two months. When the UNC troops concluded the successful attacks in mid-October, the cost in casualties was high, with the U.S. 2nd Division alone suffering more than 6,000 during the offensive.

Determined to sustain pressure on the enemy, Van Fleet also conducted a modest advance of about six miles on a line roughly from Munsan-ni on the west to Kumsong in the central sector of the front. Three U.S. divisions—the 1st Cavalry, 3rd Infantry, and 25th Infantry—the British 1st Commonwealth Division, and the ROK 1st Division participated in this offensive during October and removed this salient in the line. Communist resistance was again intense and the 1st Cavalry Division took more than 2,900 of the 4,000 casualties suffered by the UNC forces in the advance.

But the punishing "elbowing forward" tactics of the Eighth Army had given the UNC the battlefield initiative and kept the enemy off balance as well as inflicting thousands of casualties on the Communist combat units. The limited offensives at the front coupled with UNC air and naval attacks helped persuade the enemy to resume the truce talks in October.

When the plenary session resumed at the new conference site at Panmunjom on 25 October, the delegates began to iron out their differences on Item 2, the military demarcation line and the demilitarized zone. Before the talks had broken off, the Communists had worked diligently for the restoration of the 38th parallel as the military demarcation line and the UNC had firmly rejected all attempts to consider a return to the old boundary line. In an effort to shake the Communist stand, Admiral Joy had offered a novel approach to solving that problem. Since the UNC controlled the sea and the air over Korea, he had contended that the enemy should compensate the UNC for giving up its sea and air superiority by surrendering additional land territory at the front. Joy's proposal to break up the overall military power into component parts and give them separate values for bargaining purposes was an interesting gamble, but it had met with swift and rude rejection by the Communists. General Nam Il had maintained that the current battle lines reflected the concentrated expression of the total military effectiveness of the UNC land, sea, and air forces. When Joy had pointed out that Japan had been defeated in World War II without a single enemy soldier setting foot on the home islands, Nam had even derided the claim that the United States had vanquished Japan at all and had insisted that the entry of the Soviet Union into the war had provided the crushing blow. Nevertheless, the Joy proposal did provide a trade-off in settling the differences between the two sides over the military demarcation line when the October sessions began.

The Communist spurning of the UNC offers to trade territory and the UNC refusal to talk about the 38th parallel finally led the conferees to accept the current battle line as the line of demarcation on 27 November. The line dipped south of the 38th parallel in the west and arced north of the parallel in the east. The Communist insistence on completing the work on the line of demarcation before taking up the other three agenda items aroused General Ridgway's suspicions. Although the UNC insisted that the line would only be valid for thirty days, it soon became apparent that the enemy intended to make the line a permanent rather than a temporary arrangement, and had, in effect, gained a de facto cease-fire, as Ridgway had predicted. Almost immediately, military operations slowed down and the Communists showed no disposition to reach swift agreement on the remaining items before the thirty-day limit expired.

Debate on Item 3—the establishment of a supervisory organization to ensure that both sides complied with the terms of the armistice—got underway in December 1951. After preliminary skirmishing, three basic questions emerged: Who would carry out the inspections behind the lines to report on violations? How much inspection would be permitted? Would the rehabilitation or construction of airfields be allowed during the armistice?

Although the Communists eventually suggested that neutral nations be named to do the inspecting, they ran into adamant opposition when they tried to designate the Soviet Union as one of their choices. Considering the major role the Soviet Union had played in supporting the North Korean and Communist Chinese military effort, the UNC refused to accept the USSR as part of a neutral nation supervisory organization.

On the question of inspection, which the Communists traditionally had opposed in the past, it was the UNC, surprisingly enough, that proposed to limit neutral inspection teams to selected ports of entry and centers of communication. General Ridgway maintained that the Communists would probably exploit the privilege of unlimited inspection for intelligence purposes and held that the neutral inspection teams could adequately check on the arrivals and departures of men and material. Since the Communists were willing to accept limited inspection, the discussions settled down to the designation of the number and location of the inspection points.

The second major stumbling block on Item 3 arose when the UNC insisted that there should be no rehabilitation or construction of airfields during the armistice. Both Ridgway and Joy contended that the enemy should not be allowed to take advantage of the truce to strengthen its air potential in North Korea. But the Communists rejected all efforts to place restrictions on airfields just as resolutely as the UNC resisted Communist attempts to name the Soviet Union as a neutral nation.

With the major differences on Item 3 reduced to two, compromise again was reached. Poland and Czechoslovakia became the Communists' nominees for the Neutral Nations Supervisory Commission, and Sweden and Switzerland were the choices by the UNC delegation to complete the membership of that group. Now that the Communists had dropped the Soviet Union from their list of candidates, the UNC withdrew its insistence on airfield restrictions.

Final agreement on Item 3 also included the acceptance of twenty neutral nation teams to carry out the inspections, with ten to be assigned to five ports of entry on each side. Replacement of materiel was to be on a one-for-one basis only and no more than 35,000 troops were to be rotated in any one month, again on a one-for-one basis. To handle all violations of the truce and the supervision and administration of the demilitarized zone, the negotiators established a military armistice commission that would operate out of Panmunjom.

While arrangements for Item 3 were well underway, the opening discussions on Item 4, the repatriation of prisoners of war, took place. Although neither the United States nor North Korea had ratified the Geneva Convention of 1949 on prisoners of war, both had agreed to abide by its stipulations. Since Article 118 of the convention clearly stated that all prisoners of war shall be released and repatriated without delay at the end of hostilities, there appeared to be little room for dispute. Yet difficulties arose at the outset on the exchange of prisoners and steadily mounted as the issue became burdened with fundamentally divisive elements. A series of conflicts broke out between the rights of the individual and those of the majority, between legal rights and human rights, and between humanitarianism and Communist pride.

The first evidence of trouble appeared just before Christmas 1951, when the two sides exchanged lists of prisoners of war. The UNC rosters contained the names of 132,000 prisoners of war in addition to another 37,000 recently reclassified as civilian internees. Since the Communists claimed that they were missing about 188,000 personnel, the UNC holdings represented about 90 percent of the Communist total. On the other hand, the Communist list contained only about 11,500 names—7,100 South Koreans and 4,400 U.N. personnel—despite their claim that they had taken 65,000 prisoners and the UNC listing 88,000 South Koreans and 11,500 U.S. troops as missing in action. The Communist list, therefore, comprised only about 12 percent of the UNC total, a remarkable disparity.

Pressed to explain the great difference between the two totals, the Communists maintained that their lists were small because they had "reeducated" and released thousands of prisoners at the front. They strongly denied that they had impressed large numbers of former South Korean military personnel into their armed forces. In addition, they decried the UNC practice of screening prisoners and reclassifying as civilian internees those reportedly impressed into North Korea's military forces.

During the early discussions on prisoners of war in late 1951, no mention was made about the principles of voluntary or forced repatriation. Army staff officers in Washington had pointed out in mid-1951 that there were many Chinese prisoners of war who had formerly served in the forces of Chiang Kai-shek, and that they and others who had demonstrated anti-Communist attitudes in the UNC prisoner of war camps would likely be severely punished if they were returned to Communist control. The possibility of offering such prisoners a choice would be not only humanitarian, but also presented interesting psychological warfare opportunities. Although the concept appealed to General Ridgway, he pointed out that once the United States openly advocated such a principle, it would be difficult, if not impossible, to abandon it.

Since Ridgway's first concern was the quick and safe return of all the prisoners held by the Communists, he was reluctant to espouse any policy that might endanger their release. On the other hand, he was willing to try a gambit that might work. If the Communists would consent to a one-for-one exchange, the UNC could withhold all prisoners unwilling to return to Communist control until all of the UNC prisoners of war had been exchanged and then could let the remaining detainees exercise an option. The enemy negotiators, however, quickly extinguished any hopes for a one-for-one exchange and insisted firmly on an all-for-all settlement.

Blocked by the Communists on this score, the UNC delegates tried another tack in the closing days of 1951, and in the process, became committed to the principle of voluntary repatriation. They proposed to accept the Communist concept that a soldier captured could upon release choose whether to return to his own army or to join the other side. Since the Communists had admitted that they had "reeducated" and released thousands of prisoners during the early stages of the war, they had already practiced "voluntary repatriation" and the UNC advocated the adoption of this policy by both sides as a means of assuring that all prisoners would be treated equitably.

When the Communists reacted vehemently to the use of their own practices, Admiral Ruthven Libby, who had replaced Admiral Burke on the delegation, solicitously reminded them that the Chinese troops, according to the enemy's own avowals, were all simply volunteers eager to fight for the Korean People's Army. If this were true, he could not understand why the Communists were worried about any of their volunteers not wanting to go home. But General Lee Sang Cho, his Communist counterpart, refused to rise to the bait and even denied any incongruities in the Communists' earlier and current positions on voluntary repatriation. General Lee, however, did recognize the somewhat distorted logic in his arguments. At one of the January meetings, while defending the Communist system of prisoner education and calling it righteous and benevolent, he became so convulsed with suppressed laughter that he could scarcely complete his remarks.

During the talks that took place in February and March 1952, the Communists remained adamantly opposed to voluntary repatriation. Their hatred of Chiang Kai-shek and fear that Chinese prisoners of war might be sent to Taiwan if not repatriated were clearly expressed in the staff meetings. Although they refused to yield on voluntary repatriation for former North Korean and Chinese soldiers, they did evidence a softer attitude on personnel who had lived in South Korea. One of the main problems at this point was that neither side had any firm idea about how many of the prisoners held by the UNC would refuse repatriation since no real screening had been carried out.

An estimate based on guesswork made in February by the UNC staff assumed that of the 132,000 in its custody, about 28,000 would not want to go home, but only 16,000 would resist repatriation. It also assumed that about half of the 20,000 Chinese prisoners would forcibly resist repatriation, since they were well-organized and led by leaders with strong pro–Chiang Kai-shek sympathies. Although the guess that 116,000 of the 132,000 would probably agree to repatriation had no basis in fact, it became critical in early April, when the Communists demonstrated an interest in securing a firm estimate of how many prisoners would be returned. Lacking any accurate figures, the UNC staff officers indicated that about 116,000 military repatriates would be involved in an exchange. Citing this figure may have been a tactical error on the part of the UNC, since the Communists accepted it as an approximate total and were led to believe that they would recover about that number of prisoners. The enemy delegation quickly suggested that both sides check their lists to secure firm figures with the evident expectation that no more than 16,000 of their captured personnel would elect to remain under UNC control.

Although the UNC teams, sought to persuade as many of the prisoners as possible to return home during the April screening period, the final results astounded both sides. Only about 70,000 of the military prisoners indicated that they would consent to repatriation without the use of force. Significantly, only a little more than 6,000 of the more than 20,000 Chinese prisoners were included in the 70,000. The Communists' first reaction to this disclosure was profound shock, swiftly followed by bitter anger. They felt that they had been deliberately deceived by the UNC for propaganda purposes. With the Communists deeply resentful, exchanges at the truce talks became acrimonious and little progress was made. The UNC offer to swap the 70,000 prisoners for the 12,000 that the Communists held was coldly rejected at the end of April. The Communists wanted at least 116,000 returned and were especially concerned about the low total of Chinese repatriates.

The enemy secured fresh ammunition for their attacks on voluntary repatriation in May 1952 when violence erupted in the UNC prisoner of war camps on the island of Koje-do, off the southern coast of South Korea. Communist prisoners seized the UNC camp commander and used him to bargain both for concessions and for damaging admissions that the prisoners had been treated inhumanely and had been subjected to forcible screening. Although these concessions were given under duress, the enemy was able to gain the propaganda initiative during the summer of 1952.

In the process of restoring order in the prisoner of war camps after this incident, the UNC carried out a more thorough screening and segregated all the prisoners desiring repatriation from those who wished to stay. By including civilian internees and South Koreans who wanted to go to North Korea, the new total came to about 83,000. When the UNC submitted the revised figures to the Communists in July, however, they were again rejected. The enemy continued to insist on the return of higher numbers and made it increasingly clear that the Chinese prisoners were the real bone of contention.

With the negotiations stalled, both General Mark W. Clark, who had replaced General Ridgway as U.N. commander, and Major General William K. Harrison, who had replaced Admiral Joy as chief UNC negotiator in May, recommended that the UNC present the Communists with several alternate proposals for the disposition of the non-repatriates. Then if the Communists refused to accept any of them, the UNC would suspend the truce talks. Such a course would demonstrate to the Communists that the UNC had reached its final bargaining position.

President Harry S. Truman approved this action in September 1952 and on the 28th, General Harrison offered the Communists three alternatives:

1. All prisoners would be brought to the demilitarized zone and checked off by Red Cross or joint military teams. They could then choose whether to be repatriated or to remain in the control of the side that detained them;

2. All prisoners desiring repatriation would be exchanged expeditiously. All non-repatriates would be brought to the de-militarized zone in small groups and would be interviewed by teams from countries not involved in the war and could then elect repatriation or non-re-patriation;

3. All prisoners desiring repatriation would be exchanged as quickly as possible. All non-repatriates would then be brought to the demilitarized zone and freed. They could then go, without screening or in-terviews, to the side of their choice.

When the Communists turned down these proposals and continued to demand full repa-triation, General Harrison declared on 8 Octo-ber that the meetings would be in recess until they accepted one of the UNC proposals or of-fered a constructive one of their own. The talk-ing stage had come to an end.

While the talks had been going on, combat at the front had been restricted in the main to limited attacks to maintain pressure on the en-emy and to seize favorable terrain. General Clark, like General Ridgway, had no desire to incur large numbers of casualties to take objec-tives that might have to be given up when an armistice was reached. Clark did authorize sev-eral larger-scale offensives to increase the pres-sure on the enemy after the truce talks went into recess, but the efforts to take the Triangle Hill complex north of Kumwha in October and No-vember proved to be costly and the approach of winter discouraged further attempts to improve the UNC battlefield positions.

Although the liaison officers continued to meet during the winter of 1952–53, they dealt mainly in complaints and alleged violations of the truce area and no progress was made in substantive matters. The advent of a Republi-can administration under President Dwight D. Eisenhower in January 1953 led to several at-tempts, including the veiled threat of the use of nuclear weapons, to increase the pressure on the enemy to end the conflict, but to little avail.

On 5 March, however, Soviet dictator Jo-seph Stalin died unexpectedly and a thaw began in East-West relations as his successors sought to consolidate their power during the transition period that followed. Evidence of the change came in late March. In the previous month General Clark had sent a routine letter to the North Korean and Chinese Communist com-manders that requested the immediate exchange of sick and wounded prisoners. Earlier attempts along this line had been fruitless and Clark held little hope that his suggestion would be accepted at that time. In the aftermath of Stalin's death, the Communist military commanders on 28 March not only accepted Clark's offer on the sick and wounded, but also opened the door for further negotiations to settle the disposition of the other prisoners as well. Two days later, Chinese Foreign Minister Chou En-lai stated that both sides should hand over any prisoners who did not wish to be repatriated to a neutral nation for disposition and set the stage for the resumption of plenary talks in mid-April.

In the meantime, the liaison officers met on 6 April to discuss the exchange of sick and wounded prisoners in a completely different and business-like atmosphere, free of recrimina-tions and rhetoric. Lists were prepared and ex-changed and arrangements were made for transporting the sick and wounded to Panmunjom for their transfer. Operation Little Switch, as it was called, took place on 20 April, when the UNC turned over 5,194 North Ko-rean and 1,030 Chinese soldiers, plus 446 civil-ian internees, to the Communists, and received 684 sick and wounded soldiers, including 149 Americans, from the enemy.

The threat of an indecisive settlement of the conflict alarmed South Korean President Syngman Rhee and he mounted a strong cam-paign in opposition, vowing to continue the war alone if necessary. Since South Korea was in no position to wage a prolonged war without U.S. assistance, the South Korean speeches and dem-onstrations proved to be more embarrassments than deterrents. The UNC and the Communists pushed ahead in the weeks after Little Switch to resolve the last remaining issues: who would take charge of the non-repatriates, how long would they be held, and what would be their final disposition if they could not be persuaded to return home?

Initially the UNC preferred Switzerland as the chief custodial nation, but the Communists had turned that choice down and instead had pressed for India as the fifth member of a Neu-tral Nations Repatriation Commission along with Switzerland, Sweden, Poland, and Czechoslovakia. The UNC had conceded on that issue, with the specification that India would provide all the military and administra-tive personnel to carry out the mission. On the other hand, the UNC proved to be less ame-nable to the Communist proposal that the non-repatriates be held for six months while the

Communist teams sought to change their minds about returning home. After some debate, the negotiators worked out a compromise period of ninety days and also agreed that there would be no more than seven men to act as explainers or persuaders for each 1,000 non-repatriates. For those who continued to resist repatriation after ninety days, their fate would be considered at a political conference to be convened after the armistice was signed. If the conference failed to resolve their disposition within thirty days, the non-repatriates would be declared civilians and be free to seek residence in another country.

As the conferees moved ever closer to a final agreement in May, South Korean agitation continued to increase. Since the non-repatriates would remain on South Korean soil during the period of explaining and Syngman Rhee opposed the selection of India as the chief custodial nation, a crisis threatened to develop unless some means could be found to reconcile the sharp differences between the United States and South Korea over the projected terms of the armistice. Basic to the settlement of these differences was the need to dispel South Korean fears that the United States might desert it if hostilities broke out again after the armistice was signed. Although the United States was reluctant to conclude a bilateral security pact while South Korean threats and pressures were in such open evidence, President Eisenhower decided at the end of May to offer such a pact to Rhee in an effort to defuse the dangerous situation.

But Rhee had placed himself in an exposed political position by stirring up South Korean emotions to a high pitch and had to take some action before he accepted the U.S. offer. On 18 June, South Korean forces guarding the prisoners of war permitted about 27,000 Korean non-repatriates to escape from their compounds; the majority of the escapees were quickly absorbed into the civilian population and were impossible to recover without South Korean cooperation. The unilateral action, although it caused an immediate uproar, did serve to relieve the pressure on Rhee to some degree and he became more responsive to U.S. arguments that the bilateral security pact would provide assurance of U.S. support in the future, and additionally that South Korea needed more time to expand and develop its armed forces. By early July he agreed not to obstruct the implementation of the armistice terms despite his continued misgivings over the long-term results.

The Communist reaction to Rhee's release of the non-repatriates in the meantime had been surprisingly mild, although they had obviously relished the UNC embarrassment over the incident. During May and June, while the final details of the truce were being worked out, they had carried out a series of offensives to improve their defensive positions along the eastern and central fronts and, in the process, to deal the South Korean units opposing them a telling blow. The heavy attacks, which did not peter out until mid-July, caused heavy casualties on both sides and may have had a sobering effect on Rhee's bellicosity.

Although the UNC could not guarantee Rhee's full observance of the armistice terms, the Communists were now ready to complete the agreement. A final demarcation line was drawn and last-minute arrangements for the transfer of prisoners, repatriates, and non-repatriates was settled. On 27 July the plenary delegates met at Panmunjom and signed eighteen copies of the truce agreement. Twelve hours later the fighting came to an end.

Shortly after the armistice was signed, the exchange of prisoners got under way. By 6 September the UNC had sent more than 75,000 repatriates to the Communists and had received more than 12,000 from the enemy. On 23 September, the UNC followed up and delivered more than 22,000 non-repatriates to the Neutral Nations Repatriation Commission in the demilitarized zone, and the Communists gave the commission more than 350 UNC non-repatriates. Communist efforts to persuade their non-repatriates to return during the ninety days granted them were largely unsuccessful and only about 600 chose to go back when the explaining period came to an end in December. The Korean non-repatriates were released in Korea and the Chinese were sent to Taiwan, with the exception of eighty-six, who elected to go to India. As for UNC non-repatriates, only twelve changed their mind; the remainder, including twenty-one Americans, were returned to Communist control in early 1954.

Since the war had never been declared, it was fitting that there should be no official ending, merely a suspension of hostilities. With the uncertainty of Syngman Rhee's intentions casting a deep shadow over the truce agreement, how long it would last was a matter for conjecture.

Perhaps the major deterrent to renewal of the conflict was the high costs in manpower and economic resources required to continue the fighting. Estimates of enemy battle losses alone came to more than 1.5 million men, and the UNC had suffered more than 500,000 casualties (including more than 142,000 Americans) just to achieve a virtual standoff. The potential costs involved in attaining a total military victory in Korea were higher than either side wished to pay in 1953 and that, in effect, was the most patent indication that the armistice would prove durable.

Walter Hermes

Bibliography

Far East Command, United Nations Command, Headquarters, Military History Section. *History of the Korean War. Korean Armistice Negotiations (July 1951–May 1952)* (n.d.).

Goodman, A.E., ed. *Negotiating While Fighting: The Diary of Admiral C. Turner Joy at the Korean Armistice Conference* (1978).

Hermes, Walter G. *Truce Tent and Fighting Front* (Office of the Chief of Military History: 1966).

Joy, C. Turner. *How Communists Negotiate* (1955).

Schnable, J.F., and R.D. Watson. *History of the Joint Chiefs of Staff*, 3, *The Korean War* (1979).

U.S. Department of State. *Foreign Relations of the United States, 1951, 7, Korea and China* (1983).

Vatcher, William H., Jr. *Panmunjom: The Story of the Korean Military Armistice Negotiations* (1958).

Armor in the Korean War

The outbreak of war in Korea found the United States armor force sadly run down from its World War II peak of quantity, if not quality. Incredibly, in June of 1950, the United States had not one tank in production. Existing tanks had to be rounded up from a wide variety of active and reserve units and hurriedly assembled in heterogeneous provisional outfits with little cohesion or training. Some M-26 Pershing tanks were actually removed from their concrete display pedestals around Fort Knox. In addition, the tanks were in poor repair, overage, and lacked a logistical support system and trained tank mechanics. The one tank that was available in some numbers and in fair condition was the M-24 Chaffee, which was completely outclassed by the superb Soviet-built T-34. The

Army's newest tank, the M-46 Patton, was simply a cobbled-up version of the M-26, with a new turret superimposed on the Pershing hull. Rushed into combat, the M-46 suffered from many technical problems that a thorough testing period would have uncovered. In addition, it was underpowered for the terrain of Korea. As late as February 1951, the 64th Tank Battalion had no less than thirty-five of its fifty-eight tanks break down on a road march, thirty of them lost because of the same problem with their engine oil coolers. The "main battle tank" of the U.S. Army of the time, the M-48 (also known as the Patton), did not enter combat in Korea until the last year of the war. Throughout the war, consequently, United States armor still relied heavily on variants of the battle-tested M-4 Sherman medium tank of World War II.

Not surprisingly, the initial commitment of United States armor in Korea was little short of disastrous, in spite of individual heroics. One of the armor lessons learned in World War II was that "the best antitank weapon is a better tank." But the North Korean armored edge was destroyed not by United States armor, but by the new 3.5-inch rocket launcher ("bazooka"), and by air power.

Nonetheless, armor played a strong role in the Korean War from the time of the breakout in mid-1950 to the armistice/cease-fire almost exactly three years later. The role of armor in the war can be divided into three periods: from the North Korean invasion of South Korea to the U.N. withdrawal from North Korea; from the U.N. withdrawal to the start of peace talks; and from the start of peace talks to the cease-fire.

There were no tanks at all in South Korea when the war broke out on 25 June 1950; on 5 July 1950, the ill-fated Task Force Smith was routed by Soviet-built T-34 tanks. During the first tank-to-tank encounter of the war, on 10 July 1950, a light tank with 3rd Battalion, 21st Regiment, did disable an enemy tank near Chonui. On the following day, however, four tanks from Company A, 78th Heavy Tank Battalion, joined soldiers of the 24th Division in a hasty retreat from the Kum River.

Infantry commanders learned tank-infantry coordination very quickly after the Kum River retreat, using tanks to help consolidate Eighth Army strength at the Naktong River, or Pusan perimeter. Thus, on 25 July 1950, Major Gordon E. Murch, commander, 2nd Battalion, 27th Regiment, used nine tanks from Company

A, 71st Tank Battalion, to cover infantry forces in the withdrawal to Taegu and the Naktong.

Acts of individual heroism slowed the advancing North Koreans, as American forces played for time to consolidate power at the Naktong. For instance, the first medium tank encounter in Korea took place near Chinju, far to the south, on 31 July 1950, when Lieutenant Samuel Fowler, with the first three Pershing "medium" tanks to arrive in Korea, delayed a North Korean assault at the Nam River; for lack of adequate fan belts, the tanks broke down and could not be driven over the Nam to safety.

At the 130-mile Naktong front, infantry, armor, and artillery learned lessons in coordination. Near Masan, to the farthest south, on 2 August, Lieutenant Colonel Gilbert Check, of 1st Battalion, 27th Regiment, employed four Sherman tanks to lead his column through an enemy envelopment to safety, foiling an enemy surprise attack at the Chindong-ni schoolhouse the next day. North of Masan, at Miryang, Lieutenant Colonel Robert Ayres, commander, 1st Battalion, 34th Regiment, led an offensive on an enemy-occupied gristmill; a light tank led Company A in freeing captured soldiers of the 34th Regiment. On 17 August the 9th Regimental Combat Team (RCT) spotted four T-34 tanks advancing between the Cloverleaf Hill and the Obong-ni Ridge east of the river. Marine bazookas and a Pershing knocked out the first tank, bazookas destroyed the second, Pershings the third, and air power the fourth. This was the first time that Pershing tank crews had disabled a T-34 head on. The enemy assault on the mountains (the Naktong Bulge) had failed by 18 August.

The first large-scale tank-to-tank encounter of the war took place at Taegu, north of Miryang. Lieutenant Colonel Gilbert Check, commander, 1st Battalion, 27th Regiment, and Lieutenant Colonel Gordon Murch, commander, 2nd Battalion, went into perimeter defense at Tabu-dong just north of Taegu. From the east side of the road to Taegu, on the night of 18 August, combined forces of eight Pershing tanks, plus bazookas and artillery, held the enemy tanks at bay.

The first United Nations counterattack had already taken place near Masan on 12 August 1950 in an attempt to seize the Chinju Pass and secure the Nam River. Task Force Kean, composed of elements of the 356th Regiment, the 5th Marine Regiment, and the 5th RCT, were withdrawing under enemy fire when three friendly tanks "appearing from nowhere" covered the withdrawal. MSG Robert Tedford led two tanks of the 25th Reconnaissance Company in an abortive attempt to drive the North Koreans back, losing his life, and posthumously being awarded the Congressional Medal of Honor. Without advance planning, the armor commanders had proved their worth on the offense within two months after the outbreak of hostilities.

Tankers also learned to defend territory without help from other forces. On 31 August 1950, Sergeant Ernest Kuoma and SFC Oscar Berry, Company A, 172d Tank Battalion, were fired on by enemy forces which were laying an underwater bridge near Agok, not far from Miryang. Kuoma and Berry successfully fired back and destroyed the bridge; for his courage, Kuoma (who the same night came upon a North Korean force posing as Americans) was awarded the Congressional Medal of Honor.

In September 1950, armor took part in the Pusan breakout. At Waegwan, just west of Taegu, on 16 September, 3rd Battalion, 23rd Regiment; Company C, 72nd Tank Battalion; and 23rd Regimental Tank Company crossed the Naktong as a task force. Sergeant George E. Vonton of the 23rd Regimental Tank Company took Hill 201 west of the Naktong on 19 September without infantry support. On 22 September, the 23rd Regiment and a platoon of 72nd Tank Battalion took Sinban-ni. Then, tank companies from the 70th Tank Battalion went with 5th, 7th, and 8th Cavalry Regiments, with 7th Cavalry encircling Tabu-dong on 23 September.

The breakout strategy as set forth by General Walton H. Walker, Eighth Army commander, included bypassing certain areas and returning later. Thus, Task Force Matthews, which included Company A, 79th Tank Battalion and the 25th Reconnaissance Company, crossed the Nam River to take the road from Chinju to Hadong. Sergeant Raymond Reiters then used one tank to take the road from Hadong northwest to Namwon, liberating the town and eighty-six American prisoners in the process, aided by two F-84 jet fighters. North Koreans ran away in all directions. Lieutenant Colonel Welborn Dolvin, commander, 89th Tank Battalion, led Task Force Dolvin from Chingu west to Hamyang from 26–28 September, and then completed the "rectangle" by taking the road from Hamyang westward to Namwon. With tanks from the 6th Medium Tank Battalion, the 24th Division then took the

South Korean town of Kumchon, gateway to Taejon, on 25 September. Two days later, the 24th took Taejon itself. With armor in the lead, task forces of armor and infantry were proving their worth in the offensive to reclaim South Korea.

Three lead tanks of Task Force Lynch on 26 September linked up with X Corps at Osan; soldiers of X Corps heard the noise and saw the flashing lights of the approaching tanks and held their fire, correctly concluding that an enemy force would advance with stealth. The rest of the task force arrived at Osan on 29 September, formally establishing the linkup of Eighth Army and X Corps, which had already landed at Inchon, the port to Seoul in northwest Korea.

In the Inchon landings, X Corps used nine tanks in 3rd Battalion, 5th Marine Regiment, to take the islands of Wolmi-do and Sowolmi-do. Three bulldozer-equipped tanks sealed enemy troops into caves. At Red Beach, on the mainland, tanks successfully overcame the T-34 tanks and continued on the road to Seoul with the 1st Battalion, 5th Marine Regiment. Company E and supporting tanks took the important Kimpo Airfield near Seoul on 18 September. Flamethrowing Pershing tanks of Company B, 1st Tank Battalion, linked up with the 1st Marine Division to overcome enemy tank forces in the South Korean capital. In a typical assault, planes strafed barricades, engineers exploded mines, and tanks demolished the barricades. By 27 September, Marines had seized the Seoul railroad station. With tanks leading 2nd Battalion, the 7th Marine Regiment pressed on to Uijongbu, north of Seoul. By 3 October 1950, the North Koreans were pushed back to the original 25 June line of assault.

The 1st Cavalry and 24th Divisions of Eighth Army now moved northward with the Republic of Korea (ROK) 1st Division and tanks from the 6th Medium Tank Battalion. Tanks dashing on the roads northward, infantry clinging to the tank decks, were a frequent sight. American tanks and soldiers of the ROK 1st Division entered the North Korean capital of Pyongyang on 19 October 1950; the North Korean military leaders had fled northward to the Yalu River.

Meantime, the 1st Marine Division landed at Wonsan, 830 sea miles from Inchon, on the eastern coast of Korea and advanced separately northward to the Yalu. A mountain ridge (the Taebaek Mountains) eighty miles wide, running from north to south, separated the 1st Marine Division and X Corps from the Eighth Army.

Major General Oliver P. Smith, commander of the 1st Marine Division, took care logistically to cover the Marine line of advance as the soldiers went northward, to the west, and to the east of Chosin (Changjin) Reservoir. By 27 November, the first Marines had reached Yudam-ni, fourteen miles north of Hagaru, which was at the base of the Chosin Reservoir. Separately, Task Force Faith, named for its commander, Lieutenant Colonel Don Faith (also known as the 32nd RCT) of the 7th Division, had advanced northward on the east side of the reservoir.

On 25 November, in a surprise attack, Chinese Communist forces cut off and destroyed much of Task Force Faith; two tanks were not enough to stage a breakout. Lieutenant Colonel Faith himself was killed by an enemy hand grenade. On the west side of the reservoir, north of Koto-ri, in Hellfire Valley, on 29 November, a task force under Britain's Lieutenant Colonel Douglas Drysdale was nearly destroyed by Chinese Communist forces. Task Force Drysdale included seventeen lead tanks, twelve rearguard tanks, a Marine company, an infantry company, and the 41st Commandos of the Royal Marines. Conflicts between Drysdale and the tank company commander prevented placement of the lead tanks within the convoy. Few of the task force escaped to tell the story.

On 1 December, Lieutenant Colonel Robert Taplett used tanks to lead 3rd Battalion, 5th Marine Regiment, in a retreat from Yudam-ni back to Hagaru. X Corps forces on 11 December reached the point of evacuation at the harbor at Hungnam.

On 25 November, at Kunu-ri, fifty miles north of Pyongyang, Company G, 9th Infantry Regiment, 2nd Division, Eighth Army, was the first to be pinned down by the new Chinese Communist offensive. Captain Frank Munoz, commander, Company G, used his company's supporting tanks to carry wounded from the west to the east bank of the Chongchon River. Tanks led the great retreat southward, repeatedly trying to break free of attempts by Chinese Communist forces to cut them off in mountain passes. The retreat lacked the systematic defensive character of the X Corps retreat from the Chosin Reservoir; when Eighth Army soldiers came into contact with the enemy it was often as prisoners rather than as defenders.

General Walton H. Walker was killed in a jeep accident on 23 December. Lieutenant General Matthew B. Ridgway took command of all ground forces in Korea on 27 December 1950.

With this change in command, armor entered a new phase in the war.

By consolidating Eighth Army and X Corps south of Seoul, Ridgway was able to launch an offensive in depth on a narrow front. On 26 January 1951, the 89th Tank Battalion and the 35th Infantry Regiment took Suwon. Then, at the battle of Chipyong-ni on 15 February 1951, a task force under Colonel Marcel Crombez (commander, 5th Cavalry Regiment) used twenty-three tanks to clear Highway 24A, placing new M-46 "Patton" tanks in the lead. Thus, he relieved beleaguered 23rd Infantry Regiment forces surrounded by Communist Chinese. The enemy ring was broken. The seventy-five-mile march back to the 38th parallel had begun. Six American and five ROK divisions formed a powerful striking force. The guns of the 89th Tank Battalion covered the 24th Regiment as it crossed the Han River to return to Seoul in mid-March 1951. Eighth Army soldiers crossed the 38th parallel in late March, but stopped well short of Pyongyang on 9 April, at the Kansas line established by the Joint Chiefs of Staff.

Some of the fiercest armor fighting was still to come. The third and final phase of armor involvement began on 17 May, in the battle named "Bunker Hill." Enemy forces struck at the right flank of the 38th Regiment; the 72nd Tank Battalion quickly struck back, fighting across the valleys near Seoul while infantry fought in the hills. The enemy attempt to counterattack and retake Seoul from the U.N. forces failed.

Armor companies served with great distinction in the battles for Bloody and Heartbreak Ridges (part of "Operation Touchdown") from 10–15 October 1951. After 2nd Division infantry assaults on the enemy front had failed, Company B, 72nd Tank Battalion, as part of Task Force Sturman rushed down the Satae-ri Valley to the east and then up and down the Mundung-ni Valley to the west of the mountain ridges, defying enemy fire. (Engineers had prepared the tank route.) The assault at Mundung-ni took the enemy by surprise. Tank company commanders proved, however, that while they could fight successfully at the bases of the mountains ridges, the infantry had to climb the ridges themselves, suffering high casualties in the process.

As peace negotiations began, the scale of fighting and the casualty rates diminished. For example, at the battle for Old Baldy (16–18 April 1953) there were only three tanks available to aid Company K, 31st Regiment, when it was attacked by enemy forces. The tanks repulsed the enemy to the west of Old Baldy, but not from the north. Four infantry companies rushed up the slope of Old Baldy's 170 yards to aid Company K at a cost of several hundred dead and wounded. Subsequently, Washington wanted casualties reduced, as victory was no longer the United States goal in the war.

All fighting ended on 27 July 1953 with the armistice and signing of the cease-fire at Panmunjom. No formal peace treaty has ever been signed, however.

The M-46 Patton, which first saw service in Korea in August 1950, provided the base for the M-47 and M-48, the second and third tanks named for Patton. The M-48 main battle tank with 90mm main gun was not introduced until 1953.

The Soviet Union's T-34/85, introduced in 1944, became the North Koreans' main battle tank. Although the newer Joseph Stalin III tank was superior to the T-34/85, the Soviets did not allocate this tank to their allies in the Korean conflict.

There were many lessons to be learned from the Korean War. As noted earlier, the United States began work on a new main battle tank. In addition, the U.S. and its allies concluded that tank-infantry coordination required more training and refinement. Communications between ground and air forces had also proved deficient. But the most significant lesson was that the United States could not suddenly improvise an armor force and expect any success in battle.

John Cranston

Bibliography

Aiken, Scott (USMC). "The 72d Tank Battalion in Operation TOUCHDOWN," *Armor* (September–October 1992).

Appleman, Roy. *South to the Naktong, North to the Yalu: June–November 1950* (Office of the Chief of Military History, Washington: 1961).

Connor, A.W., Jr. "The Armor Debacle in Korea, 1950: Implications for Today," *Parameters* (Summer 1992).

Hastings, Max. *The Korean War*, (1987).

Hermes, Walter G. *Truce Tent and Fighting Front*, (Office of the Chief of Military History, Washington: 1988).

Schnabel, James F. *Policy and Direction: The First Year*, (Office of the Chief of Military History, Washington: 1972).

Toland, John. *In Mortal Combat: Korea, 1950–1953* (1991).

Whelan, Richard. *Drawing the Line: The Korean War, 1950–1953* (1990).

See also BAZOOKA VS. TANK

Army, Chinese Communist
See PEOPLE'S LIBERATION/VOLUNTEER ARMY

Army, North Korean People's
See KOREAN PEOPLE'S ARMY

Army, U.S., Cavalry Units
See CAVALRY UNITS, U.S. ARMY

Army, U.S., Civil Affairs and Military Government
See CIVIL AFFAIRS AND MILITARY GOVERNMENT, U.S. ARMY

Army, U.S., Corps of Engineers
See ENGINEERS IN THE KOREAN WAR

Army, U.S., Signal Corps
See SIGNAL CORPS, U.S. ARMY

Artillery in the Korean War
World War II ended on a contradictory note with respect to the future of artillery. On the one hand, nearly all the victors emerged from the war with an unshakable belief in the power of massive conventional fire. On the other hand, the advent of the nuclear weapon seemed to indicate that conventional wars, with their "puny," cannon-fired, high-explosive shells, were a thing of the past. Caught between those two poles, artillery tactics and technology languished for several years.

The Korean War opened with mobile and fluid operations. When the pace of the war started to slow down after the start of truce talks, the role of artillery increased. As stagnation eventually set in after 1950, greater firepower was seen as the key to maintaining the strategic deadlock in what was at first supposed to have been a short war. The stagnation also brought a return to a type of artillery operations not seen since World War I. Artillery positions themselves came under direct ground attack far more frequently than in World War II, and artillery units faced the problem of delivering fire support while trying to defend themselves at the same time. Artillerymen responded by digging in and fortifying their positions in much the same manner as in World War I. They also made far greater use of close defensive fire than in either world war. Older firing techniques were resurrected and updated. The famous "Box Barrage" of World War I was reborn as "Flash Fire"—a horseshoe-shaped concentration close around the fronts and sides of friendly outposts, designed to stop an enemy assault in its tracks.

The terrain in Korea compounded the problems for artillerymen on both sides. The rice paddies in the flatlands made poor gun positions. In summer they were too wet and soft to hold the guns and absorb the recoil. In winter they were firm enough, but the open areas were too exposed and the frozen water-soaked ground was almost impossible to dig into. The hills and mountains provided somewhat better natural cover, but that ground was very difficult to dig into. Often it was hard to find one patch of level ground big enough to place a single gun, let alone an entire battery. The varying heights and angles of cant of the guns within a given battery, added to the wildly varying heights of targets in highland areas, made the fire direction solution very difficult. The lack of accurate maps for many areas also compounded the complexities of the gunnery problem.

U.S. and U.N. Artillery
For the most part, the United Nations forces used the same artillery weapons the United States had at the end of World War II (see table 1). In 1951, the United States introduced an upgraded version of its heavy 4.2-inch mortar that had been so effective in World War II. The British sometimes employed the 4.2s in separate batteries, using them like field guns, rather than the infantry battalion close support weapons they were designed to be. Units of the Commonwealth Division also used the British 25-pounder MK-4 gun/howitzer of World War II vintage. The mainstay of U.N. divisional artillery was the venerable M-2A1 105mm towed howitzer. In its original version, first tested in 1932, it was designed to be towed by horses. By 1950, it was considered an obsolete relic; yet it served, and served well, throughout the Korean War, through Vietnam (very slightly updated as the M-101A1), and was

TABLE 1

Artillery Used by United Nations Forces
(all U.S. except for British*)

Model	Type	Caliber	Crew Size	Max. Rate of Fire (rds/min)	Round Weight (kg)	Gun Weight (kg)	Max. Range (m)
M-42 (1953)	Anti-Aircraft Twin SP Gun	40 mm	4	120/bbl	.96	22,500	1,000 (ceiling)
M-8 (1927)	Pack Howitzer	76 mm	4	22	6.25	653	8,500
MK-4* (1935)	25 Pounder Towed Gun/ Howitzer	88 mm	6	5	11.3	1,741	12,250
M-2A1 (1938)	Towed Howitzer	105 mm	8	8	14.9	2,220	11,200
M-30 (1951)	Mortar	4.2 in.	6	25	11.2	100	5,420
M-1 (1941)	Towed Howitzer	155 mm	11	2	43.2	5,800	14,600
M-2 (1938)	Towed Gun	155 mm	14	1	57.6	13,880	23,500
M-2 (1940)	Towed Howitzer	8 in.	14	1/2	90.7	13,471	16,800

still in service with the U.S. Army at the start of the 1990s.

Virtually every U.S. commander in Korea continually urged Washington to send more artillery. General Douglas MacArthur in particular became very upset early in the war when he received only about one-third of the non-divisional artillery he had requested. Then, as now, the heavier non-divisional guns were the primary means through which the higher echelon commanders (corps and army level) influenced the outcome of battle. MacArthur's experiences in World War II had convinced him that for an attacking force to succeed against a prepared and determined enemy, a one-to-one ratio of divisional to non-divisional artillery was required. Nothing that happened during the Korean War changed MacArthur's mind on that point.

U.S./U.N. commanders never had as many guns as they wanted, and ammunition often ran short. Nonetheless, they still managed to shoot massive amounts. Between June 1950 and December 1952, U.N. artillery and mortars expended 1,132,000 tons—as much as all the artillery ammo shot by the U.S. in World War II in the Pacific and Mediterranean theaters combined. By December 1952, the U.N. was firing nineteen rounds for every one the Communist forces fired. Even so, the effectiveness estimates ran to something like three tons (182 rounds of 105mm, for example) of artillery ammo for each Communist casualty.

The Korean War saw the introduction of many artillery tactics and techniques that were later used during the Vietnam War and are still part of today's Army doctrine. Perhaps the single greatest advancement in fire direction methods was the introduction of the target grid—a rotating overlay on the firing chart that graphically converted corrections relative to the forward observer's point of view to that of the guns. The target grid sharply decreased the time required to compute correction data, and the simplified graphic technique eliminated potential mathematical errors. The target grid is still the standard method in fire direction centers (FDCs) not equipped with computers.

Certain categories of targets are better attacked with an air burst, as opposed to a surface burst—troops in the open, for example. When the target called for an air burst, U.S./U.N. artillery made extensive use of the variable time (VT) fuse, first developed during World War II and still in use. The VT fuse is a proximity device that uses radio waves to trigger a detonation at a uniform twenty-meter height-of-burst (the optimal height for shrapnel effect). While standard time fuses can be set for a twenty-meter, or any other height-of-burst, it takes several rounds to adjust them. The considerably more expensive VT fuse gives a perfect twenty-meter burst, first time, every time. For that reason the standard time fuse was hardly used in Korea. On many occasions the guns fired with VT fuses directly over U.N. bunkers that were being overrun. The shrapnel would sweep the Communist troops off the outside of the bunker, while the U.N. troops inside would be safe from the red-hot fragments.

On the other side of the coin, Communist bunkers and fortifications proved especially difficult targets. The 105mm and 155mm howitzers used high-angle fire against the bunkers in order to drop the rounds straight down on the roof, which was usually weaker than the front and sides. This too was an old World War I technique. For the most part, however, these light and medium guns were ineffective in this role, and "bunker-busting" became almost the exclusive domain of the heavy eight-inch howitzers (about 203mm). Using concrete-piercing delay fuses, the eight-inchers fired directly into their targets from very close ranges. The delay fuse ensured that the round had the time to bury itself deep in the bunker wall before it went off.

Two important organizational changes occurred in U.S. artillery units during Korea. The typical divisional firing battery was increased from four to six guns. American artillery had used six-gun batteries at one time, but switched to four-gun batteries sometime after the War of 1812. The six-gun battery became the standard firing unit during most of Korea and all of Vietnam.

The birth of the fire support coordination center (FSCC) was the second key change. Prior to World War II, artillery was almost the only supporting weapon for ground combat operations. World War II experience, however, showed a clear need for some single agency to coordinate the supporting fires of artillery, infantry mortars, ground support aircraft, and (when available) naval gunfire. The solution to the problem was an FSCC to eliminate overlapping coverage, make sure gaps didn't occur, and to make sure artillery didn't inadvertently shoot down any aircraft that were trying to support the same troops at the same time. Run by the senior field artillery officer at each echelon from regiment to corps, the FSCC was composed of liaison teams from every fire support agency involved in the fight. The FSCC concept, first tested in Korea, remains a standard fixture to this day.

Artillery must be massed if it is to be at all effective. The guns themselves need not be physically grouped on the ground, but the effects of their fire must be massed in the target area. Three batteries firing one round per gun at the same time are far more effective than one battery firing three rounds per gun, one after the other. For these reasons, the United States had developed the time on target (TOT) technique during World War II, and refined it practically to an art in Korea. In TOT fire, any number of firing units are given the same target and the designated time (the TOT) for their rounds to impact. The FDC of the headquarters controlling the mission gives a time mark via radio or telephone, at which point stopwatches are started at each participating firing unit. Each FDC computes the firing data and time of flight of the rounds for its own unit. The guns in each battery fire at the designated TOT time, minus the time of flight. All rounds arrive at the target at the same instant. The procedure is entirely silent prior to that point. The effect in the target area is devastating, particularly when all the guns of a division or even an entire corps fire. There is no warning, and almost no escape, assuming initial target location data is correct.

U.S./U.N. artillery fire produced mixed results at different times. During the fighting around Bloody Ridge in August and September 1951, the artillery of the U.S. 2nd Infantry Division fired 153,000 rounds, and the 15th Field Artillery set a record for U.S. light battalions by pumping out 14,425 rounds in a twenty-four-hour period. The results, however, were moderate at best; in large part because much of the ammunition was wasted in ineffective high-angle fire by light and medium guns against bunkers.

What became known as the "Wonju Shoot" was probably the single most lethal use of artillery of the war. Early on 14 February 1951, four Chinese divisions (197th, 198th, 119th, and 120th) massed to attack positions held by the U.S. 2nd Division. When they launched their attack in broad daylight, they were first spotted by Lieutenant Lee R. Hartell, an aerial observer from the 15th Field Artillery. Hartell called for continuous fire from his own battalion. What he got was the artillery of the entire 2nd Division, plus additional guns from X Corps. Hartell remained in the air for several hours directing the fire, and final casualty estimates placed the Chinese dead at 5,000, with perhaps three times that many wounded. (Six months after the Wonju Shoot, Hartell was serving as a forward observer on the ground when he was killed while calling in a Flash Fire mission, winning the Congressional Medal of Honor in the process.)

North Korean and Chinese Artillery

The North Korean and Chinese forces were equipped with pre- and early World War II Soviet guns (see table 2). These weapons had simple and rugged designs and, for the most part, they outranged the U.S. guns of comparable caliber. When the war started, the North Koreans had more than 1,600 guns, about three times what the South Koreans could muster. When the Chinese entered the war they were weak in artillery at first, but by the spring of 1952 they employed almost 900 guns in Korea. In one day in September 1952, more than 45,000 Communist shells fell on the Eighth Army front.

The Chinese and North Koreans also inherited their fire support doctrine from the Soviets. While the United States and most Western armies regard artillery as an arm which exists to support the maneuver forces, the Communists saw the relationship as being the reverse. They believed that massed artillery could capture and hold ground by itself. The primary role of the maneuver forces was to exploit the effects of massed fire. The Chinese and North Korean infantry actually advanced in their own artillery fire, rather than just following closely behind. The difference in these opposing doctrines is more than merely semantic. The Communist concept was sound, assuming the guns can be supplied with the huge quantities of ammunition needed to make it work. But that was always a problem on the Communist side in Korea.

The North Koreans handled their artillery very well. But in addition to insufficient ammo, they also lacked the communications systems necessary for the rapid massing and shifting of fire. Even so, they were able to produce firepower comparable to World War II densities on certain occasions; Taejon Airfield on 16 July 1950, for example. Throughout the course of the war, approximately 35 percent of the U.N. troops killed and 75 percent of those wounded fell to Communist artillery fire. And it may be hard to credit, but by the end of the war, the Communists had more artillery in Korea than did the U.N. forces. But the enemy also had far fewer shells to fire, thanks to U.N. air and sea interdiction.

The Influence of Korea

As a result of the experience in Korea, the United States started placing more emphasis on self-propelled rather than towed guns. An artillery battery is most vulnerable to attack when it is moving, and the U.N. forces lost a great many guns that way. Self-propelled guns reduce that vulnerability somewhat by increasing mobility and providing a limited amount

TABLE 2

Soviet Artillery Used by North Korean and Chinese Communist Forces

Model	Type (all towed)	Caliber	Crew Size	Max. Rate of Fire (rds/min)	Round Weight (kg)	Gun Weight (kg)	Max. Range (m)
M-1939	Anti-Aircraft Gun	37 mm	8	180	.7	2,050	1,000 (ceiling)
M-1942	Anti-Tank Gun	45 mm	6	25	1.4	570	4,400
ZIS-3 (1942)	Divisional Gun	76 mm	7	20	6.2	1,116	13,800
M-1937	Mortar	82 mm	5	25	4	56	3,000
KS-18 (1944)	Anti-Aircraft Gun	85 mm	7	20	9.5	4,500	3,000 (ceiling)
M-1938	Mortar	120 mm	6	9	15.4	522	5,700
A-19 (1937)	Field Gun	122 mm	9	6	25.5	7,117	20,800
M-30 (1938)	Howitzer	122 mm	8	6	21.8	2,500	11,800

of armored protection. In response to the need to defend firing positions from ground attack, the United States also developed the 105mm antipersonnel round that fired thousands of nail-like flechettes directly into the ranks of the attackers. This was a return to the concept of the old canister round, which had fallen into disuse sometime after the Civil War. The antipersonnel round later became famous in Vietnam as the "beehive round."

The United States emerged from Korea more convinced than ever of the power of massed artillery. General Matthew B. Ridgway graphically noted: ". . . artillery has been and remains the great killer of Communists. It remains the great saver of soldiers, American and Allied. There is a direct relation between piles of shells and piles of corpses. The bigger the former, the smaller the latter." Noting this heavy American reliance on firepower in Korea, as well as in World War II and Vietnam, several military analysts have pointed to an inconsistency between American tactical doctrine and actual American practice vis-à-vis the primacy of firepower in relation to maneuver.

The United States carried the "bullets, not bodies" philosophy, so firmly entrenched in Korea, directly into the Vietnam War. And while this concept had its merits in a conventional if limited war like Korea, it caused severe problems for the United States in the unconventional counterinsurgency warfare of Vietnam.

David T. Zabecki

Bibliography
Bailey, J.B.A. *Field Artillery and Firepower* (Oxford: 1989).
Boatner, Mark M. III. "Countering Communist Artillery," *Combat Forces Journal* (September 1953).
Cocklin, Robert F. "Artillery in Korea," *Combat Forces Journal* (August 1951).
Comparato, Frank E. *Age of Great Guns* (Harrisburg: 1964).
Schaad, Carl W. "Fire Support Coordination," *Combat Forces Journal* (September 1952).

Australia and the Korean War
One of the first U.N. member nations to commit forces to the fighting in Korea, Australia played a small but significant role both in the U.N. agencies and within the overall British Commonwealth organization which fought as part of the United Nations Command (UNC).

Australian involvement in Korean affairs predated the outbreak of war. Australia was represented on both the U.N. Temporary Commission on Korea (UNTCOK) and its successor, the U.N. Commission on Korea (UNCOK), and its delegate played an active role in observing the elections of May 1948 in the south, which hardened the division of the country. At this stage, the Australian government was often highly critical of those political groups which had achieved power around Syngman Rhee, and of U.S. policy in supporting them. The Australian representative on UNCOK, A.B. Jamieson, was instructed to absent himself from the country during the ceremonies marking the inauguration of the southern Republic of Korea (ROK) in August 1948. Even after the outbreak of war, the Australian government emphasized the United Nations role in maintaining collective security rather than support for Rhee's government when justifying the commitment of Australian forces.

In March 1950, UNCOK had requested the secretary-general of the United Nations to provide eight field observers to monitor the military situation along the 38th parallel, but by May only two had arrived, Squadron Leader R.J. Rankin and Major F.S.B. Peach, both provided by Australia. Their report, released on 24 June (one day before the North Korean invasion), following a series of reconnaissance trips along the parallel between 9–23 June, provided important first-hand evidence in support of the belief that the war was a consequence of North Korean aggression. They advised that the ROK Army was lightly armed and equipped and incapable of serious or sustained offensive action northward. They also, somewhat obtusely, reported on the absence of "unusual activity" on the part of North Korean forces which might "indicate any imminent change in the general situation on the parallel." The report was tabled at a meeting of UNCOK in Seoul on 26 July and a précis cabled to the secretary-general and reproduced as Security Council document S/1507. Given further consideration by UNCOK on 29 June, the conclusions of which were cabled to the Security Council as well, the report strongly influenced the U.N. resolutions branding the North Korean invasion an act of aggression, and from this all other aspects of U.N. involvement flowed.

Australia subsequently committed air, ground, and naval units to the UNC, which fought independently of each other and whose involvement will be dealt with separately below. In addition, Australians continued to play an important role in the U.N. commissions, notably the U.N. Commission for the Unification and Rehabilitation of Korea (UNCURK). The Australian representative, James Plimsoll, was able to exert some moderating influence on Rhee, whose authoritarian methods and openly revanchist intentions caused the Australian government considerable disquiet. In May 1952, Plimsoll took the lead in upbraiding Rhee over the declaration of martial law and the arrest of members of the national assembly, while UNCURK maintained some influence over the South Korean police and prison administration. Australia played a minor role in the U.N. itself, generally in support of American policy. In Korea itself there were points of divergence. In December 1950, Australia backed U.K. Prime Minister Clement Attlee's concerns during discussions with U.S. President Harry S. Truman over use of atomic weapons, and over suggestions that the United States, in response to Chinese intervention in the war, retaliate against targets within China. As a consequence of its involvement, the Australian government derived a number of tangible benefits which helped to cement its role in the Western alliance and establish its security relationship with the United States.

The first Australian combat unit committed to the fighting was the Royal Australian Air Force's No. 77 Squadron, based in Japan as part of the British Commonwealth Occupation Force (BCOF) and equipped with piston-engine P-51 Mustangs. The remaining units of BCOF were preparing to return to Australia when the war began, were understrength and run-down as a consequence of long years of occupation duty, and the Australian government hesitated initially over deploying these forces into combat. Indeed, General Douglas MacArthur gained the early use of 77 Squadron only by putting public pressure on the Australian government as a result of making his request for their employment known to journalists traveling with him. The squadron was employed in fighter-interceptor and ground support roles beginning on 2 July; the years of occupation duty as part of the American Far East Air Force (FEAF) proved a bonus, since the Australian pilots were thoroughly familiar with American tactics, organization, and procedures. This enabled them to fit smoothly into the U.N. air effort; it did not save them from the customary accidents of war, as when a flight of Australian aircraft attacked a South Korean train carrying ROK soldiers and American troops of the 24th Infantry Division on the second day of operational flying. This was a result of failings in the system of target allocation, and plagued U.S. units equally until rectified gradually as a result of experience and the initiative of higher authority.

The appearance of modern, Soviet-supplied MIG-15 fighters in November 1950 reduced the value of the Australian squadron, since the Mustang was now hopelessly outclassed. The Australian government would have preferred to reequip with the American F-86A Sabre, but these were not available due to heavy demand from the USAF, and the RAAF settled instead on the British Meteor 8. This was unfortunate, because the Meteor, although a jet lighter, was not suitable as a front-line interceptor either, and as a result, 77 Squadron was deployed to fighter-sweep and ground attack roles for the rest of the war.

In addition to base and maintenance squadrons, the RAAF also fielded No. 36 Transport Squadron, which flew C-47 Dakotas, as well as No. 30 Communications Flight. These were organized as No. 91 Composite Wing, RAAF. This represented the highest command level exercised by RAAF officers during the war, since USAF authorities were extremely reluctant to include officers of other services in their command and control structure.

Like the Air Force, units of the Royal Australian Navy (RAN) were deployed for service in Korean waters from the early days of the war. And like its air and ground counterparts, the initial elements of the Australian naval commitment were on occupation duties in Japan. On 29 June, the Australian government authorized the use of the frigate HMAS *Shoalhaven* and the destroyer HMAS *Bataan*, then in Japanese waters, to relieve the former. The *Shoalhaven's* return to Australia was deferred in consequence, and the two ships joined the British Commonwealth naval force which formed the West Coast Support Group (Task Group 96.8). In late August, the destroyer HMAS *Warramunga* relieved the *Shoalhaven*, which then resumed its interrupted return to Australia. For the remainder of the war, the RAN was to maintain two destroyers or frigates on station in Korean waters.

In October 1951, the Australian naval presence was augmented by the addition of an aircraft carrier, HMAS *Sydney*, with its complement of two piston-engine squadrons of Sea Furies and one of Fireflies, organized as the 20th Carrier Air Group. The Australian carrier

A

remained in Korean waters until February 1952, replacing the British carrier HMS *Glory*, which was undergoing a refit in Australia. At this time Australia possessed only one aircraft carrier, acquired from the British soon after World War II, and the *Sydney's* deployment represented the first occasion on which Australia's newly developed maritime aviation capability was exercised.

The major Australian commitment in Korea, as in all Australia's wars, was provided by the Army, and yet again the origins of the force lay in the Australian involvement in the occupation of Japan. In May 1950, the Australian government had decided to withdraw the remaining elements of its understrength infantry battalion, the 3rd Battalion of the Royal Australian Regiment (3 RAR), which numbered between 500 and 550 men on an establishment of 960, together with base and administrative units. Initially, the government intended to continue the withdrawal of ground forces, but on 26 July, the acting prime minister, Arthur Fadden, announced that Australia would supply an Army contingent for service with the United Nations. The size and type of force were not specified. The main pressure for an Australian force came from the external affairs minister, Percy Spender, who believed that prompt government support of the American position, both in the United Nations itself and by more practical measures, would help his attempts to negotiate a binding security agreement with the United States.

Because of the peculiarities of the Defense Act, Australian regular soldiers had to volunteer for specified overseas service. Soldiers in 3 RAR began doing so on 30 July, but the unit was so badly understrength at this point that the Australian commander-in-chief of BCOF, Lieutenant General Sir Horace Robertson, insisted to his government that the unit not be deployed on active service until it had been brought up to war establishment and had completed some necessary unit training. As a result, the battalion did not reach Korea until 28 September, where it was attached to the British 27th Infantry Brigade, which had reached the Pusan perimeter a month previously and which now became the 27th Commonwealth Brigade.

The Australian battalion took part in the pursuit of the defeated North Korean forces across the 38th parallel, advancing as far north as Pakchon before the advent into the war of the Chinese forced the UNC to retreat in some disorder. During this phase of the war the Austra-

lian and British battalions often found themselves acting as rearguards for withdrawing American and Korean forces; it became widely known that the American divisional and corps commanders under whom the 27th Brigade operated relied increasingly on these volunteer troops for difficult and dangerous roles. Following the resumption of offensive activities under General Matthew B. Ridgway's command in January 1951, the Australian battalion moved northward again until it came into position northeast of Seoul in April. Brought forward hurriedly from reserve in the face of the Chinese "Fifth Phase" offensive, the 27th Brigade, further augmented at this time by a Canadian infantry battalion and a New Zealand artillery regiment, fought a major successful action against a Chinese division at Kapyong. After further fighting in May, the redesignated 28th Commonwealth Brigade was withdrawn from the line to be integrated into the 1st Commonwealth Division, formed with the 25th Canadian and 29th British Brigades. The Australian units fought as part of this formation for the rest of the war.

"Operation Commando" in October saw the Australian battalion take a leading part in the fighting to extend the Commonwealth Division's positions along the Jamestown line. At about the same time, the Australian government announced its decision to commit a second battalion to Korea in the face of repeated requests from the Truman administration for the augmentation of U.N. forces by contributing nations. The 1st Battalion, Royal Australian Regiment, arrived in Korea in April 1952, and was brigaded with its sister unit; following standard practice in British pattern armies, the command of the brigade now passed to the Australians, since they now fielded the preponderant force in the brigade. In March 1953, after a one-year tour, 1 RAR was relieved by 2 RAR; 3 RAR remained on active service throughout the war and into the armistice period, only returning to Australia in October 1954.

The major consequence for Australia of involvement in the Korean War was the signing of the Australia–New Zealand–United States (ANZUS) Treaty in San Francisco on 1 September 1951. As noted previously, Spender had argued in Cabinet that prompt and effective support of U.S. policy in Korea would greatly strengthen the case for concluding a binding security agreement with the Truman administration; this was an outcome that had been pursued with notable lack of success by

Spender's Labor Party predecessor, H.V. Evatt, after 1945. The prime minister of the day, R.G. Menzies, had expressed doubts as to both the necessity and possibility of attaining it. By adroit diplomacy and an insistence that a security treaty was the price of a "soft" peace treaty with the Japanese, which the Americans had been advocating strongly for some time, Spender convinced an unwilling U.S. administration wary of multilateral security arrangements to largely accede to his wishes. In an important sense, the ANZUS Treaty had little to do with the Korean War, since it was not a direct reward for Australian support there, but there can be little doubt that the ready offers of Australian assistance helped Spender's case, just as they smoothed the path for Australia's application to the World Bank for a $250 million loan which, unusually, was granted without tying it to any specific projects.

Involvement in the Korean War made little impact in Australia itself, especially after late 1951 when the fighting degenerated into a prolonged period of static warfare which accompanied the interminable truce talks at Panmunjom. The forces sent to Korea were entirely regular and volunteer, the actions in which they took part were notably successful, and casualties were low. Total casualties for all services were 1,584, with 339 killed; twenty-nine Australians were taken prisoner by the Chinese and North Koreans. Involvement in the war did demonstrate how far the Australian services had run down in the few short years since the end of World War II; in 1945, Australia had fielded six infantry divisions in the Pacific, as well as large air and naval forces both there and in Europe. But in 1952, it could just manage to maintain two infantry battalions on active service together with small air and naval contributions. The Korean War also marked the high point of Commonwealth military cooperation, and although Australian forces were to fight alongside British and Commonwealth forces in Malaya and Borneo in the 1950s and 1960s, the reorientation of Australian defense and foreign policy toward the U.S. alliance was given a considerable boost as a result of the Korean War.

Jeffrey Grey

Bibliography

Bartlett, Norman, ed. *With the Australians in Korea* (Australian War Memorial, Canberra: 1954).

Grey, Jeffrey. *The Commonwealth Armies and the Korean War: An Alliance Study* (Manchester University Press, Manchester: 1988).

McCormack, Gavan. *Cold War/Hot War: An Australian Perspective on the Korean War* (Hall and Iremonger, Sydney: 1983).

Odgers, George. *Across the Parallel: The Australian 77th Squadron with the United States Air Force in the Korean War* (Heinemann, Melbourne: 1952).

O'Neill, Robert. *Australia in the Korean War 1950–53*, 2 vols: *Strategy and Diplomacy* (Australian Government Publishing Service, Canberra: 1981); *Combat Operations* (Australian Government Publishing Service, Canberra: 1985).

A

B

Bacteriological Warfare

Communist allegations that American military personnel conducted germ warfare in Korea became a major propaganda issue of the Korean War. The Communists were abetted in their efforts by naturally caused epidemics during the war which made their accusations seem credible.

North Korea's foreign minister first asserted in May 1951 that U.S. troops were purposefully spreading smallpox germs. In June, China joined its ally, charging that the United States was guilty of bacteriological warfare. The Soviet Union supported the charges, claiming that the United States deployed bombs and artillery shells that contained bacterial warfare agents such as beetles, lice, and ticks. These initial accusations occurred simultaneously with the refusal of repatriation by many UN-held Communist prisoners.

During the war Communist medical services collapsed. A natural environment for disease already existed in Korea, and wartime conditions only accelerated its spread. The war's rapid movement up and down the peninsula expedited the dissemination of diseases which, in peacetime, usually stagnated in a confined area. The climatic extremes of intense cold and heat provided an environment for various strains of viruses and bacteria to thrive. The crowded nature of Korea's population, exacerbated by thousands of foreign troops and refugees, possibly introduced new strains of disease, as well as aiding their spread. Most Koreans were not immune (or vaccinated) to potential disease threats. Human wastes were used as fertilizer, and a vast variety of insects lived on the peninsula; many Koreans were infected with worms or other parasites. And when water supplies were damaged during air raids or ground movements, a vital facet of public health was seriously impaired.

The Communists faked photographs and exhibits of insects and vector-launching apparatus in order to support their allegations. These statements and exhibits were convincing, but the United States denied the accusations, stating the charge and exhibits were merely propaganda to conceal naturally occurring epidemics that the Communists could not control due to poor public health systems.

During World War II, Japan had allowed Lieutenant General Shiro Ishii to experiment in Manchuria with plague. The American government offered Ishii immunity in return for cooperation in the development of germ warfare. This protection made Asian Communists deeply suspicious of American intentions.

In truth, germ warfare seemed an attractive technique for the American military to acquire and develop. Experimental laboratories had been established at Camp Detrick in Frederick, Maryland. Both China and the Soviet Union were aware of this development and were afraid future germ warfare techniques would be deployed against them. In October 1950, Secretary of Defense George C. Marshall approved the production of diseases for weapons because Pentagon officers feared that North Korea and China themselves might initiate biological attacks, and Marshall wanted to have a retaliatory weapon. Former Secretary of Defense Louis Johnson conceded that the United States had biological weapons for use in Korea if necessary. The Communists took his statements and spread embellished versions in the Asian and Eastern European press.

U.N. soldiers also spread rumors of enemy germ warfare; in October 1950, soldiers of the 7th Division witnessed Koreans throwing brown powder in a stream and saw dead fish rise to the surface. But the powder was merely an herbal substance used by peasants to stun fish for easy harvesting. When U.N. forces entered Pyongyang in November 1950, germ cultures at Kim Il Sung Medical College were examined, and the institute's staff was interrogated. Other North Korean laboratories were examined for possible germ warfare research. To investigate North Korean reports of plague, Brigadier General Crawford F. Sams, General Douglas MacArthur's chief of public health and welfare, interrogated Communist agents, finding contradictions in their descriptions of diseases.

In February 1951, both Peking Radio and the *People's Daily* reported that Koreans had witnessed American aircraft drop insects that resulted in cases of cholera. In March, the Communists alleged that American artillery had been used to shoot typhus germs across the Imjin River, and that the U.S. Army had sent infected animals and vectors to four locations.

Kim Il Sung issued an emergency decree, calling for the National Extraordinary Anti-Epidemic Committee, the ministry of public health, and the Army medical bureau to destroy insects and initiate an anti-epidemic campaign. North Koreans were advised to adopt a systematic plan to squelch diseases; they cleaned privies, killed rats and flies, avoided raw food, and boiled water. In every month, six clean-up days were randomly scheduled, and the anti-epidemic committee performed daily inspections and reported cases of disease.

The North Koreans stated the United States was responsible for 3,500 cases of smallpox in civilians, and demanded that U.N. commanders Matthew B. Ridgway and Douglas MacArthur be tried for these "crimes." This escalation of germ warfare allegations occurred during the beginning of the stalemate in the summer of 1951. During the truce talks concerning prisoners, the issue of voluntary repatriation particularly distressed the Communists. The impasse on the field metamorphosed into a war of words. The Communists hoped to obscure the prisoner issue. The Allies' resistance to disease, compared to how quickly enemy soldiers succumbed, aided the Communists in their allegations that the Americans were to blame for disease distribution.

In an effort to turn Asians against the United Nations, the North Koreans claimed that Americans were using Communist prisoners in atomic bomb tests in the South Pacific.

On 2 February 1952, the Soviet ambassador to the United Nations, Jacob Malik, claimed that the U.S. forces were using bullets filled with toxic gas in attacks against Communist troops and civilians. In that month, Communist radio stations also relayed messages alleging that the American soldiers were poisoning wells. The Communists claimed that the U.S. soldiers used lepers to spread germs, in addition to dropping germ-infested rats from aircraft. In 1952, the Communists began ostentatiously inoculating U.N. prisoners and indoctrinating them with intensive germ warfare lectures, solicitously stressing that the vaccine would prevent them from being infected by diseases deployed by American pilots.

In March 1952, a Communist "front," the International Association of Democratic Lawyers, agreed to judge the germ warfare allegations. Its members did not question the validity of any items or testimony the Communists gave. Lacking technical knowledge and objectivity, they ruled against the United States, and the Soviet Union announced the results of the committee to the United Nations. The Soviet Union reiterated the accusations at the U.N. Disarmament Commission and implemented large-scale publicity of the accusations. The CIA reported that most non-Communist people were skeptical of the allegations, but that some did accept the claims.

The United States demanded an international investigation of the allegations to reveal that the Communists had no proof. The Moscow-supported World Peace Council investigated the charges, but the Communists refused to allow either the International Red Cross or the U.N. World Health Organization to explore the issue. International Red Cross leaders appealed to the North Koreans and Chinese to let specialists chosen by the Red Cross, including scientists from Asian Red Crosses, examine the evidence. The Communists refused.

At a meeting in Oslo, Norway, an investigatory committee was hand-picked by Dr. Kuo Mo Jo, president of the Chinese Academy and Chinese Peace Commission. The Communists decided to delay the investigation until summer because they realized they lacked convincing evidence; statements were extorted from American pilots during the spring.

United States prisoners were coerced or "brainwashed" into making public statements affirming the Communists' germ warfare allegations. In May 1952, two imprisoned pilots, after being isolated, interrogated, threatened with trial as war criminals, and promised repatriation only if they confessed, confessed to dropping germ bombs. The Communists embellished and took the pilots' confessions out of context, splicing recordings and rewording statements. In addition to the confessions, the Communists exhibited shells of psychological leaflet bombs, claiming they were examples of germ bombs which had been refitted to contain insects instead of leaflets.

The International Scientific Commission for the Investigation of the Facts Concerning Bacterial Warfare in Korea and China scrutinized the charges, studying evidence and reports, visiting alleged sites, and interviewing American pilots. The commission analyzed pathological studies of Koreans who had died of anthrax and said they found plague organisms in human fleas.

In addition, statements associating insects with flights of American warplanes were examined. Examples of peasant testimony included a story about a couple who died after eating clams; the previous night, warplanes were heard flying near the creek. A second story included allegations of planes dropping paper parachutes with contaminated rats. Although many of the vectors that the Communists claimed the United States were using were incapable of spreading diseases or were non-biting, the commission concluded that some germ warfare techniques were secret and might not be transferred through bites.

The commission did not consider significant information such as how varied altitudes and topographical conditions eliminated the chance of the insects existing at named sites. They believed the fabricated tales of the source of diseases present in Korea. On 18 September 1952, the committee released a 700-page report from Peking. The document contained detailed transcripts of testimony, analyses, and conclusions, but according to the scientists themselves, was not based on scientific methods.

On 23 April 1953, the U.N. General Assembly named a five-power commission to investigate germ warfare, but when the armistice was signed, the Communists were no longer interested in the question.

The Korean War germ warfare charges were initiated by the Communists to conceal the fact that they could not control epidemics because of the exigencies of wartime conditions and lack of effective medical care. The Communists manipulated the charge into a propaganda condemnation of the United States, and diverted attention from the refusal of thousands of their compatriots to return to their motherlands.

Ironically, Communist public health drastically improved as a direct result of incidents during the germ warfare accusations, compensating for losses in other wartime arenas.

Elizabeth Schafer

Bibliography

Cowdrey, Albert E. *The Medic's War, United States Army in the Korean War* (GPO, Washington: 1987, 1990).

———. "'Germ Warfare' and Public Health in the Korean Conflict," *Journal of the History of Medicine and Allied Sciences,* 39 (April 1984).

Harris, Robert, and Jeremy Paxman. *A Higher Form of Killing: The Secret Story of Chemical and Biological Warfare* (1982).

Winokur, George. "The Germ Warfare Statements: A Synthesis of Method of and the Extortion of False Confessions," *Journal of Nervous and Mental Diseases,* 122 (July 1955).

Barr, David G. (1895–1970)

Born in Nanfalia, Alabama, on 16 June 1895, David Goodwin Barr attended Alabama Presbyterian College for three years before leaving school to enlist in the Army when the United States entered World War I. He was commissioned a second lieutenant in the infantry after graduating from officer candidate school, and in 1918 he went to France, where he earned a Silver Star for valor while serving in the 1st Division.

Remaining in the Army after the war, Barr graduated from the Infantry School in 1921, the Tank School in 1924, and the Army War College in 1939. During World War II, he held a series of staff positions in the United States and in the European and Mediterranean theaters, finishing the war with the rank of major general, the prestigious job of chief of staff of the Sixth Army Group, and the reputation of a highly intelligent and practical officer.

At the end of 1947, Barr was named head of the United States Military Advisory Group in China, which was responsible for assisting the Nationalist Chinese in their war against the Chinese Communists, a thankless assignment. Later he was appointed director of the Joint United States Military Advisory Group–China.

Throughout 1948, Barr and Generalissimo Chiang Kai-shek disagreed over Nationalist strategy; and after the Nationalist Army was decisively defeated in Manchuria, Barr attributed the debacle to "the world's worst leadership." Convinced that the "complete defeat of the Nationalist Army" was "inevitable," he emphatically opposed any further American aid to salvage the Nationalist cause. President Harry S. Truman, however, chose to continue arms shipments. But on Barr's recommendation he recalled the advisory group in January 1949 in anticipation of the final Communist victory.

After his China assignment, Barr became commander of the 7th Division, part of the American occupation army in Japan. In the weeks following the outbreak of the Korean War in June 1950, Barr hurriedly rebuilt the division after it had been stripped of many of its best officers and men to beef up other American units and had it ready to participate in the Inchon invasion in September 1950. Notwithstanding this accomplishment and his distinguished record, Barr was not suited to command the division in battle. He had no meaningful experience as a battlefield leader, and his "rumpled and round" appearance and courtly and friendly demeanor later led even his aide-de-camp to remark that "he didn't look or act the part of a commanding general."

The American triumphs in the fall of 1950, including the 7th Division's arrival at the Yalu River after a 200-mile march through North Korea east of the Chosin Reservoir, obscured Barr's defects. However, they became readily apparent when the Chinese Communists launched a massive offensive against United Nations forces at the end of November 1950. Plagued by unsecured flanks, the wide dispersal of its units, and an inadequate supply line, Barr's division was ravaged by the Chinese onslaught. During the ensuing American retreat out of North Korea, Barr repeatedly clashed with Major General Edward M. Almond, the prickly commander of X Corps, over tactics and command arrangements, and did not hold up well under stress. He "worried about everything," but let his deputy essentially command the division, and was reduced to tears after hearing of the virtual destruction of one of its task forces.

Following the American defeat in North Korea, General Matthew B. Ridgway, commander of the Eighth Army, concluded that Barr lacked "offensive spirit" and sacked him

as part of a wholesale housecleaning of front-line generals. Barr returned to the United States in early 1951 to become commander of the Armored School at Fort Knox, Kentucky, a post he occupied until a heart attack compelled his retirement later that year. He died at Falls Church, Virginia, on 26 September 1970.

John Kennedy Ohl

Bibliography

Appleman, Roy E. *East of Chosin: Entrapment and Breakout in Korea, 1950* (Texas A & M University Press, College Station: 1987).

———. *South to the Naktong, North to the Yalu: June–November 1950* (Office of the Chief of Military History, Washington: 1961).

Blair, Clay. *The Forgotten War: America in Korea, 1950–1953* (Times Books, New York: 1987).

Department of State. *United States Relations with China* (GPO, Washington: 1949).

Senate Armed Services and Foreign Relations Committees. *Hearings on the Military Situation in the Far East*, 82d Congress, 1st sess. (GPO, Washington: 1951).

See also CHIANG KAI-SHEK

Bazooka vs. Tank

At the opening of the Korean War, the standard U.S. Army and Marine Corps antitank weapon was the M1 2.36-inch rocket launcher, popularly known as the "bazooka." A two-man weapon, the bazooka fired a 3.4-pound rocket at a muzzle velocity of 270 feet (83 meters) per second. Its effective range was 182 yards (200 meters), and its maximum range was 700 yards (640 meters). The rocket had a high-explosive antitank (HEAT) warhead that would penetrate five to six inches (127–152mm) of armor, and was thus, in theory, capable of penetrating the armor of a Soviet T-34 tank, whose maximum armor was 90mm thick.

In practice, the 2.36-inch rocket launcher had several serious problems, the most egregious of which had been its inability to penetrate heavier German armor apparent since the early days of World War II; Brigadier General James Gavin, commander of the 82nd Airborne Division, noted officially the "vast superiority" of the German antitank weapon (*panzerfaust*) over the bazooka. A historian noted the bazooka's inability to counter German panther tanks, "a fact observed and reported by scores of field commanders" at the time.

Thus it should have come as no surprise that the bazooka proved unable to stop the onslaught of North Korean T-34/84 tanks that poured into South Korea in June 1950. Although the enemy had only 150 tanks, they seemed to form a juggernaut that shrugged off South Korean U.S.-supplied 57mm antitank and bazooka rounds without effect. Not only were their rocket launchers obsolete, the rounds they fired were usually so old that they did not explode.

Although it could not help the troops of Task Force Smith, a new 3.5-inch "super bazooka" could indeed stop the T-34. Its ammunition had been in production a scant fifteen days when the war started. General Douglas MacArthur, Far East commander, formally requested the new weapon on 3 July. The first shipment of the new rocket launchers, along with a team of instructors, arrived in Taejon on 12 July. A period of intense and frenzied training followed. It was none too soon; a fierce North Korean attack struck Taejon on 20 July. On that day, the regimental commander of the 23rd Infantry supervised the first "kill" credited to the new weapon. Supposedly, on that one day, ten enemy tanks were destroyed by the 3.5-inch bazooka, while artillery accounted for a mere two. Through arrogance or ignorance, the North Koreans continued to send their tanks singly into the closely packed city, enabling bazooka teams to destroy them piecemeal. The most famous incident of the battle for Taejon was the destruction of a T-34 by a team under the supervision of the 24th Infantry Division commander, Major General William F. Dean. This led to Dean's oft-quoted but not entirely accurate remark, "I got me a tank." Dean later pointed out that an unescorted tank in a city defended by troops equipped with the 3.5-inch bazooka "should be a dead duck." But Dean's men were still suffering from the effects of soft Japanese occupation life, and outnumbered, fell back from the city. Dean himself was captured after fleeing the overrun city.

The 3.5-inch bazooka did have several limitations. It was less effective in open country. There were also numerous occasions where its rounds failed to penetrate enemy armor. The best means of stopping a T-34 tank, at least in open country in Korea, seemed to lie in a combination of 75mm recoilless rifles, the 90mm gun of the U.S. Pershing tank, and 105mm howitzers, all using armor-piercing rounds, and the 3.5-inch bazooka.

Still, the new bazooka took a fearsome toll of North Korea's once-irresistible T-34 tank force. At the beginning of the war, U.S. forces had no ground weapon that could be counted on to destroy enemy armor. Two months later, they could almost take their pick. For the remainder of that conflict, Communist armor posed no serious hazard to U.N. forces.

Spencer Tucker

Bibliography

Appleman, Roy E. *South to the Nakton, North to the Yalu* (Office of the Chief of Military History, Washington: 1961).

Blair, Clay. *The Forgotten War; Americans in Korea, 1950–1953* (Times Books, New York: 1987).

Rees, David, ed. *The Korean War: History and Tactics* (New York: 1984).

Tunis, Edwin. *Weapons* (New York: 1954).

Correspondence from U.S. Army Jefferson Proving Ground, Missouri with author. 1993.

See also ARMOR IN THE KOREAN WAR

Big Switch

See OPERATIONS BIG AND LITTLE SWITCH

Bradley, Omar N. (1893–1981)

Born in Clark, Missouri, Omar Nelson Bradley was the first chairman of the Joint Chiefs of Staff (1949–1953), active in this capacity during the Korean War. He had fought in Germany during World War II, commanding the Twelfth Army Group. A graduate of West Point in 1915, he went on to be commandant of the Infantry School at Fort Benning, Georgia, as World War II broke out. Bradley commanded forces in North Africa, contributing to the fall of Tunisia, then led the invasion of Sicily. Later he was transferred to Great Britain, where he aided in plans for the invasion of Normandy. His forces liberated Paris in August 1944. He was given command of the Twelfth Army Group, the largest U.S. Army group ever assembled, and his forces continued to fight in France, Belgium, Luxembourg, the Netherlands, Germany, and Czechoslovakia until V-E Day on May 8, 1945. Shortly before the Korean War's outbreak, Bradley served as administrator of veteran's affairs, and chief of staff of the Army for eighteen months in 1948–1949. He was chosen as the first chairman of the Joint Chiefs of Staff (JCS) after President Harry S. Truman's reorganization of the military in 1949. His relationship with the commander-in-chief, Far Eastern command, Douglas MacArthur, had remained distant (he had not seen MacArthur since his West Point days in 1922), and he had not visited MacArthur in Japan during the occupation, nor had MacArthur come to Washington. Bradley traveled to Japan (29 January–10 February 1950) with the Joint Chiefs of Staff and appraised MacArthur as having an obsession for self-glorification and a contempt for the judgment of his superiors, in short, a megalomaniac. Bradley oversaw the U.S. strategic plan in the Far East after the fall of China to the Communists in 1949, and which continued after the Korean War erupted. This was a policy of defending Japan and Okinawa, using them as platforms for mounting a strategic air defensive, and as naval bases to control the seas. The Philippine Islands air and naval bases supported this same strategy. Bradley, however, had placed the threat of Communism in Europe ahead of the threat in the Far East. MacArthur would have reversed these priorities. Korea did not feature in this strategy.

Bradley was an architect of the military aspects of the Japanese peace treaty which kept Japan demilitarized and encouraged the role of the U.S. military in defending Japan and Okinawa as our first line of defense in Asia. Bradley and the joint chiefs had consistently postponed signing of the peace treaty with Japan, believing Japan still lay open to Communist infiltration and military attack. He drew the parameters under which the United States might evacuate Japan and saw to the maintenance of the military bases the United States needed to defend its Asian interests, and had these terms grafted to the peace treaty. Bradley had originally planned secretly to rearm the Japanese; MacArthur sought to keep Japan disarmed, and the State Department later agreed.

Prior to the outbreak of the Korean War, the Joint Chiefs of Staff had little strategic interest in Korea, but Bradley disagreed with Secretary of State Dean Acheson's comments, made 12 January 1950 to the National Press Club in Washington, that Korea was outside the defensive perimeter of the United States. To counterbalance the growing North Korean Army, supplied by the Soviet Union, the Joint Chiefs of Staff had built up the Army of Syngman Rhee, and had done so to a strength of 100,000 men.

However, this force was lacking in tanks, heavy artillery, ammunition, and large-scale unit training. And after the fall of mainland China to the Communists in 1949, the JCS had reappraised their policy on Formosa (Taiwan), desiring to aid and defend the island, but Dean Acheson and the State Department disagreed. Just on the eve of the outbreak of the Korean War, however, Bradley, the JCS, in agreement with MacArthur, determined to ask President Truman for aid to Chiang Kai-shek and support for Formosa's defense as an unsinkable aircraft carrier. Convincing the president, Bradley reversed the hands-off policy in regard to Formosa and Chiang Kai-shek. For military purposes, Bradley and the JCS would have also preferred to hold on to Japan longer and delay the peace treaty, encouraged by MacArthur and Acheson; nonetheless, the treaty was signed in 1951. In regard to Indochina, Bradley believed that the Chinese Communists intended to step-up aid to Ho Chi Minh, and advanced what was later called the "domino principle," the concept that if Indochina fell to Soviet-dominated communism, this would precipitate the fall of the weak Thai and Burmese governments, as they would probably take immediate steps to orient themselves with Communist China and the USSR. If this occurred, the Communists could advance next to Malaya, Indonesia, and India.

On 25 June 1950, when the Korean War broke out, Bradley did not call a meeting of the JCS, believing the South Koreans could handle the situation, and confident that South Korea would not fall to the North Korean invasion unless the "Russians actively participate." But he did urge the defense of Formosa. Bradley met with President Truman that night at Blair House (because the White House was being remodeled). Decisions were made to rush military supplies to the ROK Army, evacuate American women and children with U.S. Air Force planes, combat North Korean tanks and planes if necessary, and defend Formosa with the Seventh Fleet. Bradley was authorized to send MacArthur to Korea on a fact-finding mission, increase aid to Indochina, and work with the United Nations to secure a cease-fire or assistance for South Korea from other nations. Bradley called the North Korean invasion an arrogant challenge to all the United Nations stood for, and the situation, in Bradley's eyes, offered an opportunity for the United States to draw the line in response to Communist aggression. Bradley attended a second meeting at Blair House on 26 June 1950, after which he authorized an order for air and naval forces to aid South Korea, and additional aid to the Philippines. On 29 June, Bradley and the JCS committed American ground troops in the Korean War in a limited manner: as service forces aiding communications, and as combat troops to secure the ports and the airbase at Pusan. Air strikes on military installations were authorized north of the 38th parallel, but were to stay well clear of the frontiers of Manchuria and the Soviet Union. Two Army divisions were then committed to the front lines, on MacArthur's urging. Bradley declined Chiang's offer of 30,000 troops, refusing to permit him to fight on the Asiatic mainland, believing he was needed to defend Formosa. Throughout the course of the war, Bradley gave various White House briefs on the situation and continuously advised the president, seeing Truman daily to brief him on the war. Bradley went to Korea only twice during the war, but made most of the military decisions emanating from Washington. Bradley was aware that Truman disliked and distrusted MacArthur, even though Truman had named MacArthur United Nations commander to defend South Korea. Bradley hand-carried most of the messages from Truman to the Pentagon to be relayed to MacArthur. Bradley was Truman's chief and most trusted military advisor.

MacArthur directed the war from Tokyo, naming General Walton H. Walker as tactical commander to lead the U.N. forces (and ROKA) on 13 July 1950. Bradley approved MacArthur's design for the Inchon landing and sent necessary additional forces and airborne divisions to facilitate the plan, which took the pressure off of the Pusan perimeter, into which the South Korean and American forces had been pushed by early August 1950. Bradley defended Formosa with the U.S. Seventh Fleet although he, Truman, and Acheson sought no close relationship with Chiang Kai-shek and his corrupt government. It was a delicate balance, not allowing too much aid, for fear that Chiang would try to return to the mainland. On 22 September 1950, Truman made Bradley a five-star general and General of the Army.

Bradley accompanied Truman to Wake Island on 15 October 1950 to meet with MacArthur. Premier Chou En-lai had already threatened on 3 October that Communist China would assist North Korea if U.N. forces crossed the 38th parallel. Communist troops began to cross the Yalu River, as MacArthur's forces moved toward Wonsan and Pyongyang, and by 26 October had claimed major victories near Onjong and Unsan. U.N. forces were in retreat, and Bradley and the JCS were in continuous discussions for sixty days—November and December 1950, a period which Bradley called the most trying of his professional career. Later, U.N. forces regained the offense, and the JCS and the National Security Council (NSC) favored an end to the war through negotiations rather than by military action alone. Bradley had supported Truman in his dismissal of MacArthur and actively monitored the peace talks at Panmunjom and the exchange of POWs, while working for President Eisenhower after his election in 1952. One of the last official acts of Bradley was as a member of the American delegation which attended the coronation of Queen Elizabeth II in June 1953. Bradley retired after the Korean War on 5 August 1953, and was awarded a fourth Distinguished Service Medal. He lived on for another twenty-eight years.

His recollections appeared in 1951 as *A Soldier's Story* and later in *A General's Life* (1983). After retirement from the Army, Bradley worked for the Bulova Watch Company, initially as head of research and development, and later as chairman of the board, resigning in 1973. In 1965, Bradley's first wife, Mary, died; Bradley later married Kitty Buhler, and together they established the Omar N. Bradley Foundation and the Omar N. Bradley Library at West Point in 1974. Bradley died of a blood clot on 8 April 1981 in New York. He had just accepted the Gold Medal Award from the National Institute of Social Sciences.

Air Force One returned Bradley's remains to Washington, D.C., and he was buried with honors at Arlington National Cemetery. Bradley should be credited with balancing the United States' commitment to Korea with its commitment to resist the Soviet challenge in Europe. He was also instrumental in ensuring that the United States did not go to war directly with mainland China.

Barbara Peterson

Bibliography

Acheson, Dean. *Present at the Creation: My Years in the State Department* (1969).
Bradley, Omar N. *A Soldier's Story* (1951).
Bradley, Omar N., and Clay Blair. *A General's Life: An Autobiography* (1983).
Condit, Kenneth W. *The History of the Joint Chiefs of Staff*, vol. II. *The Test of War 1950–1953* (1988).

Schnabel, James F., and Robert J. Watson. *The History of the Joint Chiefs of Staff,* vol. III *The Korean War* (Washington: 1972–79).

See also JOINT CHIEFS OF STAFF AND THE RELIEF OF GENERAL DOUGLAS MACARTHUR

Brainwashing, or *Xinao*

Throughout the course of the Korean War (1950–1953), nearly 13,000 United Nations (U.N.) soldiers were captured and held as prisoners of war by the Chinese and North Koreans. Slightly more than 10,000 of these prisoners of war (POWs) were members of the American armed forces. By the end of the Korean War it was learned that about 15 percent of the Americans had supposedly collaborated with the enemy and that only about 5 percent had resisted enemy attempts to indoctrinate them for propaganda purposes. All POWs were subjected by their captors to varying degrees of systematic psychological techniques of thought reform to accept Communist doctrine. One of these techniques, *xinao*, or "brainwashing," was predicated upon an erratically applied system of rewards and punishments in combination with techniques for disrupting social organization to "reeducate" POWs during their captivity.

The initial treatment of a POW depended on whether the captors were North Koreans or Chinese. The North Koreans were typically harsh and brutal. The Chinese, on the other hand, were somewhat better supplied with food and clothing, and in line with their overall indoctrination policy often tried to create an atmosphere of friendliness and leniency. When a U.N. soldier was captured he was often treated as if he had been "liberated." The friendly attitude of the Chinese soldier and his emphasis on "peace" was the first and perhaps most significant step in making the POW receptive to the formal moral indoctrination which was to come later.

Outright indoctrination was not attempted at first, although Communist propaganda leaflets were circulated among the POWs and certain activities such as singing Communist songs were required. The POWs were segregated by race/ethnicity, nationality, and rank, in violation of the Geneva accords, and organized into companies, platoons, and squads after they arrived at their respective prison camps. The POWs were not permitted any form of formal organization that would reinforce their group identity and collective behavior, except as it might serve

to strengthen their captors' efforts to remove such internal support mechanisms. This was partially achieved through the control of information whereby their captors were able to create an information bias concerning personal matters and daily events at the local, national, or international levels. Personal contacts with visitors from outside the POW camp were of little value to the men because most visitors to the camps were Communist correspondents. Their captors also attempted to undermine personal contacts by weakening the means of consensual validation between the POWs.

First of all, men were separated by race/ethnicity as well as by rank. The purpose of racial/ethnic segregation appeared to be to put special indoctrination pressure on members of certain minorities, especially blacks. The segregation by rank, however, appeared to be a systematic attempt to undermine the internal structure of the POW groups by removing its leaders. Not only were formal and informal groups which might have supported resistance activity systematically broken up, but there was persistent emphasis on undermining all friendships, emotional bonds, and such group expressions as religious services. Furthermore, POW informers, unknown to the other prisoners, provided the Chinese with further information about POW activities and helped to create a feeling of general distrust among the men. Under these conditions most men realized that the only completely safe course was to withdraw from all intimate interaction with other POWs. The effects of this social isolation were manifold. Many POWs were prevented from validating their beliefs, attitudes, and values through meaningful interaction with one another during a period when virtually all outside information was censored and frequently distorted by prison authorities.

Direct attacks on POW beliefs, attitudes, and values consisted primarily of daily lectures lasting between two and three hours, accompanied occasionally by the distribution of propaganda leaflets and the showing of films to reinforce the content(s) of the lecture's subject matter. This technique was bolstered by another similar technique involving the use of "testimonials" from POWs who were ostensibly supporting Communist enterprises. These included peace petitions, radio appeals, speeches, and confessions. The use of such testimonials had a double effect in that it weakened group ties still further while presenting pro-Communist arguments.

Indirect attacks on POW beliefs, attitudes, and values consisted of creating a set of conditions in which each POW was encouraged to participate in ways that would make it more likely for him to accept some of the new points of view. This was accomplished through group discussion sessions regarding military and non-military subjects lasting for periods of two hours or more after scheduled lectures, to thoroughly "discuss," in effect to rationalize, a series of predetermined conclusions. To ensure that this method was being properly utilized, the POWs were forced to write detailed autobiographies followed by intense interrogation. A further technique was to have the POW write out the question and then the answer. If he refused to write it voluntarily, he was asked to copy it from another's notebook. Not realizing that this copied material could be used as "evidence" to show that he had given information of his own volition, the POW inadvertently placed himself in a position to be blackmailed, since he would have a difficult time proving that he had merely copied the material.

Another effective technique for getting POWs to question their own beliefs and values was to make them confess publicly to wrongdoing and to "criticize" themselves. Throughout the time that the men were imprisoned, they were required to go through these rituals over and over again, no matter how trivial the offense. Such public self-effacement was not only a humiliating and degrading experience, but it set a bad precedent for the conduct of other men who had been attempting to resist getting caught in this net. One other technique involved enforced idleness or isolation, which was used as an opportunity the indoctrinate POWs with Communist literature, including books and articles by Western authors who directly or indirectly attacked capitalism and other Western institutions and systems.

Lastly, through collaboration, circumstances or techniques were imposed on POWs which tended to elicit new kinds of behavior not consistent with old beliefs, attitudes, and values. Collaboration was encouraged by a system of rewards and incentives on the one hand, and threats and punishments on the other. In the case of the former, a tendency toward "cooperation" was quickly followed by an increase in material rewards, and promises for the future. The Chinese also used symbolic rewards, which were in many ways more effective than material ones. Such symbolic rewards included special privileges in the prison camp, rank and status in the prison camp hierarchy, and more rewards in the future. Perhaps the most important of the privileges was freedom of movement in and around the prison camp. Essentially, this "lenient policy" applied only to those men whom the Chinese hoped they could use in their enterprise.

While the probability of collaborative behavior could be increased through the use of various rewards, it was usually necessary to use negative or painful stimulation to decrease the probability of unacceptable behavior. In most cases, threats of punishment were used when POWs refused to "cooperate." Actual punishment was meted out for more aggressive resistance. Of these, the only one that was implemented with any degree of consistency was imprisonment, which sometimes involved long periods of solitary confinement. There is also evidence that the Chinese sometimes used mock executions to elicit cooperation by first creating a state of high anxiety and then a state of grateful relief. There is not any evidence that the Chinese used any drugs, hypnotic methods, or offered sex to elicit information, confessions, or collaborative behavior. Some cases of severe physical torture were reported, but their incidence is difficult to estimate.

There were several general principles associated with all of the above-mentioned psychological techniques of brainwashing: repetition, pacing, participation, use of meaningful contexts, rewards and punishments, principles of propaganda and suggestion, and miscellaneous "tricks." In essence, the POW experience in the various prison camps can be viewed as a series of problems which each man had to solve for himself in order to remain alive and well-integrated. Foremost was the problem of physical privation which powerfully motivated each man to improve his living conditions. A second problem was to overcome the fears of nonrepatriation, death, torture, or reprisals. A third problem was how to maintain some kind of cognitive integration, a consistent outlook on life, under a set of conditions where basic values and beliefs were strongly undermined and where systematic confusion about each man's role in life was created. A fourth problem was to maintain a valid position in a group, to maintain friendship ties and concern for others under conditions of mutual distrust, lack of leadership, and systematically created social disorganization.

The Chinese created a set of conditions in which collaboration and the acceptance of Communism led to a resolution of conflicts in all these areas. We can say that the Chinese were successful in eliciting and controlling certain kinds of behavior in the POW population. They were less successful in changing the beliefs of the POWs. This lack of success, however, might have been due to the inefficiency of a program of indoctrination which could have been highly effective had it been better-supported by adequate information and better trained personnel.

In summary, it is important to realize that while other despotic regimes attempted by brutal measures to reduce their prisoners to a mass of docile slaves, the Chinese attempted by using their "lenient policy" and by treating POWs as men in need of "education," to obtain converts who would actively support the Communist point of view. Only those POWs who showed themselves to be "backward" or "reactionary" in their inability to see the fundamental "truths" of Communism were treated punitively. Chinese psychological methodology employed a combination of all of these techniques simultaneously to gain complete control over significant portions of the physical and social environment of a group of people. In order to understand and evaluate this attempt to create ideological uniformity, it is necessary to view the techniques cited in terms of a sociopsychological model which does justice to the complexity of this combination. Attempts to conceptualize the process of "brainwashing" in terms of a simple conditioning or learning model ignore the most important factor: the simultaneous application of many techniques of social and behavioral control.

Despite sensational journalistic charges in the postwar years, "brainwashing" did not seem to have "taken" among its recipients. The calm and balanced report of Alfred Biderman has never received its due reward. In sober retrospect, it can be said that most American POWs did not collaborate with the enemy. And the supposedly stouter resistance offered by other U.N. prisoners was primarily due to their ranks holding a much smaller proportion of conscripts, and the fact that the overwhelming majority of Americans were captured in the first six months of the war, when the possibility of capture was not even being considered. Further, in the conflict's earliest months, the Americans were taken by the far more brutal North Koreans. The Chinese were more likely to attempt to "reeducate" their captives. (Some American POWs later claimed that the worst Chinese "atrocity" ever inflicted on them was the terminal boredom

induced by the incessant and compulsory lectures in "Scientific Socialism.")

John William Schiffeler

Bibliography

Biderman, A.D. *March to Calumny: The Story of American POWs in the Korean War* (1963).

Cunningham, Cyril. "The Origins and Development of Communist Prisoner-of-War Policies," *Journal of the Royal United Services Institution* (March 1974.)

Grey, J. "Commonwealth Prisoners of War and British Policy During the Korean War," *Ibid.* (Spring 1988).

Schein, Edgar H. "Some Observations on the Chinese Indoctrination Program for Prisoners of War," Defense Technical Information Center, Cameron Station, Alexandria, VA (October 1955).

Schein, Edgar H. "Brainwashing," *Encyclopaedia Britannica*, (1968), vol. IV.

See also PRISONER OF WAR (POW); PSYCHOLOGICAL WARFARE

British Contribution

Britain was the first to join the United States in defense of the Republic of Korea (ROK) in June 1950. This was due to the determination of Prime Minister Clement Attlee and Foreign Secretary Ernest Bevin, mindful of appeasement in the 1930s, to stem aggression wherever it was manifested. Britain was already America's principal ally in NATO, then forming.

A strong squadron of the RN Far East Fleet, including a light carrier, was sent at once to Korean waters, and this complement was maintained there throughout the war, responsible for maritime security of the western coastline. Royal Air Force Sunderland patrol aircraft, based in Hong Kong but detached to Japan, complemented its operations. Royal Air Force pilots were seconded to squadrons of the U.S. Fifth Air Force.

In August, a light force of troops was rushed from Hong Kong to join the hard-pressed land command. This was reinforced by an Australian battalion and an Indian field ambulance unit, forming the 27th Commonwealth Brigade. It entered action in the Naktong bridgehead before taking a leading role in the advance to the Yalu. The 29th Brigade Group joined it from the United Kingdom in November 1950, and both were involved in sharp rearguard actions during the withdrawal from North Korea. The 27th opened a gate for the U.S. 2nd division as it ran the gauntlet from Kunu-ri. The 29th checked Chinese forces attempting to infiltrate into the northwest quarter of Seoul in early January 1951. Meantime, the British 41st Royal Marine Commandos, earlier employed in raiding along the North Korean coast, took part in the operations of the U.S. 1st Marine Division at the Chosin Reservoir.

During the opening of the Chinese "Fifth Phase" offensive in late April 1951, the 29th Brigade on the Imjin River was targeted specifically by the Chinese commander in chief for elimination; the brigade held ground of strategic importance. Despite severe losses, it held firm, losing one battalion, the Glosters, which fought in isolation until it was overwhelmed. General James Van Fleet remarked that this action "saved Seoul and saved the Eighth Army." The 27th Brigade was similarly targeted by the Chinese on the central front. British, Australian, Canadian, and New Zealand troops denied the Chinese access to the Pukhan valley at Kapyong during the same period.

In July 1951, the 1st British Commonwealth Division was formed, swelling British troop numbers to about 14,000 in Korea, excluding the Commonwealth contingents. The division remained in the line for the remainder of the war, principally on the Samichon, resisting some ferocious attempts to break its line. Thus, the United Kingdom (UK) contribution to force levels totaled more than 60,000 over the three years, far exceeding that of any other participant, the United States apart, among United Nations forces. UK casualties exceeded 4,000.

Britain was also America's closest political partner in the war: almost every major policy initiative on Korea during 1950 and 1951 was the product of consensus, despite important differences of outlook. The British were anxious not to provoke a Chinese attack on Hong Kong and Malaya, but, more importantly, believed that Communist China could be coaxed from dependence on the Soviet Union in the manner of Yugoslavia. A British diplomatic mission was in Beijing as the war began to negotiate formal intergovernmental relations with Mao Tsetung's regime. Still, this policy did not extend to admission of the Peking regime to a U.N. Security Council seat while it was reinforcing aggression in Korea. U.S. President Harry S. Truman and Attlee agreed that China must not receive any reward for agreeing to a cease-fire.

Equally, while Britain disagreed with American consideration of a total economic blockade of China, it subscribed to a ban on trade contributing directly or indirectly to war manufactures. This was the effect of the policy adopted by the United Nations in May 1951.

Dean Acheson and Dean Rusk had unique working relationships both with Bevin (who died in April 1951) and the British ambassador in Washington, Sir Oliver Franks, valued as a mediator by both sides during the Truman-Attlee talks in December 1950. These dealt primarily with war policy and anxieties about the containment of General Douglas MacArthur. But they also included consideration of the circumstances in which atomic weapons might be used in the struggle. President Truman promised the British prime minister that he would not use them without consulting him, a promise later found to be in breach of the McMahon Act. Nevertheless, the president remarked that he had given his word and did not feel he would break it, even though reference to this matter was necessarily omitted from the final communique issued to the international press.

Later, Britain alone was assured of consultation prior to retaliatory strikes should China launch bombing attacks from Manchuria against U.N. airfields. There was greater confidence in London in the judgment and restraint of the commander in chief when General Matthew B. Ridgway succeeded General MacArthur in April 1951. Some of the latter's supporters blamed British influence for his dismissal, but they were in error.

When Communist prisoners rioted on Koje Island, British (and Canadian) troops were sent in May 1952 to assist in restoring order. Though horrified at the lax security in the camps, the British government (by then under Winston Churchill) supported its American partners despite international criticism.

Britain left the protracted armistice negotiations to the United States, the principal in the field, but Churchill was assured by President Dwight D. Eisenhower and Secretary of State John Foster Dulles that any return to offensive action would be discussed with him in advance. The alliance struck in World War II, revived in NATO, was enhanced by common cause in the Korean War.

Anthony Farrar-Hockley

Bibliography

Farrar-Hockley, Anthony. *The British Part in the Korean War*, 2 vols. (London: 1990).

Grey, J. *The Commonwealth Armies and the Korean War* (Manchester and New York: 1988).

Rees, D. *Korea, the Limited War* (London and New York: 1964).

See also GREAT BRITAIN AND THE KOREAN WAR; ROYAL NAVY; UNITED KINGDOM

Broadcast News Coverage of the Korean War

Broadcast news of the Korean War was distributed to Americans primarily by AM radio stations, just as war news had been broadcast during World War II; but the number of radio stations in America had more than doubled between the end of World War II and the beginning of the Korean War. At the close of World War II there were 960 AM stations and fifty FM stations broadcasting in America. By 1950, there were 2,300 AM radio stations, 760 FM radio stations, and 109 television stations operating in the United States. Television networks were not national in scope because the telephone lines used to relay audio news to radio stations were not adequate to supply quality video to television stations, and the number of microwave relay stations which could send quality video to television stations across the country were still few. (There were, of course, no satellites for global broadcasting, and even United States coast-to-coast telecasting was not available until 1951.) Edward R. Murrow of CBS did use some film from Korean battle zones for his new CBS television series, *See It Now*.

In the United States there were four national radio networks at the beginning of World War II—two owned by NBC, one by CBS, and one by the Mutual Broadcasting System. In 1943, the U.S. Supreme Court ruled that NBC and CBS together monopolized the radio network business in America and ordered NBC to sell one of its radio networks. Late that year NBC did so, and this network was renamed the American Broadcasting Company in 1945. There was thus more diversity in ownership of network radio during the Korean War than during World War II, but both ABC and Mutual had quite modest news budgets compared to NBC and CBS. Thus most Americans tuned into NBC and CBS for broadcast war news, although one ABC news reporter, Lou Cioffi, became well known when he was wounded in action and was awarded a purple heart.

In 1936, during the early months of the Spanish Civil War, Hans Von (H.V.) Kaltenborn of CBS pioneered the transmission of live news reports from battle zones back to network radio newsrooms in New York via shortwave radio. The American public later eagerly listened to these nightly reports during World War II. Live radio reports of battle actions were once again popular during the early months of the Korean conflict, but these came to a swift end on 20 December 1950, when General Douglas MacArthur ordered that all war correspondent reports from Japan and Korea be censored. Live news reporting was obviously impossible in the face of prior censorship.

The Korean War could not have come at a worse time for American broadcasters. Beginning in 1949, television began to erode the audience for radio stations and networks; radio networks had less money to spend for war news than earlier. Television news was still in its infancy, and television coverage of the war was sketchy at best. The regularly scheduled network TV news broadcasts relied almost exclusively on film and even copy furnished by the armed forces, and provided little commentary and less criticism.

Donald McBride

Bibliography

Berke, Emily. "A Study of Radio News Broadcasts Since the Advent of Television" (master's thesis, Pennsylvania State University, 1956).

Duncan, Joe Turner. "A Study of the Impact of Television Upon the National Radio Networks: 1948–1960" (doctoral dissertation, University of Michigan, 1965).

"Edward R. Murrow." *Current Biography* (1953), pp. 449–450.

"The First 50 Years of Broadcasting." *Broadcasting* (2 March 1981), pp. 93–97.

"The First 50 Years of Broadcasting." *Broadcasting* (3 March 1991), pp. 161–165.

See also FILM, TELEVISION, AND LITERATURE OF THE KOREAN WAR; PRESS (WESTERN) AND THE KOREAN WAR

Canada in the Korean War, 1951–1953

For Canada the Korean War was not a welcome event, but it was an obligation that the country could not forsake. Canada had been at the forefront in the creation of the United Nations and NATO and an early promoter of the creation of a peacekeeping international military. But when the United States gained a U.N. resolution condemning the invasion of South Korea by the North, Canada was uncertain of the extent of its participation. The combination of an American imperative to stabilize Korea by collective action with pressure to realize the making of a U.N. international force left little room to maneuver. Canada had come out of World War II chastened by the exploitation of its forces in support of Great Britain. But it had also asserted itself as a player in the shaping of the postwar world. Canada realized that partnership in the enterprise meant greater participation in the United Nations and closer alliance with the United States as leader of the West. As one of the leaders in creating the North Atlantic Treaty Organization (NATO) to enforce stability in Europe, Canada learned that alliances meant obligations, which in world hot spots such as Korea left little room for picking and choosing positions.

The excitement of creating a community of nations and the restructuring of alliances did not foreshadow anything more than a peacekeeping mission in Korea, which had been divided at the 38th parallel at the end of World War II. The idea that in so remote a place, a "hermit nation," there would be an all-out brutal war with broad ideological overtones was unthinkable. From a field exercise in political muscle-flexing, it became the testing ground of the protagonists of the Cold War. When hostilities began on June 25, 1950, Prime Minister Louis St. Laurent and his secretary for external affairs, Lester Pearson, were both on vacation away from Ottawa. Pearson had to be notified by his secretary personally since he had no telephone in his cottage. He in turn had to find a pay phone to call St. Laurent in St. Patrice. The prime minister recognized that the United States would have to take the lead to defend South Korea but that the United Nations had to play a major role in order to prevent a possible global conflict.

The United States anticipated this concern by calling for the convening of the U.N. Security Council to take up the issue of the invasion. A Soviet boycott of the meeting by Jacob Malik in protest against the seating of the Nationalist China representative gave the United States a decided advantage. Though Canada was not a member of the Security Council, its ambassador, John Holmes, sat as an observer of the emergency session. Holmes filed a report with Pearson, but there was uncertainty about whether the United States would take unilateral action. There was evidence that Korea was considered to be outside the American defense perimeter. Secretary Pearson notified Parliament that given passage of the U.N. resolution condemning the invasion, he anticipated U.N. action against North Korea. However, to the press, Pearson made some off-the-record suggestions that the United States and the United Nations would not exercise military reprisals against North Korea. He did not know that on this same evening of June 26, President Harry S. Truman was in conference with the Joint Chiefs of Staff, the four military secretaries, and the State Department establishment led by Secretary Dean Acheson. Truman was unequivocal in his orders to General Douglas MacArthur, supreme commander of the Far East in Tokyo, to evacuate all American nationals and authorizing him to utilize air power south of the 38th parallel to insure the safety of the evacuation. He also ordered him to transport supplies and ammunition to the South Korean forces and to take control of the U.S. Seventh Fleet en route from the Philippines. A quick response from General MacArthur was not encouraging about South Korea's ability to resist. Truman ordered his defense secretary to call MacArthur and give orders to provide air and naval support south of the 38th parallel and to move the fleet to the Formosa Strait to provide a buffer between the mainland of China and the island of Formosa. He also approved a statement that "the action in Korea would be reported to the United Nations in whose name it would be taken." Stanley Woodward, American ambassador to Canada, notified Pearson of the action, which caught Pearson by surprise. His main concern was the precipitous unilateral action of the United States that had now taken responsibility under the umbrella of the U.N. resolution, which called for a cessation of hostilities and a withdrawal of invading forces. The second U.N. resolution, which recommended U.N. members furnish aid to South Korea to repel the aggressors came on June 27, after the United States had already taken action.

Canada was soon in the mix as Secretary Acheson asked whether Canada would be making physical contributions to the conflict. The Canadian Cabinet had suggested three destroyers and an air transport squadron, but the government was biding its time awaiting indications as to what other U.N. member nations would do. On June 29, the Secretariat asked Canada to supply military observers to join the U.N. commission on Korea. Two military officers were selected to report to Korea on July 24, the first of a much larger involvement of Canada in the Korean War.

Debate in the House of Commons was well under way before these two men were dispatched. The prime minister carefully distanced his government from any thought that Canada was in direct alliance with the United States. He declared that reaction to the invasion was the sense of the United Nations and that Canada could not shirk its responsibility under that charter. The leader of the opposition Progressive Conservatives, George Drew, joined with the government view in an eloquent speech in support of the United Nations and its responsibility to take action. They were soon to realize that Canada's austere defense budgets following

World War II had stripped the military of its vitality. There were less than 48,000 personnel on active duty as late as April 1950. The military budget had dropped to below $400 million, down from the high of almost $3 billion in World War II. Both political and military opinion was predicated on the notion that future wars would be general in nature and involve all western nations. No thought was given to isolated conflicts such as Korea seemed to represent. An imagined armageddon between the total forces of communism and democratic republics paralyzed military thought in Canada as it did elsewhere.

Canada was under external and internal pressures to provide a meaningful contribution to the developing war in Korea. The United States was literally calling on Canada's interest in collective security. Politically, Canada's government believed in U.N. joint action in defense of independent nations and in the concern that should it not participate, its carefully developed status as a force in the United Nations would be dissipated. By mid-July it became an issue of how much more Canada would contribute beyond the three destroyers and a transport squadron already committed. The Canadian press was becoming increasingly "hawkish" on greater involvement. The United States on July 27 pointedly requested that Canada provide a brigade component, but the government delayed addressing the request. Beyond the increasing criticism of the government's inaction by the press, the St. Laurent government's concerns were agitated by the fact that Great Britain and two Commonwealth nations, Australia and New Zealand, were offering ground forces. Great Britain was also making inquiries about what Canada intended to offer. The government sought some deliberate shelter in the protocol that the United Nations would need to establish what they wanted. Since the House of Commons was out of session, the dilemma over what decision to be made and to whom to respond heightened.

However, there was no doubt that action by the United Kingdom inspired Canada to take more forceful action. Discussions between the Ministry of Defense and the general staff revolved around the question of where troops could be gotten. The military came away with the idea that a force must be raised apart from and outside the army on active duty. Army headquarters was to consider creating a volunteer force of battalion strength for short-term enlistment to be guaranteed overseas duty. The announcement of the official creation of the special force was made on August 7. The prime minister's rationale for creating a unique unit rested on the premise that the regular forces had been designed for duty under obligations for North American defense.

The new Canadian Army special force strength was set at 7,065 to be drawn from a recruitment pool of former veterans, the reserves, and the general public. Regular Army volunteers would be taken only when needed to complete units. Though the new unit was regarded as part of the regular military, they were signed to a minimum of eighteen months with extensions to be determined by emergency conditions. Standards of enlistment, including restrictions on allowances for married enlistees, were lowered. Recruitment of the new force was to begin on August 9, 1950, two days after a general announcement to the nation. Both the military and the public were confused by this condition. Recruiting stations were not prepared to meet the demand for haste in processing recruits, and as early as August 8 long lines of young men between eighteen and twenty-five were crowding stations.

The enthusiasm of recruits was encouraged by Prime Minister St. Laurent's speech of August 7 which held out the promise of adventure. Unemployment was a mixed factor at best in that the new unit attracted people who were "at liberty" from job responsibility. But the provinces of Ontario, Quebec, and the prairie provinces of Alberta, Manitoba, and Saskatchewan, which had negligible unemployment, attracted 11,000 of 15,000 applicants by September 1, 1950. The defense ministry insisted on speeding up the processing of recruits by limiting interviews to five to ten minutes. This encouraged haphazard results, as men with personal, psychological, and physical problems slipped through to become eventual headaches for the force. By August 18, the twelve national recruiting depots met their required total of 7,065. The government asked that enlistments continue to a maximum of 9,970 for all ranks. This enlargement of numbers was to guarantee that there would be reserves to sustain the unit both in training and in eventual action. The extra men were important during the training phase. By March 31, 1951, when recruitment ended, 36 percent of the total special force had been discharged as unfit or had deserted. (All but 501 of 1,521 of the deserters had been captured.) The weeding out of almost one-fourth of the force early on ensured a quality fighting force,

one that was to prove itself in the months to come. The new force contained a large number of men who had seen previous service and many were former noncommissioned officers or had skills useful in the army. Less than 60 percent of the recruits were fresh to the military.

To command the new Canadian infantry brigade and prepare it for service in Korea, Brigadier J.M. Rockingham was coaxed from civilian life to volunteer as commander of the unique band of "soldiers of fortune." The entire unit was called the 25th Infantry Brigade and by August 10, 1950, Rockingham set about selecting combat and staff commanders who had volunteered but who possessed wartime experience. Wherever there was no suitable volunteer, Rockingham was allowed to select from a list of regular Army. To satisfy command needs for three battalions of infantry, one regiment of artillery, a field ambulance, a transportation company, an infantry workshop, and two field repair detachments, a large contingent of junior officers from the active, regular army were required. These units were sent to training camps throughout Canada and finally, as winter approached, to Fort Lewis, Washington, to complete unified training and prepare for embarkation.

The logistical problems of training and equipping the new force became confusing, when Great Britain suggested that Canada join with it and other former colonies to form the Commonwealth Division. Britain suggested that British supplies and equipment be used exclusively by this division as well as by the Turkish contingent. The United States, as the host and leader of the armed forces in Korea, naturally sought leadership in supplying arms and materiel to the combined army. Canada wanted to rely on its own resources whenever possible. It did, however, prefer to align with the Commonwealth countries in the field. Certain American weaponry such as the bazooka and vehicles were agreed upon, however. Once in Korea, only the Scandinavian countries and Canada accommodated themselves readily to foodstuffs which were predominantly American.

The overall plan to train the brigade in smaller units and then transfer the entire force to Okinawa for battalion exercises required a collective embarkation point. These plans were changed because the war seemed to be going well for the U.N. forces during the early fall of 1950. The suggestion was made that if Canadian troops were needed at all, no more than a battalion might be sent. It was determined that collective training would take place at Fort Lewis and that the 2nd Battalion, Princess Patricia Canadian Light Infantry, commanded by Lieutenant Colonel J.R. Stone alone would go to Korea. His unit spent only four days at Fort Lewis before sailing for Korea with 927 men on November 25. Since it had undergone almost no advanced training, it was assumed that this would be taken care of when the unit reached Korea. This was not to be as the war took a new turn. The Chinese threatened to enter the war if General Douglas MacArthur's forces continued their advance north of the 38th parallel. By the time the Canadian contingent arrived in Japan on December 14, China had joined the war. On December 18 the battalion was in Pusan and ordered to move south of Seoul to complete training. Lieutenant Colonel Stone protested both to his government and to General Walton Walker, the Eighth Army commander, two days later. Walker wanted the Canadians to join the British 29th Infantry north of Seoul and in line of the enemy advance. The harried General Walker believed that the state of Canadian training was on par with many of his own troops prior to going into action. Though he was probably correct, Stone had his own agenda. The issue became moot, however, when General Walker was killed in a jeep accident on December 23.

General Matthew B. Ridgway, the new Eighth Army commander, accepted an eight-week training interval for the Canadians. By January 13, the battalion was in action and had received its first casualty from sniper fire believed coming from guerrilla bands in South Korea. Exactly a month later, it was assigned to the front to join a British brigade, the 27th Commonwealth. It was the beginning of an involvement in the war that saw the main force of the Canadian 25th Brigade arrive in Pusan during the first week in May, and by May 11 was continuing training. The unit had arrived with a tremendous store of vehicles and equipment. They were sent to the front in support of the 28th British Commonwealth Brigade to form a line with various elements of American and ROK armies which were continuing a counteroffensive back northward over the 38th parallel once again. Canada's involvement would last through the entire war until an armistice was achieved on July 27, 1953. Some 22,000 Canadians would see service in the Canadian Army and another 3,600 in the Navy. Three hundred and ten officers and men lost their lives in combat and another 1,202 were wounded. Ninety-one more died from other causes related to their service and thirty-three men, including two officers and an Air Force pilot, were captured. The Royal Canadian Air Force attached to the U.S. Fifth Air Force provided twenty fighter pilots as well as technical officers. This group was credited with destroying and/or damaging twenty Russian-built fighter jets. Nine American medals, including the first Distinguished Flying Cross to a Canadian since World War I, were won by the air contingent. Meanwhile, the Canadian Air Transport Command delivered 13,000 passengers and 7 million pounds of air freight during its service in support of the U.N. forces. One hundred forty-six officers and 151 enlisted men were decorated or received commendations. The bulk of the major awards, except in six instances (these being regimental sergeants-major and one regimental quartermaster sergeant), went to officers. One woman officer, Nurse Lieutenant J.I. MacDonald, received the Associate of the Royal Red Cross citation while another, Captain E.B. Pense, was awarded the Royal Red Cross commendation. Awards such as The George Medal, Military Medal, and British Empire Medal, as well as Distinguished Conduct Medals, were reserved exclusively for enlisted personnel. American awards to Canadians were all won by officers. A curious omission in the awards seems to lie in the fact that the original commander of the Princess Patricia Battalion, Lieutenant Colonel Stone, is not listed in the awards roster.

The Canadians had mixed relations with the Americans, who at first appeared bent on keeping them separate from the British who eventually melded them into their division. Supply, however, was less of a problem as boots, foul weather gear, and weaponry from the U.S. forces became readily available. The venerable British Bren automatic rifle on which Canadians were trained held preference over the American Browning automatic rifle (BAR), however. With strict orders that the Canadian component had to be sustained as a distinct force under Canadian authority, strains naturally developed as Eighth Army commanders sought to utilize battalion-strength units where needed, regardless of their parent regiment or brigade. The Canadian Navy contingent did not have these problems since each ship was a self-contained unit. The destroyers worked well with the Americans in support of the Inchon landings and in patrolling and providing cover during the retreat after China entered the war.

The most stressful of Canadian-American relations in the war developed almost simultaneously during spring 1952. The U.N. was being charged with the use of bacteriological warfare, a charge that was disruptive to the peace negotiations as well as disturbing to other nations who knew little of what was going on in the war. A former missionary of the Canadian United Church, Dr. James G. Endicott, sent word from China to External Affairs about having knowledge of the use of germ warfare from "personal investigations." During a press conference which was broadcast over Peking radio, Endicott claimed that Canada was involved in that infected insects were bred for American use at the Suffield Experimental Station in Alberta. Endicott later retracted this charge but continued to accuse Americans of bacteriological warfare. The Canadian government condemned the charges and Secretary Lester Pearson was pressed to ventilate the issue. He refused to meet with Endicott, who was indulging himself in a smear campaign with Communist sympathizer overtones. China and North Korea both refused to have the issue investigated by the International Red Cross or the World Health Organization. Three experts in entomology from Canada found no evidence supporting Endicott's charges. The Pearson strategy was to deny Endicott any larger pulpit than he could secure by himself. The political opposition was satisfied that Canada was clean in the matter and that the matter at most might be looked into as a criminal charge. Endicott made public addresses in several large venues in Toronto, receiving wide coverage, but public opinion was overwhelmingly against him. Again thoughts turned to bring charges against Endicott by the House of Commons, but Parliament went into recess and the matter died.

In Korea, however, the Communist charge had some affect, and especially on the huge numbers in allied prisoner of war (POW) compounds. The largest contingent, numbering more than 130,000, were held at Koje-do, a barren rocky island. The camp was poorly structured and managed, and prisoners were kept in compounds of 5,000 or more, but administration was lax and POWs soon created their own internal management structure. The Communist and anti-Communist ideologues in the camps maintained strict discipline and a belligerent attitude toward their captors. Weapons, radios, and propaganda all found their way into the compounds. The militant leaders meted out summary punishments and torture within the camp. Serious uprisings had begun in February and continued into the spring. Troops on prison duty were generally untrained and often panicked and fired on the prisoners in order to maintain control. The North Korean and Chinese governments both seized on this as evidence of atrocities being committed. Almost simultaneous with the arrival of General Mark Clark as General Ridgway's replacement as supreme commander, the prisoners captured the commandant of the camp and held him hostage. His replacement acceded to all the demands of the prisoners, including an admission of atrocities, in order to gain his colleague's release. General Clark was outraged and reduced both brigadiers to colonel and made Brigadier General Haydon Boatner new commandant.

The situation was both a physical and a political embarrassment to the United States, particularly since it was the sole administrator of the camp. General Clark's headquarters made a decision to spread responsibility for administration of the camp. The Canadian Brigade was ordered to dispatch units to the camp for prison duty. Canada's officers had no opportunity to clear the matter with their government and the U.N. command made no attempt to notify the Canadian civil authorities. The British Shropshires were also assigned to the same duty, an action that caused protest in London that the Americans were engaging in attempts to spread the blame for their own incompetence during the spring uprising. The Canadians were dismayed and embarrassed at what they considered shabby treatment by the Americans. However, they carried out their duty without further incident as they took over security of one of the compounds. By July 14, the Canadian company was back with the rest of its brigade. But the Canadian government recalled the Canadian commander of mission in Japan, who was ordered home and forced into retirement for failing to report quickly enough the American assignment of Canadian troops to the prison.

The Canadian 25th Infantry returned to the stalemated war, patrolling north of the 38th parallel and providing security along the Imjin River. For the Canadians, as for the U.N. forces generally, the last half of the war saw the greatest number of casualties on both sides. Nondescript outposts and hills without names, only numbers, had to be taken or held, often at large human cost, and the Canadians more than held their own. When peace finally came on July 27,

C

1953, the British units detached themselves from the area, leaving the Canadian contingent to cover and patrol the former divisional responsibility. It was not until the winter of 1954 that all but one battalion-strength force was withdrawn. In the spring of 1955, the remaining third of the forces was returned to Canada, leaving behind only some 500 auxiliary personnel. These were withdrawn in June 1957, and Canada was finally free of its Korean obligation. But the monetary costs were large, estimated at more than a billion dollars in direct and indirect costs. The country paid considerable dues for loyalty and duty to the cause of collective security, a cause for which Canada went on to become an ardent proponent and practitioner.

Jack J. Cardoso

Bibliography

Cable, Malcolm W., and Frank A. Manson. *The Sea War in Korea* (United States Naval Institute, Annapolis: 1957).

Holmes, John W. *The Shaping of Peace: Canada and the Search for World Order*, Vol. 2 (1982).

Leckie, Robert. *Conflict: The History of the Korean War, 1950–53* (1962).

Munro, John A., and Alex I. Inglis, eds. *Mike: The Memoirs of the Right Honourable Lester B. Pearson*, Vol. 2 (1973).

Stairs, Denis. *Diplomacy of Constraint: Canada, the Korean War, and the United States* (1974).

Thorgrimsson, Thor, and E.C. Russell. *Canadian Naval Operations in Korean Waters, 1950–1955* (1965).

Wood, Herbert Fairlie. *Strange Battleground: Official History of the Canadian Army in Korea* (1966).

Cavalry Units, U.S. Army

The "First Team," officially known as the 1st Cavalry Division, and consisting of the 5th, 7th, and 8th Regiments, landed in Korea on 18 July 1950. The 1st Cav at first considered that its tour in Korea would last approximately the six weeks necessary to push the North Koreans out of South Korea; instead, the division fought for seventeen grueling months.

Originally established in the nineteenth century and comprised of horse soldiers and their mounts, the cavalry had been motorized early in World War II. However, the division retained its cavalry designation and traditions such as the cavalry uniform patch depicting a horsehead on a field divided by a diagonal slash. The troops also occasionally wore the old cavalryman's cross-sabre insignia and traditional yellow scarf, and sang the horse soldier's song, "GarryOwen."

The 1st Cav, organized in 1921, consisted of regiments that had participated in the late-nineteenth-century Indian Wars. In World War II, the division, as infantry, fought in the Southwest Pacific, and was then stationed as an occupation force in Japan when the Korean War began.

The 1st Cav was General Douglas MacArthur's favorite division during World War II and the Japanese occupation. He was particularly impressed with the 7th Regiment and insisted that this regiment, wearing traditional apparel, serve as his color guard. The 1st was considered combat ready and was originally assigned the preeminent role in advance plans for the Inchon landings.

But at the time of the North Korean attack across the 38th parallel, the 1st was in reality severely weakened; its three regiments fought at the reduced strength of two battalions each, with a total of 11,000 division troopers. This was about 7,500 short of its assigned manpower; a deficiency that the ill-advised transfer of nearly 100 prisoners from the divisional stockade did little to redress. Finally, the division was also short in equipment and leadership. Most of the regimental commanders were elderly but inexperienced, selected by cronies in order to advance in rank to a general's star.

The division landed unopposed at Pohang on 18 July and traveled north to reinforce and relieve the weary 24th Infantry Division at Yongdon; the 24th had been mauled severely at Taejon several weeks earlier. The cavalry was also assigned to block the North Koreans away from Taegu, and as a result found itself thrust into the battles of the Naktong River–Pusan perimeter.

The North Koreans hit the separated battalions of the 8th Regiment on 23 July. The 5th Regiment commander was hindered by battle shock and impaired hearing while his battalion commanders put in a disappointing performance or were soon medevaced. The regiment lost 275 casualties.

The poorly trained troops suffered from the high heat and humidity and were confused by the lack of a front line, as the enemy swept around strongpoints or melded with refugees to gain rear blocking positions. The 7th Regiment tried to help, but soon withdrew in chaos.

Understandably, General Walton H. Walker, Eighth Army commander, expressed his disappointment to the 1st's commander, Major General Hobart Gay. Gay came to blame Walker for throwing inexperienced outnumbered troops into combat without sufficient equipment, and claimed that his own idea was to deploy his regiments slowly once they were up to their full strengths in trained troops and equipment. This was certainly an unrealistic concept in those desperate first months of the war.

Gay, fearful that his men would be encircled, decided to withdraw to Kumchon, and eventually back to the Naktong River, defending the region from Waegwan to Yongpo. After a humiliating series of defeats, the division seemed to pull itself together. The 1st Battalion of the 7th Regiment aided the 5th Regiment in killing 700 of an estimated 1,000 enemy attempting to cross the river. Two North Korean divisions, the 3rd and the 10th, were almost destroyed by the cavalry in the northwest sector. The 1st was also bolstered by the arrival of more men and equipment, as were all U.S. units as they fought to hold the Pusan perimeter.

But once again the cavalry fell apart, this time at the "Bowling Alley" (a straight stretch of road running through a narrow valley some 13 miles northwest of Taegu. Armor-piercing shells ricocheted down the valley from enemy tanks with thunderous reverberations) suffering hundreds of casualties. But the 1st Cav's capture of Hills 314 and 902 probably saved Taegu, temporary capital of the Republic of Korea, although these actions cost about two-thirds of the cavalrymen engaged.

In the Bowling Alley, Gay ordered the 7th to strike out, but regimental commander Cecil Nist's deliberateness slowed the advance, causing Gay to fire him and name William Harris as regimental commander. The cavalry captured Colonel Lee Hak Ku, the North Korea People's Army 13th Division's chief of staff, who divulged vital intelligence about further enemy moves. Walker decided the 1st Cav would attack northwest to Sangju, then to Osan to link with X Corps, in the wake of the Inchon Landings behind North Korean lines.

Harris's 7th Cavalry led the drive north. Known as Task Force Lynch, for James Lynch's 3rd Battalion, the troops moved out, followed by the other two regiments. As they traveled north, South Korean crowds cheered them on.

Divided and in unfamiliar territory, the cavalry met enemy resistance above Chonan. After being detected by their headlights, Lynch ordered the men to drive on in darkness and destroy enemy tanks. On 27 September they managed to move through Osan and join with the 31st Infantry. The cavalry, as part of the U.S. Eighth Army, linked up with X Corps on 27 September.

After Seoul was recaptured, the 1st Cavalry prepared to advance to Pyongyang as part of I Corps. It moved through Seoul to relieve X Corps and prepared for attack across the 38th parallel. However, most of the troops realized their forces were understrength and exhausted.

The 5th Cavalry Regiment led the cavalry across the Imjin River under heavy fire from stiffening North Korean forces. The 7th pushed forward and the enemy now fled. The cavalry thus laid the groundwork for other U.N. troops to move into the sector. Cavalry troops crossed the 38th parallel on 9 October 1950.

The cavalry realized that it lacked adequate strength and supplies to overtake and trap the North Koreans. The British Commonwealth Brigade was attached to the 1st Cavalry Division, and Gay, seeking redemption for previous failures, wanted to take Sariwon so that the cavalry would have the distinction of reaching Pyongyang first. Both the 5th and 7th Cavalry Regiments were moving at night in an attempt to be the first U.N. troops in the North Korean capital.

Marcel Crombez, commander of the 5th, believing he had been overshadowed by the 7th and that Harris was purposefully blocking him on the roads leading north, began circumventing the 7th without notifying Harris. As a result the 5th was mistaken for the enemy, and the 7th fired on them; the 5th returned fire, sparking a fratricidal battle. More positively, the commander of the 7th Regiment convinced 2,500 North Korean troops that his command consisted of Soviet "allies" and duped the befuddled enemy into surrender.

After some unseemly jockeying for the honor, ROK troops actually entered Pyongyang first, but a cavalry regimental commander was named mayor of the enemy's capital, perhaps in compensation. The 1st Cavalry Division prepared to fight to the Yalu River, considering that the mission before them would be quick and easy. They crossed the Chongchon River and were the first U.S. unit to encounter Chinese Communist forces on 1 November. The Chinese cavalry rode hardy Mongolian ponies, some of which the American cavalry were able to capture to transport supplies over the harsh terrain. The 8th Regiment, commanded by Hallett Edson, and still wearing summer uniforms, falsely believed their mission in Korea was almost finished. Fires, apparently set by the enemy to conceal movement, frightened Gay into trying to consolidate his division, especially reinforcing the vulnerable 8th.

On 1 November 1950, 20,000 Chinese troops decimated the exposed 8th Cavalry Regiment at Unsan; the 8th was shattered and demoralized by the blaring whistles and bugles and by surprise attacks in the dark. Running out of ammunition and divided by the enemy, the 8th's battalions were surrounded. After fighting hand-to-hand, the survivors fled. In the 1st Battalion, 265 of 800 Americans were killed or captured. At dawn the 5th Cavalry Regiment initiated a rescue mission but suffered 350 casualties. Milburn told Gay to pull the 1st Cavalry Division below the Chongchon River. Estimates revealed that more than 600 of the 8th's Third Battalion's 800 men were dead. Stragglers wandered into camp, severely demoralized. Gay then removed Edson from command. The 8th was unable to return immediately to combat, and Raymond D. Palmer, the new commander, was ordered to rebuild it. The 5th was also pulled out of combat to be refitted. The 7th Regiment had yet to encounter Chinese forces.

After recuperation from the disaster at Unsan, the 1st Cavalry Division moved above the Chongchon to gain forward positions. At a Thanksgiving celebration designed to rebuild morale and boost cavalry enthusiasm, parades and ceremonies were held emphasizing cavalry traditions and heritage. Medals were presented, and the 35th Infantry retrieved most of the 8th's lost equipment and jeeps at Unsan. The remaining cavalry forces assembled at Sunchon to bolster the right of the Commonwealth Brigade and to reinforce ROK II Corps soldiers to counterattack the Chinese.

On 29 November the 1st Cavalry Division was deployed east of Sunchon to establish roadblocks, but enemy troops disguised as refugees managed to sneak through. However, in a crucial action, the 1st Cavalry Division's and ROK's blocking maneuvers against the Chinese allowed the 2nd Division to withdraw through Sunchon and prevent U.N. forces from being encircled. The 1st Cavalry Division remained exposed, without sufficient rations, still wearing summer clothing, and suffering low morale, anger, and frustration. The 7th gained the

Argyll Battalion and the 3rd Battalion from the 8th Regiment. Because the enemy paused to regroup and supply, the cavalry at this time did not meet much Chinese resistance.

After retreating from the Chongchon River area, in mid-December the 1st Cav entered the reserves. The newly arrived Greek Battalion was added to the 7th Cavalry Regiment. Crombez returned as commander of the 5th Regiment, and Lieutenant Commander Harold K. Johnson (later chief of staff of the Army) replaced Palmer. After Walker's death in a jeep accident, his replacement, General Matthew Ridgway, decided that Gay should be removed from command and replaced him with Gay's former artillery chief, Major General Charles D. Palmer.

In January 1951 the cavalry was positioned near the Han River as U.N. troops retreated. General Palmer was ordered to take any measures necessary to keep traffic flowing, and the 8th Cavalry Regiment was chosen to lead Task Force Johnson, a reconnaissance mission, for confidence building. Johnson explained that after the disaster at Unsan the Eighth Cav had only been used "in a gingerly sort of way." Believing that a victory was necessary for the 3rd Battalion, Johnson chose it for the lead battalion in the attack. The 8th Cavalry performed well, its morale improved, and the mission revealed no strong enemy positions near the front lines.

In the offensive known as Thunderbolt on January 25, the cavalry led another attack. Palmer was strict in matters of readiness and equipment and the 7th and 8th led the attack. The 5th remained in reserve. The troops performed well at first, but near Inchon the 8th engaged in hand-to-hand fighting on 26 January. Palmer, basing his concern on past performances, feared the 8th was unreliable and had the 5th replace that regiment.

The 5th and 7th Regiments engaged Chinese forces on January 28 and 29 and continued pushing toward the Han in early February where they were on the left flank of IX Corps, then withdrew between IX Corps and the Marines. The cavalry suffered setbacks during the Chinese attacks, and air support probably saved the day at Chipyong-ni.

In Task Force Crombez's operation to rescue the 23rd Infantry, the 5th Regiment's commander, to his troop's dismay, used Sherman tanks with infantry riding outside where the Chinese could fire on them with mortar and machine guns. Crombez ordered an advance, leaving wounded and stranded soldiers to the mercy of the Chinese. In spite of this controversial mission, Ridgway supported Crombez (and awarded him a citation) for what he considered his innovative offensive spirit.

But the cavalry did relieve Chipyong-ni, and assembled on the right flank of the 24th Division for the IX Corps assault. Colonel Robert Blanchard replaced the exhausted Lieutenant Commander Peter Clainos as commander of the 8th Cavalry Regiment. According to Blanchard, "The Eighth Cav. was a challenge. They still had not recovered from Unsan. They were always looking over their shoulders. I had to overcome this. I had to retrain the regiment, send them on patrols so they could get used to being shot at, even show them how to properly organize a field kitchen and cook." He also complained about the attached Thai unit, stating the unprepared foreign soldiers had to be extensively trained in order to enter combat. Still, the cavalry continued to disappoint: The 7th was severely fatigued after fighting for Hill 578 at Mugam, and typhus forced a quarantine of its 1st Battalion. Both it and the 8th were placed in reserve for recuperation.

In Operations Killer and Ripper, the cavalry was reinforced by a Canadian battalion, but muddy roads and a scarcity of bridges delayed movement. MacArthur visited the cavalry, which was experiencing numerous turnovers in command at the battalion and company level. Presumably unaware of the turmoil, MacArthur returned to Suwon and gave a speech extolling the cavalry's fitness to defeat the enemy.

From March 15 to 16 the cavalry marched toward the Hongchon River to flush the enemy from nearby hills and then entered the deserted city of Chunchon. They continued the attack toward line Kansas where the 1st Marines would relieve them. The cavalry reserves crossed the Soyang River toward the Hwachon Reservoir then traversed the 38th parallel and were the first above Chunchon, where the enemy responded fiercely. In April, the 5th Cavalry Regiment was brought out of reserve, but its mission was hindered by floods unleashed when the Chinese opened the Hwachon Dam. The 7th was ordered to capture the dam, but were checked by the enemy when they tried to cross the reservoir in assault boats. The 7th was then put in reserve with the other regiments of the 1st Cavalry Division.

In late April the cavalry again was defending Seoul. As part of I Corps defense, the 5th Cavalry Regiment moved to Kypyong on April 24 to block the Chinese. The 7th and 8th Regiments went to I Corps to fill the gap in front. The 5th reinforced positions so that the 24th Division could withdraw. The 1st then filled the gap on the left end of line Lincoln when British forces withdrew while the 5th stayed at Kapyong. The 1st Cavalry Division secured Uijongbu on May 6, 1951.

The cavalry then moved north of the old Kansas line toward the Imjin and Hantan Rivers, planning to take Chorwon and Kumwha in the Iron Triangle. On June 9 the cavalry discovered that Chorwon was deserted and occupied the city. In July the cavalry experienced complete turnover when Palmer rotated out, as well as Blanchard and Crombez. Colonel Dan Gilmer remained in command, staying on until he was forced out when an investigation revealed his ineptitude for combat command.

In October 1951 the new division commander, Major General Thomas L. Harrold, led the 1st Cavalry Division in Operation Commando, beginning October 3. The enemy focused its resistance on the cavalry, which had to fight for every inch gained. The 139th and 141st Division of the Chinese 47th Army were deeply entrenched in bunkers. Field artillery battalions supported the cavalry against the enemy's fierce defense. The cavalry moved toward line Jamestown and on October 5 the 8th Cavalry Regiment crested Hill 418; the 7th gained Hills 313, 334, 287, and 347, securing the high ground on the northeast half of the Jamestown line for the 1st Cavalry Division.

The 5th Cavalry continued to battle the enemy, experiencing little success. By October 12 the 8th took Hill 272; on October 15, in Operation Polecharge, the 5th Cavalry Regiment and its Belgian battalion took Hill 346, and three days later Hill 230. On October 19 the 1st Cavalry Division seized Jamestown line and dug in while the enemy retreated. This success for the cavalry was possible because the Chinese had depleted their supplies, ammunition, and men, and were forced to withdraw. The Chinese suffered 16,000 casualties and the cavalry lost 2,900 men in some of the most bitter fighting of the war.

In December 1951 the splintered 1st Cavalry Division was replaced by the 45th Infantry Division and returned to Japan as a reserve unit. The ROK cavalry, using both horse and mechanized cavalry, had aided the American cavalry throughout the war, especially against guerrillas in Operation Ratkiller.

In the 1st Cavalry Division's bitter war 16,498 men were killed or wounded compared to 4,055 casualties throughout World War II. Cavalrymen were presented various awards such as a Presidential Unit Citation, for their actions at Waegwan and Taegu, and the Medal of Honor. However, the failures of the 1st Cavalry Division revealed the commanding officers' errors and misunderstanding of how to employ the cavalry, especially by Walker and Milburn, in addition to catastrophes spawned by regimental commanders' professional aspirations and infighting. The 1st Cavalry Division remained in the Far East until 1965 when it returned to the U.S. to be the first airmobile division in the U.S. Army.

Elizabeth Schafer

Bibliography

Appleman, Roy B. *South to the Naktong, North to the Yalu* (1961).

Blair, Clay. *The Forgotten War: America in Korea, 1950–1953* (1988).

Blumenson, Martin. "Task Force Crombez, Eighth U.S. Army Korea" (Military History Section, 3rd Historical Detachment, n.d.).

Chandler, Melbourne C. *Of GarryOwen in Glory: The History of the 7th U.S. Cavalry* (1960).

———. *The First Team: The First Cavalry Division in Korea* (1952).

Hermes, Walter G. *Truce Tent and Fighting Front* (1966).

Hoyt, Edwin. *The Pusan Perimeter* (1984).

Central Intelligence Agency (CIA)

In January 1946, President Harry S. Truman issued an executive order creating the Central Intelligence Group led by a director of central intelligence (DCI). The unit was given statutory recognition and renamed the Central Intelligence Agency (CIA) as part of the National Security Act of 1947. The CIA was charged with advising the National Security Council and coordinating the production and dissemination of foreign intelligence inside the government. Despite the mystique and aura of mystery that would surround the agency in later years, the CIA initially had few friends and many enemies—it lacked the prestige, authority, human assets, and technological means to accomplish its assigned duties. Before 1949, the CIA did not have an independent budget and the armed forces refused to share information with the upstart agency.

Some animosity resulted from the CIA's rank amateurism. Because many of its agents had experience with clandestine military missions in the Office of Strategic Services (OSS) during World War II, the CIA developed a marked inclination for covert action at the expense of information gathering and analysis. In addition, the CIA had few assets in Asia because General Douglas MacArthur had excluded the OSS from the Pacific theater during World War II. When forced to permit a three-man CIA station to open in Japan, the American shogun refused to share government office space with them—they operated out of a hotel room The CIA slighted Asian developments and seriously discounted the idea of military "adventurism" by Communist powers. In the six months before the Korean War began, CIA estimates hardly mentioned the peninsula.

Thus in June 1950, the CIA and the Truman administration were caught almost completely off guard by the North Korean attack on South Korea. The CIA was criticized (justifiably) for having failed to anticipate the North Korean invasion. President Truman held the CIA and DCI Admiral Roscoe Hillenkoetter in such low regard that he did not even invite the director to the emergency staff meetings taking place in the days after the North Korean invasion. In October, Truman accepted Hillenkoetter's resignation and appointed a new, dynamic DCI, General Walter Bedell Smith.

After General MacArthur's forces landed at Inchon and the U.N. offensive began to sweep across the 38th parallel, the agency was ordered to determine whether the People's Republic of China (PRC) or USSR would enter the war. The CIA warned that both had the military capability to intervene, but dismissed the probability of intervention by either power. If anything, intelligence estimates reinforced fears of Soviet moves against Western Europe. Although the CIA was well aware of what America's adversaries could do, it had no idea of what they actually might do; it knew their capabilities, but could not discover their intentions.

The CIA (and the service intelligence agencies) forwarded reports of combat between small units of U.N. and Chinese forces in October and November 1950, but did not detect two entire army groups (IX and XIII) of the People's Liberation Army (PLA) as they crossed into North Korea. U.N. forces were not aware of the 300,000 PLA "volunteers" bearing down on them until the massive Communist counter-offensive that began at Thanksgiving time. Even after PLA intervention, the CIA insisted that Chinese soldiers were not up to professional standards and that PLA ranks were composed of unmotivated, untrained draftees. In fact, the thirty PLA divisions facing U.N. troops were mostly battle-hardened veterans of the long Chinese civil war. They lacked only the massive firepower and the modern logistics system that U.N. troops had at their disposal. U.N. soldiers learned quickly not to underestimate their Chinese opponents—and to ignore intelligence estimates to the contrary.

Nonetheless, CIA operations in Asia grew rapidly during the war, despite objections from MacArthur and his successors. The agency organized evasion and escape routes for downed American fliers, trained 1,200 Korean refugees to fight as guerrillas behind enemy lines, maintained two "fishing fleets" masquerading as black marketeers to transport agents, supply partisans, and search for downed fliers, and took proprietary control of civil air transport to fly agents and equipment into North Korea. With the aid of the Far East Air Force, the CIA inserted agents into the PRC and the Asiatic Soviet Union itself (to what effect, if any, remains unknown).

The war was a watershed for the CIA. Although there were some propaganda and psychological warfare operations, the primary emphasis of the CIA in the Korean War, and elsewhere thereafter, was covert military action and espionage. Under the forceful direction of DCI Smith, the agency was six times larger in 1953 than it had been in 1946, and had adopted the basic structure, orientation, and size it would retain for the next twenty years. Smith formed deputy directorates for administration, intelligence (analysis), and plans (DDP), the latter a euphemism for covert action. Led by OSS veteran Allen W. Dulles, the DDP commanded a disproportionate share of the CIA's budget, manpower, and resources—by 1952 it received 74 percent of the agency's budget and 60 percent of its personnel. Allen Dulles became DCI before the end of the war; the clandestine wing has dominated the CIA ever since.

David M. Esposito

Bibliography

Ameringer, Charles. *U.S. Foreign Intelligence: The Secret Side of American History* (1990).

Darling, Arthur. *The Central Intelligence Agency* (1990).

Goulden, Joseph. *Korea: The Untold Story of the War* (1983).

Leary, William, ed. *The Central Intelligence Agency* (1984).

Marchetti, Victor, and John Marks. *The CIA and the Cult of Intelligence* (1974).

Chae Byung Duk (1917–1950)

In January of 1946, Chae Byung Duk, a native of Pyongyang, later the capital of the Democratic People's Republic of Korea (North Korea), was commissioned a Second Lieutenant in the Army of the Republic of Korea (ROK). Chae had already attained the rank of major in the Imperial Japanese Army in World War II, although he did not see combat. For reasons that are not today entirely clear, Chae rapidly made his way up the ladder of promotion, and was appointed chief of staff of the ROK Army on 10 April 1949. In October of that year he retired due to "personal conflicts," but in April of the following year he was reappointed, only to be removed from his position of chairman of the ROK Joint Chiefs of Staff, again for personal political reasons. General Chae, bearing his 245 pounds on a five-foot, six-inch frame, was amiably known as "Fat Chae" by his U.S. military allies, and was an easily recognizable convivial fixture at innumerable prewar military parties.

At the outbreak of war, General Chae became a commander of the South Korean Interim Armed Forces. He was as surprised as anyone else at the North Korean attack across the 38th parallel on 25 June 1950. He quickly developed a plan to launch the next day a counterattack in the Uijongbu corridor. His plan called for the Seventh ROK Division to attack on the left. The plan was flawed and unrealistic in two respects. First, the ROK Second Division was in Taejon, ninety miles to the south, and could hardly be completely on the scene by the next morning to support the 2nd Division. Secondly, the North Korean advance was armor-tipped; the ROK Army had no armor and very little artillery.

Brigadier General Lee Hyong Koon, commanding the 2nd Division, understandably objected to Chae's plan. General Lee's objections and those of Chae's U.S. military advisory group were rejected, and the counterattack was launched the morning of 26 June. The troops of the 2nd Division who made it to Uijongbu established defensive positions three kilometers northeast of the city, but they could not hold back the armored enemy columns. The enemy pushed past Uijongbu and on 27 June were advancing on Seoul itself. By the end of that day the defenses of the ROK capital were crumbling. Refugees were fleeing the city and the ROK Army planned to evacuate to new positions south of the Han River. However, the premature destruction of the dual highway bridges over the Han early on the morning of the 28th destroyed any hopes for an orderly withdrawal. Just who had ordered this bungled demolition has never been established. Some American advisors believed that Chae had issued the order to his chief engineer; others believed the vice minister of defense was responsible. The former was summarily executed.

General Chae was relieved on 30 June, but he did not fade away. When U.S. forces arrived at Chinju in July, General Chae was there to offer his advice and volunteered to join them in combat. The former chief of staff of the Republic of Korea requested permission to accompany the 3rd Battalion of the 29th Infantry Regiment, which had been ordered to seize the town of Hadong. Chae was allowed to go along as an interpreter and guide.

On 27 July the 3rd Battalion was nearing Hadong when a group of unidentified soldiers approached the U.S. position. Chae shouted to the column, some 100 meters distant, to identify themselves. But the approaching troops jumped into ditches and opened fire, as did the Americans. Chae was hit and instantly killed by enemy machine gun fire.

Chae Byung Duk was posthumously promoted to lieutenant general. While there was general agreement that Chae had personified so much that was wrong with the ROK Army in the first months of the war, many also concluded that his brave end had redeemed his memory.

James E. Dillard

Bibliography

Appleman, Roy. *South to the Naktong, North to the Yalu; June–November, 1950* (Office of the Chief of Military History, Washington: 1961).

Blair, Clay. *The Forgotten War: America in Korea, 1950–1953* (1987).

Republic of Korea. *History of U.N. Forces in the Korean War*, Vol. IV (Ministry of National Defense: Seoul, 1975).

Chaplains in the Korean War

Chaplains from fifteen U.N. nations served in the Korean War. Korea, traditionally a Buddhist country, was first visited by Roman Catholic missionaries in the eighteenth century; in the following two centuries other foreign churches sent their missionaries to the "hermit kingdom." Despite the Japanese occupation, more than one million Koreans had identified themselves as Christians before the outbreak of war in 1950.

U.S. Chaplains' ties with the Korean population during the American occupation of 1945–1949 provided a basis for their humanitarian and military service during the war. Approximately 1,600 U.S. chaplains served during the Korean War, with nearly 300 the maximum strength at any one time. In addition to military chaplains, civilians from the United States and Korean volunteers acted as auxiliary chaplains.

Chaplains serving in the Korean War filled a variety of roles. Their primary duty, of course, was to minister to U.S. servicemen's spiritual needs. They organized Sunday morning nondenominational services. As one chaplain remarked about the lack of denominational exactness, "When they bring them in on a litter covered with mud, blood-soaked, with fear and shock on their faces, you can't tell what they are until you look at their dog tags."

Major General Ivan Bennett served as U.N. command chaplain, and Major General Roy H. Parker as Far East command chaplain and chief of chaplains. Parker, who was under the command of General Douglas MacArthur, initially suggested that chaplains volunteer for service, instead of World War II reservists being ordered to active duty. But recently released men were indeed drafted into the chaplain service, due to personnel shortages. Bennett succeeded Parker as Far East command chaplain and chief of chaplains, bringing effective leadership to the office. Bennett knew how to negotiate with senior military officers to acquire, by one means or another, necessary equipment and funding. Parker was, in turn, succeeded by James T. Wilson.

Many U.S. servicemen were apathetic to religion when they first arrived in Korea, and due to the unfamiliar cultural environment, exhibited attitudes, morale, and morals often different from that of the soldiers in World War II's "crusade." Chaplains in Korea had their work cut out for them, but as a result of their ministrations, many soldiers found a more definite religious faith.

Chaplains were also responsible for troop morale. They counseled soldiers suffering from fear, loneliness, and fatigue, and comforted men who had no mail or who had received bad news from home. They advised men who wished to marry Korean women how to cope with the pressures from domestic and American cultures, and performed the marriage ceremony.

Often attached to mobile hospitals or at the front, chaplains comforted the wounded and performed the last rites. They served as liaison for the Red Cross, receiving and transferring messages to and from home. They were also to be found on the U.N. hospital ships and in the U.S. military hospitals in Japan. In camps they held memorial services for those lost in each military engagement, built chapels, or in their hardest duty, wrote to the next of kin of the fallen. More positively, they also wrote to reassure loved ones of the condition of wounded troops. They devised sports and recreation activities, maintained circulating libraries and gave lectures, and often served as camp photographers. Education about hygiene and venereal disease was also part of the duties of these obviously overworked troopers.

Usually moving from unit to unit, chaplains held religious services wherever possible, sometimes from the hood of a jeep. Their travel across the difficult terrain of Korea was no easy matter, encumbered as it was by field organs, Bibles, hymnbooks, leaflets, and altars.

Chaplains did not confine their services to their military charges. Those who had previously worked in Korea were usually fluent in the language. They could thus serve as conduits between Koreans and U.N. soldiers. Military chaplains somehow found the time to function as missionaries to Korean civilians and prisoners of war, prompting conversions to Christianity in numerous cases. U.N. chaplains were often invited to preach in local Korean churches. Sometimes, to the surprise of local Koreans who had their hands full simply with personal and family survival, U.S. chaplains embraced orphans, lepers, and refugees, soliciting financial support for the building of orphanages, hospitals, churches, and living areas. Working with enthusiastic American soldiers, they gathered food, clothes, toys, shoes, and Christmas gifts for their charges. At Inchon, for example, chaplains initiated the construction and maintenance of a home for war widows.

Two U.S. Roman Catholic chaplains established a chaplain corps in April of 1951 to minister to ROK troops. Their salaries paid from U.S. churches, Korean Christian chaplains ministered to ROK military personnel to the end of the war and afterward.

Chaplains were hardly immune to the hazards of war. They seemed to have been singled out by the North Koreans as particular "enemies of the people." Of the four U.S. chaplains known to have been held in enemy camps, none survived. At least two vanished after last being reported devotedly staying behind with U.S. wounded in the face of enemy advances. By the time of the armistice in 1953, thirteen chaplains had been killed as a result of enemy action, six in the disastrous first month of the war; and twenty-six had been wounded. No less than twenty-two chaplains were awarded the nation's second highest military medal, the Silver Star.

An undetermined number of chaplains remained in a civilian capacity after the war to minister to the needs of a war-battered people and aid in the reconstruction of their country.

Elizabeth Schafer

Bibliography

Bennett, Ivan L. "The ROK Army Chaplaincy," *Korean Survey*, 4 (1955).

Hess, Dean E. *Battle Hymn* (1956).

Hourihan, William. *Pro Deo et Patria: A Brief History of the United States Army Chaplain Corps*, U.S. Army Chaplain Center and School (July 1991).

Muller, John H. *Wearing the Cross in Korea* (1954).

Parker, Roy H. "Religion at Work," *Chaplain*, 9 (1952).

U.S. Department of the Navy. *The History of the Chaplain Corps, United States Navy*. Vol. 6, *During the Korean War, 17 June, 1950–27 June 1954* (1960).

Venzke, Roger. *Confidence in Battle, Inspiration in Peace: The United States Army Chaplaincy, 1945–1975* (1977).

Chiang Kai-shek (1887–1975)

Chiang Kai-shek, Chinese Nationalist leader, was born in Fenghua, Chechiang province, 31 October 1887. Chiang's father was a local merchant who died when Chiang was eight. Having spent a year in a Chinese military academy, in 1907 Chiang went to Tokyo to attend the Japanese Army Military State College. While in Japan, Chiang took part in revolutionary activities led by Sun Yat-sen. In 1924, when Sun set up a military academy near Canton in southern

C

China, Chiang was appointed commandant of the school.

After Sun's death, Chiang assumed leadership of the Nationalist party. In 1926 he launched a northern expedition against warlords, which in two years achieved China's unity, a fragile unification destroyed by the Japanese occupation of Manchuria in 1931. During the war against the Japanese from 1937 to 1945, Chiang was China's generalissimo.

The war with the Japanese weakened Chiang's forces and corruption eroded his government's legitimacy. In the war with the Communists that followed, in spite of heavy American aid, Chiang lost mainland China by 1949.

The Korean War proved to be a gift to Chiang, who had retreated to the island province of Taiwan. On 27 June 1950, President Harry Truman, reversing his earlier decision not to become further involved in the Chinese civil war, ordered full support to Chiang and instructed the U.S. Seventh Fleet to "neutralize" the Taiwan Strait to prevent possible attacks from the mainland. Chiang offered to send his troops to fight in Korea, an idea supported by Douglas MacArthur. The offer, however, was turned down by the U.S. Joint Chiefs of Staff. At the end of July 1950 Chiang received MacArthur in Taipei. The two discussed the possibilities of military cooperation, but nothing concrete came of the meeting and no Nationalist forces ever fought in Korea. But fervent anti-communism and the indubitable fact that he was an enemy of the Communist Chinese gave added legitimacy to his regime and opened the floodgates of U.S. aid. In the decades to follow, Chiang's regime became progressively less brutal and eventually opened to something close to democracy. In addition, the island republic's economy boomed by the 1970s, until by the 1980s its gold reserves actually surpassed those of the United States.

Chiang was the president of the Republic of China on Taiwan until his death on 5 April 1975.

Jing Li

Bibliography
Crozier, Brian, with Eric Chou. *The Man Who Lost China: The First Full Biography of Chiang Kai-shek* (1976).
Furuya, Keiji. *Chiang Kai-shek: His Life and Times*, abridged English edition by Chun-ming Chang (1981).
Morwood, William. *Duel for the Middle Kingdom: The Struggle Between Chiang Kai-shek and Mao Tse-tung for Control of China* (1980).
Payne, Robert. *Chiang Kai-shek* (1969).

China and Chinese Decision Making in the Korean War

As hostilities began on the Korean peninsula in late June 1950, the Chinese Communist leadership was deeply involved in the complex processes of domestic political consolidation and foreign policy formation associated with the formal establishment of the People's Republic of China on 1 October 1949. The Chinese civil war continued in remote areas in the southwestern provinces and in some coastal districts; the Communist leadership had already committed itself to two major military campaigns within China proper while also acting as a supportive observer of the Vietminh's military challenge to French rule in Indochina as elsewhere. In the week immediately preceding the outbreak of war in Korea, the Communist Chinese central legislative body, the National Committee of the Chinese People's Political Consultative Conference, approved a complex and potentially socially disruptive land redistribution program, the Agrarian Reform Law, to be applied in areas recently brought under Communist control. Most historians of the Korean conflict now agree, based on assessments of China's domestic instability at the time and a growing catalogue of information on its apparent diplomatic and military unpreparedness for direct engagement in Korea during 1950, that the Chinese leadership was unwilling to actively support North Korea at the onset of the Korean War.

Once the opening hostilities across the 38th parallel had attracted direct U.S. and United Nations military support for the South Korean regime, which was formalized in presidential directives and a U.N. Security Council resolution on 27 June 1950, Beijing was compelled to include the Korean conflict in its global and regional strategic planning as well as in the calculus of its domestic military and economic development programs.

In the middle of 1950 the newly established Chinese Communist government was just completing the military occupation of the southwestern provinces of the country; Yunnan province, for example, had only seen the first arrival of main force People's Liberation Army (PLA) forces in February. The political consolidation of the new regime in the southern provinces, where Communist party organizations had been weak since the mid-1930s, required enormous military and manpower resources; tens of thousands of internal security and political education teams, as well as regular army units, poured into the south in the spring of 1950. At the same time senior planners in Beijing had other objectives which would also draw on the government's thinly stretched reserves. As a continuation of the civil war against the Nationalists, Beijing determined during the spring of 1950 to launch a series on amphibious assaults on Nationalist-held offshore islands, including the Nationalist government's stronghold on Taiwan. As part of this strategy, in March and April 1950, Hainan Island was successfully invaded by Communist troops, and Beijing publicly announced its intention to carry out similar amphibious operations against Taiwan. Eager to fully unify all of the territory traditionally claimed as Chinese, Communist leaders also began planning for a major land invasion of the semi-autonomous Central Asian territory of Tibet.

The hostilities in Korea and the United States response appear to have forced the Chinese Communist leadership to interrupt or revise at least some elements of these plans. U.S. intelligence reports indicated that under the Communists' island recovery program, an assault on Taiwan could be initiated as early as July 1950. President Harry S. Truman's 27 June 1950 order to the U.S. Seventh Fleet to "neutralize" the Taiwan Straits, issued as a warning to Beijing not to attack Taiwan, had two immediate effects: it not only forced Beijing to reconsider its timetable for the Taiwan operation, but apparently also convinced the Communist leadership that the Korean situation could not be viewed as a local conflict, but was instead an international crisis that could, depending on the nature of the American involvement on behalf of South Korea, develop into a serious strategic threat to the Chinese Communist regime itself.

Within days of Truman's action, Beijing ordered a substantial redeployment of Communist troops from the central coastal provinces near the Taiwan Straits, where they had been preparing for the planned assault on Taiwan, to China's northeastern provinces near the Korean peninsula. Military and political leadership meetings were convened in Beijing to evaluate the changing strategic situation and to prepare new contingency plans for Chinese involvement in both Taiwan and the rapidly developing conflict in Korea. Unlike the Taiwan and Korean theaters, however, Sichuan province and Tibet were relatively insulated from international attention, and planning for a major offensive operation to establish and consolidate Communist military authority there continued during the summer of 1950. The invasion, involving chiefly the Second Field Army of the PLA under Liu Bocheng, entered its final preparatory stages during the crucial September–October 1950 period, when MacArthur's Inchon landing and a U.N. offensive resulted in the recapture of Seoul and then in the crossing of the 38th parallel by U.N. forces. By the time that U.N. intelligence had revealed the presence of Chinese Communist armed forces in Korean territory, the invasion of Tibet was already under way. The opening of the offensive was marked by the official Communist news agency's announcement on 24 October 1950 that a "political liberation directive" had been issued to Communist armed forces in the southwest authorizing their movement into Tibet. Thus less than a year after the conclusion of its lengthy war against the Nationalists, the Chinese Communists calmly contemplated an invasion of Tibet and war against the United States.

Of the factors informing the Chinese decision to dispatch ground forces into Korean territory to assist the embattled North Korean regime during October 1950, none was more compelling than Mao Zedong's realization that the U.S. military presence on the Chinese border with Korea could readily develop into a direct Sino-American military engagement on Chinese territory. American air superiority and nuclear weapons capability, although still limited to relatively unsophisticated delivery systems, could be relied on to give U.S. forces such tactical superiority that their use might result in American victories that could rapidly detach whole Chinese provinces from effective Communist control; the end result could be the diminution, if not the total dissolution, of the new Communist government's authority. In this situation, it is now known, the Chinese leadership sought assurances of Soviet military support, especially antiaircraft defense systems and the deployment of Soviet air power in the China-Korea theater. After obtaining authoritative information from Moscow probably on 13 October 1950, that Stalin had refused to approve the participation of Soviet Air Force units in the conflict, Mao decided to render direct military assistance, including ground troops, in support of the North Korean forces. The decision came as North Korean troops fell back toward the Chinese-Korean border under the pressure of U.N. land-air offensives in central Korea following U.N. commander Douglas MacArthur's successful amphibious landing at Inchon.

U.S. intelligence reports had, of course, considered in advance the possibility of direct Chinese intervention, but it appears that Chinese ground troops still were able to cross the border into North Korea in battalion and division strength before MacArthur and his staff learned of their presence. The introduction of Chinese troops, which grew in number to more than 300,000 within the first three weeks of their deployment, immediately affected the progress of the U.N. offensive: by mid-November Allied forces were stalled north of Pyongyang. The original operational plan of the Chinese Communist military leadership, now cooperating directly with North Korean commanders, was principally defensive: its goals were to establish three static lines of well-positioned defensive forces between Pyongyang and the Chinese border and to delay any offensive action until training could be improved and Soviet equipment obtained. However, as U.N. forces advanced toward these lines and sought avenues of approach to the Yalu River, which formed the border with Chinese territory, the U.N. troops had split into relatively small groups, each with separate logistics systems and with little opportunity for obtaining battlefield support or troop reinforcements. Chinese commanders, seizing what they rightly believed was an excellent opportunity to stage massive attacks on the divided U.N. forces, abandoned their original operational objectives and rapidly adopted an offensive battle plan. By the end of the month the overwhelming number of Chinese troops, as well as the configurations of the enemy forces resulting from their earlier rapid advances into North Korean territory, allowed the Communists to halt the Allied advance and to develop their own offensive program, recapturing first Pyongyang and then Seoul.

The Chinese Communist leadership attempted to create the impression that its participation in the conflict was driven by the spontaneous demands of the Chinese people; it labeled the forces sent into Korea the "Chinese People's Volunteers" (CPV) and gave extensive publicity to domestic war bond drives and anti-American protest organizations, all of which it claimed had developed without official intervention by the Communist authorities. This political circumlocution notwithstanding, the central leadership in Beijing maintained direct control over domestic programs related to the war, as it did over the troop dispositions, logistics systems, and tactics of the "People's Volunteers" themselves. The domestic political consequences of the Korean conflict were never far from the leadership's thinking about the war. The military forces sent into Korea came from all five of the Communist field armies and included many potentially politically unreliable soldiers who had fought for the Nationalists during the Chinese Civil War but had been absorbed into Communist units. It has been argued that chief Communist party leader Mao Zedong (or Tse-Tung) used the opportunity presented by selective deployment to the Korean theater to undermine the growing domestic political influence of field army commanders who in 1949 and 1950 were consolidating their positions as regional leaders within the new regime.

Mao's choice as principal commander of the CPV forces was Marshal Peng Dehuai, a skilled strategist who had played a key role in the military success of the Communist forces during the Chinese civil war. Peng conceptualized his strategy in Korea in terms similar to those arising from his experiences in the 1930s and 1940s against the better-equipped Nationalist forces: even in the absence of advanced weaponry, sheer force of numbers and the intense political training of the troops could give a strategic advantage to the Communist combatants. Peng obtained impressive successes by continuing to increase the number of CPV forces in Korea, especially during November–December 1950, when the CPV drove U.N. forces not only away from the Chinese border but south of the 38th parallel and into South Korea, and seized the Republic of Korea capital, Seoul. In early January 1951, Peng secretly informed his subordinates that the CPV offensive actions were part of a series of offensive campaigns which would continue into the spring.

The political leadership in Beijing, however, aware of the financial and political stresses accompanying the war and acknowledging that substantial Soviet aid was not likely to materialize, was already poising itself for an early negotiated conclusion to the conflict on the basis of Peng's early successes. On 17 January 1951, the Chinese leadership publicly issued a statement of demands that could, it said, form the basis of a cease-fire agreement in Korea; the terms, which reveal how international political issues beyond the actual military conflict in Korea dominated Beijing's agenda at the time, included complete withdrawal of all foreign troops from the Korean peninsula, and cessation of U.S. military assistance of all kinds to the United Nations. The demands were rejected by the United States, as perhaps Mao Zedong and his advisers anticipated they would be, but the episode illustrates that tensions existed between the objectives of Chinese military commanders on the ground in Korea and those of Communist party leaders in Beijing.

When U.N. forces recovered Seoul again on 14 March 1951, and then recrossed the 38th parallel on 25 March, political-military tensions within the leadership of the U.N. coalition also emerged. United Nations military operations had been revitalized by the appointment of General Matthew Ridgway as the principal field commander under U.N. commander General Douglas MacArthur, and MacArthur publicly announced that he intended to enter Chinese territory to prosecute the conflict. This statement was followed immediately by large-scale U.N. bombing runs on the bridges over the Yalu River between China and North Korea and by the movement of elements of the U.S. Seventh Fleet from the Taiwan Straits toward southeastern coastal China and Hainan Island. MacArthur's aggressiveness provoked not only his dismissal as U.N. commander by President Truman on 11 April 1951, but also renewed offensive campaigns by the growing CPV forces. By 24 April, CPV troops had recrossed the 38th parallel at several key points.

If Truman's dismissal of MacArthur signaled that the United States was unwilling at that point to use military force inside Chinese territory, the Chinese offensive demonstrated again that the Beijing leadership was unwilling to accept the presence of U.S.-led United Nations forces directly on its border with North Korea. In the absence of significant direct Soviet assistance, however, Chinese military strategy had to continue to rely upon large-scale assaults against U.N. positions by concentrated but relatively under-equipped CPV forces. In May 1951, Peng Dehuai ordered new sustained attacks involving tens of thousands of CPV forces with no supportive air cover. The "human wave" tactics employed by local commanders were met by U.N. aerial operations and intact defensive lines and led to extremely heavy Chinese casualties; press reports at the time indicated that five days' fighting around the 38th parallel resulted in as many as 50,000 CPV casualties.

The Chinese political leadership in Beijing had by this time begun to assess the broad effects of its increasingly expensive engagement in the Korean conflict on its own potentially divisive domestic programs, especially land and currency reform, anti-corruption campaigns, and industrial sector reorganization. The war was also seen as delaying Mao's plans for gaining greater control over China's intellectuals and interfering with his programs for reducing the professionalization of the military. In June 1951, Mao and his supporters, apparently bitterly disappointed over the Soviet leadership's failure directly to assist the Chinese and Korean Communist war effort, sought a new avenue for reducing the immediate intensity of hostilities while simultaneously preserving the buffer area between Chinese territory and U.N. forces gained during the CPV's latest costly offensives. The Soviet Union's representative to the United Nations, Jacob A. Malik, signaled in a broadcast in June that negotiations on a cease-fire in Korea might be possible without specific preconditions; the move came at a time when CPV forces were actively engaged in intensive combat operations in central Korea. Instead of circumventing his military commanders' plans, it appears that Mao now sought to take full advantage of them. In the prevailing political and military climate, the signal was viewed by the U.N. coalition's leaders not as illustration of Beijing's weakness but as an opportunity to stabilize what was also for the U.N. side the increasingly costly and dangerous Korean theater of the Cold War.

Cease-fire negotiations opened on 10 July 1951 in the small village of Kaesong, which had been demilitarized by agreement of the local U.N. and Communist commanders. The agenda for these talks was dominated by both sides' demands for immediate repatriation of prisoners of war (POWs); both sides were reluctant to provide a full accounting of the POWs held and to return those POWs who claimed asylum from their home countries on the basis of ideological estrangement. The Chinese commanders also introduced accusations of U.N. use of biological weapons and abuse of Chinese and Korean POWs in the cease-fire talks; these charges prolonged the negotiations, which continued until the summer of 1953. The Chinese leadership used these negotiating tactics in order to make the broadest possible political use of the cease-fire negotiations, hoping to counteract or at least minimize the effects of China's exclusion from virtually all other international forums where it might express political criticism, or alternatively where it might engage in constructive dialogue with representatives of the United States. Although local military clashes continued throughout the period of the Kaesong and Panmunjom talks, the most serious engagements taking place in the autumn of 1951, neither side re-escalated the confrontation in a way that substantially altered the distribution of forces in Korea.

The death of Joseph Stalin on 6 March 1953 and the instability within Soviet leadership which followed appear to have offered Beijing an opportunity finally to extract itself from the Korean conflict and devote greater attention to the pressing domestic consolidation and production problems exacerbated by years of war. Indeed, Chinese decision making with regard to its support for North Korea during 1953 reflected the general pattern in its foreign policy at the time; Beijing began to deemphasize armed struggle against its ideological adversaries and to focus on domestic development and "peaceful coexistence" in international affairs. On 28 March 1953, following the return to Beijing of a high-level delegation to Stalin's funeral in Moscow, the Communist representatives at the talks on Korea agreed to an exchange of sick and wounded prisoners and proposed a resumption of the armistice negotiations. After a series of eleventh-hour offensives by the Communists, primarily designed to demonstrate the inability of the Rhee regime to survive without U.S. military assistance, an armistice agreement was finally signed on 27 July. By November 1953 the Chinese and North Korean leaderships had publicly signaled a shift from primarily military to economic and political forms of cooperation by signing a ten-year Sino-Korean economic and cultural agreement under which China agreed to provide funds for the reconstruction of North Korean industry; bilateral currency and trade agreements soon followed.

The Chinese Communists had saved the North Korean regime and had carried the brunt of the war for more than two years. They had appropriated no Korean assets, forced no unfavorable treaties on North Korea, and certainly made no demands for territorial "adjustments" in their favor. And all Chinese troops were withdrawn from Korea in 1958, although U.S. troops remained in South Korea.

All of this was in distinct contrast to that of the Soviet "liberators" of Eastern Europe or of Manchuria in 1945, or of the Chinese themselves in their brutal invasion and occupation of Tibet. Even granted that Chinese intervention in the Korean War was impelled by a sense of self-preservation, it would still be difficult to find a better historical example of national altruism.

Laura M. Calkins

Bibliography
Ascoli, Max, Charles Wertenbaker, and Philip Horton. "The China Lobby," *The Reporter*, 6 (5, 29 April 1952).
Backrach, Stanley. *The Committee of One Million* (1976).
Caridi, Ronald. *The Korean War and American Politics: The Republican Party as a Case Study* (1968).
"The China Lobby: A Case Study." *Congressional Quarterly*, *Weekly Report* (Special Supplement), 9 (29 June 1951).
Cohen, Warren. *America's Response to China* (1971).
———. *The Chinese Connection* (1978).
Dobbs, Charles M. *The Unwanted Symbol: American Foreign Policy, the Cold War, and Korea, 1945–1950* (1981).
Koen, Ross. *The China Lobby in American Politics* (1960, 1970).
Purifoy, Lewis. *Harry Truman's China Policy: McCarthyism and the Diplomacy of Hysteria, 1947–51* (1976).

See also MANCHURIA, PEOPLE'S LIBERATION/VOLUNTEER ARMY

China Lobby and the Korean War

The China Lobby was not a lobby in the strict sense of the concept of a permanent organization dedicated to pressuring governmental officials, but was rather a collection of individuals, associations, and businesses that supported the strongest possible U.S. backing of the Chinese Nationalist regime of Chiang Kai-shek during the thirty years following World War II.

The lobby can be divided into three groups: (1) Kuomingtang (KMT) officials and associates, (2) the China bloc in Congress, and (3) private American citizens who worked as individuals and within various small advocacy organizations. The three groups cohabited the same small world but had entirely different agendas. Sometimes one group coordinated its actions with the actions of another group, but more often each went its own way. The American China bloc and private-citizen advocates defined a Manichaean world of good versus evil. There could be no middle ground; those who did not fight for the good were part of the evil force of communism, or at least under its influence.

KMT officials, including the Soong family, used American anxiety to make money by unethical, if not illegal, means. Throughout the 1940s, KMT officials such as T.V. Soong and H.H. K'ung were highly successful in working with certain U.S. officials to acquire military aid and economic assistance for the beleaguered Nationalist regime; the American advocacy groups had less success, however, in holding public attention until the advent of the Korean War in June 1950. The China Lobby exploited the Korean conflict to pressure the U.S. government to underwrite the Nationalist rump government on Taiwan and place the island under the American military umbrella as part of the "Great Crescent" from the Aleutians to India.

From 1942 to 1950, KMT officials in Washington used their influence to obtain billions of dollars in loans, guarantees, gold, gold certificates, military hardware, and services. Because of inadequate accounting, a significant portion of U.S. aid was siphoned off into private hands. Initially, the U.S. government placed the Nationalist officials under restrictions on the resale of gold certificates. However, since few such restrictions were placed on Americans working as KMT agents, the KMT found it useful to contract with individuals and private companies that used bribes and kickbacks as the major means to obtain the unobtainable. With its position deteriorating in the civil war with the Chinese Communists, the KMT hired Commerce International-China, Inc. (CIC) in 1948 to obtain American tanks, planes, and artillery shells at greatly reduced prices.

In the early summer of 1950, CIC's attempt to acquire twenty-five F-51 fighter aircraft collided with the plans of General P.T. Mow and Colonel V. S. Hsiang, the Nationalist Chinese Air Force procurement officers in Washington. Although Mow and Hsiang argued that the planes had not been properly inspected before purchase, CIC officials had not offered large enough bribes to the two officers, who believed that the U.S. government would not permit the sale while American troops were engaged in major military operations in Korea. After months of charges and countercharges leveled

in the press, Mow and Hsiang fled the country, and CIC concluded the sale of F-51s to Taiwan at a reduced price.

Simultaneously, Commerce International-China established a special operations force headed by Charles M. Cooke, USN (ret.), ostensibly to train Nationalist troops in the defense of Taiwan. Cooke, however, proved to be much more effective in obtaining Navy 3-inch shells from General Douglas MacArthur's headquarters in Japan. Just prior to the beginning of the Korean conflict, Cooke obtained more than 38,000 shells for $3 per shell (list price: $39) and also obtained "without authorization at no cost" 40,000 20mm and 40mm shells.

With American troops hard-pressed on the Korean peninsula in the late summer of 1950, Cooke continued to purchase an additional 50,400 shells for the defense of Taiwan. During the same time, the U.S. Army Ordnance Department sold 200 M-5 tanks (retail: $29,000) for $500 per unit. When U.S. State Department officials suggested that Taiwan might wish to purchase additional tanks, KMT officials assured the Americans that Taiwan was obtaining all the tanks it could handle through other channels.

While KMT officials and the CIC manipulated the American procurement system, the China bloc in Congress worked hard to keep the cause of the KMT before the public. Using the issue of a worldwide as well as a domestic Communist conspiracy, the China bloc, led by Senator William Knowland and Congressman Walter Judd, argued that the U.S. government must support all anti-Communist regimes in Asia and Europe. The bloc favored a strong American presence in Japan under the leadership of Douglas MacArthur; however, the group blocked all military and economic aid bills to Europe unless linked to aid to China, Korea, and French Indochina.

In 1948, the bloc called for $125 million in aid to the Nationalist regime but was forced to accept a broader package that included all of East Asia. One year later, the Nationalist government fled the mainland to its final bastion on Taiwan. Both the China bloc and advocacy groups demanded to know "who lost China" to the Communists. Bitter about its defeat in 1948, the Republican party blamed the "leftist-dominated" administration of Harry Truman. While the China bloc pressured the administration to release more funds for Nationalists, the American China Policy Association and Frederick McKee's Commit-

C

tee to Defend America by Aiding Anti-Communist China, inundated the national and local press with stories about the bloody new Chinese Communist regime and essays which called for the resignation of several influential figures in the administration, including Secretary of State Dean Acheson and certain employees of the State Department.

Boxed into a corner, Acheson suggested that a new U.S. policy must "wait until the dust settles," but was less willing to allow the People's Liberation Army (PLA) to conquer Taiwan. More recent evidence suggests that Acheson looked at both Korea and Taiwan as logical places for raw materials and food stuffs for industrial Japan. Though several China lobbyists argued along similar lines, they stressed the need to utilize Japan, South Korea, and Nationalist China as the barricade to further Communist expansion.

To the China Lobby, East Asia was only a major front in a global war against Soviet-dominated communism. As the powerful leader of the Free World, the United States must be prepared to support all anti-Communist regimes and, if necessary, provide direct military support of threatened states. When North Korea crossed the 38th parallel, the China Lobby applauded Truman's initial reaction. Acclaim quickly changed to derision when PLA "volunteers" forced U.N. troops to retreat in December 1950. The China bloc and advocates argued that the Truman administration had restricted MacArthur's forces from winning the conflict.

After MacArthur was fired as commander of U.S. forces in Korea by President Truman in April 1951, the China Lobby reached its zenith of influence. With the war stalemated, the lobby found in Senator Joseph McCarthy a voice which could not be stifled. Feeding McCarthy data from their files, the China Lobby destroyed much of the Truman administration's credibility and paved the way for a Republican victory in 1952.

The China Lobby asserted that only the Nationalist regime on Taiwan had a legitimate right to a seat on the U.N. Security Council. With the involvement by PLA volunteers in the Korean conflict, the Truman administration saw no possibility of altering policy to admit the Chinese Communist regime to the United Nations. Once the policy was in place, successive administrations saw no advantage in changing policy until a decade later when American troops were bogged down in another Asian conflict. Though successive administrations debated the issue through secret memos, no president was willing to face the brunt of attacks from a generation of Americans who had lost sons in Korea to Communist Chinese troops. Until Vietnam, a significant segment of the American public was bitter about what was perceived as the misuse of the U.S. military and would have defined as near treason any serious discussion about the recognition of the People's Republic of China.

Part of a larger atmosphere of anti-Communism in the postwar era, the China Lobby contributed greatly to overall American anxiety. The U.S. reaction to the North Korean invasion must be placed within the context of popular perceptions of an extreme Communist threat. The Korean problem was within the sphere of the United Nations; however, the Truman administration and the China Lobby reacted as if America's defensive perimeter had been breached and that a U.S. military response was all that could save the Free World. To the China Lobby, South Korea was not an indefensible peninsula but rather another Munich crisis. For them the Free World's failure to defend Czechoslovakia in 1938 led directly to World War II. With the advent of nuclear weapons, the Free World could no longer afford to allow another non-Communist state to fall to a totalitarianism system.

Thomas E. Graham

Bibliography

Ascoli, Max, Charles Wertenbaker, and Philip Horton. "The China Lobby" *Reporter*, 6 (5, 29, April 1952).

Backrach, Stanley. *The Committee of One Million* (1976).

Caridi, Ronald. *The Korean War and American Politics: The Republican Party as a Case Study* (1968).

Caute, David. *The Great Fear: The Anti-Communist Purge Under Truman and Eisenhower* (1978).

"The China Lobby: A Case Study." *Congressional Quarterly, Weekly Report* (Special Supplement), 9 (29 June 1951).

Cohen, Warren. *America's Response to China* (1971).

———. *The Chinese Connection* (1978).

Cotton, James. *Asian Frontier Nationalism: Owen Lattimore and the American Foreign Policy Debate* (1989).

Dobbs, Charles M. *The Unwanted Symbol: American Foreign Policy, the Cold War, and Korea, 1945–50* (1981).

Dulles, Foster Rhea. *American Foreign Policy Toward Communist China, 1949–69.* (1972).

Koen, Ross. *The China Lobby in American Politics* (1960, 1974).

Levin, Murray. *Political Hysteria in America* (New York: 1971).

Purifoy, Lewis C. *Harry Truman's China Policy: McCarthyism and the Diplomacy of Hysteria, 1947–51* (1976).

Chongchon River, Battle of

When Chinese Communist forces (CCF) joined North Korean troops in October 1950, the Chongchon River served as a crucial military boundary. The Chongchon, described as shallow, broad, and swift, flowed southwest into the Yellow Sea; although its water was chilly, its riverbed was solid, facilitating fording. Surrounded by hills, the Chongchon was sixty miles south of the Manchurian border and fifty miles north of Pyongyang, the North Korean capital. After capturing Pyongyang, the U.S. Eighth Army command wanted to secure the Chongchon and its bridges as the last major water barrier before reaching the Yalu River.

As the Eighth Army moved through North Korea, most officers and men presumed that the war was concluding and that when the enemy was pushed to the Yalu, peace would be attained before winter. When these forces crossed the Chongchon, they repaired bridges, unaware of the threat posed by the CCF.

Chinese troops began harassing U.N. forces, threatening the trek to the Yalu. On 1 November, forces at Unsan retreated when attacked by the CCF; out of ammunition and confused, the U.N. troops withdrew south of the Chongchon in early November. The advancing enemy troops, sequestered in the mountains, did not attack again, and U.N. forces recrossed the Chongchon to the northern bank.

U.N. military leaders, unsure of the plans of the commander of the Northeast People's Liberation Army, General Lin Piao, concluded that his objective was either to regain Pyongyang or to halt the U.N. advance across the Chongchon River, the latter seeming more plausible. At strategic meetings, U.N. military commanders determined that the I Corps would hold a defensive position at the Chongchon. They would gain a bridgehead at Sinanju, north of the river, allowing the Eighth Army to implement offensive measures and protect passages.

Withdrawal to the Chongchon and the awareness of an expanded war were demoralizing to U.N. forces. The men lacked adequate supplies of wire and working radios for consistent communications and subsisted on depleted supplies of weapons, clothes, and food, much of which had been discarded when they thought the war would "be over by Christmas."

By late November the Chongchon River was partially frozen. Although General Douglas MacArthur had initiated his "home by Christmas" offensive on November 24, 1950, within the next three days CCF forces ruined U.N. plans, forcing a retreat to south of the 38th parallel.

The initial Chinese target was three ROK divisions on the Eighth Army's right flank; when these units withdrew under heavy fire, their flank was left exposed and vulnerable to Chinese attack. The Chinese then sought to isolate General Walton H. Walker's Eighth Army and U.N. forces from southern reinforcements and push them to the coast.

On the evening of November 25, the Chinese crossed the Chongchon. They ambushed the 25th Division, spread on both sides of the river as they withdrew across it, as well as the 2nd Division. The latter caught the full strength of the attack. This surprise assault overwhelmed the unprepared troops who were unaware that the enemy was nearby, had not dug in, and were gathered near campfires seeking warmth.

Prior to the attack, sentries at outposts had heard "an unusual amount of noise across the river." Blinded by the darkness, they were suspicious that enemy troops were moving into position and reported this speculation to battalion headquarters but were rebuffed by officers stating that only friendly troops were supposed to be near the Chongchon. Concerned that their warnings were dismissed, the troops at their outposts continued to hear extraordinary noise and contacted other units whose officers repeated they were hearing U.N. patrols west of the river returning to camp.

Unconvinced, the alert sentries requested permission to fire in the direction where they heard the noises, but were denied. Although enemy machine gun fire peppered the troops, their commanders failed to comprehend the reality of the situation, and conflicting reports confused matters, preventing proper defense of the river. As a result, the infantry did not support artillery positions when requested, and the Chinese captured these gun positions and fell on the infantry. Enemy flares lit up the sky as U.N. troops fled the enemy through fields of frozen corn stubble. In an attempt to demoralize the troops the Chinese blared signal bugles and whistles and shouted American profanity.

One soldier of a 9th Infantry heavy mortar company remembered that it was "every man for himself." Many U.S. soldiers were angered that they had been denied the opportunity to hit the enemy first, possibly spoiling his attack. Jimmy Marks of A Battery of the 61st Field Artillery Battalion explained: "We had come out second best on the Chongchon. We felt betrayed. Our outpost had wanted to open fire and, just moments before the Chinese plowed into us, was told to hold its fire." U.N. troops attempted to remove artillery before the enemy could capture it, but most equipment was immobilized in the frozen ground.

The wind chill exacerbated battle conditions during the frosty pre-dawn hours. During the next days, Allied forces rallied but were unable to cross the river to gain defensible positions; the fighting was described as savage and desperate. The Turkish Brigade suffered high casualties trying to prevent the CCF from surrounding the 2nd Division. Men retreated to rear units, telling of the attack and awaiting news of the heavy casualties.

A survivor of the 61st Field Artillery Battalion remembered "the agony of meeting each incoming little group of survivors and learning who wouldn't be coming back. Even now, it is extremely upsetting to me." On jammed roads to Seoul, survivors of the Chongchon ambush retreated. The Chinese soon seized Pyongyang, and U.N. forces withdrew south of the 38th parallel.

U.N. soldiers expressed disbelief and disgust in their leaders' lack of command during the Chinese attack at Chongchon. In the longest military retreat in American history, the U.S. Eighth Army almost disintegrated as it hurried in splintered groups to safety. Communist forces also suffered casualties at the Chongchon, but the most damage was inflicted on the U.N. forces, who were decimated in manpower and equipment. As the media reacted with gloomy predictions and analyses, the not-so-confident U.N. commanders and soldiers questioned how long they could survive in Korea with the incalculable factor of Chinese forces in the war. The disaster on the Chongchon had rendered fatuous any further thoughts of "home by Christmas."

Elizabeth Schafer

Bibliography

Alexander, Bevin. *Korea: The First War We Lost* (1986).

Appleman, Roy E. *Disaster in Korea: The Chinese Confront MacArthur* (1989).

Blackely, M.E. "Disaster Along the Ch'ongch'on: Intelligence Breakdown in Korea," *Military Intelligence*, 34 (July-September 1992).

Hoyt, Edwin P. *The Bloody Road to Panmunjom* (1985).

Knox, Donald. *The Korean War, Pusan to Chosin: An Oral History* (1985).

Marshall, S.L.A. *The River and the Gauntlet: Defeat of the Eighth Army by the Chinese Communist Forces, November 1950 in the Battle of the Chongchon River, Korea* (1970).

Church, John H. (1892–1953)

Born near Glen Iron, Pennsylvania, on June 28, 1892, John Huston Church graduated from Bucknell Academy in 1909 and attended New York University for three years. When the United States entered World War I in the spring of 1917, he was appointed a second lieutenant in the infantry reserve. In December 1917, Church went to France, and in 1918, while serving with the 28th Infantry Regiment, he saw heavy fighting in the Cantigny, Montdidier-Noyon, Aisne-Marne, and Meuse-Argonne operations, and was wounded twice. Electing to remain in the military after the war, Church was commissioned a captain in the regular Army in 1920. Between the world wars he rose to the rank of lieutenant colonel, held various assignments with infantry units, and graduated from the Infantry School in 1921 and the Command and General Staff School in 1937.

During World War II, Church, as chief of staff of the 45th Division, was in the thick of the fighting in the Sicily and Salerno landings in 1943. Named commander of the 157th Infantry Regiment in September 1943, he participated in the Anzio and southern France landings in 1944. In October 1944, Church, who had been promoted to the rank of brigadier general two months earlier, became assistant commander of the 84th Division; and in February 1945, he was wounded for a third time while commanding "Task Force Church" as it spearheaded the Ninth Army's advance into Germany.

Following the deactivation of the 84th Division in January 1946 Church commanded replacement centers in the United States before going to Japan in 1949 to serve with the Far East command.

After North Korea invaded the Republic of Korea (South Korea) on June 25, 1950, General Douglas MacArthur, the Far East commander, sent Church, as commander of GHQ Advance Command and Liaison Group (ADCOM), to South Korea on June 27 to assess the situation and to instill a fighting spirit in South Korean soldiers and officials. Finding South Korea in chaos, Church advised MacArthur on June 28 that American troops would be needed to restore the original boundary between the two Koreas, and then practically assumed direction of the crumbling defense of South Korea until the arrival of American troops in early July. Thereupon he held the position of deputy commander of American Army forces in Korea until the opening of the Eighth Army's headquarters in South Korea on July 13 left him without a job.

Promoted to the rank of major general on July 18, 1950, Church was given command of the 24th Division on July 22. He succeeded Major General William Dean, who had been captured after the disastrous American defeat at Taejon. Notwithstanding his considerable combat experience and a record of heroism that included the Distinguished Service Cross, the Silver Star, the Bronze Star, and a host of other medals, Church was a poor choice to command the division, which was desperately in need of remanning and refitting after two weeks of fierce fighting.

Fifty-eight years of age, emaciated, almost crippled by arthritis, and taciturn by nature, he was not up to the physical rigors of command and in the opinion of many of his subordinates was calm almost to the point of lethargy.

At the beginning of August 1950, Church's hastily rebuilt 24th Division was thrust into the furious defense of the Pusan perimeter. During the first battle of the Naktong Bulge, Church reacted slowly to the North Korean attacks across the Naktong River and at times seemed unable "to issue a concise and positive order," causing him in one instance to squander his only available major reinforcements. Forced by enemy infiltrators and artillery fire to move his division headquarters fifteen miles to the rear, Church was exhausted and nearly at wit's end after several days of hard fighting. To save the situation, Lieutenant General Walton H. Walker, commander of the Eighth Army, assigned the 1st Provisional Marine Brigade to

Church; and with its assistance, he virtually destroyed the North Korean 4th Division and eventually eliminated the enemy bridgehead across the Naktong.

Church had regularly violated doctrine during the Naktong battle, required more Eighth Army reserves than he should have to win it, and was not as aggressive as he should have been. Nevertheless, Walker, despite misgivings, continued him in command of the 24th Division through the breakout of the Eighth Army from the Pusan perimeter, its drive through North Korea toward the Yalu River, and its retreat from North Korea after the battle of the Chongchon River. But in early 1951, Lieutenant General Matthew B. Ridgway, Walker's replacement as commander of the Eighth Army, decided that Church was too frail and sickly to remain in command of the division and relieved him as part of a shakeup of the Army's top generals. Church thereafter commanded the Infantry Center at Fort Benning, Georgia, until his retirement in June 1952. He died in Washington, D.C., on November 3, 1953, only four months after the close of the war that had taken so much out of him.

John Kennedy Ohl

Bibliography

Alexander, Bevin. *Korea: The First War We Lost* (New York: 1986).

Appleman, Roy E. *South to the Naktong, North to the Yalu: June-November 1950* (Office of the Chief of Military History, Washington: 1961).

Blair, Clay. *The Forgotten War: America in Korea, 1950–1953* (1987).

Hoyt, Edwin P. *Pusan Perimeter: Korea 1950* (1984)

Robertson, William Glen. *Counter-Attack on the Naktong, 1950* (Combat Studies Institute, Fort Leavenworth, KS: 1985).

Schnabel, James. *Policy and Direction: The First Year* (Center of Military History, Washington: 1972).

Civil Affairs and Military Government, U.S. Army

At the time of the Korean War, U.S. Army Civil Affairs was defined as "the activities of a government of an area under military occupation and of its inhabitants, except those of an organized military character. Control of such civil affairs is the control of civilian activities in such an area by the armed forces" (*Joint Chiefs of*

Staff Dictionary of United States Military Terms for Joint Usage). Civil Affairs (CA) performed this mission magnificently in World War II, laying the foundations for European and Japanese recovery after the war. (Through the Korean War period, the terms "civil affairs" and "military government" were often used interchangeably.)

In the Korean War, civil affairs troops found themselves, for the first time, involved with a subsistence economy in which fertilizers and draft animals were more important than electricity and railroads. Also, for the first time, they were more involved in specifically civil affairs activities as opposed to military government. Furthermore, they had to deal, after 1948, with a functioning government punctilious about its sovereignty.

Although Korea's Japanese overlords had made appreciable progress since about 1932 in industrializing Korea, most of this development had come in the hydroelectricity and mineral-rich north; the economy of the Republic of (South) Korea remained predominately agricultural, although it had almost three times the population of North Korea. What industry there was in the south was controlled to the end of World War II by a Japanese managerial, technical, and governing class that represented less than 3 percent of the population of the entire Korean peninsula. Industry in southern Korea was concentrated in Seoul, Pusan, and Taegu, with minor development at Taejon and Kwangju.

But the overwhelming majority of South Koreans were farmers, agricultural laborers, shopkeepers, and craftsmen, although there was a surprisingly well-represented class of professionals whom the Japanese had allowed to flourish so long as they made no attempt to enter the higher ranks of industry or government. In 1945, therefore, the Japanese economic legacy consisted of respectable rail and communications networks, the most developed hydroelectric complex in Asia, a scattering of small to medium-size factories, and a well-educated professional class superimposed upon an overwhelmingly agrarian society steeped in an ancient, proud, and united culture.

This was the economy and the polity that the United States Army encountered when it entered southern Korea in September of 1945. Much to the dismay of practically all Koreans of whatever political persuasion or class, their nation was artificially divided in half and occupied by the Soviet Union to the north and the United States to the south. Although Korea had been one of the earliest victims of Japanese aggression, it was to be treated in the immediate post–World War II years as almost a province of the hated Japan.

Although the American Army made sincere efforts to govern justly and humanely, the mere fact of military government was a bitter burden for Koreans in the first three postwar years. The retention of Japanese technicians and even lower-level government workers in the first postwar months added to that burden. Strikes, riots, and demonstrations marred the earlier months of the American occupation of South Korea. Communism made some inroads among the strongly nationalist professional classes and even with the peasants, who were also attracted by the Soviet military government's expulsion of the Japanese, shooting of landlords, and redistribution of land. By contrast, the American authorities did next to nothing to alleviate southern Korea's oppressive landlord system and widespread poverty. When American military government turned over authority to the new Republic of Korea (ROK) in August 1948, it seemed to many Koreans that military government had midwifed an authoritarian regime that would do little or nothing to alleviate social and economic misery. Nonetheless, the fledgling Republic of Korea had made appreciable economic advances by 1950.

The coming of the Korean War brought in U.S. Army Civil Affairs in place of military government. CA troops found themselves involved in the control of refugees, supervision of public health and safety, evacuation of friendly native personnel, restoration of public utilities, the reestablishment of civil government and of liaison with local governments, the regulation and rehabilitation of public transportation and communications, the establishment of anti-inflation policies by regulating wages and prices, and the promotion of public safety.

Unfortunately, civil affairs responsibility during the Korean War was widely diffused, resulting in a lack of focus and follow-through. Counting U.N. and American civilian and military agencies, there were literally dozens of officially recognized organizations responsible for civil affairs in Korea during the war. For example, within the Eighth Army alone, seven different units had varying degrees of direct relationship with different Republic of Korea authorities. A likely explanation, if not excuse, for this confusing state of affairs is the fact that the Republic of Korea was an internationally recognized sovereign state, and CA projects could not simply be ordered into effect without consulting at some length through different levels of the ROK government.

Civil Affairs in the Korean War dates officially from the United Nations Security Council resolution of 31 July 1950 which requested the U.N. command to exercise responsibility for civilian relief and support. The United Nations' commander in Korea, General Douglas MacArthur, appointed Brigadier General Crawford F. Sams as chief of his general headquarters public health and welfare section. The Republic of Korea president, Syngman Rhee, made personnel of this section members of the existing Central Relief Committee, which was composed of his Cabinet ministers concerned with refugee problems. In addition, each U.S. Army corps and division had attached civil assistance sections to serve in the immediate combat zone. The United Nations Civil Assistance Command, Korea (UNCAK) served in those areas outside the war zones but under U.N. control. UNCAK was divided into three major divisions: supply, economics, and civil administration, and served basically as a national headquarters that paralleled ROK provincial and local governments.

Perhaps bearing in mind that Koreans often associated civil affairs with U.S. military government of recent unhappy memory, Lieutenant General Walton Walker, Eighth Army commander, had created a special staff section to plan and implement civil affairs, originally entitled the "Civil Assistance Section." This section was elevated in November 1950 to a command, the U.N. Civil Assistance Command, Korea. This command retained its authority until the end of hostilities.

The Eighth Army, through UNCAK, determined, in coordination with the ROK government and other involved agencies, the types and quantities of civilian supplies required at any time for civil affairs. A list of these items was then forwarded to U.N. general headquarters, Tokyo, for screening, revision, and the establishment of priorities and phasing. The revised list was then forwarded to the Department of the Army in Washington for final action.

To provide for longer-term civil affairs, Eighth Army in 1950 established an economic division within UNCAK, which in turn set up a similar section in each provincial team. These units were to assist the ROK government in such economic programs as providing raw material and equipment, agricultural and fish-eries support and advice, and to develop essential industries, mines, power plants, transportation facilities, and public services. For the most part, the U.N. command believed that it would prove more beneficial to furnish raw materials and semifinished products to its Korean ally, to be finished in Korean plants, rather than to furnish finished products or to aid in the construction of new manufacturing plants.

At the United Nations level, the organizational situation was hardly more clear. In addition to UNCAK, the U.N. General Assembly on 7 October 1950 established the U.N. Commission for the Unification and Rehabilitation of Korea (UNCURK), which assumed the functions of the former, prewar United Nations Commission on Korea. UNCURK was charged with representing the U.N. in bringing about a unified, independent, and democratic government for all Korea, as well as having relief and rehabilitation responsibilities. Further complicating matters, two months later the U.N. also established the U.N. Korean Reconstruction Agency (UNKRA) to carry out UNCURK directives.

The earliest large-scale civil affairs demands in Korea were for the relief of refugees. By September 1950, estimates of war refugees in the Pusan area ranged from 300,000 up to 3.5 million. Thus there was an immediate need for clothing, soap, emergency rations, bedding, household effects, and preventive medical measures. Despite some initial delay, these needs were in large part met. Other early requirements included the provision of sanitary and water facilities in the camps, particularly after an outbreak of smallpox. By the time of the U.N. breakout from the Pusan perimeter, the refugee situation, at least in the camps, had passed from emergency status to continuing tragedy.

The movement of refugees to safety also proved to be one of the most important of CA activities through the first year of the war. Those who came south from the fighting lines or from fear of Communist oppression had to be checked by intelligence, given emergency care, and forwarded to camps, usually in the Pusan area. But the evacuation by sea of refugees from North Korea by the retreating X Corps was of an altogether greater magnitude. The Hungnam evacuation of all civilians who had compromised themselves with the Americans or South Koreans was an obvious necessity. But X Corps commander Major General Edward M. Almond also ruled that his command would assist all civilians who wished to leave. In all, 98,100 men, women, and children (not counting babies carried on the backs of their parents) were evacuated in what was the greatest purely civilian maritime evacuation of modern times. These refugees were brought by sea to Pusan, where they added to that vital port's already vastly overcrowded condition.

The restoration of civil government by the U.S. Army first took place when the port city of Inchon was turned over in September 1950 to a new mayor who replaced a predecessor who had fled during the North Korean invasion and never returned. Until that month, U.N. forces had either been in retreat or making their stand along the Pusan perimeter, from which civilians had been removed. The Inchon installation marked a temporary turn of the tide, and the U.S. Army's assistance in the establishment or reestablishment of ROK civil authority from its capital, Seoul, to North Korea's seat of power, Pyongyang. All of this, of course, went into reverse with the U.N. retreat from North Korea and south of Seoul. After the recapture of the South Korean capital and the establishment of civil authority once again, battle lines hardened, and any necessity for further establishment of civil authority was over.

With the U.N. crossing of the 38th parallel in October 1950, the United States found itself, for the first and only time, responsible for the civil affairs of a recently Communist territory. The U.N. command (UNC) explicitly refused to impose a complete government on its occupied area of the Democratic People's Republic of Korea (DPRK). Rather, it hoped to insure peace and security, leading to the unification of the Korean peninsula. With that goal in mind, the UNC retained most local North Korean officials at their posts, although the inhabitants would remain under the control of corps, division, and logistical commands in the first phase of occupation policy. Refugees and the indigenous population could receive direct relief assistance. Occupation courts were established and discriminatory laws and regulations abrogated, as was the dominant and privileged status of the Korean Workers' (Communist) Party. Economically, the needs of the U.N. military forces came first, but North Korea was much less damaged by the war at this stage, so that the problems of refugees, destruction of facilities, and disruption of labor were not so severe as they had been in the south. U.N. troops seemed on the whole to have been well-behaved, although there was the inevitable looting and black market operations, particularly among the poorly paid ROK troops. U.N. forces were particularly gratified by their occupation of the DPRK capital, Pyongyang; numerous U.S. military government personnel had their smiling photographs taken in offices still dominated by large portraits of Kim Il Sung and Joseph Stalin.

It was not to last. The massive incursion of Chinese forces in November 1950 threw U.N. forces rather precipitously out of North Korea by the end of 1950. Civil Affairs personnel now faced a truly monumental refugee problem as tens of thousands of North Koreans fled their homeland. In addition to the massive evacuation of civilians through Hungnam, CA personnel also eased the plight of inland refugees by stockpiling food and rice straw at strategic river crossings, as well as providing inoculations and DDT dusting. Uncounted lives were saved by the efforts of U.S. Army Civil Affairs in those days of fear, uprooting, hunger, and numbing cold. No less than 100,000 refugees fled southward from South Pyongyang province alone. In the month of December, 200,000 refugees from North Korea entered South Korea. Considering the brief tenure of U.S. Army Civil Affairs in North Korea, CA's major accomplishment in those days may well have been refugee relief.

CA and its refugee charges had little time to rest when entering South Korea, however. With the Chinese hard on their heels, U.N. forces evacuated Seoul again. But this evacuation was more orderly than the chaotic affair of June 1950, despite far worse weather. All who wanted to flee Seoul were able, by one way or another, to cross the Han River and continue southward. CA continued to provide emergency feeding stations, and in order to prevent the clogging of roads and railways and milling about the vital cities of Taejon, Taegu, and Pusan, as many as possible of the wandering populations were funneled into the Cholla provinces in southwest Korea, and there given semi-permanent shelter. Later, as the battlefield stabilized, ROK authorities attempted to move these large body of refugees to official facilities by force, without great success.

The last major refugee problem involved the determination of many refugees to return to newly recovered Seoul or to their farms in the general vicinity of the 38th parallel as U.N. forces once again moved northward, but this time far more cautiously, and not deeply into North Korea. These migrants often flowed northward, oblivious to any U.N. concerns that they might interfere with military operations.

By the spring of 1951, UNCAK finally had the personnel and equipment to handle its responsibilities on a relatively routine basis, and was no longer hampered by any great swings in the battle lines. The emergency period was finally over.

For all the good and lasting work of U.S. Army Civil Affairs in Korea, the subject is hardly mentioned in any of the official Army volumes on the war, and then only in relation to activities during the prewar military occupation, or to a few wartime civilian evacuations. Yet it could be maintained that without the assistance of U.S. Army Civil Affairs and the work of their ROK counterparts, not only would the suffering of Koreans have been much greater, but the amazing recovery and rise to world economic power of the Republic of Korea would have been severely retarded.

Stanley Sandler

Bibliography

Dougherty, William E., and Marshall Andrews. "A Review of US Historical Experience with Civil Affairs, 1776–1954" (Special Study ORO-TP-29, Johns Hopkins University, Baltimore: 1961).

Kissinger, Henry, and C.D. Stolzenbach. *Civil Affairs in Korea, 1950–51* (Special Study ORO-TP-184, Johns Hopkins University, Baltimore: n.d. [c. 1953]).

U.S. Army John F. Kennedy Special Warfare Center, "Case Study of Civil Affairs Operations: Mid-Intensity Conflict" (Korea Text 1, Fort Bragg, NC: n.d.).

Clark, Mark W. (1896–1984)

General Mark Wayne Clark served as commander of United Nations forces in Korea from May 12, 1952, to October 7, 1953, and signed the military armistice agreement on behalf of the United Nations command with the North Korean Army and the Chinese People's Volunteers at Munsan-ni, Korea, on July 27, 1953. The son of a career infantry officer, Clark was born in Madison Barracks, New York, and spent much of his youth in the Chicago suburb of Highland Park, near Fort Sheridan. With the assistance of his aunt, Zettie Marshall (the mother of General George C. Marshall), Clark secured, at age seventeen, an early appointment to the United States Military Academy. A tall, lean, and often sickly youth, Clark failed to distinguish himself at West Point as either an athlete or scholar, graduating 110th in a class

of 139 in 1917. Following graduation he was commissioned a second lieutenant and assigned to the infantry. Severe health problems, which troubled him throughout his youth, caused him to be hospitalized and set him behind his classmates. Nevertheless, he was promoted to captain in August 1917 and saw action with the 11th Infantry in France, where he was wounded in action and later decorated for bravery.

Returning to the United States in 1919, Clark held various peacetime assignments, speaking on the Chautauqua circuit in 1921, and assuming posts in the office of the assistant secretary of war (1929–33), where he served as an instructor. Clark graduated from the Command and General Staff School at Fort Leavenworth, Kansas, in 1935 and served as deputy chief of staff for the Civilian Conservation Corps, VII Corps area at Omaha, Nebraska, prior to entering the Army War College, from which he graduated in 1937.

In 1940, as World War II approached, Clark, a lieutenant colonel assigned to Fort Lewis, Washington, was on the verge of meteoric rise, in part due to his close acquaintance with General George C. Marshall and his longtime friendship with Dwight D. Eisenhower. In August 1941, Clark was named assistant chief of staff for operations of the general headquarters, U.S. Army, and a month after the American entry into the war, Clark was appointed deputy chief of staff of Army ground forces, and less than six months later, chief of staff. In October 1942, Clark became deputy commander in chief of the Allied forces in the North African theater and subsequently planned the invasion of North Africa. Prior to the invasion he made a secret trip by submarine to the North African coast to meet with friendly French officers in the German-occupied territories. Clark's personal account of this dramatic and dangerous rendezvous brought him considerable public attention. As deputy commander of Anglo-American invasion forces, Clark took into protective custody the opportunistic Admiral Jean Francois Darlan, the highest-ranking French officer in French North Africa, and induced him to repudiate the Vichy government.

In 1943, Clark commanded the Fifth Army in the Italian campaign, the first to be activated in the European theater, leading the force in the capture of Naples on October 1, 1943, and Rome on June 4, 1944. As commander of the 15th Army Group, comprised of American and British forces, he accepted the surrender of German forces in Italy and Austria in May

C

1945. In June of that year he was appointed commander in chief of the U.S. occupation forces in Austria, and U.S. high commissioner for Austria. He served as deputy to the U.S. secretary of state in 1947 and attended the negotiations for an Austrian treaty with the Council of Foreign Ministers in London and Moscow. In June 1947 Clark returned home and assumed command of the Sixth Army, headquartered at the Presidio in San Francisco, and two years later was named chief of army field forces.

At the end of World War II, Clark stood with Generals Eisenhower, George Patton, and Omar Bradley as a leading American commander in the European theater. While he was much admired by his personal staff, others found him self-seeking, vainglorious, arrogant, and too concerned about gaining publicity. In his private correspondence General Patton referred to him as an "s.o.b." and "too damned slick." In 1948, his superior, General Jacob L. Devers, chief of Army field forces, evaluated Clark as "a cold, distinguished, conceited, selfish, clever, intellectual, resourceful officer .... Very ambitious." The general also noted that Clark "secures excellent results quickly" and gave him a "superior" performance rating. Although he held some of his British wartime counterparts in contempt, Clark managed to impress Churchill and other European leaders. Charles DeGaulle, oddly, called him "simple and direct," and Clark's blunt appraisal of the Soviets and his well-publicized calls for greater American military preparedness in the early years of the Cold War earned him more admirers than critics during his service in Austria.

Following the removal of General Douglas MacArthur, Clark was named on April 30, 1952, commander in chief, United Nations command, and commanding general, United States Army forces Far East, succeeding Lieutenant General Matthew B. Ridgway. Clark had visited Korea in February 1951 as chief of Army field forces to observe combat conditions and meet with then Eighth Army commander Ridgway, a West Point classmate. Ridgway urged Clark to intensify training in night combat, and after his return to the United States, Clark experimented with the use of searchlights and flares.

On his arrival in Tokyo to take command in May 1952, Clark was confronted with the military deadlock on the front lines, roughly along the 38th parallel, stalled armistice negotiations with the North Koreans and their Chi-

nese allies, and a complicated and explosive prisoner of war (POW) situation. Clark advocated an offensive that would have included attacks on bases across the Yalu River, but his plan, which would have widened the war, was not approved. Faced with an enemy of superior numbers, Clark determined that U.S. lines could not withstand "being dented" by an enemy who was willing to make great sacrifices in manpower. When "dented," Clark had U.S. forces "roll with the punch" and then follow with a counterattack to take strategic positions. Meanwhile, the prisoner exchange issue, which had caused a suspension in the armistice talks, was complicated by Communist agents within the U.N. prisoner of war camps. The month Clark took command, Chinese and North Korean prisoners at Koje Island rioted and took Brigadier General Francis T. Dodd captive. Clark noted "I hadn't bothered to ask anyone in Washington about POWs, because my experience had been with old fashioned wars .... Never had I experienced a situation in which prisoners remained combatants and carried out orders smuggled out to them from the enemy High Command." Clark approved use of overwhelming force to clear out the POW compounds, and "broke" two general officers responsible for bad judgment during the riots.

Following his election to the presidency, Dwight Eisenhower, as promised during his campaign, went to Korea on December 2–5, 1952, accompanied by General Omar N. Bradley and secretary of defense-designate Charles Wilson. Clark had prepared a "broad plan" for victory, but the president-elect never gave him the opportunity to present it. To a disappointed Clark it appeared that Eisenhower would seek an "honorable truce" once in office.

Early in 1953 Clark was authorized to bomb the North Korean capital, Pyongyang, hydroelectric plants along the Yalu River, and other targets previously prohibited. Pyongyang was for all intents and purposes leveled. The air attacks on the North Korean hydroelectric system deprived that nation of electric power for two weeks. Clark persevered in the air raids in the face of muted protests from the British and French. His main purpose was to keep pressure on the Communists to sign an armistice more on U.N. terms.

On February 22, Clark, with approval from Washington, wrote to Kim Il Sung and Peng Dehuai proposing the exchange of sick and wounded prisoners. His adversaries, perhaps disheartened by the death of Stalin on March 5th and the prospect of a frustrated U.S. turning to atomic weapons, agreed to the exchange and suggested that this first move could "lead to the smooth settlement of the entire question of prisoners of war." On April 2, the Communists agreed to Clark's offer of a meeting of liaison groups and, in a reversal of their earlier stand, acceded to the use of a "neutral state" to ensure a just solution to the question of repatriation. The liaison groups met on April 6 and Operation Little Switch began on April 20. Six days later the first plenary session at Panmunjom since the previous October was held.

Clark now faced the task of persuading a reluctant President Syngman Rhee of South Korea to accept a compromise settlement. On April 27, Clark flew from headquarters in Tokyo to Seoul for a series of meetings with the strong-willed South Korean leader. Two days earlier, Rhee's ambassador in Washington had told Eisenhower that Rhee would withdraw Republic of Korea forces from Clark's U.N. command if an armistice allowed Chinese to remain south of the Yalu. Rhee was unresponsive to Clark's analysis that neither side had won the war. On May 12 Clark found Rhee still strongly opposed to a truce. Nevertheless, on May 25 the final offer of the United Nations command was presented at Panmunjom.

Clark offered Rhee security assurances, U.S. financial aid, and military assistance to build the ROK Army to twenty divisions. As the date for concluding the armistice approached, Rhee made a last desperate move to disrupt the agreement. On June 18 he ordered 27,000 Communist prisoners who were awaiting a neutral party to determine their status to be released into the South Korean countryside. Yet, despite Communist protestations, diplomacy prevailed, Rhee was issued a stern reprimand by his American allies, and the agreement held. On July 27, 1952, at the 159th plenary session, an armistice agreement was formalized. Believing himself to be the first U.S. commander to agree to an armistice without victory, Clark signed the peace documents at UNC advance headquarters at Munsan-ni, stating afterwards, "I cannot find it in me to exalt at this hour."

Clark relinquished his Far East command on October 7, 1953, and retired from the service at the end of that month. He accepted the presidency of The Citadel in Charleston, South Carolina, a post he held until his retirement in 1965, when he was named president emeritus.

In 1954, he had been appointed by former president Herbert Hoover to chair a task force to investigate the Central Intelligence Agency and other intelligence organizations of the U.S. government. He wrote his memoirs, *From the Danube to the Yalu* (1954), and spoke frequently on the threat of communism and the need for greater United States military preparedness. In the 1960s he renewed the friendship with Eisenhower that had been strained during the Korean War.

Michael J. Devine

Bibliography

General Clark's papers (more than sixty boxes) are located at The Citadel.

Blumenson, Martin. *Mark Clark: The Last of the Great World War II Commanders* (1984).

Clark, Mark W. *Limited War* (The Citadel, Charleston: n.d.)

Holt, Daniel D. "An Unlikely Partnership and Service: Dwight Eisenhower, Mark Clark, and the Philippines," *Kansas History* (Autumn 1990).

Kaufman, Burton I. *The Korean War: Challenges in Crisis, Credibility, and Command* (1986).

Rees, David. *Korea: The Limited War* (1964).

Saxon, Wolfgang. "Conqueror of Rome," *New York Times* (April 17, 1984).

Collins, J. Lawton (1896–1987)

J(oseph) Lawton Collins, U.S. Army officer, army chief of staff, was considered by his contemporaries both a soldier's soldier and a general's general, and enjoyed an outstanding reputation as a combat officer and as a first-rate military planner and administrator.

Born in New Orleans, Louisiana, on May 1, 1896, Collins graduated from the U.S. Military Academy in 1917, but missed combat in World War I. Following two stateside assignments, he went to Germany in 1919 as part of the occupation forces. Two years later he returned to West Point, where he served as a chemistry instructor for four years. In the next dozen years, he was a student or a teacher in various service schools before going to the Philippine Islands. In 1936 he attended the Army Industrial College and Army War College, after which he joined the faculty of the latter. Although the short, stocky, good-looking Collins was always a well-organized, articulate individual with great interpersonal skills, he was, on the eve of World War II, considered a good, but by no means extraordinary, officer.

World War II saw Collins's fortune rise quickly. In 1942 he became commanding general of the 25th Infantry Division, and in January 1943 he led that unit as it drove the Japanese off Guadalcanal. It was at that time that he earned the nickname, "Lightning Joe." Next it was on to New Georgia where his earlier success was repeated. In December 1943 he was given command of the VII Corps, which he led onto Utah Beach on D-Day and then across Europe until it joined with Soviet forces at the Elbe River in April 1945. By this time the heavily decorated infantry officer had risen to the rank of lieutenant general. Several postwar assignments in Washington, D.C., were followed by appointment as deputy chief of staff in 1947, vice chief of staff in 1948, and after receiving his fourth star, chief of staff of the Army on August 16, 1949—a position he held throughout the Korean War.

As the U.S. Army's highest ranking officer, he was responsible for the supply, training, and functioning of all Army forces and for their operational command when sent into combat. Collins quickly found that his aggressiveness on the battlefield could not be used as effectively on the political battlefields of Washington. Because of considerable interservice rivalry, he was forced to walk a treacherous path among the leaders of the different military services and their congressional advocates.

The Army chief of staff's influence on events in Korea was exerted through the Joint Chiefs of Staff (JCS), composed of its chairman, General Omar Bradley, Air Force chief of staff General Hoyt Vandenberg, chief of naval operations Admiral Forrest Sherman, and Collins. That body was responsible to Secretary of Defense Louis Johnson, and later George Marshall, and ultimately to President Harry S. Truman for U.S. military around the world.

Prior to the North Korean attack, Collins joined the other chiefs in the assessment that Korea was not of strategic importance to the U.S. and therefore should not, in the event of attack, be defended by U.S. forces. It was that position which explains his initial reluctance to support U.S. involvement at the June 25 Blair House conference. At that same meeting, he indicated he did not feel that air and naval forces would be able to halt the North Korean forces. Yet a day later he supported use of U.S. air and naval forces against the aggression. On June 30, Collins, after a telecommunications

conference with General Douglas MacArthur in Japan, came to the conclusion that U.S. ground forces should be committed to battle. Based on that recommendation, and that of all other major advisors, Truman made the decision.

Although U.S. involvement was under the umbrella of the United Nations, the command structure was set up in such a way that the war was, in reality, run by the United States. As the U.S. military presence increased in Korea, so did the influence of the JCS, in that the president had designated it as his agent for Korea. While the JCS was responsible for proposing policy and implementing the commander in chief's orders, the operations in Korea were predominantly those of the Army; thus Collins became the primary planner, coordinator, and implementer of military action. Consequently, at the JCS meetings during the war, Collins generally took the lead.

Early in the conflict much of Collins's time was spent setting up the unified U.N. command and establishing a U.N. fighting force. These activities were extremely complicated because of the president's desire to have as many nations as possible represented in the force, as opposed to the JCS desire to have only those forces that could make a militarily significant contribution. No issue, however, was more difficult than meeting the manpower needs of the Army. When the war started, there were only 592,000 troops on active duty, but within two years, there were nearly 1.6 million, more than a two and a half-fold increase. Matters were further complicated because individuals drafted or called to active duty were, by law, limited to serving twenty-one months. Thus soldiers were trained, sent to Korea for approximately a year, and returned to civilian life. This rapid turnover created constant training and supply problems. Because of the pressing needs for more soldiers, many National Guard and reserve units and inactive reservists were called up. Such decisions generated much criticism from those affected by Collins's recommendations.

Several weeks into the war, General MacArthur informed Collins of his planned invasion at Inchon. From the beginning Collins opposed the move, and while he remained skeptical, he ultimately agreed to the action out of a firm conviction that such decisions should be those of the theater commander. From that time on, Collins was troubled by MacArthur's arrogance and contempt for the Washington establishment. While Collins agreed with MacArthur's position of advancing into North

Korea to destroy the Communist forces, he was alarmed by MacArthur's failure to adhere to warnings about sending U.S. forces to the Yalu River. For such reasons, plus a fear that MacArthur's actions might widen the war, Collins supported President Truman's April 1951 decision to relieve MacArthur.

As the conflict turned into a stalemate in 1951 and 1952, Collins, who was accustomed to the no-holds-barred combat of World War II, grew increasingly frustrated, and thus it was not surprising that in the spring of 1953 he supported use of nuclear weapons to bring the war to an end. In the last two years he successfully saw that manpower needs were met, that racial integration of units became a reality, that troops were adequately trained and supplied, and that Congress provided the funds needed by the Army to carry on the fighting. The latter became increasingly difficult as public support for the conflict waned. On August 15, 1953, less than three weeks after the armistice, Collins concluded his service as chief of staff. He subsequently served as the U.S. representative to the NATO military committee and as special envoy to South Vietnam before retiring in 1956. In later years he always maintained that Korea was a victory for the U.S. because the purpose had been to halt Communist aggression and that had been accomplished. He remained in Washington, D.C., until his death on September 12, 1987. Collins's tenure as chief of staff has been blighted in history by a perception that he did not adopt a more firm line against his subordinate, General Mac-Arthur, and his public disagreement with administration policy as laid down by the JCS. But Collins should also be remembered for his successes in securing adequate funding for the Army, for his meeting of manpower needs (at whatever political cost), his good faith and successful racial integration of the Army, and for seeing to the adequate training and supply of U.S. troops worldwide during the last two years of the war.

Keith D. McFarland

Bibliography
Bradley, Omar, with Clay Blair. *A General's Life* (1983).
Collins, J. Lawton. *Lightning Joe: An Autobiography* (1979).
———. *War in Peacetime: The History and Lessons of Korea* (1969).
Ridgway, Matthew. *The Korean War* (1967).
Schnabel, James F., and Robert J. Watson. *The History of the Joint Chiefs of Staff: The Joint Chiefs of Staff and National Policy*, Vol. III, *The Korean War* (1979).

Combat Cargo Command, U.S. Air Force

At the time of the North Korean invasion 25 June 1950, U.S. Air Force airlift capacity in the Far East consisted solely of the undermanned 374th Troop Carrier Wing. Equipped with four-engine C-54 transports and responsible for air transport throughout the theater, the 374th had two squadrons based outside Tokyo, one at Tachikawa and one in the Philippines. Initially, the wing's transports were used to evacuate diplomats, military advisers, military dependents, and other U.S. personnel from Korea. While this emergency evacuation was taking place, the Far East Air Force (FEAF) gathered C-47s and deskbound pilots from units throughout the theater and assigned them to the 21st Troop Carrier Squadron. Based in southern Japan, the newly formed "Kyushu Gypsies" flew elements of the 24th Infantry Division from Itazuki to Korea during the earliest days of the conflict.

Following a series of sharp engagements against superior North Korean forces, the battered American and South Korean units were forced into a defensive perimeter around the port of Pusan. As none of the three airstrips in the perimeter could accommodate C-54s, the main burden of supplying the hard-pressed troops fell to the "Gypsies." The C-54s flew cargo and personnel from Tachikawa to Ashiya on the southern tip of Kyushu, then C-47s took over, landing on the perimeter's airstrips or air-dropping supplies to front-line troops.

Operating procedures for the Korean airlift tended to be *ad hoc*. With inadequate or nonexistent radio navigational aids and poor communications, transport pilots had to rely on contact flying. After crossing the Straits of Tsushima, pilots would approach the Korean coast at low level, identify the Naktong River near Pusan by spotting discolored sea water, then follow the river northward until locating the railroad tracks that would take them to Taegu, the perimeter's forward airstrip. This seat-of-the-pants procedure worked, but the airlift's efficiency suffered.

On 23 August 1950, Air Force headquarters advised Lieutenant General George E. Stratemeyer, FEAF's commander, that Major General William H. Tunner could be made available to conduct airlift operations. Stratemeyer promptly accepted. Tunner, who happened to be in Japan on an inspection tour of the trans-Pacific airlift, returned to the United States, quickly assembled a group of key officers and airmen, and reported back for duty nine days later.

The Air Force's premier airlift specialist, Tunner was the ideal choice to bring order to the theater's eager but inefficient air transport operations. Tunner had learned his trade during World War II as commander of the India-China Division of Air Transport Command. Under his driving leadership, tonnage carried over the treacherous India-China "Hump" route had risen spectacularly. During 1948–49, he had applied his skills to the Berlin Airlift as head of the Combined Airlift Task Force, again with impressive results. Known as "Terrible Tunner" and "Whilly the Whip," the impatient, coldly efficient, chain-smoking airlifter often boasted that "We can carry anything, anywhere, any time."

On 10 September 1950, Tunner activated Combat Cargo Command (Provisional) at Ashiya. The CCC, which reported directly to FEAF headquarters, assumed operational control over the 374th Troop Carrier Wing and 21st Troop Carrier Squadron. It also controlled the Curtiss C-46s of the 1st Troop Carrier Group and the Fairchild C-119 "Flying Boxcars" of the newly arrived 314th Troop Carrier Wing.

Tunner and his staff patterned operations on the model of the Berlin Airlift, with an emphasis on increased efficiency. The CCC provided a weekly statement of airlift capacity to the Far East Air Priority Board, which represented the interests of all services. The board then allocated this capacity based on the tactical situation in Korea. The CCC's transport movement control center would hold a daily traffic movement conference in the office of the director of traffic, where the next day's requirements would be discussed. Aircraft would be matched to loads and flights scheduled. Pilots would fly designated airways at specific altitudes on a rigid timetable, sending progress reports back to movement control center. Standardized procedures meant increased efficiency, which could be measured by the dramatic increase in daily tonnage that took place in September.

Five days after CCC took control of airlift operations, General Douglas MacArthur's forces landed at Inchon. Although all went well at first, it soon became clear that MacArthur had underestimated the difficulties of supplying the invasion force through the port of Inchon. Fortunately, he was able to call on CCC to fill the supply gap. On September 19, nine C-54s and twenty-three C-119s landed at Seoul's newly captured Kimpo Airfield and established an airhead. Round-the-clock operations began the next day, with 225 tons of vitally needed cargo soon arriving on a daily basis. The command even transported a complete pontoon bridge to span the Han River; it inadvertently had been left behind when the invasion fleet sailed from Japan.

In early October, as United Nations forces moved northward in pursuit of the fleeing enemy, CCC prepared for a major airborne operation. A pet project of General MacArthur's, the airborne assault was designed to trap major North Korean units and to free American prisoners of war (POWs). Plans called for the 1st and 3rd Battalions of the 187th Regimental Combat Team to be dropped at a critical road junction near the village of Sukchon thirty-five miles north of Pyongyang. At the same time, the 2nd Battalion would descend fifteen miles further east, near Sunchon.

After a delay of several hours due to bad weather, the drop took place between 1400 and 1500 hours on October 20. Seventy-five C-119s and forty C-47s disgorged 2,860 paratroopers and 301 tons of cargo over the Korean countryside as Generals MacArthur and Tunner circled overhead. Following the drop, MacArthur landed at Pyongyang, congratulated Tunner, and awarded him the Distinguished Service Cross. MacArthur then held a press conference where he hailed the operation as a brilliant tactical stroke that had cut off 30,000 enemy troops.

Certainly, the drop had been accomplished with great skill. However, it did not achieve its objective. Contrary to MacArthur's assertions, all enemy units, except for a single regiment, had already moved north of the Sukchon-Sunchon area, taking with them American POWs.

The CCC continued to support the northern advance during October and November, carrying supplies needed for tactical operations as far forward as possible. Tunner's airlifters grew increasingly efficient as standardized procedures became widely accepted. On October 24, CCC set a new record, hauling 1,687 tons to Korea. The next day it topped that, carrying 1,767 tons. More than 90 percent of the tonnage, mainly rations and gasoline, went to northern Korea.

The situation in Korea changed drastically in late November as the Chinese intervened in force. On November 28, Chinese troops shattered the South Korean II Corps, exposing the right flank of the Eighth Army. The CCC launched a major effort on November 29–30, flying more than 700 wounded out of Sinanju in less than twenty-four hours.

As the Eighth Army withdrew southward, the fate of X Corps units, surrounded by some 100,000 Chinese in the Chosin Reservoir area, commanded America's attention. For twelve days, CCC gave highest priority to support the 20,000 men of the 1st Marine Division and two battalions of the Army's 7th Infantry Division as they struggled to escape the Chinese trap.

The drama of the Chosin Reservoir campaign opened on the night of November 27–29, when the Chinese tried to overrun advance Marine elements at Yudam-ni on the southwest corner of the reservoir. Simultaneously, Army units to the east came under heavy attack. On November 28, CCC made an emergency drop of ten tons of ammunition to the Marines and sixteen tons to Army units. The following day, with an airdrop supply system in place, fifteen C-119s and seventeen C-47s dropped more than 117 tons to the beleaguered forces around the reservoir.

On the afternoon of November 30, the badly exposed units began to fight their way back to Hagaru-ri, a destroyed village and Marine strongpoint located 1 mile south of the reservoir. Captain Eugene R. Hering, divisional surgeon, reported on December 1 to Major General Oliver P. Smith, commander of the 1st Marine Division, that there were 600 casualties at Hagaru-ri, with 900 more expected as forward units reached the perimeter. As it turned out, Hering had underestimated the situation: there were nearly three times that number of casualties to be evacuated.

Marine engineers had been attempting to carve an airstrip out of the frozen ground at Hagaru-ri. Although only 40 percent completed, Smith authorized the trial use of the landing area. The first C-47 landed on the 2,900 by 50-foot strip at 1430 hours and departed thirty minutes later with twenty-four wounded. Three more aircraft landed in the afternoon, including the first (and only) mission flown by a Navy four-engine transport. One C-47 broke its landing gear on touchdown and had to be destroyed. The other two airplanes carried out another sixty casualties.

Airlift operations got underway in earnest on December 2, when C-47s of the 21st Troop Carrier Squadron and 1st Marine Air Wing evacuated 914 wounded to Yonpo, where they were taken by C-54s to hospitals in Japan. With the "Gypsies" doing most of the flying, another 2,000 casualties came out on December 3 and 4. On December 5, the last day of the Hagaru-ri operation, 1,400 wounded reached safety. In all, some 4,312 casualties (by Marine count) were flown out of Hagaru-ri between 1 and 5 December in one of the most hazardous and successful airlift operations of any war.

The remaining Marine and Army troops had a long way to go to reach safety at Hamhung, sixty road miles away. On December 6, forward units left Hagaru-ri to rejoin the rest of the 1st Marine Division at Koto-ri. As the column fought its way along the twisting mountain roads, Marine planners grew concerned about the condition of the road south of Koto-ri. A key bridge across Funchilin Pass had been destroyed, and there was no way to bypass the 1,500-foot chasm. After examining the situation by air, Marine engineers concluded that the gap could be spanned by four sections of M-2 steel treadway bridge. The problem was how to get the bridge to the Marines. Although a bridge had never before been dropped by air, there was no choice except to try. Tunner's "anything, anywhere, any time" boast was about to be put to its most demanding test.

On the afternoon of December 6, CCC made a trial drop of a bridge section—18 feet long and weighing 2,900 pounds—with disastrous results. Supported by twenty-four-foot parachutes, the section bored a sizable hole in the ground. However, a second trial with forty-eight-foot parachutes gave promise of success. That night, CCC riggers attached two large parachutes to eight sections of treadway bridge. The next morning three C-119s flying at 800 feet placed three bridge sections into a 300-yard drop zone at Koto-ri. Five additional sections were dropped at noon. Although one section was damaged and one fell behind Chinese lines, Marine engineers now had what they needed. On December 8, as the withdrawal from Koto-ri began, they spanned the chasm. Two days later, the epic of Chosin ended when the column joined with a relief force from Hamhung at Chinhung-ni.

The CCC, which had dropped 1,580 tons of supplies to nearly frozen Marine and Army troops between November 28 and December 10, had no time to rest. During the period De-

C

cember 13 to 17, Tunner's transports flew out of Yonpo some 2,406 tons of supplies and more than 4,000 personnel in the most concentrated airlift of the war. In scenes reminiscent of the Berlin Airlift, a steady stream of C-46s, C-47s, C-54s, and C-119s landed and took off at intervals of two to three minutes.

As the Chinese pressed south, CCC continued to rush supplies to front-line units and to evacuate wounded. Between December 16 and 31, it airlifted 6,436 patients to Japan. During the first twenty-four days of January, CCC brought out another 10,489 casualties and delivered 12,486 tons of supplies to Korea.

On 25 January 1951, the provisional Combat Cargo Command became the 315 Air Division (Combat Cargo). Shortly thereafter, General Tunner returned to the United States, his organizational tasks completed. As the front in Korea stabilized in April, cargo operations settled into a routine.

The CCC left an impressive record. In little more than four months, Tunner's airlifters flew 32,632 sorties, carried 130,170 tons of cargo, and recorded 32.78 billion ton-miles. They evacuated 72,960 patients in Korea and Japan, with only one casualty dead on arrival. Indeed, air evacuation of wounded came of age at this time.

William Leary

Bibliography

Combat Cargo Command. "Historical Report, 10 September 1950–24 January 1951," 4 vols. (unpublished document, U.S. Air Force Historical Research Center, Maxwell AFB, AL: n.d.).

Futrell, Robert Frank. *The United States Air Force in Korea, 1950–1953* (1961).

Key, William G. "Combat Cargo: Korea, 1950–51," *Pegasus*, 17 (November 1951).

"The Moving Man," *Time*, 56 (December 18, 1950).

Thompson, Annis G. *The Greatest Airlift: The Story of Combat Cargo* (1954).

Tunner, William H. *Over the Hump* (1964).

Communications

Communications were so important in the Korean War that on at least one occasion, in early September 1950, General Walton H. Walker, Eighth Army commander, had to withdraw his headquarters back nearly to Pusan on the east coast almost solely to protect his signal equipment. Had the Eighth Army's Teletype equipment been captured or destroyed in the face of the enemy advance, there would have been no replacement in the entire Far East.

Throughout the war, high U.N. commanders could communicate directly with the Pentagon in Washington, D.C. At the lower levels of command, tactics pivoted on communications because units had to cover such large areas.

At the onset of the war in June 1950, allotted radios, all of which were of World War II vintage and most of which were obsolete, were in extremely short supply. Batteries were also hard to find, and in many early engagements U.N. forces were forced to rely on runners, many of whom were captured or simply disappeared.

The most vital communications link was that between Japan and Korea, built by the Japanese during their occupation of Korea. With the Japanese withdrawal in 1945, this link began to deteriorate, although the Radio Corporation of America (RCA) had established an international radio station in Seoul with circuits for telegraph and telephone links to the Philippines, the U.S., and Hong Kong. In 1948 the South Korean ministry of communications bought the station and in 1950 also purchased RCA's civilian communication system.

Still, the United States was not at all prepared to supply South Korea with communications for war, and new equipment was not slated to become available until 1952. Ironically, Japan, Korea's former exploiter, offered relief. To fill the gap, the U.S. Army Signal Corps renovated the Army command and administrative network to enable the Far East command to reach the U.S. speedily. Circuits were increased from single to multi-channel, with the six-channel single-side-band being enhanced to twelve channels. This expanded capacity established especially good communications between Tokyo and the U.S. West Coast.

An on-line encrypted teletypewriter gave quick and secure communication between the chief of transportation and ports so that troops and equipment could be deployed relatively quickly. By August 1951 the Signal Corps technical service logistical reporting network gave daily reports to chiefs of technical services on depot supply inventories. The Japan logistical command signal section helped the system integrate the commercial long-line telephone and high-frequency radio relay system. In that same year, the U.S. Army in Japan was using no less than 53,600 telephones.

Initially, signal equipment was procured from depots in Japan, which unfortunately did not have enough switchboards or terminals of its own. Shipments from the U.S. would take several weeks and would not reach combat troops in time. Japanese manufacturers were able to provide crucial supplies while the Army awaited shipments from the U.S. However, commanders had no system of formal authorization to issue communications equipment, and radios and telephones were often mistakenly supplied to locations were they were needed the least.

The U.S. Army Signal Corps chief signal officer was responsible for the use of communications to secure supplies and to route them to their correct destination; the Corps was responsible also for basic communications such as radio, wire, and radar, as well as still, motion picture, and aerial photography.

The basic communications equipment used by U.S. ground forces in Korea were the SCR-300 radio set, the EE-8 telephone, the SB-18/GT telephone switchboard, the teletypewriter set EE-98, signal generator I-72, and the PE95 power unit. Field radios and regimental switchboards were heavy and bulky and often had to be abandoned in the early days of the retreat to the Pusan perimeter. This equipment often could not be replaced.

The weight of U.S. ground communications in World War II had been recognized as excessive, but not a serious problem. However, in Korea, the mountainous terrain made the reduction of size and weight a priority. At the corps engineering laboratories at Fort Monmouth, New Jersey, a strong effort was undertaken to achieve "miniaturization, ruggedization, and reliability." These efforts were successful, and the backs of soldiers and porters in Korea were eventually eased. For example, a twenty-two-pound switchboard with double-capacity lines was half the weight and one-third the size of its predecessor. Field wire was reduced from 135 to forty pounds per mile and proved cheaper to manufacture, easier to store, and able to carry more messages over longer distances. A portable teletypewriter that had weighed 225 pounds was reduced to forty-five pounds and one-fourth the size.

The transistor, developed in the Bell labs in 1948, was used in war for the first time. Requiring much less electricity than vacuum tubes, and far smaller, the transistor reduced the need for the heavy battery packs and gasoline-powered generators previously required to heat the fila-

ments in vacuum tubes. The transistor was also simpler, more reliable, and did not produce heat, thus enormously simplifying maintenance. The standard converter used to change radio impulses for radio-teletypewriter equipment weighed 100 pounds and used 175 watts; the new transistor converter was scaled down to ten pounds and used a mere 1.75 watts.

Batteries, however, remained a problem throughout the war, although not so dire as in the first months. A battery that could work for thirty days in peacetime lasted only two or three days in combat. A major problem was that batteries could not be stored in advance of their use because they quickly deteriorated.

Japanese contractors were recruited, but their products were inferior to American-manufactured units and had an even shorter shelf life. Still, they helped fill the gap. Other communications equipment in perennial short supply were tuners, wires, and resistors. Scavengers from the poverty-stricken civil population also played havoc with U.N. forces communications, stealing wire, and other equipment.

Telephones did not advance so abruptly as did electronic communications in this war. The standard EE-8 field telephone connected wire-hooked switchboards to headquarters, field hospitals, etc., and provided a link to Seoul, Tokyo, and even family in the United States. Wiring was the same as in World War II. This was exhausting work, often lasting several days, and skilled personnel for this task were scarce; even commanding officers were known to help in stringing lines. There also never seemed to be enough skilled splicers, and American civilians were actually brought into the field for this work, at a higher salary than that of a U.S. Army colonel.

The Signal Corps was responsible for repairing the lines. As U.N. troops advanced, lines were hastily spliced. In retreat, they usually did not destroy wire or stations, at least within the ROK, confident that they would return and would need these facilities. Unfortunately, the resourceful enemy was quite likely to splice these same lines and tap Allied signals.

The famous Mukden cable was an essential artery of communication for the U.N. forces. Serving as Korea's primary telephone/telegraph system, it had been built by the Japanese before World War II. It ran from Pusan to Seoul and then on to Pyongyang and Mukden, Manchuria. Consisting of twenty interlocked wires, the cable relied on numerous repeater stations, and was buried one meter beneath the main north–south highway. Thus the Mukden cable did not suffer appreciable damage except where Allied bombing cratered the highway, and remained in use throughout the war by both sides within their respective territories.

Nonetheless, VHF (very high frequency) radio became the backbone of U.N. military communications. It could follow troops over mountains and rivers, from ship to shore, and keep up with the movement of infantry, providing clear and reliable reception. VHF radio did require relay stations, which were placed on high, often remote and usually inaccessible areas, to increase range; the security of these stations was sometimes a problem. While within the Pusan perimeter, frequency-modulated (FM) radio signals had often been interfered with by the surrounding hills. VHF radio operators quickly learned to let the hills work for them, bouncing radio waves off the heights, a technique not taught in Signal Corps schools.

Radio was put to good use by U.N. forces to direct artillery fire. Throughout the war the U.S. could flexibly control its artillery fire, quickly changing targets as required. The Communist forces did not have this option, lacking such refined communications, and had to resort to prearranged fire. U.S. forces could relatively easily predict and locate the enemy's static artillery fire, although it always remained a serious threat.

U.N. forces were informed and entertained by an Armed Forces Radio Service station known as Gypsy, which broadcast recorded and live transmissions. The Communists responded with their own radio efforts, broadcasting first from newly captured Seoul ("Seoul City Sue"), as well as from Pyongyang. The comparative merits of each side's propaganda broadcasts were hotly debated throughout the war. Another morale service was provided by Special Services, which allowed GIs to call home from the combat zone, as well as relaying entertainment electronically through recordings or directly from Tokyo or stateside.

A special signal service was long-range radar, with stations at Pusan and on the coast of Japan. The U.S. Coast Guard cooperated with U.N. forces in Korea and Japan to utilize the radar efficiently to monitor the coastline.

The Korean Communications Zone (KCOMZ) was established by the Eighth Army in July 1952. KCOMZ was responsible for supporting combat operations, procuring supplies and military equipment imports and deliveries in addition to a wide variety of other tasks ranging from medical aid to engineering assistance. It also provided a crucial operational and political link between U.N. forces and the ROK government.

Foreign correspondents were provided communications through telephone lines to Tokyo, Teletype, and radio, in addition to courier aircraft, jeeps, and helicopters that carried their pouches of news stories and photographs.

By contrast, Communist military communications were primitive. The North Korean Army opened the war with few radios and scavenged what they could from abandoned or seized U.N. electronic equipment. Couriers were used at all levels, with radios reserved for regimental and higher commands. Telephones and signal flares were used at the battalion level, while companies relied on bugles, and platoons used whistles.

The multinational nature of the U.N. effort in Korea created its own problems. Not only did each national force rely on its native language for communication, it also had its own operations methods, using different frequency ranges and procedures. The U.N. forces communications were eventually integrated by the expedient of issuing U.S. equipment and instructions on its use, and assigning a liaison officer who could speak English.

Aerial photography, both still and moving, was extended during the war, providing intelligence and help in mapping and target acquisition. Mobile darkrooms enabled units on occasion to have finished photos within two hours after the initial request.

Combat cameramen were active in capturing still and motion picture records of the war; the Army Motion Picture Depository in New York City received approximately 61,000 stills and one-third of a million feet of motion-picture film in one fifteen-month period from 1951 to 1952.

Without communications, U.N. commanders in Korea would simply have been unable to supply, coordinate, or deploy their troops as well as they did and would probably have lost the war in the first few months. Specifically, air-ground communications made possible the U.N. air strikes that blunted the North Korean drive for Pusan and victory.

Although communications were at first inadequate, innovations during the war vastly improved matters. By the final year of the Korean War U.N. forces communications had compressed a decade's progress into three years.

Elizabeth Schafer

Bibliography
Huston, James A. *Guns and Butter, Powder and Rice: U.S. Army Logistics in the Korean War* (1989).

Jennings, Gary. "The KCOMZ Story," *Army Information Digest* (October 1953).

Purkiser, Herman L. "What's New in Signals?" *Military Review*, 31 (1952).

Vale, Charles F. "Combat Through the Camera's Eye," *Army Information Digest* (March 1953).

Zahl, Harold A. "Toward Lighter Signal Equipment," *Army Information Digest* (June 1953).

See also SIGNAL CORPS, U.S. ARMY

Corps of Engineers, U.S. Army

See ENGINEERS IN THE KOREAN WAR

Coulter, John B. (1891–1983)

Born in San Antonio, Texas, on April 27, 1891, John Breitling Coulter graduated from the West Texas Military Academy in San Antonio in 1911 and was commissioned as a second lieutenant of cavalry in the United States Army in 1912. During the next four years he served with the 14th Cavalry Regiment along the Mexican border, and in 1916 he participated in the Pershing punitive expedition into Mexico. In World War I, Coulter was an aide to the commander of the 42nd Division and saw action as a battalion commander in the St. Mihiel operation. Between the world wars he held numerous posts in cavalry units, was attached to the military intelligence division at Army headquarters in Washington, D.C., and graduated from the Cavalry School in 1922, the Command and General Staff School in 1927, the Army War College in 1933, and the Naval War College in 1934.

Coulter, who was promoted to the rank of major general in March 1943, spent most of World War II with the 85th Division, first as assistant division commander and later as commander. In March 1944, after extensive training in the United States and North Africa, the division was sent to Italy. There Coulter led it through to the end of the war from Anzio to the Brenner Pass and earned a reputation as an expert in mountain warfare. Following assignments in the United States, Coulter went to Korea in January 1948 to command the 7th Division; and from June 1948 to January

1949, was deputy commander of American forces in Korea. He then was named commander of the I Corps in Japan, and when it was deactivated in early 1950, became deputy commander of the Fifth Army, headquartered in Chicago, Illinois.

After the invasion of South Korea at the end of June 1950, General Douglas MacArthur, commander of United Nations forces in Korea, brought Coulter back to Korea to command the I Corps, upon the establishment of a corps organization in the American Eighth Army. Arriving in South Korea with a small command staff on August 13, Coulter immediately began studies for a breakout effort from the Pusan perimeter. Two weeks later, Lieutenant General Walton H. Walker, commander of the Eighth Army, dispatched Coulter to command the crumbling South Korean front along the east coast of South Korea. Heading the makeshift Task Force Jackson (the Republic of Korea I Corps and miscellaneous American forces), Coulter eventually had to remove the commander of the ROK I Corps and a ROK division commander to restore order to the "hysterical" ROK command and to call on Walker for additional American units to stem the North Korean advance. Walker praised Coulter for his ability to get the ROKs to stand and fight, but he was not pleased with his overall generalship; in Walker's opinion, Coulter had unwisely dispersed his American reinforcements. Moreover, Coulter's "insistent and frequent" pleas for more help antagonized Walker at a time when he was desperately trying to find troops to plug holes all along the crisis-ridden perimeter.

Doubtful that Coulter was sufficiently aggressive to lead the breakout from the perimeter, Walker, on September 11, 1950, gave command of the I Corps, which was to spearhead the Eighth Army's counterattack, to Major General Frank W. Milburn and switched Coulter to the command of IX Corps. For all practical purposes, Walker's action relegated Coulter to a back seat during the liberation of South Korea. The IX Corps did not become operational until a week after the I Corps went on the offensive on September 16, and thereafter it devoted most of its energy to mopping up bypassed enemy units and securing the supply lines from the perimeter. This pattern continued after the Eighth Army moved beyond the 38th parallel into North Korea in October 1950 and advanced to the Chongchon River.

During the battle of the Chongchon River at the end of November 1950, Coulter's IX Corps, which consisted of the American 2nd and 25th Divisions, and the ROK II Corps bore the brunt of the devastating Chinese Communist onslaught against the Eighth Army. Like Walker, Coulter initially viewed the Chinese assault as a "local problem," and then misjudged the ability of the Turkish Brigade to protect the right flank of the Eighth Army after the ROKs disintegrated. On November 30, the day the retreating 2nd Division had to run a murderous Chinese fireblock and roadblock along the Kunu-ri–Sunchon road to escape annihilation, Coulter was not near the scene of crisis, having already moved his headquarters to the rear at Pyongyang earlier in the day. Failing to keep abreast of the dangerous situation confronting the 2nd Division, he did not send sufficient reserves to help the division break through the Chinese trap or authorize it to use a different and safer escape route from Kunuri, contributing to the disaster that befell his division.

Out of favor because of the Kunu-ri disaster, Coulter in early 1951 was "kicked upstairs" after Lieutenant General Matthew B. Ridgway, Walker's replacement as Eighth Army commander, concluded that he needed a "whole new team" in the top ranks of the IX Corps to help turn around the dispirited Eighth Army. Promoted to the rank of lieutenant general, Coulter was designated deputy commander of the Eighth Army and assigned the responsibility for Ridgway's liaison with the South Korean Army and with South Korean President Syngman Rhee, whom Coulter knew well from his prewar tour in Korea. Later that year Coulter returned to the United States, and at the end of January 1952 he retired from the Army.

Shortly afterward, Coulter was named the Washington office representative of the United Nations Korean Reconstruction Agency (UNKRA), which directed U.N. efforts to rebuild Korea. The next year he was appointed head of the agency with the rank of assistant secretary general of the United Nations, a job he held until 1958. Under Coulter's direction the UNKRA spent $130 million on industry, roads, schools, housing, and agriculture to get the war-racked South Korean economy back on its feet. In recognition of Coulter's work, the South Korean government in 1959 erected a statue of him in Seoul. Coulter also served as U.N. Secretary General Dag Hammarskjold's adviser on peacekeeping forces during the 1956 Middle East crisis. He died in Washington on March 6, 1983.

John Kennedy Ohl

Bibliography

Appleman, Roy E. *Disaster in Korea: The Chinese Confront MacArthur* (1989).

———. *South to the Naktong, North to the Yalu: June-November 1950* (Office of the Chief of Military History, Washington: 1961).

Blair, Clay. *The Forgotten War: America in Korea, 1950–1953* (1987).

Fisher, E. *Cassino to the Alps* (Center of Military History, Washington: 1977).

Hoyt, Edwin P. *The Pusan Perimeter* (1988).

D

Dean, William F. (1899–1981)

The eldest of four children of a dentist, William Frishe Dean was born in Carlyle, Illinois, on August 1, 1899.

Failing to gain entrance to West Point and prevented by his mother from enlisting in the army during World War I, he enrolled at the University of California (Berkeley) in 1918. Dean graduated in 1922, and the following year, having been commissioned as a second lieutenant in the infantry reserve in 1921, he received a commission in the regular Army. Between 1923 and 1941 Dean rose to the rank of lieutenant colonel, took courses at the Command and General Staff College and the Army Industrial College, and graduated from the Army War College.

During World War II, Dean, promoted to the rank of major general in 1943, held desk jobs in Washington, D.C., until early 1944, when he was made assistant commander of the Europe-bound 44th Division. In December 1944 he won the Distinguished Service Cross for personally leading "an infantry platoon through one concentration of enemy fire after another" to destroy "opposing batteries." That same month he was made the division commander, leading it in its victorious drive across Germany in the spring of 1945.

Immediately after the war Dean was assigned to the Command and General Staff College. In 1947 he was appointed military governor for South Korea, a post he occupied until elections were held in 1948 and the Republic of Korea (ROK) was established. After briefly commanding the 7th Division during its relocation from Korea to Japan, Dean was named chief of staff of the Eighth Army, the occupation army in Japan. An unpretentious man and "more of a doer than a talker," Dean thoroughly disliked staff work, considering himself a "simple, down-to-earth" infantryman who belonged with troops. In October 1949, after a "sudden transfer" left vacant the command of the 24th Division, he gladly assumed it.

When President Harry S. Truman in June 1950 committed American forces to the defense of South Korea against the North Korean invasion, Dean's division was the first element of the American Army thrown into the fight. Underequipped, undermanned, and undertrained, it had grown soft in the distractions and doldrums of occupation duty and was rated the least combat ready of the four American divisions in Japan. Yet it was chosen to led the American reinforcement, largely because of Dean. He was the only division commander in Japan who had commanded troops in combat or knew South Korea well, and his superiors believed that his "can-do" spirit and reputation as a tough disciplinarian suited him for the frenetic task of rushing American troops into battle.

In the first week of July the 24th Division deployed to South Korea, Dean himself arriving on July 3. Over the next seventeen days he engaged the onrushing North Koreans in five major holding actions while falling back nearly 100 miles, culminating on July 19–20 in the disastrous battle for the city of Taejon, the most important communications center in southwestern Korea. Confronted by superior North Korean strength in infantry and armor and beset by atrocious communications, low morale, inadequate firepower, and poor performance by the 34th Infantry Regiment, the 24th Division was practically shattered by the time it was driven from Taejon, losing 30 percent of its 16,000 men as the North Koreans continually pierced its defenses with armor and enveloped its flanks with infantry.

Dean's generalship during these catastrophic days has been criticized, particularly his decision to stay with the front-line troops during the battle for Taejon rather than at the division headquarters in the rear. As a result, he later forthrightly admitted, "I was too close to the trees to see the forest, and therefore was at the time blind to the envelopment that the North Koreans were engineering." But given the difficult conditions he faced, Dean did as well as could be expected with a division only days removed from easy occupation duty, and bought badly needed time for other American divisions to deploy to Korea. Moreover, at Taejon he showed he was a fighter at a time when the shaky American troops desperately needed inspired leadership. Frustrated by the daily crises and believing that a general should lead by example as well as manage, Dean reverted to the role of a combat infantryman and took to the streets of Taejon with a bazooka team on July 20 to stalk the feared North Korean T-34 tanks. Under his direction, the team eventually destroyed one at close range. Later that day, as North Koreans overran Taejon, Dean remained to the last, helping to organize the survivors fleeing the burning city.

The defeat at Taejon did not end Dean's ordeal. On the night of July 20–21 an enemy roadblock forced Dean's party to abandon their vehicles and take to the hills in their attempt to return to friendly lines. When he went off into the dark to fetch water for the wounded, he, rather improbably, fell down a steep slope and was knocked unconscious. Suffering from a broken shoulder and separated from his men, Dean wandered through the hills of Korea for the next thirty-six days to reach safety, all the time dodging North Korean patrols and most of the time alone. Finally, having lost sixty pounds and barely able to stand, Dean was betrayed to the North Koreans by "friendly" South Koreans on August 25, 1950. He became the Communists' highest ranking American prisoner of war, although for some unknown reason they kept his capture a secret until the end of 1951. In the meantime, the American government, needing heroes in a period of defeat and frustration, awarded Dean the Congressional Medal of Honor for bravery during the defense and evacuation of Taejon.

For three years Dean endured the threat of torture and death at the hands of his captors. Ill and subjected to brainwashing, he remained "unbreakable" and even attempted suicide out of the fear that he might disclose information

or make statements that might help the enemy. Released on September 4, 1953, six weeks after the armistice, Dean was astonished to learn that he was regarded as a hero; and with customary modesty, he said he was just "a dog-faced soldier" who deserved only "a wooden star." The American people felt differently, especially after the publication in 1954 of Dean's self-deprecating and warm account of his torment and endurance, *General Dean's Story*.

In January 1954, Dean became deputy commanding general of the Sixth Army, headquartered at the Presidio in San Francisco, California. He retired in 1955 and lived in Berkeley until his death on August 25, 1981.

John Kennedy Ohl

Bibliography

Alexander, Bevin. *Korea: The First War We Lost* (1986).

Appleman, Roy E. *South to the Naktong, North to the Yalu: June-November 1950* (Office of the Chief of Military History, Washington: 1961).

Blair, Clay. *The Forgotten War: America in Korea, 1950–1953* (1987).

Dean, William F., and William L. Worden. *General Dean's Story* (1963).

Flint, Roy K. "Task Force Smith and the 24th Division: Delay and Withdrawal, 5–19 July 1950," in Charles E. Heller and William A. Stofft, eds., *America's First Battles, 1776–1965* (1986).

Defectors

Despite its hard-fought, bitter nature, Korea was an "ideological" war, one more concerned with propaganda than with territory. Obviously, success on the battlefield could be quickly translated into favorable media attention, but even the losers could wring sympathy for a stand against "godless communism" or, on the other hand, "American imperialism." The question of the defectors or non-returned POWs of the Korean War serves as an illustrative example.

The news that twenty-one Americans had refused to return to their homeland came as a shock to the American public. Commissions were assembled to determine why any American soldier would elect to remain in a Communist country. The discipline of the U.S. Army was called into question and a new "Code of Conduct" was adopted by 1955 to guide future U.S. POWs in their behavior toward their captors. The disheartening news of the American defectors came when "McCarthyism" was at its peak, and many Americans truly feared a communist takeover through subversion or infiltration. Communists had allegedly been uncovered in many American government institutions, and now, with the tales of American collaboration in the prison camps and the undeniable fact of twenty-one (two subsequently returned of the twenty-three) soldier defectors, it seemed that even the U.S. Army shared in the rot.

But the various investigators, journalists, commissions, and boards all neglected the obvious fact that in most of America's wars some American prisoners have collaborated with the enemy. Furthermore, in this ideological struggle, U.N. POWs were now pawns in the struggle between East and West. For many the incentive for collaboration was simple survival. The conditions in the prison camps were extremely primitive and the North Koreans particularly ruthless and brutal. To gain meager privileges, some POWs turned "progressive" and allowed themselves to be used in anti-Western activities such as broadcasting and signing petitions. Some, unfortunately, went further and reported on their fellow captives who displayed "reactionary attitudes."

Some indication of just how hard life was in the Communist prison camps is seen in the fact that no less than 38 percent of U.S. POWs died in those camps. By way of contrast, 3.8 percent of American troops held by the Germans in World War II died in captivity. If all of those missing but believed captured are added to the death toll, the figure comes closer to 58 percent. Nonetheless, the fact remains that the vast majority of U.S. troops acquitted themselves well in captivity, sensational contemporary tales to the contrary notwithstanding.

POWs from the Communist side eventually proved to be the main stumbling block in the armistice negotiations. The huge number of Chinese and North Korean POW defectors was an embarrassment to both Communist nations, which had proclaimed the vast superiority of their social and economic systems to those of the "poverty-stricken" West. But it must also be noted that the conditions in the camps bordered on pandemonium, at least before the Koje riots of May 1952. Communist and anti-communist partisans fought for control of the compounds, while lackadaisical and ill-trained U.N. guards stood by. Some apologists for the Communist side (including some who should know better),

have contended that conditions were about as bad in the U.N. camps as in those of the Communists. The death rates from both sides should demonstrate the preposterousness of such claims, not to mention the vast disparity in the numbers of defectors.

The U.N. commitment to voluntary repatriation complicated and delayed the armistice talks to the point of impasse for almost two years. On 8 June 1953, Syngman Rhee, president of the Republic of Korea, broke the deadlock by unilaterally throwing open the compounds and allowing the POWs to scatter into the South Korean countryside. This action outraged the Communists, but it did bring matters to a head, and on 27 July 1953 the armistice was signed. On 5 August 75,823 prisoners were released to the Communists in Operation Big Switch and the Communists turned over 12,773 U.N. prisoners, 3,597 of whom were Americans.

On 23 September, the 14,704 Chinese and 7,900 North Korean prisoners who had refused repatriation were released to the custody of the Neutral Nations Repatriation Commission in the Demilitarized Zone. There they were interrogated by representatives of their respective governments and given a final opportunity to recant and return to their homelands under a promise of amnesty. A final 137 agreed to repatriation. On 21 January 1954, after months of delay, the 22,467 remaining POWs were released by the commission. The Chinese, with fanfare and slogans, marched off to join the Nationalists on Taiwan, while the North Koreans simply assimilated themselves into the general South Korean population.

Of the U.N. POWs, 349 elected not to return home. Of these, 327 were Koreans who were thought to be sympathetic to the Communist claim that they had simply fought for the unification of their homeland, or to have been "infiltrated" into the Republic of Korea from North Korea either before or during the war. One Briton, a Royal Marine, also held out against returning home. (He had been considered something of a barracks radical by his fellows well before the war.) The twenty-three Americans who had refused repatriation were given one last chance to reconsider, and two did agree to return. Over the decades, about half of the twenty-one have returned home to live in anonymity. With the end of the war, the POWs, repatriatees and defectors alike, ceased to have any propaganda value, but the questioning of the values and moral fiber of a generation of

American men continued for at least a decade afterward.

Donald D. Leopard

Bibliography

Biderman, A.D. *March to Calumny* (1963).

Goulden. Joseph C. *Korea, the Untold Story of the War* (1982).

Hastings., Max. *The Korean War* (1987).

Kinkead, Eugene. *In Every War But One* (1981).

Pasley, Virginia Schmitz. *21 Stayed: The Story of the American GI's Who Chose Communist China—Who They Were and Why They Stayed* (1955).

Stokesbury, James L. *A Short History of the Korean War* (1988).

White, William L. *The Captives of Korea: An Unofficial White Paper on the Treatment of War Prisoners, Our Treatment of Theirs: Their Treatment of Ours* (1957).

See also BRAINWASHING, OR *Xinao;* PRISONER OF WAR (POW) QUESTION

Demilitarized Zone

The Korean Demilitarized Zone (DMZ) has its origins in the 1945 division of Korea at the 38th parallel for post–World War II occupation by American and Soviet forces to accept Japanese surrenders and reinstall indigenous governments. The arbitrary boundary, selected quickly and randomly from a National Geographic map by American military officers, was not meant to be a permanent political border. On July 27, 1953, when the DMZ, a product of the Korean armistice, was conclusively etched, closely following troop positions near the 38th parallel, the hurriedly selected line in 1945 became an established geopolitical boundary that symbolized the division of democracy from communism in the Third World.

A demilitarized zone was a necessary condition for the seeking of truce talks and a cease-fire. Both the Communists and allies desired a DMZ with a military demarcation line (MDL) to separate the two political and military spheres. On June 23, 1951, Jacob Malik, Soviet ambassador to the U.N., initiated talk about a DMZ. He suggested the southern boundary would be the 38th parallel, but U.N. commanders unrealistically demanded a line fifty miles above the parallel.

The truce talks at Kaesong in the summer of 1951 pivoted on the question of the DMZ.

Both sides agreed that a DMZ and MDL were basic requirements for the signing of an armistice and ceasing hostilities, and both favored a wide buffer zone. However, neither group could agree on the definition of the DMZ.

General Matthew B. Ridgway wanted a defensible boundary and preferred that the line be designated by military attainments on the field. North Korean General Nam Il insisted that "We hold firmly that the 38th parallel should be made the military demarcation line between both sides and that both sides withdraw ten kilometers from the 38th parallel in order to establish a demilitarized zone." He argued that the 38th parallel was a historical border, alluding to the Communists' interpretation that the war began because the 38th had been violated (although he did not mention that the North Koreans were the violators). Nam Il continued his argument by stating the military line could not be the MDL because "no stable battle lines exist before an armistice is agreed upon and implemented."

U.S. delegate Admiral C. Turner Joy rebutted Nam Il's argument, stating that the 38th parallel should not be the the MDL just because that was where the war started. He provided a hypothetical question to the Communists as an example of their logic. He asked them that if the truce talks had begun in the summer of 1950 when the U.N. forces were compressed behind the Naktong River whether they would have wanted the historical 38th parallel as the MDL. He argued that the 38th parallel had been selected as a border in 1945 only to accept Japanese surrender. He emphasized that it was never meant to be a permanent political divider.

The U.N. commanders realized the 38th was indefensible as a MDL because it made no military sense. The U.N. delegates wanted the MDL to have "certain military realities."

Admiral Joy advocated a cease-fire with ground forces in their current places to establish the DMZ, then withdrawal of all military forces. Nam Il called his suggestion "naive and illogical" and claimed that the three lines, the northern and southern DMZ boundaries as well as MDL on the U.N. map, were randomly selected and unworthy of the Communists' consideration. Joy refuted by stating that the DMZ was created according to geography and military positions; he said the lines revealed the existing military situation, and its outline could easily be recognized by terrain features. He emphasized that both sides would have accessible defensive positions available near the proposed DMZ.

Ten sessions focused on the DMZ. Joy proposed moving on 3 and returning to the DMZ issue later, but the Communists refused. Joy stressed that the U.N. position was flexible but insisted the MDL be determined by battle positions and stated that the allies would not discuss any possibility of the 38th parallel as the MDL. Nam Il countered that the U.N. could break the deadlock by simply approving the 38th as the MDL. Joy recommended that a subcommittee be formed to discuss and seek a solution, and Nam Il agreed.

On August 17, 1951, the subcommittee first met; however, on the 22nd, the Communists ended the truce talks when they claimed the U.N. forces had bombed the Kaesong neutral zone. One small success of the meeting, however, was that both negotiating sides realized the other's demands were adjustable.

In the field, General James Van Fleet, Eighth Army commander, wanted the MDL to be along the line of contact, with a slight withdrawal to establish a buffer zone. He suggested a limited offensive to begin in September 1951 to improve U.N. positions. Among military engagements to seek this objective, UN troops fought in the Punchbowl, gaining Bloody Ridge and Heartbreak Ridge.

On October 22 the war-flattened village of Panmunjom was named as the new site for truce talks. Officials erected tents for necessary negotiation buildings, and three days later discussion of Item 2 resumed, and the U.N. delegates asked the Communists for their proposal. The Communists responded that they did not have one. Major General Henry Hodes, a U.N. negotiator, suggested a four-kilometer-wide zone based on battle positions at that time be established as the DMZ, including Kaesong in the Seoul security zone. North Korean Major General Lee Sang Cho responded that the idea was "unjust and unreasonable."

Meanwhile Van Fleet's troops were seeking territorial gains in the Iron Triangle. On October 27, Ridgway ordered him to cease the military attacks because the truce talks might be affected, and if the U.N. were forced to make concessions regarding the MDL, the commanders did not want to lose men unnecessarily to gain territory that might ultimately be lost.

On October 31, General Cho finally agreed that the DMZ would be based on the battle line and recommended that troops should withdraw two kilometers from the line of contact. The Communists, however, rejected the proposal to include Kaesong in the DMZ. On November 5 the U.N. accepted the four kilometer-wide DMZ centered on the line of contact. They reminded the Communists that fighting had continued during the negotiations and requested that the MDL be the actual line at the time the armistice was signed.

The U.N. command advised that a staff officers committee of three representatives from each side be formed to agree on the contact line, but the Communists disagreed, demanding that the MDL should be finalized during negotiations before discussions of Item 3 began. The Communists accepted the line of contact on the field at that point, claiming that the U.N. command was trying to avoid an end to hostilities. The U.N. delegates responded that they did not want a useless DMZ they could not defend or which would not reflect the military situation during the war. Also, the U.N. negotiators realized that they needed the DMZ as a bargaining tool to pressure the Communists on other items to be negotiated.

On November 17, the U.N. command agreed that the present line would be acceptable as the MDL on the provision that the armistice would be signed within thirty days. The Communists accepted this offer, and staff officers began determining the MDL. Ten days later, Item 2 was officially ratified, and the Communists began to build defenses to prevent any moving of the line back. The MDL was first marked on November 27; the allies warned that, if the Communists did not sign on time, the MDL would be redrawn to reflect line of contact when the armistice was officially signed.

The Communists did not sign by December, and the fighting continued for one and a half years. Any agreement was frustrated over the question of the forceable repatriation of POWs. In June 1953, another tentative agreement was made concerning the DMZ when the war's end seemed imminent, but before signing on July 27, the Communists demanded the MDL be redrawn to reflect their gains in the offensive they began on July 13–14 against ROK forces to strengthen their positions. Minor changes were made on both sides on the line of contact.

The final MDL was determined militarily, not geographically, reflecting the front lines as of July 27, 1953. The U.N. command tried to achieve a line that would provide maximum defense and discourage any renewed aggression. The final MDL stretches slightly south of the

38th parallel on the west coast, south of Kaesong, through Panmunjom and the center of the Iron Triangle, and north of the Punchbowl, meeting the east coast above the 38th parallel. Officially, the four-kilometer buffer zone was designed "to prevent the occurrence of incidents which might lead to a resumption of hostilities."

Within seventy-two hours of signing, the Communists withdrew north, and the allies pulled to the south, removing all military forces. They also had to dislodge all military supplies, equipment, mines, trip wires, and other hazards, informing officials of other potentially dangerous conditions. Above all, both sides were to respect the neutrality of the DMZ.

Both sides agreed that no hostile acts would be initiated or performed in or through the DMZ. They also agreed that they would not bring in armed forces except as arranged. No one, military or civilian, was allowed to cross the MDL unless they had obtained permission from the Military Armistice Commission (MAC), a joint Communist-U.N. group created to investigate and monitor activities in the DMZ. To cross the MDL also required permission of authorities from both North and South Korea.

The delegates had devoted sixty-five sessions and 186.6 hours to deciding the location of the MDL and the DMZ. Panmunjom, also known as the Joint Security Area (JSA), was named as the site of prisoner transfer. Basically, both sides were responsible for transporting their prisoners to the DMZ where the prisoners were allowed to choose whether to be repatriated to their country of origin in an interview by a neutral intermediary. Each prisoner was identified and his name checked on rolls of both sides; the prisoner then elected to choose into whose custody he wished to be transferred. The named country was responsible for removing the prisoner from the DMZ.

A Neutral Nations Repatriation Commission (NNRC) headquarters was established in the JSA, and each side was expected to provide logistical support for the NNRC. The NNRC was responsible for those who rejected repatriation to their native country. Sick and injured prisoners were exchanged first in Operation Little Switch. Operation Big Switch exchanged the other prisoners. ROK President Syngman Rhee refused to allow the Indian custodial force in South Korea because India had declined to send combat troops to help defend his country; the Indians flew in and out of the DMZ in helicopters, carrying prisoners.

The MAC administered (and continues to do so) the DMZ according to the armistice agreement. The delegates mutually agreed that an armed police force including Communist soldiers and ROK and U.N. guards would patrol their sector. MAC would be responsible for all activity in the DMZ.

Today, 1,291 yellow signs with messages in Korean/English on the southern side and Korean/Chinese facing north, mark the 151 miles of the MDL. Entrances to the DMZ are also plainly marked with wooden signs in all three languages as well as by blue obelisks with U.N. symbols on the southern boundary.

There have been approximately 2,000 incidents between North Korean and Allied units in the DMZ, and more than fifty Allied soldiers have been killed in the JSA and DMZ since 1953. (No Communist troops have been known to have been killed.) Several examples of North Korean aggression include an attack on Camp Bonifas in August 1967 and the August 18, 1976, murder of two American officers assisting in a tree-trimming mission.

Rice fields are tended by the few peasants who still live near the DMZ. Rusted tanks and vehicles remain in place where they were abandoned during the war. The bare mountains, once stripped of trees by the Japanese, have been reforested. Because no hunting is allowed in the DMZ and pollution is minimal, wildlife thrives. Endangered species, such as the Manchurian crane, enjoy the DMZ's sanctuary. The DMZ exists as a strangely peaceful yet potentially explosive belt partitioning Korea into two radically different economic, social, and political spheres.

Elizabeth Schafer

Bibliography

Hermes, Walter G. *Truce Tent and Fighting Front* (Office of the Chief of Military History: 1966).

Kirkbride, Wayne A. *DMZ: A Story of the Panmunjom Axe Murder* (1984).

———. *Panmunjom: Facts About the Korean DMZ* (1985).

Poole, W.S. *History of the Joint Chiefs of Staff*, 4, *The Joint Chiefs of Staff and National Policy, 1950–1952* (1979).

U.S. State Department. *Foreign Relations of the United States*, 1951, vol. 7: *Korea and China* (1983).

Vatcher, William H., Jr. *Panmunjom: The Story of the Korean Military Armistice Negotiations* (1958).

Democratic People's Republic of Korea
See NORTH KOREA

Dulles, John Foster (1888–1959)

John Foster Dulles, born on 25 February 1888, is known today primarily for his tenure as secretary of state under President Dwight D. Eisenhower. He constructed many elements of U.S. Cold War policy and initiatives, such as the Japanese Peace Treaty and the central treaty organization (CENTO). Dulles came from a long line of distinguished government officers, including his uncle by marriage, Robert Lansing, secretary of state for Woodrow Wilson. His maternal grandfather, John Watson Foster, was secretary of state under Benjamin Harrison. Seeking to follow in the footsteps of his distinguished relatives, Dulles attended Princeton and George Washington universities and the Sorbonne. In 1911, he entered law practice in New York and engaged in several quasi-diplomatic missions to the second Hague Peace Conference of 1907 and the Versailles Peace Conference, 1918–1919.

In the late 1930s Dulles's religious feelings quickened, and he came to believe in a combination of international "institutional mechanisms" and the Christian gospel as an antidote to war and unrest. In 1940, he chaired the Commission on A Just and Durable Peace for the Federal Council of Churches. By the end of World War II, Dulles had become recognized as a leading Republican spokesman on foreign policy issues, and served on several bipartisan delegations.

In 1948, Dulles was widely touted as the next secretary of state in the "new Dewey administration," a forecast upset by that November's election of President Harry S. Truman. Further disappointment was in store when he lost his bid for reelection as a Senator from New York, for a seat to which he had been appointed to fill out the term of the late Senator Robert F. Wagner, Sr. He then returned to writing and authored *War or Peace* in 1950, a critical assessment of the American containment policy then in much favor among the more sophisticated in the Washington/New York foreign policy establishment.

Despite Dulles's strong Republican credentials, President Truman, needing to garner GOP support for his Far East policy, appointed him as special representative to negotiate a treaty of peace with Japan. Dulles completed this task with skill and dispatch. He not only negotiated peace with Japan (which hardly had much say in the matter at the time), but also sorted out equitably the disposition of the lands conquered by the Japanese in World War II. He further saw to it that although the Soviet Union retained the Kuril Islands and southern Sakhalin, the U.S. continued to exercise control over the Ryukyu, Bonin, Marianas, and Caroline Islands and maintained military base rights in Japan and Okinawa. Domestically, Dulles proved effective in convincing the Joint Chiefs of Staff of the necessity for giving up control of Japan. (The JCS apparently had plans secretly to rearm the Japanese.)

Dulles enthusiastically supported Truman's decision to intervene in the Korean War, a support that appeared in print a mere five days after the North Korean invasion. Typically, Dulles termed Truman's decision as "courageous, righteous, and in the national interest" in his *New York Times* article characteristically entitled "To Save Humanity from the Deep Abyss." But by 1952, Dulles was just as characteristically denouncing Truman's containment policy as "negative, futile, and immoral."

With his impeccable Republican credentials and his triumph in negotiating the Japanese peace treaty, Dulles was the inevitable choice by President-elect Eisenhower as secretary of state. The two soon forged a close personal bond, although the president frequently felt constrained to moderate his secretary's more perfervid evulsions. Although both called publicly for the "roll back" of communism, and the "liberation" of those held captive by its "despotism and godless terrorism," Eisenhower cautioned his secretary of state to add the phrase "by all peaceful means." Alas, there was to be no roll back or liberation, and the new administration settled for a near-status quo antebellum truce in Korea, and later did nothing except protest the Soviet crushing of Hungary's attempt to liberate itself from communism.

The new Eisenhower administration is credited generally with ending the Korean War by quietly letting the Communists know that it was seriously contemplating an extension of the war and even the use of nuclear weapons. Here was an early example of that "brinksmanship" that was to prove so controversial a part of Dulles's dealings with the Soviet Union as secretary of state. But the death of Joseph Stalin in March 1953 seems to have had much to do with weakening Communist resolution to continue the struggle.

Dulles and Eisenhower in some ways proved as tough with their ROK ally as with the Communists. As ROK President Syngman Rhee planned to sabotage the truce talks at Panmunjom, the Joint Chiefs of Staff, with Dulles's compliance, drew up a contingency plan to overthrow Rhee if this were deemed necessary to keep the truce talks going.

Dulles retained the respect and affection of Eisenhower to the end of his life. He never moderated his moral anti-communism, and claimed to be perfectly willing to "go to the brink" of nuclear war to demonstrate America's resolution against Communist aggression. But he seemed to lack a sure touch in dealing with non-Communist Third World nationalism. He revealed little understanding of the roots of poverty and the sense of injustice that so often aided the rise to power of Third World demagogues of whom he did not approve. Dulles attempted to arrive at solutions for their unrest through Christian principles, seemingly perpetual travel, military aid, and a treaty or pact committing the United States. Although the American public seemed to agree wholeheartedly with Dulles's anti-communism, he was hardly an endearing figure with his grim appearance accentuated by his dark clothing, his lugubrious expressions, and his forebodings of the near future. A jibe of the time gave the declension of the adjective "dull" as "Dull, Duller, Dulles."

John Foster Dulles died on 24 May 1959 after a long and courageous struggle with cancer.

Barbara Peterson

Bibliography

Acheson, Dean. *Present at the Creation: My Years in the State Department* (1969).

Devine, Michael J. "The Diplomacy of Righteousness: The Legacy of John W. Foster," in Kenneth W. Thompson, ed., *Traditions and Values: American Diplomacy, 1945 to the Present* (1984).

Dulles, Foster Rhea. *America's Rise to World Power, 1898–1954* (1955).

Gerson, Louis L. "John Foster Dulles" in Robert Ferrell, ed., *The American Secretaries of State and Their Diplomacy*, 17 (1967).

Gould-Adams, Richard. *The Time of Power: A Reappraisal of John Foster Dulles.*

Guhin, Michael A. *John Foster Dulles: A Statesman and His Times* (1972)

Hoopes, Townsend. *The Devil and John Foster Dulles* (1973).

John Foster Dulles Oral History Project, Princeton University.

See also STATE DEPARTMENT, U.S.

E

Eisenhower, Dwight D. (1890–1969)

Dwight David "Ike" Eisenhower, American soldier, leader of Allied forces in Europe during World War II, and thirty-fourth president of the United States, was born in Denison, Texas, and graduated from the U.S. Military Academy with the class of 1915, the "Class the Stars Fell On." Rising slowly through the officer ranks, Eisenhower served as company commander of a tank training center at Gettysburg, Pennsylvania, during World War I, never seeing combat. (Some have speculated that this great commander, undoubtedly much to his disgust, was never under hostile fire.) In 1926, he graduated from the Command and General Staff School at Fort Leavenworth, Kansas, and two years later, now marked for high command, from the Army War College. He served as military assistant in Washington, first as an aide to the assistant secretary of war from 1929 to 1933, and for the following two years as a special assistant to the Army chief of staff, General Douglas MacArthur. (Later, Eisenhower would wryly contend that he had "studied dramatics" under MacArthur.)

Eisenhower reached the rank of colonel only in March 1941, yet three months later he was named chief of staff of the Third Army, and in September of the same year was promoted to brigadier general. By that time his rapid advancement and impressive record had brought him to the attention of the chief of staff of the Army, General George C. Marshall.

Eisenhower continued his rapid advancement. From his position as chief of the war plans division of the War Department, Eisenhower was named in June of 1942 to command U.S. forces in the European theater of operations. On November 7th of that year he initiated the successful invasion of French North Africa. In January of the following year he was named by President Franklin D. Roosevelt to conduct the invasion of Sicily and Italy. In late November 1943 he took command of the Allied troop buildup in the United Kingdom, and on 6 June 1944 gave the signal for the successful Allied D-Day invasion of the Continent. In December 1944, Eisenhower was promoted to the five-star rank of General of the Army. He ended the war as undoubtedly the most popular of the great American commanders of World War II, and already his name was being bandied about as presidential material, although no one really knew his political affiliations, if any.

Although "Ike" often spoke of retirement in the immediate postwar years, the American public had other ideas. In 1948 he accepted the presidency of Columbia University, a somewhat odd position for a soldier not known for his bookishness. In the autumn of the same year he published his war memoirs. *Crusade in Europe*, which is reliably reported to have earned him about $1 million, thanks to a favorable tax ruling.

In December 1950, as part of the great rearmament buildup in the wake of the Korean War, President Harry S. Truman appointed Eisenhower to command the forces of the North Atlantic Treaty Organization (NATO). But in June 1952, the ever-popular "Ike" resigned from the Army and returned to the U.S. to run for president as a Republican.

A major tactic of Eisenhower's campaign was to criticize the Democratic administration for its conduct of the Korean War, and in a dramatic announcement shortly before the November elections he pledged to "Go to Korea." That promise, coming at a time of profound warweariness for Americans, clinched his election, although it would be difficult to imagine "Ike" losing in 1952 or at any other time. (It is also difficult to understand why President Harry Truman never seemed to have thought of this tactic during the first two and one-half years of the war when he was president.)

President-elect Eisenhower dutifully flew to Korea one month after his victory over Adlai Stevenson. There he heard out the plans of U.N. commander General Mark Clark and ROK President Syngman Rhee to win the stalemated war by expanding it. But he spent more time in the lines, listening to the troops. While a dramatic gesture, Eisenhower's trip to Korea had far less to do with the ending of the war six months later than the death of Stalin and the leaked consideration by the U.S. administration of bombing and blockading the Chinese mainland, and perhaps even the employing of nuclear weapons. It is difficult to determine just how serious Eisenhower and Dulles were in their consideration of the nuclear option. A howl of execration had arisen from America's allies over the mere bombing of North Korean hydroelectric plants south of the Yalu in June of 1952. The breaking of the nuclear "tabu" (as Dulles termed it), that is, the use of nuclear weapons once again solely by the United States and once again solely against Asians would have represented an unimaginable moral disaster for America. Fortunately this "thinking out loud" within the new administration progressed no further than the contingency plan stage.

Far more significant than either Ike's trip to Korea or the supposed threat of the use of nuclear weapons in Korea was the welcomed death of Joseph Stalin on 5 March 1953. A new, unsteady Soviet leadership, a China that had amply demonstrated its power, and a battered North Korea all had their reasons for wishing to end the Korean War on a more or less status quo basis. And there was no stomach among the American people or their government for the vastly increased military and diplomatic effort that a war to victory would have required. The armistice ending the Korean War was signed in Panmunjom on 27 July 1953. There was absolutely no celebration over this peace, but the American public was relieved, and Ike quietly received the credit.

Through Eisenhower's two administrations (he defeated Stevenson again in 1956), he strengthened government welfare programs, created the Department of Health, Education, and Welfare, broadened the Social Security system, increased the minimum wage (to the dis-

gust of conservatives), pushed a major overhaul of the nation's federal tax system, reached an agreement with Canada to cooperate in building the St. Lawrence Seaway, and began a thirteen-year interstate highway program (the latter two projects in more recent years considered something of a mixed blessing as the nation's railways and public transit systems declined).

In national defense, Eisenhower moved to rely far more on the airborne nuclear deterrent in place of conventional military forces, but he continued the policy of the containment of communism begun under the Truman administration, again causing uneasiness among conservatives who favored a policy of "roll back." He also initiated the "Eisenhower Doctrine" that pledged aid to any Middle Eastern nation threatened by communism. Many felt that his finest hour was his support of the United Nations during the Suez Crisis of 1956 to effect the withdrawal of British, French, and Israeli forces from Egypt, an event that even at the time was recognized as spelling the end of the British Empire. Eisenhower sent troops into Lebanon in July of 1958 to stabilize its political situation and warn off the ambitious Egyptian dictator, Gamal Nasser.

In September 1957, Eisenhower also sent troops to Little Rock, Arkansas, to enforce school desegregation in the wake of the U.S. Supreme Court's 1954 landmark decision outlawing racial segregation in the nation's public school system. Nonetheless, he remained lukewarm in his commitment to racial equality, and gave only limited support to desegregation of the armed forces.

On 17 January 1961, Eisenhower gave his farewell speech as president and public citizen, a speech remembered almost entirely for his warning of a "military-industrial complex" that could get out of hand. He retired to his beloved farm near Gettysburg (where he reportedly had trouble at first using a dial telephone; when he had had to make his own calls there were no dial phones, and when dial phones were in use he was of sufficient rank that an aide made all his calls). Dwight Eisenhower, the most popular American figure of his century, died of heart failure on 28 March 1969.

More often than not excoriated by liberal and academic opinion, the Eisenhower years after about a decade began to assume something of the patina of a "golden age," primarily for what he did not do. Like Truman, he did not expand the Korean War and he rejected the nuclear option. Even Ike's obfuscatory circumlocution, an occasion for some hilarity at the time, came to be interpreted as his clever way of diverting difficult questions that he had no intention of answering.

Gary A. Donaldson

Bibliography
Ambrose, Stephen. *Eisenhower: Soldier, General of the Army, President-Elect* (1983).
————. *Eisenhower: The President* (1985).
Divine, Robert A. *Eisenhower and the Cold War* (1981).
Donovan, Robert J. *Eisenhower: The Inside Story* (1956).
Lee, R. Alton. *Dwight D. Eisenhower: Soldier and Statesman* (1981).

Engineers in the Korean War
To understand the role of the Army engineers in the Korean War is to understand the perverse nature of combat; the engineers built, fought, destroyed, and built again.

The Army Corps of Engineers has an illustrious history. It was first organized in December 1776 when Congress authorized George Washington "to raise and collect" a corps of engineers on a six-month trial basis. The corps endured and Engineers were involved in all the wars that the United States fought. By World War II, a fourteen-week course at Fort Belvoir, Virginia, was established for inductees who had no prior military training. This course consisted of six weeks of basic infantry training followed by eight weeks of individual training in such engineering techniques as mines, explosives and demolitions, fixed and floating bridges, camouflage and concealment, and map and aerial photo reading.

Just one month before the North Koreans crossed the 38th parallel to invade South Korea on 25 June 1950, LOGEX 50 was held at Fort Belvoir. An exercise to train officers of the technical and administrative service schools in interservice planning and operations in an active theater, LOGEX 50 simulated an invasion of continental Europe by the enemy, thus following the Army tradition of "re-fighting the last war." The engineers used tactics not particularly applicable to the terrain in Korea.

But when fighting broke out in Korea, President Harry S. Truman was quick to pledge U.S. support despite the fact that the armed forces were depleted and often poorly trained. Officers from the general headquarters of the Far East command who were sent to Korea at the outbreak of the war found a number of engineering problems. The biggest concern was setting up a reliable supply route to bring in ammunition. Road reconnaissance had to be established to locate the North Koreans. It was imperative to set up roadblocks and install minefields to stop the advance of the enemy. Yet the Republic of Korea (ROK) Army, assisted by U.S. forces, was successful in delaying the enemy enough to make sure there was enough ground left for a United Nations forces beachhead.

Thus from the very beginning the engineers were an important force in the Korean War. As was true in previous wars, the engineers' military mission was twofold: to expedite and assist the movement of troops, and to obstruct and make difficult any movement by the enemy. The engineers also had to be prepared to fight in combat when necessary.

The 3rd Engineer Combat Battalion of the 24th Infantry Division was the first to practice its skills in an actual war zone in Korea. The 3rd Engineers had been stationed in Japan and received word on 1 July that they would be shipped out to Korea. They began arriving in Pusan on 5 July. The troops were headed to Taejon in a forlorn effort to halt the North Korean onslaught.

For the 3rd Engineers the period from July 5 to 22 was crucial. Facing both enemy opposition and natural obstacles, the engineers managed to make fourteen reconnaissances, work on two airstrips, repair twenty-five roads, build a bridge, destroy fifty-six highway bridges, and lay both antitank and antipersonnel minefields on the Kum River. Combat engineers were the last U.S. troops to cross the Kum.

In July, the 2nd Division Engineers, the last remaining uncommitted unit of the 2nd Infantry Division, was sent to help defend Yongsan, thirty-nine miles northwest of Pusan. The 2nd Division had been the first ground troops to arrive in Korea directly from the United States. Their arrival in late July and early August did much to take the pressure off the battle-weary 24th Division.

And the 2nd soon took on heavy fighting itself. On 31 August, three enemy divisions broke through the defensive positions of the 2nd Division at the Naktong River perimeter. The 2nd Engineer Battalion had two hours' notice to get ready for combat. Then, at 5:00 A.M. on 2 September, the North Koreans attacked Yongsan. When the attack finally broke six hours later, the 2nd Engineers still held their position above the Yongsan-Miryang road and had kept the enemy from getting through. The engineers continued to function as infantry through 16 September to keep the main U.N. supply route open.

The 2nd Engineer Special Brigade assisted MacArthur's landing at Inchon, arriving offshore at Inchon on 15 September—D-Day. Almost immediately the brigade lost the support units it was promised and the engineers were left with the responsibility of keeping the cargo moving. Since both the port and the city were filled with thousands of Korean refugees it was easy for the enemy to infiltrate. Sniper fire was common. The brigade had to stretch its own troops to provide military police to root out the snipers.

But the Inchon invasion was a success, and U.N. forces broke out of the Pusan perimeter and headed north toward the Naktong River. The Eighth Army believed that it had weathered the worst of the fight and MacArthur promised that the troops would be home for Christmas.

The crossing of the Naktong River in September 1950 had been a major job for the Army engineers. This crossing was an integral part of the Eighth Army's plan to break out of the Pusan perimeter and head north. There were actually four crossings of the Naktong and the engineers had to manage these crossings "with a minimum of equipment [by enemy standards] and a maximum of improvisation," all the while meeting stubborn resistance from the North Koreans.

The 3rd Engineers reconnoitered the crossing area, gathered assault boats, and coordinated with the infantry the tactical employment of troops and equipment to be used in the crossings. On 18 September the 38th Infantry's 2nd Battalion made the first permanent crossing of the Naktong, two days ahead of division schedule. The next day the 3rd Battalion crossed, bringing with it tanks, artillery, and heavy mortars. The crossings were generally carried out under heavy enemy fire, and the engineers suffered as much as the infantry. The Naktong crossings were a triumph for the engineers. With this experience they were now seasoned veterans.

Following the Inchon invasion, the engineers did some building. Company C of the 2nd Engineers was assigned the task of building a supply bridge over the Kum River. In this "unique example" of civilian Korean cooperation, 500 to 600 Koreans worked without pay to help move thirty-three tons of bridging material, 2,500 sand-filled rice bags, and 1,852 yards of sand that were moved and placed by hand. The Korean civilians seemed as anxious as the engineers to keep the U.N. troops supplied.

This building did not, however, represent a lull in the fighting, for MacArthur's prediction that the troops would be home for Christmas did not come true. As the Eighth Army pushed northward after its breakout from the Pusan perimeter, it found itself fighting more and more Communist Chinese troops. Just after Thanksgiving, U.N. troops were ordered to retreat and head south to establish a new defensive perimeter. This withdrawal caused an abrupt change in engineering duties. For most of that autumn the engineers had helped the U.N. troops advance; they improved roads and built bridges. Now, in late November, they were faced with the "equally important but less relished task" of setting up obstacles to slow down the enemy. The duties of the engineers at this point were threefold: to keep at least one good withdrawal route open for the retreat of each corps, to make demolitions to delay the enemy, and to destroy all military equipment and supplies that could fall into the hands of the enemy.

At times this was a chaotic situation. One corporal with the 2nd Engineers, a tracked vehicle mechanic, recalled that during the retreat south, "I and five others were ordered to take the only roadgrader left south. Got lost for a month or better. Never changed clothes, never washed. Result was body lice and frostbite in both feet."

The 2nd Division bore the brunt of the Chinese attack around Pyongyang, the capital of North Korea. The 2nd Engineers were committed as a rear guard to hold the roads open so the divisional artillery could get out. The engineers were attacked from all sides and when they finally pulled out of the battle, half of their officers had either been killed or were missing, half of the men were casualties, and all of their equipment was gone. In the end, no unit of the 2nd Division was "more badly hurt or gave a better account of itself" than the 2nd Engineers.

The engineers were also instrumental in the evacuation of more than 10,000 troops (plus 90,000 civilians) through the port of Hungnam in North Korea. X Corps issued the order on 9 December and the evacuation was successfully completed on Christmas Eve. Moving the troops from the Chosin Reservoir down to the sea provided maximum challenge for the engineers. They had to keep the road free enough from obstacles so the U.N. troops could move quickly, but they also had to put as many obstacles in the road as possible in case the enemy were closely pursuing. X Corps had two engineering combat battalions and an engineering construction battalion—neither at full strength—for the work.

The goal of the engineers was to complete a two-way road with bypasses around every bridge and side-hill cut that the enemy could blow up. During the construction phase, enemy interference was mostly concentrated on ambushing vehicles and blowing up bridges. The engineers were less successful in properly placing demolitions along the route to slow down the enemy. This was not crucial, however, because the enemy did not pursue as closely as anticipated.

The engineers also prepared the Hungnam perimeter to withstand an enemy attack while the U.N. forces were evacuated. As the Marines and 7th Division withdrew south, the 3rd Division was left responsible for the final defense. Some of the engineers directly supported the divisions on the line and other engineers prepared charges further back. These duties were taken over by the infantry as they drew into smaller perimeters.

The U.N. forces also made provisions for Korean civilians to be evacuated. At Hungnam, "hard realities" of war were tempered by consideration for the destitute and homeless people, but at the risk of jeopardizing the major evacuation. The great mass of refugees impeded the loading process and posed certain security problems because there was always the possibility of sabotage and espionage.

On New Year's Day 1951 the Chinese launched a major offensive south of the 38th parallel. The 3rd Engineers received orders on 3 January to support the 19th Infantry which was located near Kandong, but the orders were rescinded and the entire division retreated south of the Han River. The Chinese again did not pursue as closely anticipated so the engineers were able to build bridges and provide general support to the infantry divisions. The engineer's biggest task was to help plan an advance through an area that had no roads. The lack of roads was compounded by rice paddies, mountainous terrain, and frozen unworkable ground. Korean civilian laborers helped build roads and the 24th Division began its advance during the first weeks of February.

This advance met heavy enemy opposition and the engineers of A and B companies were told to prepare themselves to provide infantry support to the 19th Infantry. A heavy snowfall made roads slippery and hazardous on the night of 8 February so the engineers worked through the night. They worked for thirty-one straight hours to keep the roads open and were also ready at all times to move into battle.

February 1951 presented the engineers with some of their biggest challenges of the war. Road problems continued throughout the month. Due to a preseasonal thaw, roads turned into quagmires of mud and flooded streams made it nearly impossible for supplies to get through. The engineers had to overcome the effects of the spring thaws and floods, and then they had to develop a series of roads that would sustain the spring military offensive in the mountain ranges. The spring offensive meant that everything that had been destroyed during the winter retreat had to be rebuilt.

During that spring offensive the 3rd Engineers adopted the slogan "Where danger goes dynamite makes the way." As the U.N. forces pushed north toward Yangpyong they met heavy resistance. During the attack the engineers had to complete most of the forward area work under small arms and 150mm artillery fire. Fortunately casualties were light. Throughout the month of March the division advance was limited on a few occasions by strong enemy action, and it depended on the engineers to open a minimum road network.

At the beginning of April, the enemy's control of the Hwachon Dam on the Pukhan River became a concern. A reconnaissance mission by the engineer section of IX Corps showed no apparent bulk demolition, but it was possible that the enemy was planning to raise the level of the reservoir and cause a flood. This flooding would interfere with the U.N. supply routes from Chunchon and would make crossings of the Pukhan uncertain. The Hwachon Dam was captured by friendly forces on 18 April but was abandoned to the enemy on 25 April during a fierce Chinese counteroffensive. In May, naval torpedo bombers destroyed some of the dam gates and in June, after IX Corps retook the dam, more of its gates were removed to keep the enemy from using it as a weapon again.

Just before the Chinese began their second spring offensive on 16 May, the 73rd Engineer Combat Battalion opened up a rebuilt bridge over the part of the Twinnan River that flows past Hoengsong. Hoengsong, located eleven miles north of the key rail and communication center of Wonju, had been fought over many times. The bridge had to be rebuilt before the summer flood waters arrived. It opened for traffic on 15 May and was used to move hundreds of tons of ammunition to meet the Chinese offensive.

The 2nd Engineers were in the thick of that fight, operating as infantry. The fighting was bitter; the Chinese were determined to exterminate the 2nd Division. But during the U.N. counteroffensive which began later in May, the 2nd Division killed ten Communists for every man it lost.

Even after truce talks began in June, the fighting, especially the battles for the ridges, continued. Neither side wanted to give up any territory that might be crucial in a settlement. The prime example of this bitter fighting was the struggle for Heartbreak Ridge, which began in the fall of 1951. The 2nd Engineers participated in Operation Touchdown by serving as infantry as well as solving the problem of how to get tanks into the area to help U.N. troops. In the early winter, a volunteer squad from the 65th Engineer Combat Battalion spent six nights putting up three specially designed prefabricated bunkers just thirty-five yards from enemy lines at what was referred to as Sandbag Castle. The engineers' activity drew heavy enemy fire, and two engineers had to stand as security guards while the bunkers were being built. After the bunkers were completed the engineers were able to supervise the infantry sandbagging and logging which was a vital part of the communication trench.

By the spring and summer of 1952 the engineers were once again engaged in building. The 44th and 62nd Engineer Construction Battalions rebuilt the Carney Bridge that stretched across the Han River and which had been destroyed during the withdrawal of 1950. The bridge was important for access to Seoul, and the engineers had to cope with replacing seven truss spans while working with water depths that averaged twenty feet. The work, which actually began in the fall of 1951, was halted during the May floods of 1952, and then finally completed the following May.

Flooding problems in the summer of 1952 also threatened supply lines to the western front. The Army Corps of Engineers had to protect nine bridges on the part of the Imjin River located in South Korea. Even though high floods in July wiped out all but three of these bridges, the engineers managed to keep supplying the fighting divisions.

Supply lines continued to be an issue into the spring of 1953. The 73rd Engineer Combat Battalion of the 19th Engineer Combat Group devised an aerial tramway in April to keep Hill 1220 supplied. Large-scale road construction was not possible at the time, but tramway kits were available and they could be quickly and easily assembled. The tramway operation was halted for a time by enemy mortar fire but the work was finally completed on 25 April. The tramway carried 1,200 pounds of supplies an hour, saving 192 man-days for each day of its operation.

After the truce was finally signed on July 27, 1953, the engineers still had work to do in Korea. Perhaps the most poignant was their role in Operation Glory, an exchange of Korean War dead. The site chosen for Glory was one mile north of the Freedom Bridge which spans the Imjin River about forty-five miles north of Seoul. Beginning on 16 August 1954, Company B of the 84th Engineer Construction Battalion built two camps, six miles of roads, six hospital tents, latrines, storage tents, and guard shelters. The work was completed in just fifteen days. It was difficult because of the near-destruction of Tangjang-ni and heavy rains. But Company B managed to carve two huge terraces out of the hillside and created a place where the Allied dead could be initially cared for and where daily memorial services could be conducted.

In the end, U.S. Army engineers proved themselves crucial to the Korean War effort. Their skills kept troops supplied, in communication, and hindered the advance of the enemy. And their combat skills were a necessary support to other fighting troops.

T.A. Kaminski

Bibliography

Appleman, Roy E. *South to the Naktong, North to the Yalu: June-November 1950* (Office of the Chief of Military History: 1961).

Hoyt, Edwin P. *The Pusan Perimeter* (1985).

Huston, James A. *Guns and Butter, Powder and Rice: U.S. Army Logistics in the Korean War* (1989).

Knox, Donald. *The Korean War* (1985).

The Military Engineer, 1950–1956.

Ethiopian Battalion

Ethiopian Emperor Haile Selassie pledged Ethiopian soldiers to the U.N. forces in Korea in order to acquire Western military assistance and to reaffirm Ethiopia's commitment to its Western allies.

The Ethiopian-Italian War of 1935–1936 was lost because of the lack of collective defense offered by the League of Nations. When the Korean War began, the emperor, viewing the conflict as again an issue of collective security, quickly agreed to send troops.

In August 1950 Haile Selassie offered 1,000 soldiers for combat in Korea. His original telegram to the American ambassador in Addis Ababa stated that he expected Ethiopian soldiers to be equipped and supplied with up-to-date weapons and equipment procured from the U.S.

Haile Selassie prepared to dispatch his Imperial guard to Korea and requested that the Kagnew Battalion be assembled within twenty-four hours. He ordered Mulugeta Bulli, a brigadier general and commander of the Imperial Guards, to choose men for the Kagnew Battalion, named in honor of Ethiopian King Menleik's war horse he had ridden to victory in the First Ethiopian-Italian War. The only African nation to send ground troops, Ethiopia's Imperial Guardsmen were professional soldiers who stood over six feet tall. Bulli was an honest and well-liked officer who did not pander to political patronage. Although ambitious, Bulli was hesitant and overly cautious. He remained in Ethiopia, and the emperor appointed Lieutenant Colonel Teshome Irgetu to command the Ethiopian Battalion in the field. The soldiers trained for eight months in Ethiopia's mountains, acclimatizing to mountain terrain and weather and preparing for combat patrol and ambush defenses.

After this intensive training period, the Ethiopian Battalion, commanded by Irgetu and Colonel Kebede Gebré, departed from Djibouti on April 16, 1951, on the American transport *General MacRae*. The emperor roused the 931 troops with a patriotic polemic.

The soldiers arrived in Pusan on May 7, 1951, where they were met by ROK President Syngman Rhee. The men were relocated to the U.N. reception center at Taegu where they were instructed in use of American Army weapons and equipment. The Ethiopian Battalion was attached to the U.S. 7th Infantry Division and fought most notably at Old Baldy and in the Pork Chop Hill area.

The Kagnew Infantry Battalion became noted as among the most fierce and toughest infantry units in Korea. On January 24, 1953, two platoons of Ethiopians took a hill south of Old Baldy, defending it against a Chinese counterattack. They endured a Chinese bombardment and abandoned the hill only when ordered.

The Ethiopians used unit, not individual, rotation, and in March 1952 a fresh unit replaced the original battalion, which returned on the same U.S. transport ship which had brought them. New troops arrived again in March 1953. Linguistic barriers posed some problems, especially in hospitals. Few if any Americans spoke the Ethiopian language of Amharic. Suspicious that medicines might have been poisoned, Ethiopian troops demanded that doctors taste all pharmaceuticals before they would swallow or apply them. The Ethiopian Battalion brought its own surgeon, a European physician trained in Germany who spoke English, to Korea. Ethiopian medical aides, litter carriers, and jeep drivers accompanied the battalion into battle.

Despite language differences, Ethiopian officers encouraged the evacuation of wounded Ethiopians through American channels because of superior medical facilities and attention. In order to prevent misunderstanding at crucial moments, most foreign soldiers, including the Ethiopians, learned basic English phrases and terminology.

In July 1952 on the Ethiopian homefront, Bulli was encouraged by militant Ethiopian officers to overthrow the emperor, as General Muhammad Neguib and Colonel Gamal Abdal Nasser had deposed the king of Egypt. That month, interested but cautious, Bulli considered expelling Haile Selassie, but his reluctance to act won him accolades from the emperor and military peers. While indecisively contemplating whether he should become Ethiopia's military dictator, Bulli argued that Ethiopia and Egypt were drastically different in many ways, especially in their monarchies; he also was impressed by the experience the Ethiopian military men in Korea were obtaining and noted that they had gained intellectual knowledge and opportunities for Ethiopia's future as well as for its military leadership.

American and British military and political leaders recognized Ethiopia's possible role as a mediator in the Middle East. American officials visited Ethiopia throughout the Korean War. Ethiopia pressed for military assistance, but the Americans rebuffed the request, stating that Ethiopia would have to wait until the war concluded. After British military aid was withdrawn, Ethiopia signed a mutual defense treaty

E

with the U.S. in 1951. The treaty promised that America would protect Ethiopia from the Soviet Union. Also, the U.S. would help the Ethiopian military adapt to American methods and equipment. In September 1952, Ethiopia and the U.S. signed another military pact in which the Americans pledged to train and equip the Ethiopian Army. An American detachment of military officers arrived in May 1953 to assist and serve as an advisory group to the ministry of defense.

Of the 3,518 Ethiopian soldiers who fought in Korea, 121 were killed in action, 536 were wounded in action, and none were captured or reported as missing in action. A financial agreement was later signed in which Ethiopia paid $42,000 for weapons retained by Ethiopian soldiers after the war.

Ethiopian troops remained in Korea until January 1965.

Elizabeth Schafer

Bibliography
Republic of Korea, Ministry of National Defense. *The History of the United Nations Forces in the Korean War* (1977).
Skordiles, Komon. *Kagnew, the Story of the Ethiopian Fighters in Korea* (1954).

F

Film, Television, and Literature of the Korean War

The Korean War was not covered directly by television as was the war in Vietnam. In fact, the fledgling television networks did not even try in most cases to replace the official coverage provided by the government. Of course, newsreels of events were available on a delayed basis in the movie theaters, as was the Hollywood version of the war presented in Korean War combat films.

Author Jeanine Basinger persuasively argues that the "format of the Korean War film is definitely a replay of the World War II combat film," utilizing time-tested devices such as the tough, veteran sergeant as hero, who now had fought in World War II instead of World War I, and a plot involving a last stand or a patrol on the move. The enemy, of course, had to be updated. The Japanese, former enemies, now became friends, with a *Nisei* (Japanese-American) frequently comprising part of the American combat coterie. The foe was clearly identified as "communism," or the Soviet Union, although Americans were actually fighting Chinese and Koreans. Such technological advances as the jet, helicopter, and psychological warfare (brainwashing) now became part of the plot. Also, the Korean War film expressed more cynicism and uncertainty about the reasons for the war and its final outcome. Korean War films frequently questioned military leadership. A responsibility motif seems to run through many of these films. The attachment of a small Korean child to the tough hero became a standard plot device, indicative of a much larger sense of responsibility and concern for one's family back home as well as the civilians caught up in the conflict. Basinger believes that, "The Korean

combat film is a forerunner to the home front's attitude toward the Vietnam War."

Korean War combat films include director Samuel Fuller's *The Steel Helmet* (1951) and *Fixed Bayonets* (1951). In the former a small Korean child named "Short Round"—a name used again much later in *Indiana Jones and the Temple of Doom*—falls under the protective wing of the American sergeant/hero. One reviewer called *The Steel Helmet* "the first fiction film in circulation on the subject of the Korean War." *Fixed Bayonets* portrays the usual mixture of American types—street-tough Irishman, proud Native American, and the coward waiting to redeem himself—fighting a seemingly hopeless rearguard action. "Nothing dirtier than a rearguard action," comments one of the soldiers. Fuller's two films are cinematically the best of the Korean War combat film genre. *A Yank in Korea* (1951) is dedicated to Private First Class John J. McCormack, whose letter to his children, written before his death, is supposed to have inspired the film. *Retreat, Hell!* (1952) follows the U.S. Marines in Korea from Inchon to Seoul and North Korea, and then back. ("Retreat, Hell!" said the colonel, "we're just attacking in another direction.") *Battle Zone* (1952), with John Hodiak and Stephen McNally as two official war photographers in love with the same Red Cross girl, offers very conventional fare. *One Minute to Zero* (1952) with Robert Mitchum and Ann Blyth shows the difference between the Korean and World War II combat film by emphasizing family, wives, romance, Korean refugees, and guerrillas. Since so much of the Korean War was on land or in the air, naval films are rare. *Submarine Command* (1952), starring William Holden, tells the story of a World War II submarine officer who left his commanding officer on deck during a crash dive. Needless to say he redeems himself in the Korean War. *Mission over Korea* (1953) is a very low budget film about the bravery of American pilots during the early stages of the war. *Sabre Jet* (1953) deals as much with the wives who wait in Japan as it does with their husbands who fly dangerous missions over Korea. *The Glory Brigade* (1953) with Victor Mature and Lee Marvin presents a United Nations spin on the war, telling the story of Greek infantrymen and U.S. Army engineers fighting their way to a dramatic helicopter rescue at the conclusion of the film.

Post-armistice films include *Men of the Fighting Lady* (1954), a documentary-style work about fliers operating from a carrier off the coast of Korea, and *Prisoner of War* (1954) with Ronald Reagan improbably volunteering to be captured to check out conditions for Americans in Korean POW camps. In 1955 came *The Bridges at Toko-Ri*, based on James Michener's novel, and *Battle Taxi,* starring Sterling Hayden as head of a helicopter rescue squadron. In *Pork Chop Hill* (1959), Gregory Peck leads an assault on a hill in Korea where the enemy is presented not only physically, but also psychologically through a constantly blaring battlefield loudspeaker. Interestingly, Lewis Milestone directed this film and it has the same sort of grittiness as his classic *All Quiet on the Western Front* (1930). Set in Korea, *All the Young Men* (1960), with Alan Ladd and Sidney Poitier, centers on the problem of race among Marines in 1951. Post–Korean War films, when they touched on the subject, seemed to dwell on the disturbed, even "brainwashed" veteran. (See "Veterans" entry.)

There were many other conventional combat films dealing with the Korean War (see Basinger for a complete filmography), and other Korean-related dramas such as *The Manchurian Candidate* (1962), but 1970 saw Robert Altman's *M*A*S*H* Film critic Judith Crist wrote regarding this comedy about a mobile Army surgical hospital in Korea, "The laughter is blood soaked and the comedy cloaks a bitter and terrible truth." Although set in Korea, *M*A*S*H* reflected attitudes inspired by the Vietnam War. Humorous references to many of the commercial Korean War films already discussed are sprinkled throughout this film. The sardonic, anti-military mood suited the country in 1970. A breakthrough film in popular culture, it was hailed as the anti-everything film with gallows humor and outrageous satire. But it had little to do with Korea.

Altman's 1970 film led to a television series of the same name which turned out to be one of the most successful and critically acclaimed shows in the history of television. The TV series did not disgrace the movie, as the writers tried to retain the sarcasm and irreverence of the Altman original. Obviously, "M*A*S*H," the TV series, capitalized on the Vietnam-era anti-war feeling of the country. Thus, for a generation of Americans, what they knew of the Korean War came filtered through the lenses of Vietnam and *M*A*S*H*. As the TV show aged, some of the comedic bit dulled, or perhaps the mood of the country shifted, but the later plots seemed to gravitate more and more to that trusted theme, Korean war orphans.

The actual war literature from the Korean War is slight in both volume and quality, a situation largely related to the war's unpopularity and the absence of a strong national commitment. War novel scholar Peter Jones believes that a shift in emphasis from World War II novels did take place with the novels of the Korean War: ". . . the enemy is no longer a group of hated individuals, he is merely another aspect of a generally hostile environment. . . . There are no speeches of exhortation, no calls to arms against the atrocities of a bestial enemy as is typical of many World War II novels." Novels such as Pat Frank's *Hold Back the Night* (1952) and Ernest Frankel's *Band of Brothers* (1958) demonstrate the centrality of "Don't let your buddy down" as the primary motivating factor in combat. The war novels of Korea show a new detachment from larger issues, a resignation to one's fate, and an air of "professionalism" where one simply did the job while waiting to go home. Even ten years after the armistice, no real reflective or thoughtful novels had surfaced, with the possible exception of Melvin Voorhee's *Show Me a Hero* about an American commander in Korea who, frustrated by politics and fate, tries to raise issues beyond just doing one's duty and not letting your comrades down.

Soldiers' memoirs and eyewitness accounts certainly constitute literature, and some representative examples would include Andrew Geer, *The New Breed* (1952), and Max Miller, *I'm Sure We've Met Before* (1951), both breathless, impressionistic, and very personal accounts of battle. Walter Karig, special deputy chief of information and a captain in the U.S. Navy, claims in the preface that Miller's book was "the first book on the Korean conflict," which speaks volumes about its purpose: sell the war by showing the American people the success attained by the U.S. Navy. More genuine and sincere, Martin Rust, *The Last Parallel, A Marine's War Journal* (1957) supplies a factual memorialization of the war but little else. The Korean War coming so soon after World War II, and then merging in the national mind with the Vietnam War, never received the necessary self-reflection through literature, or film, leaving a small impression on the national memory, that makes it still the least understood of America's wars.

Richard Voeltz

Bibliography

Basinger, Jeanine. *The World War II Combat Film, Anatomy of a Genre* (1986).

Biskind, Peter. *Seeing Is Believing: How Hollywood Taught Us to Stop Worrying and Love the Fifties* (1983).

Gitlin, Todd. *Inside Prime Time* (1983).

See also BROADCAST NEWS COVERAGE OF THE KOREAN WAR; PRESS (WESTERN) AND THE KOREAN WAR

First Clash: U.S. vs. North Korea

In the rain-soaked predawn darkness of Sunday, June 25, 1950, the armed forces of Communist North Korea crossed the 38th parallel and invaded the Republic of Korea. The Korean War had begun.

That afternoon, U.S. troops on occupation duty in Japan were placed on alert. News from Korea was spotty and inaccurate. On Monday, Lieutenant Colonel William S. Fultz, commanding the 507th Anti Aircraft Artillery Automatic Weapon Battalion at Camp McGill in southern Japan, was ordered by the commanding general, Fifth Air Force, to organize an anti-aircraft detachment from the 507th for "an air transported mission." Although the exact destination and further details were secret, most of the men in the battalion volunteered for assignment with the detachment. As events developed, this unit (called Detachment X) would fire the first U.S. Army shots of the Korean War.

The detachment would man four M-55, quadruple-mounted .50 caliber machine guns. Three officers and thirty-two enlisted men were selected for the assignment.

Early Thursday morning, June 29, all was in readiness; men, ammunition, and equipment were loaded aboard C-54 transports. Lieutenant Colonel Fultz gave last-minute instructions to the detachment commander, Captain Frank J. McCabe, and his assistant, Second Lieutenant Joseph V. Bailey.

In a briefing just prior to departure, Major Stanley J. Paciorek, battalion executive officer, told detachment members that their mission was to establish air defense of an airfield in Korea and that particulars would be given them once the situation was sized up on the spot.

Kimpo Airfield near Seoul had been lost to the North Koreans on the 27th. The bridges over the Han River just south of Seoul were destroyed early on the morning of the 28th. Shortly after 0900 hours on the 29th, the transports came in for a touchdown at the Suwon Airfield about twenty miles south of Seoul. A C-54 lay burning at the end of the runway, a grim reminder of an earlier enemy fighter attack. The fire at the end of the runway and the threat of further attacks made speed essential.

The men swung into action so rapidly that many did not have time to remove their "Mae West" life jackets. The M-55s were unloaded from each plane as it rolled to a stop on the field. With the assistance of Korean soldiers, the weapons were emplaced in primary positions in record time.

No sooner were the guns in position than the C-54 *Bataan*, with General Douglas MacArthur, U.S. Far Eastern commander, and his inspection staff arrived.

As the sun was dropping behind the hills at 1615 hours, in the distance there appeared what most of the men at the gun positions thought were P-51 "Mustangs"—four of them. They soon proved otherwise. Most members of the detachment found difficulty in distinguishing between the North Korean Yak-9 fighters and the American P-51 Mustangs and were obliged to depend largely on the hostile action of the airplane before taking them under fire.

"Looking toward the town about four miles away we heard an explosion, and seconds later we caught it," recounted Sergeant Melvin E. Tyra.

> The four planes approached the strip from the northeast at about fourteen hundred feet. They formed with a pair in front followed by the other two in single file and power-glided on our position area, in an apparent attempt to destroy planes parked near the runway. They made four passes, dropping three medium-light bombs, and strafed the field

at each pass. One of the attacking fighter planes hit by gunfire crashed beyond the field. The second, obviously crippled, was losing altitude as he left the area. I labeled it a probable, and its destruction was confirmed a short time later by South Korean rural police who reported finding the wreck close to the place where it was last seen.

But a C-47 transport on the edge of the airfield was destroyed in this action.

One of the planes dived on Sergeant Sidney T. Holman's gun section and attacked it by dropping bombs in trail, while a row of cannon shells tore up the earth on both sides of the gun section. Sergeant Hasse received a crease in his helmet and immediately after pulling the operating handle of his machine gun, Private Harland S. Scoville saw it shot away. Private First Class Thomas Merante suffered a broken leg from a piece of concrete thrown from the runway by a bomb explosion—the first U.S. soldier wounded in Korea. This attacking plane was later also destroyed and the pilot, a major in the North Korean Air Force, was captured by the police. At no time during the action did any men of the detachment leave the guns.

Crews continued to improve gun positions and all was quiet until 2000 hours when a "dusk patrol" of three North Korean fighters came over on two strafing passes. The guns went into action again but no kills were made. The fighters, now more wary of the ack-ack, fired only short bursts and were driven off after two passes.

Shortly after 1300 hours on the 30th, five more aircraft appeared. Three were F-80s, but two, several hundred feet below, looked like F-51s. The two lower planes peeled off and strafed the airfield. The anti-aircraft guns immediately took them under fire, but no kills were made. The enemy planes splattered the area with 23mm cannon shells that burst upon impact, spraying pellets. One of these pellets slightly wounded Private First Class Lawrence E. Rogers. The F-80s gave chase and shot down both of the strafers.

By 2115 hours, Lieutenant Bailey received word from Advance Command, General Headquarters, Far East Command, (ADCOM GHQ FEC) to prepare to evacuate the airstrip. (ADCOM GHQ had been at Suwon since June 28 under the command of Brigadier General John H. Church.) It was also learned that the South Korean line had been penetrated by

North Korean ground forces, and the encirclement of Suwon was imminent.

Orders were relayed to the gun sections to prepare for the movement, and three trucks were obtained from South Korean Army personnel at the field to evacuate the detachment south to a new location. Guns were rendered inoperable, as ordered, and the convoy moved out quietly without lights. The trucks moved some fifteen miles down the highway, picking their way through Korean civilian vehicles and people that crowded the roadway, all going in the same direction.

During their stay at the new headquarters location near Taejon that lasted until the night of July 2, members of the detachment worked with other personnel to secure the airstrip. At 2000 hours that night the detachment received word that they were to be airlifted back to Japan for re-equipping and returned to action. The detachment had participated in the first organized U.S. ground combat action in Korea six days before Task Force Smith.

Hubert L. Koker

Bibliography
Appleman, Roy. *South to the Naktong, North to the Yalu, United States Army in the Korean War* (Office of the Chief of Military History, Washington: 1961).
Det. A. 507th AAA AW Battalion, After-Action Report; 30 June–3 July 1950.

See also OPPOSING FORCES ON THE EVE OF WAR

French Battalion
Although diplomatic relations between the United States and France were cordial but often strained, the two nations had traditionally cooperated militarily. France had sent troops that significantly aided the colonists' cause in the American Revolution, and American troops in France enabled that country to emerge victorious in both world wars. Near the end of World War II, France had offered to send an Army corps of two support units to help defeat Japan, but because Japan capitulated soon after, French forces were not needed.

On June 27, 1950, when President Harry S. Truman sent U.S. military forces to Korea, he also allocated increased aid and a military assistance team to France and the "Associated States of Indochina" to counter the Vietminh rebels led by Ho Chi Minh. Although the

Indochina colonies and Vietnam required the majority of France's military, as a U.N. member, France contributed combat troops, consisting of an infantry battalion and a gunboat, to Korea.

On July 22, 1950, the Pleven government approved sending the frigate RFS *La Grandiere*, of the French Far Eastern Fleet in Indochina, to Japan for the allies to use in naval operations. During the war, sailors on *La Grandiere* navigated with other U.N. vessels, patrolling the coast near Wonsan and enforcing the blockade. One month later, the independent Premier Bataillon Français de l' O.N.U. (also called the Boeuf O.N.U. and Bataillon de Corée) was established.

Volunteers, including active army personnel, reserves, paratroopers, and French Foreign Legion veterans from France, Africa, Madagascar, and Indochina signed up for a tour in Korea. They traveled to the Sarthe department where they trained at Camp d'Auvours. On September 18, the minister of war appointed General de Corps d'Armee Magrin Vernerrey (well-known as a Legionnaire who adopted the *nom de guerre* Lieutenant General Ralph Monclar) as commander of the French forces in Korea. Influenced by working closely with General Charles de Gaulle during World War II, Monclar was also a World War I veteran who had been crippled by battle wounds and required a cane. To his men, who attempted to imitate him, he seemed fearless.

In Korea, Monclar had a staff of seven senior officers and twenty-seven enlisted men for a headquarters to accompany the combat battalion and observe military conditions firsthand. Somewhat grandiose as compared to similar but smaller battalion U.S. headquarters, the French maintained a large staff in case an entire French division were to be deployed to Korea. American officers were surprised at the calm environment at the French Battalion headquarters, where Monclar studied documents wearing informal attire and slippers, and scenes painted by his operations officer of supply drops adorned the walls. Champagne was served in crystal glasses, and tables were draped with linen cloths. To American officials viewing Monclar's camp, the French did not seem to comprehend fully the urgency of the war.

For conformity, Monclar organized the French Battalion as similarly to a typical U.S. infantry battalion as possible. After training at Camp d'Auvours from September 1 to October 25, the French Battalion boarded the troopship SS *Athos II*, an aged converted World War I German liner, at Marseilles. Camp d'Auvours was maintained as a permanent training site for reinforcements to be sent to Korea every two months for casualty replacement.

After a thirty-five-day trip, the troopship docked at Pusan on November 29 and supplies and equipment were unloaded. France's 1,043 volunteers disembarked early the next morning. Described by American soldiers as being "half-wild Algerians," the French quickly adapted to their new environment. They enjoyed drinking, smoking, and joking while waiting to be sent to the front. Although there was a dearth of translators, most French soldiers knew a smattering of English, and there were few problems in communications.

The French Battalion was transported on a troop train to the U.N. reception center in Taegu where they were provided with weapons and supplies. For the winter campaign they were issued arctic shoes. They also became acquainted with American weaponry such as the recoilless rifle and fitted their own bayonets to U.S.-issue guns. They sharpened their American bayonets into needle-sharp spears.

Monclar disliked the use of indirect fire, massed fire support, and night attacks and was occasionally rebuked by American officers who asserted that his tactics were often inappropriate and resulted in heavier casualties for the French Battalion than necessary, hinting that different, and often conflicting, military approaches in the field could possibly threaten U.S.-French relations. For example, New Zealand chief of general staff Major General K.L. Stewart noted "On at least one occasion the French fixed bayonets and charged a heavily fortified hill without waiting for the artillery to complete its work."

After acclimatizing at Taegu for eleven days, the French Battalion moved to Suwon where they were attached to what was renamed the U.S. 23rd Regimental Combat Team, part of the U.S. 2nd Infantry Division. Their prior experience in Asian, African, and European wars would make them effective, professional soldiers.

The French advocated the use of bayonet charges, as did the Turkish Brigade, and General Matthew B. Ridgway, commander of the Eighth Army, approved of this aggressive technique, stating that both the Turkish Brigade and French Battalion were inspiring. The French also used a technique by which they dug two series of ditches, crouching in the second row and waiting for the Chinese to attack and leap in the first row. At that point the French would surprise them with a mass bayonet thrust.

In January 1951, the French Battalion suffered its first casualties during enemy action at Wonju. Interspersed with American units, they made a bayonet charge on January 10, 1951, repelling the Chinese.

At Twin Tunnels (railroad tunnels southeast of Chipyong-ni) on February 1–2, the unit won a U.S. Presidential Unit Citation for bravery, as well as a French Army unit award. They held Hill 453 in hand-to-hand confrontations, then repulsed the enemy with a bayonet charge, shrilly screaming as they raced uphill. From February 3 to 16 the French fought at Chipyong-ni, where again they bravely attacked bayonet-bearing Chinese with grenades, bayonets, and a hand-cranked siren. In addition to repelling the Chinese, the French Battalion blew up enemy supply centers. Again they received the U.S. Presidential Unit Citation, General Douglas MacArthur presenting the awards in person.

The U.S. Presidential Unit Citation was awarded yet a third time to the French Battalion for their courage at Hongchon, where from March 3 to 5 the French alone secured Hill 1037, suffering forty men killed and 200 wounded.

At Heartbreak Ridge the French Battalion supported other units and prevented flank attacks by the enemy. The battalion, known by the code name "Icicle," was directly commanded by Commandant Merle de Beaufond and his deputy, General Maurice L. Barthélémy, a wounded veteran of World War II (his left arm was paralyzed) and active participant in the French Resistance. With five companies consisting of a heavy weapons company and supply and service company as well as three infantry companies (code names Xavier, Yvonne, Zoé), the French Battalion moved to a new position, replacing the U.S. 2nd Battalion, 23rd Regimental Combat Team, on Hill 931. The French achieved success with bayonet charges that repelled the Chinese, and with similar tactics by other U.N. units, Heartbreak Ridge was won. Among the French Battalion's other notable military achievements in the final phases of the war was holding Arrowhead Ridge (Hill 281) for four days.

Unlike U.S. units, French battalions were rotated as units and replaced with fresh troops. The original battalion departed in the winter of 1951, and each year another battalion left and was restored. This change of troops was a factor in the high morale of the French in Korea. The French forces' strength peaked at 1,185 soldiers; they also had a company of Korean soldiers commanded by Captain Robert Goupil, who had extensive experience working in Asia.

During the Korean War, the French forces reached a maximum of thirty-nine officers, 172 noncommissioned officers, and 8,060 enlisted personnel. Of French Army and naval personnel, 262 died, 1,008 were wounded in action, nine were missing in action, and ten were exchanged as prisoners of war (POW). The condition of these repatriates was remarkably vigorous because the Chinese had shrewdly picked them to be cooks in the POW camps, providing them access to more or less ample food.

Within France an anti-American movement had developed by early 1952. Many French citizens blamed MacArthur's aggressiveness for the Chinese entrance in the war, and criticized the American control of the war, concluding that the Korean War had become simply Americans versus Communists and not a true world effort.

Even the more mainstream French press portrayed Americans as McCarthyites and rabid advocates of detonating an atomic bomb in Korea. As a result of pressure by French Communists and further frustration in Indochina, France gradually turned to a policy of neutralism in Korea as the conflict dwindled to its conclusion.

When the Korean armistice was signed in July 1953, the French had been fighting the Vietminh for seven years. The battle-hardened veterans of the Bataillon de Corée, still wearing 2nd U.S. Infantry Division patches on their uniforms, sailed for Indochina. They arrived on November 19, 1953, and were known as the Korea Regiment. They joined the Commando Beregol and Bataillon de Marche of the 43d Colonial Infantry and a group of the 10th Colonial Artillery to form the Groupement Mobile Nr. 100 (GM 100). Commanders in Indochina noted that the French Battalion in Korea had become accustomed to, and overrelied on, such luxuries as helicopter evacuation and massive artillery and air support that were not available in Indochina. Many of the Korean veterans were killed at Dien Bien Phu or in ambushes near Pleiku and Ban Me Thut. Survivors who remained in military service later participated in the war in Algeria.

Elizabeth Schafer

Bibliography

Bergot, E. *Bataillon de Corée: Les Volontaires Français, 1950–1953* (1983).

Boatner, Mark M. "The French Battalion at Arrowhead (Korea—October 1952)," *Revue Historique de l'Armee* (1954).

Hinshaw, Arned L. *Heartbreak Ridge: Korea, 1951* (1984).

Le Mire, Oliver. *L'Assault de Crevecoeur* (1955).

Martin, Harold H. "Who Said the French Won't Fight," *Saturday Evening Post* (1951).

Republic of Korea, Ministry of National Defense. *The History of the United Nations Forces in the Korean War* (1977).

F

G

Gay, Hobart R. (1894–1983)

The son of a farmer, Hobart Raymond Gay was born in Rockport, Illinois, on 16 May 1894. He graduated from Knox College in 1917 and was commissioned in the Army as a second lieutenant of cavalry later that year. From 1917 to 1923, Gay served with the 7th Cavalry Regiment along the Mexican border, and from 1923 to 1929, he was assigned to the Cavalry School, first as a student and then as an instructor. Nicknamed "Hap" (short for "Happy") because of an inclination for joking and jesting, Gay was blinded in one eye during a polo match in 1929 and was "sidetracked" into quartermaster duties until World War II. He officially transferred to the Quartermaster Corps in June 1934 and graduated from the Quartermaster School in 1939.

During World War II, Gay was at the right hand of Lieutenant General George S. Patton, a good friend since 1938. Completely devoted to Patton and adopting some of his "techniques and mannerisms," Gay was Patton's chief of staff during Patton's command of the I Armored Corps in the North African campaign, the Seventh Army in the Sicilian campaign, and the Third Army in the European theater of operations in the last year of the war. "Average in every respect—except in Patton's eyes," Gay did not impress many American generals as a "world beater," and in March 1944, General Dwight D. Eisenhower, supreme commander of the Allied Expeditionary Forces, insisted that Patton replace Gay as his chief of staff because he did not have the "presence" to represent Patton adequately at higher headquarters. However, Patton considered Gay a superb staff officer who had run the details of his headquarters with "exceptional efficiency," and a splendid companion. As a result, in December 1944

he persuaded Eisenhower to permit him to restore Gay as his chief of staff. Promoted to the rank of major general in March 1945, Gay was, in fact, traveling in the same automobile with Patton when the latter was fatally injured in a traffic accident in December 1945.

After holding a variety of assignments with the American occupation forces in Europe and serving as commanding general of the military district of Washington, D.C., Gay, in September 1949, was appointed commander of the 1st Cavalry Division in Japan. Between 14 July and 22 July 1950, he deployed his division to South Korea to join the United Nations forces resisting the North Korean aggression. Understrength, ill-equipped, short of experienced noncommissioned officers, and plagued by aged leadership at the regimental level, the 1st Cavalry Division, like the other American divisions sent to Korea in 1950, performed poorly in its initial operation, the defense of the Taejon–Taegu highway. Fearful that their positions would be encircled and destroyed when the North Koreans attacked them in the vicinity of Yongdong, many of Gay's men "bugged out" (broke and ran under fire); and Gay, concerned about his communications with Taegu, ordered a retreat. Lieutenant General Walton H. Walker, commander of the U.S. Eighth Army, was "disappointed" by the showing of the 1st Cavalry Division and criticized Gay's leadership in a tense meeting at Gay's headquarters on 29 July. Later Gay admitted that his experience in Europe during World War II centered on offensive operations while this operation was defensive, and "he didn't know what to do about it."

In August and September 1950, Gay, now thoroughly bloodied as a division commander in this new type of war, played a prominent role in the defense of the Pusan perimeter, shattering several North Korean divisions and saving Taegu. Following the Inchon invasion on 15 September 1950, and the subsequent breakout of the Eighth Army with the X Corps near Osan, south of Seoul, South Korea, the 1st Cavalry moved northward. After U.N. forces crossed the 38th parallel, the dividing line between North and South Korea, in early October 1950, Gay spearheaded the attack into Pyongyang, the capital of North Korea, and helped seize the city on 19 and 20 October. Two weeks later, Gay's 8th Cavalry Regiment was badly mauled by the Chinese Communists at Unsan after Major General Frank W. Milburn, commander of the I Corps, refused his request to withdraw the regiment from an exposed salient. Gay's desperate effort to rescue one of the regiment's trapped battalions was stymied by a Chinese roadblock; and on Milburn's instructions, Gay, in what he described as the most painful order he ever had to issue, called off the rescue mission and left the beleaguered battalion to its fate.

At the end of November 1950, Gay's division saw heavy fighting when the Chinese decisively defeated the Eighth Army in the battle of the Chongchon River and forced its retreat from North Korea. In early 1951, Gay was relieved of his command as part of the plan of Lieutenant General Matthew B. Ridgway, Walker's successor as Eighth Army commander, to rebuild the fighting spirit of the demoralized Army by rotating home many of its division commanders and replacing them with younger and more energetic officers. Returning to the United States in February 1951, Gay was successively assigned as deputy commander of the Fourth Army, commander of the VI Corps, commander of the III Corps, and commander of the Fifth Army until his retirement, with the rank of lieutenant general, in August 1955. He then was named superintendent of the New Mexico Military Institute, a post he held until 1963. Gay died in El Paso, Texas, on 19 August 1983.

John Kennedy Ohl

Bibliography

Alexander, Bevin. *Korea: The First War We Lost* (Hippocrene Books, New York: 1986).

Appleman, Roy E. *South to the Nakton, North to the Yalu: June–November 1950* (Office of the Chief of Military History, Washington: 1961).

Blair, Clay. *The Forgotten War: America in Korea, 1950–1953* (Times Books, New York: 1987).

Blumenson, Martin. *The Patton Papers*, Vol. 2, *1940–1945* (Houghton-Mifflin, Boston: 1974).

Hoyt, Edwin P. *Pusan Perimeter: Korea 1950* (Stein and Day, New York: 1984).

Geneva Conference of 1954

Between April 26 and June 15, 1954, delegates representing the major powers participating in the Korean War met at Geneva to seek "a peaceful settlement of the Korean question."

During the negotiations at Panmunjom, the U.N. and Communist delegates had agreed that a political conference discussing Korean reunification should be held as soon as possible. The U.S. representatives suggested that the conference should occur at Panmunjom approximately three months after the truce was signed. On August 28, 1953, the U.N. General Assembly approved the Korean armistice and supported the organization of a political conference in which U.N. forces and the North Koreans would be present. The assembly suggested that the Soviet Union be invited to attend.

In October 1953 the U.S. sent Ambassador Arthur H. Dean to Panmunjom to negotiate a place and time for the conference, but the Communists resisted, insisting that the Soviet Union and India be represented as neutral, and departed, leaving a small American delegation at Panmunjom in case the Communists altered their request. The Communists declined to relinquish their demand, and the delegates continued to attempt to arrange a location and time.

On February 18, 1954, the foreign ministers of the U.S., United Kingdom, France, and the Soviet Union met at the Berlin Conference to discuss concerns in Germany and Austria. They agreed to assemble in Geneva to resolve the problem of Korean unification. In Berlin, the Soviets opposed holding free elections in their zone, and allied leaders realized they would have only a slight chance of the Soviets consenting to permit free elections throughout Korea.

Despite this discouraging foreshadowing, the allies prepared for the Geneva Conference. From February to April they planned; the Swiss agreed to organize local arrangements and security; the U.N. offered the Palais des Nations for the allies to meet in; and the allies organized separate secretariats for delegates because the Soviets requested that a joint one not be established. Peace and rehabilitation in Indochina was scheduled to be discussed in a separate phase of the conference.

On February 26, the U.S. State Department sent invitations to U.N. member countries that had sent troops to Korea; the Soviet Union was responsible for inviting North Korea and China. Among the participating nations were Australia, Belgium, Canada, Colombia, Ethiopia, Greece, Luxembourg, the Netherlands, New Zealand, the Philippines, Thailand, and Turkey. The Union of South Africa, pressured over its domestic policy of apartheid, chose not to attend.

The Geneva Conference was closed to the press. The official languages were English, French, Russian, Chinese, and Korean. Anthony Eden, United Kingdom secretary of state, and V.M. Molotov, Soviet minister of foreign affairs, resolved the matter of seating delegates by agreeing the groups would be in alphabetical order according to the English spelling of their country's name. The allies did not want China's foreign minister, Chou En-lai, or North Korean Marshal Nam Il to chair the conference, but when they asked the Swiss president to preside, he refused.

The Geneva Conference consisted of fifteen general meetings (April 26–30; May 3, 4, 7, 11, 13, 22, 28; June 5, 11, 15), and one restricted meeting (held on May 1). Discussion usually began after 3:00 P.M. and continued for several hours.

The Allied delegates agreed on two basic principles to resolve Korean unification based on their common experiences while fighting the Communists in Korea. First, the delegates insisted that a unified Korean government must be based on free elections in which voters had a genuine chance to express their political desires. Second, the delegates wanted the Communists to acknowledge and affirm the U.N.'s authority to supervise these elections.

On April 28th U.S. Secretary of State John Foster Dulles requested that Chinese troops withdraw from Korea so that the proposed elections could be free of coercion. The Communists refused this request as well as that of elections being held only in the North; they demanded peninsula-wide elections. Chinese Foreign Minister Chou En-lai pressed for an all-Korean election with no foreign interference, implying that all U.N. troops be removed from Korea before the elections.

The restricted session, chaired by Eden, began on May 1. Delegates from North and South Korea, United Kingdom, France, Communist China, the Soviet Union, and U.S. met privately. They examined the proposals for unification, but unable to reconcile in a smaller debate, returned to the general sessions.

Realizing that the Communists would probably not agree to U.N. demands because they were similar to those made at Berlin and because no conclusive decisions had been made yet, Dulles left Geneva. U.S. Undersecretary of State Walter Bedell Smith assumed leadership of the American delegation. On the 3rd Smith stated the Communist attempts to have unanimity in the all-Korean commission were in fact a "built-in veto." The Communists did not mention the U.N. in any of their proposals nor did they establish a role for the U.N. in the reunification process.

The Communists' basic proposals were unacceptable to the allies. On May 13 Eden explained that "These proposals impose conditions which would enable the elections to be held only after a long and complicated series of delays." On May 22 North Korean delegate Nam Il clarified the Communist demands by stating social organizations would be represented in the commission and that proportional representation would be achieved by creating districts from which representatives were selected based on population. The allies realized the Communists would still have veto powers and could limit the representatives of social groups and districts to individuals who shared their political stance.

On June 5 North Korea and China rejected a South Korean proposal for providing the U.N. a supervisory role, considering it a foreign intruder and belligerent. Chou En-lai reiterated his May 22 statement that a neutral nations supervisory commission be formed to observe Korean elections, ensure equal representation, and insist on unanimity.

The Soviet draft resolution iterated the Communists' position that a free election, with a secret ballot and universal suffrage, should be implemented. The resolution stated the all-Korean legislature would be based on population in the North and South but that exact composition and duties would be discussed in the future. It also suggested that troops withdraw before the election, again allocating details to future debate. Future debate was pigeonholed for an international committee to supervise the composition and management of the all-Korea assembly and unification, as well as to ensure that other powers respected their obligation to maintain peace in Korea.

G

Arguing that a neutral nations supervisory commission would not be a feasible solution because of the Communists' veto power, the allies suggested that the Communists accept the U.N. commission already in Korea: the U.N. Commission for the Unification and Rehabilitation of Korea (UNCURK).

On June 11 Chou En-lai and Nam Il declared that the previous neutral nations supervisory commission had been a failure due to U.S. policies. They continued to reject the U.N. and support Molotov's plan.

The Communists used a variety of diversionary tactics throughout the conference, attacking the allies on various charges of retaining Chinese prisoners who had not elected repatriation and criticizing American foreign policy.

On June 15 the final session of the Geneva Conference commenced. The Communists' delegates tried to prolong the meeting with proposals unconnected to unification. Nam Il demanded that foreign troops leave Korea, the reduction of Korean armies to 100,000 men each, and the establishment of an all-Korean commission, in addition to seeking unification. Chou En-lai suggested that discussion of unification continue in restricted sessions where representatives from Communist China, the Soviet Union, United Kingdom, U.S., France, and North and South Korea would gather. Molotov supported Nam Il and drafted a statement that the countries should exhibit no threatening actions once the issue of Korea unification was solved; the allies responded that they could not accept the Communists' insistence that the U.N. not supervise unification and stated that the armistice would protect the peace in Korea until an international political consensus could be attained.

The final "Declaration by the Sixteen" was signed by all Allied delegations. It noted that the Communists would not accept the two basic principles sought and continued exhibiting negative behavior that had existed since the U.N. tried to unify Korea in 1947. The allies concluded that it was better "to face the fact of our disagreement than to raise false hopes and mislead the peoples of the world into believing that there is agreement where there is none." They agreed that it was infeasible to continue negotiations at Geneva and informed the U.N. of the proceedings. In their declaration, the allies documented the U.N.'s authority to reaffirm collective security, outlined the Communists' repudiation of that international body, and iterated the need for free elections in Korea.

The Communists replied that the allies were responsible for terminating the negotiations at Geneva, and Chou En-lai blamed the U.S. for purposely blocking the peaceful unification of Korea. The Communists introduced a resolution that the delegates at Geneva would continue seeking the goal of Korean unification and sought to determine a place and time to resume talks. They requested a vote on their proposal, but Eden noted no voting procedure had been established and that the resolution could only be put in Geneva's written records.

The Geneva Conference concluded on the 15th with the Communist delegates refusing to compromise on the two basic issues presented by the allies as primary factors for settlement: free elections with proportionate population representative of North and South, and recognition of the U.N.'s right to oversee peaceful unification.

After two months of negotiations, neither side was willing to accept the other's proposals, nor were they willing to compromise. Because the Communist delegates attacked the credibility of the U.N., the U.N. delegates at Geneva realized that further discussion of methods of reunification would be fruitless.

The primary responsibility for Korean unification reverted to the U.N. which continues, somewhat discouraged, to seek acceptable formulas for reunification. In the eyes of the U.N., the South Korean government was a legitimate government because its elections were observed by the U.N. Although the Korean people long for reunion, North Korea has steadfastly refused to all U.N. officials to monitor free elections. The armistice remains in effect, and only time would tell whether the admission in 1991 of both Koreas to the U.N. represented a tangible step toward reunification.

Elizabeth Schafer

Bibliography

Brands, H.W. "The Dwight D. Eisenhower Administration, Syngman Rhee, and the 'other' Geneva Conference of 1954," *Pacific Historical Review* (February 1987).

Hermes, Walter G. *Truce Tent and Fighting Front, U.S. Army in the Korean War* (Office of the Chief of Military History, Washington: 1966).

O'Neill, Robert. *Australia in the Korean War 1950–53*, 2 vols. (1985).

Randle, Robert F. *Geneva 1954: The Settlement of the Indochinese War* (1969).

U.S. Department of State. *The Korean Problem at the Geneva Conference, April 26–June 15, 1954* (1954).

Great Britain and the Korean War

The United Kingdom's relationship with the United States was basic to its foreign policy during the period of the Korean War as it was during the entire post–World War II era. Only in the 1960s and 1970s did that "special relationship" diminish somewhat. The principal architect of British immediate postwar foreign policy was Ernest Bevin (1881–1951), who served as foreign secretary for almost the entire tenure of the Attlee Labor government. Bevin envisioned a rebuilt and more united Europe that could better resist any potential expansion on the Continent by the Soviet Union. The crusty Bevin, a former dockworker and committed socialist, yielded to no one in his opposition to communism, either of the Soviet variety or within his trade union constituency.

Despite the special relationship, NATO, and Labor's commitment to building its "better world," it was the socialist government which embarked on the creation of an independent nuclear deterrent for the UK. The fruits of this policy were not garnered until after the Labor government left office—with the detonation of Britain's first atomic bomb in 1952, and its premier hydrogen bomb in 1957. Yet because of the awesome destructiveness of these weapons, it seemed unlikely that they would ever be used. Furthermore, a nuclear weapons program appeared to many Britons as profoundly irrelevant to the problems of a crumbling empire, postwar reconstruction, equitable distribution of wealth, modernization, and inflation.

Relations with the United States were strained in the 1950s by Great Britain's recognition of the new Communist regime on mainland China, although the U.S. was able to persuade its NATO ally to recognize both the People's Republic of China (Communist) and the Republic of China (Nationalist).

Soon after the invasion of the Republic of Korea (South Korea) by the Democratic People's Republic of Korea (North Korea), the Attlee Labor government, to the astonishment of many Laborites, gave the Americans its full support, promising British forces and substantial naval aid to South Korea. This move by Attlee and Bevin was made easier by the Soviet boycott of the U.N. Security Council, enabling the Americans to assemble a broad-based United Nations coalition to repel aggression. Great Britain's contribution to U.N. forces could thus be interpreted as in keeping with the idealistic goals of the world body and not as interfering in a Korean civil war or as supinely truckling to America's reflexive anti-communism. The latter two interpretations of the Korean War were quite common in Great Britain at the time and afterward. Indeed, pro- and anti-Americanism were among the very few sentiments in the 1950s that cut across British lines of class and station.

Not surprisingly, a sharp split sundered the Attlee moderate faction from the Labor's left wing led by the eloquent Aneurin Bevan, minister of health. On 14 July 1950 a motion was tabled calling for immediate mediation of the Korean conflict, withdrawal of U.S. forces from Formosa (Taiwan), and the admission of Communist China to the U.N. Prime Minister Attlee himself hoped for a negotiated peace, and privately expressed great uneasiness about General Douglas MacArthur's later extending of military operations to the very border of China and his advocating the bombing of Manchuria. He was also convinced, on good evidence, that the United States was contemplating the use of nuclear weapons in Korea. Attlee flew to Washington in January of 1951, at the time when Chinese Communist armies seemed fully capable of overrunning the entire Korean peninsula, to press his case against doing anything that could provoke a full-blown war. On his return to London, the prime minister could report to a nervous House of Commons that the U.S. also wished to avoid a general war with China. In the parliamentary elections scheduled for the fall of that year Attlee could portray himself as almost single-handedly preventing the Americans from using nuclear weapons in Korea.

The Attlee government's greatest crisis during the period of the Korean War, however, was the resignation of Aneurin Bevan from the Cabinet on 22 April 1951, as a result of the imposition of charges for national health program spectacles and dentures. It was particularly galling to Bevan and his followers that these charges, small as they were, would be imposed to fund British rearmament. For them, the touchstone of true socialism was absolutely "free" medical care. (From the start, of course, this service was paid for out of general taxation and special levies. It is today by far the largest single charge on the UK's budget.) Bevan had already opposed the government's support of a U.S. resolution in the U.N. condemning Communist China as the aggressor in Korea, and imposing sanctions against the Communist state. Bevin, on the other hand, was far more concerned with the "special relationship" and with Europe. Despite Attlee's supposed foreign policy triumphs in restraining the "impetuous" Americans and Labor's portrayal of Churchill as a "warmonger," Labor lost ground. Paradoxically, the resignation of the firebrand Bevan (who had denounced the conservatives as "lower than vermin" in the 1950 campaign) paved the way for the narrow victory in October 1951 of the vile Tories. The British electorate pivoted far more on domestic questions, the result of a general weariness after six years of socialist austerity and exhortation. Certainly the removal of General MacArthur by President Harry S. Truman had relieved the worst fears of the electorate about any expansion of the Korean War. The new foreign secretary, Anthony Eden, waiting in the wings for Churchill to retire, fully supported American policy in the prosecution of the war, but also was convinced that most Britons still supported only a contained conflict.

The worst Anglo-American crisis during the Churchill regime came in the wake of the U.S. bombing of North Korean hydroelectric plants just south of the Yalu River in June of 1952. This action was considered an expansion of the war and was attacked in the media and Parliament with a bitterness that seems overwrought today, particularly in light of the realization that the extent and conditions of the war changed in no way after the raids. The British government was on somewhat firmer ground in its muted objection to the lack of any consultation between allies. But the aerial attacks certainly provided ammunition for the Bevin wing of the now-opposition Labor party, which could excoriate the Tories all the more for truckling yet again to the "warmongers."

Yet for all the stresses induced by the Korean War, probably nothing did more lasting damage to the "special relationship" than the unmasking of a series of Soviet spies or agents of influence in Great Britain in the early 1950s. Atom scientists Alan Nunn May and Klaus Fuchs were given long prison sentences, and another atom scientist, Bruno Pontecorvo, de-fected to the Soviet Union, as did two notorious scapegrace diplomats, Guy Burgess and Donald MacLean. All of these highly placed Britons had long been under suspicion by U.S. intelligence services, as was the double agent, Kim Philby, now often referred to as the "Spy of the Century." While the more apocalyptic fantasies of the Macarthyite era were to be discounted, British intelligence had almost automatically denigrated American warnings. The Americans would not forget.

While it did not directly impinge upon the Korean War, the death of King George VI on 6 February 1952, did represent a watershed in postwar British life. The "Old King" was only 56 when he died, prematurely worn down by his labors through World War II and the postwar years of austerity (as well as by his lifelong addiction to tobacco). His reign was always to be associated with years of trial and sacrifice. His daughter and successor, the beautiful young Queen Elizabeth II, reigned over a nation that shed its empire, but enjoyed vastly increased domestic prosperity in the years characterized by Conservative Prime Minister Harold Macmillan as those in which "You never had it so good." In those later years, as far as Great Britain was concerned, the Korean War quickly receded into oblivion.

Richard Voeltz

Bibliography
Bullock, Alan. *Ernest Bevin* (1984).
Campbell, J. *Nye Bevan and the Mirage of British Socialism, 1929–956* (1987).
Douglas, Roy. *World Crisis and British Decline 1945–1956* (1986).
Northredge, F.S. *Descent from Power: British Foreign Policy 1945–1973* (1974).
Sissons, M., and Philip French, eds. *Age of Austerity* (1963).

See also BRITISH CONTRIBUTION; ROYAL NAVY; UNITED KINGDOM

Greek Forces in the Korean War

"Korea is the Greece of the Far East," U.S. President Harry S. Truman declared shortly after he heard the news of the North Korean invasion of South Korea. American leaders viewed Greece as an example of how the U.S. was able to help vulnerable nations resist Communist aggressors. Believing that a series of countries were threatened by communism, Truman sought a policy of containment to prove to the Soviets that they would be unable to control either Greece or Korea.

Contributing an infantry battalion and an air transport squadron and pilots, Greece, a charter U.N. member, participated in the Korean War to express support for the U.N. and to reinforce ties with allies—especially the U.S.—which had provided military and economic aid to the devastated nation in the late 1940s.

During World War II, Greece had been occupied by German and Italian forces, and an active resistance movement surfaced; after liberation, civil war erupted in Greece when Communist guerrillas in northern Greece, aided by Soviet-influenced Albania, Bulgaria, and Yugoslavia, which also claimed territory on their borders with Greece, rose against the Athens government.

The U.S. and Great Britain considered Greece a vital base in the Mediterranean from which they could contain Soviet expansion. Great Britain, which was granted administrative hegemony of Greece after the war, was unable to continue financial support. In 1947, the U.S., under the auspices of the Truman Doctrine, began shipments of supplies and military advisors to Greece to help government military forces and provide relief for civilians. European nations also contributed to the Greek cause.

General James A. Van Fleet was ordered to Greece in 1948 where he assessed, reorganized, and reinvigorated the weak Greek Army. Soon thereafter, Marshal Josip Tito of Yugoslavia broke with Stalin and closed the Yugoslavian-Greek border, over which many guerrillas had slipped into northern Greece. As a result of Van Fleet's leadership, the revitalized Greek Army began an offensive that crippled the enemy's effort. By October 1949 rebel forces admitted defeat.

In October 1950, Greece sent an infantry battalion commanded by Dionyssios G. Arbouzis to Korea. Originally the Greeks had planned to send a brigade, but in autumn the Korean War seemed to be ending, and the Greek force was reduced to a regular battalion of the Greek Army. Arbouzis was an effective leader who, twenty years later, in 1974, reached the rank of four-star general and was named commander in chief of Greek armed forces. Battalion officers were selected on the basis of their fluency in English. Most of the Greek soldiers were combat veterans of their civil war.

Greece also dispatched elements of the Royal Hellenic Air Force, which arrived on November 26, 1950, and donated C-47 Skytrain transports to the U.S. Air Force 21st Troop Carrier Squadron. Greek pilots were collectively awarded the U.S. Presidential Unit Citation for actions over the Chosin Reservoir.

Arriving in Pusan on December 9, 1950, the 940 men of the Greek Battalion joined the U.S. 7th Cavalry Regiment of the 1st Cavalry Division, serving with that regiment for the majority of the war. When they arrived, the Eighth Army, which was retreating from the Yalu River, desperately needed their strength. The Greek Battalion brought valuable battle experience from fighting Communist guerrillas in their own country.

The Greeks, because of the terrain in their native land, easily acclimated to Korea's mountainous topography and bitter weather. Also, the soldiers were highly skilled in using American weapons, with which they had trained and become familiar, as well with American methods of waging war, during the Greek civil war.

The Greeks were under the overall command of Major General Charles D. Palmer, commanding general of the 1st Cavalry Division. Colonel John Daskalopoules served as communications officer of the Greek Battalion when it was attached to the 7th Cavalry.

The men of the 7th Cavalry Regiment welcomed the Greeks, appreciating their added manpower. Although the Greek Battalion did not have many translators, there were few problems translating orders. The Greeks learned basic words or pantomimes for crucial terms denoting terrain, equipment, and military maneuvers. Soon after their arrival, the Greek Battalion was placed on the central sector of the line held by General John B. Coulter.

On the night of January 29, 1951, approximately 3,000 Chinese soldiers attacked the Greek Battalion on Hill 381. In their first major action in Korea, the Greeks repelled the Chinese by using grenades, bayonets, rifle butts, and, when their ammunition supply was exhausted, bare hands to hold the hill and prevent the enemy from surrounding nearby troops.

In 1952, a Greek company helped to move prisoners and break Communist resistance in the prisoner camp on Koje Island.

The Greeks brought their own doctors, dentists, litter bearers, and aides, but most often sent their wounded through U.S. hospitals. The Greeks were particularly interested in the welfare of Korean civilians, and possibly because of the kidnapping of Greek children during their civil war, treated Korean children with great kindness, including the feeding, clothing, and sheltering of Korean orphans. An unusual facet of Greek participation was that, like the Turks, they had wide feet, and most boots allotted to them were too small. They often had to slice the leather in order to squeeze in their feet. Like most U.N. participants, the Greeks had special menu requests for breads, spices, and other staples of their diet.

Greek forces peaked with 1,263 Greek soldiers. Greek Battalion casualties totaled 174 dead and 153 wounded. Two Greek POWs were repatriated at the end of hostilities.

A postwar South Korea–Greece association was formed in order for the two countries to develop closer cultural ties. In the 1950s and 1960s, Presidents Eisenhower, Kennedy, and Johnson used the precedent of American military instruction during the civil war in Greece (and subsequent Greek support of the U.N. alliance in Korea) as an example and rationale—predicting ultimate victory—for U.S. intervention against Communist forces in Vietnam.

Elizabeth Schafer

Bibliography

Chandler, Melbourn C. *Of GarryOwen in Glory: The History of the 7th U.S. Cavalry* (1960).

Jones, Howard. *"A New Kind of War": America's Global Strategy and the Truman Doctrine in Greece* (1989).

Martin, Harold H. "The Greeks Know How to Die," *Saturday Evening Post* (1951): 26–27, 83–84.

Republic of Korea, Ministry of National Defense. *The History of the United Nations Forces in the Korean War*, 3 (1974).

Royal Greek Embassy, Information Service on Greece's Stand on the Korean Question (1951).

Gromyko, Andrei A. (1909–1989)

Andrei Gromyko, whose political and diplomatic career spanned almost the entire period of Soviet rule, was born of humble Russian parents in the village of Old Gromyki near Minsk in what today is independent Russia. Taking advantage of opportunities created by the social transformation accompanying Soviet power, Gromyko joined the Communist party at a young age, studied political economy, and

gained his Ph.D. from Moscow University. Considered a bright and obedient party member by his peers, Gromyko, on the eve of World War II, was sent by Stalin to Washington as second in command to Soviet Ambassador Maxim Litvinov. In 1943, Gromyko replaced Litvinov, becoming a key player in the unfolding diplomacy of the Allied powers, and attending the Big Three meetings at Teheran, Yalta, and Potsdam. In 1946, Gromyko was designated by Moscow as permanent representative to the United Nations, leaving that post in 1952 to become ambassador to the United Kingdom. In 1957 Gromyko became Soviet foreign minister, in 1973 a full member of the ruling Politburo, and in 1985 Chairman of the Supreme Soviet (president of the USSR).

During his lengthy period of service, Gromyko's role was more as a negotiator and proponent of Soviet policy than as one of its originators. In his memoirs, Gromyko recalls that following the invasion of South Korea he prepared instructions that the Soviet representative return to meetings of the Security Council so as to block any American resolutions requesting troops. Stalin, however, personally rejected this action, ordering Soviet representatives not to attend. As Gromyko cryptically notes: "On this occasion, Stalin, guided for once by emotion, had not made the best decision." Despite his lengthy time in service and numerous writings in Russian, little has appeared in English by or about this important Soviet diplomat. In 1989, having resigned his position as president the preceding year, Andrei Gromyko died. No major Soviet figure attended his funeral.

Ian A. Horwood

Bibliography

Anreev, G. Economist (pseudonym for Andrei Gromyko). *Eksport amerikanskogo Kapitala* (*The Export of American Capital*) (1957).

Gromyko, Andrei. *Memoirs* (1989).

———. *Pamiatnoe* (*Memoirs*), 2 vols. (1988).

Rubinstein, Alvin Z. *Soviet Foreign Policy Since World War II: Imperial and Global* (1981).

Taubman, William. *Stalin's American Policy: From Entente to Detente to Cold War* (1982).

H

Heartbreak Ridge

Heartbreak Ridge was the site of the last major U.N. offensive of the Korean War. After truce talks were adjourned and Bloody Ridge was won in September 1951, United Nations Commander in Chief Matthew Ridgway ordered Major General Clovis E. Byers, X Corps commander, to secure Heartbreak Ridge, and the 2nd U.S. Infantry Division (Indianhead Division) was assigned to accomplish this task. Its three infantry regiments—the 9th, 23rd, 38th—now designated regimental combat teams because of attached battalions—Thai (9th), French (23rd), and Netherlands (38th)—were involved.

Heartbreak's 3,000-foot ridgeline consisted of three peaks: Hill 894 was three miles from Bloody Ridge; Hill 931, the tallest peak, was 1,300 yards north; and 2,100 yards further was Hill 851. Between the needle-sharp peaks were deep valleys: in the east, Satae-ri, and to the west, Mundung-ni. They were intersected by streams and were crucial sites for tactical maneuvers. Roads on Heartbreak Ridge were blocked by boulders and enemy obstructions.

The hills' western slopes were smoother, facilitating travel, but the enemy had entrenched in deep bunkers fortified with timber and machine guns. Well prepared to encounter U.N. forces, North Koreans of the 6th Division, commanded by General Hong Nim, and reinforced by the 12th Division, were ready for battle.

At division headquarters, Brigadier General Thomas E. de Shazo, acting division commander, believed the enemy bunkers would be quickly destroyed by artillery and decided to use only the 23rd Infantry Regiment, with the 9th providing limited support and the 38th in reserve. On Thursday, September 13, the troops left Hill 702, traveling to Samtae-dong. Artillery fired on the North Koreans for forty-five minutes with minimal effect. The 3rd Battalion worked on Hill 851 while the 2nd proceeded to Hills 931 and 894, enduring mortar and machine gun fire all day and digging into the rocky ground at night.

The next morning, the 23rd pushed through the thick fog for the crest of Hills 931/851, experiencing heavy mortar attacks and digging in for the night only a few hundred yards from their previous position. During the night the 2nd Battalion reached the 3rd. On September 15 the 3rd Battalion's I, L, and K Companies pressed up the steep, rocky hills, harassed by gunfire that forced them to stop two hundred feet from the crest. The 2nd tried to divert the enemy fire, digging in for the third night of battle. Hill 894 was secured within eight hours of combat.

At dawn on the next day, artillery knocked out enemy positions, and North Korean troops counterattacked for fifteen minutes, using burp guns, but were repulsed. Nim replaced his 1st Regiment with a group of fresh troops from the 13th. Talking to a reporter, Colonel James Y. Adams lamented that his troops' losses were "such a heartbreak for me," thus giving the ridge its name.

On September 17 enemy action increased but was repulsed. Ammunition was depleted, and soldiers resorted to fistfighting. Flamethrowers were also available but were limited by distance and terrain. U.N. troops finally reached the top of Hill 851 and dug in.

During the night, North Korean infantry struck and separated the U.N. troops. The Communist troops received fresh replacements, while the U.N. forces suffered from depleted manpower and ineffective communication when lines were cut by the enemy. On September 19 the attack continued on Hill 931.

Although the Allied forces continued to use airpower and artillery, Adams realized that the enemy had the advantage in manpower and supplies and the benefit of being firmly in place on the ridgeline. He also was aware that the enemy bunkers would be difficult to destroy. Adams requested that the 23rd be withdrawn but was refused. De Shazo told him he would order a drop of rations, supplies, and ammunition, but "My reputation is at stake. Your feet are to the fire. Go take that damn hill." The U.N. troops endured periodic enemy fire and were resupplied.

On the 22nd, the 1st and 2nd gained Hill 931 but were driven from its top four times. This movement continued on the next day, and on the fifth attempt they surmounted the enemy, maintaining their position. Reinforcements arrived during the next two days, but the lack of sufficient ammunition forced the troops once again to withdraw.

On September 26, the French unsuccessfully tried to take Hill 931. Adams discussed the situation with French Battalion General Ralph Monclar and Commandant Oliver Le Mire, who asserted that the U.N. forces needed to approach the enemy through the Mundung-ni Valley and cut North Korean communication and supply lines as well as their access to reinforcements. Adams advised the French that attacking the interior would only result in losing more men.

At a meeting of the French military officers, Adams remarked that continuing previous strategies on Heartbreak Ridge would be suicidal, and the uncoordinated attacks ended. From September 27 to 28 mortar and artillery fire were heavily used, and the 1st relieved the 3rd. Ridgway commended Adams for his moral courage in dropping impractical tactics. But the battle for Heartbreak Ridge was not over. Between October 1 to 5, the forces were resupplied and prepared ambushes; patrols caught prisoners, who provided intelligence information. Because tanks and infantry would go to Mundung-ni, on the 2nd engineers began to clear the roads, using mine detectors, and dropped communication lines from the air.

The 23rd Regimental Task Force Sturman was moved in to soften the enemy in Satae-ri Valley. On the 3rd, eight enemy bunkers were destroyed. Warplanes strafed enemy positions. On the next day Task Force Sturman participated in a firefight with the North Korean 19th Regiment. Reconnaissance patrols located and targeted enemy bunkers, while warplanes bombed and sealed the fluorspar mine which the Communists had used for supplies and to conceal reserve troops. Reserve supplies of ammunition also arrived, and Navy Corsair pilots dropped napalm, searing the enemy, its equipment, and shelters.

At 2100 hours on the night of the 5th, the three regiments simultaneously began action. By the next day the 1st Battalion took Hill 728. The 9th worked on Hill 867, but progress was slow. Hill 931 was taken by the 23rd. By the 7th, Hill 967 was secured, and the troops focused on getting Hill 851.

The North Koreans counterattacked on the 8th, and on the following day, a Chinese prisoner stated that Chinese forces would arrive by October 12. Allied officers ordered fighter bombers to hit enemy bunkers with napalm and bombs. By the early morning of the 10th, Lieutenant Colonel Joseph Jarvis led his 72nd Tank Battalion to the rear of the Communists. The French also began movement, and by the morning of the 12th, the American and French forces, in a bayonet charge, joined to secure Hill 851.

In winning Heartbreak Ridge the Fifth Air Force dropped 250 tons of bombs. The enemy was well entrenched, explaining why the battle for Heartbreak Ridge continued so long and resulted in heavy bloodshed. Also, the cold weather and craggy terrain hindered the attacking allies. On Heartbreak Ridge the 2nd Division suffered 3,700 casualties, including 597 killed, 3,064 wounded, and 84 missing. One-half of the casualties (1,832) were from the 23rd and the French Battalion. Allied personnel estimated that 25,000 enemy soldiers were casualties, counted the bodies of 1,473 killed, and speculated another 8,938 died and that 14,204 were wounded. A total of 6,060 prisoners were taken.

Truce talks resumed on October 25. On November 3, the NKPA 14th Regiment attacked the 160th Infantry Regiment and 40th Infantry Division defending Heartbreak Ridge. The North Korean troops were defeated, and U.N. forces remained in control of Heartbreak Ridge until the war's end:

The North Koreans knew Heartbreak Ridge as Height 1211 and considered it the most difficult battle of the war. By winning Heartbreak Ridge, U.N. troops secured a portion of the 38th parallel that defined the final demarcation line when the armistice was signed in 1953.

Elizabeth Schafer

Bibliography

Craven, V.E. "Operation Touchdown Won Heartbreak Ridge," *Combat Forces Journal* (December 1953).

Freeman, Sam. "Tankers at Heartbreak," *Armor* (September-October 1952).

Hermes, Walter G. *Truce Tent and Fighting Front, U.S. Army in the Korean War* (Office of the Chief of Military History, Washington: 1969).

Hinshaw, Arned L. *Heartbreak Ridge: Korea, 1951* (1989).

Williamson, E.C., et al. *Heartbreak Ridge, September–October 1951*, 2nd Division, Eighth United States Army Korea, Military History Section (n.d.).

Helicopters in the Korean War

Helicopters served a vital role in medical evacuation and transport missions during the Korean War. Originally conceptualized during the Renaissance by Leonardo da Vinci, the first successful helicopter was a twin-rotor craft created by German engineer Heinrich Focke in 1936. The next year Igor Sikorsky introduced his single-rotor craft. A few helicopters were used experimentally in World War II for observation and reconnaissance.

In July 1950 a detachment of the 3rd Air Rescue Squadron arrived in Korea to rescue downed pilots, but few pilots were shot down, and when Army units began requesting aid, helicopter pilots began recovering Army casualties that field ambulances could not reach. The Army Surgeon General consulted with General Douglas MacArthur, who recognized that helicopters were needed for use as ambulances, and two helicopter ambulance companies were formed and attached to the 8076th Mobile Army Surgical Hospital (MASH).

Helicopter evacuation transcended traditional removal methods in which vehicles and human carriers required tedious hours to carry casualties to hospitals; many died in the process. Helicopters quickly delivered wounded from the front directly to a MASH. The mountainous Korean topography and the lack of adequate roads made the helicopter a welcomed mode of transportation and evacuation. Helicopters had great maneuverability, flying vertically, backwards, and sideways, and were able to hover low enough to load casualties and take off and land almost anywhere.

Known by such nicknames as "choppers," "eggbeaters," "whirlybirds," and "airedales," helicopters were flown by a single pilot and had two external pods to carry wounded. One additional patient could ride inside if physically able and if there were sufficient lift. Helicopters took the most critically wounded soldiers to the MASH to be stabilized. They provided smooth trips that did not jar injuries; the rapidity of helicopter flights lowered death caused by shock, a frequent factor in World War II.

This swift evacuation was a morale builder, as soldiers realized wounds did not mean long, arduous treks across the Korean terrain or death from complicating factors. In World War II, it often took twelve to fifteen hours to transport casualties; in Korea it took only four to six hours for helicopters to evacuate the most critically injured. In World War II, 28 percent of wounded American soldiers died; in Korea, helicopters reduced this statistic so that only 22 percent of casualties perished. Because of access to helicopter evacuation, hospitals were able to remain in one location longer and provide post-operative care instead of constantly relocating to be near casualties.

Pilots learned by trial and error. Helicopter limitations included an inability to fly at night or in bad weather and heavy winds. They could not land on slopes, and they had a limited range and altitude; they flew worst in the summer when warm, thin air provided minimal lift.

Pilots realized the risks and fragility of helicopters but many broke the rules in order to retrieve casualties or deliver supplies. For example, night flying and flying under fire were prohibited. Also, there were no lighted instrumentation panels or radios; pilots willing to risk these flights to remove wounded flew at night with flashlights between their legs to see their controls. Guerrillas and Communist soldiers harassed helicopters with small arm and artillery fire. Several helicopter pilots received citations for bravery and heroism while recovering casualties. Ground troops had to cooperate by giving accurate coordinates and weather conditions to pilots in preflight telephone instructions and by providing marked panels or smoke grenades to facilitate landing.

Most helicopter pilots had no medical training, and the wounded carried by helicopter received no medical treatment or care in transit; at first it was impossible to administer intravenous solutions. Pilots innovated methods to heat patients by covering the engine with plastic sheets so that warm air generated by the motor was trapped in the litter pods. Pod covers were built for wind deflection. Plasma could be administered to the patients when plastic tubes and a rubber bulb flow regulator were placed in the cabin.

The Marines also used helicopters for medical evacuation. More than 10,000 Marines were transported by helicopters during the war to hospitals or hospital ships. In August 1951 the Marines also began using fifteen ten-seat Sikorsky HRS-1 cargo helicopters. On September 13, 1951, the HRS-1 performed the first aerial resupply operation; in two and one-half hours pilots transported 18,848 pounds of gear (equivalent to one day's worth of supplies) and seventy-four Marines a distance of seven miles.

In January 1951, three Army helicopter detachments arrived in Korea with helicopters, pilots, and mechanics. The Army intended to relieve the Air Force of primary responsibility for evacuation of casualties from battlefields. But, as a result, infighting between the Army and Air Force developed.

The 1st Helicopter Detachment was established only on paper until December 1952 when it was abolished and replaced by Helicopter Detachment 8190th Army Unit. In March 1951, the 2nd Helicopter Detachment (later named the Helicopter Detachment 8191st Army Unit) based four helicopters with the 8055th MASH. The 3rd Helicopter Detachment (which became the Helicopter Detachment 8192nd Army Unit), and the 4th Helicopter Detachment (the Helicopter Detachment 8193d Army Unit) had numbers of their machines based with MASHs.

In November 1951 helicopters were first used for battlefield movement of combat forces, taking 950 troops to the front and returning to the rear with an equivalent group. The Bell 47 Sioux was used for communication. Among other helicopters used in Korea were the Hiller UH-12 Raven OH-23, HTE, for observation; the Piasecki (Vertol) PV-17, HRP-1 "Flying Banana," which had twin tandem rotors and was used first by the Navy and Marines, being able to carry ten troops; the large capacity Piasecki (Vertol) PV-18 Retriever, Army Mule, HUP-1, 2, 3, H-25 was first used in Korea in 1953; and the Sikorsky S-55 was used by the Army and Marines to move troops and supplies to mountain peaks.

Other helicopter usages evolved from various incidents. Helicopters were used to lay communications lines, detect mines, and in search and rescue missions; they performed similar support tasks that balloons in the Civil War and

World War I had done for reconnaissance. Helicopters carried film and news stories to news bureaus. Commanders considered helicopters to be status symbols and rode them to observe battles and travel to troops. Entertainers and high-ranking officials were delivered via helicopter. Military police flashed floodlights from helicopters for security missions, observing refugees and civilians and looking for possible guerrilla activity.

Helicopters had their disadvantages, and accidents were not uncommon. Major General Bryant Moore died of a heart attack after the helicopter in which he was a passenger plunged into the Han River. The shortage of helicopters and their extreme vulnerability was constantly a problem for adequate evacuation services.

Helicopters were expensive to maintain. Qualified mechanics were rare and parts shortages resulted in lack of transport for supply and evacuation. Helicopter pilots and mechanics required extensive and expensive training. Some critics stated the actual number of wounded carried by helicopters was small. Helicopters could usually carry only two patients per trip, costing ten times as much as a ground ambulance that could carry five patients. In the winter pilots could carry three patients because of the improved lift. However, most supporters argued that helicopter use was justified by the survival rate among casualties.

By November 1, 1951, more than 8,000 wounded soldiers had been evacuated by helicopter. On one year IX Corps pilots flew 1,500 critical cases, saving many lives that might have been lost through ground transportation delays and lack of access to physicians during the most pivotal time of injury; helicopters also carried whole blood, supplies, and medical equipment to forward battalion aid stations. From January to December 1951 helicopters carried 5,040 casualties. In 1952 they carried 7,923. In the final seven months of the war, 4,735 wounded soldiers were transported by helicopter.

In the spring of 1953, the Army began using the H-19, which provided large cargo space for short-haul transport of men and supplies, carrying wounded inside on return flights. On board, the wounded could receive medical attention during the flight.

Delegates rode helicopters to the peace talks at Kaesong and Panmunjom. During Operation Little Switch, H-10 cargo helicopters flew repatriated prisoners from Freedom Village to hospitals for medical inspection and identity checks, and then to the airport at Seoul for flights home. Helicopters performed a similar role at Operation Big Switch.

More than 20,000 casualties were evacuated by helicopters during the Korean War. The infant helicopter had matured.

Elizabeth Schafer

Bibliography

Kitchens, John W. "Cargo Helicopters in the Korean Conflict," Parts 1 & 2, *Army Aviation Digest* (January–February 1993).

Marion, F.L. "The Grand Experiment: Detachment F's Helicopter Combat Operations in Korea, 1950–1953," *Air Power History* (Summer 1993).

Martin, M.T. "Medical Aspects of Helicopter Air Evacuation," *Journal of Aviation Medicine* (1952).

Matheny, Charles W. "What Helicopters Can Do for Us," *Combat Forces Journal* (1951).

Montross, Lynn. *Cavalry of the Sky: The Story of U.S. Marine Combat Helicopters* (1954).

Mundson, Kenneth, and Alec Lumsden. *Combat Helicopters Since 1942* (1986).

Pogue, L. Welch. "The Significance of the Helicopter," *Technical Review* (1952).

United States Army Forces, Far East. Eighth United States Army Korea (EUSAK) Military History Section, 8th Historical Detachment. *Helicopter Evacuation.* Prepared by First Lieutenant John Mewha (n.d.).

See also MEDICAL SERVICE IN THE KOREAN WAR

Historiography of the Korean War

Like most conflicts, the Korean War was an ambivalent and uncertain affair for all participants whether Korean, Chinese, or American. The tide of battle moved back and forth dramatically, yet in the end, both sides accepted deadlock. Final victory in this first of several "ideological" wars proved elusive and, despite claims on all sides, no one achieved decisive success either militarily or politically. The outcome was, at best, unclear, and most of the written history, at least in the West, reflects this fact. Not surprisingly, the war has given rise to varying historical interpretations. The issues are far from settled, even as the Cold War has drawn to a close. At the same time, the war was the occasion for an intensive ongoing endeavor in official military history. The historical services of the several branches of the American military, working largely from their experience in World War II, pursued innovative and vigorous programs to publish scholarly and fairly objective histories of their participation in the war.

The root causes of the Korean conflict have evoked considerable historical debate. The most widely cited background study to the conflict is Bruce Cumings's two-volume work entitled *The Origins of the Korean War.* Based on Korean as well as American sources, it examines the general political and social unrest in Korea during the years after World War II and leading up to the eruption of hostilities in June 1950. Though mindful of the diplomatic and ideological dimensions, Cumings has drawn special attention to the domestic roots of the conflict, the civil and revolutionary struggle within the country. Cumings is not one to give the United States or South Korea the benefit of any doubt. Peter Lowe's *The Origins of the Korean War,* on the other hand, takes what is perhaps the more traditional approach and emphasizes the global setting of the war. Simply put, what was the place of Korea within the framework of the Cold War? In the process he deftly moves the discussion beyond the concerns of the United States and the United Nations to an exploration of North Korean, Chinese, and Soviet motivation and behavior.

Korea: The Limited War, written by David Rees and published in 1964, is a classic survey of American military participation. Some of the issues that Rees discusses—the doctrine of a limited war, the role of strategic bombing, "brainwashing," and Communist propaganda—reflect the concerns of an earlier generation. The more recent work of Joseph C. Goulden, *Korea: The Untold Story of the War,* utilizes substantial newly declassified materials from the National Archives. The records of the Joint Chiefs of Staff figure prominently. Among Goulden's predominant, if not particularly new, themes are his sharp criticisms of General Douglas MacArthur and what the author characterizes as the indecisiveness of the joint chiefs.

Donald Knox has written a two-volume oral history, *The Korean War.* Drawing on the testimony and letters of ordinary U.S. Army and Marine combatants, Knox offers a fine portrait of the common soldier—his suffering and courage, doubts and confusion. Weary fighting, bitter weather, and recurrent frustration were the hallmark of the Korean ordeal. These personal memories allow Knox to convey the realities of social history and offer an engaging portrait of the human experience of war.

Martin Russ, a young enlisted man who served with the 1st Marine Division, has written a frank and occasionally humorous memoir entitled *The Last Parallel*. Along similar lines, *Unit Pride* by John McAleer and Billy Dickson is an exaggerated yet telling personal account. Cast as a novel, it evokes the literature that emerged from the trench warfare of 1914–1918. The book depicts, for example, the brutal disregard which soldiers often had for "gooks," and offers a graphic account of the human wave attacks which so unnerved the American forces.

Although Clay Blair's *The Forgotten War: America in Korea, 1950–1953* is a popular history, it does raise important issues. The absence of a clear and convincing consensus among the American people compounded the problems associated with raising, training, and fielding an army composed mainly of young and inexperienced draftees. What was the relationship between a lack of strong popular home support and the ability to fight in a distant and largely unknown land? At the very least, the notion of a limited war with limited aims seemed alien to a nation that had only recently achieved total victory over Germany and Japan.

The various uniformed services undertook to write multivolume official histories detailing their role in the war. The Historical Division, Headquarters, U.S. Marine Corps, began publication of a five-volume history shortly after the war's conclusion. It is a straightforward operational analysis, concentrating on such matters as the fighting along the Pusan perimeter, the Inchon landing, and the Chosin Reservoir campaign. These volumes provide an excellent history of the tactical movements of the various Marine units, but do not always fully integrate the Marine experience with the fighting elsewhere in the peninsula.

James A. Field's *History of the United States Naval Operations in Korea* is based on official sources. Besides a thorough description of routine naval operations such as coastal patrols, off-shore bombardments and minesweeping, Field presents a detailed analysis of the air strikes and close air support by Navy aircraft operating from carriers in the Sea of Japan. He also emphasizes the failure of the Navy and the Air Force to establish effective joint operational control.

Robert F. Futrell compiled a similar volume for the U.S. Air Force. Korea was the first war in which the Air Force operated as an independent entity. Futrell's *The United States Air Force in Korea, 1950–1953* stresses the emergence of what might loosely be termed a managerial style, or at a minimum, the procedures for organization and command. American air superiority is, naturally enough, one of Futrell's principal themes. He also devotes considerable attention to the Air Force's interdiction efforts and support of ground forces.

The U.S. Army pursued what was perhaps the most ambitious of these official histories of the war. The Office of the Chief of Military History (redesignated the Center of Military History in 1973) embarked upon a five-volume history of the war. The project was modest in comparison to the ninety-six volumes originally envisaged for the Army history of World War II. Still, coverage was comprehensive. The first book appeared in 1961, the last in 1990. All five volumes treat a wide range of issues relating to policy, strategy, and operations, and are based on the official primary military and diplomatic records.

Roy E. Appleman's *South to the Naktong: North to the Yalu* examines in great detail the dramatic first five months of fighting. It moves from the initial defeats to the precarious Pusan perimeter, through the daring landing at Inchon, to the drive into North Korea toward the Yalu River. Walter G. Hermes's *Truce Tent and Fighting Front* looks at the tedious last phases of the war as the truce talks dragged on at Panmunjom while prisoners of war rioted at Koje Island and the front lines became a bloody, frustrating stalemate along the 38th parallel. A final volume by Billy C. Mossman, *Ebb and Flow*, traces the fast-paced and fluid military developments through July 1951. It describes Chinese entry into the war and the process by which the People's Liberation Army pushed U.N. troops south of Seoul before being stopped. Mossman's volume, obviously out of historical chronology with its predecessors, was published only in 1990, after much delay.

There are several additional volumes in the Army series. James F. Schnabel, *Policy and Direction: The First Year*, displays a more encompassing theme and synthetic focus. It examines the policies, command methods, and high-level political and military decisions of the U.S. Army. Schnabel relies mainly on the records of the Far East command in Tokyo and the Joint Chiefs of Staff in Washington. Robert K. Sawyer, *Military Advisors in Korea: KMAG in Peace and War*, charts the critical work of U.S. military advisors before and during the war. Albert E. Cowdrey, *The Medics' War*, underscores the extraordinary advances in medical services that have become part of the popular lore surrounding the Korean War. He analyzes such matters as helicopter evacuation, the care of prisoners and refugees, medical processing in prisoners and refugees, medical processing in prisoner of war exchanges, and the operation of medical companies and surgical hospitals.

The Army, in another innovative step, dispatched a total of nine historical detachments to Korea. They were mostly three-man teams whose purpose was to conduct interviews, gather historical materials on the battlefield, and write preliminary accounts of key actions. These detachments prepared nearly 150 separate typescript historical manuscripts that are now housed at the U.S. Army Center of Military History in Washington. The published Army histories relied heavily on these excellent sources.

One aim of the Army history program was to balance the overarching concerns of policy and strategy with accounts of small unit actions and reports focusing on lower-ranking enlisted men and noncommissioned officers. Many of these monographs center on individual and closely defined combat engagements, reconstructing them in precise detail through interviews with participants and research in unit records. They are complete with maps, orders, and photographs. The studies include accounts of squads, platoons, and companies as they conducted raiding patrols and night defensive maneuvers, attacks and counterattacks, assaults and withdrawals. The Army's historical detachments, for example, put together ten of the nineteen accounts in Russell A. Gugeler's *Combat Actions in Korea*.

Other reports centered on far larger operations. They include a four-volume study of Operation Little Switch, a major repatriation enterprise; a two-volume narrative report on Operation Clam-Up, a deployment designed to capture Chinese soldiers; and a lengthy report on the fighting along the famous Heartbreak Ridge during September and October 1951.

Still other projects dwelt on the technical aspects of warfare. There was, for instance, a report on graves registration, another on offshore procurement problems, and several studies of helicopter operations. The Army field historians prepared descriptions of hospitals and dental services, the use of flamethrowers and smoke generators, the employment of radio equipment, the winterizing of water points, the repair of tidal locks, and the destruction and demolition of various installations as a part of the withdrawal from North Korea. Finally, a few studies were of a wholly encompassing and overarching nature. They treated such matters as inter-Allied cooperation and coordination during combat operations, general personnel and logistical problems, and the order of battle for both the U.S. Eighth Army and the Republic of Korea forces.

Several of these narrative reports have become set pieces used time and again by historians, both academic and popular. Bevin Alexander, himself an Army combat historian in Korea, made full use of them for *Korea: The First War We Lost*. More recently, Clay Blair did the same in *The Forgotten War*. Among the better known accounts is that on the intense fighting with the Chinese at Chipyong-ni in February 1951. Others focus on Operation Tomahawk and the battle of Bloody Ridge later in the same year. These materials will continue to be a valuable source of information and documentation for a thorough examination of the U.S. Army's conduct of the war.

Our understanding of the conflict remains tentative, however, since historians continue to work without significant documentation from the other side. Max Hastings, in *The Korean War*, attempts to redress the balance by including the oral testimony of Korean and Chinese veterans. On the other hand, so long as the Chinese and North Korean archives remain closed, the essential problem will persist. In truth, South Korea has also been restrictive in barring access to its archival records.

Officially, both Peking and Pyongyang viewed the war in terms of American "aggression" and "imperialism." The People's Republic of China, only recently victorious in its civil war, felt threatened by the American march into North Korea and emphasized, in addition, the necessity of coming to the aid of a socialist neighbor and ally. Ultimately the war assumed a heroic and patriotic quality for many Chinese. It was for some an honor to fight there, and even civilians were sometimes anxious to contribute to the war effort. Unfortunately, neither China nor North Korea (or South Korea for that matter) has permitted historians to begin the dispassionate investigation which is so critical to a proper comprehension of events along the far northern rim of the Pacific during the early 1950s.

Raymond A. Mentzer

Bibliography

Alexander, Bevin. *Korea: The First War We Lost* (1986).

Appleman, Roy E. *South to the Naktong: North to the Yalu; June-November 1950, U.S. Army in the Korean War* (1961).

Blair, Clay. *The Forgotten War: America in Korea, 1950–1953* (1987).

Blakeley, I. *U.S. Marine Corps Operations in Korea, 1950–53*, 5 vols. (U.S. Marine Corps Historical Branch, Washington: 1954–1972), L. Montross and N.A. Canzona, *The Pusan Perimeter*. Vol. 2, L. Montross and N.A. Canzona, *The Inchon-Seoul Operation*. Vol. 3, L. Montross and N.A. Canzona, *The Chosin Reservoir Campaign*. Vol. 4, L. Montross, H.D. Kuokka, and N.W. Hicks, *The East Central Front*. Vol. 5, P. Meid and J.M. Yingling, *Operations in West Korea*.

Cowdrey, Albert E. *The Medics' War* (U. S. Army Center of Military History, Washington: 1987).

Cumings, Bruce. *The Origins of the Korean War*, 1, *Liberation and the Emergence of Separate Regimes*, 2, *The Roaring of the Cataract 1947–1950* (1981–1992).

Far East Headquarters U.S. Army Forces, Military History Detachment, 8086 Army Unit. "A Chronology of the Historical Detachments in Korea," October 1950 to January 1954: n.d.).

Field, James A. *History of the United States Naval Operations in Korea* (Office of the Chief of Naval History: 1962).

Futrell, Robert F. *The United States Air Force in Korea, 1950–1953* (Office of the Chief of Air Force History: 1961, revised edition 1983).

Goulden, Joseph C. *Korea: The Untold Story of the War* (1982).

Gugeler, Russell A. *Combat Actions in Korea* (Office of the Chief of Military History, 1954).

Hastings, Max. *The Korean War* (1987).

Hermes, Walter G. *Truce Tent and Fighting Front* (Office of the Chief of Military History, 1966).

Knox, Donald. *The Korean War*, 1, *An Oral History*, 2, *Uncertain Victory* (1985–1988).

Lowe, Peter. *The Origins of the Korean War* (1988).

McAleer, John, and Billy Dickson. *Unit Pride* (1981).

Mentzer, Raymond A., Jr. "Research from the Battlefield: Military History Detachments in Wartime Korea," *Army History* 19 (Summer 1991).

Mossman, Billy C. *Ebb and Flow: November 1950-July 1951, U.S. Army in the Korean War* (Center of Military History, Washington: 1990).

Rees, David. *Korea: The Limited War* (1964).

Russ, Martin. *The Last Parallel: A Marine's War Journal* (1957).

Sawyer, Robert K. *Military Advisors in Korea: KMAG in Peace and War* (Office of the Chief of Military History, Washington: 1962).

Schnabel, James F. *Policy and Direction: The First Year* (Office of the Chief of Military History, Washington: 1972).

West, Philip. "Interpreting the Korean War," *Journal of Military History*, 53 (1989).

Hodge, John R. (1893–1963)

Lieutenant General John Reed Hodge was the commander of the U.S. Armed Forces in Korea (USAFIK) during the period of military occupation from September 1945 until the formal establishment of the Republic of Korea (ROK) in August 1948. Born in Golconda, Illinois, he attended Southern Illinois Teachers' College from 1912 to 1913 before enrolling at the University of Illinois to study architectural engineering. After the U.S. declared war on Germany in April 1917, Hodge began his military career at Fort Sheridan's Advanced Officers Training School, earning an infantry reserve commission in August 1917. He traveled to France as part of the advanced detachment of the 5th Infantry Division, but after additional training, joined the 61st Infantry as a signal and liaison officer. During the St. Mihiel and Meuse-Argonne offensives, Hodge saw combat as a company commander. After World War I, he was a professor of military science and tactics at Mississippi A&M College.

Hodge went to Infantry School in 1925, joined the 27th Infantry in Hawaii the following year, and served with the 18th Infantry beginning in 1929. From 1932 to 1936, he attended the Chemical Warfare School, Command and General Staff School, the Army War College, and Air Corps Tactical School. After serving with the

23d Division as a battalion commander, Major Hodge spent five years on the War Department general staff. In 1941 he was plans and training officer and then chief of staff for the 7th Army Corps. After Pearl Harbor, Brigadier General Hodge became assistant commander of the 25th "Tropic Lightning" Infantry Division and fought at Guadalcanal before assuming command of the American Division in April 1943. Wounded at Bougainville, he also saw heavy action in the Solomons. In April 1944, Hodge became commander of the XXIV Corps, a unit formed to conduct amphibious operations against the Japanese in the Marianas and the Carolines. After a change in strategy, his unit fought with distinction at Leyte and on Okinawa. During World War II, Hodge earned a reputation as a "soldier's soldier," sharing hardships with his troops at the front.

During August 1945, the War Department separated Hodge and his XXIV Corps from the Tenth Army and instructed it to occupy Korea south of the 38th parallel for the purpose of accepting the surrender of half of an estimated 375,000 Japanese troops. He received no detailed guidelines for the occupation from Washington for six months, making more difficult his task of responding to the revolutionary climate existing in Korea on his arrival. From the outset, Hodge's highest priority was preserving law and order. Because he lacked administrative training, political experience, or familiarity with Korean history and culture, he committed numerous errors while occupation commander. (If he did not actually say early in the occupation that, "To me Japs and Koreans are the same breed of cat," it is significant that he was widely believed to have done so, and to have thus caused deep offense).

Acting on instructions, Hodge at first retained Japanese administrative personnel, but removed them after angry Korean protests. More significant was his reliance on wealthy and conservative Korean landlords and businessmen, including some who had collaborated with the Japanese. Unable to achieve progress toward ending the partition at the 38th parallel, Hodge worried constantly about Soviet occupation of northern Korea and the threat it posed to his command. Simple, blunt, and direct in approach, he advocated early U.S. military withdrawal from Korea and was a persistent opponent of trusteeship.

Hodge neither understood nor dealt effectively with the challenge of Korean political factionalism. Shortly after his arrival, he requested a meeting with two representatives from each party and was understandably shocked when 1,200 Koreans responded to his invitation. Hoping to promote political stability, Hodge then assisted Syngman Rhee and other Korean conservative exile leaders in their return to Korea in late 1945. Instead, political turmoil and violence increased and, in desperation, Hodge suggested his own recall, offering to serve as a "sacrificial goat." Ignoring Rhee's demand to hold quick elections for a separate government in the South, he then tried to fashion a moderate political coalition in 1946. In another major blunder, Hodge proceeded to undermine the moderates but without placating the conservatives. Rhee never forgave Hodge, and was instrumental in the general's relief and return to the United States. Following his recall, Hodge assumed various posts until his appointment as commander of Army field forces in June 1952, a post he held until his retirement the next year.

James I. Matray

Bibliography

Cumings, Bruce. *The Origins of the Korean War* (1981).
Dobbs, C.M. *The Unwanted Symbol* (1981).
Matray, J.I. *The Reluctant Crusade* (Honolulu, 1985).

Hoge, William M. (1894–1979)

The son of a principal of a military school and later the co-owner of another military school, William Morris Hoge graduated from the United States Military Academy at West Point in 1916. Commissioned in the Corps of Engineers, Hoge served with the 7th Engineers Regiment during World War I in France. There he fought in the St. Mihiel and Meuse-Argonne offensives, rose to the command of a battalion, and earned the Distinguished Service Cross and the Silver Star for bravery. Between the world wars, Hoge held engineer assignments in the United States and the Philippines and graduated from the Massachusetts Institute of Technology with a bachelor's degree in civil engineering in 1922, and from the Command and General Staff School in 1928.

After the United States entered World War II, Hoge was given the difficult job of building the northern section of the military road across northwest Canada to Alaska (later known as the ALCAN Highway). Transferred from this work in September 1942, Hoge was successively assigned to the 9th Armored Division, the 4th Engineer Special Brigade, and the 5th Engineer Special Brigade until the spring of 1944. On D-Day, now holding the rank of brigadier general, he commanded the Provisional Engineer Special Brigade Group, which landed with the assault divisions on Omaha beach, Normandy, and established and operated the beachhead. In October 1944, Hoge assumed command of Combat Command B of the 9th Armored Division and led it through tough fighting around St. Vith in the Battle of the Bulge. During the final stages of the war in Europe, Hoge's tank and infantry forces seized the Ludendorff railroad bridge across the Thine River at Remagen, Germany, providing the allies with their first bridgehead east of the Rhine. By the war's end he was commanding the 4th Armored Division with the rank of major general and spearheading the American Third Army's drive across Germany into Czechoslovakia.

Following World War II, Hoge commanded the Engineer Center at Fort Belvoir, Virginia, and American forces in Trieste. When Major General Bryant E. Moore, commander of the IX Corps, died suddenly in February 1951, Lieutenant General Matthew B. Ridgway, commander of the Eighth Army and an old and close friend, summoned Hoge to Korea as Moore's replacement. As commander of the IX Corps until November 1951, Hoge displayed the intelligence, tenacity, and aggressiveness for which he had become famous during World War II in the battles in central Korea that resulted in the stabilization of the fighting near the 38th parallel. Hoge was blistering in his criticism of ROK Army leadership after the successive debacles that befell the 6th ROK division during the Chinese 1951 spring offensive. This criticism was endorsed by Generals Ridgway and Van Fleet and made it impossible for ROK President Syngman Rhee to obtain his requested ten new South Korean divisions. Thereafter, Hoge commanded the Fourth Army in San Antonio, Texas, the Seventh Army in Germany, and American ground forces in Europe before retiring in 1955 as a four-star general. After retiring, Hoge served as chairman of the board for Interlake Iron Company in Cleveland, Ohio. He died at Fort Leavenworth, Kansas, on October 29, 1979.

John Kennedy Ohl

Bibliography

Blair, Clay. *The Forgotten War: America in Korea, 1950–1953* (1987).

Cole, Hugh M. *The Ardennes: Battle of the Bulge* (Office of the Chief of Military History, Washington: 1965).

Greenwood, John T. "General Bill Hoge and the Alaska Highway," in *The Alaska Highway: Papers of the 40th Anniversary Symposium*, ed. by Kenneth Coates (Vancouver, BC: 1982).

MacDonald, Charles B. *The Last Offensive* (Office of the Chief of Military History, Washington: 1973).

Mossman, Billy C. *Ebb and Flow, November 1950–July 1951, United States Army in the Korean War* (1990).

Home Front, U.S.

When President Harry S. Truman committed U.S. military forces to the Korean War, the nation united behind its chief executive. Five days after the invasion of South Korea by North Korea on 25 June 1950, Truman had made the momentous decision to send U.S. ground troops to the aid of the Republic of Korea (ROK). (The commitment of supplies, air, and naval forces was almost a foregone conclusion given the blatant nature of the attack on what was a U.N.-recognized sovereign nation and a near ally of the U.S.) By the end of that conflict Truman's popularity, as judged by the public opinion polls, had reached a record low. Most of this deterioration was, of course, due to the fact that the war, to quite literally everyone's surprise (including the "experts"), lasted for three years and ended with no U.S. victory.

At home the domestic counterpart of the Cold War and the new "hot war" in Korea was Red Scare II. (The first such scare came in 1919–1920, during the administration of Woodrow Wilson, when hundreds of radicals, in the wake of the Bolshevik Revolution and domestic bombings, were rounded up by the authorities or irate citizens, imprisoned, often abused, or even sent "back to Russia where they belong!") With American troops fighting in Korea against Communist forces, the Cold War naturally reached its apex during the Korean War. That war, coupled to such other overseas events as the "loss" of China (1949), the Czech coup (1948), and the Berlin Blockade (1948–1949), brought many Americans to the conclusion that the Communist world was in aggressive opposition to the values of the Free World.

The second red scare had its post–World War II origins in a number of espionage rumors that had led President Truman to issue an executive order in March 1947 that called for federal government officials to sign a loyalty oath or be fired. Clearly, the president's move was political; the growing anti-Communist movement in the country was being politicized by the Republicans, and as the 1948 elections approached, Truman feared being labeled as the candidate who was "soft on communism." Truman's strong anti-Communist stance, however, added to the intensity of the growing Cold War internationally and accelerated anti-Communist fears at home.

American anti-communism was further fueled when the Soviets detonated an atomic "device" in August of 1949, several years before the event was expected by the "experts," ending America's four-year monopoly on "The Bomb." Truman's response was to authorize the development of the even more fearsome hydrogen bomb. To most Americans, the loss of the nuclear monopoly demonstrated that Communist influence and power was expanding rapidly. And it seemed obvious that the only way the "backward" Soviet Union could have carried out its nuclear scientific feat was through espionage.

Thus by early 1950, the fear of communism had turned into something that in some quarters resembled panic. In that year a number of very visible court cases brought the Communist "threat" home to Americans.

Alger Hiss was convicted in early 1950 for lying to a grand jury as to his part in a prewar Communist spy ring. Hiss, president of the prestigious Carnegie Endowment for International Peace, had served in several federal government positions and was a member of the American delegation to the Yalta Conference (where he alone in that delegation noted the sweet reasonableness of the Soviets). The case originated in 1948, when Whittaker Chambers, a self-confessed and somewhat seedy Soviet agent before becoming an editor at *Time* magazine, told the House Un-American Activities Committee (HUAC) that Hiss had given him a number of secret documents in the late 1930s. Hiss stoutly denied the charges and sued Chambers for libel; Chambers responded by producing the documents in question. Hiss was tried for perjury (not for spying—the statute of limitations had rendered prosecution for espionage impossible), but for most Americans Hiss was in reality convicted of spying for the Soviet Union.

The Hiss case had at least two major consequences. First, it raised Representative Richard M. Nixon to national prominence. As a member of HUAC, Nixon spearheaded the congressional investigation that ultimately led to Hiss's conviction in 1950. Nixon made good use of his successes against the forces of communism to win election to the Senate in 1948. Four years later, when the Republicans were searching for a running mate for Dwight D. Eisenhower, Nixon seemed ideal at a time when Americans were embattled against communism in Korea. Second, the Hiss-Chambers case wounded the Democratic party and the Truman administration. Hiss had been a New Dealer, and a State Department official under Roosevelt and then Truman.

In 1950 Congress passed the McCarran Internal Security Act over Truman's veto. The act made it illegal "to perform any act which would substantially contribute to . . . the establishment of a totalitarian dictatorship." Truman characterized the bill as an "absurdity," having more in common with Moscow than with Washington. Even though the president might share the blame for originating the red scare, by 1950 he stood nearly alone in his opposition to the tactics of McCarthy in what was perhaps his own "finest hour." He often accused McCarthy of practicing the "big lie" and, accurately enough, termed him a "political gangster."

Over the ensuing decades the evidence indicates strongly that there were few Communists or even "fellow travelers" in the United States after 1948, and probably none in important positions. Certainly not one Communist was unmasked and convicted because of McCarthy's accusations. Yet in an indication of the temper of the times, the attorney general of an administration accused of being "soft on communism" improbably claimed that "Communists are everywhere—in factories, offices, butcher shops, on street corners, in private business, and each carried in himself the germs of death for society." Little wonder if Americans took to scrutinizing their butcher or hustling past street corner loungers.

As a result of the Hiss case, the "loss" of China, and the Soviet bomb, not to mention the Czech coup or the Berlin Blockade and war in Korea, the Republicans were able to make anti-communism into a political issue that had the potential to inflict a staggering blow to the Democrats.

Truman's attempts to limit the war to Korea were not helped by the apocalyptic imaginings and near-hysterical outbursts of not only General Douglas MacArthur, but by congressmen of both parties and commentators

H

who should have known better. These fears reached a climax in late 1950 with the Chinese Communist intervention across the Yalu River. Congressman F. Edward Hébert of Louisiana, for example, wrote Truman in early December 1950 that the nation was in "what I believe to be the Gethsemane of our existence," and Truman himself a few days later confided to his diary that "it looks like World War III is near." Early the following year Speaker of the House Sam Rayburn warned of "maybe the beginning of World War III." Normally sober military analyst Hanson W. Baldwin argued that the United States faced "the greatest danger in our history." To Baldwin, "Western Civilization and our American way of life" were imperiled as never before. *Colliers* magazine elaborated on these fears later in the year with a series of sensational fantasy accounts of a near-future Soviet-U.S. nuclear war that would leave Washington in ruins.

If the apocalypse tarried, the Republicans counted on burying the Democrats in the 1952 elections under "Communism, Korea, and Corruption," as the Republicans alliteratively put it. The GOP charged their opponents with being "soft on communism," "losing China," and generally allowing the "worldwide Communist conspiracy" to spread in the postwar years. "Corruption" was first uncovered in the Reconstruction Finance Corporation, where "five percenters" took gifts for assistance in securing lucrative government contracts; the payoffs seem to have been more in goods than money, and included mink coats and freezers. Perhaps most infuriating to Americans, who generally enjoyed one of the world's best tax compliance records, was the revelation of widespread corruption in the Internal Revenue Service itself.

About as damaging to the Democrats were the riveting televised hearings on organized crime conducted by Democratic Tennessee Senator Estes Kefauver. The Kefauver Committee began its investigations by examining the nation's organized crime syndicates, but in the process it turned up relationships between Democratic party leaders and a number of notorious crime figures.

Truman's only culpability lay in his not acting quickly enough to cut the party's losses and pushing to bring the malefactors to justice. But the Republicans could point out, of course, that it was Truman who had in most cases appointed those malefactors in the first place. By the summer of 1952, "the mess in Washington" was a phrase that reverberated nationwide.

As if this were not enough for the hapless Truman administration, the Korean War remained a seemingly intractable problem. American soldiers continued to fight and die on the Asian mainland in a war far from home that was bogged down in mud, snow, and negotiations. While the war fueled the economy and reduced unemployment, it also ignited inflation, a nemesis of the Truman administration since 1945. Truman reacted by controlling wages and prices through the establishment of a number of World War II–type regulatory agencies such as the Office of Price Stabilization. But even this effort later gave Republicans the opportunity to charge that, once again, the Democrats had "socialistic" designs on the economy.

Nonetheless, Truman's anti-inflation initiatives were relatively successful after the first year of the war until the U.S. Steel strike of 1952 threatened to unleash an inflationary cycle, strangling the economy and hampering the war effort. Truman's response was characteristically both impulsive and decisive. Moving to take over the steel mills, he relied on what he believed to be the authority of his war powers in time of emergency, particularly the authority to seize a significant industry that refused to give priority to war production. But the Supreme Court found against Truman on the grounds that the situation in 1952 was based on a labor dispute and not a question of war production.

As the 1952 elections approached, many believed that Truman would run for a third term. (He had filled out Franklin Roosevelt's unique third term, and at any rate the two-term limiting twenty-second Amendment to the U.S. Constitution charitably exempted the incumbent president.) But as early as 1950 Truman had written in his diary that renomination was not in his plans. In fact, renomination in 1952 would have been difficult for the president, and clearly his election would have proven nearly impossible—despite the memory of the glorious miracle victory of 1948. By 1952, the administration's liabilities were enormous, and the president's popularity at record lows in the polls.

Such was the charged atmosphere for the presidential elections of 1952. Most conservative Republicans wanted Senator Robert A. Taft of Ohio because of his integrity and his isolationism. The Eastern liberal/internationalists in the party strongly supported General Dwight Eisenhower, then head of NATO. "Ike" did have strong credentials: war hero, no political record (there had been some uncertainty earlier as to whether the nonvoting "Ike" was a Republican, Democrat, or independent), and hence no political enemies. But the conservative Republicans, even if they personally liked "Ike," distrusted his supporters—liberal, Eastern internationalists like Thomas Dewey (who had already lost two elections for them in 1944 and 1948) and Senator Hugh Scott of Pennsylvania. But the GOP convention almost grudgingly nominated Eisenhower, realizing that he was their best chance of winning. The general ran a fairly clean campaign, a major feat given the heated atmosphere of 1952. Nonetheless, he refused to repudiate McCarthy's even more outrageous charges, such as that Ike's wartime superior, the impeccable General George C. Marshall, was somehow soft on communism. (Eisenhower lamely confided to his intimates that "I won't get in the gutter with that guy.")

The real low-road was taken by Ike's running mate, Richard Nixon, who, being young, bellicose, and a professional politician, could offset Ike's age, charm, and political innocence. Nixon hammered away at what he termed the Democrats' "twenty years of treason." But he soon found his own virtue called into question when it was charged that he had taken illegal campaign money. Nixon responded by going on television, baring his soul and wallet, claiming rather bizarrely that his wife owned a "Republican cloth coat" (a mink coat had been one of the bribes featured in the Truman administration's scandals), and noting that they drove a 1952 Oldsmobile. But come what may, the two Nixon daughters would never give up their adorable cocker spaniel, "Checkers," which was indeed a gift. Perhaps this was all beside the point, but it was very effective theater. Nixon concluded, to Ike's apparent consternation, by exhorting his viewers to phone in their votes as to whether he should stay on the ticket. The decision was thus cleverly taken out of Ike's hands, and the public overwhelmingly phoned in their votes for Nixon to stay on. Ike summoned Nixon, whom he hardly knew, to his presence, and greeted his running mate with the words, "You're my boy," at which Nixon fell on Ike's shoulder and dissolved in public tears.

The unenviable task of running against Eisenhower in 1952 fell to the democratic governor of Illinois, Adlai Stevenson. Stevenson was in many ways an attractive candidate, articulate and intelligent. But he had serious problems in trying to defend Truman's record without becoming identified with it. He could also never shake the anti-intellectual animosities he aroused by his urbane wit and delivery. He and his followers were "eggheads," "longhairs" (the latter hardly fitting the bald Stevenson). There were also ugly undertones, with references to "Harvard lace-liberals," Stevenson was termed "Adelade" and accused of using "teacup words." No one ever accused Eisenhower of being an intellectual or questioned his manhood.

Eisenhower became the inevitable winner when he proclaimed that "I shall go to Korea." Stevenson was boxed in and could hardly reply "me too." By late 1952 Americans were sullenly sick of Korea. Whatever Eisenhower would do about the war afterward, the point to most voters was that he was ready to do something besides talk interminably with the enemy at Panmunjom. In fact, most Americans by then were apparently even ready to contemplate using "The Bomb" if that was what it would take to end the war and "Communist Aggression." Here they seemed to be following the unpublicized contingency plans of their federal government, of both Truman and Eisenhower.

Eisenhower indeed went to Korea, and then settled for an armistice that formalized the battlefield stalemate. After the unconditional surrenders of America's enemies that ended World War II, the armistice of 27 July 1953 was disappointing indeed. Yet Americans were so weary of the war that there was hardly a murmur of complaint throughout the nation. Whether it was ended by bombing China or by a truce seemed to make little difference. The election of Eisenhower and the negotiated ending of the war in Korea made the doctrines of the containment of communism, as opposed to "victory," less suspect as being "un-American." McCarthy himself barely survived the end of the war, being censured by the Senate a little more than a year after the armistice was signed. In 1957 he died of drink and disappointment.

Yet relatively little of the crises and thunder of these tumultuous years touched Americans profoundly. Only the young were directly affected by the Korean War, and many of these escaped military service altogether through an iniquitous system of collegiate educational deferments that saw many a young man claim a previously unsuspected interest in lengthy and abstruse graduate school work. Certainly very few Americans were affected by McCarthyism; only the merest handful were pro-Communist or liberal or bold enough to attract the atten-

H

tions of local superpatriots or ideological vigilantes. No rationing was ever introduced during the war, and higher taxes and inflation were more than counterbalanced by the wartime employment boom. Americans went about their business relatively untroubled by events overseas or in Washington, D.C. They were far more affected, albeit almost without realizing it, by the most significant development in America during the second half of the twentieth century, the suburbanization of their nation.

Constantly exhorted by public figures to realize that they lived in uniquely challenging times, Americans remained nonetheless resolutely attached to their status quo. For example, they seemed convinced of their nation's "progress" on "the race question." Only the U.S. armed forces realized by the early 1950s that racial segregation, let alone racial discrimination, was impossible in a modern society and put an end to this blight a full decade before the rest of the nation.

The younger generation of the early 1950s was seemingly characterized by silence or apathy for the rest of the decade. Its values were strongly middle-class, even middle-aged, symbolized by its choice of heroes through a *Life* magazine survey of 1950: Lincoln, Franklin Roosevelt, Roy Rogers, Joe DiMaggio, Babe Ruth, MacArthur, Florence Nightingale, Doris Day, and Sister Elizabeth Kenny.

Intellectuals read David Reisman's *The Lonely Crowd* and debated its argument that nineteenth-century Americans had been "inner-directed," full of ambition and guided by external goals of success and respectability while the twentieth-century American was supposedly soft, pliant, and shapeless, his individualism almost gone. From his school training on, the new American had become "other-directed," reluctant to go against the group. The modern American was a conformist. The fact that the word "conformist" was almost always used pejoratively in the 1950s casts some doubt on at least the latter half of Reisman's thesis, but it enlivened "serious" contemporary literature and faculty-room conversations.

The average American household spent four and one-half hours a day viewing television by 1950. In that year, the highest rated TV program was the *Texaco Star Theater*; in 1951 it was *Arthur Godfrey's Talent Scouts*, and in 1952–1953, CBS's phenomenal *I Love Lucy*. The Korean War obtruded minimally on television programming, but the wartime year of 1951 did witness the technological feat of coast-to-coast TV broadcasting, inaugurated, appropriately enough, by Edward R. Murrow's news program, *See It Now*. (Perhaps less portentously, in 1951 Swanson and Sons introduced the first frozen "TV dinner.") And 14 June 1951 saw the unveiling of the world's first commercial computer, designed for the U.S. Census Bureau—UNIVAC I. This was a fabulously expensive and complex electronic monster with a control panel described by a reporter as "a contraption that looks like a combination [of] pipe organ console, a linotype machine and a telephone switchboard," controlled by a "Buck Rogers typewriter." Inexpensive hand-held computers that could do everything UNIVAC could and more were unimaginable in 1951, and decades in the future.

If most Americans during the Korean War seemed characterized by apathy and a lack of critical inquiry, it should be remembered that every adult citizen of that time had passed through the Great Depression and World War II. They were assured that "The American Way of Life" had survived those fiery trials and was, if anything, better and the stronger for it. It would take more than the trumpeted apocalyptic threat of global communism or a second-class war in far-off Korea to shake such assurance.

Gary A. Donaldson/Richard Voeltz

Bibliography
Chafe, W.H. *The Unfinished Journey* (1986).
Diggins, John Patrick. *The Proud Decades: America in War and Peace, 1941–1960* (1988).
Donovan, Robert J. *Tumultuous Years: The Presidency of Harry S. Truman, 1949–1953* (1982).
Gaddis, John L. *Strategies of Containment: A Critical Appraisal of Post War American Security Policy* (1982).
Hart, J. *When the Going Was Good: American Life in the Fifties* (1982).
O'Neill, W.L. *American High: The Years of Confidence, 1945–1960* (1968).
Reichard, G.W. *Politics as Usual: The Age of Truman and Eisenhower* (1988).

I

Inchon Landings, 1950

The amphibious assault at Inchon on 15 September 1950 was General Douglas MacArthur's Korean War masterstroke. Quickly planned despite opposition from his superiors in Washington, it was a brilliant military coup that turned the tide of the war, temporarily. MacArthur, as United Nations Commander in Korea actually had begun to envision this end run behind enemy lines in the dispiriting early days of the war when South Korean troops were in full retreat from Seoul in the face of the North Korean initial invasion.

By early August of 1950 UN troops were restricted to the Pusan perimeter. Even as those forces endeavored to blunt the enemy offensives to secure the vital port of Pusan, MacArthur was preparing to open a second front, believing that this was preferable to a frontal breakout along the perimeter. An attack elsewhere would present the North Koreans with a two-front war. MacArthur was confident that his forces could hold the perimeter and so began to divert resources for an invasion force. He also activated X Corps under the command of his prickly Chief of Staff Edward Almond.

The point selected for the invasion was Inchon, Korea's second largest port, and only fifteen miles from Seoul. This area was the most important road and rail hub in Korea and a vital link in the main NKA supply line to their forces along the Pusan perimeter. Cutting that line at Inchon would starve NKA forces to the south. Kimpo Airfield, near Inchon-Seoul was also one of the few hard-surfaced airfields in all of Korea. In addition, the capture of Seoul would be a severe psychological and political blow for the North Koreans, and the sort of grand gesture that so appealed to the UN Commander. As MacArthur's intelligence chief grandiloquently

put it: "MacArthur courageously set his eyes on a greater goal; to salvage the reputation of Allied Arms, to bring into sharper focus the colossal threat of Imperialist Mongoloid pan-Slavism under the guise of Communism, and to smash its current challenge in one great blow." (Charles Willoughby, *MacArthur*, 347–348).

MacArthur initially planned to put his 1st Cavalry Division ashore at Inchon as early as July 22. Events overtook this, and planning was abandoned on July 10. That same day MacArthur met in Tokyo with Lieutenant-General Lemuel Shepherd, commander of the Pacific Fleet Marine Force. With JCS approval, Shepherd said the whole 1st Marine Division could be in Korea within six weeks and in action by September 15. MacArthur immediately requested the two remaining regiments of the division. Its 5th Regiment, about to sail from San Diego, was already earmarked for action along the Perimeter where it would be redesignated the 1st Provisional Marine Brigade. At first the JCS agreed to send only the 1st regiment but, on August 10, it allowed MacArthur the 7th as well; however, only the 1st and 5th were at Inchon on D-Day.

Planning for the Inchon Invasion, code-named Operation Chromite, (originally Operation Bluehearts) began on August 12 and was completed in only one month. It was carried out by the inter-service Joint Strategic Plans and Operations Group, under control of the Operations Division of the Far East Command. The Special Planning Staff of JSPOG emerged as the nucleus of the staff of X Corps. The corps was activated on August 26, the same day that MacArthur appointed Major General Edward M. Almond, his chief of staff, to command it. Low morale in the Eighth Army may have led MacArthur to divide military authority in Korea; X Corps was entirely separate from Eighth Army, a decision that would have unfortunate subsequent repercussions.

Objectives of the operation were: neutralization of Wolmi-do, the fortified island controlling access to Inchon harbor (regarded as essential by the Marines to protect the subsequent assault on Inchon); the landing at Inchon and capture of the city; seizure of Kimpo Airfield; and, finally, the capture of Seoul.

The only real opposition to the idea of a second front came from Eighth Army. Its staff was strongly opposed to weakening the Perimeter and believed that if reinforcements intended for X Corps were sent to them they could defeat the North Koreans without what appeared a risky grandstand play. Apart from EUSAK there was general agreement on a second front, but not on the place; only MacArthur favored Inchon.

The Joint Chiefs of Staff and most of MacArthur's subordinate commanders, including all the key Navy and Marine commanders in the Far East, opposed Inchon. Both the tide and terrain made the operation extremely hazardous. Tidal shifts at Inchon were sudden and dramatic; the range of spring tides was from an average of twenty-three feet to a maximum of thirty-three. At ebb tide the harbor turned into mud flats, extending as far as three miles from the shoreline. While most landing craft drew twenty-three feet, the LSTs—considered vital in getting heavy equipment to the shore quickly—drew twenty-nine feet. The Navy estimated that there was a very narrow range around two dates, September 15 and October 11, when the spring tides would be high enough to let the LSTs gain Inchon. Even then they would have only a three-hour period on each tide in which to enter or leave the port. This meant that supplies could be landed during only 6 hours each 24 hour period. Flying Fish channel was narrow, winding, and studded with reefs and shoals; its five-knot current was also a problem. One sunken ship here would block all traffic. There were no beaches, only twelve-foot sea walls that would have to be scaled. The Marines would have to take Wolmi-do eleven hours in advance of the assault on Inchon. At the landing site in Inchon itself there were few cargo-handling facilities. Undamaged, Inchon had a capacity of 6,000 tons a day, only ten percent that of Pusan. Also, steep hills from the water would allow enemy defenders to fire down on the attackers. All of these conditions precluded a night assembly of the invasion force; the main landing would have to take place in the evening, with only two hours of daylight to secure a perimeter ashore.

Suggestions were made for landing either at Kunsan to the south or Chinnampo to the north. But Kunsan was too close to the Pusan perimeter; and Chinnampo, Pyongyang's port, was too far north. Posung-Myon, thirty miles south of Inchon, was rejected because it had an inadequate road net from the beaches.

MacArthur met with his critics in a final dramatic meeting in Tokyo's Dai-Ichi building on August 23. His commanders, Lieutenant-General G.E. Stratemeyer, Vice-Admiral C. Turner Joy, and General Almond were there. Army Chief of Staff General J. Lawton Collins and Chief of Naval Operations Admiral Forrest P. Sherman were on hand from Washington to express "grave reservations" by the JCS to the operation. The Navy and Marine contingent included Admiral Arthur Radford, Commander in Chief Pacific CINCPAC; Vice-Admiral A.D. Struble; and Rear Admiral James H. Doyle; Generals Shepherd and Oliver P. Smith were there for the Marines.

Doyle, an expert on amphibious operations, began the meeting by listing Navy objections. "The best I can say is that Inchon is not impossible," he concluded. General Collins expressed reservations about withdrawing the Marine Brigade from Pusan perimeter and the possibility that, once ashore, X Corps might be pinned down at Inchon. He preferred Kunsan.

Finally, MacArthur spoke for about forty-five minutes. He said he recognized the hazards but had confidence in the Navy and Marines to overcome them. To inject reinforcements on the Pusan perimeter might risk stalemate. An envelopment from a landing at Kunsan would be too narrow. The fact that the enemy did not anticipate an assault at Inchon would help assure its success: "The very arguments you have made as to the impracticabilities involved will tend to ensure for me the element of surprise. For the enemy commander will reason that no one would be so brash as to make such an attempt. . . ." If the war in Korea was lost the fate of Europe would be jeopardized. He concluded dramatically, "I can almost hear the ticking of the second hand of destiny. We must act now or we will die. . . .We shall land at Inchon, and I shall crush them."

Although some senior officers at the briefing remained unconvinced, it was the turning point in the debate. General Shepherd made one subsequent futile effort to persuade MacArthur to choose Posung-Myon, where Navy frogmen had landed and found beach conditions suitable.

On August 28 MacArthur received formal approval from the JCS for the Inchon landing. The Chiefs took the unusual precaution of securing the written approval of President Truman for the operation; this undoubtedly reflected fears that, if the operation were unsuccessful, they would be held responsible. There is no indication that Truman ever believed it might fail.

The major units of X Corps were two divisions: the 7th Infantry and the 1st Marine. Support units were the 92nd and 96th Field Artillery Battalions (155mm howitzers); the 50th Antiaircraft Artillery Battalion; the 19th Engineer Combat Group; and the 2nd Engineer Special Brigade. The 7th was the one remaining division of Eighth Army not sent to Korea from Japan. Commanded by Major-General David G. Barr, it was seriously understrength and was augmented by all available reinforcements, including Koreans. More than 8,600 Korean recruits arrived in Japan before the division embarked for Inchon; approximately 100 were assigned to each rifle company and artillery battery. The 7th Division strength on embarkation was 24,815 men, including the Koreans. The 1st Marine Division, commanded by Major-General O.P. Smith, was made a heavy division with the addition of the Marine Brigade, redesignated the 5th Marines. On invasion day the 1st Marine Division numbered 25,040 men, including 2,760 Army troops and 2,786 Korean marines attached; with the 7th Marines, organic Marine strength increased by 4,000 men. General Walker was upset that the Brigade would be withdrawn from the line with the North Koreans planning a new assault against the Perimeter in early September. He secured agreement that it would be released only at the last possible moment and that a regiment of the 7th Army Division would be kept in Pusan Harbor as long as possible to act as a floating reserve.

The marines considered it vital that Inchon be successful, for many questioned the Corps' viability. A year before, General Omar Bradley had observed that large-scale amphibious landings were a thing of the past. As General Shepherd put it, "The Marine Corps was fighting for its very existence."

Over 200 agents inserted into the Inchon area reported approximately 500 North Korean Army troops on Wolmi-do, 1,500 around Inchon, and another 500 at Kimpo Airfield. There were, however, major reinforcements only a few hours away, in the southeast.

The final Inchon plan was ready by September 4. On D-Day the tides would be at 0659 and 1919 with a maximum of thirty-one feet of water in the evening. A battalion landing team of 5th Marines was to be put ashore on the morning tide at Green Beach on Wolmi-do at 0630. The major landings would be at 1730 that evening, at Red Beach, Inchon's sea front, and at Blue Beach, three miles to the southeast, in order to command rail and road lines from Seoul. Eight LSTs would follow the assault force with heavy equipment and landing teams.

Deception to confuse the enemy as to the intended landing site included bombardment of Chinnampo by a British naval task force and a landing party put ashore at Kunsan from a British frigate. Miraculously, although the destination of Inchon was not closely held, apparently no word of it got to the enemy command. In fact, around Tokyo, Operation Chromite was known as "operation common knowledge."

Joint Task Force Seven, commanded by Admiral Struble (on the cruiser *Rochester*), was the naval force organized for the Inchon landings. Rear Admiral Doyle, second in command, was on the command ship *Mount McKinley*. Each of seven subordinate task forces was assigned specific objectives. More than 230 ships took part in the operation.

The armada of vessels carrying nearly 70,000 men was a makeshift affair. It included ships from Australia, Canada, New Zealand, France, Holland, and Great Britain. Marine aircraft from two escort carriers, naval aircraft from the *Boxer*, and British aircraft from a light Royal Navy carrier were to provide air support over the landing area. Thirty-seven of forty-seven LSTs in the invasion had been nastily recalled from Japanese merchant service, and were manned by Japanese crews.

Loading was delayed for thirty-six hours by the 110 mph winds of Typhoon Jane on September 3. There was some damage but deadlines were met. On September 13, the Task Force, now at sea, was assaulted by typhoon Kezia with 60 mph winds on September 13, although, again, no serious damage resulted.

The convoy reached the Inchon Narrows just before dawn on September 15, the fifth day of air and naval bombardment of Wolmi-do. The naval Gunfire Support Group was made up of four cruisers and six destroyers. At 0633 the 5th Marines went ashore, MacArthur observ-

I

ing the landing from the bridge of the *Mount McKinley*. Resistance was light; the American flag was raised on Radio Hill at 0655 and Wolmi-do and nearby Sowolmi-do were both secured by noon. A total of 108 enemy were killed; 136 were captured. Approximately 100 more who refused to surrender were sealed in caves by tank dozers. Marine casualties were only seventeen wounded.

The Marines requested permission to continue their advance across the four-hundred-yard causeway to Inchon, but were refused. The invaders were now cut off from the fleet by a vast sea of mud. There was little enemy fire from Inchon and covering aircraft could detect no enemy reinforcements en route.

At 1430 the cruisers and destroyers in the invasion force began a shore bombardment of Inchon. Enemy fire was sporadic and light. At 1645 the first wave of landing craft left the transports for Inchon. At 1731 the first Americans climbed up ladders onto the seawall. As on Wolmi-do, most of the defenders were still in a state of shock from the bombardment.

The sun was setting and visibility was further inhibited by smoke and drizzle. Careful plans went awry and were forgotten as the landing craft made for the waterfront. Some in the second wave grounded and the men were forced to wade ashore, but within six hours the Marines were firmly lodged in Inchon. Eight specially loaded LSTs also made it to the seawall, where they disgorged jeeps, trucks, tanks, and supplies.

The Marine landing force sustained casualties on D-Day of 20 KIA, 1 missing, and 174 wounded. On the morning of the 16th, 1st and 5th regiments linked up ashore and began the drive east to Seoul; the ROK Marines were left behind to mop up Inchon. Early on September 17 a column of six enemy T-34s and 200 infantry was ambushed by 5th Marines. By the night of the 17th much of Kimpo airfield had been taken; by the 18th it was completely in Marine hands. That same day, the 7th Infantry Division started landing at Inchon; and on the 21st, the remaining Marine regiment, the 7th, disembarked. By the end of the 19th, 5th Marines had cleared the entire south bank of the Han River on their front; they crossed the river a day later but were soon slowed by determined enemy resistance. The 1st Regiment encountered difficult fighting with a regiment of the NKA 18th division on the 22nd, before it too reached the Han.

On September 16, a day after the Inchon invasion, General Walker's Eighth Army began its breakout along the Pusan perimeter and drove north. The Inchon and Pusan forces made contact on 26 September at Osan, site of America's disastrous first land battle of the war.

MacArthur and Almond were determined to capture Seoul on 25 September, which would have been three months to the day after the North Korean invasion. Almond had made it clear to General Smith that the city must fall by that date. But the U.S. flag, soon to be replaced by that of the UN, was not raised over the capitol building by the 5th Marines until the afternoon of 27 September (although Almond had prematurely announced, just before midnight on the 25th, that the city had fallen. On 29 September MacArthur presided over an emotional ceremony in the gutted capitol building marking the liberation of Seoul and the return of the Rhee government.

The victory of the Inchon-Seoul campaign greatly increased MacArthur's self-confidence (if he were in need of such an increase). He now tended to dismiss any reservations from Washington about his plans. The North Korean Army was so badly beaten that he was certain that the war for Korea had been won and that it was just a matter of mopping up. He did not, of course, anticipate the massive Chinese intervention that would in a matter of weeks tarnish his Inchon glory.

The following decades have also seen some criticism of MacArthur's "master stroke." Professor Karl Larew has even claimed that Inchon was unnecessary. Eighth Army was already strong enough to break out of its Pusan perimeter bonds by the middle of September, and with the addition of Inchon-diverted X Corps, would have likely rolled up the North Koreans. Larew further claims that the diversion of X Corps actually weakened Eighth Army at the Perimeter. Finally, Inchon in some ways proved a psychological disaster. Its overwhelming success gave the U.N. Command "swelled heads" and vastly strengthened the calls for total victory. In fact, it could even be argued that the Inchon landings were not all that much of a risk. Even if the U.N. armada were stranded on the mudflats by some misadventure or scheduling foul-up, how much good would that have done the enemy? The U.N. by September 1950 had complete control of the air. Whatever element of surprise still existed for "Operation Common Knowledge" would have been lost, but protected by its overwhelming air cover, it is difficult to see how the North Koreans could have foiled this powerful amphibious force.

Withal, the Inchon landings were a brilliant success, almost flawlessly executed. For almost four decades these landings remained the only unambiguously successful, large-scale U.S. combat operation.

Spencer Tucker

Bibliography

Field, James A. *History of United States Naval Operations: Korea* (Office of Naval History, Washington: 1962).

Heinl, R.D. "The Inchon Landing (September 1950): A Case Study in Amphibious Planning" *Naval War College Review* 19 (May 1967).

Larew, K.G. "Inchon Not a Stroke of Genius or Even Necessary," *Army* (December 1988).

Montross, Lynn, and Nicholas Canzona. *The Inchon-Seoul Operation*, 2, of *U.S. Marine Corps Operations in Korea* (USMC Historical Branch, Washington: 1954–1957

Pirnie, Bruce. "The Inchon Landing: How Great Was the Risk?" *Joint Perspectives* 3 (Summer 1982).

Indian 60th Field Ambulance and Surgical Unit

When the United Nations Security Council denounced North Korea's aggression on June 25, 1950, and demanded a cease-fire at the 38th parallel, India's prime minister, Jawaharlal Nehru, following a nonalignment policy, instructed the Indian representative to the Security Council, Sir Bengal N. Rau, to support the resolution. Without further advice from Nehru, Sir Bengal also approved the second resolution, calling for collective action to counter the aggression. The Indian Parliament unanimously approved Rau's voting for U.N. support of South Korea.

Despite this diplomatic backing, India refused to commit military forces. Nehru considered the Korean conflict as basically the United States versus the Soviet Union and did not want to align with either side. Denouncing aggression, Nehru criticized North Korea, but insisted that he would not contribute to any expansion of the war. His goal was to secure a peaceful solution. Some contemporaries considered India's independent route as selfish, with Nehru concerned only for India's welfare, but diplomatic peers admired his tenacity in attempting not to antagonize either Eastern or Western powers.

India's army was small, poorly equipped, and overwhelmed by domestic concerns, and Nehru did not have troops available to send to Korea. He sought to attain neutrality while offering moral support to the U.N. forces, stating that India would be friendly to all countries who reciprocated.

As a concession for not supplying troops or equipment and to show some commitment to the Commonwealth, Nehru agreed to send the Indian 60th Field Ambulance and Surgical Unit in a humanitarian gesture reminiscent of the Mahatma Gandhi's humane policies. The 60th served the 27th British Commonwealth Brigade (later renamed the 28th Commonwealth Brigade). The unit arrived in Pusan on November 20, 1950, with 346 men and seventeen officers. Unlike other medical units, the Indian 60th Field Ambulance and Surgical Unit was split into two groups, with Lieutenant Colonel A.G. Rangaraj commanding the auxiliary to the main Commonwealth troops in battle zones and Major N.B. Banerjee overseeing medical aides in a ROK hospital at the rear in Taegu. Medical support personnel were needed both at the front and rear because the first winter was a critical time of the war.

Commander Rangaraj arrived with his men in Pyongyang in early December 1950. The Indian ambulance unit approached Pyongyang at the same time the Eighth Army was evacuating that city. Rangaraj, realizing that he had approximately six months' worth of medical supplies—a valuable and scarce commodity in Korea—on the troop train, urgently insisted that American forces aid him in securing the pharmaceuticals and supplies. American officers refused, claiming they had no transport, that no engines were available to pull the train to safety, and ordered him to destroy the medical goods.

Rangaraj resisted these orders and directed a scouting party to hunt for a working engine. The reconnaissance group found an engine and even more fortunately also located ample wood for fuel. Several of Rangaraj's men were able to drive the engine, maneuvering the supplies out of Pyongyang just before the last bridge over the Taedong River was destroyed.

The 60th formally joined the 27th Brigade on December 14, providing crucial medical support previously often unavailable. Before the Indian medical professionals arrived, each battalion had been responsible for evacuation. The Indians went into combat zones to treat the wounded; they also trained local citizens to work in hospitals and attempted to improve conditions, food, and medicine for Korean civilians.

Nehru had been upset when U.N. forces crossed the 38th parallel, although he was silent when the late 1950 Communist offensive took them once again across the parallel. Afraid that China would enter the war as the Indian ambassador in Peking had been warned, Nehru requested a cease-fire and demilitarized zone. Trying to appease China, Nehru declined to label China officially as an aggressor because he feared this rhetorical identification would only prolong the war. He also supported Communist China being included on the U.N. Security Council. When the U.N. did not heed his advice, Nehru claimed "The military mind has taken over." India continued to attempt to improve relations with China, serving as a mediator. Nehru also believed that Stalin perpetuated the war in order to weaken China, keeping that country subordinate to the Soviet Union.

Rangaraj led the Indian 60th until February 27, 1953, when he was replaced by Lieutenant Colonel M.B.K. Nair, who served until February 9, 1954. The Indians, who were proficient and highly regarded, made a significant contribution toward mitigating conditions for the wounded. Although they did not billet with forward units, the Indians evacuated casualties, working under artillery and mortar fire and bravely treating patients. Night casualties were often routed to the Indians instead of a MASH unit, and the Indians transported patients by jeep ambulance from camps to hospitals.

The Indians risked battle hazards and other dangers, as when a 60th ambulance was blown up by mines in May 1951. Throughout the Korean War the Indians performed an estimated 2,324 surgical operations on 195,000 outpatients and 20,000 inpatients, as well as providing nearly 5,000 dental examinations. Among the awards cited to the Indians were the Korean "Chungmu" and Distinguished Service Medal, several Indian awards, and American Bronze Stars. A total of 627 tributes were accumulated by the unit from its arrival in 1950 until its discharge on February 23, 1954.

The Indian 60th Field Ambulance and Surgical Unit remained above politics and was warmly regarded by U.N. forces and Korean civilians alike.

Elizabeth Schafer

Bibliography

Bowles, Chester. *Ambassador's Report* (1954).

Cowdrey, Albert E. *The Medic's War* (1987).

Dayal, Shiv. *India's Role in the Korean Question* (1959).

Nanda, B.R. *Indian Foreign Policy: The Nehru Years* (1976).

Republic of Korea Ministry of National Defense. *The History of the United Nations Forces in the Korean War* (1977).

Sheean, Vincent. "The Case for India," *Foreign Affairs*, 30 (October 1951).

Soward, F.H. "The Korean Crisis and the Commonwealth," *Pacific Affairs*, 24 (June 1951).

See also MEDICAL SERVICE IN THE KOREAN WAR

Indochina and the Korean War

The Korean War revolutionized American strategy by transforming the Cold War from a politico-economic struggle in Europe into a military struggle as well for the control of Asia. The parallel wars in Korea and Indochina became linked in a single effort to "contain Communism." By July 1952, Assistant Secretary of State for Far Eastern Affairs John Allison was declaring that "the struggle in Indochina is an integral part of the worldwide resistance to Communist attempts at conquest and subversion."

Indochinese nationalists (Vietminh) had declared their independence of France in September 1945. France nonetheless managed to reestablish control of much of its Far Eastern empire during 1946, and fighting broke out in November 1946. The Cold War pushed the United States, which had originally sympathized with the nationalists, into supporting France in Asia as part of an effort to support France in Europe. In February 1950 the United States recognized the anti-Communist client of the French, Bao Dai. Indochina got the lion's share of economic aid allotted to Southeast Asia even before the outbreak of the Korean War, although Secretary of State Dean Acheson also hoped that a "genuine nationalism" could be cultivated in the region.

However, the Korean War intensified efforts to shore up a key position in the containment of what American officials now took to be a generalized Communist aggression. The Chinese Communist victory in fall 1949 had put their forces on the frontiers of Indochina. The initiation of armistice negotiations in Korea (July 1951) aroused concern in Washington and Paris that Chinese troops freed from fighting in the north would soon make their presence felt in Indochina. A constant fear that China would increase its level of support to the Vietminh lurked behind all the optimistic assessments of the Indochina situation offered by French and American officials.

To counter this danger, the Americans pursued a dual policy. On the one hand, American officials recognized that anticolonialism would provide local forces for the war against the French, which could forestall direct Chinese intervention. The Americans pressed the French to mobilize Indochinese nationalism against Communism by granting real political independence to Vietnam, Laos, and Cambodia. The U.S. also pressed the French to shift responsibility for the war onto the shoulders of local national armies of these states in order to reduce the colonial character of the struggle against the Vietminh.

On the other hand, they sought to organize a more effective French military effort through the provision of military aid and by an increasingly close consultation on strategy. American aid poured in on a scale unparalleled in the rest of Southeast Asia, rising from one-sixth of the cost of the war in 1951 to one-third in 1952 to just over half in 1953 to about three-quarters in 1954. The aid became all the more necessary as the war came close to exhausting France's economic and military resources at a time when that country formed an essential part of the Western alliance.

The essential problem lay in the inability of the French to win a decisive victory. American diplomatic pressure since November 1950 had encouraged the French to formulate more effective strategies to deal with the insurgency. None had succeeded. A new round of American studies (September 1953) produced a comprehensive plan for victory. France accepted this program, then assigned its implementation to General Henre-Eugene Navarre. The "Navarre Plan" called for increased recruitment of local forces to support a joint campaign designed to break the power of the Vietminh within two years. The French made it clear that the "Navarre Plan" would form their last effort before turning either to negotiations or transferring responsibility to the Americans. American leaders grasped all the more eagerly at Navarre's confident statements that the Vietminh would be beaten in 1955 in that President Dwight D. Eisenhower had explicitly stated in February of 1954 his reluctance to send American forces to war in Indochina. Unwilling to send its own troops and unwilling to negotiate, the United States could only hope that an exhausted, overmatched French colonial army which lacked national support for its efforts could defeat the Vietminh.

The house of cards came down in a rush in spring 1954. On 20 November 1953, as part of Navarre's effort to defeat the main elements of the Vietminh, French airborne forces seized a position at Dienbienphu in the northwestern highlands as a base for forward operations. In March and May 1954, Vietminh forces besieged and captured the French base, where the cream of the French colonial army had been marshaled to seek a decisive battle. Although American leaders had come to see Vietnam as a keystone of the American security system in the Far East that had been created since the outbreak of the Korean War, a lack of public support kept the United States from directly intervening in a struggle that might well turn into another limited war of the sort which had developed in Korea. Instead, the Eisenhower administration refused to sign the Geneva accords ending French rule, sponsored the creation of a treaty system integrating South Vietnam, Cambodia, and Laos into the American security sphere, and diverted much of the financial aid once supplied to the French war effort directly to the anti-Communist regime created in Saigon, which had also refused to sign the Geneva agreements. For their part, the Soviet Union and the People's Republic of China supplied the Communist regiment in Hanoi. Thus the American entanglement in the Vietnam War, begun as part of the Cold War and expanded as part of the Korean War, would be deepened throughout the following decades.

John S. Hill

Bibliography

Gardner, Lloyd C. *Approaching Vietnam: From World War II through Dienbienphu, 1941–1954* (1988).

Short, Anthony. *The Origins of the Vietnam War* (1989).

Wall, Irwin M. *The United States and the Making of Postwar France, 1945–1954* (1991).

Intelligence in the Korean War

See WILLOUGHBY, CHARLES A. (1882–1972)

J

Johnson, Louis A. (1891–1966)

Louis Arthur Johnson, lawyer and secretary of defense, 1949–1950, was born in Roanoke, Virginia on January 10, 1891. Following his 1912 graduation with a degree in law from the University of Virginia, he began practicing in Clarksburg, West Virginia. In time, his law firm, Steptoe and Johnson, became one of the largest and most influential in the nation. During World War I he saw action in France as a captain in the infantry. In the 1920s and early 1930s he was extremely active in the American Legion, becoming state commander and ultimately, in 1932, national commander. His Legion activities were instrumental in his becoming well-versed in national defense issues. From 1937 to mid-1940, he served in the War Department as assistant secretary of war. In that position he played a major role in initiating and implementing the industrial preparedness plans that were so successful in World War II. Even his harshest critics credited his mobilization planning with significantly improving America's war industrial power.

Johnson, arrogant, outspoken, and ambitious, was always at the center of controversy. Such was the case at the War Department where he conducted a well-publicized feud with Secretary of War Harry Woodring. That controversy became so disruptive that in 1940 President Franklin D. Roosevelt dismissed both Woodring and Johnson.

In 1948, Johnson took what many considered as one of the most difficult jobs in the country, finance chairman of the Democratic National Committee, which meant raising campaign funds for incumbent President Harry S. Truman, who everyone thought was doomed to defeat. Johnson succeeded in raising the necessary campaign funds, and when Truman pulled off the political upset of the century, Johnson was clearly in line for a major political payoff. He made it clear what he wanted, and on March 2, 1949, the president announced Johnson would replace James Forrestal as secretary of defense. He assumed the post on March 28.

In his new position, Johnson faced two major challenges: unification of the armed forces and implementation of the president's austerity program. Johnson, who was the second secretary of defense, assumed leadership of a military establishment created just two years earlier by the National Security Act of 1947. Under that structure the secretary had Cabinet status but presided over three equal executive departments—Army, Navy, and the newly established Air Force. The Navy was suspicious of Johnson because of his long-time advocacy of air power, and well they should have been. In late April 1949 he canceled construction of the USS *United States*, the new super aircraft carrier. That action not only led to the resignation of Secretary of the Navy John L. Sullivan, but sparked a controversy over the roles, responsibilities, and budgets of the respective armed services. Johnson's budget cuts were in response to President Truman's mandate that the total defense budget would have to be less than $15 billion per year, and preferably $13 billion. As a result of Johnson's cuts, the size of the armed forces was reduced by 190,000, to 1,460,000, many military installations were closed, ships were mothballed, and training cut back. In instituting the cuts, Johnson reduced the budgets of all the services, but the Navy suffered the most. A major consequence of the secretary's unification and economy moves was "The Revolt of the Admirals." The "revolt" saw a number of high-ranking career naval officers publicly charge that Secretary of Defense Johnson and the

Army and Air Force were out to weaken, if not destroy, the Navy and Marines. Following lengthy congressional hearings in August and October 1949, Johnson, the Army, and Air Force were vindicated. As secretary, Johnson was also instrumental in bringing about racial integration of the armed forces, the expansion of the nation's atomic arsenal, the development of the hydrogen bomb, and the creation of the Military Sea Transportation Service.

Johnson's disputes were not limited to those in the Defense Department. He was also in constant conflict with the State Department. That feud resulted from both personal friction—Johnson did not like nor get along with Secretary of State Dean Acheson—and Far Eastern policy differences—Johnson supported aid to Nationalist China, while Acheson did not. In June 1950, Johnson and Chairman of the Joint Chiefs of Staff General Omar N. Bradley spent two weeks in the Far East visiting military installations and commanders, including General Douglas MacArthur. They returned on June 24, feeling that things were running smoothly in the Pacific. Around 10:00 P.M., Johnson received word from a reporter that North Korea had launched a major attack against the South. Johnson indicated he had not received such a report and therefore could not comment. Shortly thereafter he received a similar report from the Pentagon duty officer. Being unable to get additional information and doubting the accuracy of such reports, since none of his Far Eastern briefings had indicated the likelihood of such an attack, Johnson delegated to Secretary of the Army Frank Pace authority to handle the situation. He then went to bed. The following morning he and General Bradley went to a previously scheduled speaking engagement in Norfolk, Virginia, leaving Secretary Pace still in charge. At that point it never entered Johnson's mind that the administration would alter its Korean policy, which he and the Joint Chiefs of Staff (JCS) fully supported, that South Korea was not of strategic importance and therefore could not, should not, and would not be defended by U.S. forces.

On the afternoon of June 25, Johnson learned that President Truman was returning to Washington and had called a meeting of his top military and civilian leaders at Blair House for that evening. After a short meeting with the services secretaries and the JCS, Johnson went to the airport to meet the president. On the way to Blair House, the president indicated his determination not to let the North Korean attack succeed, and Johnson then voiced his support for that position. In the discussion that evening, Johnson initially took the position that the security of the U.S. was more dependent upon what happened on Formosa than on what took placed in Korea. He also expressed opposition to sending U.S. ground forces but did support sending military supplies to South Korea to carry out the U.N. call to halt the aggression.

The next evening, with the situation continuing to deteriorate, Johnson agreed to the State Department's recommendation that U.S. air and naval forces be used to halt the attack. Johnson iterated his desire that U.S. ground forces not be used. He also added that if Chinese or Soviet forces entered the conflict the U.S. should withdraw because this was not the place to get into a conflict with those nations. Over the next several days, however, Johnson and his staff worked on many contingency plans for U.S. response should the Soviet Union decide to use the crisis to push its advantage in locations around the globe. On the 29th, Johnson came to accept the view of the JCS that if South Korea were to be saved, U.S. ground troops would need to be committed. This change resulted in part from his feeling that Communist success in Korea would endanger other nations in the area, including Formosa and Japan. Furthermore, he felt this was a major test for the U.N., and the U.S. should be supportive if the world organization was to reach its potential as a force for world order.

After U.S. entry into the conflict, many of Johnson's responsibilities, such as procurement, establishment, and strengthening of NATO forces and public relations remained essentially the same as before the war, but many others, such as appropriations, manpower needs, the Japanese Peace Treaty, and rearmament of West Germany assumed new and more complex dimensions. Still other problems, such as establishment of the U.N. military command and securing Allied support for the U.N. operation, were completely new. Johnson played a major role in assuring that while the conflict was officially being waged as a U.N. action, in reality it was the U.S. that, rather literally, was calling the shots. Johnson spent much of his time trying to carry out the president's wish to have as many nations as possible represented in the U.N. command and still meet the JCS desire to accept only forces that would enhance the command's fighting ability. Once the war began, Johnson usually met with the president at least once a day to present the assessments and views of the JCS and to put forth his own views. Johnson was not a profound military thinker, and he realized that; therefore, on military matters, he tended to defer to the JCS. The chiefs felt Johnson presented their views to the president accurately and forcefully.

It was ironic that in the summer of 1950 Johnson became increasingly involved in the buildup of the U.S. military forces that he had been busy dismantling—in the name of economy—for the past fifteen months. Since the president delegated to the secretary of defense the authority to call up National Guard and reserve units and individuals in the inactive reserves, it was Johnson who caught much of the heat when such action was taken. In the first two months of the conflict, Johnson was responsible for calling up 404 reserve units, 205 National Guard outfits, and more than 250,000 men. The demand for more manpower was accompanied by the need for more supplies and equipment, and Johnson found himself, in July and August, actively supporting supplemental appropriations of some $12 billion—nearly doubling the annual defense appropriations. Many pro-military congressmen were upset that Johnson, who had so easily wielded the economy axe, now came forward to claim that nothing was too good for the nation's men in uniform as they moved to stop Communist aggression in Korea.

The war did not go well for the U.N. forces in July and early August, as the North Koreans advanced steadily southward toward the port city of Pusan. The situation stabilized somewhat in late August, but what U.N. commander General Douglas MacArthur was planning was a masterstroke that would dramatically reverse the tide of the war. That venture was to be the surprise attack at Inchon. Johnson first learned of MacArthur's plans for Inchon in mid-July, and he was supportive from the beginning. This was one case where Johnson was not in agreement with the JCS. The chiefs remained skeptical. On September 15, 1950, the successful Inchon invasion was carried out, but Johnson could not savor the shared triumph; three days earlier he had been fired by President Truman.

As the war expanded in July and August so had Johnson's difficulties. His problems were: (1) increasing criticism of him, the Defense Department, and the president over the poor showing of U.S. military forces in Korea; (2) growing conflict between him and Acheson, especially over the administration's Formosa policy, and (3) his increasing tendency to resort to political intrigue to undermine Acheson and the State Department and to promote himself.

As the bad military news flowed unremittingly out of Korea in the summer of 1950, newsmen and the public began to speculate as to what had gone wrong. While the president ultimately endured much criticism, such was not originally the case; in time of crisis the nation usually rallied behind its commander in chief. Thus, as poorly equipped and poorly trained American soldiers began to die, the secretary of defense became a convenient scapegoat. By late August many congressmen and editorial writers were calling for Johnson's replacement. As public criticism of the war effort grew, so did Johnson's personal and ideological conflict with Acheson. Acheson (and the president) believed in keeping a safe distance from Chinese Nationalists, whereas Johnson wanted to develop closer ties with Chiang Kai-shek and his regime on Formosa (Taiwan). On this issue, Johnson was taking a position strongly held by General MacArthur and most Republicans. Furthermore, it became a political liability in the upcoming congressional elections; some, in fact, believed that he was in secret communication with top Republicans.

President Truman called Johnson to the White House on September 12, 1950 to demand his resignation. Johnson tearfully pleaded for the president to reconsider, but Truman was adamant, and Johnson resigned on September 19, to be replaced by the olympian World War II "Architect of Victory," George C. Marshall.

In his last months in office, Johnson had become increasingly choleric, even irrational. Truman confided to his diary that Johnson was "the most ego maniac (sic) I've ever come in contact with—and I've seen a lot." Acheson, admittedly no friend, thought him mentally unbalanced. And soon after his resignation Johnson was successfully operated on for a brain tumor. It is truly sobering to reflect that America's first two secretaries of defense, James V. Forrestal and Louis A. Johnson, in a time of great international challenge, were mentally ill.

Keith D. McFarland

Bibliography

Condit, Doris M. *History of the Office of the Secretary of Defense*, 2, *The Test of War, 1950–1952* (1988).

Poole, Walter S. *The History of the Joint Chiefs of Staff: The Joint Chiefs of Staff and National Policy*, 4, 1950–1952 (1979).

Rearden, Steve L. *History of the Office of the Secretary of Defense*, 1, *The Formative Years, 1947–1950* (1984).

Schnabel, James F. *U.S. Army in the Korean War, Policy and Direction: The First Years* (1972).

———, and Robert J. Watson. *The History of the Joint Chiefs of Staff: The Joint Chiefs of Staff and National Policy*, 3, *The Korean War* (1979).

Joint Chiefs of Staff and the Relief of General Douglas MacArthur

On 10 April 1951, in an unprecedented move which turned the Free World's attention from the Korean battlefield to the United States political arena, President Harry S. Truman divested General Douglas MacArthur of his several military commands as supreme commander, Allied powers in Japan (SCAP; commander in chief, Far East (CINCFE); commander in chief, United Nations command (CINCUNC); and commanding general, United States Army forces, Far East (CG AFFE). The president named General Matthew B. Ridgway, incumbent commanding general, Eighth U.S. Army in Korea (CG EUSAK), to succeed MacArthur in all these positions. The abrupt dismissal of the widely admired MacArthur appeared to a segment of the American public as an arbitrary action that demeaned one of America's greatest living military heroes. It had far-reaching consequences and brought about a divisive and partisan inquiry into the conduct of the Korean War, even as that war continued unabated.

The president was assailed vociferously by General MacArthur's supporters. He was even burned in effigy, and Republican Congressmen discussed the possibility of impeaching him. Inept handling of administrative details (General MacArthur learned of his relief from his wife, who had heard of it from an aide, who had picked up the news on a radio broadcast) added insult to what his supporters considered injury, and further fueled their indignation.

President Truman had intended no gratuitous affront to General MacArthur, nor did he decide to fire the prestigious military hero of World Wars I and II on the spur of the moment. The nation's chief executive took this action only after long and grave consideration, and in close consultation with his key advisors, including the Joint Chiefs of Staff (JCS). He

did so only after MacArthur's own actions had convinced the president that he was deliberately undercutting the national policy toward Korea, that he was defying presidential authority, ignoring presidential directives as a matter of his own policy, and that he had left the president no alternatives but to capitulate or fire him.

From early in the war, MacArthur had issued statements making clear his disagreement with the president's Korean policies, and had on at least three occasions violated presidential directives passed to him by the JCS. President Truman had been reluctant to take drastic action because of MacArthur's prestige. He had, instead, continued to spell out his directives in very clear terms, given MacArthur mild warnings, and had even sent emissaries to Tokyo to explain the reasoning behind his directives and policies. None of these measures proved effective, and as the war continued to intensify, General MacArthur's transgressions continued and became, in the president's view, more egregious. He continued expressing in public his dissatisfaction and disagreement with the president's stewardship of the Korean War, and when it suited his purposes, ignoring his orders. For this, General MacArthur paid a heavy price and ended his military career.

The Formosan Misunderstanding

The first glimmer of discord between President Truman and General MacArthur appeared in July 1950 in connection with the national policy toward Formosa (Taiwan) and the Chinese Nationalist government under General Chiang Kai-shek, which had fled to the offshore island in 1949. On 29 June, implementing the president's orders, the JCS ordered MacArthur to defend Formosa, and reaffirmed that for this purpose the U.S. Seventh Fleet was under his operational control. United States policy toward Formosa was under intensive study in Washington at the time the war broke out. The president's greatest concern was the greatly increased danger of a general war with the Soviet Union because of the outbreak of hostilities in the Far East. General MacArthur flew to Formosa on 31 July, where he conferred with Chiang Kai-shek for two days. Washington had been apprehensive about this trip but had not opposed it. Unfortunately for relationships between MacArthur and the president, MacArthur did not render any report of his visit for almost a week. In the meantime, the press speculated that MacArthur had made secret agreements and had taken the trip without Washington's knowledge. Rumors also spread in official Washington that Mac-Arthur planned to transfer fighter squadrons to Formosa. These reports were untrue, but they caused much nervousness among Washington officials who could not judge their validity. Chiang Kai-shek intensified this concern by a vague public statement hinting that he and MacArthur had made a number of secret agreements. President Truman had no way of knowing exactly what had taken place in Formosa, but he was trying to convince the Communists that the United States had no designs on Formosa or the mainland and wished only to neutralize the area. Accordingly, he instructed Secretary of Defense Louis A. Johnson to send a stern warning to MacArthur saying, "No one other than the President as Commander-in-Chief has the authority to order or authorize preventive action against concentrations on the [Chinese] mainland. The most vital national interest requires that no action of ours precipitate general war or give excuse to others to do so."

General MacArthur replied that he understood the directive and that he was operating exactly according to his instructions. On 7 August he finally reported on his meeting with Chiang Kai-shek, whom, he said, had agreed to cooperation with the United States. American military activity would be limited to reconnaissance of coastal areas of China and the Formosan straits and familiarization flights by U.S. planes, to include landing and refueling on Formosa.

President Truman sent Ambassador Averell Harriman to Tokyo later in August. On his return, Harriman reported that MacArthur had not exceeded his military authority in visiting Formosa. His report did, however, reflect a skepticism about how wholeheartedly Mac-Arthur was supporting the presidential policy toward Formosa. The president announced that he was satisfied with MacArthur's performance. For his part, General MacArthur charged that anyone who even hinted at friction between himself and his superior was guilty of "sly insinuations, brash speculations, and bold misstatements."

Evident in this situation was a sharp dichotomy of views between General MacArthur and the president. President Truman was determined that no action of the United States would trigger a general war. General MacArthur, on the other hand, seemed intent on the immedi-ate situation facing his command and revealed no concern at the consequences of his actions or statements.

The VFW Incident

President Truman had publicly denied Beijing's charge that the United States intended to seize Formosa. He was angered, therefore, when in late August, General MacArthur addressed a letter to the National Encampment of the Veterans of Foreign Wars (VFW) insisting that the United States must retain control of Formosa at any cost, calling it an "unsinkable aircraft carrier and submarine tender." He spoke scathingly of those who advocated "appeasement and defeatism in the Pacific."

MacArthur's public expressions evoked a strong reaction from President Truman. According to Secretary of Defense Johnson, the president was so indignant over the letter, which had been transmitted through Army facilities, that he discussed with him, on 26 August 1950, the advisability of relieving MacArthur. Truman decided not to do so, but directed Johnson to order MacArthur to withdraw his statement. MacArthur protested that his letter actually supported the president's policies and since it had already been widely disseminated in advance press releases its withdrawal would be "a grave mistake." He also pointed out that the views he expressed were "purely my personal ones," as if he could separate his official and personal public statements. Nonetheless, he was ordered to withdraw his letter. The president revealed his own sensitivity to General Mac-Arthur's prestige and influence when he softened this order somewhat by transmitting to the general messages which he had sent to the U.N. setting forth U.S. policy on Formosa and telling MacArthur, "I am sure when you read this . . . you will understand why my action . . . was necessary."

Truman's concerns over the letter were justified. Following the appearance of Mac-Arthur's "withdrawn" statement in *U.S. News and World Report* on 1 September, the Soviet Ambassador to the United Nations charged that General MacArthur had, "with cynical candor," informed the world that the United States intended "at all costs" to turn Formosa into a U.S. base in the Far East. Unhappily, the Formosan fiasco marked the beginning of a series of similar actions by MacArthur that were to weaken progressively, and to the breaking point, President Truman's patience with his recalcitrant commander. General Omar N. Bradley, chairman of the JCS, testified later that the VFW letter was the first in a sequence of events that was to lead ultimately to MacArthur's dismissal.

MacArthur Reacts to Defeat

For the next two months, General MacArthur refrained from criticizing publicly the president's policies. In fact, when President Truman summoned him to Wake Island in mid-October, he stated that no commander in the history of war had ever had more complete and adequate support than he'd had from "all agencies in Washington." When later in the month he found that his current operating directive was not in accord with his plans for advancing into North Korea, he ignored it, and ordered all of his forces, not just the Republic of Korea Army (ROKA), to advance to the Chinese border. He avoided criticizing the directive, however.

On 6 November, in reaction to early signs of Chinese intervention, General MacArthur once again violated his directives by ordering the bombing of the Yalu River bridges, even though on 29 June the JCS had ordered him to stay well back from the Chinese and Soviet borders in his air operations. When the JCS suggested on 9 November that, in light of new developments his mission might have to be changed, he disagreed sharply, and his mission was not changed. On the very eve of the Chinese Communist attack against his forces on 25 November, the JCS again suggested that he check his attack to a line short of the Yalu. Again his reaction was violent disagreement. Yet at no time in this crucial November period did MacArthur publicly criticize his directives and, indeed, denied that Washington had ever suggested that he stop at any line short of the international boundaries.

The crushing Chinese onslaught of 25 November forced a costly, headlong retreat of U.N. forces to below the 38th parallel and turned the prospect of victory into the prospect of their being driven ignominiously from Korea. Reacting to humiliating defeat, General MacArthur spoke out in his own defense, publicly claiming he had been forced to operate under an enormous handicap "without precedent in military history." He went further and charged that selfish European interests were causing Washington to withhold support from his forces. Because these statements came at a time when the United States was doing its best to reassure its uneasy allies that MacArthur's rashness would not involve the West in a large-scale war with China, they caused consternation and concern among the president and his advisors.

The JCS viewed MacArthur's blaming his defeat on operational restrictions as a reflection on the president, who had imposed those restrictions. They could not help but note also that MacArthur was at least partially responsible for his own predicament, since he had persuaded the president to allow him to advance to the borders by his great confidence that the Chinese would not, or could not, intervene effectively.

President Truman was angered by MacArthur's public charges. He stated later that he should have relieved General MacArthur at this point, but claimed that he did not want to go against a man down on his luck. He castigated MacArthur, nonetheless, when he recalled in his memoirs that MacArthur had, within four days and in four different ways, blamed his defeat on Washington's orders to limit the hostilities in Korea.

As a direct consequence of these statements, President Truman issued a directive on 5 December that ordered government officials to clear all public statements on political matters with the Department of State and all statements on military affairs with the Department of Defense. This directive was addressed to heads of all executive departments, but was aimed specifically at General MacArthur.

Throughout December 1950 and January 1951, MacArthur proposed certain measures: bombing of the mainland, blockade of China and other drastic actions, that would carry the war to China's mainland. He did so forcefully, but always through official channels. In mid-February, however, he changed tack and began airing his views and recommendations in public. In a press statement on 13 February, MacArthur argued that unless he was allowed to reduce Chinese superiority, ostensibly through air attacks on their "sanctuary," that he could not even consider major operations north of the 38th parallel. In another blast at the national policy, or supposed lack of it, he charged on 7 March that he required guidance based on decisions that must be provided on "the highest international levels." Neither of these statements had been cleared in Washington and thus violated the 5 December presidential directive, a violation which did not go unnoticed in Washington.

What may have been the culminating factor in the president's decision to relieve MacArthur was the latter's 24 March 1951 call on enemy leaders to negotiate with him, ridiculing of Chinese military power, and threatening an expansion of the war outside Korea should they not negotiate. This not only flouted the U.N. policy of confining the war to Korea, but completely vitiated the initiative which the president had been preparing to take in his planned call on the enemy to negotiate, a copy of which had been furnished General MacArthur. President Truman considered this a defiance of his orders as commander in chief and a challenge to his authority. Truman recalled later that at this point he felt he could no longer tolerate MacArthur's insubordination. He took no action to relieve MacArthur, however, until another incident, relatively minor in comparison, snapped his patience. On 5 April 1951, Congressman Joseph W. Martin, House of Representatives minority leader, made public the contents of a letter which General MacArthur had written him containing a relatively mild commentary on American foreign policy. The letter, which had not been cleared as required by the December directive, was merely a reiteration of his views that the Asian theater was fully as important as the European theater and that the United States must continue the fight in Korea until victory was achieved. The president's annoyance at this violation was undoubtedly exacerbated by the fact that Congressman Martin was a Republican and a strong political rival.

Thus was set in motion the series of meetings and consultations between the president and his principal advisors that was to lead to MacArthur's firing. The first session, called by the president on 6 April, included Ambassador Harriman, Secretary of State Dean Acheson, Secretary of Defense George C. Marshall, and chairman of the JCS General Omar Bradley. Harriman told the president that he should have relieved MacArthur in 1949 when he had begged off returning to the United States when the president had asked him, pleading press of business. Secretary Marshall, concerned over the effect which MacArthur's dismissal might have on pending military appropriations, advised caution. General Bradley felt MacArthur had been insubordinate and deserved to be relieved, but deferred a final recommendation until he had talked with General J. Lawton Collins, Army chief of staff. Secretary Acheson believed that MacArthur should be relieved, but wanted this done only after a unanimous decision to do so by the JCS. President Truman had already decided to relieve MacArthur, but kept this to himself for the time being. He instructed his four top advisers to return the next day. Secretary Marshall was told to study all messages exchanged between Washington and General MacArthur over the past two years.

At the meeting on 7 April, General Marshall told the president that, after reading the messages, he agreed with Harriman that MacArthur should have been relieved in 1949. At the conclusion of this meeting, President Truman instructed General Bradley to obtain the consensus of the other members of the JCS and to be prepared to make a final recommendation on 9 April.

The JCS and General MacArthur

All members of the JCS were considerably junior to General MacArthur. General Bradley had been a major when the latter was a brigadier general in World War I. General Collins and Admiral Forrest Sherman, chief of naval operations, 1917 graduates of West Point and Annapolis, respectively, had been very junior officers when MacArthur was superintendent at West Point. Collins had taught there at the time but had little contact with MacArthur. General Hoyt Vandenberg, Air Force chief of staff, had been a cadet when MacArthur was superintendent. This disparity in rank and its effect within the military system was apparent in communications between Washington and Tokyo, with MacArthur sometimes addressing the JCS in a tolerant tone with an occasional hint of condescension. The JCS, on the other hand, couched their messages in language calculated not to offend so senior an officer as MacArthur, and only rarely spoke to him in a decisive and firm manner.

The JCS role in MacArthur's dismissal was in strict keeping with their statutory responsibilities as principal advisers to the commander in chief. While each of the members was aware of the president's growing displeasure over MacArthur's statements and actions, none of them knew that he was thinking of dismissal proceedings until the incident of the Martin letter brought the issue into the open.

That the JCS were suspicious of General MacArthur's judgment is well illustrated by their withholding from him the knowledge that the president had granted him authority to attack air bases in Manchuria and China if the Soviets launched a major air attack against his command. They feared, according to General Bradley, that he might "make a premature decision in carrying it out."

Before his meeting with the president on 5 April, General Bradley had appraised the JCS of the president's reaction to the Martin letter. He alerted them to be ready with their recommendations. The JCS met on the afternoon of 8 April and discussed the military aspects of MacArthur's relief. All agreed that from the military viewpoint, MacArthur should be relieved. General Collins held that MacArthur did not believe in the United Nations basic Korean policies and that the president, as commander in chief, was entitled to have a field commander more in sympathy with these policies and "more responsive to the will of the President. . . ." He pointed specifically to MacArthur's violation of the president's order that public statements on foreign policy be cleared. Admiral Sherman maintained that if the United States were to limit the conflict to Korea and avoid World War III, "we must have a Commander in whom we can confide and on whom we can rely." The JCS agreed that, if the president did not remove MacArthur, General Marshall, whose prestige was at least equal to that of MacArthur, should send him a letter pointing out to him the difficult position in which he was placing President Truman. Generals Bradley and Marshall drafted such a letter jointly, but it was never sent. General Bradley summed up the agreed JCS position by writing on 24 April that the JCS were all concerned that "if General MacArthur was not relieved, a large segment of our people would charge that civil authorities no longer controlled the military."

On 9 April 1951, having received the recommendations of his top advisors, the president announced his decision to relieve General MacArthur of all his commands. He ordered a message sent to Secretary of the Army Frank Pace, who was in Korea at the time, instructing him to deliver the news of his relief to MacArthur in person at the U.S. Embassy in Tokyo. This was to be done at 1000, 12 April, Tokyo time (2000, 11 April, Washington time). A failure in communications facilities between Washington and Korea prevented Secretary Pace from receiving the president's instructions in time. When, late on 10 April (Washington time), it appeared that the *Chicago Tribune* intended to print the story prematurely, the president ordered the transmission of the official notification moved up by almost twenty hours. However, the official notification did not reach General MacArthur until thirty minutes after he had been told of his dismissal by his wife.

The official message from the president to General MacArthur read as follows: "I deeply regret that it becomes my duty as President and Commander in Chief of the United States Military Forces to replace you as Supreme Commander, Allied Powers; Commander in Chief, United Nations Command; Commander in Chief, Far East; and Commanding General United States Army, Far East. You will turn over your commands, effective at once, to Lieutenant General Matthew B. Ridgway."

MacArthur received a hero's welcome on his return to the United States. Two Senate committees held joint hearings to investigate his relief by the president. These hearings began on 3 May 1951 and lasted almost two months. General MacArthur and all the president's principal civilian and military advisors, including members of the JCS, testified at these hearings. Aside from serving to generate an excellent body of documentation for historians, the hearings had little positive effect, reached no agreed findings, and, in the end, changed nothing. Secretary of State Dean Acheson summed up his judgment of the hearings by noting that they "exhausted both committees, bored the press and the public, publicized a considerable amount of classified material, and successfully defused the explosive 'MacArthur issue.'"

James F. Schnable

Bibliography

Collins, J. Lawton. *War in Peacetime* (1969).
Schnable, James F. *Policy and Direction: The First Year* (United States Army in the Korean War, Office of the Chief of Military History, Department of the Army, Washington: 1972).
Schnable, James F., and Robert J. Watson. *The Korean War (The History of the Joint Chiefs of Staff,* The Joint Chiefs of Staff, Washington: n.d.).
Truman, Harry S. *Memoirs, Vol. II, Years of Trial and Hope* (1956); *Military Situation in the Far East*, Hearings before the Committee on Armed Services and the Committee on Foreign Relations, U.S. Senate, 82d Congress, First Session, Washington: 1951).

See also MACARTHUR, DOUGLAS

Joy, C. Turner (1895–1956)

Charles Turner Joy was born in St. Louis, Missouri, on February 17, 1895. Appointed to the United States Naval Academy (USNA) with the class of 1916, he was commissioned an ensign and assigned to the battleship USS *Pennsylvania* on graduation. After earning a graduate degree in ordnance engineering from the University of Michigan and completing several ordnance-related assignments, Joy took command of his first ship, the destroyer USS *Litchfield*, in 1933. Following assignment to the USNA in 1937 as head of the department of ordnance and gunnery, he participated in eleven naval combat engagements in the Pacific theater during World War II, including Bougainville, Rennell Island, Guadalcanal, Attu, Saipan, the Philippines Sea, Formosa, and Okinawa. When hostilities ended in August 1945, Joy was in command of amphibious forces training in the United States for the planned invasion of the Japanese mainland. He then held such assignments as commander, Yangtze Task Force, and commander, Naval Proving Ground. In 1949 the admiral took part in the American occupation of Japan as commander of naval forces, Far East. When war unexpectedly erupted in Korea on June 25, 1950, Joy believed his naval resources inadequate to meet the challenges posed by the North Korean invasion of the South. Yet, through skillful coordination of the rapidly expanding American (and later United Nations) naval assets, the admiral was able to support friendly combat forces during the hectic opening weeks of the conflict. Concerns over a Communist Chinese invasion of Formosa (Taiwan) and possible intervention by Soviet submarines in the waters surrounding Korea forced Joy to look beyond strictly tactical considerations—escalation into a global conflict weighed heavily on the admiral. Compounding these concerns was General Douglas MacArthur's proposed amphibious operation at Inchon. Believing such an employment of forces was not feasible due to the hazardous sea approaches to Inchon, Joy and his staff nevertheless became totally committed to the project once it became apparent there were no other alternatives. The stunning success of "Operation Chromite" at Inchon and the ability to overcome the multitude of demands required of Allied naval assets during the first six months of fighting were tributes to Joy's leadership and direction. As a result, the U.N. naval forces were prepared when Communist China intervened in the late fall of 1950. The following summer, when fighting stagnated and negotiations opened, Joy was chosen to serve as senior delegate and chief of the United Nations command delegation to the Korean armistice conference. In addition to his proven leadership and years of Far Eastern experience, General Matthew B. Ridgway likely selected Joy because his calm and unhurried manner inspired confidence in both superior and subordinate. Yet the admiral and his team of negotiators, limited by the United Nations to discussion and resolution of strictly military matters relating only to Korea, were hampered by shifts in fundamental negotiating positions dictated by the United Nations. While such modifications sought to prevent an impasse, Joy believed they furthered Communist delay of serious negotiations in the hope of gaining further concessions. Negotiations languished after the admiral put the final United Nations command package proposal on the table in April 1952. Frustrated by lack of progress, Joy requested reassignment and was tendered the position of thirty-seventh superintendent of the USNA. Yet only one month after taking command at Annapolis the admiral was diagnosed with leukemia. He completed his tour as superintendent and retired from active duty in July 1954. Succumbing to the disease, C. Turner Joy died in San Diego, California, in June 1956.

William E. Fischer, Jr.

Bibliography

Field, James A. *History of United States Naval Operations: Korea* (1962).

Hermes, Walter G. *Truce Tent and Fighting Front, 2, United States Army in the Korean War* (1966).

Joy, C. Turner. *Negotiating While Fighting: The Diary of Admiral C. Turner Joy at the Korean Armistice Conference* (1978).

———. *How Communists Negotiate* (1955).

Republic of Korea, Ministry of Defense, *The History of the United Nations Forces in the Korean War*, 7 Vols. (1972–77).

K

KATUSA (Korean Augmentation to the U.S. Army)

On August 15, 1950, the Far East command directed the Eighth U.S. Army to employ Korean recruits in American divisions in Korea and in the 7th Infantry Division, which was preparing for movement to Korea. Each company or battery was to receive 100 Koreans. The Koreans were to be part of the ROK Army, to be paid by the ROK government, but they would be fed and equipped by their American unit. Each augmentation soldier was to be paired with an American in a "buddy" system. The 7th Infantry Division, which had been greatly depleted by the three divisions preceding it to Korea, was to receive 8,625 KATUSAs. This large replacement force would arrive at the 7th Division camps in Japan only three weeks before the division's landing at Inchon.

The program was initially too drastic. Many of the Koreans were simply seized off the streets. To have expected these raw recruits, many just schoolboys who could not speak English, to be ready for combat in three weeks was unrealistic. This hasty program demonstrated its shortcomings during the fighting withdrawal from North Korea a few months later. The KATUSAs were unprepared for combat and could not be effectively used by the 7th Division. Not surprisingly, these poorly trained recruits were easily demoralized and many hid in foxholes, never firing their weapons. Early problems with the KATUSA program contributed to the breakdown of the "buddy system" in some of the American divisions. The 1st Cavalry and the 2nd Infantry Division maintained the buddy arrangement, with American soldiers training the recruits in weapons use and American tactics. In the 24th Division, however, the Koreans were placed in separate squads and platoons. These Korean squads proved effective in specialized tasks such as guarding, scouting, and patrolling. They were also employed to move heavy weapons over the tough Korean terrain. In addition, they taught American soldiers how to camouflage with straw and natural elements. The reluctance of U.S. units to accept KATUSAs kept the program from reaching its planned level. In June 1951 there were 12,718 Korean augmentation soldiers. However, with improved training, combat effectiveness was enhanced and plans drawn up for expansion. The new goal was to assign 2,500 to each of the eight American divisions, or a total of 27,000. This number was basically reached in late 1952 when 20,000 KATUSAs were in divisions and the remainder in combat support units. When properly trained and supported, the KATUSA and ROK soldiers and units proved equal to U.S. soldiers and units. KATUSA strength declined after the armistice and in July 1971, following the reduction of U.S. ground forces in Korea, stabilized at about 7,000. The program, however, continues to the present day.

D. Colt Denfield

Bibliography

Appleman, Roy. *South to the Naktong, North to the Yalu: June–November, 1950* (1961).

Blair, Clay. *The Forgotten War: America in Korea, 1950–1953* (1987).

Hermes, Walter. *Truce Tent and Fighting Front, United States Army in the Korean War* (Office of the Chief of Military History, Washington: 1966).

Mossman, Billy. *Ebb and Flow: November 1950–July 1951 United States Army in* the Korean War (Center of Military History, Washington: 1990).

Skaggs, D.C. The KATUSA Experiment: The Integration of Korean Nationals into the U.S. Army, 1950–1965 (1974).

Stanton, Shelby. American's Tenth Legion, X Corps in Korea, 1950 (Novato, CA: 1989).

Kean, William B. (1897–1981)

Born in Buffalo, New York, on July 9, 1897, William Benjamin Kean entered the United States Military Academy at West Point in June 1917. After completing a crash course instituted by America's entry into World War I, he graduated in November 1918 and was commissioned a second lieutenant in the infantry. Recalled to West Point as "student officers" a month later, Kean and his classmates were regraduated in June 1919. Between 1919 and 1941 Kean rose to the rank of lieutenant colonel and graduated from the Infantry School and the Command and General Staff School. At the outset of World War II Kean was assigned to the office of the chief of infantry. There he impressed Brigadier General Omar Bradley, then attached to the G-1 division of the War Department general staff, as a tough-minded, tireless worker who possessed exceptional analytical ability. When Bradley was named commander of the 28th Division in 1942, he took Kean along as his chief of staff. For the next two years Kean remained as Bradley's chief of staff as Bradley's importance grew, serving as his chief of staff in the II Corps during the Tunisian and Sicilian campaigns in 1943 and as his chief of staff in the First Army during the Normandy campaign in 1944. Curt and often abrasive with his underlings, Kean ruled Bradley's staff with an "iron fist" and was irreverently known behind his back as "Captain Bligh." But he also excelled as a manager, and following Bradley's appointment as commander of the Twelfth Army Group in the summer of 1944, Bradley left Kean, who had been promoted to major general in June 1944, as chief of staff in the First Army "to keep a fire lit" under its new and pallid commander, Courtney B. Hodges. In this capacity Kean was "a tower of strength" during the early days of the Battle of the Bulge when the Germans delivered a strong blow to the First Army. After World War II Kean commanded the 5th Division at Fort Jackson, South Carolina, and beginning in August 1948, the 25th Division in Japan. Between July 10 and July 15, 1950, Kean's division deployed to South Korea to join the United Nations forces resisting the North Korean invasion. During the next two and one-half months Kean, in his first combat command, led the 25th Division through fierce fighting to slow the North Korean drive toward Pusan and in the subsequent breakout of the U.S. Eighth Army from the Pusan perimeter. Like the other American divisions thrown into the desperate defense of South Korea in the summer of 1950, the 25th Division, understrength and ill-prepared for battle after years of soft occupation duty in Japan, initially failed to appreciably slow the North Korean advance, prompting Eighth Army commander Lieutenant General Walton H. Walker to "chew out" Kean for the division's poor performance. However, in early September, Kean, displaying tactical brilliance and decisive leadership, virtually destroyed the North Korean 6th and 7th Divisions during the North Korean "Great Naktong Offensive" and, through spectacular armored spearheads, cleared southwest Korea of the defeated North Koreans. Kean blamed his division's early difficulties on the tendency of the 24th Infantry Regiment, a black regiment, to "bug out" (break and run under fire), although he acknowledged that individual black soldiers had demonstrated competency and courage. Subscribing to the widespread Army view that "Negroes won't fight," he said that the regiment was so unreliable that its presence threatened the entire United Nations effort in Korea and recommended that Walker disband it and reassign its troops as fillers in white units at the ratio of one to ten. While many black officers and men disagreed with Kean's indictment of the 24th Infantry, it became the generally accepted version of the regiment's fighting ability and significantly contributed to the flurry of charges and countercharges about blacks as soldiers that echoed for years after the Korean War. In late November 1950, Kean's division fought in the battle of the Chongchon River in which the Chinese Communists decisively defeated the Eighth Army and forced its withdrawal from North Korea; and in early 1951, the division played a prominent role in the Eighth Army's operations in South Korea to stop the Chinese advance and stabilize the United Nations position. For the most part the 25th Division performed well in these engagements under Kean's leadership. But the heavy fighting it had seen since the previous July had worn Kean down, and in February 1951, Lieutenant General Matthew B. Ridgway, recently named commander of the Eighth Army, relieved him as part of a general shakeup of the Army's front-line generals. Before leaving Korea, Kean complied with the request of Ridgway, who had embraced his view on the performance of the 24th Infantry, to propose officially the elimination of black units and the integration of white and black troops. Later that year Ridgway used Kean's proposal to help win Washington's approval for the complete desegregation of the Far Eastern command. Following his return to the United States, Kean in March 1951 assumed command of the III Corps at Camp Roberts, California. In July 1952 he was appointed commanding general of the Fifth Army at Chicago, Illinois, and a month later was promoted to lieutenant general. Kean retired from the Army in September 1954 and then served as executive director of the Chicago Housing Authority until August 1957. He died on March 10, 1981, in Altamonte Springs, Florida.

John Kennedy Ohl

Bibliography

Appleman, Roy E. *Disaster in Korea; The Chinese Confront MacArthur* (1989).
———. *South to the Naktong, North to the Yalu: June-November 1950, United States Army in the Korean War* (Office of the Chief of Military History, Washington: 1961).
Blair, Clay. *The Forgotten War: America in Korea, 1950–1953* (1987).
Bradley, Omar, with Clay Blair. *A General's Life* (1983).
Marshall, S.L.A. *The River and the Gauntlet* (1953).

Keiser, Laurence B. (1895–1969)

The son of a prominent physician, Laurence Bolton Keiser, nicknamed "Dutch," was born in Philadelphia, Pennsylvania, on June 1, 1895. He graduated from the United States Military Academy at West Point on April 20, 1917, two weeks after the United States entered World War I, and was commissioned a second lieutenant in the infantry. A year later Keiser went to France and at age twenty-three became a battalion commander in the 5th Division and was awarded a Silver Star for gallantry during the Meuse-Argonne offensive. Between the world wars Keiser completed the company officers

and the advanced course at the Infantry School, was an instructor at West Point, and in 1939 graduated from the Command and General Staff College.

During World War II, Keiser, promoted to the rank of brigadier general in January 1944, held staff posts in the United States and briefly in North Africa and Italy. He finished the war in Texas as chief of staff of the Fourth Army, lagging behind many of his West Point classmates in rank and accomplishments. From 1946 to 1948 Keiser served in China with the United States advisory group. In January 1949 he was appointed assistant commander of the 2nd Division at Fort Lewis, Washington, and in February 1950, he was promoted to the rank of major general and named commander of the division as a "capstone" to his "thwarted career."

After the outbreak of the Korean War in June 1950, Keiser's division was dispatched to South Korea. In August and September 1950, it saw heavy fighting in the defense of the Pusan perimeter and in the American Eighth Army's subsequent pursuit of the North Korean Army after the Inchon invasion rendered the North Korean position in South Korea untenable. During these actions, Keiser, who had not commanded troops in battle since 1918, did not impress his superiors or his subordinates as an energetic leader. He tended to remain in his command post, only rarely leaving it to visit front-line units, and relied on his assistant division commander to be his "eyes and ears" in the field.

In October and November 1950, Keiser's division participated in the United Nations drive through North Korea toward the Yalu River. At the end of November it was destroyed as an effective fighting force when the Chinese Communists intervened in the war and launched a devastating offensive against the Eighth Army along the Chongchon River in northwestern Korea. Threatened by enemy troops bearing down on his front, flank, and rear, Keiser fought a desperate rearguard action in the Kunu-ri area while protecting the right flank of the retreating Eighth Army. When the 2nd Division withdrew from Kunu-ri on November 30, it had to run a formidable Chinese gauntlet stretching six miles along the thirty-mile-long road from Kunu-ri south to Sunchon. Unknown to Keiser, two Chinese regiments had occupied the high ground overlooking the road, and they decimated Keiser's 7,000-man force as it attempted to reach safety

K

in a mad dash that degenerated into a case of every unit, and often every individual, for itself or himself. Barely 4,000 men escaped the ambush, and much of the division's equipment was lost.

Suffering from a bad cold, Keiser displayed great personal courage amid the chaos. On several occasions as he made his way through the gauntlet he left his jeep to organize his demoralized and exhausted troops into some kind of meaningful resistance, and he regularly returned enemy fire with his own rifle. Physically and emotionally drained by the ordeal, Keiser was relieved of his command in early December 1950 by Lieutenant General Walton H. Walker, commander of the Eighth Army. Ostensibly Keiser was relieved for medical reasons, but actually he was relieved because Walker considered him responsible for the disaster that had engulfed his division.

Largely because of faulty battlefield intelligence, Keiser had grossly underestimated the strength of the Chinese position on November 30, and he, or his staff officers, committed a number of tactical errors in handling the division's withdrawal. Nevertheless, Keiser was not completely responsible for the disaster, for he was poorly served by higher authority. His superiors, Walker and Major General John B. Coulter, commander of the U.S. IXth Corps, failed to keep in close touch with the unfolding battle and did not send an adequate force from their reserves to help Keiser or grant him authority to utilize a different and safer route in his withdrawal from Kunu-ri.

His reputation tarnished by the Kunu-ri disaster, Keiser returned to the United States in early 1951 and assumed command of the 5th Division. Following his retirement from the Army in 1953, he lived in San Francisco, California, until his death on October 20, 1969.

John Kennedy Ohl

Bibliography

Appleman, Roy E. *Disaster in Korea: The Chinese Confront MacArthur* (1989).

———. *South to the Naktong, North to the Yalu: June-November 1950, United States Army in the Korean War* (Office of the Chief of Military History, Washington: 1961).

Blair, Clay. *The Forgotten War: America in Korea, 1950–1953* (1987).

Fehrenbach, T.R. *This Kind of War* (1963).

Marshall, S.L.A. *The River and the Gauntlet* (1953).

Kim Il Sung (1912–1994)

Kim was president of the Republic of North Korea (ROK) and general secretary of the Committee of the Korean Workers party. The propaganda needs of Kim's cult of personality have often distorted his origins and especially his reputation as a Korean patriot. Those who search for a historically accurate version of Kim's life and early career must be cautious in evaluating sources.

Born Kim Song-ju at Magyongdae, near Pyongyang, he was the eldest son of Kim Hyong-jik and Kang Pan-sok. He began school in Manchuria at Badaogu Elementary School (1919–1923). He returned to Korea and attended Changdok Elementary School in Pyongyang (1923–1925), but resumed his studies in Manchuria in 1925. His formal education ended in 1929 when he was expelled from middle school and imprisoned by the Japanese for participation in illegal activities.

In the spring of 1930, on his release from jail, Kim associated with guerrilla bands who mobilized to oppose Japanese invaders in Manchuria. It was at this time that Kim's understanding of communism was probably deepened by his association with a Communist Chinese guerrilla, Wei Zhengmin. It was also during this period of anti-Japanese activity that he adopted the pseudonym "Kim Il Sung." Although other Korean guerrillas would have the same name, there seems to be no doubt that the later president of North Korea and the anti-Japanese revolutionary of the 1930s were one and the same person.

Kim's partisan activities in the 1930s positioned him for political leadership in the future North Korean state. Moreover, his exploits served as the basis for the later cult of personality that would envelop him. Kim would later claim that he formed the Korean People's Revolutionary Army in April 1932, the forerunner of the Korean People's Army. Whether this is true or not, Kim rose to prominence as he engaged in a series of skirmishes and battles with the Japanese in Manchuria. In November 1938, he came to head a branch of the Northeast Anti-Japanese United Army, a joint force which had earlier drawn together the scattered Chinese and Korean guerrillas in Manchuria. In March 1940, Kim's guerrillas inflicted a defeat on Japanese police forces in near Kaspen, Yanggang-do province. An intense Japanese counter-campaign severely crippled guerrilla resistance and in 1941 sent Kim Il Sung into exile in the Soviet maritime province. Although he would be hailed as a Korean hero, Kim apparently never opposed the Japanese on Korean soil.

From 1941–1945, Kim trained with other Korean partisans (later known as Soviet Koreans) at Okeanskaya Field School near Vladivostok. During this five-year period he married Kim Chong-suk and on February 6, 1942, his son, Kim Jong Il, was born. Kim wore a Soviet uniform and apparently participated in occasional raids against the Japanese in Manchuria. Stalin was ambivalent toward these Soviet Koreans and his treatment of them was a reflection of the shifting nature of larger Soviet policy in the Far East. On the one hand, Stalin apparently purged a number of the Soviet Koreans before the end of the war, yet when the Soviets occupied Korea north of the 38th parallel, they took many of these Soviet Koreans with them. Kim Il Sung joined the contingent in the North in late September 1945.

From August 1945 until February 1946, Soviet policy toward occupied North Korea was somewhat ambivalent. Initially, they worked with a medley of Communists and nationalists under the leadership of Cho Man-sik. In February 1946, after the breakdown in negotiations over a trusteeship in Korea, the Soviets began to draw the North into what one historian calls "a quasi-colonial relationship." Kim Il Sung became an integral part of this Soviet strategy. On February 8, 1946, Soviet occupation authorities established the North Korean Provisional People's Committee and appointed Kim Il Sung as its head. With the assistance of Soviet authorities, North Korea created a Communist party structure, instituted political and economic reforms, silenced opposition press, and created the Korean People's Army. Cho Man-sik was placed under house arrest and opposition forces were given only token representation in the government. Kim used Soviet support to best the three factions that stood in his path to absolute control: indigenous Communists led by Pak Hong-yong, returned revolutionaries from China (also known as the Yenan group) led by Kim Du Bong, and the Soviet Koreans who returned as he did with the Soviet occupation forces. Kim's ultimate success was guaranteed by Soviet support, but also because his rivals were divided. Korean Communists were surreptitiously headquartered in distant Seoul and not all supported Pak Hong-yong; nor did all the Yenan group support Kim Du Bong. The Soviet Koreans were not a cohesive group and many of them supported Kim. With Soviet help, a merger of the New Demo-

cratic Party and the North Korean Communist Party was effected. Using his base of strength among the Soviet Koreans, Kim attacked indigenous communists such as O Ki-sop. In this the Yenan group remained neutral. After the failure of the Soviets and Americans to establish a unified governing body in Korea, a general election was held in the south in May 1948 under United Nations supervision, and a government, the Republic of Korea, was established there. On September 9, 1948, the Democratic People's Republic of Korea was proclaimed in the North with Kim Il Sung as its head. South Korean Communist, Pak Hong-yong who had fled to the north was appointed vice-premier. Both governments claimed jurisdiction over the entire territory of Korea.

At the end of 1948, the Soviets withdrew their occupation forces. Kim spent the years 1948–1950 building up the North Korean military to a fighting strength of 120,000. He continued to receive support and assistance from Soviet sources although it seems unlikely that he received "permission" from Stalin to attack South Korea in June 1950. Kim's plans for the reunification of Korea went awry when large-scale United Nations intervention in behalf of the south turned back his earlier military successes and threatened to conquer all of North Korea. Only intervention from Communist China saved the embattled North Korean leader and restored the Korean peninsula to the status quo ante bellum. As a result of this near disaster, internal challenges to Kim's leadership developed which sought to replace him with Pak Hong-yong. After the signing of the Korean armistice in July 1953, Kim reestablished his power and purged North Korea of opposition to his regime. Pak Hong-yong was expelled from the party and in late 1955 put on trial before the Supreme People's Assembly accused of espionage, being an American sympathizer, and conspiracy. He was found guilty and executed. With the assistance of loans from the Soviets and the Chinese, Kim launched a three-year economic plan (1954–1956) which completely nationalized North Korean industry. He also began the collectivization of North Korean agriculture.

During the post–Korean War era Kim moved to solidify his hold on North Korea. He imposed a more thorough-going control over the Communist party and accelerated the process of state socialization. Not only did he reconstruct the war-shattered country, but launched a period of phenomenal economic growth with a program of industrialization and construction of showcase buildings and monuments. The ideological underpinning of this vast effort was first articulated by Kim in September 1955 when he laid out the principles of *chuch'e* or *juche*. *Chuch'e's* most salient feature is its emphasis on self-reliance. Building on the homogeneity of Korean society and its tradition as the "hermit kingdom," Kim has proved to be an Asian variant of Yugoslavia's Marshal Tito, successfully adapting (and even abandoning) Marxist-Leninist categories to Korean realities. *Chuch'e* is essentially an assertion of Korean nationalism. In the view of one scholar, Kim was able to modernize Korea while at the same time eschewing modernity. Moreover, he selectively used elements of the once regnant Confucian social structure to build a cult of personality and a dynastic leadership. On his death in July 1994, the "Great Leader" (Kim) was replaced by his son, Kim Jong Il, the "Dear Leader."

In striking this distinctive pose for Korean communism, Kim walked a delicate path between his two chief patrons, China and the Soviet Union. Reliant on both for financial aid and for military security, Kim kept the nation neutral in the Sino-Soviet difficulties of the 1950s. In 1962, Kim cautiously edged toward the Chinese and away from the Soviets. However, during China's cultural revolution (1966–1976) he lurched back again toward the Soviets. The events surrounding the collapse of communism in Eastern Europe and the Soviet Union pushed Kim back toward the Chinese.

The end of the Cold War posed serious questions regarding the long-term prospects of Kim Il Sung's regime. Three features of the collapse of communism had special significance on the discussion of North Korea's future: the reunification of Germany, the violent demise of the personality cult of the Ceauşescu family in Romania, and the economic pressures on Russia and China which have strained their ability to support client states. Although Russian and Chinese pressures forced him into some conciliatory gestures toward South Korea, in the main, Kim was able to confound pundits and prognosticators that his regime was next for liberalization and ultimately for reunification. Reunification with the South and integration into the world community seems more remote than ever, especially in the wake of North Korea's development of nuclear weapons. Kim's cult of personality seemed to have a genuine base in Korean society and weathered the repeated attacks and derision of Western journalists. Even his son's succession seems to have been accomplished smoothly. Kim Il Sung proved to be a resilient and adept leader, successfully drawing on the strengths of Korean nationalism to solidify his home base while conducting a skillful foreign policy with his two giant neighbors.

Steven M. Avella

Bibliography
Baik Bong. *Kim Il Sung, Biography*. 3 vols. (1969).
Cumings, Bruce. *The Origin of the Korean War: Liberation and the Emergence of Separate Regimes, 1945–1947* (1981).
Dae-Sook Suh. *Kim Il Sung The North Korean Leader* (1988).
Koh, B.C., "North Korea in 1988: The Fortieth Anniversary," *Asian Survey*, XXIX (January 1989): 39–45.
Phipps, John. "North Korea—Will It Be the 'Great Leader's' Turn Next?" (The Crisis of Marxism-Leninism, part 6) in *Government and Opposition* 26 (Winter 1991): 44–55.

Kimpo Airfield

Located northwest of Seoul, Kimpo Airfield was a vital asset for the transport of supplies and troops during the Korean War. The field had been improved during the American occupation after World War II, and was consequently the most modern in Korea, north or south. It and Suwon Airfield (the latter twenty miles south of Seoul) were the only fields suitable for high-performance aircraft.

Kimpo was used initially for the evacuation of civilians at the outbreak of hostilities in June 1950. On the afternoon of 25 June, North Korean Yak fighter aircraft buzzed and strafed Kimpo in an effort to disrupt this evacuation; they damaged the control tower, fuel pumps, and a four-engine C-54 U.S. Air Force Military Air Transport Service (MATS) transport. That night, six more enemy fighters strafed the field and completely destroyed the C-54. The following day, full-scale evacuation began from Kimpo, with the U.S. Air Force using aircraft flown in from Japan. Several hundred civilians, mostly U.S., were airlifted to Japan during the next three days. The USAF 8th Fighter Wing offered protection, flying over the field, and, as a result, no refugees were even injured by enemy attack. In fact, USAF F-82 "Twin Mustang" piston-engine fighters shot down seven enemy fighters on the 27th without loss to themselves.

The Republic of Korea (ROK) Air Force based aircraft both at Kimpo and Suwon, evacuating the aircraft as the North Koreans approached. On 29 June, a B-29 mission was mounted to destroy the facilities at Kimpo to prevent their use by the enemy. During this mission, the bombers were harassed by North Korean fighters, but suffered no losses.

Despite this attack, by 15 July, reports indicated that enemy aircraft were now based at Kimpo. A concerned General Douglas MacArthur and Lieutenant General Earle E. Partridge, U.S. Far East Air Force commander, sent USAF fighters on a strafing mission. B-29s also bombed the runways. Yet within a month the North Koreans had repaired the damage. So, on 4 August, Fifth Air Force fighters again strafed Kimpo aircraft and cratered its runways.

Kimpo was a prime objective in the planning for the Inchon landings. On 17 September, U.S. Marines captured Kimpo, and two days later the first C-54 landed at the airfield, followed by eight more, and twenty-three C-119 "Flying Boxcars" loaded with supplies and men. The Far East Air Force's Combat Cargo Command quickly organized an around-the-clock airlift, and specially trained USAF cargo handling teams expedited the work. By October, both Kimpo and Suwon were bases for fighter-bomber groups. The 811th Engineer Aviation Battalion arrived in late September to fill in the innumerable bomb craters, covering them at least temporarily with pierced steel planks. (Unfortunately, naval aircraft sometimes caught their tailhooks in the planking, causing damage to both planes and planking.)

As the war moved into North Korea, the pace of activity at Kimpo became nearly frantic. The base required more than 60,000 gallons of jet fuel daily, delivered by pipeline, train, and truck. Inadequate electronic equipment interrupted communications regularly. In the midst of this activity, "Operation Christmas Kidlift" airlifted war orphans from Kimpo to Cheju-do island.

Most U.S. troops flew from Ashiya Air Base, Japan, to Kimpo, and then to smaller airfields, or took ground transport to their units. Kimpo was also the primary base for jet fighter missions to the Yalu River area, 200 miles to the north.

In January 1951, when the Chinese Fourth Field Army reached Seoul, Allied engineers destroyed stores, equipment, and buildings at Kimpo. The Chinese reached the field, but only temporarily. By 10 February, U.S. Army I Corps had regained battered Kimpo. From then on Kimpo stayed in Allied hands.

For the rest of the war, Kimpo was a target for harassing raids by enemy aircraft, which were almost totally absent elsewhere in South Korea. By now, most Allied aircraft were based in Japan for logistical and operational reasons, although Australian Air Force No. 77 Squadron remained at Kimpo.

"Dentist" radar was installed at Kimpo to give warning of enemy aircraft approaching. Yet in August 1951, four MIGs overflew the airfield with impunity. The following month a Soviet-built enemy PO-2 biplane evaded detection and dropped two bombs, damaging some Sabre jets before being shot down, one of the few such "hecklers" to meet this fate.

Kimpo's runways were resurfaced and lengthened in 1952, and searchlights positioned around the perimeter. Kimpo was declared a "gun defended area" and airspace was restricted at night to aircraft cleared by the tower. Interceptors monitored Kimpo's airspace, noting planes higher than 2,000 feet and traveling faster than 160 miles per hour. (This monitoring, of course, missed the slow and low-flying PO-2s, and helps to account for their relative immunity.) And yet even in June 1953, Kimpo was subject to nightly enemy attacks. North Korean pilots added insult to injury by dropping propaganda leaflets over Kimpo and Seoul.

Less than one month after the armistice, a North Korean pilot defected from Pyongyang landing his MIG-15 at Kimpo and collected the $100,000 that United Nations commander General Mark Clark had offered for receipt of an intact MIG. (It remains unclear if the pilot defected for the money; he claimed never to have heard of the offer.)

After the armistice, Kimpo remained a major military base, but in later years developed also into a hub for international and domestic civil aviation.

Elizabeth Schafer

Bibliography

Futrell, Robert F. *The United States Air Force in Korea 1950-1953* (1961).

Hallion, Richard P. *The Naval Air War in Korea* (1986).

Huston, James A. *Guns and Butter, Powder and Rice: U.S. Army Logistics in the Korean War* (1989).

Jackson, Robert. *Air War Over Korea* (1973).

K

O'Neill, Arthur C. "Flight to Freedom," *Aerospace History* 16 (1969): 19-20.

Thompson, Captain Annis G. *The Greatest Airlift: The Story of Combat Cargo* (1954).

KMAG (Korean Military Advisory Group)

With the departure of U.S. Army occupation forces, KMAG was activated on 1 July 1949 as the official U.S. Army organization for training the fledgling armed forces of the Republic of Korea (ROK). Such training had been in progress ever since American military forces had occupied the southern half of the Korean peninsula in September 1945.

Such training had labored under severe difficulties. Korea was hardly a high priority for the Pentagon, and the better American personnel were often drawn off for use by General Douglas MacArthur's Japan occupation forces. (Those forces were enjoying lotus-land duty, some of the most undemanding assignments ever given to American arms. The lack of hard training would make itself felt disastrously in the first months on Korean battlefields.) Those soldiers detailed to Korea often resented their assignment to this hard-scrabble backwater instead of the green pastures of occupied Japan. The land yielded few resources, except for a population unusually well-educated for the Asian mainland. Favoritism, factionism, and corruption were rampant. The Koreans had not known self-government since the Japanese seizure of Korea in 1910 and had endured a brutal occupation in which very few of them had advanced to any position of responsibility. The government of the newly organized ROK, under the old patriot, Syngman Rhee, was anything but a model of democracy, and American advisors had to walk a fine line between advancing Korean military personnel on their merits and making some allowances for the wishes of what was, after all, a sovereign government after 1948.

Over all KMAG's work there loomed the brooding presence of the Democratic People's Republic of [North] Korea (DPRK), a Stalinist cult-nation, whose Radio Pyongyang made no secret of its nation's "mission" to throw out the "landlords, capitalists, and imperialists" of the ROK. Very little was known of North Korea's military; the main threat to the ROK was believed to come from a North Korean–instigated uprising in the South. Indeed, communism had a certain appeal across some segments of the ROK. Intellectuals and patriots resented the arrogance and cultural insensitivity shown at least in the early days of the American occupation, particularly in the retention of hated Japanese police and technicians. Some leftist South Koreans were attracted to North Korea's bloody purges of landlords, bankers, etc. Some South Koreans simply believed North Korean propaganda that things were better run in a nation free from government corruption, policy brutality, or economic exploitation.

It was against this seething background the KMAG found itself in limited combat two years before any of MacArthur's troops found themselves embattled on the same peninsula. On 19 October 1948, the ROK 14th Regiment at Yosu mutinied, spreading the uprising rapidly to the towns of Sunchon, Posong, Polgyo-ri, and Kwangyang, an indication of widespread dissatisfaction with the Rhee regime. At least two KMAG advisors were captured by the rebels, but managed to escape. Two other advisors managed to rally part of a loyal regiment and halt the rebellion's progress until the arrival of reinforcements and the brutal breaking of the rebellion. Although the Yosu Rebellion was suppressed, many of the mutineers escaped into the mountains to conduct guerrilla war, while the South continued to be plagued by a series of smaller-scale disturbances, as well as cross-border raids from the North. From May to November, there were no less than 400 separate engagements between North and South Korean armed forces along their mutual border, with heavy casualties on both sides, and the ROK Army (ROKA) was involved in nearly three antiguerrilla actions per day over roughly the same period of time.

Thus it was only natural that the ROKA would be trained as a counterinsurgency force, rather than to repel a full-scale invasion from the North, whose Army was not believed to possess armor or heavy artillery. KMAG advisors were exhorted to be just that—advisors. They could not command, but were teamed with Korean counterparts to be available at all times for advice. But the constant mobilization of ROKA forces to put down insurgencies stretched the ROKA to its limits. Training schools were set up at the urging of KMAG, including an officer academy, an ordnance school, a signal school, etc. KMAG advice and training was not limited to land forces; a Korean Coast Guard was established, and KMAG helped to train the national police and (reluctantly) a very small ROK Air Force. In all, the

KMAG training and advising program was adequate enough, considering the mission for which it was training, the constraints of strictly limited budgets, and having to work with a regime punctilious about its sovereignty. Even so, on the eve of war, KMAG estimated that the ROKA, with the ammunition and equipment on hand, could fight a defensive action for no more than fifteen days. It warned presciently, "Korea is threatened with the same disaster that befell China." In the words of the KMAG commander, Brigadier General William Lynn Roberts, "Time ran out."

From the beginning of the North Korean invasion of South Korea on 25 June 1950, KMAG was involved in full-scale war. KMAG managed to extricate its advisors from overrun areas without loss, arrange for the evacuation of U.S. civilians, and help to organize the defense of the ROK in a fast-deteriorating situation. The next few months were desperate ones for KMAG, forced to drop its advisory role and take to the field where its personnel virtually commanded ROK units in a situation of haste and expediency. ROKA casualties were enormous in the first days; almost half of the Army had been killed, captured, or wounded, and equipment losses were even more severe, although that Army had never been given heavy artillery or armor in the first place. Most KMAG advisors found themselves in the field, isolated, eating Korean rations, begging or borrowing their tentage, communications, and gasoline where they could, and working hard to overcome the language barrier with sign language and sketches drawn in the dust for shocked survivor and raw recruit alike. But ROKA units broke and retreated with disheartening frequency. Many KMAG advisors openly wondered, "Why do their Koreans fight so much better than our Koreans?" and half-seriously claimed that KMAG's initials in truth stood for "Kiss My A _ _ Goodbye." Wretchedly trained as it was, manpower was about the only resource in relatively plentiful supply, and KMAG was somehow able to establish training centers during the retreat to the Pusan perimeter to give some sort of elementary training to the flood of recruits.

In the summer of 1951, KMAG was reorganized to become an operational major subordinate command of Eighth Army, rather than a special staff section. Although it now provided advisors down to the battalion level, its main focus was on the improving of the ROK Army. President Rhee seemed merely to want the Army expanded, but a disastrous defeat suffered by one of his division at the hands of an inferior North Korean force clinched the American argument of quality before quantity. The primary ROKA need remained better leadership and training. To that end, KMAG convinced the ROK government and Eighth Army of the need for a training command to coordinate all the instructional activities for the ROKA.

As the pace of fighting slackened after the beginning of armistice talks in the summer of 1951, KMAG now had time to stimulate the growth of existing training facilities and to establish new ones, all the while focusing on the basic needs of leadership and training. Each ROKA division could now be pulled out of the line at different times and be sent to a training camp for nine weeks of basic training. Equipment also now became available to improve training and make it more realistic. By the middle of 1952, the pattern of KMAG training for the rest of the war had been set. In addition to the ROKA divisional refresher training, increasing numbers of specialists were being produced, as well as combat and service support troops, all required for an Army that would double in numbers of personnel and divisions in the near future.

Stanley Sandler

Bibliography

Appleman, R.E. *South to the Naktong, North to the Yalu* (Office of the Chief of Military History, Washington: 1961).
Hall, T.A. "KMAG and the 7th Division," *Infantry*, 79 (November–December 1989).
Noble, H.J. *Embassy at War* (Seattle: 1975).
Sawyer, Robert K., and Walter G. Hermes, eds. *Military Advisors in Korea: KMAG in Peace and War* (Office of the Chief of Military History, Washington: 1962).

Korea and the United States to 1945

At about the same time that small bands of Asiatics whose descendants Christopher Columbus would mistakenly identify as Indians were somehow traversing the Bering Strait from Siberia to present-day Alaska—probably between 30,000 and 20,000 B.C.—equally small bands of tribespeople (whose forebears had been kinspeople of the forebears of the North American "Indians") began making their way from present-day Manchuria across the Yalu and Tumen Rivers into the rugged Korean peninsula. At length, sometime around 2,000 B.C., a minuscule kingdom took form in north central Korea. It was known as Chosen—"land of the morning calm." Across the centuries that followed, kingdoms and dynasties came and went in the land the Occidentals would come to know as Korea. And some of them left rich legacies of artistic and intellectual achievement. But when thirteen British colonies along the Atlantic coast of North America established the independence of the United States of America in the last quarter of the eighteenth century, only a handful of citizens of the new republic, it seems fair to say, knew anything at all about Korea, a long-suffering country that had endured intermittent devastation at the hands of rapacious neighbors, that had been a tributary state of the Ch'ing dynasty of China for more than 200 years. In subsequent decades, Korea remained virtually unknown to Americans. Geographies and histories published in the United States during those years usually mentioned Korea only in passing, if they mentioned it at all. Fairly typical was the entry in J.E. Worcester's *An Epitome of Modern Geography*, published in 1820: "Corea is a small kingdom tributary to China, but is little known. King-kitao Seoul is the chief town."

Animated by what historians have identified as a "spread-eagle" impulse, Americans by the 1840s were taking increased interest in the world beyond their shores and borders, and in July 1844, American diplomat Caleb Cushing affixed his signature to a treaty establishing commercial relations between the United States and China. A few weeks after the Senate consented to Cushing's treaty, in February 1845, Zadock Pratt, Democrat of New York, offered amendments to a bill pending in the House of Representatives. Those amendments urged the federal government to undertake to establish commercial relations with the empire of Japan and the kingdom of Korea. Read and tabled, Congressman Pratt's resolution passed into oblivion when the Twenty-eighth Congress expired.

Less than a decade later, in 1854, Commodore Matthew C. Perry of the United States compelled the leaders of Japan to accept a trade treaty with the North American republic. But officials in Washington betrayed no interest in Korea. Then, in June 1866, the American schooner *Surprise* foundered in the Yellow Sea off Korea's northwest coast. Crewmen of the *Surprise* made their way to the Korean shore in small boats, and within a short time were trundled across forbidding mountain passes and over the Yalu to neighboring Manchuria. Two months after abandoning the *Surprise*, the castaways were delivered to the American consul at Yingtsze on Liaotung Bay. The consul thereupon arranged their return to the United States.

At the same time that the crewmen of the *Surprise* were making their way across the mountains to northwestern Korea to Manchuria in August 1866, the Crew of the American schooner *General Sherman*, under charter by a British firm, sailed from Chefoo on China's Shantung peninsula—destination Korea and a very different fate. The ostensible purpose of the voyage was to exchange trade goods. The *General Sherman* entered the Tacdong River, then moved upstream toward Pyongyang, only to become hopelessly stuck in the mud of the riverbed when the water level fell dramatically. Apparently on order of authorities in Seoul, Korean soldiers, some armed with muskets, others with bows and arrows, attacked the schooner. Heavily armed, the *General Sherman* crew held off the attackers, but after four days the Koreans overwhelmed and burned the stricken vessel.

Although rumors abounded, the precise fate of the *General Sherman*, its three American officers, two British subjects who were aboard, and its crew of fifteen or twenty Chinese and Malays remained a mystery outside Korea. To resolve the mystery, Commander Robert W. Shufeldt, in January 1867, guided the USS *Wachusett* from China across the Yellow Sea to the west coast of Korea. Foul weather compelled him to return to China before it was possible to receive a reply to a polite letter he had sent to the Korean king inquiring about the fate of the *General Sherman* and its crew. More than a year later, in spring of 1868, Commander John C. Febiger of the USS *Shenandoah* sailed from China to the mouth of the Taedong, communicated with local authorities, and at length received a letter prepared the previous year in response to Shufeldt's inquiry. The document explained that a local mob, under extreme provocation, had destroyed the *General Sherman* and killed every man on board.

Two years after Febiger's return from Korea, in 1870, Secretary of State Hamilton Fish instructed Frederick F. Low, the United States minister to China, to proceed for Korea the purpose of securing a treaty for the protection of shipwrecked seamen who might find themselves stranded on the shores of what Occidentals sometimes referred to as "the hermit kingdom." He also instructed Low, should the opportunity appear favorable, to strive to negotiate a commercial treaty with Korea. Accordingly, in May 1871, Low boarded the USS *Colorado* at the Japanese port of Nagasaki, and accompanied by a squadron of warships and gunboats, set sail for Korea. The flotilla dropped anchor near Chemulp'o (present-day Inchon), whereupon Low and his aides made contact with local officials. The officials reported that the Korean king sought friendly relations, but did not wish to negotiate commercial treaties. Then, on June 1, 1870, four steam launches accompanied by two gunboats to make observations and take soundings, proceeded up the Yom-ha (or, in the Occidental lexicon, the Salée River), the narrow passage that separates the Korean mainland from the large island of Kanghwa (at the mouth of the Han River). On rounding a sharp point in the passage, the flotilla came under fire by Korean shore batteries. After the guns of the American gunboats had silenced the batteries, the flotilla, unscathed, returned to the anchorage.

When Korean authorities failed to disavow the attack of June 1, Low ordered a punitive attack on the Korean fortifications along the Yom-ha. On June 1, 1871, two gunboats, an assortment of steam launches, and boats towed by the launches moved up an improvised company of sailors armed with rifles. Moving from one fortification to the next, the Americans, over the next two days, captured and destroyed five forts, killed about 250 Koreans, and took several prisoners. Three Americans died in the action, three were wounded. The destruction of Korean fortifications along the Yom-ha notwithstanding, authorities in Seoul persisted in their refusal to enter negotiations with Low. The Low mission a failure, the United States flotilla, on July 3, 1871, weighed anchor and sailed away.

Five years later, in 1876, a flotilla of Japanese warships, after the fashion of Commodore Perry's expedition to secluded Japan two decades before, sailed menacingly along the west coast of Korea. Intimidated by the show of Japanese power, the government in Seoul accepted the Treaty of Kanghwa, which provided that Japan and Korea would exchange envoys and allow one another's nationals to conduct business and trade without restriction within their respective borders. Then, in December 1878, a fleet of American warships under command of the aforementioned Robert Shufeldt (now Commodore Shufeldt) departed Norfolk

on the first leg of a round-the-world cruise, the purpose of which was to bring about an expansion of American trade in Africa and Asia. On reaching the Far East, Shufeldt, with assistance by the Japanese, set about to negotiate a commercial treaty with Korea. His enterprise again met frustration. But at length, in summer of 1880, Shufeldt accepted an invitation by the Chinese viceroy in Beijing to visit China, which of course was the suzerain of Korea.

After discussions with the viceroy in Tientsin, Shufeldt returned to America, whereupon the viceroy prevailed upon authorities in Seoul to accept a treaty with the United States. When Shufeldt returned to the Far East the following year, he and the viceroy, meeting in Beijing, negotiated a treaty that would bind the United States and Korea. A short time later the Koreans agreed to the terms and in May of 1882 the American commodore sailed across the Yellow Sea aboard the USS *Swatara*, and on a hillside near Chemulp'o he and emissaries of the royal court in Seoul put their hands to a treaty of peace, amity, commerce, and navigation, the first article at which provided that "if other Powers deal unjustly or oppressively with either Government, the other will exert their good offices, on being informed of the case, to bring about an amicable arrangement, thus showing their friendly feelings." Over the next few years, Great Britain, Germany, France, and Russia negotiated similar treaties with the one-time hermit kingdom.

The first American minister to Korea, Lucius M. Foote, arrived in Seoul in 1883. During his sixteen-month tenure as minister, Foote arranged for a delegation of Koreans to travel to the United States. Treated with manifest cordiality on their arrival in America, the delegates were received in Washington by President Chester A. Arthur. Foote also prepared the way for two American trading companies to set up operations in Korea. He helped Thomas Alva Edison secure an exclusive franchise to install electric light and telephone systems in the country. And he opened the door of his legation to Horace N. Allen, a Presbyterian medical missionary, and before long, Allen and other missionaries from the United States and elsewhere, ignoring laws that forbade such practice, were actively striving to convert Koreans to Christianity. As Allen gained the confidence of King Kojong of Korea, his interests gravitated increasingly to diplomacy, and in 1897 he became the United States minister to Korea. Until his recall in 1905, Allen helped American corporations and entrepreneurs acquire concessions in Korea in a variety of fields, including electric power, railroading, pearls, and gold mining.

Korea, meanwhile, became caught up in the crosscurrents of the rivalries of larger neighbors, and following a war in 1895 in which the Japanese thrashed the Chinese it ceased to be a tributary state of China, only to fall under the domination of Japan. Before long, however Imperial Russia set about to challenge Japan's primacy in Korea and on Manchuria's Liaotung peninsula, and the outcome, in 1904–1905, was the Russo-Japanese War. During the latter war, the Japanese tightened their grip on Korea. They did so with the support of U.S. President Theodore Roosevelt, a man who admired the Japanese and held Koreans in utter contempt. Indeed, in July 1905, Roosevelt's secretary of war, William Howard Taft, proposed during a conversation with Japanese Prime Minister Taro Katsura that Japan establish suzerainty over Korea. That is, he proposed that Japan effect the demise of a nation-state whose freedom from injustice and oppression by other powers the United States had pledged to support by diplomatic initiative ("on being informed" of said injustice and oppression) in the Treaty of Chemulp'o of 1882.

Having turned aside a petition urging that he intercede on behalf of Korean independence by invoking the Chemulp'o treaty—a petition that was presented to him in person at his estate on Long Island by two youthful Korean emissaries, one of whom was the twenty-nine-year-old Syngman Rhee—Roosevelt, in September 1905, arranged the Treaty of Portsmouth ending the Russo-Japanese War. In one clause of the latter treaty, the imperial government of Russia agreed "not to interfere or place obstacles in the way of any measure of direction, protection, and supervision which the Imperial Government of Japan may deem necessary to adopt in Korea." Less than three months later, in November 1905, the Japanese coerced Emperor (formerly King) Kojong into accepting a treaty by which Korea became a protectorate—in truth, a colony—of Japan. A few days after Kojong signed the treaty, Homer B. Hulbert, an American confidant of the Korean monarch, arrived in Washington with a secret appeal by the emperor urging that the United States, in accordance with the treaty of 1882, exercise its good offices to rescue Korea from the clutches of Japan. Roosevelt turned aside Kojong's appeal.

During the years that followed, Japan tightened its grip on Korea with the acquiescence of the United States, which in 1908, via the so-called Root-Takahira agreement, endorsed the status quo in Northeast Asia, that is, recognized Japan's primacy in Korea and southern Manchuria. Then, in 1910, Japan completed its conquest of the ancient land of the morning calm by annexing it and making it an integral part of the Japanese empire. Still, Korean nationalists, including perhaps 6,000 Koreans who had migrated to Hawaii and the United States, kept alive the dream of an independent Korea. They gained a measure of notoriety in the United States in 1908 when one of their number fatally wounded Durham White Stevens, a long-time employee of the Japanese government, at a railroad station in San Francisco.

Of larger interest perhaps was the memorial dispatched to President Woodrow Wilson in December 1918, on the eve of the Paris Peace Conference (one month after the battlefield armistice terminating the Great War), by three representatives of the Korea National Association, an organization that claimed to speak for Koreans in the United States, Hawaii, Mexico, China, and Russia. One of the authors of the memorial was Syngman Rhee, a student and protégé of Wilson several years before when Wilson was president of Princeton University. After essaying Korean grievances against Japan, the memorial argued that, inasmuch as the treaty of Chemulp'o of 1882 had never been abrogated, the United States had a moral obligation "to aid the Koreans in their aspirations for self-determination." Wilson, like Roosevelt, ignored the memorial and when Rhee sought to travel to Paris to make a personal appeal to his former mentor the State Department denied him a passport on the ground that he was now a Japanese subject and hence must apply for a Japanese passport!

A short time later, in March 1919, Rhee made public a letter that he and another Korean nationalist had forwarded to President Wilson urging that the League of Nations, soon to be organized, assume mandatory responsibility for Korea until such time as the League should decide that the old hermit kingdom was prepared to be independent. In the following month, April 1919, Rhee was the central personality in a Korean congress that met for three days in Philadelphia to publicize Japan's alleged misrule in Korea. And in that same month, Korean nationalists from Korea, Japan, America, and elsewhere converged on Shanghai, proclaimed a provisional government for an independent Korea, and elected Rhee the fledgling government-in-exile's first president.

Meanwhile, Koreans in Korea were astir, and the outcome, in March and April of 1919, was nationwide demonstrations and riots protesting Japanese rule of their ancient nation. The purpose of this so-called Mansei Revolution was transparent: to prevail upon the people of the United States and their president to press the Japanese to accept the principle of national self-determination with respect to Korea. Alas, the people of the United States and their president took scant notice of the tumultuous events unfolding in Korea in spring of 1919. Rather, they were absorbed by goings-on in Paris, where Wilson and the leaders of Britain, France, and Italy were redrawing the map of Europe.

During the two decades that followed, a handful of American churchpeople who oversaw and supported the activities of Christian (mostly Protestant) missionaries who continued to toil in the vineyard of Korea—under close observation by the Japanese—kept abreast of goings-on in the onetime hermit kingdom. Otherwise, Korea seldom if ever intruded into the thoughts of most Americans. Only rarely did a news story or magazine article touching on Korea find its way into print in the United States. Syngman Rhee's attempt to win again a hearing on behalf of Korean independence during the Washington Conference of 1921–1922 attracted little attention. It was rare that an official in Washington was willing to grant an audience to Rhee, who in 1939, after living in Hawaii for many years, took up residence in the American capital. As the United States and Japan edged toward war in 1941, he published a book entitled *Japan Inside Out*, which argued that Japanese expansionism in Asia constituted a threat to free peoples everywhere, but it sparked little interest.

But then, on December 7, 1941, the Japanese unleashed their attack on Pearl Harbor, and the following day the United States declared war on Japan. Leaders of the Korean government-in-exile were ecstatic. Kim Ku, the leader of Korean nationalists in Chungking dispatched a cable to Washington pledging that the Korean provisional government would do everything in its power to assist the United States in overcoming the Japanese, while Rhee set about to lobby officials in Washington to recognize the provisional government as the legal political agent of the Korean nation. To the disappointment of

Rhee and other exiled chieftains, the recognition they sought was not forthcoming. Spokesmen in the State Department believed it would be unconscionable for the victorious allies at the end of the war to impose on the Korean people a provisional government that they had not chosen—one comprised of men who had been absent from Korea for more than two decades and had long since lost touch with political currents in their homeland. Of larger moment perhaps, leaders in Washington were conscious of historic Soviet interests in Northeast Asia, knew that Korean Communists who expected to compete for political influence in postwar Korea were living under the protection of the Soviets, and feared that recognition of the provisional government might weaken the military coalition of the Westerly powers and the Soviet behemoth.

Meanwhile, Generalissimo Chiang Kai-shek of China came to fear that the Soviets would exploit unrest in Korea at the end of the Pacific war to the detriment of China. Accordingly, in 1943, he prevailed on Franklin D. Roosevelt and Winston Churchill to join him in proclaiming support for Korean independence. The outcome was a pledge, issued in a communiqué at the end of the so-called Cairo Conference in the autumn of 1943, that China, the United States, and Britain, "mindful of the enslavement of the people of Korea, are determined that in due course Korea shall become free and independent." Leaders of the Soviet Union subsequently consented to the substance of the communiqué. Because of its "in due course" language, intimating as it did that Korea would not achieve immediate independence at the end of the war, but rather would be under the governance of some sort of trusteeship established by the victorious powers, the Cairo declaration came under vigorous—and fruitless—attack by Kim Ku, Syngman Rhee, and other Korean exiles.

Their attention riveted on the drive of Allied armies into Germany and the amphibious operations of American task forces in the Central and Southwest Pacific, the leaders of the United States gave only intermittent thought to Korea in the year and a half that followed the Cairo communiqué. Then, in July 1945, as American forces deployed for an amphibious assault on the Japanese home islands, officials in Washington directed General Douglas MacArthur, recently appointed commander in chief of all United States Army Forces in the Pacific, to prepare for the occupation of Korea

K

as well as Japan. On August 6–9, 1945, American nuclear bombs devastated the Japanese cities of Hiroshima and Nagasaki and the Soviet Union entered the Pacific war. On August 10, the leaders of Imperial Japan, the longtime oppressor of Korea, requested terms of surrender.

John Edward Wilz

Bibliography

Deuchler, Martina. *Confucian Gentlemen and Barbarian Envoys: The Opening of Korea, 1875–1882* (1977).

Harringtoll, Fred Harvey. *God, Mammon, and the Japanese: Dr. Horace N. Allen and Korean-American Relations, 1884–1905.* (1944).

Oliver, Robert T. *Syngman Rhee: The Man Behind the Myth* (1955).

Woo-keun Han. *The History of Korea* (1971).

Yur-bok Lee. *Diplomatic Relations between the United States and Korea, 1866–1887* (1970).

Korea and the United States, 1945–1950

As the war in the Pacific was moving to a climax in the summer of 1945, Soviet dictator Joseph Stalin agreed to an arrangement proposed by President Harry S. Truman whereby the Soviets would accept the surrender of Japanese forces in Korea from the Yalu and Tumen Rivers down to the 38th parallel, while the Americans would accept the surrender of enemy forces below that line. A short time later, in the closing days of August, troops of the Red Army, looting and raping as they proceeded southward, reached the 38th parallel. The Soviets thereupon cut railways, roads, and telephone lines, then set about to curtail the movement of people and commodities between the two halves of Korea. After turning the parallel into a fortified frontier, they established a Communist administration for northern Korea, its capital in Pyongyang, and placed that administration under the headship of Kim Il Sung, a comparatively youthful Korean Communist who had led Korean patriots in guerrilla operations against the Japanese in Manchuria from 1932 to 1941 before fleeing to the maritime province of the Soviet Union. Clearly, the current chieftains in the Kremlin, no less than their tsarist predecessors a half-century before, viewed Korea as an area of large importance in terms of the strategic interests of their Eurasian empire.

Under the command of Lieutenant General John R. Hodge, United States troops arrived in southern Korea during the first week of September of 1945. They quickly found themselves to be the occupiers of a country (or half of a country) in which the economy was in disarray and the political situation tense. Their mission? That was not entirely clear. Indeed, it was not until the middle of October that General Hodge received a directive spelling out the "ultimate objective" of the United States with respect to Korea. That objective was eventual restoration of Korea's national independence. During an interim period, however, the Soviet Union and the United States would administer the affairs of Korea. At length, administration of the country would pass to a trusteeship presided over by China, Great Britain, the Soviet Union, and the United States. Finally, at some undetermined time, Korea would achieve full independence and become a member of the United Nations.

Demanding immediate independence for their long-suffering homeland, most Koreans, including Syngman Rhee and Kim Ku, for many years the leaders of a Korean government-in-exile who returned to Korea in October 1945, took a jaundiced view of the trusteeship conception. And when the Soviet Union and the United States, in December 1945, drew up an agreement providing for a five-year trusteeship for Korea, thousands of Koreans took to the streets of Seoul and other cities in the American zone of occupation in riotous demonstrations. Undeterred by the objections of Koreans, the occupying powers set about to fashion a precise formula for the administration of a unified a Korea by a trusteeship. Their discussions yielded little save recrimination. As General Hodge reported in February 1946 to his superior, General Douglas MacArthur, the commander in chief of United States armed forces in the Far East, "My best guess now is that north and south Korea will never be really united until the Russians are sure that the whole will be soundly communistic." In their zone of occupation, meanwhile, the Soviets set about to organize and train a Communist military force comprising scores of thousands of youthful Koreans.

From the perspective of the United States, the situation in Korea only worsened as the months of 1946 unfolded. Syngman Rhee and other non-Communist nationalists continued to rail against the Soviet-American plan to place Korea under a trusteeship. To generate discord and unrest in the American zone of occupation, Communists undertook a campaign of harassment and disruption and organized demonstrations against the occupiers of southern Korea. At length, in May 1947, emissaries of the Soviet Union and the United States resumed negotiations aimed at working out a trusteeship formula. As in the past, the Soviets determined that a trusteeship must facilitate an eventual takeover of all of Korea by Communists, the Americans that it must prepare the way for a freely elected government which, in their view, would doubtless be non-Communist (inasmuch as it was an article of the American credo during those years that, given a free choice, the people of no nation would opt for rule by Communists). Accordingly, the negotiations quickly deadlocked.

By the summer of 1947, of course, American leaders had come to realize that the United States was in the grip of what would come to be referred to as a Cold War with the Soviet empire. And the previous spring, the prestigious journal *Foreign Affairs* had published George F. Kennan's celebrated "X-article" setting out the argument that the Western democracies must contain Soviet power. The Cold War and the containment conception notwithstanding, policy planners in the State Department, in early September of 1947, reached an almost unanimous conclusion that, in the matter of Korea, the best course for the United States would be to abandon the Koreans to their fate. A fortnight later, the Joint Chiefs of Staff reported that "from the standpoint of military security, the United States has little strategic interest in maintaining the present troops and bases in Korea." In the event of a general war in the Far East, they explained, the 45,000-man American force presently deployed in the peninsula would be a military liability. And in the event of "violent disorders" inside southern Korea, that force might be compelled to make a humiliating retreat from the peninsula. The conclusion was transparent: the joint chiefs wanted to withdraw United States troops from southern Korea.

In the last days of September 1947, the State Department, now presided over by General George C. Marshall, passed to the United Nations a Soviet proposal that all foreign troops be withdrawn from Korea forthwith, and an American recommendation that a freely elected government be established for the entire peninsula. That the U.N. would prove unequal to the task of working out an acceptable formula for establishing a freely elected government for all of the country was a foregone conclusion. But that mattered little. What Marshall and the policy planners in Washington were most anxious to accomplish was the withdrawal of United States forces from Korea with a minimum of ill effects. Or as George Kennan, the director of the State Department's policy planning staff, subsequently observed in a memorandum, the aim of the Washington government was "to get the best bargain we can" regarding Korea. Six weeks later, in mid-November 1947, the General Assembly of the U.N., over Soviet objections, approved an American-sponsored resolution providing that a single government should be organized for all of Korea. An election to choose representatives whose mandate would be to fashion a constitution for the new government should take place throughout the peninsula no later than March 31, 1948.

Policy planners in Washington were under no illusion that the Soviets would allow the people of northern Korea to participate in the U.N. enterprise to establish a democratic government for the entire Korean nation. Hence they recommended that if, as expected, the Soviets refused to permit elections above the 38th parallel, the United States should press for elections below that line—elections that would result in the establishment of an independent government for southern Korea. They proposed that the inauguration of the new government for southern Korea take place on August 15, 1948, after which date the withdrawal of United States forces from the peninsula would commence. Agreeing that a Soviet-sponsored takeover of southern Korea in the wake of the withdrawal of American troops would damage American prestige and interests across the entire world, the planners proposed that the United States provide economic and military assistance to the new South Korean republic.

Was economic and military assistance apt to save a South Korean republic from the Communists after the removal of United States forces? The Joint Chiefs of Staff did not think it would. According to the chiefs, in a memorandum prepared in February 1948, "eventual domination of Korea by the U.S.S.R. will have to be accepted as a probability if U.S. troops are withdrawn." Did such a probability move the joint chiefs to revise their view about the desirability of withdrawing American forces from southern Korea? It did not. The chiefs still wanted those forces out of Korea "at the earliest practicable date."

During the weeks that followed, officials in Washington, their attention concentrated on the coup in Prague that delivered Czechoslovakia to the Soviet empire, the debate in Congress over the Marshall Plan of economic assistance to the struggling democracies of Western Europe, and Soviet harassment of the overland access routes of the Western powers to their occupation zones in Berlin, continued to assess their government's Korean policy. The outcome, in spring of 1948, was a paper by the National Security Council (NSC-8) which, when approved by President Harry S. Truman a short time later, became the basic statement of American policy regarding Korea. The essential conclusion of NSC-8 was that the United States should help the south Koreans build up their economy and armed forces, but beyond that it would be up to them to secure their fledgling state against the Communists. Clearly, the overbearing purpose of the United States with respect to Korea was to disengage from the peninsula as gracefully as possible.

Meanwhile, in January 1948, a U.N. commission had made its way to the Far East to arrange for the establishment of a freely elected government for all of Korea in accord with the U.N. resolution of the previous November. When the Soviets, to nobody's surprise, refused to admit the commissioners to northern Korea, the commissioners, on instructions from U.N. headquarters in New York, set about to arrange elections in southern Korea only. Those arrangements made, an estimated 95.2 percent of southern Korea's eligible voters, on May 10, 1948, trooped to polling places and elected representatives to a National Assembly. The National Assembly, in July 1948, drafted a constitution for the Republic of Korea (ROK), a state which in theory would include northern Korea, but whose writ obviously would not run beyond the 38th parallel, and then elected Syngman Rhee to be the first president of the new republic. The inauguration of the ROK (South Korea) took place on August 15, 1948, an oppressively hot day in Seoul. A principal speaker during the elaborate ceremony was General MacArthur, and in his rich baritone the grandiloquent warrior-statesman announced that the "artificial barrier" dividing Korea "must and will be torn down."

Less than a month later, in early September 1948, Communists in northern Korea established the Democratic People's Republic of (North) Korea (DPRK) and designated Kim Il Sung the first premier of the Kremlin's newest client state. Like its counterpart in Seoul, the new government in Pyongyang claimed jurisdiction over the entire peninsula. Over the next four months, the Soviets withdrew all of their troops from North Korea, but left behind an increasingly well-trained and well-equipped North Korean Army.

Meanwhile, in the weeks following Syngman Rhee's inauguration as president of the ROK, the withdrawal of United States troops from South Korea got under way. But then in January 1949, officials in Washington asked General MacArthur to evaluate the probable impact of an early withdrawal of the remaining American troops from South Korea. In his reply the general did not respond directly, but his thinking was perfectly clear. The threat of an invasion from the North, he explained, was apt to hang over South Korea during the foreseeable future. Could the South Koreans turn back such an invasion? No. Should the United States commit military forces to bolster the South Koreans in the event of an invasion? Also no. The remaining American troops ought to be withdrawn from the peninsula as soon as possible, say by May 10, 1949. MacArthur went on to say that the Japanese must be conditioned to the prospect of Soviet domination of all of the East Asian mainland, and that the prestige of the United States in the area must rest on its ability to control the sea lanes of the Western Pacific and maintain assorted island bases.

Two months later, on March 23, 1949, President Truman approved NSC-8/2, essentially a reiteration of NSC-8 of the previous year except that it set a date for the withdrawal of the last United States troops from South Korea (save for a small group of American military personnel that would advise and instruct the South Korean Army): June 30, 1949. Unnerved that the ROK was about to lose the shield against invasion from the North provided by American troops, President Rhee, on learning of Washington intention to remove its remaining forces from his republic, made an impassioned appeal for a pledge of American support in the event the North Koreans unleashed an invasion over the 38th parallel. Washington declined to make such a pledge.

The anguish of Rhee and other South Koreans notwithstanding, the last American combat troops moved out of South Korea in June 1949. And as they bade farewell to the ancient land of the morning calm, officials in the Pentagon weighed actions that the United States might take should a North Korean invasion of the ROK come to pass in the near future. They set out their views in a paper that was transmitted to the State Department on June 27, 1949.

The authors of this paper believed that in the event of an invasion of South Korea, the United States would be compelled to make some sort of response. But what kind of response? Assuredly not a unilateral reintroduction of American combat forces in Korea. Such a move, even if inspiring anti-Communists across the world, would commit the United States "to a unilateral course of action and responsibility in Korea from which it so recently has struggled to extricate itself." It would, moreover, place unacceptable demands on American manpower and resources, and might lead to a long and costly involvement of American forces in an undeclared war. Rather, the United States should respond to a Communist invasion of South Korea by evacuating American nationals from South Korea and submitting the matter of the invasion to the Security Council of the U.N. for emergency consideration as a threat to the general peace. If the Soviets refrained from exercising their veto, it might be possible for the world organization to dispatch a task force comprising military units of the United States and other nations to restore law and order south of the 38th parallel. The enthusiasm of America's military leaders for a U.N.-sponsored "police action" (a term actually used in the paper) in Korea was nil. "This course of action is unsound militarily and should be considered only . . . if it becomes apparent that all other methods have failed." And it was a course that absolutely should not be taken without "complete cooperation and full participation by other member nations."

On the day after the last United States combat troops departed Korea, June 30, 1949, General MacArthur, whose only visit to Korea since the end of the Pacific war had taken place on the ROK's aforementioned independence day in August 1948, relinquished all command responsibilities in Korea. Still, MacArthur would find himself temporarily involved with Korea in the event of an attack across the 38th parallel by the armed forces of North Korea or a large-scale uprising by South Koreans against the government in Seoul. His involvement would not be particularly dramatic. In accord with Plan Chow Chow of July 1949, the general's Far East command would evacuate to Japan all American civilian and military personnel who were in Korea at the time, as well as designated foreign nationals. Should a "general emergency" come to pass, i.e., an outbreak of hostilities involving the United States and the Soviet Union, Americans in South Korea would be on their own, presumably because ships and planes would not be available for evacuation purposes. What should be the course of action if American combat units deployed in the Far East to counter an attack on South Korea in the improbable event that the U.N. Security Council sanctioned it and other U.N. members agreed to dispatch forces? Plan Chow Chow included no provision whatever for such deployment.

Had leaders in Seoul known that MacArthur's contingency plans for military operations in the Far East included no provision for reintroducing American forces in Korea, they doubtless would have been more upset than they were. And they continued to be upset, as Rhee's special representative, Dr. Pyung Ok Chough, explained in a conversation with Secretary of State Dean Acheson in Washington on July 11, 1949. Chough also told Acheson that what the South Koreans wanted was a specific guarantee that the United States would move to the defense of the ROK in the event of an armed attack against it. Acheson replied that such a specific commitment by Washington was out of the question.

Rebuffed in his effort to secure an American commitment to defend South Korea, Rhee now sought to persuade Washington to provide increased quantities of military equipment for his armed forces. In an impassioned letter to President Truman dated August 20, 1949, he expressed his conviction that the North Koreans intended to invade the ROK in the near future. Only if the United States stepped up its shipments of arms and ammunition, he said, would the South Koreans stand a chance of repelling the northerners. Truman replied a month later. Observing that South Korea might receive additional support under military assistance legislation pending in Congress, he made it clear that the United States had no intention of providing aid on the scale requested by Rhee. "This government feels that the security of the Republic of Korea can best be served by the development of an efficient, compact Korean force rather than by amassing large military forces which would be an insupportable burden on the economy of the country." Truman's explanation was disingenuous. In truth, the American president feared that the irascible and irrepressible Rhee, if provided the requisite implements of war by the United States, might break the uneasy peace in the Far East by ordering the armed forces of the ROK to undertake an invasion of North Korea.

Moved no doubt by the momentous events unfolding in China, officials in Washington meanwhile had begun—incredibly for the first time—to work out an overall American policy for the Far East. Hitherto the United States had fashioned policy for the area on a country by country basis. The outcome was NSC-48/2, approved by President Truman on December 30, 1949. The central purpose of American policy in the Far East, the top secret document made manifest, was to prevent the expansion of Communist power eastward from the Asian mainland into the Pacific. To achieve that purpose, the United States would continue to rely on its bastions in the Philippines, the Ryukyus, and Japan. As for South Korea, mentioned almost in passing, Washington should continue to provide economic, military, and technical assistance.

A fortnight after Truman approved NSC-48/2, on January 12, 1950, Secretary Acheson spoke to the National Press Club in Washington on the subject of American policy in Asia. The Asian policy of the United States was a subject of concern to many Americans in those first weeks after the Communists had completed their conquest of China. In the course of his remarks Acheson sketched America's defensive perimeter in the Far East. In accord with NSC-48/2, the line moved from the Aleutian Islands through Japan to the Ryukyus, to the Philippines. Should an attack occur in other areas (South Korea?), the secretary explained, "the initial reliance must be on the people attacked to resist it and then upon the commitments of the entire civilized world under the Charter of the United Nations, which so far has not proved a weak reed to lean on by any people who are determined to protect their independence against outside aggression." What would happen if the victim of aggression on the other side of the American defensive perimeter in the Far East could not hold back the aggressor—and if a Soviet veto or a general unwillingness by U.N. members to act prevented the world organization from making an armed intervention on behalf of the victim, Acheson did not say. But the secretary's inference seemed clear: the United States had no intention of acting unilaterally to counter aggression on the other side of the defensive perimeter it had marked out in the Far East.

What interpretation the Soviets and North Koreans put on Acheson's remarks of January 12 is impossible to say for certain. But the secretary's speech set off alarm bells in Seoul. Assistant Secretary of State for Far Eastern Affairs, Dean Rusk, observed a few months later that in the aftermath of the speech the State Department "was subjected to a barrage of representations from the South Korean government and its representatives designed to elicit from the U.S. a commitment to extend its defense line in the Far East to include South Korea." Washington turned aside the South Korean appeals.

Still, recent events were casting a long shadow across America's position in the world and causing leaders in Washington to conclude that the time had come to reassess the country's foreign and military policies. The shadow-casting events were the completion of the Communist conquest of China and the detonation of an atomic weapon by the Soviet Union. Indeed, President Truman appended a directive mandating a reassessment of America's foreign and military policies to his order of January 31, 1950, directing the Atomic Energy Commission to perfect a hydrogen or "super" bomb. The result, in April 1950, was another top secret paper, NSC-68, put together in the Departments of State and Defense under the supervision of Paul Nitze of the State Department's policy planning staff.

Repetitious and pedestrian, NSC-68 assuredly was no literary masterpiece. And abounding as it did with hyperbole, it scarcely offered a dispassionate analysis of America's diplomatic and military problems. The document asserted that the Soviet Union, animated by a new fanatical faith, was seeking to impose absolute authority over the rest of the world. According to NSC-68, "The issues that face us are momentous, involving the fulfillment or destruction not only of this Republic but of civilization itself." NSC-68 did not state categorically that the United States ought to deploy its armed forces to meet aggressive moves by the Soviet Union or its satellites or clients against one of the lesser non-Communist countries, say South Korea. But it expressed the conviction that Washington should view any such moves with utmost seriousness. Asserted the document, "The assault on free institutions is world-wide now, and in the context of the present polarization of power a defeat of free institutions anywhere is a defeat everywhere."

Because it had allowed its conventional, that is, nonnuclear forces to deteriorate, NSC-68 complained, the United States had no choice at assorted pressure points across the world between capitulation to Soviet or Soviet-supported aggression and precipitating a global (and, presumably, atomic) war. "Instead of appearing strong and resolute we are continually at the verge of appearing and being alternately irresolute and desperate." Many pages later NSC-68 proclaimed that "the Soviet Union has consistently pursued a bold foreign policy, modified only when its probing revealed a determination and an ability of the free world to resist encroachment upon it." The conclusion was transparent: the United States must build up its military strength as quickly as possible. Wrote the authors of NSC-68, "It is necessary to have the military power to deter, if possible, Soviet expansion, and to defeat, if necessary, aggressive Soviet or Soviet-directed actions of a limited or total character." To counter limited actions, the United States needed to strengthen its conventional forces to a point where it was not so dependent on atomic weapons. But to meet the threat of total war, the country should produce and stockpile thermonuclear or hydrogen weapons in the event such super weapons were perfected.

NSC-68 clearly indicated a new determination by the United States to "stand up" to Soviet or Soviet-supported expansion across the entire world, not just in Western and Southeastern Europe—a determination to give new substance to the celebrated Truman Doctrine of 1947 whereby, according to the thirty-second president, it was to be the policy of the United States "to support free peoples who are resisting attempted subjugation by armed minorities or by outside pressure." NSC-68 had the unflinching support of Secretary Acheson, who had kept in close touch with its drafting and who later recalled that it was discussed with Truman during a National Security Council meeting on April 25, 1950, and became national policy.

As matters turned out, the leaders of the United States were slow to apply their new perceptions, that is the perceptions spelled out in NSC-68, to specific problem areas. Thus there was no apparent change in Washington's policy vis-à-vis South Korea. The State Department *Bulletin* in March 1950 published a statement by Acheson given to the Senate Foreign Relations Committee at the same time that NSC-68 was taking form. Regarding Korea, the secretary did not take the opportunity to suggest that the United States, in accord with new perspectives, might respond most vigorously to any Communist aggression against South Korea. Rather, he said that there was good reason to hope that the ROK could survive and prosper, then added, "This, of course, cannot be guaranteed."

Two months later, in May 1950, *U.S. News & World Report,* a weekly news magazine, published an interview by an unnamed reporter with the chairman of the Senate Foreign Relations Committee, Tom Connally of Texas. Asked if he thought "the suggestion" (the source of which suggestion was not given) that the United States ought to abandon South Korea should receive serious consideration, Connally replied, "I'm afraid it's going to happen, that is, the abandonment of South Korea, whether we want it to or not." He explained that the United States was appropriating money to help South Korea, but the Soviet Union could overrun the country whenever it wished. Asked if South Korea was essential to America's defensive strategy, the senator answered, "No. Of course, any position like that is of some strategic importance, but I don't think it is very greatly important. It has been testified before us that Japan, Okinawa, and the Philippines make the chain of defenses which is absolutely necessary. And, of course, any additional territory along that area would be that much more, but it's not absolutely essential."

A public statement of what political and military leaders in Washington had been saying in secret for more than two years, Connally's remarks touched off a reaction in Seoul. In an obvious attempt to calm the South Koreans, Secretary Acheson told a news conference on May 3, 1950, that his department had continually stressed the importance of South Korea. He went on to say that the United States had cooperated with other nations to establish the ROK, and that Washington was presently providing the South Koreans with "very substantial" economic and military assistance. Two days later, the United States ambassador to the Rhee government, John J. Muccio, was quoted as saying that there could be no doubt of the eagerness of the United States to maintain the independence of the ROK. But neither the secretary nor the ambassador offered any hint that the United States might rally to the defense of Syngman Rhee's republic in the event of a North Korean invasion.

Meanwhile, there was no relaxation of Communist pressure on the ROK. Communist guerrillas continued their high level of disruptive activity across South Korea during the first months of 1950, and daily intelligence summaries prepared in MacArthur's headquarters in Tokyo in that period were sprinkled with reports of bloody clashes between guerrillas and government troops. Guerrilla activity was not the only manifestation of the continuing Communist threat to the security of the ROK. Armed clashes between ROK and North Korean troops along the 38th parallel took place in early 1950 at a rate of several per week. More ominously, MacArthur's intelligence section, in the first week of January 1950, evaluated reports that an invasion of South Korea might occur the following March or April. Two months later, in March 1950, it considered a prescient report that the North Korean People's Army, reinforced by Korean troops who recently had fought in China's civil war, would invade South Korea in June of 1950.

Was an invasion indeed imminent? MacArthur's intelligence people did not think so. In late March of 1950, they conceded that the North Koreans might be prepared to invade South Korea during the weeks ahead, and certainly would be prepared to undertake an invasion in the following autumn. But they surmised that the Soviets, who they believed were orchestrating all Communist activities in the Far East, were not apt to order an invasion pending the outcome of current Communist operations in Southeast Asia. If the Communists were checked or beaten in Southeast Asia, they concluded, the Soviets might order an invasion of South Korea.

In the unlikely event of an early invasion from the north, would the armed forces of the ROK be able to stop the Communist intruders? Individuals who were in a position to assess the capabilities of the rival Korean armies were less than sanguine about the ability of the South Koreans to withstand a Communist drive over the 38th parallel. Writing in March 1950, Brigadier General William L. Roberts, commander of the United States Military Advisory Group to the Republic of Korea (KMAG), expressed the view that the South Korean Army was capable of an excellent initial performance against the North Koreans, particularly if American advisors were on hand to provide guidance. But because North Koreans would give the southerners "a bloody nose," Roberts thought, the people of South Korea probably would follow the apparent winner in the conflict, whereupon the ROK "would be gobbled up to be added to the rest of Red Asia." In a message to the secretary of state in mid-June

1950, Ambassador Muccio struck a similar note. According to Muccio, the South Korean Army was well-trained, had good morale and effective leadership, and was equipped with excellent small arms. But because they had a decided superiority in aircraft, tanks, and heavy artillery, the North Koreans were preponderantly stronger. A fortnight earlier, on June 1, 1950, the intelligence section of the Far East Air Force (FEAF) had concluded that the North Koreans had sufficient military power to undertake a war against South Korea any time they chose. The outcome of such a war? "South Korea will fall before a North Korean invasion. . . . "

The Central Intelligence Agency was slightly more optimistic. In a memorandum dated June 19, 1950, the CIA asserted that the North Korean Army, as presently constituted, could capture the upper reaches of South Korea, including Seoul. But there was no certainty that, without the active intervention of Soviet or Chinese military units, the North Koreans could take all of South Korea. Above the 38th parallel, in Pyongyang, the leaders of North Korea apparently concurred with Roberts and the intelligence analysts of the FEAF.

If Nikita Khrushchev's published reminiscences are authentic and accurate, the North Korean premier, Kim Il Sung, traveled to Moscow in late 1949 to confer with Stalin. In Khrushchev's words, Kim "wanted to prod South Korea with the point of a bayonet," that is, wanted to undertake an invasion of South Korea. An armed move against southern Korea, Kim argued, would touch off a popular uprising against Syngman Rhee's government. The outcome would be a unified and Communist Korea. According to Khrushchev, Stalin told Kim to go back to Pyongyang, think over his proposals and make some calculations, then return to Moscow with a concrete plan. Kim did as Stalin directed, returned to Moscow with his plan (presumably in early 1950), and told Stalin that he was absolutely sure that an invasion of South Korea would succeed. Fearing an intervention by the United States, Stalin was hesitant, but decided that a swift stroke by the North Koreans would forestall any military move by the Americans to rescue the ROK. (At some point in that period, Khrushchev recalled, Stalin solicited Mao Zedong's opinion of Kim's proposed adventure. Surmising that the United States would not undertake a military intervention on behalf of South Korea, Mao endorsed the plan for an invasion.) Khrushchev also remembered a spirited dinner at Stalin's dacha during one of Kim's visits, presumably the second. Kim spoke expansively of the benefits that would result from a Communist conquest of South Korea. "We wished every success to Kim Il Sung," Khrushchev recalled, "and toasted the whole North Korean leadership, looking forward to the day when their struggle would be won." Unbeknownst to Kim and his hosts, of course, leaders of the United States, as the drafting and adoption of NSC-68 demonstrate, were at that very time edging to the conclusion that the security and interests of the United States might require an armed response to Soviet or Soviet-sponsored aggression even in such a peripheral area of the world as the Korean peninsula.

Their movement undetected by the United States intelligence apparatus, North Korean Army units began to deploy for the invasion of the ROK in mid-June 1950. Then, at approximately 4:00 A.M., Sunday, June 25, North Korean infantrymen, supported by intensive artillery fire, moved across the western end of the 38th parallel in the Ongjin Peninsula. Over the next hour, from Ongjin to the Sea of Japan, other North Korean assault troops likewise crossed the parallel. At 10:00 A.M. (9:00 P.M., Saturday, June 24, in Washington), Ambassador Muccio reported the attack to the State Department. A short time later, Secretary Acheson, who was spending the weekend at his farm in Maryland, passed the news to President Truman.

John Edward Wilz

Bibliography

Cumings, Bruce. *The Origins of the Korean War: Liberation and the Emergence of Separate Regimes, 1945–1947* (1981).

Dobbs, Charles M. *The Unwanted Symbol: American Foreign Policy, the Cold War, and Korea, 1945–1950* (1981).

Foot, Rosemary. *The Wrong War: American Policy and the Dimensions of the Korea Conflict, 1950–1953* (1985).

Matray, James I. *The Reluctant Crusade: American Foreign Policy in Korea, 1941–1950* (1985).

Sandusky, Michael C. *America's Parallel* (1983).

Schnabel, James F. *United States Army in the Korean War*, I, *Policy and Direction: The First Year* (1972).

Simmons, Robert R. *The Strained Alliance: Peking, P'yongyang, Moscow, and the Politics of the Korean Civil War* (1975).

Stueck, William W., Jr. *The Road to Confrontation: American Policy toward China and Korea, 1947–1950* (1981).

Korean Augmentation to the U.S. Army
See KATUSA

Korean Military Advisory Group
See KMAG

Korean People's (North Korean) Air Force

The Korean People's Air Force (KPAF) had its origins in a group called the Korean Aviation Society, which was organized in August–September 1945 at Sinuiju Airfield by Colonel Lee Hwal, a Korean who had served in the Japanese Air Force. The society, which was patterned after the volunteer paramilitary aviation clubs of the Soviet Union, began its active training program in October 1945 under the supervision of Soviet advisors and Koreans trained in Japan and China. In 1946, the society assumed military status and was moved to Pyongyang to become the aviation section of the newly formed Korean People's Army Military Academy. In November 1948, the aviation section was redesignated the Korean Air Regiment. The birth of the air regiment occasioned no immediate change in troop strength but did involve a structural reorganization, which resulted in a two-battalion organization. The newly created Air Force, by virtue of this reorganization, was elevated to a position of equality with the Korean People's Army and Navy under the ministry of national defense.

The final phase in the development of the Korean People's Air Force was apparently ushered in with the expansion of the air regiment into an air division during January 1950. In the course of this reorganization, the 1st Battalion of the air regiment became a fighter regiment, composed of three battalions. Meanwhile, the 2nd Battalion was transformed into a ground attack regiment, likewise composed of three battalions. Also organized at this time was a training regiment composed of three battalions: the 1st Battalion (fighter training) stationed at Pyongyang Air Base, the 2nd (ground attack training), and the 3rd (mechanics and communications training) Battalions shared the facilities of Yonpo Airfield with the ground attack regiment. Additionally, two technical battalions charged with housekeeping and supply functions were organized and assigned to the rear services of the air division headquarters at Pyongyang.

By April 1950, the air division consisted of approximately 1,675 officers and men, including 76 pilot officers, 364 nonrated officers, 875 enlisted men, and 360 cadets. The number of aircraft held by the air division had risen from 115 to 178 with the receipt of sixty-three Soviet aircraft on 15 April 1950. This total is believed to have included seventy-eight Yak fighters, thirty PO-2 primary and Yak-18 advanced trainers, and seventy IL-10 ground attack bombers.

The combat record of the Korean People's Air Force prior to the intervention of the Communist Chinese forces is characterized by its extreme brevity. Reported acts of aggressive air action until 1 July 1950 consisted of two strafing attacks, one each on 29 and 30 June, by six fighters and four attack bombers on Suwon Airfield, an attack by four Yak-9 aircraft on two USAF F-80s, and a pass by one Yak-9 on a mission of B-29 bombers. Attacks mounted by the KPAF during the month of July were equally unimpressive. On 2 July, ten KPAF planes purportedly strafed and dropped leaflets on Suwon Airfield, and on 6 July, four Yak-9 fighters strafed Osan. On 7 July an unknown number of aircraft dropped eight bombs on Hyopchon. A short flurry of KPAF air activity occurred during the two-day period of 11–12 July, during which conventional single-engine fighters engaged in the following encounters: three aircraft fired on an F-80 mission; two aircraft shot down an L-4 liaison plane; two Yak-9 fighters attacked a B-29 over Seoul; and two Yak-9 aircraft made several passes at a flight of USAF F-80 fighters. The last significant offensive action of the KPAF involved air attacks and a leaflet drop over Taejon on the night of 17 or 18 July 1950 by Yak-9s. There is no evidence to indicate that the KPAF engaged in any significant offensive action after this date, other than nighttime PO-2 "heckler" missions.

The failure of the Korean People's Air Force to initiate more than token aggressive or defensive action in spite of the impressive number of aircraft of fairly modern design, that it possessed at the outbreak of hostilities can probably be attributed to the fact that intervention by UNC forces precluded the successful accomplishment of the assigned mission. Un-able to cope with a major air power, the KPAF apparently decided to conserve hard-to-replace aviation personnel until the time when their employment would have a better change of influencing the overall tactical situation. In any event, the methodical UNC bombing of KPAF air facilities in the initial phases of the war inflicted a fatal blow to the KPAF's air potential. The available evidence indicates that at least 152 aircraft were destroyed on the ground between the beginning of the war and September 1950. Pyongyang Airfield was rendered practically useless by a UNC bombing attack in the middle of August, and all facilities had to be moved underground because of daily air attacks. For all practical purposes, damaged aircraft were put out of action permanently, since they could only be repaired by "cannibalizing" other damaged planes.

After the intervention of the People's Republic of China (PRC), military bases in Manchuria were made available to KPAF. In this sanctuary, the KPAF was rebuilt with Soviet technical guidance, aircraft, and related equipment. This process was significantly aided by the fact that at the time the war began, an estimated 1,400 personnel of the KPAF were receiving aviation training outside Korea; of these, approximately 300 were in Manchuria, while the remainder were in the USSR. The major centers for KPAF activity within Manchuria were at Harbin and Kirin airfields.

Although never a serious threat, one area in which the KPAF did enjoy some measure of success during the latter part of the war was with its nighttime "heckler" raids. During these raids a single aircraft (typically a PO-2) would fly back and forth over UNC lines at night and drop small bombs at irregular times.

Almost immediately after the signing of the 1953 armistice agreement, those KPAF elements in Manchuria reoccupied airfields throughout North Korea.

Joseph S. Bermudez, Jr.

Bibliography

Defense Intelligence Agency. "North Korea Rebuilds Air Facility Network" [Declassified], *Defense Intelligence Digest* (March 1964), pp. 25–27.
———. "North Korean Air Force" [Declassified], *Defense Intelligence Digest* (October 1969), pp. 21–23.
"Enemy Light Plane Raids in Korea," *ONI Review*, Vol. 8, No. 8 (August 1953), pp. 378–379.

Futrell, R.F. *The United States Air Force in Korea, 1950–1953* (Office of Air Force History, 1983).

GHQ, FEC, MIS, GS. *ATIS Research Supplement—Interrogation Reports,* 100 (30 April 1951), pp. 2–18.

USAF, HQ FEAF. *FEAF Intelligence Roundup* (various issues 1951–1954).

Korean People's (North Korean) Army

The Korean People's Army (KPA) that attacked across the 38th parallel on 25 June 1950 evolved primarily from two distinct and competing political/military groups known as the "Yenan" and "Kapsan" "Bans" (power-holding groups). The Yenan Ban consisted of those Koreans who, in general, were followers of Mao Zedong and who had fought with the Communist Chinese forces during both World War II and the Chinese civil war. The major leaders within the Yenan Ban were Kim Du Bong and Kim Mu Chong. The Kapsan Ban was formed primarily from Korean anti-Japanese partisans who had fled from the Japanese to the Soviet Union, and a number of Soviet citizens of Korean ancestry. The major leader within the Kapsan Ban was Kim Il Sung.

The Yenan Ban's origins date to 1939 and the Yenan area that Mao Zedong had retreated to during the "Long March." It was here that a handful of Koreans formed the Korean Volunteer Army (KVA). The KVA's ranks were filled by Koreans who had been conscripted into, and then deserted from, the Imperial Japanese Army. Approximately 2,500 of these troops would eventually fight with the Chinese Communist forces against the Japanese during World War II. Immediately following the Japanese surrender in 1945, these troops, under the command of Kim Mu Chong, attempted to return to their homeland and establish an independent nation. The majority were, however, initially denied entry into their country by the Soviet Army which had occupied Korea in order to accept the surrender of Japanese forces north of the 38th parallel. These troops were then persuaded to continue to assist the Chinese Communist forces in their war against the Nationalist Chinese forces of Chiang Kai-shek. The Soviets were motivated not only by their desire to assist Mao Zedong and the Chinese Communist forces; but also to keep this well-equipped, trained, and politically indoctrinated force out of Korea, thereby facilitating the consolidation of northern Korea's leadership within the hands of their own candidate—Kim Il Sung, and his "Kapsan" Ban (Kim had just returned to Korea in August 1945).

The history of the Kapsan Ban is essentially the history of Kim Il Sung, former president of the Democratic People's Republic of Korea, general secretary of the Korean Worker's Party, and commander in chief of the Korean People's Army, who died in 1994. Kim, during the mid-1930s, was the leader of a small band of Korean guerrillas who were active against the Japanese in eastern Manchuria and northern Korea. On June 4, 1937, a battle took place between guerrillas and Japanese troops near the town of Kapsan, Yanggang-do province, close to the Manchurian border. During this battle two companies of Japanese troops were allegedly wiped out; a very significant victory for the guerrillas, and hence the source of the "Kapsan Ban" name. Kim was active in guerrilla operations until 1939, when he and his troops were driven out by the Japanese and fled to Soviet territory. Here Kim was recruited by Soviet military intelligence and was given command of the 88th Special Independent Sniper Brigade in July 1942. The mission of this unit was to collect military information on the Japanese troops occupying Korea and Manchuria. (Even though designated a brigade it was in reality a multiracial battalion-level unit composed of approximately 600 Chinese, Koreans, and Soviets.) In September 1945, shortly after the Soviet occupation of Korea, the Korean contingent of the 88th returned to Korea through the port of Wonsan and under Kim's command. Under the direction of the Soviets, Kim and his companions established a Communist government in northern Korea.

During late 1946, officers' training schools and centers were established under the supervision of the Soviets to begin the serious work of establishing the Korean People's Army and internal security forces. With the establishment of these centers and schools, members of the Kapsan Ban and KVA were systematically returned, trained, equipped, and organized first into border and railroad constabularies and then into regular military units.

The border and railroad constabularies were security forces deployed mainly along the 38th parallel and along the railroads of northern Korea. Trained, armed, and equipped as infantry, these constabularies were commanded by officers who were, for the most part, members of the Kapsan Ban, and their membership was drawn largely from Communist groups. The constabularies were trained, advised, and supervised by the Soviets. At least two of the border constabulary brigades were later expanded to divisions in July 1950.

The Korean People's Army had as its core the veteran troops of the KVA. Officially activated in February 1948, the KPA's organization training, equipment, and growth actually took place during the 1945–50 period. Three of its divisions, the 5th, 6th, and 7th, were composed primarily of ex-KVA troops. Two other divisions each had a regiment composed of such veterans. These North Korean units, and all those activated later, were trained (or retrained) according to the North Korean version of Soviet tactical doctrine and were primarily armed and equipped by the USSR.

By June 1950, North Korea, with full Soviet assistance in all phases of preparation, had developed a ground force estimated at 135,000 men, organized—under one army and two corps headquarters—into ten regular infantry divisions, one armored brigade, five border constabulary brigades, and all the necessary combat service support and combat support elements.

Organization

At the beginning of the war a typical KPA infantry division had 11,000 men and was organized along the lines of the World War II Soviet infantry division with the following exceptions: the KPA unit had an additional self-propelled artillery unit, a signal battalion instead of a company, a replacement battalion instead of a company, and lacked a chemical warfare company. Most divisions were equipped with Soviet equipment, although there were some notable examples of Japanese, Chinese, and U.S. equipment. A typical KPA infantry division was organized into:

- Headquarters
- Three rifle regiments
- Artillery regiment
- Self-propelled artillery battalion
- Antitank battalion
- Engineer battalion
- Signal battalion
- Training battalion
- Reconnaissance company
- Divisional rear services:
  Medical battalion
  Transport company
  Supply services

The sole armored unit in the KPA at the beginning of the war was the 105th Tank Brigade (later the 105th "Seoul" Tank Division) but its small size was more than countered by the fact that the ROK Army lacked any armor. It entered the war with a personnel strength of approximately 6,000, organized along the lines of the World War II Soviet tank division with the following exceptions: the overall strength of the KPA unit was approximately 50 percent less than that of its Soviet counterpart (6,000 vs. 11,500) and it did not include a heavy tank regiment, rocket launcher battalion, mortar regiment, or antiaircraft regiment. It was entirely equipped with Soviet tanks (approximately 120 T-34/85 medium tanks and sixteen SU-76 self-propelled guns), vehicles, and weapons. The 105th was organized into:

- Headquarters
- 107th, 109th, and 203rd Tank Regiments
- 206th Mechanized Infantry Regiment
- 308th Armored Battalion
- 303rd Reconnaissance Battalion
- 202nd Signal Battalion
- Engineer battalion
- Divisional rear services:
  403rd Medical Battalion
  Ordnance battalion
  Transport company
  Supply services
- 849th Antitank Regiment (organized and attached to the division after hostilities started)

The Korean War

On Sunday, 25 June 1950, the Korean People's Army invaded South Korea, and steadily pushed the Republic of Korea Army (ROKA) and reinforcing United States units southward, finally cornering them within the Pusan perimeter. The Inchon landing on 15 September 1950 turned the tide of battle and forced the KPA to flee north in disarray. The People's Republic of China (PRC) entered the war in October 1950, and it was this force that constituted the bulk of the opposition against the United Nations command (UNC) until the end of the fighting in July 1953. What follows are brief unit histories for the more significant divisions of the Korean People's Army during the war.

1st Infantry Division

September 1946	Organized at Kaechon as the 1st Peace Preservation Officer Training School.
February 1948	Redesignated the 1st Infantry Division.
20 June 1950	Moved south to the 38th parallel.
25 June 1950	Invaded the ROK as part of I Corps.
11 July 1950	Transferred to II Corps.
November 1950	Reorganized under III Corps and committed against UNC units in the Hungnam perimeter.
1951	Involved in combat in the Pyongchang and Yanggu areas.
July 1952	Withdrawn from the front line and assigned to III Corps where it assumed a reserve and training mission.
November 1952	Recommitted to combat where it suffered heavy casualties.
January 1953	Relieved by the 37th Infantry Division and assumed a training mission.
May 1953	Redeployed on the front line relieving the 45th Infantry Division.

2nd Infantry Division   *"Seoul Guards Division"*

1946	Organized at Nanam as the 2nd Peace Preservation Officer Training School.
February 1948	Redesignated the 2nd Infantry Division.
January 1950	Received training in assault tactics.
June 1950–March 1951	Invaded the ROK in the central sector. The division suffered heavy casualties and was withdrawn from combat. It was then reorganized and resupplied.
April 1951–July 1953	Recommitted to combat in eastern sector.

3rd Infantry Division   *"Seoul Guards Division"*

October 1948	Organized at Pyongyang from the 3rd Independent Brigade, a regiment of the 2nd Division, and personnel in training centers.
June–September 1950	Invaded the ROK as part of I Corps. Assisted in the capture of Seoul for which it was awarded the title of "Seoul Guards Division." Moved south and engaged in the Pusan perimeter fighting.
October 1950	Withdrew to Chakang province, North Korea, and reorganized.
November–December 1950	Operated under III Corps in Hungnam perimeter.
January 1951	Moved to Wonsan area and subordinated to VII Corps.
Summer 1951	Provided replacement troops to front-line units.
January 1953	Recommitted to combat in eastern sector.

4th Infantry Division   *"Kim Chaek, Seoul Guards Division"*

February 1948	Activated from elements of the 4th Brigade.
October 1948–June 1950	Underwent basic and mountain warfare training.
28 June 1950	Committed to combat. Assisted in the capture of Seoul for which it was awarded the title of "Seoul Division."
July–August 1950	Moved south and engaged in combat on the Pusan perimeter. Assisted in the capture of Taejon for which it was awarded the title of "Guards."
September–October 1950	The division conducted a fighting withdrawal to North Korea while fighting behind UNC lines as guerrillas. For its fighting withdrawal it was awarded the title of "Kim Chaek."
January 1951	Under control of the IV Corps, the division moved to Pyongyang and reorganized.

March 1951– 1953	The division remained in the Pyongyang area constructing defensive positions, training, and occasionally conducting rear repair work.

5th Infantry Division

August 1949	Activated from Korean veterans of the 164th Infantry Division, 55th Communist Chinese Army.
June– August 1950	Invaded the ROK and fought on the eastern coast of Korea under II Corps.
September– November 1950	Forced to withdraw to North Korea while suffering heavy casualties.
December 1950	Reconstituted under control of IV Corps.
January 1951	Moved to Pyongyang area.
1952–1953	Moved to Nampo area with the mission of defending the south and west flanks of Pyongyang.

6th Infantry Division   *"Guards Division"*

25 July 1949	Activated at Sinuiju from Korean veterans of the 164th Infantry Division, 56th Communist Chinese Army.
September 1949– May 1950	Conducted tactical field training.
25 June– August 1950	Invaded the ROK by attacking and clearing the Ongjin peninsula, then moved south to seize Inchon. For these actions it was awarded the title of "Guards." Fought on the southern flank of the Pusan perimeter where it suffered heavy casualties.
September– October 1950	Forced to withdraw to North Korea where it was reorganized.
November 1950– January 1951	Captured Wonju, assigned to V Corps, and subsequently withdrawn to Hongchon to reorganize.
February– July 1951	Recommitted and fought in the central sector.
August– October 1951	Became V Corps reserve where it received replacements and trained. With the relief of the V Corps by the 68th Communist Chinese Army, the division moved to the Wonsan area.
November 1951–1953	Underwent reorganization and training in the Wonsan area. Assigned the mission of defending the Wonsan area from amphibious assault.

7th Infantry Division

3 July 1950	Activated at Haeju from the 7th Border Constabulary Guard Brigade and local conscripts.
28 July– August 1950	Secured the city of Yosu on the southwest coast of the ROK. Attempted to repel amphibious landings of ROK Marines, but was forced to withdraw to Chinju.
September– December 1950	Forced to withdraw to North Korea. Engaged in guerrilla warfare behind UNC lines.
January– March 1951	Fought under V Corps in the Yanggu-Hoengsong-Wonju area.
March 1951– December 1952	Withdrawn from combat and assigned to the VII Corps where it was reorganized and participated in training.
January 1953	Assumed coastal defense mission on the east coast of North Korea.

8th Infantry Division

1 July 1950	Activated at Kangnung from the 1st Border Constabulary Guard Brigade.
July– August 1950	Fought on the northeastern flank of the Pusan perimeter where it suffered heavy casualties.

September–December 1950	Remnants of the division withdrew to the Chosan area near the Yalu River where it recruited and trained additional personnel.
January–March 1951	Fought under I Corps in the Seoul area. Suffered heavy casualties and then withdrew from the area.
March–June 1951	Fought in the Munsan-ni area. Replaced by Communist Chinese Army elements and withdrew west of the Yesong River for rest and reorganization.
July–October 1951	Displaced to the Sinchon area where it was involved in training.
November 1951–July 1952	The division relieved the 18th Infantry Division VI Corps on the east coast where it assumed a coastal defense mission.
August–December 1952	Relieved the 47th Infantry Division on the front line in the eastern sector.
January–August 1953	Relieved by the 3rd Infantry Division, VII Corps. It underwent training and built fortifications. Moved to the Kaesong area.

9th Infantry Division

1 July 1950	Activated at Kaesong from the 3rd Border Constabulary Guard Brigade.
11 July–12 August 1950	Engaged in guarding the city, and the area south of Kaesong.
25 August–15 September 1950	The division, less the 87th Infantry Regiment, attacked across the Naktong River (Pusan perimeter); so decimated by UNC attacks that it was forced to retreat westward.
20 September–14 December 1950	Withdrew to North Korea where it was reorganized under II Corps.
15 December–15 May 1951	Crossed south over the 38th parallel under II Corps with the mission of severing supply and communication lines in the area east of Taejon. It failed in this mission.
16 May–August 1951	The division moved to the western front and became subordinate to VI Corps. Remained in defensive positions in the Yonan area.
August 1951–January 1953	Moved to the east coast to defensive positions in the Kosong area. Became subordinate to I Corps on inactivation of the VI Corps.
January–August 1953	Relieved by the 7th Infantry Division, VII Corps, after which it moved to the western sector.

10th Infantry Division "Guards Division"

March–July 1950	Formed from the 4th, 5th, and 6th training classes of the 2nd Democratic Young Men's Training Center. Engaged in basic and advanced training.
August–December 1950	Attacked across the Naktong River (Pusan perimeter) under I Corps. Suffered heavy casualties and forced to withdraw to North Korea. Engaged in combat and was awarded the title of "Guards" for its actions.
December 1950–March 1951	Shifted east with the II Corps to Yanggu area. Infiltrated south to within thirty miles of Taegu where it was stopped and sealed off by UNC forces. It then reverted to guerrilla operations. Remnants of the division succeeded in withdrawing north of UNC lines.
April 1951–May 1952	Reorganized under IV Corps as a mechanized division; received tanks from both the 105th Tank and the 17th Mechanized Divisions. Reorganized and trained while defending the coasts in the IV Corps northern area.
May 1952–53	Again reorganized as an infantry division, losing its tanks.

12th Infantry Division "Andong Division"

| June–September | Activated from former 7th Infantry Division elements, it fought under |

1951	II Corps in the eastern sector. The division captured the city of Andong after a bloody battle, for which it was awarded the title "Andong." Fought on the northeastern flank of the Pusan perimeter, where it suffered heavy casualties.
16 September–November 1950	Remnants of the division were forced to withdraw to the northwest coast of Korea. The division, as such, then ceased to exist.
18 November 1950–June 1951	A new 12th Infantry Division was activated under V Corps from former members of the 7th, 9th, and 12th Infantry Divisions. Fought under V Corps and suffered heavy casualties.
June 1951–53	Withdrew from contact to reorganize and train. Recommitted in late July 1951. Moved to defensive positions on the east coast in the Chunhung-ni area when the V Corps was relieved by the 68th Communist Chinese Army in October 1951.

13th Infantry Division

June 1950	Activated from personnel of the Democratic Youth Training Corps and attacked south across the 38th parallel.
July 1950	Engaged in combat under the II Corps. The division displayed poor fighting capabilities and was almost completely disorganized.
August–October 1950	Reorganized and recommitted. The division sustained many casualties and many high-ranking officers surrendered, including the division chief of staff. This division had the worst combat record of all KPA divisions.
November 1950	Withdrawn from contact, and resupplied and reorganized.
March 1951–July 1953	Recommitted to combat and remained until the armistice.

15th Infantry Division

June 1950	Activated from personnel of the 3rd People's Training Center in Hoeryong and from the Democratic Youth Training Center at Najin.
4 July–5 September 1953	Committed to combat. Fought under II Corps on the northeastern flank of the Pusan perimeter. Suffered severe casualties and loss of materiel in an attack on Yongchon.
6 September 1950–August 1951	Withdrew to the Chunchon area under constant attack. Relieved by the 45th Infantry Division, III Corps in July 1951. Trained and received replacements.
September 1951–January 1952	Recommitted to combat, and relieved the 13th Infantry Division, II Corps. Remained on line until relieved by the 45th Infantry Division, III Corps.
July 1952–53	Relieved the 13th and 27th Infantry Divisions, II Corps on line in the eastern sector.

27th Infantry Division

August–November 1950	Organized as the 27th Brigade at Kumchon. The brigade withdrew to the north in complete disorder when UNC forces advanced on Kumchon.
December 1950–January 1951	Formed as the 27th Infantry Division. Fought as guerrillas under II Corps. Attached to V Corps and crossed the 38th parallel in the Yanggu area.
January 1951–March 1951	Reverted to III Corps control. Engaged in combat until III Corps broke contact and withdrew to the Hoeyang area and reorganized.
May 1951–October 1955	Fought on the eastern sector under II Corps until September 1951. Relieved by the 13th Infantry Division, II Corps. Rested and reorganized until it relieved the 2nd Infantry Division, II Corps in

November 1951. Prepared defensive positions and resisted limited UNC probes until relieved by the 50th Infantry Regiment, 1st Infantry Division, III Corps in July 1952.

November
1952–53   Moved to the Wonsan area with II Corps.

37th Infantry Division

September 1950–   Existence reported in September 1950. It was trained and organized
September 1952   under VII Corps in Chilin province, Manchuria. Entered Korea
                          with the VII Corps in late January 1951 and proceeded to the
                          Wonsan area. Assumed a coastal defense mission and had no
                          combat.

October–   Relieved by elements of the II Corps. Moved to the Marhwi-ri area.
December 1952

January–   Relieved the 1st Infantry Division, III Corps on line in the eastern sec-
August 1953   tor and assumed a defensive role. Relieved by elements of the 15th
                          Division, III Corps.

45th Infantry Division

August–   Formed in the Nampo area where it trained and had a coastal defense
December 1950   mission. Routed by UNC forces in October, it withdrew to
                          Manchuria.

January–   Reconstituted under VIII Corps in eastern sector. Fought until April
May 1951   when it suffered heavy losses in personnel and equipment.
                          Withdrew to the Kumgang Mountain area for rest, reorganization,
                          and training.

July–   Relieved the 15th Infantry Division, III Corps in the eastern sector.
August 1951   Later it was relieved by elements from the VI Corps.

August 1951–   III Corps reserve, involved in training.
January 1952

January 1952–53   Recommitted to combat, again relieving the 15th Infantry Division, III
                          Corps in the eastern sector.

46th Infantry Division

August 1950–   The division was activated in the Chinnampo area. Due to UNC action
January 1951   the division was forced to withdraw to Manchuria where it was
                          reconstituted from remnants and new recruits.

February–   Assumed defensive positions under VIII Corps in the Hamhung areas.
October 1951   Transferred to VII Corps on the inactivation of the VIII Corps.

November   Transferred in place to the V Corps, its mission of coastal defense in the
1951–1953   Hamhung area continued.

47th Infantry Division

August 1950–   Organized originally in Sinuiju, but subsequently reorganized and
November 1950   equipped with recent conscripts, newly trained officers, and new
                          weapons in October 1950. Proceeded to Kusong under I Corps.
                          Forced to withdraw to Sakahu.

December 1950–   Proceeded to Seoul where it assumed a defensive mission.
March 1951

March–   Withdrew from Seoul with I Corps and prepared for offensive action.
November 1951   Attacked across the Imjin River, but was repulsed by a UNC
                          counterattack. Withdrew west of the Yesong River. Received
                          replacements and conducted training. Moved to Yonan area where
                          it engaged in a coastal defense mission.

December 1951–   Relieved the 19th Infantry Division, VI Corps in eastern sector and
August 1952   assigned a defensive mission.

August 1952– 1953	Relieved by the 8th Infantry Division, I Corps, and moved to Tongchon area on the east coast for coastal defense duty.

105th Tank Division   *"Seoul Division"*

May 1947– June 1950	Formed as the 15th Tank Training Regiment during May 1947 in the town of Sadong near Pyongyang. In May 1949, the 15th Tank Training Regiment was deactivated and its personnel, most of whom were promoted to officer grade, were transferred to the newly activated 105th Tank Brigade. Moved south to positions north of the 38th parallel.
25 June 1950– 1 October 1950	Committed to combat. Assisted in the capture of Seoul for which it was awarded the title of "Seoul Division." One tank regiment was attached to the 3rd Infantry Division for the invasion. On 16 July the remaining regiments were detached from the division to support the attack south and operations against the Pusan perimeter. On 10 September 1950 units of the 105th were ordered to assemble in the vicinity of Kumchon to regroup and receive replacements. A few days after the Inchon landing, the 105th was ordered northwest to Suwon to repel UNC forces. Before it had a chance to make an orderly withdrawal, the division was heavily engaged by UNC forces driving from the south. The remaining elements withdrew to North Korea.
1 October 1950– July 1953	The remnants of the 105th that managed to reach the North were reorganized in the Sakchu area during October 1950, while rear service elements of the division withdrew across the Yalu River into Manchuria. On 6 November 1950 the remaining combat elements of the 105th were recommitted under the I Corps in support of an attack by Chinese troops, but were quickly forced to withdraw again. Following in the wake of the Chinese advance against UNC forces, the shattered 105th proceeded south to the Sukchon area where it began reorganizing and was subsequently placed under the IV Corps. During mid-1951 small elements of the division moved southward into the vicinity of Sariwon; however, the bulk of the division remained in the Sukchon-Anju area. Here the division remained until the end of the war.

Korean People's (North Korean) Navy

Officially, the Korean People's Navy (KPN) was established in 1948, at the same time as the Korean People's Army. In reality, however, the KPN began as an outgrowth of a small Soviet-sponsored coastal defense force organized shortly after World War II. This was later reorganized as the Korean Coast Guard during 1946, and finally the KPN in February 1948. On 25 June 1950 the combat strength of the KPN was organized into three naval squadrons, the 1st Squadron (Chongjin), the 2nd Squadron (Wonsan), and the 3rd Squadron (Chinnampo). The majority of the afloat strength of the KPN between 1945 and 1950 consisted of Soviet-designed craft, most notably a number of P-4 motor torpedo boats, ex-Japanese minesweepers, and ex-U.S. ships.

Although the KPN was virtually destroyed early in the Korean War, it was able to conduct numerous small amphibious landings along both coasts of the Republic of Korea (South Korea) during the first days of the war. The most successful of these was the landing of the 766th Marine Regiment along the southeastern coast of the ROK. The only known naval battle involving KPN combatants occurred during the early morning hours of 2 July 1950 when four P-4 torpedo boats from the 2nd Naval Squadron escorting ten small freighters from Wonsan to Chumunjin encountered U.S. Navy warships. In the ensuing battle all four torpedo boats were destroyed in quick succession before they could fire a single torpedo. Throughout the war the KPN's only demonstrated ability was its successful deployment of massive defensive naval minefields outside major port cities, most notably Wonsan, Hamhung, Chongjin, and Chinnampo.

After the first weeks of the war, in order to preserve what little remaining strength it possessed, the KPN withdrew the majority of its forces to the territorial waters of the Communist Chinese (3rd Squadron) and the Soviet Union (1st and 2nd Squadrons). As with the KPAF, immediately after the signing of the 1953 armistice agreement, those KPN elements in the People's Republic of China and USSR returned to the major ports of North Korea.

Joseph S. Bermudez, Jr.

Bibliography

Defense Intelligence Agency, "North Korea Rebuilds Air Facility Network" (Declassified), *Defense Intelligence Digest* (1964).

Defense Intelligence Agency, "North Korean Air Force" (Declassified), *Defense Intelligence Digest* (1969).

"Enemy Light Plane Raids in Korea," *The ONI Review* (1953).

Futrell, R.F. *The United States Air Force in Korea, 1950–1953* (1983).

GHQ, FIC, MIS, GS, *ATIS Research Supplement—Interrogation Reports*, 100 (1951).

USAF, HQ FEAF, *FEAF Intelligence Roundup* (1951–1954).

U.S. Army, *ATIS Research Supplement*, No. 3, FEC, G2, 15 November 1950.

———. No. 104, FEC, G2, 1951.

———. *Daily Intelligence Summaries and Periodic Intelligence Reports*, HQ, FEC & EUSA, MIS, G2, 1951, various issues, 1950–1953.

———. *History of the North Korean Army*, 31 July 1952.

———. *North Korean Armed Forces*, DA Pamphlet 30–52, 11 July 1962.

———. *Order of Battle Handbook: Chinese Communist Forces, Korea and the North Korean Army*, HQ, FEC & EUSA, ACS-G2 (1 October 1955).

———. *Tables of Organization and Equipment of the North Korean Army*, HQ, FEC & EUSA, ACS-G2 (1 July 1957).

K

L

Lin Piao (1907–1971?)

Lin Piao was born in Ung Kung, Hupeh province, the son of a factory owner ruined by high taxation. When he turned eighteen and was completing study at the Whampoa Military Academy, he changed his name from Lin Yu Yung ("fostering demeanor") to Lin Piao ("tiger cat"). Such a decision fitted well with the career choice young Lin had made. Whampoa had been founded by Chiang Kai-shek at the behest of Sun Yat-sen after the latter had sent Chiang to study political and military science in the Soviet Union. At Whampoa, Lin studied military science under Chiang and politics under Chou En-lai, each of whom were subsidized by the Soviets. On the death of Sun, Chiang and the Communists allied against the feudal warlords. Lin rose from company commander to the command of a regiment by the age of twenty, only to suffer from the Koumintang Army's purge of all Communists. He and other young commanders rebelled in the Nanching uprising of 1 August 1927, that marked the birth of the Chinese People's Army. After the famous "Long March," the survivors regrouped in the northern mountains and there planned the "liberation" of China. Lin proved himself time and again against the Nationalists as well as the Japanese. His work at the Red Army academy at Yenan and his articles on military tactics became legendary. He abolished the professional military caste system, ended the use of insignia and rank, and abolished all special privileges as he worked to de-Russify the People's Army. Despite his frail build and undistinguished gaunt and pale features (most likely a result of his long-term tuberculosis), his cool, distant nature and enigmatic disposition lent an aura and dignity to his name. He was ever a favorite of Mao Zedong, but there is no evidence that he ever sought to replace him. Lin fought in more than 100 major battles against the Nationalists and the Japanese and never suffered physical harm.

In the Chinese civil war of 1945–1949, Lin had liberated Manchuria by 1947, then took his army south and defeated the Nationalist forces at Beijing and Tunjim, achieving final victory on the eve of the Korean War. At the age of forty-two, Lin Piao, with an army of over one million, was the dominant figure in the freshly minted Chinese People's Liberation Army.

Early in the Korean War, Lin had argued before Mao and the Communist Party Central Committee that the Chinese Army needed further training before facing the Americans, particularly with the latter's air power. But General Peng Dehuai was eager for engagement, which he saw as a logical extension of the war of liberation. It was Peng who on 5 October 1950, took command of a part of Lin's 4th field army called the XIII Army Group. This new army was massive in and of itself, with its twelve divisions of 10,000 infantry each, a regiment of cavalry, and five regiments of artillery. Between 13 and 25 October, this force of more than 130,000 moved into North Korea under the very eyes of U.S. aerial reconnaissance. This occurred at the very moment when General Douglas MacArthur was assuring President Harry S. Truman on Wake Island that the Chinese would not intervene and that the Korean War was for all intents and purposes over. But Lin was already reinforcing General Peng with still more divisions that by Thanksgiving would bring the Chinese forces to 300,000. They marched by night, dispersing by day into the ravines, valleys, and forests of North Korea, with only donkeys and mules to help in hauling heavy ordnance. Their reward was the rout of the U.N. forces from all of North Korea.

But when the Chinese entered South Korea, their supply lines were tenuously extended and under constant air attack, while U.N. lines were shortened. The Americans were on the offensive by early 1951, while Chinese and North Korean forces were at their lowest ebb of the war and racked with disease. The U.N. command was able to establish a battle line that was not much different from the old 38th parallel demarcation line that held to the end of the war.

After the Korean War (in which he supposedly lost a son), Lin was believed to be the anointed successor of the venerable Mao. But in September 1971, the Chinese government announced that Lin, his wife, and his aides had been killed in a plane crash in Outer Mongolia. Not for another two years was Lin mentioned by name, then it was as a "bourgeois careerist, conspirator, counter-revolutionary double-dealer, renegade and traitor from the Party and the leader of an anti-Party clique." The long-dead Lin was expelled from the party. There has been informed speculation that Lin, a seasoned hater of the United States and the most orthodox of Marxist-Leninists, opposed the developing rapprochement between China and the United States, and was fleeing to the Soviet Union when he met his mysterious end. To compound the mystery, Mongolian party leaders declared in 1990 that Lin's body was not in the crashed plane found in 1971.

Jack J. Cardoso

Bibliography

Goulden, Joseph. *Korea: The Untold Story of the War* (1982).
Hastings, Max. *The Korean War* (1986).
"Lin Piao." *Current Biography* (1967).
Snow, Edgar. *Red Star Over China* (1968).
Sung An Tai. *The Lin Piao Affair* (1974).
Terrill, Ross. *Mao* (1980).

Little Switch

See OPERATIONS BIG AND LITTLE SWITCH

Logistics, U.S.

The reaction of the United States to the North Korean attack across the 38th parallel on 25 June 1950 was something like a microcosm of American involvement in World War II. At first President Harry S. Truman and his advisors hoped that logistic support for the forces of the Republic of Korea (South Korea) would be enough. That hope lasted less than two days. The next step was to order naval and air forces of the United States into action to ensure the delivery of supplies. On 29 June, the president authorized General Douglas MacArthur, commander in chief of the Far East command, with headquarters in Tokyo, to use certain Army forces to furnish essential logistic services and to defend port facilities and an airport in the Pusan area at the southeast tip of the Korean peninsula. One day later, and with United Nations backing, Truman announced that Army forces were being committed to ground combat in Korea.

Less than twelve hours after receiving authority to commit ground forces, MacArthur had an infantry battalion of the 24th Division, poorly prepared as it was, on the way from Japan by air. Landing near Pusan on 1 July, the battalion moved northward by railway and truck to Osan, and met the enemy on 5 July about twenty miles south of Seoul. Reinforcements followed as quickly as possible, but nothing could stem the Communist tide until it had rolled South Korean and U.S. forces into a beachhead perimeter extending little more than fifty miles from Pusan.

Direct reinforcements were moving from the United States. On 8 July the 2nd Division, then training at Fort Lewis, Washington, was alerted for overseas movement with 25 July as the target date for first elements of the division to begin loading. Supplies and equipment had to be sent from all over the country to fill the division's authorized requirements. In addition to its full table of organization equipment it would carry a sixty-day supply of ammunition, above its basic load. With all this, the schedule was moved forward.

On 17 July—just nine days after the first warning, and eight days ahead of the original target date, the 2nd Battalion of the 9th Infantry moved by Greyhound buses to the pier at Tacoma to board a Navy transport. Soon the 2nd Division's train of some twenty-one ships extended all the way across the Pacific from Puget Sound to Pusan. On 5 August the 1st Battalion Combat Team, 9th Infantry, was moving into the front near Yongsan while the last ship, carrying division headquarters and special troops, was departing Tacoma. The last tactical elements arrived at Pusan on August 20. Undoubtedly the 2nd Division had made the quickest preparation and movement of an entire infantry division at full strength and equipment from home station to overseas battlefield in Army history.

Others were soon to follow. The 3rd Division, with units in various parts of the country, assembled at Camp Stoneman, California, and less one regiment that stayed at Fort Benning, Georgia, sailed from San Francisco 30 August–2 September. The 65th (Puerto Rican) Infantry which would become the division's third regiment, sailed from San Juan, Puerto Rico, in two transports on 26 and 27 August. One arrived in Pusan on 22 September; the other broke down en route and the troops had to transfer to another ship at Pearl Harbor, and did not arrive at Pusan until 1 October.

All this movement had to be coordinated with the movement of a Marine division (less one combat team) to Korea while a second was moving across the United States to the West Coast.

Meanwhile there were spectacular developments in Korea itself. In mid-August Far East command had directed the Japan logistical command to stage units and prepare supplies for a daring amphibious assault at Inchon, far up the west coast of the Korean peninsula opposite the capital city of Seoul. The X Corps, made up of the 1st Marine Division, the 7th Infantry Division, and special and logistic support units, would make the attack. Within the next month more than 260 vessels were collected in Japanese waters to carry this force from Kobe and Yokohama. On 3 September a typhoon struck Kobe and threatened to disrupt the whole operation. But soldiers, sailors, Marines, and Japanese civilians worked feverishly to get preparations back on schedule. The initial contingent was ready to go on schedule, 10 September. At Yokohama, the 7th Division, brought up to strength with 8,000 South Korean soldiers, was a day late, and because of a shortage of shipping, supporting units were three to five or more days late. Still the Yokohama port handled 100,000 tons of cargo in three days' time. The assault force itself went forward on schedule and landed at Inchon on 15 September with complete success. Within a week some 50,000 troops, 5,000 vehicles, and 20,000 tons of cargo were ashore.

Concurrently the Eighth Army had broken out of its Pusan perimeter and was streaming northward. While the Eighth Army and South Korean forces continued their rapid advances north of the 38th parallel, the X corps returned to the sea and moved around the peninsula for landings far up on the east coast. The 1st Marine Division and the 2nd Engineer Special Brigade outloaded at Inchon and sailed around to Wonsan. The 7th Division and supporting elements moved by truck and rail all the way back to Pusan, where they boarded ships for a landing in the area of Iwon, 178 miles (by road) north and east of Wonsan. The Marine force left Inchon on 15 October and arrived off Wonsan five days later, but then had to stand offshore for another six days while naval mines were cleared. South Korean ground forces already had overrun the area so that an "administrative" landing was possible. On 29 October the 7th Division, with South Korean units attached, landed unopposed on the beaches of Iwon. By the end of the month both Inchon and Wonsan were receiving supplies by sea, the rail line and the highway had been opened to Pyongyang, and air shipments were being delivered to Pyongyang, Sinanju, Wonsan, and Hungnam.

Within the next three weeks units of the Eighth Army were pushing across the Chongchon River in the northwest, and in the extreme northeast, a few Marines, U.S. Army forces, and South Koreans of X Corps were at the Yalu River/Manchurian border and approaching the border north of the Chosin Reservoir and north of Chonongjin on the coast. The end of the war appeared to be in sight.

But Chinese "volunteers" struck with great force and surprise against both the Eighth Army in the west and the X Corps in the northeast. After a South Korean corps collapsed on the Eighth Army's right flank, other units of that army began a withdrawal that turned into a flight. In six days of withdrawal and fighting against Chinese roadblocks in its rear, the 2nd Division alone suffered more than 4,000 casualties and lost most of its weapons and equipment.

The X Corps was able to fight a more orderly withdrawal and then defend an arc around the port of Hungnam to permit the greatest evacuation by sea in U.S. military history. Corps set up a tent city to provide some shelter against the bitterly cold winds and icy snow for troops as they awaited their turns to board ship. Some units boarded at Songjin and some at Wonsan, but most left from Hungnam itself. There, docks accommodated seven ships, and ten LST's could be loaded on the beaches simultaneously. The Navy brought in 114 ships of various kinds. They carried away 105,000 troops, 6,900 Korean and Japanese laborers, 18,000 vehicles, 350,000 tons of bulk cargo, and 98,100 refugees in the course of about two weeks. Another 3,600 men, 196 vehicles, and 1,300 tons of supplies went out by airlift. Most of the military evacuees went to Pusan to prepare to fight another day.

Back in Washington, Lieutenant General Thomas B. Larkin, G-4 (logistics) on the Army general staff, and his deputy, Major General William O. Reeder, on hearing the news of the disastrous situation, determined to do something quickly to help. If whole units were losing their equipment, they reasoned, why not take the table of organization and equipment of an infantry division as the measure of items to be shipped, and send at once all the equipment needed to outfit an entire infantry division? There would be no waiting for requisitions, no query to the theater about its needs, no waiting for status of equipment reports. Getting to work on the plan on Saturday night, 2 December, Reeder set up a schedule for four ships to be on berth each at San Francisco and Seattle by 5 December; deadline for arrival of equipment at the ports would be midnight, 8 December, and the ships were to sail on Saturday, the 9th. Depots as far east as St. Louis and Chicago would have to load their railroad cars by Tuesday night, the 5th, to have them reach the ports by special train before the deadline, and depots in the East, around New York, Philadelphia, and Baltimore, would have to turn their loaded cars over to the railroads by that time to go by express trains. By 7 December 2,000 tons of equipment had been loaded into the ships, another 5,000 tons were at the ports, and 25,000 tons were en route. As it turned out, only three ships were needed at each port, and with the exception of one that remained one day for the arrival of an air shipment from the East Coast, all sailed on schedule.

Concurrently the Far East command had been developing an emergency shipment of its own from stocks in Japan to Hungnam to replenish the X Corps. But when it developed that the X Corps had to evacuate from Hungnam, that shipment was redirected to Pusan. Then, to avoid adding further to the congestion at Pusan, the special shipment from the United States was redirected to Yokohama.

Most of the supplies that went to Korea during the first several months of combat were from continental reserves made up largely of World War II surplus stocks. The first phase of the Korean War had little impact on industrial mobilization in the United States. The second phase, i.e., the Chinese intervention, did. As soon as he learned of the extent of that intervention, Secretary of the Army Frank Pace directed the Army staff to "pull out all the stops" in the procurement program. Still, he resisted pressures for a large-scale mobilization of manpower. For the first time in American military history, he was applying the principle that material mobilization should have precedence over manpower mobilization.

On 15 December President Truman established an Office of Defense Mobilization with Charles E. Wilson, president of General Motors, as its head. That evening the president went before the nation on a radio and television broadcast to announce an increase in the armed forces from 2.5 million to 3.5 million, wage and price controls in essential areas, and a step-up in military production that would provide a five-fold increase in the production of aircraft, a four-fold increase in the production of tanks, and that would multiply the output of electronic equipment by four-and-one-half times, all within a year. The next day he issued a proclamation of national emergency that would bring into force national emergency clauses in scores of laws, old and new.

Several other top-level decisions and assumptions governed mobilization for the Korean War. One was that Korea must be regarded in a worldwide setting—requirements for security in Europe could not be ignored in meeting requirements for the Far East. A second was that while material mobilization should take precedence, and industrial production should be stepped up significantly, it would not be a total effort, and it should be accomplished with the least possible dislocation of the domestic economy. Closely related to this was a policy of building a broad production base, to be prepared for the long haul in the Cold War. A decision of the secretary of defense over the objections of the secretary of the army was to base military budget guidelines on the assumption of an early termination of the conflict. This meant that the costs of the war could be provided for only in a series of emergency appropriations.

In Korea the bitter winter retreat of United Nations forces, mingled with the flight of refugees, continued southward. On 4 and 5 January, Seoul and Inchon fell once more to the Communists. Then Lieutenant General Matthew B. Ridgway, who had arrived to take command of the Eighth Army after the death of Lieutenant General Walton H. Walker in a jeep accident, took up the task of regaining the offensive. Soon his forces were able to stabilize a position fifty to sixty miles south of the 38th parallel, and before the end of the month they were striking back. Seoul again fell to the Eighth Army on 15

March, and U.N. troops recrossed the 38th parallel in force on 3 April. Once more the Chinese launched a heavy counteroffensive. They threatened but did not recapture Seoul. But American supply officers moved all ammunition, gasoline, and grain (intended for civil assistance) as rapidly as possible by rail to supply points in the South. All other cargo in the Inchon port area, including salvage vehicles, was backloaded onto ships. One ammunition ship and one tanker remained in the harbor for discharge if needed while the other loaded ships sailed for Pusan. By 1 May the situation had stabilized so that resupply could be resumed at Inchon.

In late May and June United Nations forces were able to establish positions fifteen to thirty-five miles north of the 38th parallel. In July, long, drawn-out negotiations for an armistice began while bitter fighting continued.

Supply from the United States had become effective quickly, but it was not nearly enough to meet all the requirements during the early months of the conflict. Fortunately, a sizable program of gathering up World War II equipment and rebuilding it in Japanese factories had begun before the outbreak of the war. Now that became a major effort. Most important was the rebuilding of vehicles—mainly 2½-ton trucks and jeeps. During the first half of 1950, fewer than 3,000 rebuilt vehicles came from the production lines; in the last six months of that year rebuilding plants turned out more than 28,000 vehicles. By that time more than 65 percent of all the vehicles being used in Korea for hauling supplies and troops had come from the rebuilding plants in Japan. Moreover, vehicles worn or damaged in Korea could now be returned to Japan to go into the rebuild plants. By 1 May 1952, the total number of general purpose vehicles rebuilt in Japan had reached 98,831. These were produced at half the cost of new vehicles, and they had the great advantage of being there, without the costly and time-consuming shipment across the Pacific.

Another ordnance rebuild program led to the turning out of more than 3,000 combat vehicles at one-fourth their new production cost. By October 1951 an engineer rebuild program was operating through eight Japanese contractors employing more than 12,000 workers in seventeen plants. More than half of the cranes, air compressors, road graders, tractors, and generators, in addition to thousands of boats and bridging, construction, water supply, and electrical equipment, as well as other items used in Korea came from the program. Other programs included the rebuilding of signal equipment, marine engines, railway rolling stock, millions of items of clothing, thousands of tents, thousands of office machines, and scores of other items.

In addition to the vast rebuild programs, Japan was the direct source of many items required in Korea—trucks, lumber, manila rope, sandbags, oil drums, railway equipment, fresh food, and other items.

Forces in Korea fought the war with World War II–type firearms. Tanks were in the midst of modification when the war began, but those that could be made available were sent off to the battle area without full testing. Shipments of tanks to the Far East, in addition to those that went with units in the two years between 1 July 1950 and 30 June 1952 included 2,139 M-26 Pershings, 1,215 M-4A3 Shermans, 850 M-46 Pattons, and 616 M-24 Chaffee light tanks.

A great deal of public attention centered on reports of ammunition shortages in Korea. But at no time were there shortages in the sense that stocks of critical items were near exhaustion. Stocks varied a great deal, but that was a relative matter.

Again, for artillery ammunition, reliance had to be on World War II leftovers. New production did not become significant until near the end of hostilities, but was important for restoring the reserves that had been depleted.

While Japan was a significant source of fresh food, the bulk of the fresh food, as well as the nonperishable canned rations for U.N. troops in Korea, came from the United States.

The soldiers' clothing and individual equipment in Korea were essentially the same as those used in World War II. The most apparent differences were items of winter clothing and in such characteristic apparel as cotton field caps and pile caps. In the early phases of operations, American soldiers fought in cotton fatigue uniforms that had been moved from one Pacific island to another after World War II, and finally stored in Japan. In winter most soldiers wore the World War II-type olive drab wool uniform with a wool undershirt and a cotton undershirt underneath if available, and perhaps a wool sweater together with a field jacket. Field overcoats and wool overcoats were available, but the troops tended to throw these away. Standard winter footgear was the shoepac worn with felt inner soles, a pair of ski socks, and a pair of cushion sole socks. The mountain sleeping bag was a favorite item although it was not available in large numbers for the first winter.

Wool "mummy" sleeping bags or wool blankets were poor substitutes.

Nearly 65 percent of the tonnage of all supplies shipped from the United States to the Far East command was petroleum products. The more than 170,000 tons each month of gasoline and oil going to Korea in April and May 1951 were 4.25 times as much as the tonnage of food supplies and more than 3.54 times the tonnage of ammunition sent during the same period. Petroleum products comprised the one class of supplies furnished by the U.S. Army for all U.N. forces—ground, sea, and air—in Korea. The Air Force was responsible for the financing and consignment to the Far East command of high-octane aviation gasoline, jet fuel, and aircraft lubricants, but the Army had responsibility for all other petroleum products and it was responsible for the distribution of all gasoline and oil, including aviation fuels and lubricants. The handling of petroleum products cut across service lines in a peculiar way. The product was owned by the respective military service; the tankers to move it were controlled by the Military Sea Transportation Service (MSTS) of the Navy; requirements were computed by the military services and the theater, and the Armed Services Petroleum Purchasing Agency acted as procurement agent for all the armed forces. Within the Army, the Quartermaster Corps had overall responsibility for petroleum supply, but construction, maintenance, and operation of pipelines and terminal facilities was a function of the Corps of Engineers, and the operation of tank cars and trucks and arrangements for air transportation and local water transportation was a function of the Transportation Corps.

Shipment of supplies and troops to the Far East overtaxed available shipping in the United States. As a measure of unification, the Military Sea Transportation Service had been established in the Navy Department. When the Korean conflict began the MSTS had a fleet (including ships turned over to it by the Army) of fifty troop transports, forty-eight tankers, twenty-five cargo ships, and fifty-one smaller craft. This provided a nucleus, but it could not begin to meet the requirements for the long trans-Pacific lines of communication. Chief reliance had to be on privately owned ships operating under MSTS charter. After obtaining eighty-seven of these, the Navy turned to the reserve fleet to bring World War II ships out of "mothballs." To meet immediate needs until those ships could be made ready, MSTS chartered thirteen foreign ships. Early in 1951 the Maritime Administration began letting contracts for a $350 million program to build fifty new, fast cargo ships.

In the Far East, Japanese resources again were essential for support of ocean shipping. Military cargo handled by Japanese ports jumped from 125,000 tons in May 1950 to nearly 1.4 million tons in September 1950, and thereafter averaged about 1.2 million tons a month. About two-thirds of the sea traffic to and from Japan went through Yokohama. Yokohama was able to handle such large quantities through a fleet of barges that could be used to unload ships when all the berths were taken. Barges would carry cargo to the docks or up canals and streams directly to the depots.

The main bottleneck to sea transportation for Korea was in Korea itself. With an excellent though small harbor, Pusan was the only port in South Korea with adequate deep-water dock facilities to handle a substantial volume of general cargo. But this it did splendidly. Its four piers and intervening quays could berth up to twenty-nine deep water ships, and in addition, twelve to fifteen LSTs could unload on the beach at the same time. The port had a discharge potential of 40,000 to 45,000 measurement tons a day, though shortages of personnel and restricted transportation to the hinterland kept actual capacity nearer 28,000 tons a day. Late in 1952 Pusan's stevedores unloaded the ten-millionth ton of military cargo to be shipped by the San Francisco port of embarkation since the beginning of the war. By this time Pusan and its outports were handling about one million tons of cargo a month. All the other ports in South Korea, of which Inchon, in spite of its extreme tidal variations, was most important, were handling about one-third that tonnage.

Transportation by air became significant in the movement of troops overseas and in the evacuation of casualties, and it was important at times for moving certain special items of high priority, but in terms of total cargo tonnage, it was almost negligible.

The rough Korean terrain was a major barrier to land transportation. Main reliance was on the railroads. After extensive repairs to tracks, building of bridges and cars, and rebuilding of steam locomotives in Japan and importing diesels, the U.S. Transportation Corps was able to get the railways of South Korea back into good service. By April 1951 more than 1,360 miles of railroad track were in use in South Korea, with 715 locomotives and 5,225 usable cars. On an average day at this time more than thirty trains were being dispatched—about twenty-five forwarding supplies to forward railheads, three or more shuttling troops, two or more evacuating casualties to the rear, and the remainder carrying supplies to distribution points or other rear area destinations. During the last year of the conflict, freight movements averaged about 1,250,000 short tons a month, and personnel movements averaged about 300,000 a month.

The limited road net in Korea restricted the use of motor trucks. Nonetheless, the total tonnage moved by trucks over the main supply routes increased steadily in 1951. By May, trucks were carrying 465,000 short tons a month. In the week ending 26 October 1952, the twenty-six truck companies assigned to Eighth Army transported 57,998 tons of supplies an average distance (one way) of twenty-six miles. In addition, those companies carried 34,337 troops a comparable distance.

An essential link in getting supplies over the rugged mountain terrain to the front line units were the Korean carrying parties. Organized as the Korean Service Corps, one company of these Korean carriers generally supported an infantry battalion, or a service corps battalion supported an infantry regiment. A carrier's outfit included light cotton shirt and trousers, perhaps an outer jacket, cap, Japanese sneakers, a wool blanket, and most important, an A-frame for mounting a backpack. A standard day's work for each carrier was supposed to be to carry fifty pounds of supplies a distance of ten miles. In covering long distances the carrier companies set up a relay system of six-mile segments.

Aerial tramways across difficult mountain valleys, and helicopters and other aircraft supplemented carrier companies in delivering supplies to inaccessible positions in the mountains.

There were virtually no pipelines in Korea before the beginning of the war, but the advantages they offered stimulated the construction of lines as soon as materials and engineer units were available. At first these were short lines to connect coastal terminals with airfields. Then in the summer of 1951, Eighth Army undertook to lay 200 miles of pipeline to deliver gasoline for motor trucks as well as fuel for aircraft. A line from Inchon to Chunchon and then to Uijongbu would release more than sixteen railway cars a day. In the week ending 25 October 1952, the Eighth Army received 916,680 gallons of motor gasoline by pipeline.

Two characteristics that most distinguished the evacuation and hospitalization of casualties in Korea from the World War II experience were the widespread use of the helicopter for evacuation of battlefield casualties and the deployment of mobile Army surgical hospitals (MASHs).

Ordinarily a rifle battalion had the support of three litter squads. It took four men to carry a litter patient. Wherever the terrain permitted, litter jeeps carried the wounded back to the battalion aid station. Often, tracked "weasels" provided an indispensable service in carrying wounded men across mud or snow. For evacuation across water, the amphibious 2^1/$_2$-ton trucks (DUKWs) were invaluable. Sometimes in difficult mountain country where no vehicles could operate, it would take all night for a litter squad to reach a wounded man and then all the next day to carry him back to the aid station. Sometimes engineers were able to rig aerial tramways for bringing down wounded men from mountain positions.

The normal evacuation chain from infantry units was by ambulance from battalion aid station to regimental collecting point and thence to the division clearing station and mobile army surgical hospital or to an evacuation hospital. Railroads were useful at times for evacuation even from forward areas. Some units used self-propelled railroad cars ("doodle bugs") for this purpose. Some improvised rail buses, that is, they fitted metal wheels with flanges on to the front and rear of the buses. These wheels could be lowered by means of a crank for operation on the railroad or raised to allow the bus to run on its regular rubber-tired wheels on roads.

More and more the helicopter came into use to cut short the evacuation chains. They would evacuate casualties from the battalion aid station, or at times from the very spot where a man had been wounded, directly to the MASH. It came to be the practice to attach a helicopter unit, made up of four helicopters, four pilots, and four mechanics, to each MASH. In the first year of the war helicopters of all services evacuated more than 3,000 patients. That winter they began evacuating a number of wounded men directly to hospital ships.

The standard mobile Army surgical hospital had been designed as a sixty-bed unit to be located with or near division clearing stations to provide surgical treatment for casualties too badly injured to be evacuated further without first having such attention. In Korea the MASHs generally were expanded to 200-bed units.

Most casualties, whether sick or wounded, went by air or ambulance and rail from clearing stations and MASHs to evacuation hospitals. Equipped to give complete general medical care, evacuation hospitals as a rule retained all patients expected to recover within thirty days; the others they prepared for further evacuation by air or ship to Japan. All of the evacuation hospitals were 400-bed, semi-mobile units. In June 1952 six of them were operating under Eighth Army.

After August 1950, most casualties were evacuated from Korea to Japan by air. General hospitals and station hospitals provided care in Japan. The general policy was that patients requiring treatment estimated at longer than 120 days should be returned to the United States (usually by air). However, in September and again in December 1950 so many casualties arrived in Japan that there were not enough doctors and nurses to care for them. This made it necessary to go to a sixty-day evacuation policy during each of those months in order to make facilities and medical personnel available for them. Thereafter, it was possible to hold to a 120-day evacuation policy.

Aircraft carrying patients from the Far East to the United States usually arrived at Travis Air Force Base, Fairfield, California, or at McClellan Air Force Base, near Sacramento, though the bigger planes sometimes flew to destinations in the interior. Thence patients went, again by air, to a hospital chosen on the basis of availability of specialized treatment, availability of beds, and proximity to the patient's home.

It was clear from the beginning of operations in Korea that the United States would have to bear the major part of the logistic support for South Korean forces. In the first few days of fighting, the South Koreans lost most of the American arms and equipment they had received under earlier military assistance programs, as whole units melted away. The Eighth Army was able to assemble only four skeletonized South Korean divisions to help hold the Pusan perimeter during August 1950. It was necessary to begin at once the task of rebuilding South Korean units. Equipment would be according to allowances under special tables of organization and equipment drawn for the Korean units. Far East command began equipping the new divisions from its own stocks and asked that additional material for that purpose be sent from the United States.

Special measures were necessary to provide a satisfactory combat ration for Korean units. The Japan logistical command quartermaster developed a special J-ration for Korean troops in combat. This ration, containing rice starch, biscuits, rice cake, fish, peas, kelp, tea, chewing gum, and condiments, provided 3,210 calories, weighed 2.3 pounds, and cost less than seventy-nine cents. (The U.S. standard C-ration provided 3,800 calories and cost about two dollars.) Assembled in the Tokyo quartermaster depot by Japanese employees, these rations were sent to Korea at the rate of about one million a month. The fiery Korean staple, kimche, was also canned and distributed to ROK troops until the potent juices ate away the cans. A second issue protected the cans with a plastic insert.

At the end of February 1953, the Republic of Korea Army had a strength of more than 411,000 officers and men plus 66,000 civilian trainees. In addition, the national police force had more than 63,000 officers and men. Now South Korean units were manning more than 60 percent of the fighting front; American units held 25 percent of the line, and other United Nations forces held the remaining 15 percent.

In three years of war, coalition forces in Korea other than those of the United States and the Republic of Korea never amounted to as much as 10 percent of the total troop strength. The United States provided one-half or more of the logistic support for those forces, but this represented a relatively insignificant fraction of the total supplies and services provided for United States and South Korean forces. But the significance of United Nations participation in the Korean operations, and of American logistic support for the forces of those countries, was not to be measured in numbers of troops alone. The problems of coordination, negotiation, financial arrangements, and accounting were as great as if troop contributions had been several times as large.

National differences in customs and tastes led to many complications in supplying U.N. forces. The American ration had to be modified to satisfy each of the national tastes or religious scruples, except for Norway, Sweden, and Canada (the Canadians provided most of their own food).

The United States furnished much of the individual clothing and equipment and small arms for forces of the other United Nations, as well as motor vehicles, electrical and signal equipment, all the gasoline and oil, nearly all of the transportation within the Far East theater, and much of the transportation between the theater and home countries.

International financial policy remained one of the great unsolved problems of modern coalition warfare. Whenever a country volunteered forces to participate in the common effort it thereby incurred a financial obligation (mostly to the United States) for their support. On the other hand those nations, including those who had voted in favor of the General Assembly resolutions on the unification of Korea and declaring Communist China an aggressor, but who furnished no troops, incurred no such financial obligation.

The total tonnage of all classes of supply sent from the United States to the Far East during the thirty-seven months of the Korean War—31.5 million tons—was 82 percent greater than the total shipped to General MacArthur's Southwest Pacific area during a like period (August 1942–August 1945) in World War II. It was more than twice the tonnage shipped from the United States in support of General John J. Pershing's American Expeditionary Force in World War I during nineteen months (June 1917–December 1918). The comptroller of the Army estimated the total cost to the Army of operations in Korea for the period 27 June 1950 to 30 June 1953 to have been over 17.2 billion. This included over 11.7 billion for supplies shipped to the Far East (excluding equipment that accompanied troops), $1,522,925,000 for contractual services in moving troops and supplies, $1,729,152,000 for the cost of installation activities in the United States and the Far East in direct support of operations in Korea, and soldiers' pay of $2,192,461,000.

The total troop strength in Korea as of June 1952 was as follows:

U.S. Army	230,000
U.S. Marine Corps (ground)	27,000
U.S. Marine Corps (air)	600
U.S. Air Force	35,000
U.N. Allied (ground)	35,000
U.N. Allied (air)	1,100
Republic of Korea Army	320,000
Republic of Korea Navy and Marines	25,800
Republic of Korea Air Force	5,400
Korean Augmentation to U.S. Army	8,200

James A. Huston

Bibliography

Far East Command, General Headquarters, Military History Section. *Logistical Problems and Their Solutions* (EUSAK, n.d.).

Flanigan, William J. "Korean War Logistics: The First Hundred Days," *Army Logistician*, 18 (1986).

Heiser, Joseph M., Jr. *A Soldier Supporting Soldiers* (Center of Military History, Washington: 1991).

Huston, James A. *Guns and Butter, Powder and Rice: U.S. Army Logistics in the Korean War* (1989).

Westover, John G. *Combat Support in Korea* (Office of the Chief of Military History, Washington: 1955).

MacArthur (in non-regulation boots and scarf) inspects U.S. troops.
Courtesy National Archives.

U.S. naval air power in Korea. WW II-vintage Corsair Navy fighter-bombers over WW II-era Essex-class carrier. Courtesy National Archives.

The "workhorse" of two wars: The immortal C-47 transport. Courtesy Air and Space Museum, Smithsonian Institution.

F9F Grumman U.S. Navy jet fighters making a carrier landing.
Courtesy U.S. Naval Institute.

Boeing B-29 bombers over North Korea early in the Korean War. (By 1951, their undersides were painted black,
a reflection of the potency of enemy antiaircraft guns.) Courtesy Air and Space Museum, Smithsonian Institution.

Commonwealth troops disembarking from USAF Douglas C-54 (DC-4) transport.
Courtesy Air and Space Museum, Smithsonian Institution.

ROK civilians being armed for defense of Taejon, July 1950.
Courtesy National Archives.

USAF North American F-86 fighter aircraft.
Courtesy Air and Space Museum, Smithsonian Institution.

As usual, the American Army did not stint on equipment. Every U.S. soldier in Korea could easily have ridden into battle. Courtesy National Archives.

The most reliable—often the only means of supply in Korea's hills—native manpower and the "A" Frame. Courtesy National Archives.

U.S. troops manhandle artillery piece up Korean hill.
Courtesy National Archives.

"Shovelling out" leaflets from a Douglas C-47 (DC-3) transport.
Courtesy Air and Space Museum, Smithsonian Institution.

ROK troops on the march.
Courtesy National Archives.

Massacred U.S. troops from early
retreat, summer, 1950.
Courtesy National Archives.

Burned-out terminal of Kimpo airfield, Seoul shortly after capture by U.S. forces, September, 1950; floodlights and antennas erected. Courtesy National Archives.

U.S. Marines go over the seawall at Inchon, September 1950. Courtesy National Archives.

Human crush of citizens of Pyongyang pick their way across wrecked bridge over the icy Taedong River, fleeing the advancing North Korean and Chinese communists, early December 1950. Courtesy National Archives.

HST signs state of national emergency, 16 December 1950.
Courtesy National Archives.

Wary replacements learn how to stay alive as they enter the line.
Courtesy National Archives.

Exploit of the U.S. Army Engineers.
Courtesy National Archives.

Troop entertainment for a division. Photo gives good indication of the size of a U.S. Army infantry division. Courtesy National Archives.

U.N. partisans and their U.S. advisors on an island off the west coast of North Korea. Courtesy R. Paschall collection.

Ambush site of U.N. convoy; work of communist guerrillas.
Courtesy National Archives.

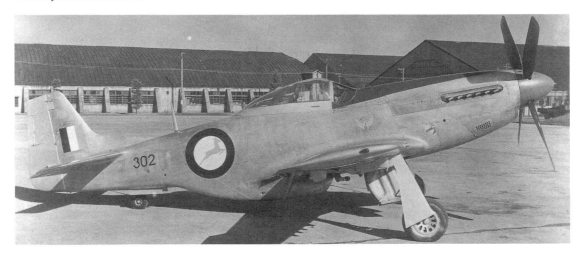

South African Air Force North American P-51 Mustang fighter.
Courtesy Air and Space Museum, Smithsonian Institution.

USAF Lockheed F-84 fighter and ground attack aircraft.
Courtesy Air and Space Museum, Smithsonian Institution.

Belgian troops in Korea write notes.
Courtesy National Archives.

The blasted terrain around "Old Baldy."
Courtesy National Archives.

Korean civilians packing U.S. Army psychological warfare leaflet bombs.
Courtesy Air and Space Museum, Smithsonian Institution.

The Korean War saw the complete racial integration of the U.S. armed forces, fully a decade before civilian
society took the step. Courtesy National Archives.

Jubilant ROK troops roll into North Korea.
Courtesy National Archives.

Haggard American prisoners of war, forced to parade through Pyongyang, summer 1950.
Courtesy Air and Space Museum, Smithsonian Institution.

U.S. Army "psywar" leaflet bundles dropped over enemy lines.
Courtesy Air and Space Museum, Smithsonian Institution.

Captured MIG-15 taking off for flight testing, closely followed by a North American F-86, the two main combatants of "Mig Alley" along the Yalu River. Courtesy Air and Space Museum, Smithsonian Institution.

Possible enemy
mortar position
on reverse slope

Friendly 40 mm.
tracer fire

Battle lines during period of near-total stalemate, 1951–1953. "Here we were and there they were."
Courtesy National Archives.

Demarcating the armistice line, Panmunjom.
Courtesy National Archives.

M

MacArthur, Douglas (1880–1964)

Douglas MacArthur, American general, was commander of Allied forces in the Southwest Pacific during World War II, commander of the Allied forces during the occupation of Japan, and commander of United Nations forces during the first nine months of the Korean War. MacArthur was born in 1880, the son of Arthur MacArthur, who had been awarded the Congressional Medal of Honor during the Civil War for his exploits at Missionary Ridge. Arthur MacArthur also served in the Indian Wars, fought in the Philippines during and after the Spanish-American War, and was appointed military governor of the Philippines. When Arthur MacArthur retired in 1906 he was the senior ranking officer in the U.S. Army.

Douglas MacArthur entered West Point in 1899, graduating four years later at the head of his class and setting the highest scholastic record at the academy in twenty-five years. His first assignment was in the Philippines, where his father had served as military governor just two years before. In 1904, he was promoted to first lieutenant and became his father's aide-de-camp in Japan.

In 1906, MacArthur was appointed aide-de-camp to President Theodore Roosevelt, and in 1913 he was appointed to the general staff under President Woodrow Wilson. The next year, MacArthur took part in the Veracruz, Mexico, expedition. By the time America entered the European war in 1917, the talented and flamboyant MacArthur had r ached the rank of major.

MacArthur helped organize the famed 42nd Infantry Division, better known as the "Rainbow Division." As a colonel, he served as the division's chief of staff. In August 1918, MacArthur was promoted to brigadier general and became commander of the Rainbow Division's 84th Infantry Brigade which he led in the St. Mihiel, Muese-Argonne, and the Sedan offensives. His exploits during the war won him a number of citations and brought him to national prominence for the first time.

Following the war, MacArthur became the superintendent at West Point, the youngest officer to ever hold that post; he remained there until 1922. Following a second tour in the Philippines, he returned to the United States in January 1925, was named commander of the 3rd Corps, and then returned to the Philippines where he served as department commander.

In 1930, MacArthur returned to the United States and was named by President Herbert Hoover as chief of staff of the Army. At age fifty, he was promoted to the rank of full general at a time when America was staunchly isolationist and military figures like MacArthur played a small part in the nation's activities. In 1932, MacArthur led a force of tanks, cavalry, and infantry against a group of 15,000 unarmed World War I veterans who had camped in Washington to petition Congress for early payment of their service bonuses. In a violent clash precipitated by orders from MacArthur, the "Bonus Army" was dispersed. For many at that time, and for historians since, the harsh treatment of the "Bonus Army" has seemed to offer insight into the mind and character of Douglas MacArthur. MacArthur later justified his actions by improbably claiming that he had thwarted a "Communist revolution."

In 1936, MacArthur was appointed military advisor to the Philippines, where he trained commonwealth military forces and prepared the Philippine government for its coming independence. In 1937, he retired from the Army, but remained in the Philippines as an advisor to its government with the rank of generalissimo and a lavish salary and perquisites.

MacArthur built up and trained Philippine forces between 1935 and 1937, but he trained them for a conventional war—an unrealistic goal. When war came, MacArthur's Philippine Army was poorly prepared to meet the crack invading Japanese Army in the field, and lacked the training to conduct the only real option open to it: guerrilla warfare. About the only positive conclusions that could be validly made about the Philippine Army of 1941–1942 was that it remained loyal, fought bravely on occasion, and in distinct contrast to other Asian "colonial" armies, it could boast native officers up to the highest ranks.

In the summer of 1941, the entire Philippine Army was inducted into the Army of the United States, and MacArthur was recalled to active duty to head the new command: United States forces in the Far East. The long-expected Japanese attack came at Clark Field, north of Manila, about eight hours after the initial Japanese attack on Pearl Harbor. Most of MacArthur's air force was destroyed on the ground by Japanese aircraft in "Pearl Harbor II."

MacArthur committed at least one serious military blunder in the early days of the Philippine campaign in his disastrous attempt to meet Japanese thrusts everywhere, a strategy based on his exaggerated estimate of the prowess of the Philippine Army. In addition, his failure to transfer the vast food stocks that had been earlier assembled for removal to the Bataan peninsula resulted in the largely unnecessary hunger that so debilitated its doomed defenders.

But MacArthur retrieved his reputation by his aggressive defense at Bataan, a defense that seemed all the more the work of a military genius when contrasted to the astonishingly quick capitulation of the other colonial powers in the area, the Dutch and British at Malaya and Singapore. Although he was criticized by some of his troops for leaving the Philippines before the inevitable surrender, his orders came directly from President Franklin D. Roosevelt, and this was one presidential order that MacArthur chose to obey.

MacArthur was evacuated by patrol torpedo (PT) boat to Australia in March where he was named supreme commander of the Southwest Pacific and began his plans to launch an attack on Japanese power in the Pacific.

After five months of preparation, MacArthur began a daring counteroffensive against the Japanese at New Guinea. Bypassing Japanese strongholds (such as Rabaul) and cutting off supplies to the enemy from the Japanese home islands to the north, MacArthur's armies leapfrogged through the Solomon, Bismarck, and Admiralty islands back toward their destination of the Philippine islands. With the support of Admiral William Halsey's forces in the South Pacific and Admiral Chester Nimitz's forces advancing across the Central Pacific, the Japanese were pushed back throughout 1943 and 1944. On October 20, 1944, MacArthur's forces invaded Leyte Island in the Philippines. In December, he was promoted to the rank of five-star General of the Army. On December 15, MacArthur seized Mindoro, and on January 9, 1945 he landed in force on Luzon. Through February and March, Allied forces gained control of a devastated Manila, and soon thereafter completed their conquest of the islands.

MacArthur was to lead American forces in the invasion of the Japanese home islands, and he was in the process of preparing for that impending and horrific operation when the atomic bomb brought an abrupt and decisive end to the war. On August 15, MacArthur was named supreme commander for the Allied powers, and in that capacity he accepted the surrender of Japan aboard the USS *Missouri* on September 2, 1945.

From his role of military leader in time of war, MacArthur moved on to a new chapter in his life as the commander of the Allied occupation of postwar Japan. He held that position until 1951, ruling Japan through a series of orders from his headquarters in Tokyo. MacArthur is credited with restoring Japan's devastated economy, placing the defeated nation's political future on a sound footing, liberalizing the government, and setting Japan on the road to democracy and postwar recovery. His rule of Japan in this period (in the name of the Allied powers) is usually considered both fair and progressive, and MacArthur claimed, a greater source of satisfaction to him than his military successes.

MacArthur tested the waters of politics in 1948 by allowing his name to be placed on Republican party primary ballots in a number of states in the spring and summer prior to the 1948 election. However, after a disastrous primary defeat in Wisconsin, MacArthur did not actively lend his name to any additional political activities.

Still another chapter in MacArthur's life opened when the armies of North Korea attacked South Korea on June 25, 1950. On July 14, the general was named to direct United Nations forces in the defense of South Korea. With the few and poorly trained troops that were then stationed in Japan, MacArthur fought a holding action against a powerful North Korean army. His forces were pushed down the Korean peninsula until a defense perimeter was finally established at the southeastern segment of the peninsula around the vital port city of Pusan.

At the end of July, MacArthur flew to Taiwan for two days of talks with Chiang Kaishek. At the end of these talks MacArthur made a vague announcement praising Chiang's anticommunism, but further stating that "arrangements have been completed for effective coordination between American forces under my command and those of the Chinese government." This sounded suspiciously as though Chinese Nationalist troops were to be introduced into the Korean fighting, which was definitely not U.S. government policy. MacArthur cavalierly refused to give details of his supposed plan to the State Department, and even waited for four days to report to the Joint Chiefs of Staff, nominally his superiors, on this important meeting.

In spite of his embattled situation along the Pusan perimeter, MacArthur nonetheless found the time to excoriate administration policy in his message to the Veterans of Foreign Wars (VFW) on 20 August. He dismissed any threat of the war's expansion by arguing that as the most knowledgeable expert on "oriental psychology" he knew that most Asians admired his "aggressive, resolute, and dynamic leadership." President Harry S. Truman forced MacArthur to withdraw the statement, but mutual ill-will continued to fester between the two leaders.

On September 15, MacArthur, now age seventy, directed the surprise amphibious landing behind enemy lines at Inchon, just west of Seoul. His plan had been opposed by most high military officers in Washington, but MacArthur was able to convince the Joint Chiefs of Staff of its feasibility and the operation succeeded famously. By the end of the month, the North Korean forces began to collapse quickly and were rolled back across the 38th parallel. On October 8, U.N. troops pushed the enemy north into North Korea and followed in hot pursuit. MacArthur was, of course, only following the directives of the president and the Joint Chiefs of Staff. The following day, he issued an ultimatum to Pyongyang, calling on the North Korean government "for the last time" to surrender immediately and inviting its people to cooperate with the U.N. in creating a "unified, independent, and democratic government of Korea." The Stalinist premier of the Democratic People's Republic of Korea (North Korea), not surprisingly, ignored such overtures. Many North Koreans collaborated with U.N. forces, for whatever reasons, and had to be evacuated when those forces withdrew.

Elements of MacArthur's command actually reached the Yalu River marking the border between China and Korea by late October. But these forces were divided into two commands, X Corps and Eighth Army, which had practically no communication with each other and which seemed to invite an enemy offensive to destroy them piecemeal. MacArthur refused to believe that the Chinese, firm allies of North Korea, would enter the war in any strength, and opened his "end the war by Christmas" offensive. (Later, and very improbably, he termed this offensive "a reconnaissance in force"; still later and even more improbably, he claimed to have "upset the enemy's timetable.") Some writers have even contended that MacArthur's intelligence was good enough that he realized that the Chinese were likely to intervene and welcomed this opportunity for a showdown with Asian communism. A more considered appraisal of the general, however, would have to conclude that he was neither that clever nor that stupid.

MacArthur's "intelligence failure" is more understandable, however, when it is remembered that his staff was responsible for information on the current enemy, that is North Korea. Determining what other nations, such as the People's Republic of China, might do was up to the Central Intelligence Agency and the State Department. The available records indicate little intelligence sharing or coordination, and blame for that failure can be apportioned all around.

On November 24, Chinese forces struck hard, and MacArthur's divided U.N. troops were pushed back across the 38th parallel in a matter of weeks. The once ebullient U.N. commander now seemed sunk in gloom and alarmism, which in numerous cases permeated the entire command by the end of the year. U.N. forces retreated to well below the 38th parallel.

The two U.N. counteroffensives of late winter and early spring 1951 were primarily the work of General Matthew B. Ridgway, General Walton H. Walker's successor as commander of Eighth Army, although MacArthur gave

M

Ridgway his blessing. But stiffening enemy resistance as their lines of communication shortened brought Operations Killer and Ripper to a halt near the 38th parallel, but with the ruins of Seoul once again in U.N. hands. MacArthur again called upon the enemy commander, this time not to sign a surrender instrument but to meet with him to negotiate a cease-fire and acceptance of U.N. objectives for Korea. This move was probably designed to forestall peace proposals about to be forwarded by the Truman administration. MacArthur may well have wished to torpedo negotiations, and if so, he succeeded.

Rebuffed by the Communists, MacArthur called for an extension of the war into China that would pave the way to victory in Korea and an end to communism in Asia. He advocated the bombing of bases in Manchuria, the blockading of the Chinese coast, and the introduction of Nationalist Chinese forces into the war. This plan was, of course, completely contrary to the policies of the Truman administration, and of the succeeding Eisenhower administration as well, for that matter. Neither, whatever their differing public expressions, had any desire to escalate the limited Korean conflict.

It should be noted also that none of MacArthur's plans for air or sea attacks stood any chance of execution; they lacked any basis in logic or in logistics, and it is surprising that so experienced a commander would forward them. The Joint Chiefs of Staff were well aware of the deficiencies of MacArthur's ideas; only later, in their testimony before various Senate committees, did they claim that his ideas ran the risk of igniting World War III.

Yet, despite the perfervid rhetoric of some of MacArthur's opponents, there is no evidence that the general had any intention of overthrowing or even challenging the American constitutional principles of civilian control of the military. MacArthur was fired for public insubordination. He also deserved at least to be quietly retired for incompetence. At any rate, MacArthur was relieved of his commands by the president on April 11, 1951.

His brilliant military career at an end, MacArthur returned to the United States for the first time in fifteen years. He received a hero's welcome at a number of cities throughout the country as he made his way to Washington. On April 19, MacArthur was invited by conservatives to address a joint session of Congress. In a memorable speech he defended his plan for

escalating the war that had led to his dismissal, concluding with a line from an old Army ballad that has since come to be associated with him: "Old soldiers never die; they just fade away."

With the exception of a brief run for the presidency in 1952 (he delivered a listless keynote address at the Republican national convention that year) MacArthur retired to a quiet private life. He died at Walter Reed Hospital in Washington on April 5, 1964, at the age of eighty-four.

History has treated MacArthur as the consummate soldier, a leader of men, but a man who could give orders better than he could take them. For most, he was the genius behind America's victory against Japan. In Korea, the legacy of MacArthur is usually expressed as much in the controversy that led to his firing as the brilliant landing at Inchon that changed for a time the entire character of the war.

Gary A. Donaldson

Bibliography

James, D.C. *The Years of MacArthur*, 3 vols. (1970, 1975, 1985).

MacArthur, Douglas. *Reminiscences* (1964).

Manchester, William. *American Caesar: Douglas MacArthur, 1880-1964* (1978).

Mossman, Billy C. *Ebb and Flow: November 1950–July 1951* (Center of Military History, Washington: 1990).

Petillo, Carol M. *Douglas MacArthur: The Philippine Years* (1981).

Rovere, Richard, and Arthur M. Schlesinger, Jr. *The MacArthur Controversy and American Foreign Policy* (1965).

See also JOINT CHIEFS OF STAFF AND THE RELIEF OF GENERAL DOUGLAS MACARTHUR

Manchuria

Manchuria is a Western term for a region of China that the Chinese call Tungpei, "the Northeast," or Tungsansheng, "the three northeastern provinces." This is an area of about 300,000 square miles, sharing borders with Mongolia on the west, with the former Soviet Union on the north and east, and with Korea on the southeast. On the south the Liaotung peninsula stretches into the Gulf of Chihli. The region is known for its fertile soil and rich deposits of coal, iron ore, oil, and fierce winters.

Historically, the Mongol-Tungus tribes inhabiting Manchuria, especially the southern part, were intermittently under the cultural influence and political control of Chinese dynasties. In the latter half of the seventeenth century, the Machus, who sprang from the Tungus tribes, conquered China proper and established the Ch'ing Dynasty that lasted till 1911, when it was replaced by the Republic of China.

In the latter half of the nineteenth and the first half of the twentieth centuries, Manchuria was a field of international rivalry. In 1858 and 1860, China had to cede to Imperial Russia all its territories beyond the Amur and Ussuri Rivers. In mid-1894, Chinese and Japanese troops clashed in Korea; overpowering the Chinese Army and Navy, the Japanese invaded Manchuria and other parts of China. Facing utter defeat, the Ch'ing government agreed to cede the Liaotung peninsula, among other concessions. This was not carried out because of Russian, German, and French protests. In the course of next the few years, Russia acquired rights to build railways in Manchuria and leases on the Liaotung peninsula, including a naval base. In 1904, Japan went to war with Russia in the region. As a result of the war, Japan took former Russian concessions in southern Manchuria. In 1931, Japanese troops drove out Chinese forces and occupied all of Manchuria. Three years later, the Japanese set up Manchukuo, a puppet government. In 1937, Japanese forces in Manchuria drove southward and started the second stage of the Sino-Japanese War.

On the Japanese surrender in 1945, Manchuria became a major battlefield in the competition between Chinese Nationalists and Communists. By the end of 1948, the Communists had wiped out the Nationalist forces in the region. With its economic power, Manchuria played an important role in the Chinese Communist victory and reconstruction.

After the Korean War broke out, the Chinese government started to concentrate forces in Manchuria. In early October 1950, the headquarters of the People's Volunteer Army (PVA) was set up in Shenyang in southern Manchuria. In mid-October the PVA started to move into Korea. During the war Manchuria served as a major base for both the Chinese and North Korean war effort.

During the Korean War, the question of Manchurian "sanctuaries" was a contentious issue between General Douglas MacArthur and his supporters and successors, and the Truman and Eisenhower administrations.

General MacArthur, commander of U.N. forces in Korea, had prohibited operations across the Chinese or Soviet borders as his troops were poised to cross the 38th parallel dividing North and South Korea in October of 1950. But by December of that year, with those troops in full retreat, the general now claimed extravagantly that such a restriction was an "enormous hardship, without precedent in military history" and the cause of his great retreat from North Korea and the subsequent military stalemate. He held to this view to the end of his life.

It was undoubtedly frustrating for U.S. pilots to actually witness the dust clouds kicked up by swarms of vulnerable Chinese MIG-15 jet fighters as they taxied out of the Manchurian airfields unmolested to do battle, and then to see them break for their off limits airfields when pressed too closely. But the Truman and Eisenhower administrations and their military advisors firmly held that the main Communist threat lay in Europe, not Asia, and that, in the often-quoted words of Chairman of the Joint Chiefs of Staff General Omar N. Bradley, a wider war in Asia "would involve us in the wrong war, at the wrong place, at the wrong time, and with the wrong enemy."

Jing Li

Bibliography

Chang, Kia-ngau. *Last Chance in Manchuria: The Diary of Chang Kia-ngau* (1988).

Chao, Kang. *The Economic Development of Manchuria: The Rise of a Frontier Economy* (1982).

Hunt, Michael H. *Frontier Defense and the Open Door: Manchuria in Chinese-American Relations, 1895–1911* (1983).

Lattimore, Owen. *Manchuria: Cradle of Conflict* (1932).

Lee, Chong-sik. *Revolutionary Struggle in Manchuria: Chinese Communism and Soviet Interest, 1922–1945* (1983).

See also CHINA AND CHINESE DECISION MAKING IN THE KOREAN WAR; PEOPLE'S LIBERATION/VOLUNTEER ARMY

Mao Tse-tung (1893–1976)

Mao Tse-tung (or Zedong), Chinese Communist leader, was born in Hsiang-t'an, Hunan province, China, on December 26, 1893. Mao grew up in a peasant family of sufficient means. From eight to thirteen he was educated in the Chinese classics. For the next two years he helped his father in the fields. In 1910 he left home to attend school. Next year, when an anti-Ch'ing Dynasty revolution broke out, Mao joined a revolutionary group but soon quit to continue his education. He took part in the May Fourth Movement of 1919, and in 1921 was one of the creators of the Chinese Communist party.

In the Nationalist-Communist coalition against warlords formed in 1924, Mao soon became known as an effective peasant organizer. When the Nationalists and the Communists split in 1927, Mao started the Autumn Harvest Uprising and set up a "Soviet Republic" in Kiangsi province.

Under persistent Nationalist attacks, in 1934 Mao's Red Army had to abandon its base area. One year later, after what is known as the "Long March," Mao and his followers reached Shensi province in northwestern China. Here, in the coming ten years, Mao refined his revolutionary theories, consolidated his leadership in the party, and while fighting in an alliance with the Nationalists against the Japanese invaders, dramatically expanded the Communist force. During this period Mao also developed his military theories which had a strong influence on the Chinese Communist Army. In the war with the Nationalists that followed the Japanese surrender, Mao's army cleared mainland China of the Nationalists by 1949, and Mao became the head of the newly founded People's Republic of China (PRC).

In early October 1950, when U.N. forces reversed the course of the Korean War, Mao decided to intervene in spite of differing opinions from some of his more wary colleagues. Although it is unknown what Mao's original plan was—to unite Korea or just to drive the U.N. forces out of North Korea—by early 1951 he had become prudent. At this time he instructed Peng Dehuai, the commander in chief of the People's Volunteer Army (PVA): "Win a quick victory if you can; if you can't, win a slow one." According to Mao, a Chinese victory would prove of enormous strategic and psychological value, but even the more likely stalemate between backward China and the mighty U.S.A. would still amount to something like a victory. In defeat, China would simply abandon its coastal provinces, as in World War II, and fight on from the interior a "protracted war."

The outcome of the war certainly enhanced the prestige of Mao as a Communist leader, though he paid a high price. Among other things, he lost his elder son, who died during an American air raid in Korea; he may also have

missed a chance to complete China's unity—a separate Taiwan remained one of his major concerns for the rest of his life.

In 1972 Mao received President Richard M. Nixon in Beijing, symbolizing the opening of a new U.S.-PRC relationship.

Mao died in Beijing on September 9, 1976, in the position of chairman of the Chinese Communist party.

Jing Li

Bibliography
Ch'en, Jerome. *Mao and the Chinese Revolution* (1965).
Chou Ching'wen. *Ten Years of Storm* (1960).
Mao Tse-tung. *Selected Readings from the Works of Mao Tse-tung* (1967).
Schram, Stuart. *Mao Tse-tung* (1967).
Snow, Edgar. *Red Star over China* (1938).
Terrill, Ross. *Mao: A Biography* (1980).

Marine Corps, U.S.
Victory in the Pacific found the Marine Corps swollen to a record strength of 485,833. Following the signing of the Japanese surrender in 1945, the Marine Corps began major initiatives regarding personnel reduction. By February 1948, demobilization had reduced the corps to 92,000 Marines.

Despite the reductions, the corps attacked on another flank, turning a problem into an opportunity. Presidential Order Number 9981 issued in 1947 officially abolished segregation in the armed forces. By 1949, recruit platoons and enlisted clubs at Parris Island Recruit Depot demonstrated full integration. During November of that same year, the corps enlisted its first black women Marines.

Budget and personnel reductions continued; total corps strength dropped to 74,279 men and women by June of 1950. The 25 June invasion of South Korea by North Korea found the corps understrength but anxious to return to combat. Commandant Clifton B. Cates immediately proposed that Marine units be sent to the Korean war zone. The commandant's offer went initially unanswered in the confusion of the moment, but as the severity of the situation in Korea became apparent, all alternatives found a receptive ear. On 2 July 1950, General Douglas MacArthur submitted a formal request for Marines, asking for a regimental combat team. In the days following, MacArthur raised his request to a full Marine division, including a Marine air wing.

On 7 July 1950, the corps activated a provisional brigade in California. The 1st Brigade sailed from San Diego for Korea on 15 July 1950. Only twelve days had passed since MacArthur's first request for help from the Marines.

On 19 July, an additional 33,000 organized Marine reserves, many World War II combat veterans, received notice to report for active duty. On 7 August, 50,000 Marines of the volunteer reserve received similar notifications. Characteristically, many former Marines and active reservists began straggling voluntarily into Camp Pendleton, California, during July to rejoin the corps.

Pusan

On 2 August 1950, the 6,500 men of the 1st Marine Brigade began debarking in Pusan. Originally ordered to Japan as the lead element in an anticipated autumn Marine amphibious landing in North Korea, the brigade received new orders at sea on 25 July. Crisis within the Pusan perimeter led to the change of plans. The North Koreans had attacked the perimeter in strength. Fearing a breakthrough, Army Lieutenant General Walton H. Walker requested reinforcements, including the Marine brigade. Thirty days after being activated, the Marines arrived in Pusan, distinctive in their camouflaged helmet covers, yellow khaki leggings, and characteristic swagger.

The Marines had sailed without individual or unit special training prior to deployment. Additionally, the brigade's three infantry battalions included two rather than the normal three rifle companies. The artillery batteries found themselves similarly short, lacking two howitzers in each of three batteries.

However, the Marines supplied their own air support, making the brigade a fully integrated air/ground team. The Marines brought observation aircraft and helicopters ashore with them. Tactical ground support would operate off escort carriers which had accompanied the Marines to Korea. Additionally, most of the officers, senior noncommissioned officers, and many of the enlisted ranks had served in combat during World War II. The 1st Marine Brigade brought a much needed sense of confidence and élan to the embattled American forces.

The brigade's commander, Brigadier General Edward A. Craig, a much decorated World War II commander, received orders to move his unit southwest from Pusan harbor.

The 1st Marine Brigade joined the United States 5th Infantry Regiment in reinforcing the Army's 25th Division. Task Force Kean, as the combined Army/Marine Corps command became known, accepted responsibility for defending the southwest sector of the Pusan perimeter. Additionally, Task Force Kean's command received orders to launch the war's first counterattack against the North Korean 6th and 7th Divisions. The Marines, holding the extreme southern (left) flank, began their advance on 7 August. In stifling heat, the Marine's attack began as scheduled. In temperatures that reached 112 degrees F., the Marine battalions leapfrogged forward, supported by air and artillery fire coordinated by lead infantry units.

By 11 August, the Marines had cleared the Taedabok Pass, pressing back to the north aggressively to reach their objective at Sachon. But on 12 August, the 3rd Battalion, 5th Marines, received orders to return to Chindong-ni to reinforce overrun Army artillery units. The Marine brigade now found itself fighting on two fronts. With the two elements separated by twenty-five miles, General Craig commanded from a helicopter. With the North Korean's 6th Division probe against the southwest corner of the Pusan perimeter halted, another crisis evolved. The Marines, again consolidated, convoyed seventy-five miles north to Miryang. Placed under the command of the U.S. 24th Infantry Division, the Marines again prepared for battle.

The North Koreans crossed the Naktong River on 6 August. The river provided a natural barrier on the western flank of the Pusan perimeter, but the river valley offered the North Koreans a gateway leading to Pusan and its harbor. Most pivotal of the terrain features was the Naktong bulge, a four-by-five-mile area east of the river and west of Miryang. Here the river bends sharply to the west where Hill 311 dominated the terrain.

At 8:00 A.M. on 17 August, the Marines joined Army units in an all-out counteroffensive into the bulge area. Supported by the Army's 9th Regimental Combat Team, the Marines attacked south of the Naktong road, advancing up No Name Ridge. Poor coordination of supporting arms and intense heat slowed the Marine attack. By noon, attacking a numerically superior, heavily entrenched foe, the 5th Marines suffered 50 percent casualties. Despite heavy losses, the attack escalated during the afternoon.

As the Marine attack continued, the legend of invincibility surrounding the Soviet T-34 tank dissolved. Using recoilless rifles and rockets, the Marines destroyed four of the lumbering armored giants during the afternoon. The next morning the Marines resumed their attack. Marine air supported the advance with precision placement of 500-pound bomb loads. Soon the Marines held the highest peak on the ridge, Hill 153. By early afternoon of 18 August, the Marines had taken Hill 207 immediately west of the ridge. From there they looked down into the four-by-five-mile area of the Naktong bulge. Below they saw the bunched North Korean People's Army (NKPA) troops scurrying toward the river and the safety beyond. Fire from artillery, air, and mortar began to fall on the panicked North Korean soldiers.

> Victory turned into slaughter when the brigade's supporting arms concentrated on the masses of Communists plunging into the river.

By 19 August, the Marines had taken Hill 311, the highest promontory in the Naktong bulge. The brigade then refitted, regrouped, and received some 800 fresh replacements. Rumors of a forthcoming amphibious landing dominated the Masan bivouac area.

The rumors, for once, proved true. Early on 15 September 1950, after heavy naval and air bombardment, the Marine landing party went ashore at Inchon. At 6:33 A.M. the 3rd Battalion, 5th Marines commanded by Lieutenant Colonel Raymond B. Murray, landed at Wolmi-do Island in the middle of Inchon harbor. In a matter of hours, the Marines overwhelmed the heavily fortified but poorly defended island. The Marines killed 400 NKPA during the brief fight with minimal American casualties. MacArthur acknowledged the letter-perfect performance of Murray's Marines. "The Navy and Marines have never shown more brightly than this morning," MacArthur messaged the fleet.

Late in the afternoon of 15 September, the tide at Inchon harbor again flooded, allowing the remainder of the Marines to come ashore. Murray's two remaining battalions struck the sea wall immediately fronting the city of Inchon in another picture-perfect attack. Three miles to the south, the 1st Marines under Colonel Lewis B. "Chesty" Puller attacked into a suburban area. Smoke and late evening haze began to obscure visibility as the Marines' amphibious tractors and landing craft slammed into the sea-walls, the Marines going up and over the walls with ladders. Confusion reigned as some elements strayed off course during the landing. Unperturbed, Colonel Puller steadied his regiment, concentrated, and began to advance. Simultaneously, the Marines on Wolmi-do Island crossed the causeway to the mainland to join their parent regiment in downtown Inchon. By midnight, 13,000 Marines, with their equipment, were ashore. Marine casualties proved light for the first day of the landing, 153 wounded and twenty-one dead.

On Saturday, 16 September, both the 1st and 5th Marines attacked at first light. Quickly the regiments linked up and cleared the city of Inchon. Inchon secured, the 5th Marines headed northwest toward Kimpo Airfield sixteen miles distant. The 1st Marines drove straight east toward Yongdungpo, twenty miles beyond the Inchon/Seoul highway. Both regiments focused on Seoul, the capital city beyond the 400-yard-wide Han River. On 22 September the 5th Marines crossed the Han and struck the northwest defenses fronting Seoul. The 1st Marines advanced through Youngdungpo and attacked directly into Seoul. The 7th Marines followed the 5th Marines in trace, pivoting on the division's left flank and shutting off the enemy's escape to the north.

Aided by Korean Marines, the lead regiment struck a force of 10,000 NKPA, defending in depth. The battle of Seoul had began.

The 5th Marines and their Korean compatriots struggled against stubborn resistance. On 25 September, the 7th Marines crossed the Han River, joining the attack just north of the 5th Marines. As dawn broke on 25 September, the Marines entered Seoul. Against savage resistance, they made steady, if painful, progress.

With the city finally taken on 28 September Marines took up defensive positions within Seoul. In October, the Marines received orders to return to Inchon. There they boarded ships and headed to Wonsan on the Korean east coast. In two weeks, the Marines had captured Inchon and Seoul. Estimates placed enemy losses at 4,692 prisoners and 13,666 dead and wounded. The Marines listed 421 dead while suffering 2,029 wounded.

Operation Yo-Yo

Flushed by victory at Inchon and Seoul, the 1st Marine Division received fresh operation orders in early October 1950. Some 21,176 Marines boarded transports at Inchon with additional

U.S. Army, Navy, and Korean Marine personnel. On 15 October, the armada sailed from Inchon, carrying a total of 30,184 troops.

As the Eighth Army attacked north, General MacArthur directed the Marines as part of Army Major General Edward M. "Ned" Almond's X Corps to seize Wonsan on the Korean eastern coast. The 1st Marine Division would then lead the attack north from Wonsan, a petroleum refining center blessed with a fine harbor and unused airfield. But the Navy found Wonsan harbor and its beach approaches ringed with magnetic mines. Finally, on 25 October, Marines began to land over Yellow and Blue beaches at Wonsan.

Simultaneously, new orders arrived from MacArthur's headquarters. General Almond relayed instructions to Marine Commander Major General Oliver P. Smith to relieve the ROK I Corps north of Wonsan. Specifically, the Marines received responsibility stretching 300 road miles to the north from Wonsan to the Yalu River and extending fifty miles to the west. MacArthur now shook off all constraints regarding troop dispositions near the Manchurian border.

With their feet finally on solid ground, the 1st Marine Division headed north and west. Marine Air Group 12 began flying close air support from Wonsan with additional support forthcoming from Marine and naval air units stationed aboard aircraft carriers steaming in the Sea of Japan to the east. But by early November, ominous reports filtered back from Marine pilots attacking Sinuiju at the western mouth of the Yalu River. They reported large numbers of Chinese trucks moving into Northwest Korea from Chinese Manchuria.

The Changjin (Chosin) Reservoir

General Smith deployed the 1st Marine Division in late October. The 5th Marines (Murray) and the 7th Marines led by Colonel Homer L. Litzenberg, Jr., moved north. The 1st Marines (Puller) remained in Wonsan, fragmenting into a variety of guard details.

Sharing little of the optimism emanating from the Army high command in late October 1950, the Marines found themselves scattered as part of X Corps along a hundred miles of northeastern Korean coast. Forewarned in late October by the heavy Chinese attacks against the Eighth Army to the west, the 7th Marines fought back resolutely when attacked by the 124th Division of the Chinese People's Liberation Army (PLA) near Sudong on 2 November.

The enemy advanced in waves of infantry during a series of night attacks. Initially fragmented, the 7th Marines consolidated and held the high ground. Chinese infantry accompanied by NKPA tanks fell back before the stubborn Marine defense. Colonel Litzenberg then rallied his regiment to the offense. During the subsequent five days, the Marines destroyed the Chinese 124th Division. As quickly as they had come, enemy survivors disappeared. Cautiously the 7th Marines continued their advance north toward the Changjin (Chosin) Reservoir. The 5th Marines followed in trace, the 1st Marines holding the lengthening division supply route linking the Americans to Wonsan and the sea.

Growing increasingly apprehensive, General Smith convinced X Corps of the need to concentrate the 1st Marine Division. Almond reluctantly agreed, allowing Smith to shift the 1st Marines north of Hamhung to join the 5th and 7th Marine regiments. But, as temperatures dropped from 32 to –8 degrees F. on 11 November, Almond again ordered a general northern advance toward the Yalu River.

The Marines had received only partial allotments of cold weather gear to offset the numbing cold and gusting winds. Some of the equipment, principally the footwear, proved ineffective. In addition, the 1st Marine Division found both flanks now exposed. To the west, massive Chinese attacks had shattered the Eighth Army. To the east, only scattered Army 7th Division forces had survived the Chinese onslaught.

Smith continued to follow the letter of Almond's order concerning a continued advance. However, the Marine general dramatically reduced the division's pace. As they pushed cautiously forward, the Marines secured their flanks and rear, outposting the high ground. Units concentrated, preparing for the inevitable.

Lying in wait, the PLA 9th Army Group, ten divisions of 100,000 battle-hardened veterans, prepared to accomplish their objective—the destruction of the 1st Marine Division. Although without air or artillery support, the Chinese held a five to one numerical advantage in personnel. Mortars, machine guns, and a few NKPA tanks complemented seasoned Chinese infantry. By 26 November, the 5th and 7th Marines entrenched near Yudam-ni, west of the Changjin Reservoir. The remainder of the division guarded the main supply route (MSR) stretching to Chinhung-ni, at the base of the mountains, forty-five miles to the south.

M

Remnants of the Chinese 124th Division had disappeared into the Taebaek Mountains, following the early November Marine offensive. Those mountains, rising from 7,000 to 8,000 feet above sea level, supplied cover for the Chinese, protecting them from the Marine air and artillery that had savaged the Communists during the fight with the 7th Marines.

U.S. Army historians estimated the 124th Division had suffered 7,000 casualties during the engagement. The Marines had killed 700 Chinese during the first night of the battle on 2–3 November, wounding additional thousands. The Marines suffered but 314 casualties. Subsequently, General Smith's continued cautious reaction to Almond's orders to advance began to pay handsome dividends.

Despite the victory over the 124th Division, Smith's concern regarding the dispersion of his units had continued to grow. By mid-November, Smith had taken the extraordinary precaution of relaying his concern to Marine Commandant Cates in Washington. Smith wrote:

> I do not like the prospect of stringing out a Marine division along a single mountain road for 120 air miles from Hamhung to the border. There is a continued splitting up of units and assignment of missions to small units which puts them out on a limb. (Blair, 415)

By 15 November, the 7th Marines reached Hagaru, just south of the Changjin Reservoir. The arrival of the Army's 3rd Division at Wonsan allowed Smith to move forward the 1st and 5th Regiments to protect his supply line.

On 27 November, the Chinese justified Smith's fears. The People's Liberation Army attacked in force. The Army's remaining 7th Division units east of the reservoir suffered grievously.

Despite the buildup of Chinese forces, Almond ordered X Corps to resume the offensive on 27 November. The Marines would serve as the spearhead, attacking west and then north from Yudam-ni on the west side of the Changjin Reservoir. The 7th Marines would lead. Considering the bitter cold, formidable terrain, and numerous Chinese, the decision to return to the offensive proved extremely ill-advised.

In brutal cold and a blinding snowstorm, the 5th Marines at Yudam-ni attacked. As the intense cold froze weapons, plasma, and can-teens, the Marine offensive shuddered to a halt. The 5th Marines absorbed heavy casualties while advancing but 1,500 meters against the Chinese.

That night, the Chinese struck the Marines in overwhelming force. The Chinese 79th and 89th Divisions assaulted the Marines' 5th and 7th Regiments at Yudam-ni from the west. Advancing beneath flare illumination and mortar fire with the characteristic accompanying cacophony of whistles and bugles, the Chinese swarmed into the Marine perimeter. The Marines fought back, killing hundreds, but by dawn, the Chinese had made appreciable gains. To the rear, the Americans found that the Chinese 59th Division had severed the Marine supply link southeast to Hagaru.

On 29 November, the Chinese continued the attacks in the area around Hagaru and Yudam-ni. Despite desperate odds and numbing cold, the Marines responded valiantly. Smith ordered the 5th Marines to hold Yudam-ni while the 7th Marines attacked toward Hagaru to open the roads.

With but one battalion of Marines holding Hagaru, General Smith also ordered the 1st Marines to Koto-ri to send reinforcements eleven miles north to Hagaru. Colonel "Chesty" Puller, commander of the 1st Marines, responded by sending a mixed force of British and Army units sprinkled with some Marine replacements. Puller named it Task Force Drysdale, after the British Marine officer designated to lead the 900-man relief force.

Disaster followed. Drysdale led a convoy of 922 men and 141 vehicles out of the 1st Marines' perimeter shortly after 9:00 A.M., heading north. By dusk, only half-way to Hagaru, heavy fire forced the convoy to halt on a broad plain ringed by wooded hills. Drysdale later called this "Hell Fire Valley." Heavy small arms, machine gun and mortar fire engulfed the column. In the resulting confusion, Drysdale lost nearly his entire force.

Holding the high ground surrounding Hagaru, the Chinese attacked in force on the night of 30 November. The next day, survivors of the Army's 7th Infantry Division, decimated east of Changjin, entered the Marines' perimeter. With supplies diminishing and the wounded increasing, the first Air Force C-47 transport plane landed on the Hagaru airstrip on 1 December. In twelve days, under severe weather and combat conditions, the Marines' 1st Engineer Battalion had built an airfield under the worst of conditions.

Almost simultaneously, General Almond ordered the withdrawal of all Marine forces to Wonsan. The distance from the 7th Marines forward outpost at Yudam-ni to the sea stretched seventy-eight miles over terrain as formidable as any in the world. Through that terrain wandered the slim, primitive road that provided the 1st Marine Division a single strand of survival. Surrounded by a nearly 100,000-man Chinese field army, the 20,000 Marines and attached units prepared to fight their way down the road leading to the sea, and safety.

Anticipating MacArthur's authorization to withdraw the Marines, General Smith had already begun to realign his forces on 29 November. Unifying command of the 5th and 7th Marines, Colonels Murray and Litzenberg began a dangerous turning movement in the face of the enemy.

Using the daylight, which allowed maximum effective air and artillery support, the 5th Marines withdrew first from their positions northwest of Yudam-ni. At 8:00 A.M. on 1 December, the Marines began their breakout. Or as General Smith so colorfully put it, they began advancing in a different direction.

In a routine that would become familiar in the days ahead, the Marines sent the main column of the 1st Marine Division south down the single strand of icy road leading to the sea. As the convoy struggled forward against flanking fire and enemy ambush, supporting units worked the high ground. Above the Marines, close air support swept the Chinese constantly with fire. As the convoy advanced from Yudam-ni only the drivers and wounded rode. The dead remained, hastily buried by Marine engineers.

Lieutenant Colonel Raymond G. Davis led his first battalion, 7th Marines, south along the ridgelines paralleling the road. In temperatures that dropped to −16 degrees Fahrenheit, Davis sought to relieve the embattled Marine company that held Fox Hill, an eminence controlling the vital Toktong Pass eight miles south of Yudam-ni.

Two hundred and forty Marines of Fox Company, 7th Marines, defended the high ground overlooking the pass. Commanded by Captain William E. Barber, the Marines held for five days in a savage fight against numerically overwhelming Chinese forces.

On 2 December, Davis's battalion relieved Fox Hill. They found the remnants of epic sacrifice. After five nights of Chinese assaults, only eighty-two of the original 240 Marines could walk. Captain Barber, who had won a Silver Star at Iwo Jima during World War II, led his men from a stretcher. But Fox Company had held the hill mass controlling the pass.

As Davis consolidated his men astride Fox Hill, Lieutenant Colonel Robert D. Taplett led the Third Battalion, 5th Marines, down the road toward the Toktong Pass. On the afternoon of 2 December, elements of Taplett's and Davis's battalion met. In three days of fighting, Taplett's rifle companies had suffered 200 casualties. The column continued to press down the road, beating back almost constant Chinese ambushes and attacks. On 4 December, the van of the Marine column reached Hagaru. During the first fifty-five hours of the breakout, the Marines traveled fourteen miles, bringing out 1,500 of their wounded. It took an additional twenty hours for the remainder of the 1st Marine Division to fight its way into the perimeter at Hagaru.

By early afternoon, 4 December, the long column of Marines and attached units coiled itself within the perimeter at Hagaru. As the 1st Marine Division rested and regrouped, the Chinese again disappeared into the mountains. Evacuation of the Americans began immediately, only the most seriously injured being placed aboard aircraft now using the Hagaru airfield.

The next stage of the Marine attack began on 6 December. With the 5th Marines screening the high ground and elements of the 1st Marines supplying rear security, the 1st Marine division advanced on Koto-ri.

Early on 6 December, the Marines assaulted East Hill, a promontory near Hagaru dominating the road south. By afternoon, that ridgeline fell to the Americans. But fierce fighting broke out subsequently just south of East Hill. The combat became the most intense of the breakout. Elements of the 5th Marines estimated killing 800 Chinese during the twenty-two-hour fire fight.

As the 5th Marines fought for the high ground, the 7th Marines attacked directly down the road. Advancing in bitter cold and fog, the Marines destroyed a series of roadblocks and strongpoints during a slow but steady advance toward Koto-ri. The following morning, 7 December, the security units at Hagaru blew the remaining supply caches and joined the withdrawal. By the morning of 8 December, the 1st Marine Division licked its wounds within the compound at Koto-ri. The Division had suffered 616 casualties during the breakout from Hagaru, including 103 dead.

M

At Koto-ri, 2,300 soldiers and 11,600 Marines readied for their final spring to safety. Ten miles of mountainous terrain, heavily defended by Chinese, separated Koto-ri from the relative safety of Chinhung-ni. Adding to the problem, the Chinese had blown the bridge at the Funchilin Pass, three and one-half miles south of Koto-ri.

Abutted against the mountains on one side and flanked by a deep chasm on the other, the 24-foot-wide crevice could not be bypassed. On 7 December, the Air Force dropped eight 2,500-pound steel M-2 treadway bridge spans into the Koto-ri perimeter. Of the eight dropped, six spans survived. Marine engineers trucked four of these to the Funchilin Pass, subsequently bridging the obstacle with Herculean efforts. The Marines completed the bridge late on 9 December. Troops and vehicles began crossing the improvised link to safety that night by flashlight.

As the Marine engineers struggled to replace the Funchilin bridge, Lieutenant Colonel Donald M. Schmuck led the 1st Battalion, 1st Marines, north from their defensive position at Chinhung-ni. On 8 December, in a heavy snowstorm, with temperatures recorded at −14 degrees Fahrenheit, Schmuck and his men attacked Hill 1081 (height given in meters, not feet.) Atop the hill, the Chinese 6th Division defended to the north, planning to stop the Marines now advancing south from Koto-ri. As temperatures dropped to −25 degrees, Schmuck's men drove the Chinese from Hill 1081 during 8 December. The next day dawned cold but clear, allowing air support for the hard pressed column of Americans. The improved visibility also revealed more Chinese astride the crest of Hill 1081.

Schmuck's battalion immediately attacked. In a no-quarter fight with the help of Marine air and artillery, the Marines dislodged the Chinese from their positions at mid-afternoon on 9 December. Simultaneously, forward elements of the 7th Marines came into view on the winding road below the hill. The Marines counted 530 Chinese dead atop Hill 1081. This proved the final Chinese effort to halt the Marine column moving south from Changjin.

Good visibility now aided Marine air and artillery support. Additionally, the numbing cold savaged the often poorly equipped Chinese troops. As the Marines pushed south, they stretched already tenuous Communist supply lines. Marines now encountered numerous frozen or freezing Chinese. Many of the enemy began to come into the Marine lines to surrender.

In fresh fallen snow, the remainder of the Marines traversed the Funchilin Pass over the improvised bridge on 9 December. Refugees and cattle joined the long column passing safely below Hill 1081, now secured by Schmuck's battalion.

Early on 10 December, the advance elements of the 1st Marine Division began entering Chinhung-ni. That afternoon the last Marine elements left Koto-ri. Puller's 1st Marines formed the rear guard. Again, only the dead and wounded rode.

By 11 December, the last elements of the 1st Marine Division arrived at the staging area at Hungnam. Seventy-five more men had died during the final phase of the breakout from Koto-ri to Hungnam.

But the 1st Marine Division had survived. A nation transfixed by the anticipated tragedy breathed a collective sigh of relief. Glory had not come without a price. From 30 November through 11 December the 1st Marine Division suffered 342 dead, 78 missing, and 1,683 wounded, a total of 2,103 battle casualties. But during their advance in a different direction, the 1st Marine Division had destroyed seven combat-tested Chinese divisions.

Operations Killer and Ripper

A lone bugler sounded taps over the fresh graves of the Marines laid to rest near Hungnam on 13 December 1950. General O.P. Smith rendered the final salute to the last of those who fell in the Changjin (Chosin) Reservoir operation. The Marine commander then boarded the USS *Bayfield* in Hungnam harbor. Two days later Smith, with the rest of the 1st Marine Division survivors, sailed south to Pusan.

Behind, the Marines left a legacy of courage and professionalism. The 1st Marine Division had destroyed a numerically overwhelming enemy, evacuated the wounded, and saved much of their equipment despite seemingly insurmountable terrain and bitterly cold weather. Soldier/historian S. L. A. Marshall emphasized the epic qualities of Marine operations near the Changjin Reservoir in the late fall and early winter of 1950:

No other operation in the American book of war quite compares with this show by the 1st Marine Division in the perfection of tactical concepts precisely executed, in the accurate estimate of the situation by leadership at all levels, and in promptness of all supporting forces.

However, there remained little time for the 1st Marine Division to savor the costly success while reorganizing its slim formations. Even as the Marines debarked at the southern Korean port city of Pusan and convoyed forty miles northwest to their new training camp at Masan, new operational orders percolated down to the division from higher headquarters.

To the north the enemy went to an all-out offensive as the new year opened. During the days that followed, Chinese and North Korean forces drove the allies past the Han River and the city of Seoul. As Communist supply lines lengthened, however, Allied airpower took a mounting toll. Lieutenant General Matthew B. Ridgway, who had replaced Eighth Army commander Walton H. Walker after that general's death in a jeep accident on 23 December 1950, now prepared to mount his own all-out offensive. Again, the 1st Marine Division would serve as the tip of the Allied spear in a general offensive.

By 9 January 1951, the 1st Marine Division took up a blocking position in the rear area immediately west of the eastern port city of Pohang. The Marines continued to refit and retrain, patrolling the rice paddies near Pohang in search of guerrillas. With the recapture of Inchon and Kimpo Airfield on 10 February, the Chinese committed additional forces to their offensive. Ridgway shifted the 1st Marine Division to a central position on the Korean northern perimeter. As the Chinese effort culminated, the Marines attacked north from Wonju on 22 February in the opening phase of Operation Killer.

Terrain slowed the Marines. But of greater concern was the loss of their Marine air support team. The 5th Air Force had assumed control of all air support. Stripped of the support that had proven the difference at Pusan, Inchon, Seoul, and the Chosin Reservoir, the Marines complained bitterly about the loss of their own air wing.

By 1 March, however, the division succeeded in crossing the rain-swollen Som River and secured the hills to the north of Huengsing. Operation Killer included forty-eight dead and 345 wounded in eight days of combat.

On 7 March, the 1st Marine Division again attacked to the north. Operation Ripper brought the Marines into the deserted Korean capital of Seoul on 15 March. Despite stiffening resistance by Chinese rearguard forces, the 1st Marine Division reached its objective at phase line Buffalo on 20 March. Joined by the 1st Korean Marine Regiment, the division took Hill 975, ending Operation Ripper.

Activity on the battleground subsided. But the Chinese continued to concentrate forces in the central Korean "Iron Triangle" area for an anticipated major spring offensive. On 22 April, the Chinese again attacked as they began their "Fifth Phase" offensive.

The Chinese Fifth Phase Offensive

The heaviest blow by the Chinese fell on the 6th ROK Division, securing the 1st Marine Division's western flank. The Korean unit collapsed, leaving a ten-mile gap exposing the 1st Marine Division. In heavy fighting, the Marines rushed forward reinforcements, extended their lines, bending but not breaking despite the Chinese pressure. As fighting ebbed and flowed across the battlefield, the Marines paid a high price in blood. During the 140-hour period the division suffered nearly 300 dead and wounded. In the face of a numerically superior enemy, the Marines shortened their lines, taking up new positions northeast of Hongchon. On 16 May, the Chinese again attacked north as the Chinese offensive culminated and the enemy retreated into the northern mountains.

By June the Marines found themselves contending with the Chinese in the broken terrain north of the 38th parallel. Combat centered on Hill 1316, called the "Punchbowl" by the Marines. In bitter fighting in which the Marines closed with the Chinese with bayonet and grenade, the 1st Marine Division suffered continued casualties. By the end of June, the Marines were dug in on the hill masses above the Punchbowl. The first year of the Korean War ended on 25 June 1951. On July 10, with the 38th parallel restored, the Korean peace talks began.

As the envoys talked, the Marines fought. The long static war began, a killing match waged along the 38th parallel that continued for two years. Although Pusan, Inchon, and the Chosin Reservoir later attracted greater attention from historians, the positional war proved extremely costly. During September of 1951 alone, the 1st Marine Division suffered 1,621 casualties in a limited offensive. These casualties increased as the gap between Marine and Air Force commanders widened.

On 17 March 1952, the Marines moved west, taking responsibility for the area above

M

the Imjin River, blocking access routes leading into the nearby capital city of Seoul. The Marines now found themselves faced by the formidable 63rd and 65th Chinese Divisions rather than the North Koreans. The Marines regularly exchanged artillery salvos, night probes, and battalion-size attacks with the skilled and dedicated Chinese. Casualties continued to mount. On 4 July 1952, all Marine units attacked the Chinese. A total of nearly 300 casualties resulted from the unsuccessful effort to storm the Chinese fortifications. As the combat increased along the Marine front during August, emergency drafts of Marine replacements left California for Korea as the killing match between the Chinese and the American Marines continued. Both sides jockeyed for position.

The Outpost Wars

The fighting in the Punchbowl area of central Korea during the late summer of 1951 ended the mobile phase of the Marines' war in Korea. The 1st Marine Brigade during 1950 had set the early tone during the critical August days inside the Pusan perimeter. The combat-tested unit had responded with spirit and professionalism when rushed from one brushfire to another. Expanded to the 1st Marine Division, the unit had performed with equal dash and valor during the Inchon, Seoul, and Changjin (Chosin) operations. The Marines had doctrinal difficulties concerning logistics and communications. During Operations Killer and Ripper in the 1951 spring offensive, the Marines obscured these doctrinal incongruities with movement. Fighting in the isolated, mountainous terrain northeast of the Punchbowl in 1951 introduced the Marines to static warfare. Most of the veterans of the first year's fighting, including General Oliver P. Smith, had rotated home by then. General Gerald C. Thomas, another Marine World War II veteran, had replaced Smith. Behind the veterans of Pusan, Inchon, Seoul, and Changjin came the last of the World War II battle-tested NCOs and officers. Trained and integrated with young recruits, the 1st Marine Division had lost none of its combat effectiveness as the fall of 1951 introduced the long Korean outpost war. But doctrinally, static warfare proved uncomfortable for the Marine Corps, both physically and emotionally.

During this period the Marines had more than doubled the skeletonized corps that answered the call to arms in June 1950. One year later the corps listed nearly 200,000 effectives under arms. But these numbers now came at the price of growing draft quotas and shortages of trained officers and noncommissioned officers. As growth accelerated promotions, veteran Marines began to worry about the quality of the corps training in the States.

As the armistice talks continued into the fall of 1951, the Marines periodically interjected new doctrinal methods applicable both to Korea and the wars the Marines knew lay beyond. Marines began ferrying both men and supplies by helicopter. Previously used only for reconnaissance and evacuation, the Marines grasped the added dimension the vertical lift of the helicopters provided. Helicopters could lift men and supplies over the ridges and valleys, mud, mines, and ambushes endemic to warfare.

The Marines settled into the numbing boredom of trench life broken by periodic training behind the lines. On 11 January 1952, Major General Thomas served his final day as commander of the 1st Marine Division. Another World War II combat commander, Major General John T. Selden replaced Thomas. On 17 March 1952, an Eighth Army realignment positioned the Marines in far western Korea above the capital city of Seoul. Repositioned, the Marines settled into the routine of artillery battery and counter-battery fire broken by an even tempo of attacks and assaults. As the peace talks continued, the Marines extended their lines 6,800 meters to the west, stretching the Marines' defensive line to the maximum. Across a narrow mountain valley the Marines prepared and waited for the inevitable Chinese probe.

Those probes and assaults by the Communists continued for two years. Forty percent of the total Marine casualties came during this period. With the cease-fire in 1953, the Chinese assaults ceased. During 1955, the First Marine Division returned to Camp Pendleton. Subsequently, during 1956, the First Marine Air Wing left Korea for the air base at Lwakuni, Japan. There the Marine Korean experience ended.

The scorecard for the Marine Corps during Korea proved mixed. The epic fights at Pusan, Inchon, Seoul, and the Chosin Reservoir insured the continued public and Congressional support the corps needed during a time of military transition. The exemplary conduct of the corps' few prisoners of war validated the tough corps training and leadership. But these costs served as investments in the future.

On the other side of the coin, the corps drafted 72,000 Marines during Korea, reducing effectiveness in the minds of many Marine veterans. Most important, the war proved costly in blood, the corps suffering 4,262 dead and 26,038 wounded during the conflict.

But overall, the Korean experience enhanced the prestige and esteem of the U.S. Marines. Three years and 30,000 casualties separated the Marines from the initial landing at Pusan and the final bloody month of the war, July 1953. During that time, the corps proved to be in step, smartly.

Mike Fisher

Bibliography

Appleman, Roy E. *South to the Naktong, North to the Yalu* (Office of the Chief of Military History, Department of the Army, Washington: 1961).

Army Historical Series, American Military History (Center of Military History, United States Army, Washington: 1989).

Blair, Clay. *The Forgotten War* (1987).

Geer, Andrew. *The New Breed: The Story of the U.S. Marines in Korea* (1952).

Millett, Allen R. *Semper Fidelis* (1980).

Moskin, J. Robert. *The Story of the U.S. Marine Corps* (1979).

Marshall, George C. (1880–1959)

General of the Army George Catlett Marshall, if not America's greatest soldier, was one of the nation's most capable and one of the great men of the twentieth century. A graduate of Virginia Military Institute, Marshall was a staff officer to General of the Armies John J. Pershing in World War I and chief of staff of the Army during World War II. On President Harry S. Truman's urging he returned to public service as special envoy to China (1945–1947) and then as secretary of state (1947–1949). In August 1950, President Truman again persuaded him to come out of retirement to replace Defense Secretary Louis Johnson, who was forced to resign on September 12, 1950, as a result of U.S. reverses and lack of military preparedness in the early days of the war in Korea.

Truman had also been upset by Johnson's feuding with other Cabinet members, especially Secretary of State Dean Acheson. The president had decided as early as late June to remove Johnson, but waited to sound out Marshall and see if his views were in accord with his own and those of Acheson regarding Korea. There was a fierce congressional fight over Marshall's confirmation as a result of hysteria over the 1949 Communist victory in China. Marshall met these personal attacks, and all others, with calm logic.

As defense secretary, Marshall's top priority was more manpower for the armed forces to meet the demands of both Korea and Europe while maintaining an adequate reserve. He secured the appointment of Anna M. Rosenberg as assistant secretary of defense for manpower and brought a major civilian architect of U.S. airpower, Robert A. Lovett, back into government service as undersecretary of defense. Marshall also restored harmony between the Defense and State Departments. Early on he established a good working relationship with the military chiefs. Chairman of the Joint Chiefs of Staff (JCS) General Omar Bradley had served under him in World War II, and the two men worked well together, as was the case with Bradley's successor, General J. Lawton Collins. Marshall also respected and worked well with Air Force Chief of Staff General Hoyt Vandenberg and Chief of Naval Operations Admiral Forrest Sherman.

The Inchon landing and the Pusan perimeter breakout preceded Marshall's confirmation as secretary of defense, but he participated in the decision authorizing MacArthur to conduct operations north of the 38th parallel. Marshall shared the view of MacArthur and the joint chiefs that he should follow up his victory. A secret "eyes only" signal from Marshall to MacArthur on September 29 declared Washington's commitment to an advance into North Korea ("We want you to feel unhampered strategically and tactically to proceed north of the 38th Parallel") but he advised against advance announcements which might precipitate a new vote in the United Nations.

For some time the top figures in the Truman administration had worried about a clash with China. Despite MacArthur's unbridled confidence at the Wake Island meeting with Truman on October 15, the Chinese had already begun to move forces into Korea. After the initial Chinese military clashes with ROK and American units at the end of October, neither Marshall nor the joint chiefs made any effort to halt MacArthur's advance. Marshall opposed MacArthur's request for permission to bomb the Yalu bridges unless the security of all his forces was directly threatened. When MacArthur predicted dire results, Truman authorized the strike. Marshall supported the recommendation from the joint chiefs authorizing pursuit of enemy aircraft into Manchurian airspace, but Allied reaction caused the proposal to be dropped. Marshall and the joint chiefs were generally supportive of MacArthur because of the traditional Pentagon

M

reluctance to supervise field commanders too closely and the fact that MacArthur was no ordinary commander.

Following the second, and massive, Chinese military intervention in late November, rather than criticize, Marshall and the joint chiefs sought ways to help the general. At the meeting of the National Security Council on November 28, Marshall agreed with the president and the joint chiefs that all-out war with China must be avoided. The United States should continue to work through the United Nations and maintain U.N. support for the war. When the JCS instructed MacArthur to withdraw X Corps from its exposed position, Marshall inserted a statement that the region northeast of the waist of Korea was to be avoided except for military operations essential to protect U.N. military security.

In the debate over what to do about the changed military situation in Korea, Marshall opposed a cease-fire with the Chinese—it would represent a "great weakness on our part"—and added that the United States could not in "all good conscience" abandon the South Koreans. When British Prime Minister Clement Attlee suggested negotiations with the Chinese, Marshall expressed opposition, arguing that it was almost impossible to negotiate with the Chinese Communists; he also expressed fear of the effects on Japan and the Philippines of concessions to the Communists. At the same time Marshall sought ways to avoid a wider war with China. When many in Congress favored an expanded war, Marshall was among the administration leaders who in February 1951 stressed the paramount importance to the United States of Western Europe.

In the April 6 meeting between Truman and his closest advisors to discuss the future of General MacArthur, Marshall characteristically urged caution. If MacArthur were recalled, military appropriations might be obstructed by Congress. Later that morning Truman asked Marshall to review all the messages between Washington and Tokyo over the past two years. When the five men met again the next morning, Marshall declared that, having read the papers, he now shared W. Averell Harriman's view that MacArthur should have been dismissed two years earlier for flouting administration directives over occupation policies for Japan. Marshall and the other men involved in the decision to sack MacArthur exhibited a considerable degree of courage given the political risks involved.

In the congressional hearings which followed the general's dismissal, Marshall defended the decision. Long-time rivals, in many ways Marshall and MacArthur represented different viewpoints: moderate conservative versus committed right-winger, Europe-first versus concentration on Asia, and limited-war versus total war. Marshall defended the concept of limited war in Korea; he hoped it would "remain limited." He said there was no easy solution to the Cold War short of another world war, the cost of which would be "beyond calculation," now that the Soviet Union possessed the atomic bomb. As a result, the administration's policy remained that of containing Communist aggression by different methods in different areas without resorting to total war. Such a policy was not always easy or popular. But the Western alliance would be kept intact, America would rearm as quickly as possible, the status quo would be maintained, and Formosa (Taiwan) would "never be allowed" to come under Communist control.

By now the Truman administration was under heavy attack. In June 1951, when Senator Joseph McCarthy demanded the resignations of Acheson and Marshall and threatened Truman with impeachment, he all but called Marshall a Communist. The unjust attacks against him may well have confirmed Marshall's decision to step down from a position he had agreed to hold only for six months to a year. In any case, McCarthy's attack practically ended Marshall's usefulness as a nonpartisan member of the administration. At Truman's request he stayed on until September 1, 1951, when he officially resigned. He was replaced by his deputy, Lovett. For Marshall it was the end of fifty years of dedicated government service.

Apart from his other services, as secretary of defense, Marshall had restored morale in the armed forces, rebuilt a cordial relationship between the Defense and State Departments, increased the size of the military, and assisted Truman in the crisis over the MacArthur firing. These were not inconsiderable achievements, and Marshall's status has grown steadily since the 1950s among historians and the military both in the U.S. and the United Kingdom.

Spencer Tucker

Bibliography
Acheson, Dean. *Present at the Creation. My Years in the State Department* (1969).

Condit, Doris M. *History of the Office of the Secretary of Defense, 2, The Test of War, 1950–1953* (Historical Office, Office of the Secretary of Defense, Washington: 1988).

Pogue, Forrest C. *George C. Marshall: Statesman, 1945–1959* (1987).

Truman, Harry S. *Years of Trial and Hope* (1956).

Marshall, S.L.A. (1900–1977)

From 1939 to 1968, Samuel Lyman Atwood Marshall was America's most widely known writer on military subjects. During World War II he had joined the U.S. Army's Office of Historical Research after a career as a military columnist with the *Detroit News*. His articles were syndicated and his reputation as analyst and critic of military matters had made him a pioneer in the field. He enjoyed privileged status at the newspaper, which allowed him to move wherever and whenever he wanted and to take on personal tasks as he chose. The *Detroit News* and Marshall both enjoyed favored status with the Defense Department and particularly with the U.S. Army. To have a reliable outlet with a national media capability was of immense value, especially in the constant struggle to gain approval for military budgets that were increasingly suspected by elected officials to be inflated.

Marshall had been careful to nurture his military bona fides since first serving in an engineering unit as part of the Texas National Guard during the final year of World War I. He had stayed in the Army reserve following the war and gained the rank of lieutenant. Throughout his life, Marshall was enamored of the officer corps. Given his authority as a correspondent, he was in a position to mix freely with commanders, and as a reserve officer he sought to embellish and enlarge his service and his rank. His service grew into an arrangement: he would be a publicist for the military, and the military would reward him with emoluments and authority. Both the Army and Marshall got more than they knew from this unwritten agreement. In Marshall the Army had a guaranteed public relations man for itself, and Marshall in turn gained entrée to the privileged sanctuary of command headquarters. He reveled in the company of heavy brass, and the field grade commanders nurtured the stocky, jowly little man with the facile pen and unlimited imagination.

He was in Korea for only three months on assignment with an Army-sponsored "think tank," most of which was spent in corps and division headquarters where he unabashedly presumed that he was sharing in the design of tactics and strategy and making a difference in the conduct of the war. He was but a quarter mile behind the jeep of General Walton H. Walker, who passed him on an icy road and then died when his jeep crashed. Even before this, he was charged by the same Walker to rally the flagging spirits of the 2nd Division and brace the backbone of its shaky new division commander. General Matthew B. Ridgway, just taking over, the Eighth Army, asked him: "Do you have anything that will help me right now?" and then charged Marshall with drawing up a plan on the illuminating of the battle zone. Nothing deterred him in his pursuits to write an analysis of the strengths and weaknesses of the Chinese in attack, to front for the Eighth Army by praising the 2nd Division despite the harrassment of the press, and to file a story praising the capabilities in combat of the partially integrated 9th Infantry Regiment at a time when the Army was still not ready to grapple with full acceptance of African American soldiers. Sharing a tent and several days of conversation with General Oliver Smith and Colonel Lewis B. "Chesty" Puller of the 1st Marine Division, he mused about the virtue of battalion over company-sized perimeters. An indefatigable writer, he was always on the lookout for the action story that would go beyond the professional assignment. He developed through his oral interviews and ostensibly personal observation the heroic stand of Captain Lewis Millett's Easy Company and then after a week's bout with pneumonia bunked down in Colonel John "Mike" Michaelis's tent and presumably planned the advance of the colonel's Wolfhound Regiment. By then it was February 1952, and he had to leave Korea to write his report. His experience with Michaelis, however, encouraged him to suggest to General Ridgway the need for some sort of engineering help to be assigned to battalions and regiments, perhaps using indigenous Korean civilian personnel.

Throughout his short stay in Korea Marshall dutifully filed newspaper copy to the *Detroit News*, laid up extra copy for his feature pieces and eventual books, as well as compiled his notes and observations which would go into making his official reports. As a full colonel in the Army reserve, a status he preferred not to make known generally, he ingratiated himself with the dominant command leadership. Young officers knew him by reputation and by his association with headquarters staff wherever he went. With his casual, almost slovenly dress, his swagger, and his colorful language, his presumption to knowing virtually everything there was to know about soldiering, he tended to overwhelm young officers. He moved in heady circles in an Army which provided him with a pulpit from which he tossed his caveats, opinions, and blarney. He was very useful to the Army, but as a former chief of staff once warned: "he could be treacherous" if he wasn't watched carefully.

Marshall was to return to Korea again in 1953 after the death of his wife. He married again in 1954 an accomplished stenographer and writer who shared his passion for the Army and for writing. For Marshall, to return to the milieu and soldiers he admired was to gain an outlet for his personal loss. His first wife had been chronically ill and needed constant care while he, with her blessing, was off on his assignments.

His final return produced his book *Pork Chop Hill* which, like his *The River and the Gauntlet*, dealt with the heroics of infantry units withdrawing in the face of great odds. Marshall was the only correspondent on the scene; the rest were covering the interminable truce talks at Panmunjom. *Pork Chop Hill* became a popular motion picture starring Gregory Peck. It was a book which Marshall suggested was definitive on the role of combat infantrymen. The war was coming to a close under command of General Mark W. Clark, whom Marshall praised despite severe reservations about Clark's experiences in the Italian campaign in World War II. Army headquarters was concerned with the problem of effective unit patrolling of the combat zone. Troop rotation policies had seemingly undercut the combat effectiveness of patrol units who were less prone to expose themselves to possible firefights and resulting wounds. Marshall instituted his interview techniques, analyzing patrols immediately after their missions and in this way guaranteeing that all members of the patrol were telling the same story in their reports.

Another task Marshall took on was to examine and explain the behavior of U.S. prisoners of war (POWs) who were being repatriated. These prisoners were at times critical of the U.S. and the war. Marshall in one instance speculated that they were often from poor homes, were carefully picked by the Chinese for their susceptibility to persuasion, and then used for propaganda purposes. They were not, however, to be regarded as representative of American soldiers generally. The ending of the war as it did was not welcomed by Marshall, who held the popular notion of total victory.

The Korean War began as Marshall was turning fifty, still a well-paid editor and columnist, a colonel in staff and administration in the Army reserve, and a consultant to the Army. His 1947 book, *Men Against Fire*, based on his World War II observations, had become part of training doctrine. The Army had revamped its weapons instruction, and the Korean War provided a field study of the impact of that change. Marshall's argument that infantrymen in World War II were reluctant to fire their weapons even in the most dire of circumstances was not reiterated in his Korean report, *Commentary on Infantry Operations and Weapons Usage in Korea, Winter of 1950–51*. Marshall reported that riflemen in Korea used their weapons far more readily, though he later criticized their failure to use hand grenades.

He also spoke of the bayonet and its employment differently in his official report. He saw it as an item quickly discarded by officers and men alike with no penalties for loss of equipment. This contrasts with his books, *Battle at Best* and *The River and the Gauntlet*, which breathlessly deal with the action of Captain Millett's company taking a heroic stand with "cold steel." Marshall included his own personal admonishments to Millett on the use of the bayonet prior to the attack. This experience is not in the official report. His after-action interview of the men in Millett's company was conducted solely by himself since his clerk-driver ostensibly went on sick leave, leaving Marshall to make his own notes. Easy Company, which had already had a Congressional Medal of Honor winner and a distinguished unit citation, would soon receive a double honor. Marshall personally wrote Captain Millett's citation before returning to the U.S., and another unit citation was bestowed.

Two other lengthy reports under auspices of the operations research office were written by Marshall. One, *Notes on Infantry Tactics*, analyzed Chinese tactics in the attack, and another, *Problems of Field Tactics in Defense Against Area Weapons*, were both well received by the Army. He also wrote short articles for *Army* magazine and *Combat Forces Jounal*, and a piece for *Harper's* magazine in the spring of 1951 which displayed to the fullest his promotional thrust on behalf of the military in Korea. Ten years after the war he produced a juvenile book, *The Military History of the Korean War*.

Marshall's interviewing techniques, which were his creation and instituted as standard practice by the Army historical section, rested on the assumption that bringing all combatants together regardless of rank would ensure that false testimony would be out of the question. He never considered that the presence of authority figures might have a deterrent effect or that unit cohesiveness would combine against outside inquiry about their performance. Marshall's development of these interviews often suggests that, as in the instance of Captain Millett's Easy Company, he himself was an on-scene observer, despite being hundreds of yards to the rear. He had a capacity for creating graphic narratives by naming names and framing individual action in dramatic mosaics of atmosphere and desperate circumstances.

It was an after-the-fact association with events or notable figures which became a passionate habit. His promotion of the military, especially the Army, ingratiated him with high command. He could be counted on never to put the Army in a bad light. If he was not able to make a direct personal association with a MacArthur, a Ridgway, a Taylor, or a Clark, he would admire them in a manner that would allow the impression that they were all his fellows, his colleagues in arms. For his part, Marshall was a man who could be counted on to give his best for the good of the Army. It is a curious outgrowth of his work that though he espoused the nobility of the individual infantryman while always reserving criticism for combat leadership, his personal relationships are universally suggestive of association solely with field grade commanders. His field notes served himself as he always associated personally with the event after the fact. This gave an immediacy to his writing while at the same time encouraging a belated scepticism which surfaced after his death in 1977.

When Marshall was dispatched to Korea during winter 1951 as a member of the contingent of historical investigators, he was to examine what might be going wrong with the war as well as put to a test some of the individual training experiences of Americans in action. Actually, the war was going fairly well when the matter of sending investigators was considered. In fact it was assumed that the war might well be over before the researchers could be sent. But the entry of the Chinese changed all that, and most U.N. units now faced a time of trial and defeat. Marshall in Korea immediately concentrated on the U.S. 2nd Division which had gone through a trial of terror in their retreat from the Yalu River. Marshall sought to put a good face on the division as well as the corps whose commander he declared to be the "best corps commander in Korea" after three months in the area, not all of which were in the same sector. Little did Marshall realize that General Ridgway's opinion of the same commander was less laudatory. Marshall quickly took up the cause of a rifle company in an isolated action from which he extrapolated that the entire battalion, regiment, division, and even corps, were fundamentally sound. Therefore any perception of a previous lack of performance was, at best, an aberration.

He determined that Easy Company of the 24th "Wolfhound" Regiment led by Captain Millett would be the focus of his study even before it became engaged! That the company had been previously commanded by Captain Reginald Desiderio, who had been killed in action and awarded the Medal of Honor, and that the unit had already received a Distinguished Unit Citation, certainly established that this particular company stood out from the rest. The design of Marshall was transparent and it was not long before the units provided him with the copy he sought to refurbish the image of the entire division and corps. This tactic of extending an argument from a base of minimal and often questionable data became virtually a guiding principle, not only in writing about the military, but also in the passion he indulged for fleshing out a romantic past for himself. He took on a lot of psychological baggage in his determined struggle for acceptance by the military community of staff officers. His claim to be the youngest commissioned officer in the American Expeditionary Force (AEF) in World War I, his name-dropping as confidante and sounding board of generals and statesmen, his notion that his ideas and methods were unique to him and that any comparisons with military analysts were erroneous, his perception of himself as a combat leader, his generalizations from minimal data, his notion that he shared and initiated combat planning with commanders in the field, his fabrication of his age and the adding of a third middle name, "Atwood," created out of whole cloth to make the nickname "SLAM" from his initials, all serve to encourage speculation about the veracity of the man.

He had truly become an American success story, but personally he could never realize enough comfort or security from his success. He had left high school without graduating and then dropped out of the College of El Paso without taking a degree. What little success he had gained in his early career came from the two years he spent in the AEF in 1917–1918. Even there he could not bear to live with the idea that he had missed action. Never an imposing figure at five feet five inches and 160 pounds, Marshall found journalism, but especially military writing, to be a box on which he could stand. The dearth of material available for public consumption and the primitive public affairs posture of the Army made for a happy association. He carefully kept up his membership in the Army reserve and shrewdly carved out small unit action as the base of his expertise, for to Marshall, all large military victories are derived from the effectiveness of small unit action, the key to which was sound combat leadership, unexceptional principles indeed. In the world of the blind, Marshall's personal vision made him king.

Jack J. Cardoso

Bibliography

Marshall, S.L.A. *Battle at Best* (1963).
———. *Bringing Up the Rear* (Marshall's autobiography) (1979).
———. "CCF in the Attack," part 1, Staff Memorandum, ORO, Eighth U.S. Army Korea (5 January 1951).
———. "CCF in the Attack," part 2, Staff Memorandum, ORO-S-34, EUSAK (27 January 1951).
———. "Commentary on Infantry Operations and Weapons Usage in Korea: Winter of 1950–51," ORO-S-4, EUSAK (2 January 1951).
———. "Notes on Infantry Tactics in Korea," ORO-T-7, EUSAK (1951).
———. *Pork Chop Hill: The American Fighting Man in Action* (1956).
———. *The River and the Gauntlet: Defeat of the 8th Army by the Chinese Communist Forces, November 1950* (1953).
Spiller, Roger J. "S.L.A. Marshall and the Ratio of Fire," *Journal of the Royal United Services Institution* (Winter 1988).
Williams, F.D.G. *SLAM: The Influence of S.L.A. Marshall on the United States Army* (U.S. Army Training and Doctrine Command, Fort Monroe, VA: 1990).

Medical Service in the Korean War

Medical support for the United Nations forces in the Korean War began with hasty improvisation, but grew over the course of the war into a mature, scientifically sophisticated system. During the course of the struggle the mobile Army surgical hospital (MASH) passed the test of battle, the helicopter was successfully integrated into the evacuation chain, and progress in the understanding and treatment of cold injury and neurosurgical problems marked notable advances in the art of military medicine.

When North Korean units crossed the 38th parallel in the rainy predawn darkness of June 25, 1950, U.S. Army medical personnel of the Far East command (FEC) were as ill-prepared as their nonmedical comrades. As American air, naval, and ground forces were committed, hasty efforts began to cobble together new field units and to strengthen those that existed by pulling personnel from the fixed hospitals. Meanwhile, in Korea, medical officers and enlisted men of the Korean Military Advisory Group (KMAG) retreated with the Republic of Korea (ROK) forces. Accompanying the first American ground troops, battalion medics of Task Force Smith set up their aid station in a muddy dugout on a ridge north of the village of Osan. When the enemy forced the unit to retreat, the wounded had to be abandoned to the enemy. The episode marked the beginning of a tragic period of recurrent withdrawals and frantic evacuations by any means available—ambulances, jeeps, airplanes, or trains.

The fighting that followed around the Pusan perimeter was intense and unrelieved, more like the European than the Pacific battles of World War II. The MASH, originally intended to provide emergency forward surgery to stabilize the severely wounded for their trip to the rear, emerged instead as a small, all-purpose hospital. Equipped and staffed to hold sixty patients at most, it was often filled with hundreds. Meant to support a single American division, each MASH in fact supported several and, as new nations joined the fighting, treated a growing range of United Nations soldiers. The few field hospitals that arrived in Korea in the first months, and the single evacuation hospital stationed at the port of Pusan, were likewise overwhelmed with wounded and sick.

Many patients who should have stayed in Korea were hastily evacuated to nearby Japan by plane or by any ship or small boat available.

As the fighting raged, General Douglas MacArthur prepared his amphibious strike behind enemy lines. The 1st Provisional Marine Brigade had already joined the fighting with an experienced brigade surgeon but a scratch force of Navy doctors who were, by and large, ill-trained and assembled in haste. When X Corps took form in Japan, the 1st Marine Division hastily assembled its own medical support as it prepared to lead the invasion at Inchon. When it went ashore in mid-September, its battle casualties were treated, according to a Navy historian, by "a casual staff of orthopedists, surgeons, and dentists." Like the Army medical personnel supporting the 7th Division, these men learned combat medicine on the job. Meanwhile, the veteran medics of the Eighth Army supported the breakout from the perimeter, finding in the aftermath—as the enemy forces dissolved—that their greatest problem was to keep up with the rapid advances that followed.

For a time in October, casualties were light as U.N. forces advanced into North Korea. Cold was increasingly intense, but the hardest labor of hospital personnel was provoked by repeated displacements. Then in late November the Chinese invasion again sent U.N. forces on a long retreat burdened by casualties. The MASH moved like birds in a windstorm, settling down only to flee again. In the operating rooms plasma froze, lights winked out as generator fuel lines clogged with ice, and surgeons worked by flashlight, the bodies of the wounded steaming as surgical knives cut them open. On the long retreat from the "Frozen Chosin," soldiers and Marines flew out as many casualties as possible, most by Army lightplanes or Air Force transports. The rest had to be carried in ambulances and trucks. Medics bound wounds with torn T-shirts and improvised urinals for immobilized patients from empty C-ration cans. But the retreat did bring shortened lines of evacuation, and the bitter experiences of 1950 left the men and women of the medical service capable veterans. In the battles of the spring, this field-toughened medical system provided capable support for Lieutenant General Matthew B. Ridgway's forces as they lost and regained Seoul, and once more penetrated North Korea.

Meanwhile, the hospitals of Japan had mirrored the changes of fortune on the battlefield. Conditions in July 1950 were close to impossible, with wounded pouring in and hospital staffs depleted of doctors, nurses, and technicians by the needs of the field. The arrival of new personnel and the apparent victory of September–October 1950 eased the pressure, only to have the severe fighting of the winter and the spring of 1951 increase it again. A program of building new hospitals and enlarging those already in existence expanded the capacity of the Army Medical Service in Japan, and a doctor draft voted by Congress in the fall of 1950 began to deliver a steady supply of youthful medical officers in the spring of the following year. Ironically, the system's strength blossomed in mid-1951 just as the onset of peace talks and hopes for an early resolution of the war reduced the influx of wounded once again. Thereafter, hard but sporadic fighting along the fortified lines that divided the peninsula made for waves of wounded, followed by troughs when available beds far outnumbered the patients.

Once the lines stabilized in Korea, the medical system was able to mark steady advances in organization, disease control, and battlefield research. Yet the abundance of resources enjoyed by some theaters in World War II never came to the Korean War. Even when the fighting was most bitter, the attention of the American government was fixed on Europe. Still, what matured in Korea was a remarkably advanced and sophisticated system of emergency medicine, with hospital ships and Military Air Transport Service (MATS) flights to shuttle serious cases to Japan and the Zone of Interior (U.S.A.).

The MASH's famous partner, the helicopter, emerged during 1950–1951 as a critical innovation and enduring image of Korean War medicine. Introduced first by the Air Force as a means of retrieving downed fliers, and developed by the Marines, helicopters quickly proved their value to Eighth Army surgeon Colonel Chauncey Dovell. Korea's hilly landscape combined with the enemy tactics of infiltration and encirclement to make the machine an essential part of the U.N. medical system. The helicopter evacuated the wounded of surrounded units, moving the most serious cases smoothly and quickly to care. Its normal route of travel was from the regimental collecting station or division clearing station to the surgical hospital. There can be no question that many of the patients it moved would have died without it. Yet the helicopter's effectiveness in a limited role, and its dramatic image—the noisy, dust-flailing arrivals and departures—caused its overall importance to be exaggerated. Medical helicopters probably carried no more than 4 percent of all hospital admissions during the Korean War, while motor ambulances and the hard-working Korean railways moved the rest.

A high-cost experimental vehicle, the helicopter would not become a routine carrier of military and civilian emergency cases for another decade. But if World War II had introduced the medevac "chopper," the Korean War conclusively demonstrated its potential.

The helicopter and the MASH together made possible one of the most important medical innovations of the Korean War. Neurosurgical cases—casualties with injuries to the brain or spinal cord—had always been particularly hard to treat under wartime conditions. The jolting of a wheeled ambulance on rutted roads often inflicted additional trauma to the patient, sometimes causing paralysis or death. In Korea, beginning in the spring of 1951, the Eighth Army made a conscious effort to better the record of World War II, when 15 percent of neurosurgical cases died. The FEC's able, abrasive neurosurgical consultant, Lieutenant Colonel Arnold M. Meirowsky, established special units at the 121st Evacuation Hospital and the 8209th MASH. Henceforth the neurosurgical casualty traveled by helicopter from the battalion aid station direct to the neurosurgical unit, by helicopter again to an airfield, and by Air Force C-54 to Tokyo. Intermediate stops and the wheeled ambulance were eliminated, and mortality fell to 8.5 percent.

Helicopter transport also played at least a peripheral role in efforts to counter the most baffling medical threat of the war—the unexpected outbreak of epidemic hemorrhagic fever in the late spring of 1951. A viral disease whose cause and carriers were unknown, the illness began its epidemic rise when U.N. forces settled down on defensive lines northeast of Seoul. Early mortality in hard-hit units reached 20 percent of those affected. After a lull in the summer, a new wave struck during the fall—a pattern of incidence that was to continue through the war. Investigations by Army laboratories, efforts at environmental control, and the establishment of a specialized treatment center at the 8228th MASH taught medics how to handle these patients and reduce mortality to an endurable 5 percent of those taken ill. But the war ended without further light on the cause of the disease or how it spread. As in the case of neurosurgical injuries, speedy evacuation and prompt and sophisticated nursing care represented the best that the medical system could offer, and hemorrhagic fever cases were among those authorized helicopter transport.

In most respects, the end of the war of movement in the summer of 1951 produced clear medical gains. Especially was this so in preventive medicine. With the troops in bunkers and rest areas behind the line, the rituals of public health—systematic immunization, examination for venereal disease, water purification, and measures to enable men to bathe, change into clean clothing, and warm themselves during cold weather—all became incomparably easier. But treatment also benefited, because the hospitals no longer had to move so frequently. After July 1951, a MASH might move two or three times a year instead of several dozen as in the war of movement. Though battles for fortified heights produced heavy influxes of wounded, slack times intervened in Korea, as in the hospitals of Japan. Medical cases tended to be seasonal, with viral disease outbreaks in the spring, enteric problems and malaria in the summer, and respiratory complaints in the winter. Reduced pressure, high technical skill, and improved antibiotics combined to halve the World War II death rate among hospital patients.

Clinical knowledge spread freely, as doctors, nurses, medical administrative officers, and technicians, both officer and enlisted, used their leisure to hone their skills. Through the consultant system, experts in many medical specialties visited the forward areas in Korea, lecturing to medical personnel and demonstrating new techniques in the MASHs and field hospitals. A variety of medical societies sprang up spontaneously, at which doctors read and criticized one another's professional papers. Teams were sent out by both surgeons general—Army and Navy—to explore diverse problems in surgery, wound treatment, and cold injury. The last, under Army Lieutenant Colonel Kenneth D. Orr, was so successful as to make the Korean War a landmark in the understanding and prevention of this ancient bane of warriors. And practical innovations in equipment followed on research. Navy experiments begun late in World War II brought to Korean battlefields the first successful body armor ever used by American infantry, saving many lives and minimizing injuries. The Army's "Mickey Mouse" boot and the snug, semicylindrical Jamesway tent were also much appreciated by the troops.

Prewar efforts to integrate the medical systems of the armed services and the international character of the war both contributed to the medical system's joint and combined character. Army hospitals treated Marines; Navy hospital ships served as mobile hospitals along the coast for Marines and soldiers; and Army and Navy hospitals shared outpatients in Japan and the Zone of Interior. Air evacuation from Korea to Japan and from Japan to the Zone of Interior was the province of the Air Force. U.N. units that were neither American nor South Korean provided their own first-echelon medical service, but evacuated to American MASHs and field hospitals. Medical units volunteered by other nations, such as the Norwegian MASH, received the wounded of all forces. British Commonwealth forces provided a more complete chain of evacuation for their own men. The South Korean medical service, poor and even barbarous at the war's opening, improved with great rapidity and by the end of the war, in the opinion of the American Army's surgeon general, was about equal to the American system in World War I. For many complex forms of treatment, ROK soldiers were sent to American hospitals, but sophisticated treatment developed also in their own army with the establishment of a Korean-staffed neurosurgical hospital.

Despite such integration, observers noted one clear distinction in medical care between the two American armed services that bore most of the nation's casualties. In mid-1951, questions arose within the Army Medical Service about the first link in the chain of evacuation—the removal of the wounded from the battlefield. Missing in action (MIA) figures reached 27 percent of the wounded for the Army, less than 3.5 percent for the Marines. One soldier was killed in action to every four wounded, compared to one to six for the Marines. Ultimately, Army statisticians were to conclude that the ratio of deaths to hits—that is, to wounded in action plus killed in action—was higher in Korea than in the European Theater of World War II, though lower than in the Pacific, and much lower than in World War II as a whole. The reason has been variously explained as a consequence of the Army's loose organization and lower esprit, compared to the Marines, and as a consequence of prewar training for Army medical officers that emphasized professional over military skills. One result of the controversy was to tighten field training in the Medical Field Service School at Fort Sam Houston, Texas; another was to bring an ambitious program of field training for medical officers to Korea under a new Eighth Army surgeon, General L. Holmes Ginn, Jr.

Other problems reflected the changing nature of the war in Korea and of the Army that fought there. The introduction of rotation in 1951 combined with the draft to bring the Army Medical Service a degree of personnel turbulence that resembled permanent revolution. Young doctors fresh from civilian life arrived at forward locations where their sophisticated skills might find little use. Their instinctive scorn of things military was matched by the attitude of enlisted draftees serving resentfully in a war that to many Americans had lost most meaning. Complaints by inspecting officers and tensions between regular officers and civilians in uniform did not, however, affect the quality of professional care in Army hospitals, which remained, even in the opinion of critics, the best in any American war to that time.

In the spring of 1953, world events began to point toward an early end of the fighting. In March, Joseph Stalin died, and Operation Little Switch brought an exchange of sick and injured prisoners of war (POWs). The signing of the armistice in July brought Operation Big Switch, the general POW exchange. Medical care for returnees was lavish, though it soon became evident that harsh conditions in the North Korean prison camps during 1950–51 had left few survivors among prisoners injured in the initial battles. The Chinese had treated prisoners better than the North Koreans, though they had exploited captured airmen for propaganda, especially in the germ warfare campaign. Psychiatric studies of former POWs provided insight into the mechanisms of survival under stress, though sensational tales of "brainwashing" were more exciting to the general public. Overall, the successes of the American medical services reflected the clinical excellence of American medicine and the nation's commitment to saving every possible life. Their failings reflected lack of preparation for war, rooted in the difficulty of the United States providing medical officers who were both able doctors and combat-ready soldiers or Marines. During the U.N. retreats that marked the first year of fighting, mastery of clinical medicine and laboratory technique proved to mean nothing to the medical officer who had to manage the rapid evacuation of helpless patients before a swiftly advancing foe. Women nurses, all of whom were volunteers, served courageously and ably in forward locations. The Navy's Hospital Corps was more successful in providing trained enlisted medics than the Army's replacement system, for the Army Medical Service was without a permanent enlisted corps.

It is also true that the Marines overall were a service better adapted than the Army to the kind of war that Korea became—a struggle without prospect of victory, whose only aim was the restoration of a rough status quo antebellum. For the Army Medical Service, at least, the war ended with a record of generally outstanding achievement, but no clear solution to the problem of how to combine medical and military professionalism within the context of a limited war.

Albert E. Cowdrey

Bibliography
Blumenson, Martin. "8087th MASH" (n.d.).
Cowdrey, Albert E. *The Medic's War* (1987, 1990).
Far East, U.S. Army Forces. Military History Detachment, "8086th Army Unit, The Regimental Medical Company in Korea," Project NO MHD-13 (n.d.).
———. "The Surgical Hospital in Korea. July 1950 to February 1953" (n.d.).
———. "'Germ Warfare' and Public Health in the Korean Conflict," *Journal of the History of Medicine and Allied Sciences* (April 1984).
———. "Development of Aeromedical Evacuation in the USAF, 1909–1960," Vol. 2, USAF Historical Division, Research Studies Institute, Air University, Maxwell AFB (Alabama: May 1960).
Pugh, H. Lamont, et al. *The History of the Medical Department of the United States Navy, 1945–1955*, NAVMED P-5057 (Washington: 1958).
———. *Recent Advances in Medicine and Surgery Based on Professional Medical Experiences in Japan and Korea, 1950–1953* (Washington: 1955).

See also INDIAN 60TH FIELD AMBULANCE AND SURGICAL UNIT; HELICOPTERS IN THE KOREAN WAR; RED CROSS, INTERNATIONAL (IRC)

Milburn, Frank W. (1892–1962)

Born in Jasper, Indiana, on 11 January 1892, Frank William Milburn graduated from the United States Military Academy at West Point in 1914 and was commissioned as a second lieutenant of infantry. Over the next twenty-eight years, Milburn, nicknamed "Shrimp" for his stature, held a series of increasingly responsible troop and staff assignments and graduated from the Infantry School in 1921 and the Command and General Staff School in 1933. He also taught military science at Montana State University from 1926 to 1931, and was an instructor at the Command and General Staff School from 1934 to 1938. After the United States entered World War II, he assumed command of the 83rd Division, and in December 1943, now holding the rank of major general, he became commander of the XXI Corps. The following October he took his corps to Europe, where he ably commanded it in France and Germany until July 1945. Milburn then commanded the V Corps at Fort Jackson, South Carolina, and the 1st Infantry Division in Germany and, beginning in August 1949, was deputy commander of American forces in Germany.

Two months after President Harry S. Truman committed American forces to the defense of the Republic of Korea in June 1950, Army chief of staff General J. Lawton Collins sent Milburn to Korea to command one of the two corps in the U.S. Eighth Army. As soon as Milburn arrived, Lieutenant General Walton H. Walker, Eighth Army commander, gave him command of the I Corps and the job of leading the breakout from the Pusan perimeter. During the last two weeks of September 1950, Milburn spearheaded the Eighth Army's drive to link up with the X Corps just south of Seoul, capital of South Korea, and then spearheaded the Eighth Army's drive into North Korea in October. In early November, he finally halted at the Chongchon River after the Chinese Communists had intervened and delivered a sharp blow against the I Corps at Unsan.

Following the defeat of the Eighth Army by the Chinese in the battle of the Chongchon River at the end of November 1950, Lieutenant General Matthew B. Ridgway, who succeeded Walker as commander, concluded that the quiet and unassuming Milburn lacked the fire he wanted in his subordinates as he struggled to turn the demoralized Army into an effective fighting force. But rather than relieve Milburn, an old and devoted friend, Ridgway decided to leave him in command of the I Corps for the time being and promote him to the rank of lieutenant general. To ensure that Milburn had the "spark of initiative" when the Eighth Army went on the offensive in January 1951, Ridgway temporarily established his forward command post at Milburn's headquarters so that he could watch over his shoulder. Milburn continued to command the I Corps through heavy fighting that eventually saw the battle line stabilize in the vicinity of the 38th parallel in the summer of 1951. Returning to the United States in July 1951, Milburn served a brief stint as inspector of the infantry in the office of the chief of Army field forces before retiring in May 1952.

During the next two years, Milburn was athletic director at Montana State University; and in 1955, he was a member of the committee that wrote the code of conduct for American military personnel captured by the enemy. The code was an outgrowth of the ill treatment of U.N. prisoners in Korea at the hands of the Communists. Milburn died in Missoula, Montana, on 25 October 1962.

John Kennedy Ohl

Bibliography

Alexander, Bein. *Korea: The First War We Lost* (Hippocrene, New York: 1986).

Appleman, Roy E. *South to the Naktong, North to the Yalu: June–November 1950* (Office of the Chief of Military History, Washington: 1961).

Blair, Clay. *The Forgotten War: America in Korea, 1950–1953* (Times Books, New York: 1987).

MacDonald, Charles B. *The Last Offensive* (Office of the Chief of Military History, Washington: 1973).

Ridgway, Matthew B. *The Korean War* (Doubleday, Garden City, NY: 1967).

Military Government

See CIVIL AFFAIRS AND MILITARY GOVERNMENT, U.S. ARMY

Muccio, John J. (1900–1989)

John J. Muccio was the first U.S. ambassador to the infant Republic of Korea (ROK) and would remain in this position until two years after the start of the Korean War. Born near Naples in Italy, his parents came to the United States when Muccio was an infant and settled in Providence, Rhode Island. World War I interrupted his college education. After serving briefly in the U.S. Army in 1918, he graduated from Brown University in 1921. That same year, he became a U.S. citizen and entered the consular service, subsequently earning an M.A. from George Washington University. In 1924, Muccio's first posting was as vice-consul in Hamburg, Germany. He served thereafter in China at Hong Kong (1926–1928), Foochow

(1928–1930), and Shanghai (1930–1934). For the next nine years, he served in Latin America as consul and second secretary in Bolivia (1935–1938), second and first secretary in Panama (1938–1940) and Nicaragua (1940–1943), and then counselor in Cuba (1943–1944). In 1945, Muccio returned to Germany as an assistant to Robert D. Murphy, U.S. political advisor on German affairs, and attended the Potsdam Conference. After a brief stay in the United States late in 1946, he spent the next year traveling throughout China and Manchuria as a member of the inspector corps of the foreign service.

In August 1948, when the U.S. accorded conditional recognition to the Republic of Korea, President Harry S. Truman appointed Muccio as his special representative to replace Lieutenant General John R. Hodge, the occupation commander, as head of the U.S. diplomatic mission in Seoul. Undoubtedly, Truman selected him because he had both experience in Asia and familiarity with the problems of military occupation and division in Germany. In March 1949, Muccio became the first U.S. ambassador to the ROK when Washington raised its mission in South Korea to embassy rank. His greatest challenge at that time was maintaining good relations with President Syngman Rhee. Previously, he had criticized the Rhee regime for its political repression, but now faced the difficult task of overcoming South Korean opposition to U.S. plans for an early military withdrawal. After negotiating an agreement providing for U.S. economic assistance to the ROK, Muccio demonstrated considerable diplomatic skill in pacifying Rhee. Subsequently, he persuaded Rhee to implement strong measures to control inflation and to hold the May 1950 national assembly elections on schedule. During the six months before the start of the Korean War, he vigorously advocated an expansion of U.S. economic and military aid for the ROK, both in private cables and in testimony before congressional committees.

It was Muccio who notified leaders in Washington of the North Korean invasion of South Korea on 25 June 1950. As the Army of the Democratic People's Republic of [North] Korea (DPRK) moved southward, he supervised the evacuation of U.S. personnel, but applied great pressure on the Rhee government to remain in Seoul. Muccio seriously considered remaining in the beleaguered capital, but left after Secretary of State Dean Acheson informed him that his capture would not serve any U.S. interests. During the retreat to the Pusan perimeter, Muccio surely performed the most important service of his long career. He consistently argued that the war was not lost and victory was indeed possible, thus reinforcing the morale of Rhee and other South Korean officials. Muccio's embassy, meanwhile, persuaded the U.S. Army to accept organized Korean combat police battalions in American divisional areas to detect infiltrators and fight as light infantry. He further helped persuade the U.S. Army to fill out its understrength battalions with Korean soldiers. Finally, Muccio served as a liaison between U.S. military leaders and the Rhee government, reducing suspicion and friction.

Following the Inchon landings and subsequent liberation of Seoul in September 1950, Muccio returned his embassy to the capital. He attended the Wake Island Conference with General Douglas MacArthur and spoke in favor of permitting the Rhee government to play an active role in the occupation of North Korea. At Wake, Truman presented him with the Medal of Merit. Muccio then traveled to Washington in late October to confer with administration officials regarding postwar U.S. policy in Korea. After Chinese military intervention abruptly upset these sanguine plans, he moved his embassy directly to Pusan where it would remain for the balance of his tenure as ambassador. With the start of armistice negotiations in July 1951, Muccio struggled unsuccessfully to persuade the Rhee government that the U.S. would never permit the Communists to conquer South Korea and that a negotiated settlement was therefore in the interests of the ROK. Similarly, his efforts to promote democracy failed, as Rhee crushed his enemies and strengthened his dictatorial rule in the South Korean political crisis of June 1952. Two months later, Ellis O. Briggs replaced Muccio, who a short time later received appointment to the U.N. Trusteeship Council. Muccio's diplomatic career ended with appointments as envoy extraordinary to Iceland (1954–1956) and ambassador to Guatemala (1959–1961), retiring with the highest rank of career minister.

James I. Matray

Bibliography
Current Biography, 1951.
Foreign Relations of the United States, 1950, VII: *Korea* (Washington, D.C.: 1976), *1951*, VII: *Korea and China* (Washington, D.C.: 1983), and *1952–1954*, XV: *Korea* (Washington, D.C.: 1984).
Matray, J.I. *The Reluctant Crusade* (Honolulu: 1985).
Muccio, John J. Oral History Interview Transcripts, Harry S. Truman Library, Independence, MO.
Noble, H.J. *Embassy at War* (Seattle: 1975).

See also STATE DEPARTMENT, U.S.

N

Napalm

Napalm, a sticky gasoline gel, was employed as a major weapon during the Korean War. In 1943, Harvard University chemistry professor Louis F. Fieser produced the petroleum gel known by an acronym derived from the aluminum naphthenic and palmitic acids it contained. American tacticians subsequently developed techniques of napalm bombing which relied on achieving air superiority.

Compared to previous incendiary weapons, napalm spread further, stuck to the target, burned longer, and was safer to its dispenser because it was dropped and detonated far below the airplane. It was also cheap to manufacture.

During World War II, the U.S. Army Air Force dropped approximately 14,000 tons of napalm, two-thirds being released in the Pacific theater. Troops found it effective because of the terror it incited. During the post–World War II era, napalm became a common weapon and was used in the Greek civil war and Indochina. The U.S. Far East Air Force used at least 32,357 tons of napalm in Korea in addition to napalm detonated by the Navy and Marines. Ironically, Japan, Korea's former oppressor, manufactured napalm for the U.N. forces.

Napalm was utilized in a variety of ways. For landmines, fifty-five-gallon drums of napalm were connected to explosive charges and detonators. Napalm was also used to burn off vegetation, to illuminate battlefields, and to force the enemy to dig tunnels and entrenchments. Napalm was considered useful in efforts to weaken morale and was expended against enemy supply centers and concentrated troops, truck and armored tank columns, and enemy gun positions.

On an *average* day, the Air Force dropped 45,000 gallons, the Navy released 12,000 gallons, and the Marines delivered 5,000 gallons to targets. Napalm's volatile mixture was improved when more precise thermometers were used to monitor its production, and in Korea, two Army companies were employed solely to mix napalm.

Pilots realized that dive-bombing was the best procedure to drop napalm. They also learned how to bounce bombs toward targets. Tanks could quickly be destroyed by napalm because fuel tanks, rubber tires, and ammunition caught fire, and the heat killed the crew. A procedure known as "Golden Rain" was developed where the napalm mixture was sprayed in the air above troops, showering them with flame.

Early in the war, in July and August 1950, problems in napalm use surfaced, including inadequate ground crews and technical failures with ignitions. These technical shortcomings were overcome in time. As U.N. troops retreated from North Korea in the winter of 1950, they implemented a scorched earth policy, aided by pilots burning enemy installation with napalm.

Where targets were too closely located to permit precision bombing, napalm was used. Five major cities in North Korea were sites for heavy napalm bombing: Pyongyang, Seishin, Rashin, Wonsan, and Chinnampo. By the end of the war, these cities had practically ceased to function above ground. Pilots focused on dropping napalm bombs to cut communications and to strike dams, factories, power plants, and industrial centers.

Napalm was effective in lowering civilian morale. It often struck civilian populations; people not only suffered horrific burns and death, but often expired from carbon monoxide poisoning or suffocation. Some correspondents attacked what they considered the United Nations indiscriminate use of napalm bombs and depicted in their news articles grotesque details of napalm casualties. In Britain, prominent individuals such as the Archbishop of York and certain religious groups publicly questioned the deployment of napalm bombs. A letter in the London *Times* criticized napalm's use as a weapon, but because of press censorship, an organized public protest denouncing napalm did not develop.

The actual effects of napalm varied. U.N. ground troops argued that napalm was an effective weapon because it caused the enemy to experience overwhelming fear. North Korean prisoners countered this viewpoint, claiming that only when they were trapped were they afraid of burning. In reality, of all the flame weapons, the Communists disliked the flamethrower the most, but flamethrowers were often ineffective because they were too heavy to carry up steep hills, and few soldiers were adequately trained to use them. Nonetheless, napalm was a horrific weapon. Literally hundreds of civilians or troops could be incinerated where they stood, their skin burned away. One GI reported hearing napalmed North Korean troops in their death agonies, although the enemy was more than a mile away. Occasionally, napalm was accidentally dropped on American troops.

Geneva Conventions throughout the twentieth century have limited chemical warfare. The International Committee of the Red Cross attempted to improve articles passed in 1949 that did not include incendiary bombs such as napalm among prohibited weapons. Draft restrictions written after the Korean War prohibited utilization of incendiary and chemical weapons in military actions, but these suggested policies were never implemented, and napalm has been used in post-Korean military conflicts. In the Vietnam War, public outrage about napalm became more pronounced because of intensive press coverage and access to information about the physical results of napalm attacks, especially visual images of vast ballooning napalm clouds and burned children. It has been pointed out by critics of U.S. military policy that the United States inflicted napalm, like nuclear bombing, primarily only upon Asians.

Elizabeth Schafer

Bibliography

Brady, James. *The Coldest War: A Memoir of Korea* (1990).

International Committee of the Red Cross. *Weapons that May Cause Unnecessary Suffering or Have Indiscriminate Effects* (1973).

Lumsden, Malvern. *Incendiary Weapons* (1975).

United Nations. *Napalm and Other Incendiary Weapons and All Aspects of Their Possible Use* (1973).

NATO, Impact of the Korean War on

The militarization of the Cold War in the Far East had three important consequences for Europe: it expanded the American commitment to Western European security through the North Atlantic Treaty Organization (NATO); it accelerated the return of West Germany to full sovereignty, and in doing so, gave a further push to European integration; and it helped to transform economic relations within the Atlantic community because of disputes over the allocation of the economic burdens among alliance members.

First, North Korea's attack on South Korea aroused an intense fear in Western Europe that a similar conflict might be engineered by the Soviets in divided Germany. The apprehension Soviet aggression in Western Europe had produced an American commitment to European security through NATO in 1949, even before the outbreak of war in Korea, but the surprising explosion of a nuclear device by the Soviets (September 1949) immediately threw established strategy—based on an American nuclear monopoly countering Soviet predominance in conventional forces—into disarray. A secret National Security Council study (NSC-68) portrayed a highly aggressive Soviet Union unlikely to be deterred by the existing containment policy, and it proposed a more aggressive strategy. Implementation of the new strategy had remained suspended as State Department Soviet specialists challenged the intellectual foundations of the study, opponents of increased defense spending attacked the economic consequences of rearmament, and many others questioned the stationing of large numbers of conventional forces and nuclear weapons in forward positions in Europe during peacetime. Meanwhile, the Soviet Union launched a propaganda campaign aimed at encouraging a latent but powerful Western European neutralism.

President Harry S. Truman's vigorous response in the Far East swept away lingering

European doubts about America's willingness to defend its allies. Truman seized upon the new state of mind on both sides of the Atlantic to implement the measures proposed in NSC-68: an integrated military command was created with Dwight D. Eisenhower as commander, four divisions of American troops were sent to Europe, the American military budget was quadrupled, American bases constructed in Europe, and a NATO secretariat organized to coordinate operations. Rather than merely helping the Europeans to help themselves, the United States now committed itself to act as a European power.

Second, the war transformed the international position of Germany and greatly improved the bargaining strength of the Germans in the face of French efforts to shackle their independence. Germany and France had traced opposing arcs since 1945 as the rebounding German economy contrasted sharply with French political, economic, and social instability. French statesmen had crafted one stratagem after another to hold Germany at a permanent disadvantage that did not correspond to the real relative strength of the two powers. France's seeming inability to set its house in order and Britain's general refusal to interest itself in Continental affairs undermined these efforts. West German Chancellor Konrad Adenauer's assertiveness in claiming German rights alarmed the French, who would have preferred more signs of contrition for past aggression.

The war caused the United States to press its European allies for a greater defense effort on their own behalf. The inadequate response by NATO led the Americans to propose (September 1950) the rearming of West Germany. Adenauer accepted this idea as a means of turning the West German people away from the temptations of neutralism. On the other hand, this idea alarmed the French, who had hoped to harness German industrial power through the pooling of their coal and steel industries (European Coal and Steel Community, May 1950). Some new device had to be found to render German military power unthreatening to the Western allies. In August 1950, the French had already proposed a range of measures to create an integrated defense force: in October 1950, French Prime Minister René Pleven suggested a European Defense Community (EDC) containing German units, rather than creation of a German Army, as the best framework for rearmament. Although neither Britain nor its Scandinavian allies favored the "Pleven Plan,"

American leaders became active supporters after an initial hesitation, and Adenauer used the fierce opposition of the German Social Democrats as a lever by which he extracted a full restoration of sovereignty as the price of West German participation.

The institutional appendages of the EDC (a common budget, a common assembly) aimed at a further extension of integration. Other provisions of the treaty made it clear that the EDC was intended more to preserve German subordination than to create an integrated Europe. Nevertheless, the effort to control a European army through a European political community seemed an important step toward supranational federation. Although both the EDC and the European Political Community failed to long survive, a decision (February 1953) to study the creation of a European common market left a more enduring legacy of this effort.

The third problem created by the war lay in sharing the economic burdens of rearmament. Industrial mobilization held the key to the military balance after the outbreak of the Korean War, so both the Atlantic alliance and the Soviets set about achieving a massive increase in their military establishments. The international economy soon transmitted the effects of the Cold War around the globe. Western statesmen found themselves confronted by the need to regulate the competitive struggle for resources among themselves while trying to achieve victory in a similar struggle with the USSR. Although American leaders were agreed on the need to subordinate every other consideration to the imperious needs of rapid rearmament, the initial plans soon proved beyond the reach of the weakened European economies, and even that of the United States.

Rearmament drove up the share of defense spending in the gross national product (GNP) of the NATO countries from 5 percent in 1950 to 8 percent in 1951. The sustainability of this effort came into almost immediate question. Even the United States proved unable to meet its commitments on deliveries of supplies to its allies. Europeans had much less of a national surplus to divert into arms, so the defense buildup bit painfully. Industrial production soon began to press against the outer limits of capacity in a number of key areas before it plateaued during 1951. Coal shortages endangered Western European industrial growth by limiting the production of steel and compelling costly energy imports from America. The boom outstripped the production of raw materials, shifting the terms of trade against industrial nations and devouring many of the gains in the balance of payments which should have resulted from increased exports of manufactured goods. Rising world demand intensified inflationary pressures within exporting and importing countries during the second half of 1951, just at the moment when postwar stabilization measures seemed to be nearing success. These developments somewhat short-circuited the West European recovery fostered by the Marshall Plan.

The ability of the NATO allies to mobilize the resources necessary to meet their own long-term targets became increasingly doubtful by mid-1952. Britain, France, and Belgium all began to scale back their rearmament efforts. By November 1952, it had become a commonplace that rearmament on the scale planned could not be squared with the preservation of an adequate standard of living. The Europeans lacked the means to meet their commitments and the United States refused to close the gap. European production remained stalled during 1952. Similarly, Congress cut the Truman administration's proposed $5.2 billion in aid to European rearmament to $4.4 billion. The two developments preserved a wide "dollar gap," even after raw materials prices had broken downward during 1951.

These frustrations heralded the advent of a new economic relationship between the members of the Atlantic alliance. Europeans and Americans now sought ways to eliminate the direct American contribution without ruining the ability of the European economies to support and defend their stability. The substitution of dollars earned from trade and American investment for aid now figured as the most attractive approach to Europe's continuing dependence. A series of American studies urged increased trade between Europe and America, the transfer of American capital and productive methods to Europe through direct foreign investment and off-shore procurement, mechanisms to regulate raw materials markets, and the creation of a currency stabilization fund as partners to European modernization and stabilization efforts. For their part, the Europeans adopted a complementary set of goals for economic policy: European modernization and stabilization, American trade liberalization, direct investment and off-shore procurement, and a stabilization of world raw materials prices. Taken together, base leases, troop pay, and off-shore procurement became an effective substitute form of aid when the Marshall Plan ended.

By putting flesh on the bare bones of the original North Atlantic treaty, by pushing Germany into an important role in the defense of Europe, by sustaining and developing efforts at European integration, by redefining economic relations, and by raising the issue of burden-sharing within the alliance, the Korean War made an important contribution to shaping both the structures and the dilemmas of the Atlantic alliance in the following decades.

John S. Hill

Bibliography

Gaddis, J.L. *Strategies of Containment* (New York: 1982).

Kaplan, Lawrence S. *NATO and the United States: The Enduring Alliance* (Twayne, Boston: 1988).

Pach, Chester J., Jr. *Arming the Free World: The Origins of the United States Military Assistance Program, 1945–1950* (University of North Carolina Press, Chapel Hill: 1991).

Urwin, Derek. *The Community of Europe: A History of European Integration Since 1945* (Longman, New York: 1991).

Wells, S.F., Jr. "Sounding the Tocsin: NSC-68 and the Soviet Threat," *International Security* (1979).

Naval Air Operations in the Korean War

The naval air war in Korea has not received the attention that it deserves. Korea constituted an important experience for naval aviation, coloring both the future employment of carrier forces and the Navy's future acquisition strategy. But beyond this, Navy and Marine air operations against North Korean and Chinese Communist forces were on such a scale and of such significance as to belie any impression that they somehow constituted a sideshow to other Air Force and United Nations air contributions. Indeed, during the war, Navy and Marine Corps airmen compiled an impressive operational record. They flew 41 percent of American combat sorties, as well as 40 percent of the American interdiction effort, 53 percent of all USN/USMC/USAF close support sorties, 36 percent of all American counter-air sorties, and 30 percent of all USN/USMC/USAF reconnaissance sorties. The Korean War had roughly four phases: the North Korean invasion, the Allied counterassault, the Chinese intervention, and the war of stalemate to the armistice. Within this framework there were essentially five phases to the Navy's air war in Korea: preserving the Pusan perimeter, supporting the Inchon landing and the drive to the Yalu, covering the retreat of U.N. forces in the face of the Communist Chinese intervention, participating in the interdiction campaign from 1951–1952, and participating in the air pressure campaign of 1952–1953. Outside this framework were, of course, a constant set of other operations including maritime and Anti-Submarine Warfare (ASW) patrol, fleet air defense and air superiority, search and rescue, tactical and strategic reconnaissance, and electronic warfare.

The advent of the Korean War found the Navy in the midst of a shaky recovery from the tumultuous months of debates on the roles and missions, the "Revolt of the Admirals," and the extensive downsizing of naval forces after World War II. The Navy was a force in transition from 1945 through the early 1950s, adjusting to the realities of the postwar world and technological changes such as the introduction of the jet airplane and the advent of the atomic bomb. But mission changes were equally challenging. In the years after V-J-Day—and lasting until the Gorshkov era—beginning in the 1960s, when the Soviet Navy began an enormous expansion, the Navy lacked a major seagoing threat. No longer could one envision using carriers in major fleet engagements at sea at Midway or the Marianas. Instead, the carrier was increasingly an element of forward presence, a symbol of far-flung power, an ostentatiously cocked revolver. Ironically, in Korean combat, the carrier would return to its pre–World War II roots, when it had been used as a mobile airfield parked (as it were) in close proximity to hostile shores. The Japanese had first employed their carriers in such a role when they conducted sustained operations against Chinese targets during the Sino-Japanese war. Operations in Korea would foreshadow the way in which the carrier was used in Vietnam more than a decade later, or for that matter in the brief Gulf War four decades later.

Naval air operations in Korea began more slowly than those of the Air Force because the ships of the Seventh Fleet were scattered among several Asiatic ports. On July 3, carrier aircraft from the USS *Valley Forge* and the British aircraft carrier HMS *Triumph* (operating in the Yellow Sea), hastily organized as Task Force 77, attacked Haeju Airfield and Pyongyang, shooting down two Yak fighters and destroying other

aircraft on the ground as well as railroad rolling stock. Then the carriers returned to Buckner Bay, Okinawa, before sallying forth to support the upcoming Pohang landing of the Army's 1st Cavalry Division to slow the tide of the North Korean advance. The Pohang landing itself came off without resistance, and afterward *Valley Forge's* airmen attacked and essentially destroyed—as confirmed by subsequent ground inspection—the Wonsan oil refinery complex, which produced approximately 500 tons of refined petroleum products per day. Both these strikes—the Pyongyang raid and the Pohang-Wonsan operation, gave a clear indication that naval air power could easily reach significant targets and do real damage, given the geographical opportunity afforded by the Korean peninsula.

As the North Korean advance continued down the Korean peninsula, the major challenge facing both the Navy and the Air Force by late July was in delivering attacks to blunt this drive and preserve the forces being gradually compressed into what became known as the "Pusan perimeter." At this point, the Navy's slower adaptation of turbojet technology after 1945 actually helped the service meet this particular challenge. Because the North Koreans had overrun most South Korean airfields, the Fifth Air Force's fighter squadrons, most of which were jet-equipped, had difficulty operating at the practical limits of their combat radius with any meaningful payload. (Korea was, of course, a war fought in the pre-air refueling era, with a few notable exceptions.) As an emergency measure, the Air Force sent a large number of older F-51 Mustangs to the Far East, but in August 1950, it largely fell to the long-endurance high-payload piston-engine aircraft such as the F4U Corsair and particularly the magnificent Douglas AD Skyraider to strike at North Korean columns in conjunction with Air Force B-26s and B-29s. In response to an emergency request for direct support by the Eighth Army (endorsed by Lieutenant General George E. Stratemeyer, the commander of the Far East Air Forces—FEAF), Task Force 77 launched its first emergency close support air strikes on July 25. These strikes revealed serious problems with interservice communication systems, notions of air power organization, and the efficacy of ground and airborne forward air control. In August, nearly 30 percent of all naval close air support (CAS) sorties had to be scratched because planes were unable to communicate with ground controllers, thanks to differing radio systems.

The communications issue was the single most important issue in the air support controversy that now erupted, though at the time (and since, as well) much attention was devoted to the theological underpinnings of "Air Force" and "Navy-Marine" notions of battlefield air support. In truth, both air support systems had their merits, and, undoubtedly, the debate that took place took on added vehemence coming as it did on the heels of the unfortunate defense debate of the late 1940s that had already strained relations between the services. When joined—and they fitted nicely, the Air Force system closely approximating contemporary notions of second-echelon battlefield air interdiction, and the Navy-Marine system dealing with threats right down to the perimeter wire— they destroyed the hopes of the Communist regimes in Pyongyang, Peking, and Moscow in a welter of shot, bombs, rockets, and napalm that littered the territory around the Pusan perimeter with the bodies of those unfortunate enough to serve the Communist cause.

But this success—most visible with hindsight—did not prevent criticism (much of it justified) about the quality of close air support furnished to the beleaguered troops within the Pusan perimeter during the bitter fighting of August and September 1950. To the Air Force, CAS was an adjunct to long-range artillery (and thus to be applied only rarely closer than 1,000 yards in front of friendly forces). To the Navy and Marines, CAS was a substitute for the lack of available heavy artillery (and thus intended for application as close as 50–200 yards in front of friendly forces); it was a product of years of small wars and Pacific experience; and it was less centrally controlled: frontline Marine TACPs could radio strike requests directly to a Marine brigade's tactical air direction center which, in turn, could contact an offshore carrier. The range limitations of Air Force jet aircraft operating from Japan forced controllers to give them priority for striking Korean targets even though, in many cases, their actual payloads were quite small; one F-80 squadron, for example, dropped only 7,500 pounds of bombs in seventeen days of constant combat operations, an average of 441 pounds per day. In contrast, one piston-engine Douglas AD Skyraider operating from a carrier could carry (on a typical sortie) 400 rounds of 20mm ammunition, three 150-gallon napalm bombs, twelve 250-pound fragmentation bombs, and

still have a four-hour endurance! To troops facing North Korean attack, the effect of seeing Navy and Marine aircraft orbiting overhead while controllers frantically tried to find targets for jets having as little as five minutes of combat fuel available before having to return to base can well be imagined, as well as the effect of seeing Corsairs and Skyraiders literally attacking right down the forward edge of battle with prodigious amounts of ordnance.

Though subsequent battlefield air support practices resulted in increased acceptance of the existing Air Force-Army system (particularly after the crises of 1950 passed and the war entered its stabilization phase in 1951), the application of CAS in Korea remained controversial. After Inchon, MacArthur affirmed that the Air Force had responsibility for coordinating tactical airpower in Korea, though the Navy and Marine Corps chafed somewhat under this arrangement.

During the operations to save Pusan, the combination of weapons carried by on-call Navy-Marine close air support aircraft proved particularly effective. The North Koreans' T-34 tanks, formidable weapons, were impervious to destruction by airborne guns except under unusual circumstances (for example, if they were carrying supplementary fuel tanks). Aerial rockets, particularly the ATAR, an antitank variation of the standard five-inch high velocity aerial rocket carrying a shaped charge warhead and rushed from emergency development at the Naval Ordnance Test Station at China Lake to Korea in less than a month, were effective, provided one flew close enough to overcome their accuracy problems. Napalm, which soon came to typify the air-ground war in Korea, was far more useful, generating a consuming fireball covering a pear-shaped area up to 275 feet long by 100 feet wide. Fragmentation bombs took a heavy toll of troops, light vehicles, and emplacements.

It is not too much to say that resolute air action—of which Navy and Marine air must receive particular recognition, for it substituted at the most critical period of the war for the unavailability of land-based air—was of decisive importance to denying Kim Il Sung the victory he so tenaciously sought. Though airpower could not win the war in Korea, it clearly did prevent North Korea from overrunning the south in the crucial opening months of the Korean War. Thereafter it was less decisive, until the closing months of the war, when it again played a major role in preventing last-minute territorial grabs.

During the Inchon-Seoul operation, naval airpower played the predominant air role, with three fast carriers (Task Force 77) and three escort carriers (Task Group 90.5 and Task Force 91) furnishing a total of nineteen fighter and attack squadrons in direct support of the 230-ship invasion force. Five long-range maritime patrol squadrons of Task Force 99 (four of which were British and American seaplanes) maintained sea watch and flew countermine sorties.

On September 15, MacArthur's forces came ashore at Inchon, as TF 77 and TG 90.5 supported the landing, flying 302 sorties that day for a loss of two aircraft. Altogether, during two weeks of Inchon-related operations, American carrier aircraft flew nearly 3,100 sorties, though at a cost of thirteen aircraft lost to North Korean flak. On September 27, X Corps and the Eighth Army linked up, a planned invasion of Wonsan proved unnecessary, and less than a month later, Pyongyang fell. Thereafter, naval air turned its attentions toward operating ever-northward as the bombline moved onward toward the Yalu. The Navy had responsibility for attacking forces, communications, and installations east of 127 degrees east longitude. So rapid was the ground advance that the service ran out of worthwhile targets, and increasingly turned its attention toward battlefield air support missions for a lack of other worthwhile things to do. Then, of course, came the shattering surprise of the Chinese intervention, which made battlefield air support absolutely critical.

On November 1, six MIG-15s crossed the Yalu and entered the war, triggering the first jet-age dogfights between American and Communist jet aircraft. The appearance of the swept-wing Soviet-built MIG-15 shocked the Navy, for its highest-performance jet fighter, the straight-wing Grumman F9F Panther, was clearly inferior. Only the better training of Navy pilots and the lethality of the Panther's 20mm gun system enabled them to offset somewhat the faster and all-around better-performing Communist plane. The same relative inferiority, of course, was true for the Air Force's Lockheed F-80, and the appearance of the MIG forced the rapid introduction of the evocative and graceful F-86 Sabre into combat. Thereafter, when operating in northwest Korea, Navy and Marine pilots largely depended on the Sabres to fend off the MIGs. This situation—exacerbated

by a mysterious overwater dogfight two years later between Soviet and Navy airmen near the carrier *Oriskany* in November 1952—goaded the Navy into subsequent development of two superlative fighters, the Vought F-8 Crusader, and the McDonnell F-4 Phantom II, both of which would be major players in the Vietnam War over a decade later. Now—really for the first time since the Korean War had begun—the Navy had to concern itself with air superiority as it battled (alongside the Air Force) to drop the Yalu bridges and prevent Chinese intervention. (In fact, some twelve divisions of Chinese troops were already in the south.) Though some spans were dropped during the two-week anti-bridge campaign, overall it was a disappointment for both services. Then, on November 25, Chinese ground forces entered combat.

Weather seriously constrained air operations against the Chinese, for snows covered land-based airfields, and the decks of carriers at sea. On November 27, despite foul conditions, TF 77's airmen began intense operations in support of retreating Allied columns, complementing the equally intensive efforts of the Fifth Air Force. Contingency plans for an emergency evacuation from Hungnam were put into effect, U.N. forces around the reservoirs began a long bitter retreat from Hagaru to Koto-ri, Hamhung, and to the port of Hungnam. Until three more carriers arrived on station, these forces could only call upon two carriers, one escort carrier, and Marine air ashore to hold the line. Further, the Eighth Army's collapse in the west was so complete that the Navy had to send strikes of Corsairs and ADs across the Korean peninsula to help out. As the crisis deepened, this division of effort could not be tolerated, and the Navy and Marines devoted their entire effort to protecting the columns making their way down from the reservoirs. The breakout began on December 1, and ended on the 11th. In the intervening time, Marine aircraft flew 1,300 sorties in direct support, and the Navy a further 860; weather severely constrained flight operations but, even so, they were extremely effective. Their presence comforted those walking out and there was never less than an average of twenty-four CAS aircraft—typically Corsairs and ADs—orbiting over the column, strafing, rocketing, and napalming Communist forces ahead, behind, and on the flanks. Air strikes combined with immediate ground attacks routed Communist ambushers, and an airborne four-engine Douglas R5D (C-54) transport hastily outfitted with communications, three controllers, and a situation room functioned as a super-Mosquito FAC orbiting the column for twelve hours at a time. Prisoner interviews confirmed that naval air attacks had severely hampered the ability of the Chinese to close with the Americans, despite the desperate condition of retreating forces, inflicting approximately 20,000 casualties from air attack. On Christmas Eve, the last vessels embarked from Hungnam bringing the sad saga of the retreat from the reservoirs to a close.

Though Seoul fell for a second time, the long retreat eventually came to an end and U.N. forces began once again to more forward. Seoul had its second liberation on March 14, 1951, and shortly thereafter the war settled into an uncomfortable stalemate, with occasionally bitter fighting along a narrow strip of land running near the 38th parallel. In the first five months of 1951, Navy and Marine aircraft flew 33,415 combat sorties, made 173,000 attack runs on enemy targets, dropped 104,145 bombs, fired 70,400 rockets, and fired 13,100,000 rounds of ammunition. Much of this effort had been devoted to battlefield air support. But now, in response to the stabilization of the front, U.N. air planners turned to interdicting Communist supply lines in a vain attempt to influence the combat along the front. After the frantic pace of operations that had characterized naval aviation in the first six months of Korea, the more deliberate nature of the interdiction war resulted in a standardization of naval operations that lasted through the armistice.

For example, at any one time, TF 77 typically consisted of three fast carriers on station, with two conducting flight operations and one replenishing at sea. A fourth carrier would be on port call in Japan, on twelve-hour recall. (The escort carriers operating in the Yellow Sea, usually consisting of American, British, and Commonwealth ships, were primarily devoted to battlefield support missions; they were much smaller as well—an American escort carrier typically carried but a single squadron of Marine Corsairs.) A battleship or heavy cruiser accompanied TF 77, as did a radar picket screen of between nine and sixteen destroyers. Each carrier could launch up to 100 sorties per summer day, and about eighty-five sorties per winter day. Ships replenished underway every fourth day, and the typical carrier air group consisted of a jet squadron (either Grumman F9F Panthers or McDonnell F2H Banshees), two prop fighter squadrons (Vought F4U Corsairs), one attack squadron (Douglas AD Skyraiders), and small detachments of specialized night fighter and attack, electronic warfare (ECM/ECCM), photo reconnaissance, and airborne early warning (AEW) aircraft, as well as a small search and rescue (SAR) helicopter. Earlier in the war, carriers operated with up to five squadrons, but it was found that four-squadron groups worked best, giving a carrier approximately eighty-one aircraft. Over time, the percentage of jet aircraft to prop aircraft changed. At the end of the war, the typical carrier operated two jet squadrons, one prop fighter (Corsair) squadron, and one Skyraider squadron. The most versatile carrier aircraft was undoubtedly the Douglas AD Skyraider, a product of the legendary designer, Ed Heinemann. It served in the attack, ECM, night attack, and AEW roles, a true multi-mission platform. Though not invulnerable to ground fire, it was considerably more survivable than the tough Corsair, and manifestly better in ground attack than the temperamental jets which, though infrequently subjected to the intense ground fire directed at the slower Corsairs and Skyraiders, were far more likely to suffer serious damage if "tapped."

But enemy fire was not the only threat facing naval aviators. In the era of the jet airplane, the straight-deck carriers, equipped with hydraulic catapults and requiring a paddle-waving landing signal officer (LSO) were anachronistic. A jet airplane that landed badly might leap a barrier, run into the planes parked forward of the "island," destroying and damaging many and possibly killing or injuring deck and aircrew alike. Such happened several times during the Korean War, accelerating adaptation of the angled deck, the steam catapult (which greatly improved takeoff performance), the Fresnel lens landing approach system, and redesigned nylon barriers. All these features, mostly pioneered by the Royal Navy, of course, were subsequently adapted to existing carriers and integrated into the new *Forrestal* class and subsequent ships after Korea. As with Vietnam later, there were instances of hangar deck fires and incidents. But unlike that war, which witnessed three disastrous fires, in Korea there was but one. *Boxer* lost nine dead, thirty injured, and eighteen aircraft damaged and destroyed to a fire in August 1952 that for a brief while seemed likely to go out of control; after temporary repairs in Yokosuka, it returned to the Sea of Japan for continued operations.

Thus, from mid-1951 on, while CAS and battlefield support remained important—particularly to the Marine aviators of the 1st Marine Air Wing—the majority of naval air operations involved strikes at targets east of a line running vertically from the Yalu down to Koksan. Indeed, Far East Air Forces (FEAF) had assigned naval aviation responsibility for interdiction attacks over essentially the entire east coast of Korea, from the Soviet and Manchurian border, and into the heartland of the country itself.

The interdiction war for both the Air Force and Navy proved a frustrating one, typified by draining losses for low gain. Nothing so characterized this air war as attacks against roads and bridges; the former were impossible really to destroy, for North Korea had essentially no paved highways, while the latter were equally difficult to destroy in the pre-precision-guided-weapon era. (Indeed, one of Korea's results was the acceleration of Navy interest in precision guided missiles which eventually led to weapons such as the Bullpup and Walleye.) Bombed roads could be filled in within hours, rail cuts could be almost equally quickly fixed, and bombed bridges could usually be bypassed or quickly repaired. Between May 1951 and the end of the year, TF 77 airmen were credited with destroying more than 700 bridges and making nearly 4,500 rail line "cuts," but, of course, much of this destruction was, in fact, the result of constantly revisiting previously "destroyed" targets. Meantime, "revisit" requirements meant that such targets became profound flak traps; by mid-1952, Allied intelligence estimated that more than half of all North Korean antiaircraft artillery was emplaced around bridges and rail lines. More significant were TF 77's destruction claims against actual hardware—which, during this time, totaled eighty-four locomotives, more than 2,000 rail cars and rolling stock, nearly 2,100 other vehicles, nearly 6,000 buildings and warehouses, and almost 250 small boats. But even so, under the stalemate conditions that governed the war in Korea, the supplies that continued to get through were more than sufficient for continued enemy combat along the front.

The frustrations of this kind of air war—which America would experience with even greater effort over North Vietnam—were caught by novelist James Michener's fine novel, *The Bridges at Toko-Ri*, based on a real anti-bridge campaign, the so-called "Battle of Carlson's Canyon." Attacks against bridges and roads gave way to attacks against rail lines, but over the length of the war, intelligence reports and analytical studies grew increasingly pessimistic. One, in December 1951, reported that while attacks had forced the Communists to devote great attention to countering interdiction strikes, it came at the price of "almost the entire" offensive effort of TF 77, 60 percent of the offensive effort of the 1st Marine Air Wing (MAW), and 95 percent of the offensive effort of the Fifth Air Force. The report continued that:

> It is doubtful whether the interdiction campaign in Korea has been as costly to the enemy as to the U.S. The enemy has lost many vehicles, much rolling stock and supplies and has suffered heavy physical destruction of property, but it is doubtful whether this has placed a greater strain on the economies of North Korea, China, and the U.S.S.R. than upon the economy of the U.S. The cost of maintaining interdiction forces in and near Korea, the cost of the hundreds of aircraft lost and the thousands of tons of munitions and supplies consumed, and the expenditure of national resources have been keenly felt. Certainly the value of the U.N. aircraft lost alone is greater than that of all the enemy's vehicles, rolling stock, and supplies destroyed. While the cost of the war assumes fantastic proportions to the U.S., the enemy largely offsets our efforts by the use of his cheapest and most useful asset, mass manpower.

A total of 384 Navy and Marine fighter and attack aircraft were lost to North Korean antiaircraft fire from the summer of 1951 through the armistice in 1953, a little over fifteen per month, on average. By mid-1951, North Korea had nearly a dozen different kinds of early warning (EW), ground-controlled-intercept (GCI), and fire control radars, ranging from Soviet models to some British and American systems shipped originally to the Soviets, and including one Japanese EW radar and—possibly—ex-Nazi *Freya* radars as well. By 1952, more than 109 individual fixed and mobile radars were in service, and Navy ECM crews concluded both that the North Koreans possessed good radar equipment and good discipline in using it. Ironically, though the means had existed since the middle of World War II to frustrate radar (namely, by chaff drops), the Navy made little use of it, with the exception of one highly successful strike against Kowon in June 1952, when two ECM ADs dropped rope chaff to confound radar-directed antiaircraft fire. The resulting antiaircraft fire was woefully inaccurate, bursting in the midst of the slowly descending chaff. But this one episode exhausted TF 77's entire chaff supply! (To be fair, it should be mentioned that the Strategic Air Command, for security reasons, did not clear its own B-29 bombers to use this decade-old counter weapon until the following September, though, unlike the Navy, the Air Force subsequently made extensive use of chaff.)

In fact, however, the greatest losses were caused by heavy machine guns and light antiaircraft cannon, typically 12.7mm, 23mm, and 37mm weapons. Of the 384 aircraft lost to North Korean antiaircraft defenses from mid-1951 onward, fully 193—just over 50 percent—were F4U Corsairs. Proving that heavier armor helped but still didn't guarantee safety, nearly 27 percent—102—were AD Skyraiders. Approximately 15 percent—fifty-seven—were F9F Panthers. Just over 8 percent—thirty-two aircraft—were a miscellaneous grouping of AUs (the ground attack variant of the F4U), F7F Tigercats, and F2H Banshees. Panther losses might appear high, but it was the Navy's primary jet fighter in Korea; in contrast, relatively few Banshees served in the war. As a rule, the speedy jets were less likely to be hit by Communist AAA, though they lacked the survivability of slower propeller-driven attackers. But the slower prop aircraft, despite their armor, were more often engaged by defenders (thus increasing their chances of a lethal hit), particularly aircraft such as the Corsair, used heavily for battlefield support as well as strike missions. The Corsair, an air-cooled radial-engine aircraft, might have been expected to have a higher survivability than the Air Force's liquid-cooled (and hence vulnerable) F-51 Mustang. In fact, insufficient oil cooler and engine protection rendered the Corsair just as susceptible as the Mustang to ground fire; in April 1951, for example, thirty were lost—the same number of F-51s lost that month on similar missions.

Not surprisingly, given the constant losses, the danger of routine flight operations, and the apparent minimal return for effort, morale of air crew suffered (a point well-made by Michener in his novel). One air group commander recollected that morale constituted:

> one of my toughest jobs . . . [a] constant battle . . . the war in Korea demanded

more competence, courage, and skill from the naval aviator than did World War II. The flying hours were longer, the days on the firing line more, the antiaircraft hazards greater, the weather worse.

In mid-1952, frustrated by the unproductivity of well-publicized interdiction efforts, U.N. air planners instead reassessed what kind of strikes might best hurt the North Korean war effort. In some respects, it calls to mind the search for the "vital centers" that planners undertook in the preparation of the Instant Thunder air campaign plan that formed the core of the Desert Storm air campaign's first phase. Central to this effort was increasingly close cooperation between the Navy and the Air Force, enhanced by strong bonds of mutual respect and friendship between key Air Force and Navy individuals, particularly Air Force Brigadier General Jacob E. Smart, and Navy Vice Admiral J.J. "Jocko" Clark. Smart believed that, while interdiction efforts should continue to ensure that the Communists could not regain the ability to undertake a war of maneuver, more precisely focused and specific joint strikes were needed to pressure them to seeking a settlement. Admittedly, there had already been some creative strikes that constituted quasi-air pressure ones, even during the "interdiction" era. For example, in May 1951, Air Group 19's ADs had torpedoed the gates of the Hwachon Dam to prevent its use by North Korea to delay advancing U.N. forces via selective flooding. Then in August 1951, Navy F2H fighters protected thirty-five B-29s attacking the Rashin (now Najin) logistical transshipment center and petroleum storage facility. In October 1951, alerted by intelligence before a pending Communist leadership meeting, ADs from *Essex* and *Antietam* attacked a major Communist conference center in Kapsan, killing more than 500 key members of the North Korean government and allegedly destroying all records of the North Korean Communist party. But it was only in the spring and summer of 1952, after the frustrations of the abortive interdiction campaign had reached their peak, that planners sought a restructuring of the air war.

In April 1952, Smart's staff drew up plans for strikes against the North Korean power generation facilities, the first phase of a more aggressive and selective air strategy. U.N. Commander General Matthew Ridgway concurred, particularly as the Panmunjom peace talks were proceeding slowly, and after he was replaced the following month by General Mark Clark, Clark likewise strongly endorsed the strikes. These first "air pressure" strikes occurred on June 23, 1952, when Navy AD dive bombers from four carriers, covered by Air Force Sabres, went deep into MIG Alley to attack the Sui-ho power generation complex. In two minutes they dropped eighty-five tons of bombs, and follow-on Air Force attacks added another 145 tons, the combined total knocking Suiho out of the war. Subsequent attacks against other generation facilities over the next day reduced North Korea's power generation capacity by 90 percent. Other joint Air Force–Navy–U.N. strikes in July and August essentially destroyed Pyongyang's military value, leaving its military centers, communications facilities, and storage facilities in ruins. Next, at Smart's suggestion, Air Force–Navy strikes went after the remnants of North Korea's mining and extractive industries, destroying production plants for processing zinc ore and magnesite shipped to the Soviet Union, and the Aoji oil refinery, located only eight miles from the Soviet frontier. By the fall of 1952, "air pressure" strikes, in contrast to the far less profitable road and rail strikes of 1951–52, were generating far more productive results, though the number of suitable targets declined rapidly.

In May 1952, during an inspection flight behind Allied lines, Jocko Clark was struck with the density and diversity of U.N. supply depots, and, particularly, their vulnerability to attack from the air. He reasoned that the Communists must have similar dumps, between the artillery line of U.N. forces, but below the bombline, and certainly not as far back as the main supply routes which had been pounded since the summer of 1951. To Clark, this was potentially the North Korean Achilles' heel—the result of all their effort to get supplies to the front must be caches well within reach of Allied airpower. Subsequent TF 77 photoreconnaissance of the area behind the Communist front-line positions confirmed Clark's suspicions. Thus was born the so-called "Cherokee" strikes, christened in honor of Clark's Native American ancestry.

The first of these strikes began on October 9, 1952, and thereafter continued through to the armistice eight-and-one-half months later. At any one time after the Cherokee strikes began, they constituted at least 50 percent of TF 77's air effort; up to three strikes per day were typically flown. Coordination of these strikes—essentially ones that would fall within the current definition of battlefield air interdiction—

proved troublesome, for there was initially the belief within the Fifth Air Force that they really were little more than a form of close air support. In fact, there were some significant differences. Unlike CAS, which typically was spontaneous and not briefed before takeoff, Cherokee strikes were thoroughly planned and prebriefed. CAS strikes usually employed no more than about eight aircraft; Cherokee strikes usually numbered about fifty. CAS weapons loads were primarily antipersonnel; Cherokee used whatever weapons were dictated by the target itself. CAS strikes loitered "on call" over the front; Cherokee strikes crossed the beach, hit the target, and then quickly went "feet wet." So large were the Cherokee strikes that they severely taxed the abilities of forward air controllers to coordinate operations within and beyond the bombline. This concern over operating within the bombline led eventually (following a mid-November conference) to a decision to move the bombline as close as 300 yards of the front (thus allowing for all Cherokee strikes to be "above" the bombline), to coordinate the strikes with the Fifth Air Force and Eighth Army, and, finally, to rely upon Mosquito FACs to mark the targets with smoke rockets.

The Cherokee strikes undoubtedly reduced the strength of front-line Communist forces, generating the first real instances where they clearly suffered from supply shortages. Numerous secondary explosions—twenty-seven in one case—accompanied Cherokee missions, indicating profitable targeting. The volume of Communist fire along the front noticeably slackened, and—for the first time in nearly two years—the Communists attempted to run risky daylight road convoys down from the Yalu to the front. Truck hunting was excellent, and night attackers—flying specialized versions of the Corsair and AD—found a plethora of targets. Indeed, General James Van Fleet suggested after the war that had the U.N. launched a ground offensive in concert with the Cherokee strikes, North Korea might well have been forced to surrender a great amount of its territory. In fact, of course, the political realities of 1952–1953 made such a speculation inconceivable.

In June and July, the North Koreans launched fierce attacks against the I and II ROK Corps, covered by bad weather that hampered the ability of Allied air to help defenders. By mid-July, in response to the Eighth Army's pleas for support against what were, in effect, human-wave assaults, Clark ordered all TF 77 efforts to go either to CAS or to Cherokee; interdiction was out. It is a measure of his concern that he saw to it that the Task Force was equipped with nuclear capability.

Fortunately, conventional means prevailed; the naval war's end came on July 27 at 9:25 P.M.—slightly more than a half-hour before the armistice—when a land-based Marine AD dropped three 2,000-pound bombs on Communist positions, a fittingly explosive finale.

On the eve of the Korean War, naval aviation had been confronted by operational and strategic challenges; a force in transition between the era of the piston-powered aircraft and the newer jets, a force under attack over its future value to national defense, a force shrinking in numbers of ships, aircraft, and personnel. By 1953, this had changed. While the number of aircraft had declined because of combat losses and retirements from 9,422 to 8,818, the latter included a much higher proportion of newer jet aircraft and new designs than had the former. In 1953, the fighter force was a jet force; in 1950 it had been a prop one. The Korean conflict had resulted in the rehabilitation of carrier aviation. In 1950, the Navy had a total of fifteen carriers, only seven of which were larger *Essex* or *Midway* fast carriers. In 1953, this had risen to thirty-four, of which seventeen were fast carriers, and larger carriers—typified by the *Forrestal*—were on the way. In 1950, the Navy had 10,401 pilots, and the Marines had 2,177; in 1953, the Navy had 18,296, and the Marines had 4,615. In 1950, naval aviation had been characterized by conventional weaponry; in 1953, TF 77's carriers were equipped with atomic weapons. In 1950, naval aviation was in disarray in the wake of the Johnson defense cuts, the cancellation of the supercarrier USS *United States*, and the "Revolt of the Admirals." In 1953, there was no question about the future viability and vitality of naval aviation.

But if carrier aviation came out of the Korean War more secure then it had been when it went in, the experience had been neither predictable nor pleasant. The Korean War was the last pre-missile, pre-smart-bomb war that the United States fought. It was not quite the last America would fight with piston-powered combat airplanes. It was also primarily a ground attack air war. For the Navy and Marines, it had been a costly and frustrating one. On average, over the length of the war, the Navy and Marines lost one airplane per day. Direct enemy action resulted in the loss of 564 aircraft, consisting of 400 fighters, 140 attack aircraft,

twelve observation airplanes, eight helicopters, three patrol planes, and one utility aircraft. Almost all the losses of fighter and attack aircraft were from ground fire; MIGs were rarely a problem, for the Sabre screen at the Yalu kept them off the Navy's and Marine Corps' more vulnerable airplanes. This does not imply that the Navy's and Marine Corps were not players in the air superiority war along the Yalu, for they were, and, in one way, important ones. FEAF relied on Marine and Navy F3D night fighters as the primary means of protecting its B-29s from predatory MIGs as they raided North Korea by night, and they scored a number of night MIG kills though not, unfortunately, without loss to themselves. Further, a number of Navy and Marine pilots shot down various Communist aircraft over the length of the war in the course of naval air strikes, and thirteen exchange pilots in Air Force fighter squadrons shot down twenty-five MIGs as well.

The post-Korean experience of the carrier confirmed the basic change in the mission of the carrier to one as a mobile airfield; already French carriers were functioning in such fashion off Indochina. In three more years, Anglo-French carriers would go to war in Suez; the 1960s and 1970s saw carriers steaming off Vietnam, and the 1980s–1990s witnessed carrier operations under such circumstances in the South Atlantic (the Falklands War), off Libya and Lebanon, Grenada, and the Red Sea and Persian Gulf.

The Korean experience drove major changes in naval weaponry and systems. First, the tendency to envision the carrier as going even more closely "in harm's way" drove ever greater efforts to extend the carrier's warning screen, resulted in greater emphasis on early warning, new generations of fighter aircraft, and both air-to-air and surface-to-air missile development. The AEW interest led to the introduction of increasingly sophisticated carrier-based airborne early warning aircraft. The unhappy experience of having to rely on Air Force Sabres to keep the MIGs at bay accelerated development of new fighters designed to secure air superiority over the fleet, notably the F-8 Crusader and the F-4 Phantom II. It might be said that the Korean experience powerfully concentrated the acquisition energies of the Navy, for after Korea, far-fetched or fanciful aircraft proposals and projects—which had abounded within the Bureau of Aeronautics before the war—were quickly dropped in favor of more realistic "real world" solutions.

(Conversely, having done well with its fighters in Korea, the Air Force went in just the opposite direction; Air Force fighters grew more distant and detached from the real world anticipated needs of the 1960s, resulting in the service—much to its chagrin—eventually having to buy large quantities of a land-based variant of the Navy's F-4).

Likewise, the recognized vulnerability of ships to air attack at jet speeds resulted in the navy prioritizing the development of sophisticated air-to-air missiles to kill threats before they arrived over the fleet. The result was the heat-seeking Sidewinder, the most successful military missile system ever developed, and the radar-guided Sparrow which, forty years after Korea, were responsible for the destruction of all the Iraqi fighters shot down in Desert Storm. This same fear, coupled with still-fresh memories of the Kamikaze menace during the latter stages of the Pacific war, stimulated a tremendous investment in surface-to-air missile development, resulting in the "Terrible T's": the Terrier, Talos, and Tartar family and their present-day successors.

The frustration of repeatedly having to revisit bridges stimulated smart weapon development, particularly the development of air-launched stand-off guided weapons. This concern carried over to accelerate interest in what would become known to later generations as "cruise missiles." In World War II, the danger of risking piloted aircraft on strikes against heavily defended targets resulted in the Navy experimenting with remotely piloted drones against Japanese fortifications. The idea was revived in Korea, where a Navy test team flew F6F Hellcat drones guided by controller aircraft into North Korean targets. An operational test and evaluation unit launched six from the *Boxer* against various bridges, tunnels, and power plants, and though the results—one hit, one abort, and four misses—were inauspicious, it encouraged continued work that culminated in the highly successful ship- and submarine-launched Tomahawk used extensively in the Gulf War.

But even more conventional aircraft weaponry underwent changes. One of the ironies of Korea had been jet aircraft designed to operate at speeds well above 500 mph carrying bulky high-drag bombs designed to be dropped at half that speed or even less. The shapes added greatly to the drag of the aircraft, reducing their range and speed, and, in addition, had somewhat unpredictable accuracy

when released at higher speeds, compromising the value of strike missions. In the post-Korean era, the Navy sponsored development of an entirely new family of streamlined bomb and fuel tank shapes to reduce drag, improve performance, and improve the predictability of bomb accuracy.

Alternately frustrated by how difficult night attack had been in Korea (where specialized night-flying versions of the Corsair and Skyraider had attempted to interdict North Korean road and rail traffic heading south) and encouraged by how productive it could be when one *did* locate enemy road convoys and trains, the navy pressed the development of new attack aircraft able to prosecute both day and night attacks.

The nature of carrier operations and equipment changed dramatically after Korea. As noted, the angled deck replaced the straight deck, bringing the era of frequent (and disastrous) deck-landing accidents to a merciful close. The steam catapult replaced hydraulic "cats," vastly improving the takeoff performance of the heavier and hotter-performing jets; mirror landing systems replaced the paddle-waving LSO, and, eventually, automated carrier landing equipment made possible the era of hands-off flight control and throttle manipulation. In-flight refueling, which revolutionized both Air Force and Navy operations, greatly enhanced combat potential and day-to-day safety and efficiency.

The relative contribution of the Navy and Marine Corps to the Korean War can best be measured by comparing their effort with that of the United States Air Force. USN/USMC airmen flew 41 percent of all combat sorties flown by USN/USMC/USAF aircrews. Tables 1 and 2 present a statistical glimpse at the contributions of the Navy and Marine Corps to the Korean War:

TABLE 1   USN/USMC/USAF Combat Sorties by Type, 1950–1953

Mission Type	USN/USMC	USAF
Interdiction	126,874	192,581
Close Air Support	65,748	57,665
Counter-Air/Air Superiority	44,607	79,928
Reconnaissance	26,757	60,971
Antisubmarine Patrol	11,856	(n/a)
Strategic Bomber Sorties	(n/a)	994
Total:	275,842	392,139
(n/a=not available)		

TABLE 2	Distribution of Combat Effort within USN/USMC and USAF	
Mission Type	USN/USMC	USAF
Interdiction	46%	49%
Close Air Support	24%	15%
Counter-Air/Air Superiority	16%	20%
Reconnaissance	10%	16%
Antisubmarine Patrol	4%	(n/a)
Strategic Bomber Sorties	(n/a)	0.2%
(n/a=not available)		

Richard P. Hallion

Bibliography

Cagle, M.M., and F.A. Manson. *The Sea War in Korea* (1957).

Field, J.A. *History of United States Naval Operations: Korea* (Office of Naval History, Washington: 1962).

Hallion, R.P. *The Naval Air War in Korea* (1986).

Navy, U.S.

The U.S. Navy's experience in the Korean conflict demonstrated once again the indispensability of naval forces to the successful conduct of war far from American shores. The fleet's overwhelming presence in the Western Pacific enabled the United States to fight a major war on the periphery of Asia, even with strong concentrations of enemy military power close by.

The United States government clearly was surprised when North Korean forces smashed their way south into the Republic of Korea on 25 June 1950. American leaders had not positioned sizable military forces in Northeast Asia because they were convinced that any challenge from the Soviet-led Communist bloc would first occur in Europe. After World War II, the Truman administration garrisoned Japan with only four Army divisions, which in 1950 were understrength and inadequately trained, and a handful of Air Force and Navy units. These forces were under the commander in chief, Far East (CINCFE), General Douglas MacArthur.

The naval component of MacArthur's Far East command (FECOM) was U.S. naval forces, Far East (NAVFE), at the outset of the war under Vice Admiral C. Turner Joy. He served with distinction as commander until his routine replacement on 4 June 1951 by Vice Admiral Robert P. Briscoe, who led the command until 1954.

On 25 June 1950, NAVFE totaled a modest strength of one light cruiser, four destroyers, four amphibious ships, one submarine, ten minesweepers, and an attached frigate from the Australian Navy. However, help was on the way. On 27 June, Admiral Arthur W. Radford, the commander in chief, U.S. Pacific Fleet, headquartered in Hawaii, transferred operational control of his Seventh Fleet, under Vice Admiral Arthur D. Struble, to NAVFE. During the next month, NAVFE also was made responsible for the direction of British Commonwealth and other United Nations naval forces, and the Republic of Korea Navy. In practice, the commander of the Seventh Fleet directed the combat operations of the major U.N. naval forces.

As is normal operating procedure in the U.S. Navy, the naval command in the Korean theater was organized by task forces. Throughout the war, COMNAVFE's major combat elements were Task Force 77, the carrier striking force; Task Force 95, the blockading and escort force; Task Force 90, the Far East amphibious force; and Task Force 96, naval forces, Japan. The latter NAVFE component carried out the antisubmarine patrol of the waters off Korea and Japan and protected the critical U.S. naval bases in Japan.

Task Force 77 was formed around the fleet's most potent ship, the aircraft carrier. The following carriers served combat tours during the war, many completing several operational tours in the theater: *Valley Forge, Bon Homme Richard, Antietam, Boxer, Lake Champlain, Kearsarge, Philippine Sea, Oriskany, Leyte Gulf, Essex,* and *Princeton.* Launched from the flight decks of these ships were piston-engined F4U Corsair, AD Skyraider, jet F9F Panther, and jet F2H Banshee aircraft. These planes and the ships from which they flew were protected from enemy planes, surface vessels, and submarines by an escorting screen of cruisers and destroyers. Task Force 77 operated for the most part in the Sea of Japan off Korea's east coast.

Task Force 95, the blockading and escort force, also employed naval power with one light carrier, *Bataan,* and four escort carriers, *Bairoko, Badoeng Strait, Rendova,* and *Sicily.* Marine air units flew from these ships and from air bases ashore.

American and other United Nations command aircraft carriers operated against Communist rear areas. Carrier planes engaged enemy aircraft, shooting down thirteen MIGs,

Yaks, and other hostile planes. Other units bombed and strafed enemy truck convoys, trains, oil refineries, and supply depots and stood by to rescue flyers downed ashore or at sea. Attack aircraft operating from carriers poised offshore provided close air support for the U.S. Eighth Army. During the summer of 1950, U.S. naval air units gave swift and effective air support to Allied ground forces fighting desperately and successfully to hold a perimeter around the key South Korean port of Pusan.

By the end of the Korean War, U.S. Navy and U.S. Marine Corps aircraft of Task Force 77, Task Force 95, and Task Force 96 had flown more than 275,000 sorties. This amounted to 100 percent of the antisubmarine patrols, 53 percent of the close air support strikes, 40 percent of the interdiction missions, 36 percent of the air-to-air sorties, and 30 percent of the reconnaissance sorties executed by U.S. Air Force, Navy, and Marine Corps aircraft. The Navy-Marine aerial assault forces dropped more than 178,000 tons of bombs, triggered over 274,000 air-to-ground rockets, and fired more than 71 million cannon rounds. While it was impossible to determine enemy losses with any precision, the American command estimated that naval air power killed 86,000 North Korean and Chinese troops and destroyed 44,000 buildings, more than 6,000 locomotives, tankers, and boxcars, 7,500 tanks and vehicles, 1,900 supply dumps, and 2,400 vessels.

The cost for this success was not cheap. Communist antiaircraft fire shot down 559 Navy and Marine planes, and enemy MIGs destroyed another five. A further 684 naval aircraft were lost to noncombat causes, for a total of 1,248.

In addition to carriers, the blockading and escort force operated naval gunfire support ships. The surface combatants that steamed with Task Force 95 included, at various times, the four powerful World War II Iowa-class battleships—*Iowa, Missouri, Wisconsin,* and *New Jersey*—and cruisers, destroyers, and rocket ships. These warships steamed along the Korean peninsula shelling enemy troop concentrations and supply caches, bridges, railways, and supply routes. These units provided indispensable fire support to ground forces and denied the enemy daytime use of the main roads running along the coasts fronting the Sea of Japan and the Yellow Sea. U.N. surface forces fired more than 4 million rounds of naval gun ammunition, in the process sinking hundreds of enemy small craft, leveling more than 3,000 buildings, and destroying 214 trucks, 108 bridges, and ninety-three supply dumps. In addition, more than 28,000 enemy soldiers died under shelling by Allied naval guns. While return fire from Communist shore batteries damaged eighty-two U.N. vessels, it did not sink one.

Admiral Joy's amphibious command was Task Force 90, which grew from a small contingent of five amphibious ships on 25 June to an armada of 112 U.S. and Allied attack transports, cargo ships, minesweepers, landing ships, patrol vessels, and other vessels on the eve of the September 1950 landing at Inchon.

Also part of the U.N. naval armada were the British carriers *Glory, Theseus, Ocean,* and *Triumph,* cruisers *Belfast, Jamaica, Birmingham, Kenya,* and *Newcastle,* destroyers *Cossack, Consort, Cockade, Comus,* and *Charity,* and other naval vessels. The Australians deployed to Korean waters the carrier *Sydney,* destroyers *Waramunga* and *Bataan,* and a host of frigates. New Zealand, Canada, Columbia, France, the Netherlands, and Thailand also dispatched destroyers and frigates to the hostile waters off the Korean peninsula.

When the war began, the 7,000-man Republic of Korea Navy, then operating with only one frigate (*Bak Soo San*), one tank landing ship, and fifteen motor minesweepers, was two years old. By July 1953, however, the United States had reinforced the fledgling navy with frigates *Kum Kang San, Apnok, Chi Ri San,* and *Sam Kak San,* additional LSTs, and other support vessels.

The fleet's mastery of the Pacific Ocean made it possible for the U.N. command to hold Korea, build up the forces hanging on, and then counterattack to regain territory lost to the North Koreans. Admiral Joy also coordinated the efforts of the Navy's Military Sea Transportation Service (MSTS), which carried out the massive sealift of troops, vehicles, equipment, and supplies from the United States to the Far Eastern theater and between Japan and Korea. Korea is almost 5,000 nautical miles from the U.S. West Coast; the distance is double that from the U.S. East Coast via the Panama Canal. Hundreds of troopships, freighters, and tankers operated by MSTS transported U.S. Army and Marine combat divisions, trucks, weapons, ammunition, and fuel to the Far East and then returned to California for more. In one instance, in September 1950, MSTS carried the Army's 187th Airborne Regimental Combat Team from California directly to besieged Pusan. During the war, MSTS transported 5 million passengers, more than 52 million tons of cargo, and 22 million long tons of petroleum, oil, and lubricants in support of the war effort.

The fleet's oilers, ammunition ships, and stores ships also supplied warships at sea, enabling U.S. and Allied naval forces to remain continuously on station in the combat theater. A major contribution to the successful support of UN forces ashore was made by hospital ships. With the first use in war of the helicopter, it was possible quickly to evacuate casualties from the battlefield to the ships, refitted with landing platforms. Because the United States had mothballed all of its hospital ships after World War II, the first such vessel to reach Korean waters was the British hospital ship *Maine*. Eventually, the U.S. Navy deployed hospital ships *Consolation, Haven*, and *Repose*. Denmark also dispatched the hospital ship *Jutlandia*.

The Navy's chief contribution at the outset of the war was to help the United Nations command avert disaster. The mobility of the Pacific Fleet and the forward basing of its major combat elements, the Seventh Fleet, enabled President Harry S. Truman to back up his decision to oppose what he saw as a challenge in Asia by the entire Communist bloc. Soon after the North Korean invasion, the president announced that the United States, as part of a United Nations coalition, would use military force to preserve the sovereignty of the Republic of Korea. He also made it clear that the use of Chinese Communist (and by implication Soviet) air and naval forces to broaden the war in Asia would be resisted. To back up this stand, he ordered the Seventh Fleet to sortie into Chinese and Korean waters. In the first week of the war, the fleet, formed around the aircraft carrier *Valley Forge*, heavy cruiser *Rochester*, eight destroyers, and three submarines, was especially busy. The fleet first paraded its strength along the Chinese coast, and then *Valley Forge* aircraft bombed airfields and rail yards in Pyongyang, North Korea, then beyond the range of the U.S. Air Force planes in Japan.

From evidence now available, it is clear that this rapid show of force deterred the Chinese Communists from executing a long-planned amphibious assault on the island of Taiwan, which was held by anti-Communist Chinese Nationalist forces. An invasion of Taiwan would have undoubtedly expanded the conflict in the Far East. Furthermore, the quick

deployment forward of U.S. naval and land-based air forces could be credited with influencing Soviet Premier Joseph Stalin to withdraw an earlier pledge of Soviet air support for the North Korean attack. Throughout the Korean War, U.S. Navy submarines and patrol aircraft were positioned between the Soviet Union and the combat theater, not only to warn of any attack, but to discourage an attack. Other submarines and patrol planes, and periodically carrier task forces, operated off the Chinese littoral in a similar deterrence role.

From the start the Navy mounted combat operations to achieve and maintain superiority at sea and in Far Eastern skies. As they would throughout the war, surface ships, submarines, carrier aircraft, and shore-based reconnaissance planes patrolled along the littoral of China and off both Korean coasts. At least partly because of this presence, at no time during the war did Beijing and Moscow use the sea or the air above it to support Communist forces fighting on the Korean peninsula.

The fleet's availability in the Western Pacific and its expeditious move to Korean waters also enabled MacArthur's Far East command to slow down Pyongyang's 1950 ground offensive, hold a precarious beachhead on the Korean peninsula, and build up forces ashore for a counteroffensive.

One of the first actions of the allies was to destroy North Korean naval offensive forces. Although the North Korean Navy operated only forty-five small vessels, they were pressed into the enemy's initial assault. Pyongyang used them to transport supplies to forces advancing along both coasts. In the early hours of the offensive, the enemy also used naval vessels for a *coup de main*, an attempt to seize Pusan with 600 troops landed near the port. Pusan was South Korea's best port and its location in southeastern Korea across from logistic support bases in Japan made it critical to the Allied cause. A North Korean success here would have doomed the Allied effort to retain a toehold in South Korea. The enemy attempt was frustrated when, late at night on 25 June, a patrol craft, the largest vessel in the South Korean Navy, intercepted and sank an enemy vessel steaming off the southeastern coast. Shortly afterward, on 2 July, U.S. cruiser *Juneau*, British cruiser *Jamaica*, and British frigate *Black Swan* intercepted a North Korean naval force of torpedo boats and motor gunboats off the east coast and sank five of the enemy vessels.

The fleet's great mobility and control of the sea enabled General MacArthur and his U.N. command to turn the tide of battle. In mid-September 1950, Admiral Struble, "dual-hatted" as commander of the Seventh Fleet and commander of Task Force 7, led an armada of 230 amphibious and other ships north to the North Korean-held port of Inchon on the west coast. In Operation Chromite, the fleet disembarked combat elements of the 1st Marine Division, reinforced with 8,600 South Korean Marines and soldiers, and the Army's 7th Infantry Division far in the enemy's rear. These forces were the major components of Army Major General Edward M. Almond's X Corps. The Communists and even most American leaders had doubted that a major amphibious operation could be successful at Inchon, where the tide ranged between twenty-three and thirty-five feet. At low tide, any attacking ships would be literally stuck in the mud. Furthermore, two fortified islands blocked access to the port of Inchon. Convinced of the physical strength of the position, however, the enemy failed to emplace strong forces at Inchon.

Following days of bombardment by carrier aircraft and shelling by the battleship *Missouri* and other naval gunfire support ships, at 0633 hours on 15 September, elements of the 5th Marine Regiment assaulted positions ashore. By the early morning hours of 16 September, the D-Day objectives had been secured. Two days later Marine aircraft began operating from the recently captured Kimpo Airfield between Inchon and Seoul. On 21 September, the 31st Regiment of the Army's 7th Infantry Division linked up with U.S. Army units which had pushed north from the perimeter at Pusan. One week later, after heavy fighting, the Marines and soldiers of the X Corps captured Seoul. The corps suffered 3,500 killed, wounded, and missing but the North Koreans lost 14,000 killed and 7,000 captured. Soon the advancing U.N. Army had driven the disintegrating North Korean People's Army from South Korean soil.

General MacArthur hoped to replicate his Inchon masterstroke on the east coast of North Korea. At Wonsan he planned to land the X Corps, reembarked in Task Force 90's ships after the capture of Seoul. The command would then push eastward for a linkup at Pyongyang with the northward advancing U.S. Eighth Army. Fast-advancing South Korean ground troops, however, secured the port of Wonsan on 10 October, one week before the scheduled amphibious landing. Furthermore, the fleet dis-covered that the enemy had sown the approaches to the port with between 2,000 and 4,000 Soviet-supplied magnetic and contact mines. Several U.S. Navy ships were sunk before the troops could be landed. This setback at Wonsan resulted from prewar cutbacks in the mine warfare force, lack of suitable equipment, and the lack of adequate attention to this threat by the Navy. Finally, on 25 October, 1st Marine Division troops began coming ashore and heading northwestward for the mountainous North Korean interior.

Despite the misfortunes at Wonsan, the Task Force 95 minesweeping force registered some successes, such as the opening of the sea channel to Chinnampo, the port serving captured Pyongyang, without the loss of a single ship.

The U.S. Navy's superiority at sea and great mobility also made it possible for U.N. forces to break off contact with the enemy and retreat to the safety of blue water when the battle soured, as in northeast Korea in the fall and winter of 1950. When the Chinese People's Liberation Army intervened in the war in November 1950, U.N. forces in the interior of North Korea found themselves outnumbered and dangerously overextended. As a result, the Allied command decided that the X Corps, then comprised of the 1st Marine Division and the Army's 3rd and 7th Infantry Divisions, and three South Korean divisions of the I and II Corps, would be evacuated by sea from the east coast ports of Hungnam and Wonsan.

Protecting the evacuation flotilla was an armada of powerful naval vessels. Fleet carriers *Philippine Sea, Valley Forge, Princeton,* and *Leyte Gulf* and three escort carriers dispatched swarms of aircraft that battered advancing enemy troops and disrupted their logistic support. Naval aviators carried out more than 1,700 sorties during only one week of the operation. At the same time, the battleship *Missouri,* cruisers *St. Paul* and *Rochester,* and a score of destroyers and rocket ships dropped a curtain of fire behind the embarking Allied troops. More than 23,000 16-inch, 8-inch, 5-inch, 3-inch rounds and rockets fell on Chinese and North Korean forces moving against the U.N. defensive perimeter. By Christmas Eve day, when Navy explosive teams destroyed the port facilities at Hungnam and then joined their comrades offshore, the Navy had withdrawn by sea 105,000 troops, 91,000 civilian refugees, 350,000 tons of cargo, and 17,500 military vehicles. Another 3,600 troops, 1,300 tons of cargo, and 196 vehicles had been airlifted out by Air Force and Marine planes. Thus, the Navy's control of the sea enabled the X Corps to live and fight another day.

Allied naval forces also maintained a United Nations sanctioned blockade of North Korea's coastlines. Not only did this prevent the enemy's use of the sea but allowed Allied vessels to move about in near-absolute freedom. Furthermore, the enemy was forced to place scarce forces in defensive positions along the length of both coasts. Periodically, the fleet mounted naval feints and demonstrations to keep the enemy unsure of Allied intentions. In one such action, Operation Decoy in October 1952, COMNAVFE compelled the Communists to rush reinforcements to the coast near Wonsan. The enemy reacted when Navy carrier aircraft, battleships, cruisers, and destroyers pounded targets ashore near Kojo and Task Force 90 simulated a landing of a 1st Cavalry Division regimental combat team. Conversely, the allies were able to put all their combat troops on or near the front line.

Control of the sea also allowed U.N. command surface ships and submarines to land U.S. Navy UDTs (underwater demolition teams), U.S. Marines, British Royal Marine commandos, South Korean commandos, and other special forces on both Korean coasts and on myriad coastal islands. These elite units destroyed enemy railways and railway tunnels, highway bridges, and supply depots. U.N. naval forces also deployed U.N. guerrillas ashore for extended operations behind Communist lines.

In a major operation, from 16 February 1951 to the end of the Korean War, the fleet denied the enemy use of the port of Wonsan by subjecting it to bombardment by air units, sometimes using airstrips on captured nearby islands, and by battleships, cruisers, and destroyers of Task Force 95. One history of the war credits this blockade with diverting 80,000 North Korean troops from duty along the fighting front to the south. It was also the longest blockade of modern times.

Sea control was especially crucial during the last two years of the war when the Communists launched numerous ground offensives to improve their negotiating position in the cease-fire talks held at Panmunjom. U.S. naval power was a significant factor in frustrating these enemy goals and persuading the enemy to sign the armistice agreement, which ended the Korean War on July 27, 1953.

A total of 1,842,000 Navy personnel served in the Korean War, a sizeable proportion of the 5,720,000 Americans who responded to the call to duty. Of these, 458 officers and men were killed in action, another 4,403 sailors died from disease or injury, and 1,576 were wounded in action during the first "limited war" of the Cold War era.

Edward J. Marolda

Bibliography

Cagle, Malcolm W., and Frank A. Manson. *The Sea War in Korea* (1957).

Field, James A. *History of United States Naval Operations: Korea* (1962).

Hallion, Richard P. *The Naval Air War in Korea* (1986).

Lott, Arnold S. *Most Dangerous Sea* (1959).

Summers, Harry G., Jr. *Korean War Almanac* (1990).

Netherlands Forces in Korea

The Netherlands, a charter member of the United Nations, contributed one infantry battalion and one destroyer to the U.N. forces fighting in the Korean War.

The destroyer HMNS *Evertsen* joined the Blockading and Escort Force of the U.S. Naval Forces Far East. As part of this nine-nation blockade and escort unit, the *Evertsen* patrolled near Wonsan and was also part of the invasion fleet at Inchon.

In order to man an infantry battalion, the Netherlands government placed advertisements in Dutch newspapers for volunteers. The recruits were a varied group: some had been resistance fighters during World War II; others had been members of the S.S. and now joined the Netherlands armed forces in order to have their Dutch citizenship reinstated. Many of the new soldiers had returned from fighting in Indonesia.

Reasons for Dutch volunteers to join were myriad. Some World War II veterans signed up because they sought further adventure, considering the postwar Netherlands too stifling. The allure of traveling to the Orient was also appealing. Other volunteers fled unemployment or unhappy homes. Many joined because they were veterans and felt their prior war experience would be beneficial. Some joined seeking glory, danger, and fame. Many simply felt that it was their duty to serve their country.

The volunteers were immersed in a commando training course at Roosendaal in Brabant, learning weapons handling and military tactics. They departed from Rotterdam in a World War II–vintage Liberty Ship converted to transport troops, and frequently stopped to load troops from England, France, and Greece. While in ports in Turkey, officers recruited men off the street to fill out the ranks of those who had disappeared while enjoying the temptations of Turkish urban life.

The advance party of the Netherlands Battalion reached Korea on 24 October 1950. The full battalion arrived at Pusan one month later on 23 November, accompanied by Dutch medical personnel for front-line aid stations. The Dutch rifle companies and heavy weapons company came from Indonesia, where they had high combat effectiveness. However, in Korea they were thrust from a warm to cold climate which at first interfered with their efficiency.

The Netherlands Battalion (better known as the Dutch Battalion)—like the French Battalion—was divided into four groups, each composed of two companies. After a period of adjustment at the U.N. reception center in Taegu—where American officers hurried to provide the Dutch with ample diets of bread and potatoes, their staple foodstuffs—the Dutch were dispersed among American troops. They were first attached to the 38th Infantry Regiment, which then was known as the 38th Regimental Combat Team.

The Dutch had wanted to be placed under the British, with whom they felt more familiar. Thirty years later, Major General George C. Stewart recalled that as part of the U.S. 2nd Infantry Division, the Dutch "had a mind of their own. If they thought their assignment (either attack or defense) made good sense they were superb—otherwise they sometimes did what they thought appropriate."

At first the Dutch performed mostly anti-guerrilla duty. While attached to the U.S. 2nd Infantry Division, the Dutch were assigned to protect flanks and provide support. They were then assigned to take over a section of the front on the 38th parallel from American Marines.

When Wonju was lost to the Chinese in January 1951, the Dutch battalion filled the gap. The battalion entered Hoengsong to reestablish the line from Osan to Samchok. The Dutch patrolled east of that area and prevented the enemy from laying mines. They experienced several brief skirmishes while on patrols. Defending Hoengsong's perimeter, the Dutch Battalion suffered a furious Chinese attack. The battalion commander, Lieutenant Colonel M.P.A. den Ouden, and four of his officers were killed in action when Chinese troops pretend-ing to be ROK soldiers needing ammunition shot the Dutch officers at close range.

The Dutch Battalion suffered more than 100 casualties within a three-day period and was given a U.S. Presidential Unit Citation for stubbornly withstanding the enemy. As a result of its stand, the withdrawal of two battalions to the south of Wonju was accomplished. The Dutch waited for the last troops to withdraw, then followed at the rear. General Matthew B. Ridgway ordered the battalion to the reserve as a result of its heavy losses.

In May 1951, the Dutch Battalion was ordered to the left of the ROK 5th and 7th Divisions, and X Corps, near Hangye-ri and No-name line, where they stood their ground under continuous attack with the support of U.N. artillery fire. However, when the 1st Battalion of the 38th Regimental Combat Team was in trouble, and the Dutch were ordered to help, they responded slowly. By the time Lieutenant Colonel W.D.H. Eekhout, the Dutch commander, ordered his men to counterattack, Hill 1051 was lost.

Disaster plagued the Dutch. During the fighting, a hovering observation helicopter's engine died, and the machine crashed onto the mountain. The Dutch focused on rescuing the crew. Battalion commander Eekhout was on Hill 1051; in addition to Eekhout, two company commanders and several staff members were slain. As darkness fell, the Dutch withdrew.

From September to October 1951, the battalion assisted in the capture of Heartbreak Ridge by artillery support and patrols. In June 1952, Dutch forces aided in moving Communist prisoners from Koje-do Island. In that same year, a financial agreement was reached in which the Dutch government agreed to pay a portion of war expenses. The following year, Dutch forces peaked at 819 soldiers.

One Dutch prisoner was exchanged in "Operation Little Switch" in April 1953. Altogether, the Netherlands sent 3,972 infantry soldiers and 1,350 naval personnel to Korea. Dutch casualties in Korea totaled 120 soldiers killed and 645 wounded. Three additional Dutch POWs were exchanged at the war's conclusion.

After the truce, the troops were moved to Tokyo for a period of rest and recuperation, and a Dutch chaplain was stationed in Tokyo to counsel the Korean veterans.

The Dutch Battalion sailed for home after the Armistice ending the Korean War, where

Queen Juliana presented service decorations. The Korean War veterans were exuberantly welcomed by their countrymen. Many Dutch Korean War veterans reenlisted for military service or migrated to more exotic places, such as Australia and New Zealand.

Elizabeth Schafer

Bibliography

Blair, Clay. *The Forgotten War: America in Korea, 1950–1953* (1988).

Ministry of National Defense, ROK. *The History of the United Nations Forces in the Korean War*, III (1977).

Montyn, Jan, and Dirk Ayelt Kooiman. *A Lamb to Slaughter* (1985).

New Zealand Forces in Korea

Historically, New Zealand had readily contributed troops to the British Commonwealth. New Zealand soldiers were well represented, in both world wars. New Zealand joined the 1950 Colombo Plan for economic support of Southeast Asia and initiated compulsory military training to reinvigorate the New Zealand Army, exhausted and depleted from World War II service.

When the Korean War began, U.S. military leaders suggested that a small New Zealand force be deployed. New Zealand Prime Minister Sir Sidney George Holland and chief of general staff Major General Sir Keith Lindsay Stewart contemplated joining forces with Australia or the Commonwealth. However, the Commonwealth experienced more factionalism than unity, and on 26 July 1950, New Zealand committed a ground force for Korea before Great Britain or Australia decided to send troops.

New Zealand officers recruited New Zealand citizens of European or Maori descent, age twenty-one to thirty-two (officers or veterans could enlist up to age forty). On December 31, 1,231 New Zealand officers and soldiers arrived in Korea. They traveled to Taegu to adjust and receive heavy equipment and military orders. The 16th Field Regiment, Royal New Zealand Artillery, commanded by Lieutenant Colonel J.W. Moodie, was attached to the 27th British Commonwealth Brigade in January 1951. The New Zealanders were to provide vital fire support for Commonwealth infantry using their own artillery, but sharing similar battle tactics with the British.

New Zealand also contributed naval forces to the U.N. Korean War effort. Beginning 1 August 1950, naval frigates HMNZS *Pukaki* and HMNZS *Tutira* sailed with the Blockading and Escort Force of the U.S. Naval Command Far East in the Yellow Sea. New Zealand naval personnel helped patrol near Wonsan. The New Zealand Navy also participated in the screening force at Inchon. The HMNZS *Taupo*, HMNZS *Totoiti*, and HMNZS *Hawea* patrolled the coast, and during 1951 and 1952, in a combined endeavor with ROK Marines and the U.S. Navy, were ordered by Admiral C. Turner Joy to bombard enemy guerrillas and insurgents on islands in the Han estuary.

New Zealand ground forces coordinated well with Australian troops. Many members of the New Zealand field regiment had not been adequately trained in technical matters to perform as gunners, and Australian artillery officers were attached to supervise their performance. New Zealand soldiers were also incorporated into Australian units to gain additional experience. The New Zealand force was particularly important at Kapyong and Maryang San where its accurate fire assured safe occupation by Allied troops.

In the first week of February 1951, the New Zealanders offered fire support to the U.S. 24th Division, helping its advance to Chuamni. In April 1951, a New Zealand transport company with headquarters and light aid detachment was sent to Korea. At this point New Zealand troops comprised about 5 percent of the Commonwealth Division.

The New Zealanders supported the 6th ROK Division in April 1951 at the U.N. line above Seoul when the Fifth Chinese offensive began. Hindered by mountainous and rugged terrain, the New Zealanders experienced difficulty transporting their equipment and were unable to provide effective support. The ROK defense collapsed, and the New Zealand troops disengaged, moving south to Kapyong, where the Commonwealth Brigade was in reserve. In their own retreat, the New Zealanders did not lose any guns. Major General William M. Hoge, U.S. IX Corps commander, reordered the New Zealanders to move forward, protected by the UK Middlesex Battalion, but again the ROKs retreated chaotically, and the New Zealand regiment again withdrew to Kapyong.

At Kapyong the U.S. 213th Field Artillery Battalion reinforced the New Zealand unit with 155mm self-propelled howitzers; the New Zealanders also worked closely with Australian defensive forces. While the New Zealanders were supporting these Australian troops, U.S.

aircraft accidentally napalmed them, destroying men and equipment and permitting the Chinese to break through the lines. Nonetheless, New Zealanders helped the Canadian Battalion by firing artillery from the rear, killing many of the advancing Chinese.

The New Zealanders played a vital support role on 24 April by shelling directly in front of the Canadian troops, foiling a Chinese advance. The assault continued until 1 May, when the New Zealanders helped the U.S. 24th Division decisively defeat the Chinese offensive and advance to the Kansas line. For their bravery, ROK President Syngman Rhee gave the 16th New Zealand Field Artillery Regiment a presidential citation. The New Zealanders also provided artillery support at the battle of Maryang San, where they fired 50,000 rounds.

As the war became protracted in 1951, the U.S. urged New Zealand and other commonwealth members to send more troops as quickly as possible. New Zealand refused to send additional forces, stating that its military forces were needed domestically. However, the New Zealanders increased their transportation force from platoon-size to a divisional company.

In July 1951, the United States suggested a joint Australian–New Zealand force to be formed with liaison officers reporting to the U.S. Department of Defense. New Zealand, however, preferred to operate within the British Commonwealth in which it would only be expected to contribute a field artillery regiment and not infantry. Within the British Commonwealth, however, New Zealand protested that it was often ignored and taken for granted. Despite this dissatisfaction, the 16th New Zealand Field Artillery, in order to limit its contribution, was merged into the 1st Commonwealth Division when the latter was established in July 1951. In late 1952, the U.N. command again requested more New Zealand troops, but the nation's leaders again refused because, based on New Zealand's population, they claimed that country had given enough men to the cause.

New Zealand volunteers were rotated individually after one year of service. In 1953, the New Zealand force reached its maximum strength of 1,389 men. A total of 3,794 New Zealanders soldiers and naval personnel served in the Korean War. Of the commitment, twenty-three died, seventy-nine were wounded, and one was repatriated in "Operation Big Switch." The Commonwealth troops, including New Zealanders, were gradually withdrawn from Korea in the years immediately following the armistice. In September 1954, with the precarious Korean armistice very much in mind, New Zealand entered the Southeast Asia Treaty Organization (SEATO) collective-defense arrangement.

The Korean War aided New Zealand domestically. An increased demand for textiles—clothing and blankets—proved profitable for New Zealand's wool growers and textile producers.

Elizabeth Schafer

Bibliography

Barclay, C.N. *The First Commonwealth Division: The Story of British Commonwealth Land Forces in Korea, 1950–1953* (1954).

Carew, Tim. *Korea: The Commonwealth at War* (1967).

Clemow, C.W.A. "New Zealand, the Commonwealth and the Korean War: A Study in Government Policy and Unofficial Opinion," (master's thesis, University of Auckland, 1967).

Grey, Jeffrey. *The Commonwealth Armies and the Korean War: An Alliance Study* (1988).

Oliver, W.H., and B.R. Williams, eds. *The Oxford History of New Zealand* (1981).

O'Neill, Robert. *Australia in the Korean War 1950–53*, 2 vols. (1985).

North Korea

North Korea, officially founded as the Democratic People's Republic of Korea (DPRK) on 9 September 1948, played the dual role of the aggressor and the defeated in the Korean War. Initiating the attack, North Korea hoped to compel the reunification of the Korean peninsula by military force. The resulting Korean War was the most devastating conflict in Korean history.

Korea had traditionally endured the influence and dominance by its northern neighbor, China. But in 1910, the "hermit kingdom" became a colony of Japan. Under the exploitative Japanese occupation, the mass of Koreans yearned for independence after World War II. Initially, the allies issued the Cairo Declaration in December 1943, suggesting the establishment of a free and independent Korea. This understanding eventually evolved into a four-power trusteeship between North Korea, the United States, Great Britain, and the Soviet Union in June 1945.

Korea, a nation and people united in race, language, and culture, was nonetheless partitioned at the conclusion of World War II. South Korea subsequently suffered political turmoil and violence through the late 1940s.

The North Korean state had its origins as a spoil of war for the Soviet Union, which was promised supervision of northern Korea in exchange for entering the war against Japan. On 11 August 1945, Colonel C.H. Bonesteel III and Dean Rusk of the Army General Staff randomly designated the 38th parallel as the division line for Allied and Soviet troops to accept Japanese surrenders. The Soviets saw the northern half of Korea as a potential client state, while the United States established its own occupation regime in the south. The Koreans themselves, not consulted in these matters, became bitter and insistent in their demands for unification.

In 1947, the United Nations General Assembly agreed on an all-Korea election with a temporary commission, UNTCOK, to regulate the proceedings. The Soviets refused to hold elections in the north, or even to allow the commission to enter its zone.

Instead, the People's Committee called a Communist-supported conference in Pyongyang to demand unification. Of the 545 delegates, 360 were southern moderate to liberal Communists who demanded the withdrawal of foreign troops. The conference especially hoped to block the U.N. election. In the south, American-supported Syngman Rhee won a somewhat free election to the office of president of the newly established Republic of Korea (ROK) in August 1948. American troops began withdrawing as soon as the South Korean elections concluded—the bulk being gone by June 1949—leaving only the 500-man Korean Military Advisory Group (KMAG) to train ROK forces in antiguerrilla and defensive operations.

Sealing the border and denouncing U.N. involvement in the south, the Soviets supported only Communist political groups and demanded that unification occur only under Communist rule.

During this formative time, Kim Il Sung reinforced his image as North Korea's savior, and henceforth, until his death in 1994, the history of North Korea was basically the history of Kim. A war hero in his thirties, Kim had been an officer in the Soviet Army during World War II and a staunch Communist. He encouraged guerrilla raids and violence against the south, training southern partisans before, during, and after the Korean War. These border incidents on

occasion were matched by the violently anti-Communist south. Serving under Soviet occupation authorities, Kim also used the bitter division of the peninsula to begin the elimination of his rivals.

In February 1948, the (North) Korean People's Army was officially founded, and in September, the Democratic People's Republic of Korea (DPRK) was established with Kim as its first premier. By June 1949, the Korean Workers' Parties from the south and the north united, with Kim Il Sung appointed chairman of the combined organization. Modeling this new party, government, and army on Soviet examples, Kim acquired leadership by controlling his opposition. When Korea was divided, many evangelical revolutionaries traveled south to Seoul, where they believed Korean Communism should be centered, leaving Kim in the north with few rivals. He was quickly considered the supreme leader of the nation and could contemplate with equanimity the withdrawal of Soviet forces by the end of 1948. He then began his most consistent policy through the subsequent years, one of self-reliance.

The number of Communist party members in northern Korea increased from 366,000 in August 1946 to 780,000 by January 1948. At least 60 percent of its members were peasants or factory workers, many active in party cells at their villages or workplaces. Kim ordered the careful compilation of party member information. More significantly, he nurtured a military buildup in the north to achieve his primary goal. However, to become militarily strong, he had to ensure that he could control North Korea's political structure.

Since the 1920s, Korea had been riddled with indigenous Korean Communist factions. Kim Il Sung, who had been in Manchuria, had not participated in these Communist movements, which the Soviets themselves denounced. Under Kim, the Soviets wanted to install their own Communist state. Soviet dictator Joseph Stalin believed he could use Kim Il Sung as a puppet to eliminate rival groups while securing North Korea.

From 1945 to 1953, a coalition of Communist groups dominated North Korea. Not until the Korean War did Kim have sufficient political strength to completely rid North Korea of his opponents. The war complicated factional strife. The three primary factions in North Korea included the domestic Communists, the Kapsans, and the Yenans. The Kapsan, or Manchurian faction of Korean revolutionaries, also called the Soviet-Koreans, had been militarily trained by the Soviets. These Koreans had gone to the Soviet Union to escape the Japanese and to foment revolutionary activities, and returned to Korea with the Soviet occupation army. This was the group with which Kim Il Sung identified himself. The Yenan, or Chinese faction, had fought in Chinese Communist-led armies. These revolutionaries had sent agents across the border to conduct anti-Japanese activity, and then returned after years of exile.

Even though Kim Il Sung's faction was in the minority, it managed to win power, due to Stalin's support. From 1945 to 1950, Kim sought an alliance with the Soviet and Chinese factions while purging domestic Communists through executions and imprisonment or forcing them to flee to South Korea. Domestic leader Hyon Chun-hyok was assassinated, and nationalist faction leader Cho Man-sik was expelled from office. The Soviet-Korea and Yenan factions cooperated at first because of their similar ideologies, but factional struggles remained.

Kim managed to control the consolidated groups because of Stalin's economic and military support. Kim chose the Soviet Union as the first country with which North Korea established official diplomatic relations, and then extended similar courtesies to Soviet satellites. Considering Stalin his mentor, Kim stated that "All the most precious and best things in the life of the Korean people are related to the name of Stalin. Stalin has become the flesh and blood of every Korean family living north of the 38th parallel and extending up to the Yalu River."

Stalin supported Kim Il Sung's dream of reunifying the Korean peninsula into a Communist state and helped and encouraged his plan for war. The Soviet Union began training North Koreans. Although the Soviet Union did not actually plan the invasion of South Korea (North Korea did), Stalin approved Kim's attack plans when he discussed them with him in 1949. Presuming that the United States would not intervene, the Soviets supported the invasion both technologically and diplomatically.

The Democratic People's Republic of (North) Korea and the Republic of (South) Korea sharply contrasted at the beginning of the Korean War. Consisting of 48,000 square miles, North Korea relied on Japanese-built industry from the occupation period. Its mountainous landmass held 9 million citizens in 1950. Pyongyang served as the industrial center of North Korea. Sixty-two percent of North Koreans were peasant farmers, tending primitive rice paddies fertilized with human wastes. In contrast, the South had 21 million residents and the best agricultural land, as well as some small industries and the majority of cities.

To combat these uneven resources, Soviet advisors (who soon exited Korea) assisted the North Korean People's Army (NKPA) and provided artillery, weapons, and aircraft. Many battle orders were issued in Russian. And North Korea adopted the Soviet doctrine of sending every man available to the front with weapons of any type.

Considering the Soviet Union an unreliable ally, Kim Il Sung on one hand sought more self-reliance, yet on the other hand protested that with more Soviet aid he could conquer the South and reunify Korea. Demanding air support, Kim was rebuffed by Stalin, who did not want the Korean conflict to escalate into a larger military confrontation with the United States. Stalin believed that the Korean War could be quickly won and that Taiwan would fall as well. After all, Mao Tse-tung had emerged almost completely victorious in China less than one year earlier.

The North Korean Army of 89,000 men, swarming across the 38th parallel, invaded South Korea in the pre-dawn hours of 25 June 1950. This invasion validated Western fears of Communist aggression that verged, at least in the United States, on something resembling panic. On the day after the invasion, Kim Il Sung broadcast on Radio Pyongyang, appealing to the North Korean populace to cooperate in the war effort even if it required sacrifices and struggles. Kim demanded that "All Korean people must stand up and join our struggle to destroy the puppet government of the traitor Syngman Rhee and its army." Stressing the goal of reunification, he exhorted North Koreans to kill "traitors," whom he defined as those who did not wholeheartedly support the war.

On the same day, he established, and headed, a seven-man military committee to coordinate all Army administrative needs. This group could also mobilize all citizens, who were expected to submit to the committee. Named supreme commander in chief, within two weeks, Kim imposed strict wartime controls over the NKPA, as well as North Korean civilians. Continuing to utilize the radio, he gave his military effort the unwieldy term the "Great Liberation War of the Korean People for Freedom and Independence."

Under General Chio Yung Kun, the NKPA quickly pushed south to the Pusan perimeter, overwhelming the ROK Army and its U.S. military ally. Within six weeks, the South Korean capital, Seoul, and 90 percent of South Korea were controlled by North Korea. In overrun areas, the NKPA established people's committees and conscripted local residents into the NKPA and the Communist party.

But North Korean victory was stymied by the swift U.N. counteroffensive at Inchon in September 1950. North Korea's Army seemingly disintegrated, and by 1 October, ROK troops had pushed retreating NKPA forces back across the 38th parallel. On October 11, Kim issued a radio message exhorting Army and Communist Korean Workers' Party members to defend their territory and attack the rear of enemy forces. North Koreans were also expected (again) to eliminate "spies and rumormongers," organize guerilla raids, and execute non-Communists. Kim then fled Pyongyang.

The commander of the 2nd Army Corps remained in the capital city as Kim escaped to Manchuria. Despite his orders, Mu-Jong then vacated Pyongyang when the enemy advanced north toward the city. Most North Korea Communists also fled or hid, well aware of their fate, at least at the hands of the retaliating South Koreans. Many cadre members cooperated with Allied forces, destroying evidence of party affiliation. Some Communists surrendered—including the highest-ranking North Korean prisoner, Colonel Li Hak Ku—only to organize future riots in U.N. prison camps such as the one at Koje Island.

Allied forces moved deeper into North Korea, with elements ultimately reaching the Yalu River. North Korean anti-Communists, including members of the suppressed Democratic Party and Youth Fraternal Party, joined the South Korean Army's effort to locate hiding Communists. During the Allied occupation of North Korea, both the Korean Workers' Party and Kim Il Sung's regime itself seemed near collapse. According to North Korean sources, Kim himself led his troops in battle, being wounded near Hamhung.

The sudden entry of Chinese Communist "volunteers" into the war in November 1950 saved North Korea. The Chinese, fearful of U.N. forces on their borders, also wanted to protect the dams and hydroelectric plants in the far north, and to preserve North Korea as a buffer state.

China suffered great losses during the war, including the death of Mao Tse-tung's son. A U.S. fleet now defended Taiwan against any Chinese attacks. During the Korean War, Kim Il Sung used the Chinese presence to gradually remove North Korea from Soviet control, later encouraging feuds between the two countries in order to obtain North Korea's political and economic independence. The Chinese Communist Army remained in North Korea for eight years. As Chinese influence increased, Soviet control declined. Military orders, once given by Soviet military advisors, were now issued by Chinese officers. The Soviets limited their aid even more, particularly in not providing air cover, which might well have tipped the scales to Communist victory during both the North Korean and Chinese drives. As it was, the uncontested air superiority of the United States made all the difference in stopping both Communist offensives.

For the rest of the war, North Korea endured devastating bombing of targets such as Pyongyang, which was flattened (underground bunkers protected vital cadres and facilities), and heavy casualties. In addition, frantic campaigns of atrocity bombings, germ warfare accusations, and "brainwashing" of prisoners seemed to do little more than provoke war-weariness. New groups challenged Kim's leadership.

But Kim used the chaotic environment to consolidate his power. Coup attempts were poorly organized, and Kim proved he could retain his leadership without strong Soviet support. He focused on domestic political rivals, eliminating Soviet-Korean partisans. Political prisoners were executed, and approximately 685,000 North Koreans moved south with U.N. forces retreating from the Chinese at the end of 1950. As the Communists regained their territory in North Korea, people's courts punished northern residents considered to be reactionaries. Internally, trials against alleged conspirators for treasonous crimes multiplied.

Kim Il Sung called the third plenum of the central committee of the Korean Workers' Party in December 1950 on the Manchurian border. He used the meeting to rectify defects he perceived in the Army and party when NKPA forces retreated north. He also used this plenum to eliminate his rival, Mu-Jong. Emphasizing the goal of unification, Kim stressed:

Our party would not connive and tolerate or so contradict the wishes of the Korean people as to allow the 38th Parallel to separate our territory into two parts.

He attributed the retreat to Army leaders who were too egotistical and cowardly and on party leaders who were too provincial and fled instead of organizing partisans. Blaming these subordinates for North Korean defeats, Kim demoted them or forced them to resign. He meted out the harshest punishment to Mu-Jong, whom he blamed for military disorder, insubordination, even manslaughter. Mu-Jong was stripped of his rank and imprisoned, never to be seen again.

Kim, who insisted that the war revealed who the true Communists were, followed the example of Stalin and resolved on a general party purge. The first members purged included nonactive members, those in hiding, and those accused of concealing their Communist convictions during the U.N. occupation. At least 450,000 of 600,000 members were expelled.

Realizing that ousted members posed a danger to the party, Kim called a conference on 1 September 1951 to assuage purges. He promised that no punitive actions would be taken against those who had committed only small errors or had merely lost their identification cards. He also resolved to recruit new members. Many local cells, however, were hesitant to readmit purged members, or recruit new members. Thus few new members or reinstated Communists were actually added to the party at the time.

One Japanese source claims that during the U.N. offensive, 150,000 civilians, mostly skilled laborers, were executed by the Communists or fled south. Often, local party cells did not consider the remaining peasants to be educated or politically aware enough to become party members, thus keeping the party isolated from the North Korean masses. Kim arranged for a fourth plenum, held in November 1951, to purge his powerful Communist rival, Ho Kai, whom he accused of poor organizational work.

Ho Kai, a Soviet-Korean, was an influential rival of Kim's. Although he had cooperated in placing Kim in charge during the Soviet occupation, Ho Kai openly criticized him. Considered an arrogant leader, Kai protested replenishing the party after seeing how many cadre had behaved during the brief U.N. occupation. About this time, the Soviets withdrew their aid, providing only moral support. In the U.N., Soviet delegate Jacob Malik called for an armistice. Kim now realized that the Soviet Union would sacrifice his goal of unification to prevent war with the United States, and would offer no troops to save North Korea. Lashing out, Kim blamed Ho Kai for the near-demise of the Communist party in North Korea. Kai committed suicide.

Kim, now free to widen party membership without criticism, ordered that age requirements be lowered and membership application processes simplified. Party membership increased to one million by the end of 1952, and members of local parties attended mandatory study meetings and lectures during their limited "free" time.

On 1 February 1952, Kim exhorted the joint conference of the chairmen of provincial, city, and county people's councils and party leaders to enact stricter control over local governments and the masses. He noted that North Koreans resented high local taxes imposed by quotas on local officials. Kim even commented that many North Koreans felt alienated by the war.

Most of North Korea's industry was destroyed. Skilled workers were dead or injured. Farmers could only work at night due to air raids. Fishing was severely limited because of the Allied naval blockade, and many citizens were deprived of adequate food, shelter, and clothing. To improve morale and appear sympathetic to the common people, Kim claimed that he too was tired of the war and its related problems, and in 1952, exempted citizens from taxes and fees for use of government facilities. He also waged a domestic war against bureaucratism in the Korean Workers' Party at all levels.

By then, with most North Korean industry and manpower crippled by the war, only Chinese and (to a lesser extent) Soviet support kept the war machine going. After cease-fire talks began in June of 1951, both sides came to agree on almost every point except the voluntary repatriation of prisoners of war. Communist China, experiencing economic strain because of its recent establishment, and fearing war with the United States, pressured Kim for an armistice. By the end of 1952, more than one million Chinese troops were in North Korea. Kim realized that alone North Korea could not continue the war and began speaking about "peaceful unification."

At the fifth plenum in December 1952, organized to consolidate party growth, Kim delivered his report, "The Organizational and Ideological Strengthening of the Party—The

Basis of Our Victory," in which he criticized favoritism in the party, particularly rebuking party officials who named friends and relatives to local party posts. Kim invited the culprits to confess. Thorough "examination meetings" were held from January to April 1953 for self-criticism and confession. Party members were also encouraged to criticize their peers and to designate spies.

The July 1953 armistice found North Korea reduced almost to rubble and ruin, but its government (i.e., Kim) remained stronger than ever. The Korean War had helped Kim Il Sung monopolize leadership by eliminating his rivals on war-related charges, but he was devastated by the failure to achieve reunification.

In a radio message immediately after the armistice was signed, Kim announced that the armistice was in reality a victorious step toward unification. He added that antiparty factions had perpetuated the war. Now it was time to reconstruct North Korea on a "solid democratic basis for peaceful unification" and to oust "American imperialism" by encouraging social revolution in the south. Kim never admitted that the war he had unleashed had been a failure.

Kim's explanation for not achieving unification emphasized those whom he claimed had conducted "antiparty" activities, especially native Communists, and other supposed party stalwarts. He expelled these from the party at the sixth plenum. As a result, Kim staged yet another purge, this time a mass decimation of indigenous Communists and former South Korean Workers' Party members, including its leader, Pak Hong-yong, and the DPRK's deputy premier and foreign minister, whom Kim considered his greatest threat. The North and South Korean Workers' Parties had merged only when forced to by the threat of Allied forces in the south. Both factions sought leadership of the DPRK. On 3 August 1953, posters plastered Pyongyang proclaiming the trial of twelve leading members of the South Korean Workers' Party, all subordinates of Pak Hong-yong, and mainly educated and literary men.

During a four-day military tribunal, the men were charged with the familiar crimes of subversion, plotting to overthrow North Korea, espionage, terrorism, propaganda, and of being American spies who had leaked secret military information to occupation forces during the autumn of 1951. The absurd charges claimed that after the ouster of Kim, the miscreants planned to start a new government with Pak Hong-yong as premier and secure the capital-

ist domination of North Korea. Needless to say, these charges were backed by no convincing evidence.

According to North Korean sources, all of the accused confessed and were executed, except for two who were imprisoned. Pak Hong-yong, who considered Kim's "peaceful unification" strategy to be appeasement, and believed Seoul should be the center of Korean communism, was executed in December 1955. He was accused of consorting with "imperialists" and profiting from public property. Ironically, the purging of these South Korean Communists made the infiltration and subversion of the south that much more difficult.

Although his attempt at a military unification of Korea had failed, Kim had forged a powerful political foundation and conquered his opposition during the war, purging his last opposition during reconstruction. The postwar period in North Korea focused on economic rebuilding and internal strengthening, promoting Kim as the nucleus, almost the deity, of North Korea. What opposition remained weakly tried to counter Kim's focus on agricultural collectivism and industrial reconstruction.

Kim Il Sung rebuilt North Korea with a variety of multiyear economic programs. Due to Soviet criticism of his industrialization plans, Kim had to rely on indigenous sources for reconstruction, building up the coal, iron, and hydroelectric industries. He emphasized Korean culture and history as he interpreted it, always stressing the north's great "victory" over the unspeakable "imperialists," and especially arousing national hatred of the United States and its involvement in the south.

North Korea was governed by the presidium of the central committee, formed by Kim Il Sung, the members of which owed their political positions to him and could easily be swayed, and an elected politburo, with Kim acting as chairman of the central committee. The committee focused on removing all native Communists from the central party, as well as assuaging the aftereffects of the purge.

Kim became especially vulnerable after Stalin's death. In February 1956, Nikita Khrushchev's de-Stalinization speech criticized some of Kim's actions during the war. That August, the Korean Workers' Party central committee held a plenum where pro-Chinese and Soviet factions actually criticized Kim's leadership and his Stalinist ways. Kim expelled these last intraparty factions in purges from August 1956 to March 1958, including Vice Premier and Minister of Machine Industry Pak Chang-ok, Vice Premier Choe Chang-ik, and Chairman of the Presidium of the Supreme People's Assembly Kim Tu-pong.

North Korean communism had emerged under Kim's dictatorship after undergoing the three stages of factional disputes: eliminating nationalists and non-Communist groups from 1945 to 1948; fabricating spy charges to discredit South Korean Communists from 1949 to 1953; and factional realignment from 1956 to 1958, purging pro-Chinese and Soviet Communists. An alliance of survivors of these groups, built on resentment of Kim Il Sung, offered only weakened resistance, mainly because possible leaders had been killed or had defected. Kim's Stalin-style purges had insured his autonomy.

In the following decades, Kim Il Sung continued purging individuals who threatened his leadership. He concentrated on strengthening his "Asian Stalinism." He also implemented Chollima, his "Flying Horse" modernization movement, quickly metamorphosing North Korea from an agrarian into an industrial nation using domestic resources and labor. He introduced his concept of *chuch'e*, or Korean self-reliance, in December 1955. *Chuch'e* became North Korea's official ideology to guide the nation in achieving political and economic independence. Kim stressed that "Establishing *chuch'e* means, in a nutshell, being the master of revolution and reconstruction in one's own country." Not an original thinker, Kim repeated these ideas copied from Communist peers that he modified for his country.

Kimilsungism developed as a term to explain Kim's unique application of Marxism-Leninism to North Korea. But it all revolved around the veneration of the all-wise, the all-powerful Kim Il Sung. Mao Tse-tung had used a similar personality cult during the Chinese Cultural Revolution to reinforce his political power, and a tradition of idolatry of oriental leaders was well entrenched.

Kim self-promotingly portrayed himself as the greatest Korean ever and as the leader of an international revolution, modestly labeling himself "the Sun of the Nation," a selfless patriot preparing for the future united Korea, a national savior, an all-wise messiah and omnipotent and infallible demigod. The controlled press perpetrated his worship as the "respected and beloved fatherly leader of the Korean people" and "the most profound revolutionary genius of all time." Rewriting history, Kim excluded other leaders. North Korean bookstores only sold books about Kim and his ideology, and references to ideologies differing from Kim's were excised from publications. Photographs were tampered with, and images (with the exception of Stalin) of Soviet leaders who had helped him in the past were removed.

The Kim Il Sung cult included thousands of monuments honoring him throughout North Korea, songs glorifying his revolutionary deeds, and schools and athletic facilities named in his honor. His portrait was ubiquitous and his birthday celebrations were considered a national holiday, one of which featured dedication of the Revolutionary Memorial Museum and a gold-coated, sixty-six-foot statue facing south. Objects Kim touched at official meetings were enshrined. Nearly everyone wore a pin emblazoned with Kim's image, and citizens were required to dedicate several hours daily to studying his ideology and works, and to take daily loyalty oaths.

Kim Il Sung was the only leader North Koreans had known since 1948. Furthermore, he established the world's first Communist dynasty by introducing his son, Kim Jong Il, into the affairs of the nation during the 1980s. Kim Il Sung died in July 1994, leaving his nation reportedly in a state of profound grief.

Elizabeth Schafer

Bibliography

An, Tai Sung. *North Korea in Transition: From Dictatorship to Dynasty* (1983).

Kiyosaki, Wayne S. *North Korea's Foreign Relations: The Politics of Accommodation, 1945–75* (1976).

Nam, Koon Woo. *The North Korean Communist Leadership, 1945–1965: A Study of Factionalism and Political Consolidation* (1974).

Suh, Dae-Sook. *Kim Il Sung: The North Korean Leader* (1988).

U.S. Army Civil Affairs School. "The Korean Handbook," (n.d.).

North Korean People's Air Force
See KOREAN PEOPLE'S AIR FORCE

North Korean People's Army
See KOREAN PEOPLE'S ARMY

North Korean People's Navy
See KOREAN PEOPLE'S NAVY

Nuclear Weapons: The Question of Their Use

The United States possessed a monopoly on atomic weapons from 1945 to 1949, when the Soviet Union detonated an A-bomb of its own. Even then, America maintained a clear nuclear supremacy—in 1950, the CIA estimated that the Soviets had no more than twenty-five aircraft capable of reaching the continental U.S. on one-way suicide missions. America, with its growing number of intercontinental bombers and atomic weapons during the Korean War, was capable of inflicting massive devastation on the Soviet Union, People's Republic of China (PRC), and North Korea, virtually without fear of atomic retaliation. However, the presence of a large Soviet army in Eastern Europe meant that atomic attacks might bring an invasion of Western Europe which tiny NATO forces could not repel. Conventional forces and nuclear weapons tended to offset each other.

Nevertheless, many high ranking officials in the Truman administration saw the Korean War as the opening Soviet gambit of World War III, and seriously considered a possible atomic attack on the USSR. Secretary of Defense Louis Johnson discussed the idea informally with friends and subordinates. Secretary of the Navy Francis Matthews took the case to the public in a speech to a cheering crowd of 100,000 in Boston. Undoubtedly, a nuclear war in Korea, at least at first, would have been popular in the United States. Former Secretary of the Air Force W. Stuart Symington urged President Harry S. Truman to send an ultimatum to the Soviets saying that any further Russian aggression would provoke an American nuclear attack. The principle of massive retaliation had numerous advocates long before it was elaborated by John Foster Dulles.

In November 1950, after the Chinese had entered the Korean War, President Truman raised the spectre of nuclear retaliation at a press conference. He said that using the bomb was under active consideration, and that it was a matter for the military, specifically the commander in the field, to decide. The idea of General Douglas MacArthur deciding where and when to unleash the U.S. nuclear arsenal caused widespread consternation abroad. Later that same day, the White House press office "clarified" Truman's statement: according to the Atomic Energy Act, only the president can authorize the employment of nuclear weapons. Within days, British Prime Minister Clement Attlee flew to the U.S. to get assurances that America would consult with its allies before it started dropping atom bombs.

In January of 1952, frustrated by Communist posturing and stubbornness at the armistice talks, Truman again toyed with the idea of an ultimatum. If the PRC and North Korea, both Soviet puppets as far as Truman was concerned, refused to negotiate in good faith, he considered threatening to bomb PRC and Soviet cities. In May, once again frustrated by interminable and fruitless armistice negotiations, Truman returned to the idea of threatening the USSR and the PRC with American atomic bombs. However, Truman never did issue the nuclear ultimatum and confined his musings to his diary.

Truman's successor, Dwight Eisenhower, also contemplated using atomic bombs to end the Korean stalemate. As far as Eisenhower was concerned, nuclear weapons simply represented a more powerful arsenal. Initially, he insouciently considered using nuclear bombs on the Korean battlefield, perhaps a test burst over one or two Communist airfields. But a lack of promising targets and serious doubts raised by some of his military advisors as to the effectiveness of nuclear weapons against entrenched opponents led Eisenhower, who as an old soldier should have been aware of these problems, to reject the tactical nuclear option.

"Ike's" National Security Council had also considered nuclear weapons to break the Korean stalemate, although how seriously will probably forever remain unclear. NSC-147 outlined options for ending the war on U.S. terms, and in subsequent discussions the question of nuclear weapons was inevitably raised. Incredibly, NSC-147 did not consider the reaction of the Soviet Union to nuclear war in Korea, which, after all, did border the Soviet maritime province; nor to the threat of global war. It was left to the Joint Chiefs of Staff to fill in that omission. Any decision to employ nuclear weapons at any time during the Korean War would hardly have provoked riots in the streets; responsible polls throughout this period show solid support for the option to "drop the bomb."

The U.N. commander in Korea from May 1952 to the signing of the armistice, General Mark W. Clark, also considered a contingency plan for a drive to the Yalu, spearheaded, inevitably, by atomic weapons as well as by Chinese Nationalist troops. It should also be noted that the Chinese Communist leaders were quite prepared to endure a U.S. nuclear offensive against their nation; they would simply abandon their coastal cities (which they apparently thought would not be a major loss) and, as in the days of the sacred "Long March," withdraw inland for protracted resistance.

Although publicly American public figures warned of "mortal peril" and of the "imminence" of World War III (see "Home Front, U.S."), by 1953 they knew privately that the nation now had hundreds of atomic bombs and the new B-47 jet bombers to drop them. Also, there were still plenty of the B-36 behemoths which could deliver two nuclear bombs apiece on intercontinental missions. And the newest transcontinental jet bomber, the B-52, was completing flight testing. The Soviets were hardly in the competition, unless they were prepared to commit national suicide.

Eisenhower supposedly was ready to order Operation Shakedown, an all-out offensive possibly including the use of nuclear weapons, in Korea. But first he may have "signaled" the Chinese and Soviet leaders of his intentions through trusted intermediaries. In addition, the more horrific aspects of NSC-147 were "leaked" to the press. The actual effect of this nuclear diplomacy will not become known until former Soviet, PRC, and North Korean archives are opened to scholars. Presumably the Chinese Communists rethought their plans to defy American nuclear weapons, airpower, and blockade and decided to settle for the status quo in Korea. But, for whatever reasons, the Communists did make concessions and the armistice was signed ending the war and bringing the world through a perilous Cold War nuclear threat.

David M. Esposito

Bibliography

Buhite, Russell, and William Hamel. "War for Peace: The Question of an American Preventive War Against the Soviet Union, 1945–1955," *Diplomatic History* 14 (1990).

Goulden, Joseph. *Korea: The Untold Story of the War* (1983).

Herken, Gregg. *The Winning Weapon* (1981).

Keefer, E.C. "Eisenhower and the End of the Korean War," *Diplomatic History* (Summer, 1989).

N

Operations Big and Little Switch

Operation Little Switch, 20 April–3 May 1953, was the exchange of sick and wounded prisoners of the Korean War. The exchange was agreed to during the truce talks at Panmunjom on 11 April, following United Nations commander in chief General Mark W. Clark's indirect approach to North Korean Premier Kim Il Sung and Chinese General Peng Dehuai, which itself had developed from initiatives at the U.N. and the International Red Cross in Geneva. The Communist side repatriated 684 U.N. sick and wounded troops, while the U.N. command (UNC) returned 1,030 Chinese and 5,194 Koreans, together with 446 civilian internees. As with everything else concerning the prisoner of war (POW) issue, the exchange was marked by strong disagreement and controversy. Returning Communist prisoners tried to embarrass their captors by rejecting rations and clothing issued to them, while sensational reports appeared in the Western press alleging that numbers of sick and wounded POWs were still being held by the Communists in spite of the exchange agreements. The contentious issue that had prolonged the war for two years, that no U.N. POW would be forcibly repatriated, remained. The surprising acceptance of this exchange may well have come as a result of uncertainty over Soviet policies after the death of Joseph Stalin.

Operation Big Switch, 5 August–23 December 1953 was the final exchange of prisoners of war by both sides, and like Little Switch was marked by controversy over voluntary repatriation and, later, by allegations of brainwashing and torture of U.N. POWs by the Communists. The issue of forced repatriation of POWs proved the major stumbling block to successful conclusion of the truce talks. Communist insistence on the return of all captured nationals held by the U.N. command was strenuously opposed by the United States and South Korean governments, although a number of the other governments who had committed forces to the U.N. command in Korea argued that the principle of voluntary repatriation should not be permitted to obstruct an early conclusion of hostilities. Eventually it was agreed that a U.N. Neutral Nations Repatriation Commission, chaired by India, would take responsibility for prisoners who had indicated a desire to remain with their captors. During a ninety-day period in which the NNRC held custody of the "non-repatriates," a series of "explanations" was provided during which the non-returnees were advised strongly to return to their home nations, generally without success.

The UNC returned 75,823 POWs (70,183 Koreans, 5,640 Chinese); the Communists repatriated 12,773 UNC POWs (7,862 Koreans, 3,597 Americans, 946 British). The vast majority of the 22,600 enemy non-repatriates were Chinese, most of them former Chinese Nationalist veterans. Only 137 Chinese agreed to return to their homeland before the expiration of the ninety-day period stipulated in the armistice agreement. Only 357 UNC prisoners indicated a desire to remain with the Communists (333 Koreans, 23 Americans, 1 Briton), and of these, two Americans and eight Koreans chose to return within the alloted time for the changing of one's mind. The UNC released all remaining former POWs thereafter, the Communists following suit a few days later.

Jeffrey Grey

Bibliography

Bernstein, Barton. "The Struggle over the Korean Armistice: Prisoners of Repatriation?" *Child of Conflict: The Korean-*

American Relationship, 1943–1953, ed. Bruce Cumings (1983).

Hermes, Walter. *Truce Tent and Fighting Front, United States Army in the Korean War* (Office of the Chief of Military History, Washington: 1966).

MacDonald, Callum. *Korea: The War Before Vietnam* (1986).

U.S. Army Forces, Far East, 8086th Army Unit, Military History Detachment. *Operation Little Switch,* 4 vols., n.d.

Opposing Forces on the Eve of War

Troop units stationed in the Far East in early 1950, like those of the rest of the United States military establishment, were the product of nearly five years of unrelenting "economizing" in manpower and budget and a public attitude favoring minimal military forces. Demobilization following Japan's surrender had been at a pace well-described by then Army Chief of Staff Dwight D. Eisenhower as "disintegration." A few months after V-J Day there were few if any combat-ready units in the U.S. Army; certainly there were none in the Far East command.

That command, under General of the Army Douglas MacArthur, covered a vast expanse of the Pacific and contiguous land masses including occupied Japan itself, the Ryukyu, Bonin, Mariana and Marshall islands, troops stationed in the Philippines and, until 1949, Korea. In 1950, MacArthur's principal combat force was the U.S. Eighth Army, stationed on the four main Japanese islands.

At the outbreak of hostilities in Korea on 25 June 1950 the Eighth Army, commanded by Lieutenant General Walton H. Walker, consisted of, with supporting units, the 1st Cavalry Division and the 7th, 24th, and 25th Infantry Divisions. The 1st Cavalry, so designated for historical reasons, actually was a standard World War II infantry division, as were the other three, and was stationed north of Tokyo. The 7th was in northern Honshu and southern Hokkaido. The 25th was based in the Kyoto-Osaka-Nara region, and the 24th on the southern main island of Kyushu. The 1st Cavalry and the 24th and 25th had been in Japan since early in the occupation period; the 7th had been deployed to Japan from its Korean stations when troops were removed from that peninsula in 1949, replacing the 11th Airborne, which was returned to the United States.

Subsequent to the beginning of the occupation, the Eighth Army had become seriously understrength through unreplaced attrition, perhaps more than had most U.S. Army units throughout the world. The Selective Service Act had been permitted to expire, to be revived only briefly during the Berlin Airlift emergency, and again allowed to expire. Neither General Walker, nor Lieutenant General Robert L. Eichelberger, who had preceded him, received what could be viewed as a fair share of enlistments. The Cold War created what were perceived as more urgent priorities. The low point in the Eighth Army's strength was reached in April 1948 when, authorized a total of 87,215, it reported only 45,561. Combat strength, including the four divisions and supporting units, was down to 26,494.

Faced with mandated troop ceilings and actual conditions, each of the twelve regiments in the divisions was placed under "reduced-strength" tables of organization with only two instead of the normal three battalions. The sole exception was the 24th Infantry of the 25th Division, which retained all three of its battalions. Each regiment's direct-support artillery battalion similarly was reduced to two firing batteries (again except for the 159th, which supported the 24th Infantry).

Under wartime-strength organization, a division was authorized a medium tank battalion and a tank company in each regiment, which also was authorized a cannon company equipped with short-range howitzers. Each of the Japan-based divisions had only a single tank company issued light tanks instead of mediums, and none of the regiments had a cannon company, nor the antitank company also authorized under war-strength tables. That a two-battalion regiment was tactically unsound was confirmed early on. Conventional doctrine called for initial commitment of two battalions with one in reserve, an impossibility under the circumstances.

By mid-1949, some rebuilding of strength had become possible under a vigorous recruiting effort in the United States, and a training program was initiated. Still, troop levels had not yet approached those authorized even under the "reduced-strength" concept by June 1950. The average rifle company, authorized 187 officers and men, went to Korea with around 125–140. The 25th Division and some other units were drained of junior officers and noncommissioned officers to augment the 24th, the first division to be committed. This was an unsatisfactory expedient; leaders in the 24th went into battle not knowing, nor being known by, their subordinates. And later, of course, the depleted units which soon followed did so without the leaders with whom they had trained.

The training program initiated in 1949 suffered under several constraints, one being the requirement for personnel to perform housekeeping, administrative, and logistical duties. While Japanese labor was employed extensively, still, soldiers from the infantry and other combat arms were operating warehouses, transportation facilities, military police detachments and other activities, few of whose functions could be interrupted to accommodate tactical training schedules.

Another handicap, and a serious one, was the severe shortage of training areas. Japan was (and is) a fearfully crowded island nation with little land available for military maneuvers. (Prior to World War II, one of the reasons for Japan's having rotated units between the home islands and Manchuria was the availability of real estate on the Asiatic mainland.) In the famine conditions following the surrender, every arable plot was desperately needed for growing rice; the arable, flat square miles required for military maneuvers simply were unavailable.

One of the areas eventually made available was at Gotemba, a former Japanese training site on the lower slopes of Mount Fuji. But it was able to accommodate only an infantry battalion at a time. As a result, no exercise above that level could be conducted and none had been up to the time of deployment to Korea.

Gotemba also is more than 300 miles from the stations of the 25th Division, one of the organizations which used it, and reachable only by rail. Trucks, tanks, fieldpieces and other impedimenta, and troops had to be loaded at their home bases, transported to Gotemba and offloaded, and the process reversed for return to bases. The schedule for the Gotemba site was so tight, with so many units needing it, that frequently more days were consumed in the loading, travel, and unloading process than were available at the location. Also because of scheduling, some units were compelled to engage in unit training (company or battalion) before they had completed individual training.

Thus the overall situation, as it was affected by personnel shortages, geography, and non-tactical limitations, was not one to favor combat-readiness. Still, it has been observed, the force deployed across the Straits of Tsushima to counter the North Korean invasion quite possibly was the closest thing to a professional army ever fielded by the United States.

Virtually all of the noncommissioned officers were combat veterans of World War II, as were most officers above the grade of first lieutenant. Because promotions after August 1945 had been practically nil, quite a few first lieutenants had, in 1950, dates of rank going back to 1943. So there was considerable experience; there just was an insufficiency in men and, as we shall see, in serviceable equipment.

The Army of the Republic of Korea (ROK) also was ill-constituted to oppose the North Korean assault. Originally established as the Korean constabulary early in the occupation period, it suffered in leadership, experience, equipment, and, probably, esprit. Some of its officers, most of them young, had served with the Japanese. However, Japanese policy did not promote Koreans to high rank, and most of the experienced ones had become casualties during the final months of World War II.

The ROK establishment, organized, trained and equipped by the United States, had been kept deliberately weak. Under President Syngman Rhee, there was considerable agitation for reunifying Korea by force. The U.S. government was apprehensive that, should the South Korean military become sufficiently strong, the U.S. might be unable to deter it from invading the North, with unfavorable political consequences, as well as virtually inevitable defeat. So the ROKs were kept on a short leash logistically. In short, while the ROK forces did not suffer the manpower shortages which plagued the Eighth Army, in 1950 the Army of the Republic of Korea was not a well-led, well-trained, nor well-equipped institution.

The North Korean Army, on the other hand, was a professional one, as was the U.S. Eighth, but better trained and equipped. It was a respectable army by any standards and, by those usually applied to Asian military organizations, a superb one. First announced as in being in February 1948, it had actually been organized and begun training more than a year earlier. Rigidly disciplined under its Soviet masters, it was organized, trained, and equipped for the mission to which it would be committed. There was some suspicion that East Germans had participated in the tactical instruction; veterans of combat in the European Theater of Operations (ETO) noted similarities in tactics.

A doctrinal shortcoming of the North Koreans was their willingness to accept casualties they could ill-afford, and their losses during the summer of 1950 were horrendous. North Korea is much less heavily populated than is the

South, and few replacements were available. While they held most of South Korea the northern forces resorted to wholesale impressment of local manpower, but with little or no time to train it.

In summary, the North Korean People's Army was an effective military machine for a short, swift campaign, which was what they expected their invasion to be. To their credit, they almost succeeded.

After the end of World War II the United States disposed of its arms and equipment with the same enthusiasm it had displayed in demobilizing its manpower. The popular view was that the war was over, none of that expensive materiel ever would be needed again, and that it should be sold for what it would bring. "Army and Navy surplus" outlets sprang up by the thousands, and every conceivable item became available for sale to the general public, some of them to be repurchased after June 1950 for several times the prices brought earlier. Jeeps and trucks especially were in demand; transportation in the United States was worn out after nearly four years during which none had been produced for civilian use. Thousands of vehicles were sold as "surplus," some of them new and in the crates in which they had been packed for shipment overseas.

Meanwhile, troop units on overseas stations, had to make do with the equipment left over from the later war, much of it in sad condition as the result of normal wear and tear and, in the Far East especially, the effects of tropical salt-air climates.

It should be remembered that all of the equipment taken to Korea by the Eighth Army, and by units which followed from other locations, was of World War II vintage. Although new generations of weapons, vehicles, communications equipment, and other items were being developed and issued in the United States, none was made available to the forces in Korea.

That General Walker had any resupply at all was largely attributable to "Operation Rollup," initiated in the Far East command in 1948. Under this program, vehicles and other items were scavenged from the various Pacific combat areas and returned to Tokyo Ordnance Depot for rebuild and reissue as replacements. Unfortunately, some of the "rebuilds" amounted to little more than replacement of rotted rubber and canvas, and paint. Some metal components were so rusted and corroded that, for example, a hard bump could break a vehicle's frame, consigning that item to salvage.

Nevertheless, the system did provide a source of replacements. During July and August 1950, some 4,000 such vehicles were processed, and by a year later as many as 46,000 had gone through the establishment.

And so, to its end in 1953, the Korean War was fought primarily with World War II equipment, and the decision to stick with it undoubtedly was correct. Mixing of the new generation materiel would have created impossible supply and maintenance problems.

As mentioned earlier, none of the divisions in the Eighth Army had a medium tank battalion, nor tank nor antitank companies in their regiments. Each division had a reconnaissance company equipped with M-24 light tanks and World War II half-tracks, and a single light (M24) tank company. There was an additional reason for limiting these units to light instead of medium tanks; the then-primitive road nets in occupied Japan could not handle the weight of M4s ("Shermans") and heavier equipment.

As a result, nothing capable of stopping the North Koreans' Soviet-supplied T-34 tanks was available. U.S. field artillery had limited success, but a howitzer is an area weapon not suited to armored warfare. Tables of organization called for infantry units to have the 3.5-inch rocket launcher, the "bazooka," but the feeble World War II 2.36-inch version was on hand and it was ineffective against the front or the sides of a T-34.

Each infantry division also was authorized, under war-strength tables, an antiaircraft artillery battalion, but under the "reduced-strength" concept, only a single firing battery was available to each. These were equipped with half-tracked vehicles, on each of which were mounted either four .50 caliber air-cooled machine guns or a 37mm gun and two .50s. Since after the first few days of the conflict the enemy had no airpower, the AAA units seldom were employed in their designed roles. However, they proved a potent defense against the "human-wave" attacks occasionally mounted by the North Koreans, and especially by the Chinese after they joined the conflict late in 1950. Since in such a capacity they consumed vast quantities of ammunition, resupply became a problem, as it did with the armored field artillery battalions that came from the States late in that same year.

As mentioned earlier, Republic of Korea (ROK) forces had been kept to low levels of readiness, partly for practical reasons and for others political. The U.S. was cautious about getting the ROK into such shape as might prompt an invasion of the North.

As a consequence, the South Korean Army was limited to only some eighty-nine World War II "infantry" howitzers in lieu of real artillery. These could fire only up to "charge 5" instead of the "charge 7" of which the regular 105mm howitzer was capable (though they used the same ammunition), and maximum range was only 7,200 yards. Armor was limited to a reported twenty-seven World War II armored cars, with no tracked vehicles. The M-8 armored car mounted a 37mm gun, completely ineffective against the North Korean T-34.

At the outbreak of hostilities a few ROK units still were armed with Japanese rifles for which no ammunition had been manufactured since 1945, and which soon had to be discarded for lack of such ammunition.

And throughout the South Korean establishment, ammunition and other supply had been kept deliberately short by the United States, again so as to discourage the possibility of an attack to the North. The result, of course, was that the South was equally unprepared to defend.

The North Korean military establishment was the creature of the Soviet Union. All of its equipment, save a few of those same Japanese rifles which were discarded when their ammunition ran out, was Soviet. And not all of it was World War II "surplus"; some items captured in 1950 bore manufacture dates of that same year.

The North Koreans had some artillery, both towed and self-propelled, but many more mortars which, of course, could be transported by manpower and so were better-suited to the limited roadnets of the Asian continent. Their only airpower, a few Soviet World War II planes, was practically eliminated by the U.S. Air Force early in the conflict. Consequently, the North Koreans' principal activities had to be limited to the hours of darkness during which they, and later their Chinese allies, were especially effective. They had to stay under cover during conditions of daylight and good weather. Darkness or bad weather and the freedom from the threat of airpower brought North Korean attacks.

The North's armor, so formidable against virtually unprotected troops, lacked an adequate recovery and maintenance capability. A breakdown of a tank frequently would necessitate that vehicle's sitting beside the road where it would become the target of U.S. airpower. Most of the North's successes with armor were accomplished early, before the Eighth Army and the Fifth Air Force were committed effectively. But as an examination of an operations map of, say, 1 September 1950, shows they came close to achieving their objective.

Carl Eigabrodt

Bibliography

Alexander, Bevin. *Korea: The First War We Lost* (1986).

Appleman, Roy E. *South to the Naktong, North to the Yalu: United States Army in the Korean War* (U.S. Army Center of Military History, 1961).

Knox, Donald. *The Korean War: Pusan to Chosin: An Oral History* (1985).

MacDonald, Callum A. *Korea: The War Before Vietnam* (1987).

Mewha, John. *Enemy Tactics,* Eighth U.S. Army Korea, Headquarters, Enemy Materiel.

Schnabel, James F. *Policy and Direction: The First Year, United States Army in the Korean War* (U.S. Army Center of Military History, 1972).

See also FIRST CLASH: U.S. AND NORTH KOREA

P

Pace, Frank, Jr. (1912–1988)

Frank Pace, Jr., lawyer and secretary of the army, 1950–1953, was born July 5, 1912, the son of prominent Little Rock, Arkansas lawyer Frank Pace and his wife, Flora Layton Pace. The junior Pace graduated from Princeton University in 1933 and went on to Harvard Law School where he was a student of Felix Frankfurter. Following graduation in 1936, he returned to Arkansas where he practiced tax law until the outbreak of World War II. In 1942 he was commissioned a second lieutenant in the U.S. Army Air Corps and for the next four years served in a variety of administrative assignments in the Air Transport Command. He was discharged in 1946 with the rank of major. It was then on to Washington, D.C., where he joined the staff of Attorney General Tom Clark as a tax specialist. He then served as executive assistant to the postmaster general before becoming the assistant director of the Bureau of the Budget (BOB).

In 1949, at the age of thirty-six, he was named by President Harry S. Truman to be director of the BOB. In that position he quickly emerged as one of the rising stars of the Truman administration, being hailed as a top-notch efficiency expert and first-rate administrator. As budget director, he instituted a performance-based budget for most federal agencies, established a management appraisal system, prepared organizational plans for simplifying more than two dozen government agencies, and produced the first "budget in brief." It was, however, his preparation, presentation, and defense of Truman's lean 1950 budget that won the president's admiration.

As an organizer and administrator, he was without equal, but his glibness, seeming irreverence for the Washington establishment, and unwillingness to play politics kept him from gaining the power base needed to be a major player on the Washington scene. It was probably those characteristics that led President Truman to tell Pace that he was a great budget director but a "lousy politician."

In April 1950, when Gordon Gray resigned as secretary of the army, Truman, without hesitation, named Pace as his successor. The president was hopeful that the Arkansasan could help Secretary of Defense Louis A. Johnson institute major cuts which could take the "fat" out of the military budget. Pace's appointment was greeted with skepticism by military leaders and supporters because of his youth (thirty-seven years old), reputation for cost cutting, and his lack of experience on defense issues. Although he was a very quick learner, even Pace later admitted that upon entering the post, his knowledge of the Army was rather limited.

Pace was in his post as civilian head of the United States Army less than nine weeks when the Korean War broke out, and while he was involved in virtually all the top strategy meetings which ultimately resulted in the commitment of U.S. combat forces, his impact on the course of events was minimal. When the North Korean attack came, the secretary initially questioned the use of U.S. ground troops before joining the chorus of military and civilian advisors in supporting intervention. In the next two and a half years, Pace was generally a strong supporter of the Joint Chiefs of Staff (JCS) on key military decisions, including reservations about the Inchon invasion, pursuit of the North Korean Army north of the 38th parallel, rotation of troops, and desegregation of Army units. He would, however, occasionally go against his chief Army advisors as he did when he favored removal of General Walton H. Walker early in the conflict. In April 1951, Pace was scheduled to personally inform General Douglas MacArthur that he was being relieved, but a premature leak to the press forestalled that plan.

Although included in most key wartime meetings with the president (including the Wake Island Conference), the Joint Chiefs of Staff and State Department officials, Pace felt that Army Chief of Staff General J. Lawton Collins frequently did not keep him adequately informed about Army operations in Korea. The secretary also believed that in strategic planning he had responsibility without adequate authority. Consequently, he advocated, albeit unsuccessfully, full Cabinet status and the right to attend National Security Council meetings.

Pace's impact as an able administrator was significant. The rapid expansion of the Army created ample opportunity for managerial leadership to meet problems of raising, training, and supplying troops. He was responsible for implementing the popular "point system" for troops in Korea. His commitment to and implementation of new procurement methods helped to overcome major supply problems, particularly of new ammunition, but not before major shortages had occurred. Even though it was wartime, he continually pressed for cost-cutting measures, thereby winning support of fiscal conservatives but angering military supporters.

In January 1953, a week before the Eisenhower administration prepared to assume control of the government, Pace resigned his Army post. For the next ten years, he was with General Dynamics Corporation, serving as executive vice-president, president, and chairman of the board. From the time he left office until his death on January 8, 1988, he served on various commissions and task forces, including appointment as the first chairman of the Corporation for Public Broadcasting.

Keith D. McFarland

Bibliography

Blair, Clay. *The Forgotten War: America in Korea, 1950–1953* (1987).
Bradley, Omar with Clay Blair. *A General's Life* (1983).
Collins, J. Lawton. *Lightning Joe: An Autobiography* (1979).
Condit, Doris M. *History of the Office of the Secretary of Defense: Vol. II, The Test of War, 1950–52* (Washington, 1988).
Schnabel, James F., and Robert J. Watson. *The History of the Joint Chiefs of Staff: The Joint Chiefs of Staff and National Policy, Vol. III, The Korean War* (1979).

Peng Dehuai (1898–1974)

Peng Dehuai, the commander in chief of the People's Volunteer (Chinese Communist) Army (PVA) from 1950–1954, was born in Hsiangt'an, Hunan province, China, 24 October 1898. Peng's father was a poor peasant, and his mother died when Peng was seven. In some bad years for the family, Peng begged for food. At ten he hired himself out, but in 1916 he joined a warlord army, and was promoted quickly for his courage. From 1926 to 1927 he participated in the North Expedition led by Chinese Nationalist leader Chiang Kai-shek. But he joined the Chinese Communist party in 1928, and later that year he and his Communist comrades in the army started the P'ingchiang Uprising. He then led his army to the Chingkangshan Mountains, where Mao Zedong's Red Army was fighting the Nationalists. He fought in the vanguard of the Red Army in the "Long March" from 1934 to 1935.

During the Sino-Japanese War between 1937 and 1945, Peng was deputy commander in chief of the Eighth Route Army, the Communist force under a Nationalist–Communist coalition. At the end of the war, he was a member of the CCP Central Committee and an alternate member of the party's Politburo. In the war with the Nationalists in the late 1940s, he commanded the People's Liberation Army in northwest China.

In early October 1950, as U.N. forces pushed toward the Sino-Korean border, Peng was appointed commander in chief of the People's Volunteer Army, the Chinese forces that were to fight in Korea. He crossed the Yalu River on 18 October. From then until January 1951, Peng launched three major offensives, driving U.N. forces back to the 38th parallel. Then Peng had to withdraw his army in the face of U.N. counterattacks and give up Seoul. After traveling to Peking to report the field situation, Peng decided to fortify and resist along the 38th parallel. The war had stabilized and Peng conducted what he termed "an active defense in position warfare," more or less what the U.N. command was committed to.

In 1951 and 1953 Peng was twice awarded the Democratic People's Republic of Korea (North Korea) National Flag Medal, First Class. He signed the armistice agreement at Panmunjom for the PVA on 27 July 1953.

On his return from Korea, Peng served as vice premier of the state council and minister of national defense. In 1955, together with nine other Chinese military leaders, he was awarded the title of marshal. His remodeling of the Chinese Army along Soviet lines after his experiences in the field in Korea put him on the wrong side at the beginning of the Sino-Soviet split. Peng was considered a straightforward, honest soldier but a mediocre strategist. But he did not pay undue heed to Marxist-Leninist theory and may have suffered from resentment caused by China's enormous manpower losses in Korea, losses incurred in military operations that had nonetheless failed to drive the "imperialists" from that neighboring nation.

To make matters worse, Peng in 1959 spoke out against Mao Zedong's radical economic policy. After a partial rehabilitation in the early 1960s, he was arrested in 1966 when the Great Cultural Revolution began. Tortured and imprisoned, his health deteriorated, and he died in a prison hospital on 29 November 1974. The Revolution had once again devoured one of its own.

Jing Li

Bibliography

Domes, Jurgen. *Peng Te-huai: The Man and the Image* (1985).
Peng Te-huai. *Memoirs of a Chinese Marshal: The Autobiographical Notes of Peng Te-huai (1898–1974)*, trans. Zheng Longpu (1984).
Snow, Edgar. *Red Star over China* (1938).
Union Research Institute, ed. *The Case of Peng Te-huai: 1959–1968* (1968).

People's Liberation/Volunteer Army

The People's Volunteer Army (PVA) was the term used by the People's Republic of China (PRC) for the Chinese troops involved in the Korean War. The use of this title instead of "People's Liberation Army," the title of the military forces of the PRC, indicated the cautious intention to avoid a full-scale conflict with the United States and the U.N. forces in Korea. (Nonetheless, the PLA leadership seemed to accept with equanimity the prospect of a U.S. blockade and even nuclear bombardment of its major cities if the Korean War had escalated beyond Korea's boundaries.) Unlike the heavily equipped (North) Korean People's Army, the People's Volunteer Army (and the PLA, for that matter), was primarily a light infantry organi-

zation. And it was in light infantry operations that it excelled.

From mid-May to mid-July of 1950, two Chinese armies were redeployed to Manchuria, the Chinese region bordering on North Korea. It cannot be stated with any certainty that these moves were connected to the situation in Korea; many of the troops were assigned to construction work, as were PLA forces in numerous other parts of a China recovering from almost continuous war since 1937.

But as the course of the Korean War turned in favor of the U.N. after the Inchon landings in September, a more serious military buildup commenced in mid-September. Peng Teh-huai was appointed commander in chief of the PVA on 5 October, just two days before U.S. forces crossed the 38th parallel. The headquarters of the PVA was established in Shenyang, a city in southern Manchuria, and in mid-October the PVA began to move quietly into Korea.

In the early stages of the war, the PVA consisted of two army groups: the 13th under Li T'ien-yu, and the 9th under Sung Shih-lun, with a total of nine armies. Normally, a Chinese army contained three divisions (units at lower levels were also triangularly organized), but some of the PVA armies were reinforced by an additional division. The average strength of a Chinese infantry division was about 9,000, that is, about half that of a U.S. Army infantry division.

Soviet Premier Joseph Stalin had agreed to provide, in addition to military equipment, air cover for the bridges across the Yalu. This latter aid was superfluous, as the PVA moved across the frozen river under the noses of unsuspecting U.S. air reconnaissance.

By western standards, the PVA was not well equipped. Its firepower was consistently inferior to that of U.N. forces; it could deploy virtually no air cover. As for logistics, it boasted two regiments with 800 heterogeneous trucks and much of its supply had to be carried by civilian laborers.

But Chinese soldiers were tough and well-disciplined, hardened by their wars with the Nationalists and the Japanese. (Many of those troops were actually Nationalist veterans impressed into the PVA.) To further offset their equipment shortcomings, the PVA utilized the strategies and tactics they had developed in those wars: concealed movement and surprise attack, closing to do battle with grenades and bayonets, marching cross-country rather than following roadways, striking at the enemy flanks, infiltrating the front, sowing confusion within enemy positions, and blocking supply lines and paths of retreat. The PVA enjoyed great success utilizing these tactics in pushing U.N. forces south of the 38th parallel late in 1950. But when that enemy consolidated its positions, the PVA found it hard to maneuver and suffered extremely high casualties from U.N. firepower.

The well-known Chinese Field Marshal Lin Piao wrote an oft-quoted pamphlet on his views of U.S. troops, *Primary Conclusions of Battle Experience at Unsan*, dealing with an occasion in which American troops were hardly at their best. He asserted that "Cut off from the rear, they abandon all their heavy weapons. . . . Their infantrymen are weak, afraid to die, and have no courage to attack or defend. They depend always on their planes, tanks, artillery. . . . When transportation comes to a standstill, the infantry loses the will to fight." The United States forces of the Korean War era have justifiably been accused of not taking their Communist enemies seriously at first; the published thoughts of Marshall Lin show that such ignorance was not all on one side. Chinese troops who believed such exaggerated denigration of their enemy would pay a heavy price at the hands of a reconstituted Eighth Army in the battles to come.

The PVA received its first major deliveries of Soviet equipment in August 1951: artillery, tanks, and unarmored vehicles. Later in the war the Chinese also built up their airpower with about 2,000 aircraft, but this had little impact on the stalemated conflict, other than in the highly publicized battles over "MIG Alley," and in the nightmares of U.S. Air Force commanders who tended to nurse apocalyptic visions of "Red" airpower out of all proportion to its true worth.

Throughout the Korean War, about 2.3 million PVA troops rotated in three groups in and out of Korea, which was about 66 percent of the CPA field forces. Thus the PRC could fight a war of attrition with its massed manpower and no fears of public outcry at heavy casualties.

No official information on total PVA casualties has ever been released by the PRC. Western sources vary in their estimates, but agree that casualties must have been heavy. Peng Teh-huai, the PVA commander in chief, later disclosed that by January 1951, the PVA had been reduced by nearly 50 percent, an incredible figure if true. A great many of these casualties may

be attributed to PVA poor supply system. For example, at the end of 1950, a single PVA army reported more than 100,000 noncombat losses. A reliable figure for PVA total casualties throughout the war would be about a third of a million. (The PRC's inability or unwillingness to produce any accurate figures speaks volumes.) The great disparity between PVA casualties and those of, for example, U.S. forces (33,000 battle deaths in a longer period of conflict) should give pause to those who extoll the "lean" PLA, compared to "road-bound" Western forces. The PVA could win initial victories against even a well-equipped but overconfident foe, but it could not sustain its offensive and its troops suffered terribly. The vast numbers of PVA surrenders and the subsequent refusal of more than 14,000 of its POWs (compared to 359 U.N. non-repatriates) to accept repatriation to the Socialist motherland indicates that poor morale was an inescapable consequence of such suffering.

At the end of 1952, the PVA was reported to have a strength of about one million. After the armistice agreements, which Peng signed for the CPVA, these numbers began to fall. The last of the PVA departed Korea in 1958, although it is still officially represented at the Panmunjom armistice meetings.

Jing Li

Bibliography

McMichael, S.R. *An Historical Perspective on Light Infantry* (U.S. Army Command and General Staff College, Combat Studies Center, Research Survey No. 6, Fort Leavenworth, KS: 1987).

Spurr, Russell. *Enter the Dragon: China's Undeclared War against the U.S. in Korea, 1950–51* (1988).

Whiting, Allen S. *China Crosses the Yalu: The Decision to Enter the Korean War* (1960).

Pork Chop Hill

Pork Chop Hill (Hill 255) represented the static front in the Korean War. Named for its unique shape, it was located on the east side of the Iron Triangle near the Yokkokchon River; it was near other hills such as Arrowhead, White Horse, and Arsenal. The Chinese Communist forces (CCF) were positioned on nearby peaks and were also entrenched in tunnels.

Pork Chop Hill was the target of Communist offensives several times during the war.

Efforts to secure the hill intensified during armistice negotiations, as the Communists urgently sought to acquire territory before a cease-fire was signed. The Allied forces were also interested in obtaining and defending the same territory to straighten the final demarcation line. Both sides were motivated by the desire to advance as far north or south into enemy territory as possible, and to strengthen their lines.

On June 6, 1952, Allied forces encountered opposition as they sought to control key outposts, including Pork Chop Hill. In a night maneuver, two platoons from I Company, 180th Infantry, finally secured the hill after combatting two Chinese platoons and enduring artillery fire for an hour. They dug in, building bunkers and laying barbed wire, mines, and communication channels. The outposts on Pork Chop Hill were reinforced with supplies and successfully repulsed Chinese advances during the following days. On June 16 Lieutenant Colonel Joseph C. Sandlin and the 179th Infantry Regiment relieved the 180th and held the hill against several attacks.

In November the Thailand Battalion guarded Pork Chop Hill and was attacked by several Chinese companies. The Chinese, armed with artillery and mortars, fired for approximately an hour before regrouping for a second advance. The Thai soldiers managed to defeat the attackers, who returned four days later, attacking from the north, east, and southwest. The Chinese stormed forward to the Thais' trenches before being repulsed. They made two more offensive efforts that night before retreating.

By spring 1953, the Korean War was a two-year-old stalemate. Pork Chop Hill symbolized the territorial aspirations of both Communist and Allied leaders in the contest for permanent geographical gains during truce negotiations for tactical or status reasons. On March 1, 1953, a patrol from the 31st Infantry Regiment, U.S. 7th Division, detected an enemy battalion preparing to attack Pork Chop Hill. Forewarned, the 31st Infantry, under the command of Colonel William B. Kern, withstood 8,000 rounds of Chinese artillery fire before the enemy departed. The winter rains and mud discouraged infantry action. Later that month the 7th Division heard rumors of an enemy attack from two deserters.

On March 23, artillery and mortar from the CCF 67th Division, 23rd Army, assaulted Pork Chop Hill while other Chinese forces hit nearby Old Baldy. The U.N. forces held Pork Chop Hill, but Old Baldy was lost. On Pork Chop Hill the men fought until their ammunition was depleted. They concentrated their forces on the hill's crest where they were resupplied. The Chinese again attacked the next morning, pinning down a company and setting bunkers on fire. Casualties littered the hill, but the fighting died down.

By April 1953 the company-size U.S. garrison on the hill was a temporary unit and not fully equipped or manned; only two rifle platoons, totalling seventy-six men of which many were absent on patrol or as outguards, were present. Rumors of an enemy attack circulated, but most men were not alerted to the possible attack.

On April 16 approximately 2,300 Communist infantry advanced toward Pork Chop Hill. Allied patrol and outguards saw them clustering in the valley and tried to warn the company via telephone, but the line was dead. They threw grenades as the enemy advanced, but the Communist artillery overwhelmed them. The Chinese took the troops' chow bunker and captured unaware men who came inside to eat. Fighting occurred in isolated pockets, with small groups of U.S. soldiers defending themselves. The dearth of information made the troops unsure of what was happening or its extent and severity. They did not realize how far the Chinese had advanced. Communication with outposts and patrols was nonexistent, and supplies dwindled.

A platoon was ordered to attack from the rear, but it became lost and never arrived; a reinforcement platoon had not been informed of the Chinese presence and, unprepared, fled through the valley as the Chinese attacked. The Chinese captured and occupied Allied trenches and bunkers; remaining U.N. soldiers hid behind natural barriers and in bunkers. They did not want to leave the bunkers, as field officers suggested, because they feared injured men in bunkers would fall into enemy hands. They reinforced and sealed bunkers and requested illumination of the hill with flares to inhibit Chinese movement. They used bayonets and even mess tin spoons to dig protective trenches inside the bunkers.

A group of men managed to surmount Pork Chop Hill as artillery fire raged, but only fourteen survived the onslaught. On April 16, the Chinese secured the hill only to be ejected two days later as the 7th Infantry Division's nine artillery battalions pounded the enemy with 77,349 rounds. Chinese artillery fired nearly as many rounds, surely something of a record for so confined an area and time.

The final assault on Pork Chop Hill was one of the last battles in the Korean War. On July 6, 1953, the Chinese attacked the 7th Infantry Division and mounted the hill's crest. The 17th Regiment reinforced troops for a counterattack that night but it failed. Another counterattack was attempted the next day with the U.N. forces withstanding the Chinese assaults. A stalemate emerged in which both sides futilely attempted to push the other off the hill. Chinese loudspeakers warned that the Communists would take no prisoners.

The U.N. command then concluded that because the Communists were willing to suffer unlimited casualties to capture and hold the hill, the sacrifices necessary to hold Pork Chop Hill for the allies did not equal its tactical worth.

On the following day, Allied soldiers were evacuated from Pork Chop Hill inside armored personnel carriers; the Chinese assumed that the carriers were merely transporting supplies and ammunition, not men. After two days passed, they realized the hill had been evacuated and advanced to secure it, tripping booby traps rigged by the 7th Division.

Truce negotiations resumed, and territorial possessions were viewed as important bargaining points. In the battles for Pork Chop Hill, the Communists used their attacks to exhibit their strength, humble U.N. troops, and improve their position on the field for the positioning of the postwar demilitarized zone. Although the Chinese were willing to take heavy casualties for Pork Chop Hill, the U.N. refused to sacrifice their troops for unclear tactical objectives. The U.N. command also realized that heavy losses suffered obviously so close to an armistice would upset the American public. Nonetheless, the U.N. suffered 300 casualties on Pork Chop Hill and Old Baldy. Estimates of 600–800 Chinese casualties are recorded. In the end, Pork Chop Hill was designated as partly inside the DMZ and partly in North Korea when the Armistice was signed on July 27, 1953.

Elizabeth Schafer

Bibliography

Hermes, Walter G. *Truce Tent and Fighting Front* (1966).

Knox, Donald, and Alfred Coppel. *The Korean War—Uncertain Victory: An Oral History* (1988).

Marshall, S.L.A. *Pork Chop Hill: The American Fighting Man in Action Korea, Spring, 1953* (1956).

Power Plants, U.N. Air Attacks on

After almost a year of fruitless negotiations, U.N. and Communist negotiators remained deadlocked. Only a renewed strategic air assault, argued Far East Air Forces (FEAF) planners, would break the stalemate. The FEAF commander, General O.P. Weyland, concurred and directed the destruction of four enemy hydroelectric complexes in the early summer of 1952. The ensuing attacks of June 23–27 destroyed 90 percent of North Korea's power generating capacity, but did not cajole Communist leaders to make any concessions at the bargaining table at Panmunjom.

In order to operate critical chemical and light metals industries in Manchuria, the Japanese spent twenty years constructing numerous hydroelectric systems in North Korea. With the advent of the Korean War, the majority of these systems remained intact. The Far East command target committee subsequently ordered air attacks against North Korean hydroelectric facilities, and on September 26, 1950, eight B-29s from the 92nd Bomb Group neutralized the Fusen complex, located in the northeast portion of the country. The nascent campaign, however, quickly came to an end. Washington remained uncertain about attacking politically sensitive targets, the power plants had only an indirect impact on North Korea's combat capabilities, and General Douglas MacArthur demanded unstinting tactical air support for his upcoming invasion of the North. As a result, the hydroelectric complexes remained again unmolested until June 1952.

General Matthew B. Ridgway, MacArthur's successor as commander in chief of United Nations command and the American Far East command, opposed large-scale strategic bombardment while peace talks were in progress. However, when General Mark W. Clark replaced Ridgway on April 28, 1952, he ordered General Weyland and Vice Admiral Robert P. Briscoe, commander of naval forces Far East, to conduct coordinated attacks against the hydroelectric centers at Fusen, Choshin, and Kyosen. On June 19, the Joint Chiefs of Staff (JCS) added Sui-ho as a target. Sui-ho was the fourth largest hydroelectric complex in the world, producing 640,000 kilowatts of power, and sat astride the Chinese-North Korean border, forty miles northeast of Antung. Because of its location it was a politically sensitive target.

The attacks began against Sui-ho at 4:00 P.M. on June 23. Because of the 250 MIG-15 fighters stationed at Antung and Ta-tung-kou,

Manchuria, eighty-four F-86 Sabres established local air superiority. Thirty-five propeller-driven AD Skyraiders from the aircraft carriers *Boxer, Princeton,* and *Philippine Sea* then attacked. (The assault marked the first appearance of Navy aircraft in "MIG Alley" since 1950.) From 4:10 to 5:00 P.M., seventy-nine F-84s and forty-five F-80s joined the attack. Within the hour, American airmen dropped 145 tons of bombs on Sui-ho at a cost of two lightly damaged planes. Navy F9F jet fighters suppressed local flak batteries while 160 MIGs, possibly thinking themselves under attack, fled from Antung and Ta-tung-kou deeper into Manchuria.

During the raid on Sui-ho, piston-engine P-51 Mustangs also struck Fusen Complexes Nos. 3 & 4, the 1st Marine Air Wing hit Choshin Nos. 3 & 4, and Navy Skyraiders, F4U prop Corsairs, and jet F9F Panthers struck Fusen Nos. 1 & 2 and the facilities at Kyosen. Navy and Air Force pilots struck the same targets over the next three days, while also adding strikes against Chosin Complexes Nos. 1 & 2.

The results of these raids were impressive. From June 23–27, the Fifth Air Force flew 730 fighter-bomber and 238 counter-air sorties without any losses. The Navy, in turn, accomplished 546 sorties in two days and lost only two aircraft. The assaults marked the first time during the Korean War that Air Force and Navy air units conducted joint operations against a single target. Within the four hydroelectric complexes attacked, eleven of thirteen plants stopped operating. North Korea experienced a two-week blackout and then restored only 10 percent of its lost capacity. It could no longer export electric power to Manchuria and Siberia. As a result, thirty out of fifty-one key Chinese industries at Port Arthur, Dairen, Funchun, and Anshan did not reach their annual production quotas.

These raids failed to change the negotiating attitude of the Communists at Panmunjom, and aroused heated protest in Great Britain. Even within the Conservative government there was indignation that the Americans had carried out the attacks without prior consultation with an ally, which, after all, had ground, naval, and air forces fighting alongside their American comrades in a war none too popular at home. The Americans, for their part, may well have refused such liaison because of their well-founded suspicion of U.K. security in the wake of the sensational defections of two British diplomats the year previous.

Subsequent to the June 1952 attacks, follow-up raids were periodically required. Sev-enth Fleet aircraft struck Chosin Nos. One and Two on September 12–13, February 15, and May 10, 1953. For the rest of the war, the lights never really went back on again in North Korea.

Peter R. Faber

Bibliography

Futrell, Robert F. *The United States Air Force in Korea 1950–1953* (Office of Air Force History, GPO, Washington: 1983).

Ridgway, Matthew. *Soldier: Memoirs of Matthew B. Ridgway* (1956).

Stewart, James T., ed. *Airpower: The Decisive Force in Korea* (1957).

Press (Western) and the Korean War

The Korean War was covered by print journalists supplemented by radio broadcasts, newsreels, and photographs. U.N. press correspondents covering the war experienced turmoil trying to work professionally and ethically while being limited by the military's protocol regarding journalists. The first U.N. correspondents in the Korean War were reporters stationed with wire services in Seoul at the time of the North Korean invasion: Keyes Beech (*Chicago Daily News*), Frank Gibney (*Time*), Burton Crane (*New York Times*), and Marguerite Higgins (*New York Herald Tribune*).

The U.N. press pool had swelled to seventy reporters by July 5, 1950. The correspondents migrated south with the troops, writing about unprepared soldiers and the lack of proper equipment. When two reporters flew to Tokyo to file stories (there were no such facilities in Korea) they were notified that they could not return because their stories would detrimentally affect the troops and home front. General Douglas MacArthur relented but emphasized that all U.N. journalists needed to act responsibly because the press played a major role in psychological warfare.

At the outbreak of hostilities there was no formal censorship in Korea. Correspondents were expected to follow voluntarily unwritten standards of journalistic conduct in order to preserve secrecy and promote the U.N. cause. MacArthur warned correspondents not to identify and reveal troop movements and locations. Despite his advice, the competitive nature of the reporters, striving to scoop their colleagues, resulted in various security breaches.

U.N. correspondents requested formal censorship with specific limitations and processes, but the military refused. On July 25, 1950, the military announced that the voluntary code also disallowed any criticism of U.N. decisions or personnel. Journalists continued to demand official censorship to clarify their role and the military persisted in its refusal, stating that it was not ready for formal inspection of news reports. Caught in the paradoxical situation of having access to stories but being unsure of what they could write, journalists also were frustrated by having to depend on the military to provide communications, transportation, and housing, which were limited and of poor quality.

The public information office of the Far East command provided information on the war through official releases which often were sketchy or biased. Telephone lines were limited, and correspondents were rationed several minutes to transmit copy, risking eavesdroppers who might steal stories. Secrecy was nonexistent unless a reporter flew directly to Tokyo or created a diversion; even carrier pigeons were used but required two weeks to fly to Tokyo. When the correspondents requested additional phone lines and equipment, the military denied them, stating that such crucial equipment was needed by military units.

By September 1950, 238 American and foreign U.N. correspondents, representing nineteen countries, reported in Korea. The maximum number of correspondents totaled 270 (as compared to 419 in Vietnam). Many were veteran correspondents of World War II. In Korea they were divided in two groups: those that scanned the front lines for stories and those who worked from headquarters.

As the war continued to worsen for the U.N. forces, the Army desired to limit the number of correspondents and access to communications in order to control what was reported. The military staged some stories. At the Inchon landing, MacArthur invited four correspondents as his personal guests on his command ship supplied with telephone connections to Tokyo to relay the military's official version of the landing.

Eventually, some war correspondents began writing analyses about the war. Some reporters questioned if the U.N. should be in South Korea or if that country should even be saved. Many journalists focused on associated war topics such as civilians and political corruption. They depicted soldiers suffering from malaise, disillusionment, homesickness, and cold. Some muckrakers exposed the widespread corruption in Syngman Rhee's government such as the police profiteering from Army supplies, operating brothels, protecting distillers of alcohol sold to the troops, and executing political prisoners.

On December 21, 1950, with U.N. forces in full retreat before the Chinese onslaught, MacArthur's headquarters announced that voluntary censorship would no longer be permitted because too many correspondents wrote articles critical of the U.N. effort. Full military censorship was implemented. Given the pamphlet *Censorship Criteria*, reporters no longer had vague ideas of what they could not print. Reporters had to use the dateline "Somewhere in Korea" and not divulge potentially embarrassing information or name a unit's arrival or existence in Korea until first mentioned in official reports. Reporters had to receive permission to write about a military action. They could not mention the nationality of troops or commanding officers. Nor could they discuss Allied or enemy casualties.

Because the military wanted news to be timely and accurate, they provided reporters twenty-four-hour access to censors from all military branches. The censors recommended deletions and revisions; photographs, newsreels, and radio broadcasts were carefully censored because they could potentially be re-captioned or dubbed by the enemy for propaganda. All news stories were examined twice in Korea and Tokyo. Reporters were often annoyed with the censors delaying publication of their stories.

Reporters sent their stories via Teletype from Korea to Tokyo, where the staff forwarded them to the reporter's home office after clearing them. Reports from foreign correspondents had to be censored by individuals fluent in that language and occasionally translated to English for publication. Many reporters relied on press pools, using dispatches penned by public information officers who cleared information from interviews that reporters were not permitted to attend.

In order to circumvent censorship, some few reporters resorted to the mail system, commercial wires, or radio lines, risking banishment. Military press briefings were held daily, including censor-cleared front-line dispatches and communiques. For interviews with dignitaries, the public information officer arranged photo shoots, approved quotes, and provided background information.

Reporters quickly realized that the censorship policies would not be lenient. By January

1951, all U.N. journalists were under military jurisdiction and were given a list of violations and possible punishments such as suspension, deportation, and court martial. The military regulations stressed security and forbade mention of Allied airpower, effect of enemy fire, criticism of Allied conduct, or derogatory remarks about the U.N. troops and their commanders. Journalists protested these restrictions, arguing that there was not much they could report except the fact that troops were in Korea. Some correspondents returned to the states to write, unrestricted by censors. Several books highly critical of the Korean War effort were written by U.N. correspondents, including I.F. Stone's *The Hidden History of the Korean War*, and Reginald Thompson's *Cry Korea*, but both were marred by leftist bias or (in the case of Thompson) persistent anti-American feeling.

MacArthur expelled at least seventeen correspondents who questioned his policies, and Ridgway was just as adamant. As a result, U.N. correspondents carefully avoided criticism of military leaders. Among topics not printed or given full attention were possible use of the atomic bomb, Allied disunity, the behavior of Allied prisoners, and the peace talks at Kaesong and later at Panmunjom.

During the prisoner exchanges, military censorship prohibited repatriates from describing their experiences in interviews in Asia, on troopships, in hospitals, and at home in an attempt to suppress facts about collaboration and confessions, a restriction that upset many correspondents.

The climax of tension between U.N. correspondents and the military high command occurred during the beginning of armistice talks in 1951. The military was angered at the reporters for not agreeing to submit fully to suggested regulations on covering the talks. At the peace talks, accredited U.N. correspondents could not speak with U.N. delegates, and were briefed by a U.S. Army officer only after the sessions concluded. U.N. reporters were not permitted to view documents or maps. Reporters resented the U.N. command's apparent distrust of their willingness or ability to write accurate copy that would not discredit the military. This disrespect for their reporting ethics and abilities angered many correspondents and resulted in confrontations with briefing officers.

As a result of the U.N. military command's attitude toward them, many U.N. correspondents relied on information from the Communist reporters Wilfred Burchett of *Ce Soir* and Alan Winnington of the *London Daily Worker*, who were attached to the Communist delegation. (The odious Burchett, who always claimed total objectivity, was later reliably reported to have visited Communist prisoner of war camps in Chinese Army uniform, haranguing U.S. POWs and threatening them if they failed to sign "confessions" or adopt a "progressive" world view. Winnington at least had the courage to be open about his convictions.) Burchett and Winnington were happy to provide information and disinformation from the other side, much to the disgust of the U.N. military high command.

The *Stars and Stripes* editor was fired when he circulated Burchett's picture of General William Dean in captivity. Ridgway prohibited contacts between U.N. and Communist correspondents, stressing that Communist correspondents threatened military security. Most U.N. correspondents ignored Ridgway, and some even strove to talk to the Communist reporters. Editors, on the whole, were supportive of the correspondents' right to sources and even sent a group of their colleagues to Japan to remonstrate with General Ridgway about the ban.

Competition was sometimes hazardous to the correspondents who took risks to acquire news. Some ten American correspondents died during the Korean War, mostly during the first year, and Frank Noel, an AP photographer, was captured by the Chinese and held prisoner for several years.

U.N. correspondents in Korea encountered a myriad of professional problems, and they were frustrated with insulting and fickle censorship policies administered and enforced by the military. Whether to reveal or conceal events in Korea became the primary issue confronting correspondents. Covering a wide range of topics, from Chinese intervention to MacArthur's dismissal, U.N. correspondents tenaciously endured the military's suspicions toward the press. The strained relationship between military and press would resurface and worsen in the Vietnam War.

Elizabeth Schafer

Bibliography
Beech, Keyes. *Tokyo and Points East* (1954).
Blumenson, Martin. *Monograph: Special Problems in the Korean Conflict* (1952).
Higgins, Marguerite. *War in Korea: The Report of a Woman Combat Correspondent* (1951).

Knightley, Phillip. *The First Casualty: From the Crimea to Vietnam: The War Correspondent as Hero, Propagandist, and Myth Maker* (1975).

Pease, Stephen E. *Psywar: Psychological Warfare in Korea, 1950–1953* (1992).

Voigtlander, Karl A. Von. "The War for Words," *Army Information Digest* (1953): 54–59.

Wiley, Noble J., Jr. "The Pen Supports the Sword," *Army Information Digest* (1953): 7–13.

See also BROADCAST NEWS COVERAGE OF THE KOREAN WAR; FILM, TELEVISION, AND LITERATURE OF THE KOREAN WAR

Prisoner of War (POW) Question

The disposition of prisoners of war (POWs) was a major source of contention during the prolonged Korean War truce talks. After prisoner exchanges began, sensational stories of collaboration by captured Americans made headlines. The treatment and behavior of Americans in captivity became one of the major stories of the Korean War era. As a result, POWs and their treatment attracted far more attention than in previous wars. Some of this new interest carried over to the POWs of the Vietnam era.

Almost all aspects of the Korean POW experience remain controversial. There are disputes over the treatment of POWs on both sides. Disagreements abound about the behavior of captured Americans. There are quarrels over the merits of voluntary versus total repatriation, and finally there are questions over how the POW issue contributed to the prolonging of the truce talks.

Being a POW was unpleasant and dangerous for the troops of all the nations that fought in Korea. The fighting that surged up and down the Korean peninsula in the first year of conflict produced many prisoners as units on both sides were overrun by enemy offensives. Neither side was adequately prepared to deal with the number of captives taken and death rates among prisoners were high. The North Koreans did not expect to encounter Americans and no provisions existed for dealing with them. When in doubt, many North Korean units simply tied the hands of the American soldiers and then shot them. After the Chinese entered the war they took control of almost all American POWs.

The Chinese had a fully developed system for dealing with prisoners that they had used extensively against both the Japanese and the Chinese Nationalists. However, the Chinese quickly learned that their system did not work with Americans and they had to develop a new POW policy. The Communist states did not accept the 1949 Geneva Convention. The Chinese called their system the Lenient Treatment Policy. During the Sino-Japanese War and the Chinese civil war, the Chinese Communists fed and treated their prisoners well (by their standards), then released them to tell their fellow soldiers that being captured by the Communists was not bad and that maybe they should all surrender at the next good opportunity. In pursuance of this idea they released a number of captured Americans soon after their entry into the war. However, the Chinese discovered that the Americans did not appreciate their treatment while POWs and there was no inclination on the part of other Americans to surrender in hope of good treatment.

In these circumstances the Chinese, like the North Koreans, saw little value in prisoners. Instead they were a burden on the Chinese supply system. The only short term use for prisoners was propaganda and in the summer of 1950 and the winter-spring of 1950–1951, when first the North Koreans and then the Chinese expected to drive the Americans off the peninsula, such propaganda was of limited value. During these periods and throughout the chaotic North Korean retreat in the fall of 1950, large numbers of U.N. prisoners were killed or died from mistreatment.

Officially the U.S. Army reported that 38 percent of all American POWs died in enemy hands, the highest death rate for American POWs since the Revolutionary War. Even the savage treatment of American POWs by the Japanese resulted in the deaths of "only" 30 percent of them. There is reason to suspect that the actual number of deaths in Communist prison camps in Korea was higher than the official figures indicate and many of those who died in the prison camps were included under the missing in action (MIA) figures.

The South Koreans, like the northerners, had no policy for prisoners and sometimes shot the North Koreans they captured. Ultimately, the U.S., as executive agent for the U.N., collected all North Korean POWs and placed them in camps. After China entered the war the U.S. gathered Chinese prisoners in the same camps. While the U.S. observed the provisions of the

1949 Geneva Convention on the treatment of prisoners, the general attitude might best be termed benign neglect. The vicious struggles for control of the North Korean and Chinese POW camps caused many deaths and additional POWs died when the U.S. forcefully reestablished control of the camps on Koje-do Island.

The North Korean and Chinese prisoners were a mixed lot. There were long-term professional Communist soldiers from both nations, heavily indoctrinated, many veterans of the fighting against Japan and the Chinese civil war. Others were civilians, from both North and South Korea, forced into the Communist forces to replace the heavy losses suffered by the North Koreans in the first three months of the war. Among the Chinese POWs were those who had served under General Joseph W. Stilwell and later Chiang Kai-shek until wholesale surrenders made them part of the People's Liberation Army. The Chinese POWs also contained recently inducted and only partially indoctrinated troops.

With the U.S. exercising minimal control over the internal situation in the POW camps, these disparate groups began to struggle for control of the camp's inmates. After the truce talks began, both the North Koreans and Chinese actually allowed key personnel to be captured so they could take charge of the POW compounds. Rival groups beat and killed their opponents in the camps while the U.S. troops supposedly in charge had no concern for or comprehension of what was happening behind the barbed wire. Only when the POWs began to display propaganda banners and make demands on the camp authorities did the U.S. command realize that they had a problem. Even then the actions of the U.S. authorities were inexcusably slow and hesitant.

The tense situation culminated in the POW seizing of a U.S. general officer and refusing to release him until he signed a paper which admitted U.S. mistreatment of the Communist POWs and promised to improve conditions. When the general's superior seemed to accept this statement, both men were later relieved and reprimanded.

The Army then sent a combat command to straighten out the matter. After putting an abrupt end to bureaucratic routine, Major General Haydon Boatner, the new commander, sent armed troops into the compounds to restore order. They did so, but killed a number of POWs in the process. In the propaganda battles being waged at the truce talks this affair was a Communist public relations gold mine. Not only did this give them an answer to U.N. charges of mistreatment of U.N. POWs, but also an invaluable face-saving explanation for the large number of their soldiers who refused to return home—they had been terrorized by the "imperialists" and forced to refuse repatriation.

When the truce talks began, the propaganda value of U.S. POWs to the Chinese increased sharply. From that time the Communists generally attempted to keep their prisoners alive while utilizing them for propaganda. The Communists saw the truce talks as a different method of keeping up the struggle, using words instead of bullets. The talks offered them a wonderful forum for propaganda. However, the discovery that large numbers of North Korean and Chinese POWs did not wish to return to their homelands remained a damaging public relations setback. The Communists worked as hard in U.N. camps as in their own POW camps to offset this unfavorable publicity. But in the end, nearly one-third of the Chinese and North Korean POWs did not return to Communist control.

It was the propaganda statements emanating from U.S. POWs in the Korean camps that first led to charges of large-scale collaboration by American POWs. Although most American POWs sought to evade the Chinese demands for material that could be used against the U.S., many were coerced into producing propaganda. Most did not consider the statements they made as harmful to the U.S. It should be noted that few, if any, gave their interrogators any information of military value. For their part, the Communists were not particularly interested in military information, preferring to deal with politics, social conditions, and economics. What they asked Americans to write or say were everyday examples of the excesses of political demagoguery implicit in the American right of free speech. While the wording might be strained to fit Communist jargon, the ideas were not unfamiliar.

Who in America of the 1930s and '40s had not heard that the Republican party was the tool of the rich, those "malefactors of great wealth," those "merchants of death" who saw in war a chance for personal profit? Charges that powerful members of the government and business stood to profit from war are a staple of American political discourse. Some American POWs saw nothing unusual in calling Harry S. Truman, a "warmonger." This could easily be expanded to charges that the U.S. and Truman started the war for "imperialistic" purposes.

In the U.S., particularly in the 1930s, attacks on "capitalists" and "imperialists" were part of normal American political rhetoric and many POWs saw no real harm in restating them in Communist jargon. The Chinese told the POWs that they were part of the proletariat being exploited by the capitalist imperialists. Therefore the Chinese, who had been exploited by these same villains, were actually their friends who sought to rescue their American brothers from the clutches of the U.S. military which exploited them for the profit of their capitalist masters, "the running dogs of Wall Street." Until the germ warfare campaign became the dominant theme of Chinese propaganda, statements by POWs attacking capitalist-imperialism was the objective of Communist pressure on POWs.

For the Communists, charges of imperialism were very useful and they sought to extract statements coupling U.S. actions in Korea with such claims from the POWs. Accusations of imperialism were both common in American political debate and useful to undermine support for the war on the U.S. home front. POW support for charges of imperialism was valuable on the Chinese home front and in the Third World. It was also useful in Western Europe and in other Communist states.

In the Communist lexicon imperialism is an inevitable consequence of capitalism, so the Chinese sought criticism of capitalism, capitalists, and imperialists from the POWs. Lenin wrote that capitalism is exploitation of the internal proletariat, while imperialism is exploitation of the external proletariat. The Chinese interpreted this to mean that any foreign trade by a capitalist country was imperialism and no POW could deny that America had extensive international trade relations.

The Chinese demanded that South Korean POWs accept ROK responsibility for starting the war at the behest of their American masters. President Syngman Rhee was a "lackey of Wall Street," a "running dog of American Imperialism." American POWs were also pressed to join in such charges although they were much less familiar with such phrases. The substantial amount of anti-Rhee, anti-ROK material provided by American POWs was used not only in Korea but in the U.S. and other countries supporting the U.N. in Korea. The Chinese believed such statements would erode support for the war in both the U.S. and Western Europe.

The Communists put heavy pressure on the prisoners to write letters or sign petitions calling for peace and opposing the U.S. effort in Korea. As almost none of the POWs had any idea of where Korea was or why they were there, they could not refute Communist claims that American capitalist warmongers started the war and wanted to continue it for personal profit. The U.S. government gave the prisoners no assistance in this matter for they feared that picturing the war as an ideological one comparable to that against the Nazis would lead to demands to expand the war, something they hoped to avoid. The government never furnished its troops with any solid rationale for fighting in Korea, while the Communists furnished them with any number of explanations, all of which suggested wrongdoing exclusively by the U.S. It was American POW contributions to the Communist "peace offensive" that led to charges of weakness and lack of patriotism.

The major Chinese propaganda operation of the Korean War was the charge that the U.S. used germ (biological) warfare in Korea. Their attempts to extract confessions from POWs of their complicity in biological warfare were intense and a number of Americans died for refusing to sign confessions. POW confessions were only a part, although an important part, of this Chinese effort to denigrate the U.S. in the Third World and reduce support for the war in the Western world. This last was almost a total failure for only a tiny minority of Americans ever took the germ warfare charges seriously, but they had and continue to have an impact on Third World nations, and to a lesser degree on Europeans. (A handful of U.S. academics, who were never in a Communist POW camp, still believe that there was something to these charges.)

The Chinese particularly sought to wring confessions of germ warfare from captured U.S. airmen. The Chinese methods included so-called brainwashing in which calculated irrational treatment caused an individual to lose contact with reality until he was no longer able to distinguish between fact and fiction. The interrogators turned lights on and off in an unpredictable manner, sleeping patterns were disrupted, and behavior that was praised one day was punished the next. The general hardships of prison life also were varied unpredictably. Some victims of this treatment became temporarily insane.

Some prisoners proved much more resistant to these procedures than others. As far as can be determined from very incomplete sources and records, between 20 and 35 percent of those interrogated died. Of the survivors about the same number confessed as held out until repatriated.

Many Communists from both Eastern and Western Europe visited the POW camps to support the Chinese charges of germ warfare. Some, such as "journalist" Wilfred Burchett actively put pressure on POWs and helped prepare "confessions" for international consumption. Others interviewed U.S. pilots and filmed conferences in which the pilots talked about their "participation" in germ warfare.

The earliest germ warfare confessions were palpably false, containing aerodynamic and biological impossibilities. The Chinese, or more likely the odious Burchett, discovered the discrepancies and rewrote the confessions to eliminate such errors and sometimes those who made them. All later confessions were carefully checked and rewritten to conform to the Chinese scenario. Once they returned to U.N. territory all those who confessed to germ warfare repudiated their signed statements. In a manner reminiscent of the soldiers who produced "imperialist" materials, the airmen said the charges were so ridiculous they did not think anyone would believe them, so they persuaded themselves that their confessions would not significantly harm the U.S.

Eugene Kinkaid, in his book *In Every War But One,* popularized the tripart division of prisoners into "progressives" (those who collaborated with their captors), "reactionaries" (those who never cooperated with the Communists), and those (80 percent) who played it cool, cooperating minimally. Varying definitions of cooperation led to substantial variations in the number in each category. Kinkaid considered anyone who did more than give name, rank, and serial number to be cooperating. A major problem with this classification is how to categorize the prisoners who died—half the total. Some commentators seemed to think that those who died of "giveupitis," belonged to the moderate collaborators because a true "reactionary" would not give the enemy the satisfaction of dying. Probably those who died included few that could be classified as "progressive" and many who were "reactionaries," all of which casts great doubt on Kinkaid's assessment that 10 percent of all prisoners were "progressives."

The whole concept of "giveupitis" is suspect. Given the conditions in the POW camps during the first winter, dying was not a sign of moral weakness. The POWs lived in unheated quarters without adequate clothing in temperatures of minus 40 degrees F. The food was inadequate, almost all had dysentery, and many had additional problems including intestinal parasites and wounds. To suggest that under these conditions men died from lack of will to survive is like saying victims of Nazi concentration camps also died from "giveupitis." To add to their suffering the POWs received hours of political harangues and indoctrination. The Chinese insisted that POW suffering was the fault of their civilian and military superiors and urged them to protest and save themselves by signing antiwar petitions. On occasion no one in a group ate until all members signed such petitions.

Some American doctors captured by the Communists first used the term "giveupitis." Many of the enlisted men were critical of the doctors, accusing them of mistreating the sick. The doctors replied they were trying to shake the men out of their lethargy, to make them feel some emotion, even anger.

To many people the only true collaborators were the twenty-one Americans who chose not to return to the U.S. after the war but to go to China. (Most of these returned to the U.S. after the Supreme Court ruled they could not be tried for offenses committed while POWs or for failing to return.) Few of these men were committed Communists; some feared they might face court-martial for actions in the POW camps. A few were opportunists who felt they were in too deep to back out. Only a few of them really believed the party line, while some who stayed lacked the mental ability to understand Communist concepts. It is worth remembering that the Chinese sought propaganda, not converts. The objective of the lectures, indoctrinations, and interrogations was useful propaganda, not bodies. Only when it became painfully apparent to the Communists that many of their POWs did not intend to return did they show an interest in persuading Americans to refuse repatriation. Whether those who refused repatriation were Communists was not an important consideration in these circumstances. Even a few Americans staying behind cushioned the ideological setback when large numbers of enemy POWs proved reluctant to return to their Communist utopias.

The POW repatriation issue surfaced early in the truce talks, but no real consideration of the matter occurred until late 1951. The tentative cease-fire line laid out on November 27, 1951, had a thirty-day limit and the POW question became the main obstacle to reaching an agreement within this time frame. The crux of the dispute was whether all POWs should be exchanged or only those who desired repatriation. The Geneva Convention of 1949, which neither side had ratified, could be read as supporting either position.

After World War II the Western powers had turned over to the Soviets large numbers of ethnic Russians and East Europeans serving in German Army units, most of whom were promptly executed. This was embarrassing to the U.S. and when Senator Joseph McCarthy charged that Communist sympathizers in the State Department had deliberately turned anti-Communists over to Stalin to be slaughtered, the administration was in no mood to open itself again to such charges. President Truman himself felt the U.S. should never again be party to such immoral behavior. Therefore the U.S. demanded, and stuck to it, that there be no forcible repatriation.

When the Communists first learned some POWs held by the U.N. did not wish to return they were not particularly concerned, and only asked how many. When they found how many of their soldiers did not wish to return they became adamant in their demand that all prisoners be returned. The Communists insisted that no POWs should be held against their will and that, given the option, all POWs wished to return home. They claimed that the U.N. coerced POWs into requesting asylum and would not agree that any of their soldiers be retained.

Only after the death of Stalin did the stalemate over the disposition of POWs break. Within a few days of that event an agreement to exchange sick and wounded sent thousands of Chinese and North Koreans home while several hundred Americans returned to U.S. custody. For the first time the American public got some indication of the heavy loss of life in the Communist camps. However, indignation at the Communists was quickly diverted by stories of collaboration by American prisoners.

It took several months more to reach a final agreement on POW exchanges. The contending parties finally agreed that all prisoners who said they did not wish to return would be turned over to neutral control (India) and their parent army could attempt to persuade them to return home. A number did reconsider, including two of the twenty-three Americans who originally

had elected not to return. The South Koreans released thousands of prisoners before turning them over to the Indians, whom the South Koreans believed favored the Communists.

On 27 July 1953 the truce took effect and prisoners on both sides began moving to the demilitarized zone for repatriation. In general, the more cooperative with the Chinese the U.S. POWs had been the sooner they were released. The "reactionaries" were the last to be freed, along with General William Dean, whom the North Koreans retained until the end. As Communist prisoners approached the exchange point they tore off their clothes and boots and threw them in the road, furnishing excellent photographic opportunities for the Communist newsmen of the almost naked conditions in which the Americans returned their captives. Some Americans gave emotional demonstrations on their release but most retained a military bearing. Those who cooperated least with their captors were usually the least demonstrative on release.

American POWs had suffered a considerably higher death rate than did other Allied prisoners, except the South Koreans. The reasons were straightforward: the Americans were the first to be captured in relatively large numbers and the North Koreans were unprepared to deal with an enemy they had not thought would even enter the war. In addition, the North Koreans and Chinese made a particular target of the Americans, knowing full well that it was U.S. intervention that had saved the Republic of Korea and American firepower that was decimating their comrades and destroying their cities. Furthermore, the American Army deployed far more conscripts to this war and deployed them earlier than did any of its non-Korean allies; these conscripts generally had less motivation and sense of comradeship on the whole than professional soldiers, particularly in a war that had become increasingly meaningless to most Americans.

Some British journalists and analysts, who should have known better, were particularly supercilious about American troop behavior in the field and in the camps. This superior attitude ill-behooved those whose army less than a decade earlier had surrendered so easily to a Japanese force less than half its size at Singapore, while Americans still held out in the Philippines. Such attitudes, fortunately, diminished as one approached the front.

Returning American POWs were given a screening and physical examination. Although the Army Medical Service claimed that these examinations were of high quality, an investigating committee disagreed and noted that the exams were cursory and turned up only obvious problems. The medics even missed cases of intestinal parasites. A more complete follow-up examination was planned for those who returned home by ship, but this shipboard exam was almost entirely of a psychological nature and directed more to uncovering possible acts of collaboration. A multiple-choice test was the main instrument used to assess the mental state of the former POWs. The psychologists seemed surprised that a group of soldiers who in many cases had been in brutal captivity for almost three years showed signs of aggression and frustration. Post-traumatic stress was an unknown condition at the time. Congress finally took action in 1975 by determining that former Korean POWs who developed any of a wide range of symptoms would have their medical problems considered service-connected, and could then be treated at government expense.

The death rates of former Korean POWs remained substantially above that expected for males of their age for the next thirty years. This higher morbidity paralleled that experienced by former prisoners of the Japanese. The returned prisoners tended to be subdued for years after their return. Public opinion held that they had failed both themselves and their country. Several hundred men believed to have been alive at the end of the war did not return, and the government contented itself with a few formal protests. There was no thought of punishing those who had murdered their fellow prisoners. The government was anxious to put the war behind it and all former POWs were required to sign a classified statement that they would not talk about mistreatment of POWs.

Not until the return of the POWs from Vietnam and the favorable treatment they received from the media together with the public concern over the missing POWs from Vietnam did Korean POWs receive sympathetic public notice. Since then former Korean POWs have held reunions and there was even some renewed interest in those Korean prisoners not returned. All but two of the twenty-one Americans that had refused repatriation have returned to the U.S.

The treatment of Americans taken captive by various groups since Vietnam parallels that of prisoners in Korea. After many years of neglect the U.S. shows increasing concern for those citizens who fall into the hands of those who ignore the Geneva Convention regarding the treatment of POWs. This is in marked contrast to the experience of the Korean POWs who were heavily criticized by their countrymen. This is most marked in the "giveupitis" claim which held the prisoners, rather than their captors, responsible for their deaths.

Jack Gifford

Bibliography

Biderman, Albert D. *March to Calumny* (1963).

Farrar-Hockley, Anthony. *The Edge of the Sword* (1954).

Kinkead, Eugene. *In Every War But One* (1959).

Weintraub, Stanley. *War in the Wards*, 2nd ed. (1976).

White, William L. *The Captives of Korea* (1957).

Prisoner of War (POW) Riots, February–December, 1952

These were a series of riots in the prison camps of the United Nations command (UNC) on the offshore islands of Koje-do and Pongam-do, South Korea, during 1952. The conflict between Communist and non-Communist prisoners for control of the compounds turned into major uprisings, initiated by the Communist prisoners while truce talks stalled for more than a year over the issue of forced repatriation. The riots were characterized by widespread violence and the capture of the prison's commandant. Worldwide publicity from the riots often overshadowed news from the Korean War theater. The media focus even contributed to a spinoff effect of riots and strikes in American penitentiaries and Soviet forced labor camps.

As long as the battlefront remained fluid, with neither side gaining permanent control, the prisoners were docile, despite the inadequacies of their confinement. But the enormous surge in the number of prisoners had caught the United Nations command unprepared. Housed in makeshift compounds, the POWs were allowed to run their internal affairs within the compounds while the UNC provided minimal camp security. In early 1951 all prisoners were evacuated to Koje-do, a small island twenty miles southwest of Pusan, where permanent compounds had been built. Although the evacuation from the mainland to the island was harsh, conditions and food did improve. However, no effort was made to segregate the Communist from the anti-Communist prisoners in the new compounds on Koje-do.

During 1951, a civil war raged in the camp compounds on Koje-do between the Communist and non-Communist prisoners. Although control often fluctuated between these two groups, the ultimate result of the clashes left the anti-Communists in charge of most compounds. Shortly after the Communists rejected proposals of voluntary repatriation at the truce talks, the first major riot broke out between the Communist prisoners and the UNC.

During the first major clash between prisoners and guards on February 18, 1952, seventy-seven POWs were killed and 140 were wounded. Smaller riots broke out in the following weeks. These conflicts were used by the Communist negotiators at Panmunjom as a basis for charging mistreatment of POWs and using force to prevent them from choosing repatriation. The February riots foreshadowed a major publicity disaster for the UNC in May, following its decision to screen the prisoners in order to determine how many favored repatriation. In fact, the screening process triggered the rebellious inmate activity after the truce talks had been reduced to the final issue of prisoner repatriation on May 2nd.

On May 7, 1952, Brigadier General Francis T. Dodd, the commander of the island prison camp, was seized by North Korean officer compound number 76 when he went to the compound after the controlling inmates refused to allow the screening. Dodd had been sent to Koje-do a couple of months before in order to prevent a repetition of the bloodshed of the February 18 riot. In Dodd's place, Brigadier General Charles F. Colson negotiated with the Communist inmate representatives. They demanded a confession of past "crimes" against POWs, a pledge to recognize Communist organizations and an agreement "to stop torturing and mistreating prisoners" to make them anti-Communists. Although Colson got the prisoners to slightly moderate their demands, he signed a compromising statement to obtain the release of Dodd on May 10. Subsequently, both American generals were reduced in rank and retired from the Army.

Dodd's capture and Colson's statement were major international news. Moscow radio stations and *Pravda* featured the story. Communist parties in Western Europe staged demonstrations. In Teheran, Communist youths triggered a riot in May that left 12 dead and 250 wounded. On May 13, the Chinese compound of 6,500 POWs on Koje-do demonstrated. Brigadier General Haydon L. ("Bull") Boatner, the fifteenth commander of the island prison camp, led an investigation which determined that the riot resulted from the death of a Chinese POW and that the UNC was partially responsible due to its lack of control in the compounds. He would quickly correct the situation that had put the UNC on the defensive in the truce negotiations.

Boatner implemented a plan during the next month that restored order in the flimsy and vastly overcrowded compounds. First, the civilians adjacent to the camp were removed. Then new and more secure compounds were built. The old compounds that had been designed to hold 4,500 prisoners averaged 6,000 prisoners in 1952; the new compounds were much smaller, separated, and easier to control.

The effort to transfer the Communist prisoners into the new compounds on June 10, 1952, triggered the last major riot on Koje-do. Using flamethrowers and tear gas, U.N. troops moved against the "iron triangle" of prisoner resistance in compounds 76–78. During the crackdown, forty-one Communist prisoners were killed and 274 were wounded. One American soldier was killed.

Boatner moved the leaders of the June riot from Koje-do compounds 76–78 to neighboring Pongam-do Island, where the final major POW riot of the Korean War occurred on December 14, 1952. It was also the bloodiest, with 85 POWs killed and 113 hospitalized.

Since the American Civil War, the United States had not faced handling such a sudden mass of POWs. But, certainly, the worst of the pandemonium in the POW camps might have been prevented had the American command noted a similarity to such problems toward the end of World War II, less than a decade earlier.

W.D. Pederson

Bibliography

Fehrenbach, T.R. *This Kind of War. A Study in Unpreparedness* (1963).

Kaufman, Burton I. *The Korean War. Challenges in Crisis, Credibility, and Command* (1986).

MacDonald, Callum A. *Korea. The War Before Vietnam* (1986).

Meyers, Samuel M., and Albert Biderman. *Mass Behavior in Battle and Captivity* (1969).

Pederson, William D. "Inmate Movements and Prison Uprisings," *Social Science Quarterly*, 59 (1978).

Psychological Warfare

In the Korean conflict, U.S. psychological warfare was a military affair, and no definitive assessment of its effect on soldiers and civilians in North Korea can be made. But a count of prisoners of war (POWs) taken by the United Nations forces revealed that about one-third claimed to have at least surrendered in part because of psychological warfare leaflets. Nearly every prisoner voluntarily taken had one or more U.N. leaflets. Psychological warfare was credited with a "nudging" effect on one's willingness to surrender, though insufficient alone to cause surrender. The Chinese enlisted men were found the most amenable to the surrender mission of psywar, and the hard-core North Korean officer corps the least inclined.

The primary purpose of psywar was to lower the morale of the enemy soldiers and to influence them to stop fighting. Less tactical and more indirect in effect was the spreading of the "true" battle picture and of the U.N. aims of peace, unification, and reconstruction.

Before the Korean conflict, details for a well-honed, coordinated operation had not been thought out carefully. Thus, only at the tactical level—the combat operation at or near the front line—did the approach taken show improvement over World War II.

When North Korea attacked South Korea, the only operational psywar troop unit in the Army was at Fort Riley, Kansas. The unit, sent to Korea in fall 1950 as the 1st Loudspeaker and Leaflet Company, was the Eighth Army's tactical propaganda unit during the war. Loudspeakers on vehicles and aircraft also disseminated propaganda.

General Matthew B. Ridgway, Eighth Army commander in Korea, was enthusiastic about psychological warfare and frequently passed along suggestions to the psychological warfare department for consideration. He once suggested he would prefer greater use of art on leaflets, especially those depicting to enemy the horrors of their comrades' deaths on the battlefields.

One such message, disseminated by artillery and aircraft bombardment, proclaimed:

Comrades! Soldiers of the North Korean Army.... U.N. airplanes are overhead prepared to strike your positions. They are loaded with rockets, napalm and MG. U.N. artillery is sighting on you. At my command they will bring you death. ... You have seen your positions littered with the burned, blackened, and shattered bodies of your buddies after our planes and artillery come down upon you. You have seen your buddies with their clothes and bodies blown limb from limb by our shells. ... Even if you are not hit directly, your nose and ears will bleed, your eardrums will be broken, your organs deranged, and your minds will cease to function. ... Raise both hands high over your head and walk in the open toward U.N. lines. ... You are guaranteed good treatment. ... Act now. You have five minutes.

Some leaflets promised medical treatment for frostbite, undermined faith in officers, and similarly instilled fear for soldiers' safety. Other themes for tactical operations told of the mounting enemy dead and the U.N. materiel superiority. Many enemy POWs claimed that the signature of General MacArthur on a surrender pass convinced them that promises of good treatment would be honored.

Secretary of the Army Frank Pace, Jr. believed Korea offered an "especial opportunity for highly profitable exploitation" of psychological warfare, and the secretary advocated "quality rather than quantity" in producing leaflets and radio broadcasts. In spring 1951, strategic plans were under way to double an effort of about 13 million propaganda leaflets a week and to augment thirteen hours of daily radio broadcasts in Korean by adding shortwave broadcasts in Chinese to Chinese troops in Korea and Manchuria. Aircraft by then were flying leaflet missions nearly every day of the week. Leaflets and loudspeakers were credited as a factor in a heavy increase in prisoners as the Korean War moved into its second year. Pace considered psywar as the "cheapest form of warfare," and Ridgway, when he moved into charge in Tokyo of the Far East command, wanted personnel of "integrity and intellectual capacity" for a psywar planning group.

The 1st Radio Broadcasting and Leaflet (RB&L) Group became the operating agency for psywar in the Far East after it arrived in Tokyo in summer 1951, some of its key personnel having been rushed over earlier to become immediately operational. Some group members were young draftees who were graduates of journalism schools. Others had art backgrounds or experience in advertising, radio, or newspapering. This background may well account for the unparalleled visual quality of U.N. Korean War leaflets. The unit had an international flavor because some of its members were native linguists. To facilitate radio and leaflet propaganda and reach all educational levels of the target audience, members of the group eventually compiled a 4,000 character Chinese-English dictionary used to produce effective propaganda material. Translators often had laughed at errors in scripts caused by the Americans' failure to understand the language nuances and the cultures of their targets. Some expensive printshop equipment shipped to Japan was stored in Yokohama because the Japanese printing industry was well developed and no need existed to set up a separate printing plant. The group supervised a radio network known as the "Voice of the United Nations" and produced millions of leaflets disseminated by aircraft and artillery shells. Its radio operations in Korea were under control of the 1st RB&L Group's Mobile Radio Broadcasting Company.

By the end of the war, more than 2.5 billion leaflets had been dropped over enemy troops and civilians in North Korea. The usual procedure was as follows:

Psywar officers in the field would decide on a drop in a particular sector. They would telephone the Tokyo psychological warfare office, giving the general content thought desirable and where the drop should occur. The Tokyo personnel took the leaflets out of existing stocks or printed them for the occasion. From the printing plant the leaflets were taken to air bases and loaded into aircraft for drops or shipped to Korea for drops by Korea-based aircraft.

Interrogation of enemy soldiers showed about one of three were to some degree influenced to surrender by the leaflets. Interrogation of civilians in North Korea and the parts of South Korea that had been occupied by Communist forces revealed that the radio programs also reached a considerable audience and stirred some civilian opposition to the red regime. Native Koreans served as announcers.

About 200,000 radio sets were in Korea before the fighting broke out, about one set per 100 people. A shortage of receivers and frequent disruptions of electrical power limited the effectiveness of radio operations. A few North Koreans owned two radios. Sometimes they would tune a radio in the front of a home to a Communist station and in another part of the house clandestinely listen to the U.N. broadcasts.

For all this apparent success, division and corps commanders had to be indoctrinated to the value of working with the psychological warfare section.

Brigadier General Robert McClure, chief of the psychological warfare division of the Army, operated out of Washington after his office was created in late 1950 after the war began. The Army, because of the impetus of the war, Cold War tensions, and Secretary Pace's persistent pressure, had created an unprecedented staff organization in the Pentagon—the office of the chief of psychological warfare. A "true believer" in psywar, McClure had emerged from World War II as the Army's expert in the new field. Under Pace, the general created a staff responsible for psychological and unconventional warfare. Despite the "hot war" in Korea, the driving factor in the Army's support was a desire for guerrilla capability in Europe to retard a Soviet invasion, if it should occur. McClure convinced the Army to create a separate Psychological Warfare Center in 1952 at Fort Bragg, N.C., from which the Army Special Forces training facilities would emerge.

McClure campaigned to improve the air support he claimed psywar lacked in its initial year in Korea. But in the ten days after the successful surprise landing at Inchon on September 15, 1950, accompanied by the simultaneous breakout from the Pusan perimeter, thirteen B-29s had bombarded the North Koreans with leaflets inviting them to surrender. Operations officers at FEAF thought the support effort excessive, but Air Force intelligence reported the missions as "highly profitable." Near Seoul on September 23, a total of 104 enemy Koreans surrendered together, each man carrying one of the "safe-conduct" passes dropped by the Superforts.

U.S. aircraft dropped warning leaflets before bombing industrial and factory areas in the North, giving workers time to flee, though some were ordered to stay on the job and not read the leaflets.

B-29 crews called the leaflet missions "paper routes." Over friendly territory, the leaflets were dropped from low-flying planes in loosely wrapped bundles that fell apart as they descended. In the beginning the leaflet bombs were extremely unreliable, more than one-third failing to open. The supply at times ran out, and because of failures the coverage was less thorough than it might have been.

Drops over hostile territory used hollow aerial bombs, each with a capacity of 45,000 4-by-5-inch leaflets. Thirty-two bombs constituted an aircraft load. The bombs were released at 15,000 feet or higher, with fuses set to open them at 1,000 feet. Standard artillery smoke shells were converted to leaflet shells and dispersed by artillery in cooperation with combat operations.

In March 1951, a psywar leaflet urged guerrillas in South Korea to give up a hopeless fight. Translated, the message warned that "the mouse has gnawed at the tiger's tail long enough." Hard-hitting cartoons were also part of a propaganda effort aimed at an enemy whose foot soldiers usually had only a smattering of elementary education.

Within twenty-four hours after President Harry S. Truman announced U.S. troops would assist the invaded Republic of South Korea, leaflets were dropped over Korea telling of the decision. And within the next twenty-four hours, radio broadcasts from Tokyo were beamed toward Korea, psywar becoming the first weapon used by the United Nations north of the 38th parallel.

Prior to the outbreak of hostilities, Major General Charles A. Willoughby, General MacArthur's assistant chief of staff, G-2, had set up a small planning group to carry out psywar in the event of an emergency. The original planning group of six had grown to thirty-five by December 1950.

Two C-47 aircraft were made available to the Eighth Army and X Corps to broadcast surrender messages over airborne loudspeakers. The Air Force had failed to develop loudspeaker aircraft before the Korean War and the two that were finally put into service had the loudspeakers mounted to project slightly from the doors, pointing to a 45-degree angle downward when the planes flew straight and level. In May 1951 the speakers were moved to the bottom of the planes so they could point them directly at the ground with less danger to the craft. Psywar staff officers were the link between the operational forces and higher headquarters.

By April 1951, psywar officers in the field tried to make greater use of tactical aircraft, and coordination efforts improved in leaflet drops, loudspeaker missions, and air missions.

In March 1953, the Fifth Air Force in cooperation with the Eighth Army began dropping a special leaflet that asked: "Where is the Communist Air Force?" The drops were made on enemy troop concentrations the Air Force attacked. Radio Seoul hammered the same theme.

On the night of April 26, 1953 two B-29s dropped more than one million leaflets along the Yalu River on the North Korea–China border, offering $50,000 and political asylum to each Russian, Chinese, and Korean pilot who would deliver his jet plane to Kimpo Airfield. The first man who delivered his plane would receive an extra $50,000. The offer became known, fittingly, as "Project Moolah" and was first conceived by a war correspondent in Seoul, according to one report; another account termed "Moolah" the product of the Harvard University Russian Research Center. Another half-million "reward" leaflets were dropped on the nights of May 10 and May 18 over Sinuiju and Uiju airfields, and radio stations beamed the "Moolah" offers in Russian, Chinese, and Korean language broadcasts.

But no Communist airman delivered a plane as a result of the "Moolah" broadcasts. A North Korean lieutenant who defected after the war with a MIG on September 21, 1953, claimed he had never heard of the $100,000 windfall he was to receive, according to Air Force intelligence. But a unit commendation issued by the Army to the 1st Radio Broadcasting and Leaflet Group in July 1954 gives the unit implied credit for the pilot delivering the undamaged MIG-15 fighter plane and cites the unit for "an ingeniously planned and capably disseminated propaganda broadcast" that materially assisted in destroying the morale of enemy troops, reducing greatly their effectiveness in combat. It may well be that the MIG pilot was reluctant to admit that he had brought over his plane and his person for crass monetary gain.

It is thought the Soviets may have withdrawn their pilots after the "Moolah" offer. An unlocated radio transmitter began to jam only Russian-language broadcasts of the reward offer, and after May 8 most MIGs sighted by Sabres bore Chinese or North Korean insignia. Earlier in the year most MIGs had borne the plain red stars of the Soviet Union.

The 98th Bomb Wing at the end of the war was using leaflet casings of about 500 pounds when loaded. About one million individual leaflets could be distributed nightly by a single B-29 Superfort. The big planes used radar to rain the leaflet clusters at night and in bad weather on towns, villages, and military billeting areas.

P

Weekly plans spelled out psywar themes for radio, leaflets, and other media. One major theme was that the Communists sought to enslave all Korea and to exploit its economy for their own gain. Another was that all the free nations of the world, through the United Nations, supported the Republic of Korea in opposing Communist aggression.

The reliance on C-47 transport aircraft as a way of disseminating leaflets and the use of voiceplanes at the tactical level were uncomplicated by enemy air or antiaircraft action.

William I. McCorkle

Bibliography

Andrews, T.G., et al. *An Investigation of Individual Factors Relating to the Effectiveness of Psychological Warfare* (1952).

Daugherty, William, in collaboration with M. Janowitz. *A Psychological Warfare Casebook* (1958).

Hansen, K.K. "Psywar in Korea," typescript, Office of the Joint Chiefs of Staff (n.d.).

Kahn, Lessing, and Julius Segal. *Psychological Warfare and Other Factors Affecting the Surrender of North Korean and Chinese Forces* (1953).

McLaurin, R., ed. *Military Propaganda: Psychological Warfare and Operations* (1982).

Mossman, Billy. *EUSAK Combat Propaganda Operations, 13 July 1950–1 September 1952*, Far East United States Army Forces, 3rd Historical Detachment (n.d.).

Pease, Stephen E. *Psywar: Psychological Warfare in Korea, 1950–1953* (1992).

See also BRAINWASHING, OR *XINAO*

Pusan Perimeter

No U.S. troops of the twentieth century, except for those involved in the forlorn defense of Bataan and Corregidor against the Japanese soon after Pearl Harbor, were so embattled as those who fought to hold the line at the Pusan perimeter against the North Koreans from early August through the middle of September 1950.

The first two months of the war, which had opened with the North Korean invasion of the Republic of Korea (ROK) on 25 June 1950, had seen a string of almost unbroken defeat and retreat for the ROK forces and their U.S. ally. American forces, routed in their first ground clash at Osan early in July, had then suffered disaster at the Kum River and had been routed again at Taejon. The only good news was the pounding the North Koreans were suffering under U.S. ground attack airpower, attacks which, indeed, had undoubtedly delayed the enemy's quickly overrunning of all of South Korea. But ROK and American troops were worn out from their near-constant retreats and morale was none too good.

By 4 August 1950, U.S. and ROK forces, at the end of their long retreat from the 38th parallel, had taken up positions along a rectangular area about 100 miles from north to south and half that width from east to west. The Naktong River, Korea's second largest, formed a moat on the western border of the perimeter. The southern border lacked any natural barrier, and was thus the scene of fierce fighting and of enemy breakthroughs barely contained. Here the battered U.N. forces would make what was widely believed to be their last stand to save the Republic of Korea (ROK) from North Korean conquest. The defense of the Pusan perimeter would be fought by the U.S. 24th and 25th Infantry Divisions, and the 1st Cavalry Division, allied to the ROK 1st, 3rd, 6th, 8th, and Capital Divisions.

Battering away at these U.N. forces were the North Korean 83rd Motorized Regiment of the 105th Armored Division (the high number should not mislead; the 105th was North Korea's only armored division); the 3rd "Seoul Guards," the 4th "Kim Chaek, Seoul Guards"; the 6th "Guards"; the 8th; the 12th "Andong"; elements of the mauled 13th Division; the 15th Division, and the 766th Independent Infantry Regiment. All had suffered heavily before arriving at the perimeter and all would endure even heavier losses in the perimeter fighting. In fact, contrary to popular reporting at the time, the U.N. now actually enjoyed a substantial superiority in manpower over the enemy: approximately 92,000 to 70,000.

Yet the outnumbered North Koreans, many of whose units were now fleshed out by conscripted South Koreans with varying degrees of commitment to the war, bereft of any air support and subjected to brutal, nearly unremitting U.N. air strikes, on several occasions nearly broke the Pusan perimeter. Such an impressive military record can be fairly attributed to the North Koreans' superior motivation in their campaign to unify Korea and their Army's brutal discipline. Finally, at least at the start of the invasion, something like one-half of the North

Korean troops had accumulated combat experience on the winning side of China's lengthy civil war, as well as in the war against Japan. American troops, by way of contrast, somewhat lacked the stomach to fight all-out for someone else's country in an undeclared so-called police action. Furthermore, U.N. troops had been in almost unbroken retreat since the beginning of the war; the enemy seemed nearly invincible both to himself and to U.N. forces. Finally, ROK soldiers, although showing a much tougher military spirit than they have been given credit for, fought under the psychological disadvantage of knowing that if their side won, Korea's division would be perpetuated. (This consideration may go some way toward answering the question often raised by GIs: "Why do 'their' Koreans fight better than 'our' Koreans?").

And yet that discipline, morale, and motivation must have been brittle. Those disciplined, highly motivated North Korean troops, when they realized that they might be trapped between U.S. X Corps troops behind their lines as a result of the Inchon invasion and the breakout of Eighth Army and ROK forces from the Pusan perimeter, would bolt and run in a retreat more precipitous than any staged by their enemies. That retreat was in the future, however, when North Korean Premier Kim Il Sung set 15 August, the fifth anniversary of the liberation of Korea from Japanese rule, as the date for the complete "liberation" of the South.

The fighting up and down the hills and mountains and across the fetid rice paddies of the perimeter was brutal for both sides. The troops fought in 110 degree heat, their boots and belts sometimes rotting away. Often casualties from heat exhaustion exceeded those inflicted by the enemy, at least among unacclimatized American troops. But the North Koreans suffered their own peculiar hell from the incinerating napalm and white phosphorous dropped on them by unopposed U.S. warplanes. They lacked medical care and were almost always hungry, ordeals that American and ROK troops usually escaped.

By early August, the North Koreans, still rolling back U.N. forces, were nonetheless at the end of an increasingly attenuated supply line, under constant air attack, relying increasingly on South Korean conscripts, and showing signs of weariness. U.N. forces, on the other hand, were being reinforced from the United States, and later from other United Nations. They now had a more or less continuous, if not very strong, line and were not so frequently routed by the standard enemy maneuver of flanking and rear attacks. Their logistics lines were now a short distance from the great supply center of Pusan. The North Koreans were like a stretched rubber band, the U.N. forces like a compressed spring. But at the time, and as late as the end of August, the fall of Pusan and the loss of the war was still an unnerving possibility.

Even before U.N. forces had moved into their positions along the perimeter, General Walton H. Walker, Eighth Army commander, had issued his controversial "Stand or Die" order:

> There will be no more retreating, withdrawal, or readjustment of the lines or any other term you choose. There is no line behind us to which we can retreat. . . . There will be no Dunkirk, no Bataan . . ., a retreat to Pusan would be one of the greatest butcheries in history. . . . Capture by these people is worse than death itself. . . . We are going to win.

In fact, as historians have pointed out, the U.N. forces had yet to retreat into the Pusan perimeter when this order was given. And even at the time the use of the term "line" was a most imprecise means to refer to the rather disconnected series of strongpoints that held the perimeter, and through which the North Koreans would time and again infiltrate. Nonetheless, after the order there was no large-scale retreat within the perimeter and many commanders reported an improved attitude among their troops. Certainly, U.N. forces began to inflict enormous casualties upon the enemy. The *New York Times* pointed out the situation at the end of July more succinctly than most: "For five weeks we have been trading space for time. The space is running out for us. The time is running out for our enemies" (*New York Times*, 29 July 1950).

The enemy proceeded to throw its troops against the U.N. lines, often achieving at least local breakthroughs. But in many cases the North Korean high command seemed to have little overall plan than to take Pusan on Kim Il Sung's 15 August deadline. After the battle of the Naktong Bulge in mid-August, for example, the 24th Division buried more than 1,200 enemy dead. Enemy prisoners reported that about one-third of their 4th Division's wounded died because of lack of medical care.

An equal threat developed to the north, where North Korean troops actually entered the small port city of Pohang-dong before being driven out. The USAF base at nearby Yonil was hurriedly evacuated, the 3rd ROK Division evacuated by sea, and for days afterwards fighting raged, as the city became a no-man's land. The enemy was finally cleared with the help of intense U.S. sea and land bombardment.

Perhaps the most dangerous North Korean thrust was at the central, or Taegu front, where the enemy 10th, 3rd, 15th, 13th and 12th Divisions, as well as elements of the 105th Armored Division crossed the Naktong and drove on the city. A few enemy rounds fell on the refugee-swollen city on 16 August, precipitating something of a civilian panic. Both the provincial and the national government left the city that day for Pusan. General Walker also evacuated his headquarters to Pusan, although this move was precipitated primarily by a concern that his mobile communication system, the only one of its type in the Far East, stood in danger of capture or destruction. More positively, it was during the enemy thrust toward Taegu that the North Korean Army lost much of its armor in battles with U.N. tanks along the so-called Bowling Alley. By the end of August, some ROK and U.S. officers were anticipating an end of the war by Thanksgiving. They were somewhat premature; for the next two weeks the U.N. command would be fighting for its survival as the enemy, drawing on its last reserves mounted desperate attacks all along the perimeter.

On one day, 3 September, for example, General Walker found himself fighting no less than five serious defensive battles simultaneously. Pohang was lost on 6 September, and Taegu remained under threat. U.S. casualties during the first two weeks of September would be the heaviest of the entire war. Despite heavy numerical superiority and overwhelming armor and artillery, not to mention complete control of the air, the U.N. forces by the middle of September had barely turned back the final series of enemy offensives around Pohang and the Kyongju corridor, in the Taegu area, and in the south. But by then the enemy was exhausted and hungry, morale was low and discipline maintained primarily by force. Any hope of taking Pusan by the 15th was gone. But no one, friend or foe, could dispute that they had done their best.

On the other hand, U.N. forces were constantly being replenished with troop replacements and equipment; the first British forces arrived in September. Although Eighth Army intelligence did not realize it, by 15 September U.S forces alone considerably outnumbered the enemy. The triumph at Inchon and the breakout from the perimeter lay just ahead.

D. Randall Beirne

Bibliography

Appleman, Roy S. *South to the Naktong, North to the Yalu, The U.S. Army in the Korean War* (1961).
James, D.C. *The Years of MacArthur, 3, Triumph and Disaster, 1945–1964* (1970).
Rees, David. *Korea: The Limited War* (1964).
Robertson, W.G. *Counterattack on the Naktong: 1950* (U.S. Army Command and General Staff College, Fort Leavenworth, KS: 1985).

Pusan Perimeter: Breakout

The breakout at the Pusan perimeter between 16 and 22 September 1950 was one of the major offensive actions of the Korean War. Its purpose was to fix and hold North Korea's main combat strength and prevent movement of its units from the Pusan perimeter to the Inchon-Seoul area. The plan called for the United States 1st Corps under General Frank Milburn and consisting of the U.S. 1st Cavalry Division, the 24th Infantry Division, the 1st ROK Division, the 27th British Brigade, and the U.S. 5th Regimental Combat Team (RCT) to break out of the perimeter at Waegwan. The main effort would be directed along the Taegu-Kumchon-Taejon-Suwon axis in order to effect a junction with the X Corps in the north. Here were two bridges which had been damaged but could eventually be used by the I Corps to cross the river. And here was the major axis for the I Corps to move to Seoul.

Hill 268 was to become the critical terrain feature in the breakout. It covered not only the Taegu highway and railroad, but also the main highway running from Waegwan south along the east bank of the Naktong River. Any attack by the United States Army toward Waewan from the south had to take Hill 268.

The North Korean forces in the area around Waegwan were three understrength infantry divisions reinforced by one armored regiment. The North Korean 3rd Division occupied the positions south and southeast of Waegwan.

Two infantry regiments, the 8th and 9th of the 3rd Division, were identified in defensive positions in the hills south of Waegwan. Covering the roadnets in the vicinity of Waegwan was the 65th Regiment of North Korea's only armored unit, the 105th Armored Division.

Further to the east and covering the main highway out of Taegu to Tabu-dong were the North Korean 1st and 13th Infantry Divisions. This area, known as "the Bowling Alley," was mountainous and well-fortified.

By 15 September, North Korean forces had fought hard to attain these strategic positions. Some units were only eight miles from Taegu. Word of the Inchon landings did not reach them until several days after the start of the U.S. and South Korean offensive from the Pusan perimeter. Even when the North Koreans heard of the Inchon landings through intercepted radio communications, these units were told to "hold at all costs."

On 16 September the 2nd Battalion of the 5th RCT first met enemy resistance south of Waegwan on the Naktong River. By the 17th, the 1st Battalion had joined it in an attack north along the river. The 3rd Battalion meanwhile turned up a right fork at this time. Rain was pouring down, and the tanks accompanying the 3rd Battalion could not keep up. The shoulders of the road weakened, causing three tanks to slip off the road into a rice paddy. The infantry of the 3rd Battalion, however, moved ahead without tanks. They were taking artillery and mortar fire when they received a radio message that they had taken a wrong turn.

The 3rd Battalion moved back down the road. Company K moved around the right side of a reservoir and Company L the left.

Hill 268 was a long prominence with entrenchments at the south end and bunkers at the north end that controlled the Taegu road. Company K attacked from Hill 160 up one finger of the south end of Hill 268. Company L attacked from Hill 160 up another finger of Hill 268 to the west. Company B of the 1st Battalion helped L Company and attacked to the west below the finger. Company I was in reserve on Hill 160 and waited until the southern crest of Hill 268 was taken before it attacked the bunkers on the north end.

When halfway up the finger of Hill 268 the three rifle platoons became pinned down by enemy rifle fire and grenades from trenches on the south end. Four men of the 2nd Platoon of Company I threw grenades at an enemy foxhole, charged over a barbed wire emplacement,

and dashed into the hole. This action apparently penetrated the enemy defensive position. The enemy then fled to the north end of Hill 268 as K Company charged up the hill.

The other two companies then went into action. Company L moved up the hill to a position on the left of K Company. Company I then passed through Companies K and L and twice assaulted the bunkers on the north end of Hill 268. Company I had ten men killed and many wounded in trying to take these bunkers and finally gave up for that day. The enemy originally had about 600 soldiers who were "diehards." Taking Hill 268 was going to be tougher than anticipated.

As the sun began to set, men from K Company crept out in the light of dusk and dragged wounded from I Company that they could reach safely. Others that could not be reached died or were killed by the enemy during the night. Finally, Company M with heavy mortars and machine guns arrived. All four companies awaited the called-for air strike that would take place early in the morning.

At dawn on the 19th, three flights of F-51s dropped napalm on the enemy bunkers on Hill 268. After the air strikes, I Company, reinforced by platoons from Companies K and L, assaulted these bunkers. The enemy in many cases again fought to the last man. When their dead were counted after the air strike and the three-company assault, between 200 and 250 bodies were found. Among the dead was a full colonel, a regimental commander of the North Korean Army. By 1200 hours, the summit and back slopes of Hill 268 were finally consolidated by the 3rd Battalion of the 5th RCT.

In the meantime, the 2nd Battalion took Waegwan from the high ground south of the town at 1430 hours. They then moved through the town to the southwest slope of Hill 303. The 1st Battalion crossed the road southwest of Waegwan at 1530 hours and moved to a defensive position to the north. These two battalions cost the North Koreans 300 dead, twelve prisoners of war, plus many mortars, machine guns, antitank guns, and one tank.

The regiment suffered 148 casualties in the nine rifle companies on the 19th, but suffered few casualties against light resistance the next day. The 1st and 2nd Battalions finally took Hill 303 (Objective Philadelphia) on the 20th of September. In this assault they received only limited resistance. That night they began crossing the Naktong River at 2035 hours. The 2nd Battalion ran into no resistance. By the morn-

P

ing of the 21st of September both battalions were across the river.

The 3rd Battalion of the 5th RCT moved on Hill 300 (Objective Boston) on the 20th and tried to cut off escaping North Korean soldiers who were now in complete disarray. By the 21st they were relieved by an advanced party of the 5th Cavalry Regiment. The 3rd Battalion then crossed the Naktong River at 1330 hours. The enemy attempted to delay this crossing for a short time by artillery and mortar fire. By 1900, however, the entire 3rd Battalion was on the high ground across the Naktong River and had prepared this position for the night.

Meanwhile, the rest of the 1st Cavalry Division was not idle. The 5th Cavalry Regiment had moved into the attack on the 17th of September along the Waegwan–Taegu road. The 1st Battalion took Hill 203 after much fighting. The 70th Tank Battalion alone lost nine tanks and one tank dozer in support of the 1st Battalion on the 18th. The 3rd Battalion of the 5th Cavalry, after several tries, finally took Hill 174 and tried to move on Hill 371. The 2nd Battalion engaged the enemy on Hill 184 and then proceeded to attack Hill 253.

The 8th Regiment, 3rd Division, refused to give up Hills 253, 300, and 371 on 18 September. On the 19th, after heavy casualties, the 1st Battalion of the 5th Cavalry and the 2nd Battalion of the 7th Cavalry Regiments together took Hills 300 and 253. The enemy on Hill 371, however, continued to resist, and all attacks failed.

The 1st and 3rd Battalions of the 7th Cavalry Regiment with the 70th Tank Battalion in support pushed northeast up the Waegwan–Taegu road. Once past Hill 300, the 1st Battalion turned off the main road and headed east toward Tabu-dong. By evening of 20 September, the 1st Battalion, with the 3rd Battalion close behind it, was four miles from Tabu-dong. Because the movement was too slow, the commander of the 7th Cavalry Regiment was replaced.

The next morning, 21 September 1950, the 1st Battalion attacked Tabu-dong, and by early afternoon it had taken the town and turned south, toward Taegu. By late afternoon it had linked up with the 8th Cavalry Regiment, which was attacking north from Taegu. The 3rd Battalion of the 7th Cavalry followed the 1st Battalion, but at Tabu-dong it turned north and set up a blocking position. The encirclement was now complete. Large elements of the North Korean 1st, 3rd, and 13th Divisions were cut off.

The breakout from the Pusan perimeter had been accomplished. The North Korean Army was cut off and in retreat. The U.S. Eighth Army under General Walton Walker, led by the I Corps, was now heading for a link-up with the X Corps at Seoul. Other than battles with escaping elements of the North Korean Army, the fight to save South Korea was over. The United States Eighth Army had completely defeated the North Korean Army and was poised for the invasion of North Korea itself.

David Kangas

Pyongyang

The city of Pyongyang, capital of the Democratic People's Republic of (North) Korea (DPRK), functioned as the northern capital in the Koryo Dynasty, A.D. 953–1392. It is the largest and oldest city in the north, located on the Taedong River, with the estuary city of Chinnampo used as its port. Pre–Korean War Pyongyang served the Japanese occupiers as an industrial and railroad center. The DPRK, a Soviet-sponsored, Stalinist regime, was based in Pyongyang when the republic was proclaimed on 9 September 1948. In 1950, the year of the outbreak of the Korean War, Pyongyang claimed almost one-half million residents.

The DPRK Premier, Kim Il Sung, had fought under the Soviets in Manchuria, developing his ideology and cementing diplomatic ties. The Soviets helped establish the Korean People's Army (KPA) and strongly supported North Korean demands for the reunification of the Korean peninsula.

After the retaking of the Republic of Korea capital, Seoul, by U.N. forces in September 1950, Pyongyang became the primary objective of the "drive northward." The U.S. Eighth Army moved toward the city from the south while U.S. X Corps landed at Wonsan to the east. But it was the ROK 1st and 7th Divisions that took the city on 19 October 1950, against only moderate resistance, much less, in fact, than the KPA's fierce resistance in Seoul. On 24 October, President Harry S. Truman, unpresciently, predicted to U.N. commander in chief General Douglas MacArthur, that Pyongyang's capture would have "a most profound influence for peace in the world."

Before evacuating the capital, government forces had executed civilians they deemed "political enemies" (although it would be difficult to imagine how many such could have remained after five years of the most intrusive totalitarian governance on earth). The Communist authorities also warned Pyongyang's citizens that U.N. forces would abuse and kill them. They were thus pleasantly surprised when Allied soldiers dispersed rations and medical supplies, not to mention candy and the exotic chewing gum. ROK soldiers did hang several North Korean soldiers and other prisoners after some had donned the ROK uniform. Allied soldiers also rifled Kim Il Sung's office as intelligence officers examined DPRK government files left behind. They also explored the city, ripping down posters of Stalin and Kim Il Sung; in too many instances such "political statements" by ROK troops and "souvenir hunting" by U.S. soldiers degenerated into sheer looting in the euphoria of victory. Some historical artifacts and national treasures were thus lost. Most U.N. troops, however, simply took the opportunity to rest from their battles and enjoy the entertainment laid on for the victorious troops, including visits by Bob Hope and Al Jolson.

A rather fortunate few U.N. troops remained as occupation forces when the U.N. command, practically oblivious to the Chinese threat, resumed its headlong drive to the Yalu and total liberation of North Korea. The occupation was marked by food shortages and irregular supplies of electricity and water. But in late November, the Chinese entered the war in force, forcing the U.N. to quickly retreat southward after suffering heavy casualties at the Chongchon River. On 3 December, Eighth Army commander General Walton H. Walker, ordered the evacuation of Pyongyang and the destruction of any war material that could not be evacuated quickly. The allies had left behind large amounts of such equipment in the city in order to be unencumbered in their drive north, and more continued to flow into the city; much of this now had to be abandoned or destroyed.

Refugees and enemy agents disguised as refugees fled south in droves, creating a chaotic situation and substantially interfering with Allied troop movements. They waded the Taedong's icy waters or bravely climbed the precariously twisted girders of blasted bridges to make their way south. U.N. troops also retreated on foot, by military vehicle and troop train. At the Allied government building, formerly Kim Il Sung's headquarters, officers packed vital documents and then abandoned the structure, leaving Stalin's portrait still hanging behind the absent premier's desk. The city then burned. (The official U.S. Army history of the Korean War that deals with this period

notes that "much of the city was afire by 0730 on 5 December," but does not state whether these fires were set deliberately or were the result of the massive destruction of U.N. stores during the evacuation.)

Enemy troops reached Pyongyang's airfields by the night of the 5th and entered the city the next morning. Propaganda teams took motion picture and still film of the smoldering city to document the ferocity of the "imperialists"; these images were widely disseminated to advance North Korea's cause.

Almost in retaliation, Allied commanders ordered heavy bombing missions over Pyongyang, and the city was eventually flattened. From 14 to 15 December the USAF dropped napalm and 175 tons of bombs. Many of these bombs were designed to explode as much as seventy-two hours after being dropped, thus maximizing casualties among the unaware. These raids were escalated in the summer of 1951, forcing the Pyongyang government and remaining citizenry underground; deep bunkers were dug, including one especially designed for Premier Kim's political meetings. Factories were also constructed underground to continue war production. Even as truce talks began, air raids continued to pound the city. Pyongyang's population dwindled to a mere 50,000. Most women and children were evacuated to China and Eastern Europe, where they generated much officially sponsored sympathy. Remaining citizens led an underground life, at least during daylight hours.

On 15 August 1951, U.N. air Operation Strangle began its attempt to cut enemy communications and supply routes by once again bombing the ruins of Pyongyang, its railway yards, and other targets in the area. But the raids were also designed to exhaust Pyongyang's citizenry as well as cause military casualties. Despite this attempt at "psychological warfare," Pyongyang's government and disciplined population continued functioning to the end of the war.

Allied air raids continued to focus on the city's factories and other facilities, including its sources of electrical power. July to August 1952, saw Operation Pressure Pump, consisting of twenty-four-hour raids on the city. Australian and South African airmen joined USAF and ROK Air Force pilots in the blitz. The raids were planned to coincide with Chinese Premier Chou En-lai's visit with a large Chinese delegation to Moscow, but were also primarily a part of U.N. commander Mark Clark's "air pressure" strategy to bring pressure to bear on the Communists at the Panmunjom truce talks. The USAF had warned civilians to avoid military sites and had dropped leaflets stating that bombing raids would occur soon. Indeed, one warning gave the inhabitants a full fifteen-minute alert. Pyongyang later reported that more than 2,000 people died in these raids, and 4,000 were wounded, including hundreds of U.N. POWs. In the most intense raid of the war, on 29 August, 6,000 persons were reported killed. (But all these figures must be handled with caution; the Kim regime was never noted for its devotion to objective truth.) What was not reported was the scuttling of numbers of Communist party cadre on any available transport after such warnings, much to the disgust of the citizens who had to endure the coming raids.) When the napalm and high-explosive raids ceased, Pyongyang resembled World War II Warsaw or Dresden, with only the shells of buildings and the remaining inhabitants to remind an observer that a city had ever existed on the site.

With not much left of Pyongyang to go after, the USAF then targeted five dams which provided the water necessary for the rice crop on which Pyongyang depended. Planned for the crucial time of the year when the rice roots required water to mature, the raiders bombed the Toksan Dam above Pyongyang, causing flash floods for twenty-seven miles below the city. Several days later, the Chasan Dam was destroyed, inundating the city and rice crops and even worrying the U.N. command that flood waters might reach Seoul.

In order to forestall charges that the civilian economy had been deliberately targeted, the U.N. command emphasized that the raids were planned only to destroy bridges, railroads, and communication lines. But many civilians had drowned in the flood waters, rendering the distinction unclear.

After the armistice (27 July 1953), the population picked through Pyongyang's rubble to begin the rebuilding of the city as a propaganda piece for the DPRK. Today, Pyongyang is an eerily quiet, immaculate, crime-free metropolis in which all scars of the Korean War have been obliterated and all citizens proclaim their conviction that they abide in a paradise made possible by the late beloved, Kim Il Sung.

Elizabeth Schafer

Bibliography

Blair, Clay. *The Forgotten War: America in Korea, 1950–1953* (1988).

Halliday, J., and Bruce Cumings. *Korea: The Unknown War* (1988).

Mossman, Billy. *Ebb and Flow: November 1950–July 1951*, United States Army in the Korean War (1990).

R

Rangers, U.S. Army

After World War II, ranger units were disbanded as part of the Army's rapid demobilization. However, at the outbreak of hostilities in Korea, it became apparent that the Army would again need this hard-hitting, unconventional warfare force. The man selected to head the ranger training program was Colonel John Gibson Van Houten. On 15 September 1950, he was instructed to begin training ranger-type units at Fort Benning, Georgia as soon as possible. The target date was 1 October with a tentative training period of six weeks.

To obtain potential rangers, Van Houten sent out a request for volunteers who were willing to accept "extremely hazardous" duty in the combat zone of the Far East. Volunteers came from a variety of sources, but many had previously served in the original ranger battalions, the Canadian–U.S. First Special Service Force, or in the Office of Strategic Services, during World War II. The 82nd Airborne Division was particularly responsive to the call. Some estimates report as many as 5,000 of these paratroopers volunteered for ranger training.

The first group of volunteers were formed into three companies and began training on 2 October. A week later they were joined by a group of black paratroopers which would eventually become the 2nd Ranger Infantry Company (Airborne), the only all-black ranger unit ever authorized by the Army.

The implementing orders had authorized a headquarters detachment and four ranger companies. Eventually a total of eight companies would be trained. Each 112-man company would be attached to an infantry division. Several ranger officers called instead for a ranger battalion which would be commanded by a lieutenant colonel and include a staff. They argued that such an organization would facilitate tactical employment and that a lieutenant colonel would have better success in dealing with other senior officers than would individual company commanders who would be only captains. However, these opinions were overruled, and on 17 December the 1st Ranger Infantry Company (Airborne) arrived in Korea where it was promptly attached to the 2nd Infantry Division. The 2nd and 4th Ranger Infantry Companies (Airborne) followed, arriving on 29 December. The 2nd Company was attached to the 7th Infantry Division, and the 4th Company served both the Eighth Army headquarters and the 1st Cavalry Division. The 3rd Ranger Infantry Company (Airborne) remained at Fort Benning to train the second cycle of companies.

Chipyong-ni

As separate units, the Ranger companies participated in a wide range of operations with various commands on all parts of the battlefield. One of the early actions was the 1st Company's participation with the 2nd Infantry Division at the battle of Chipyong-ni. Prior to this action, the Chinese had experienced unchecked success, and General Matthew B. Ridgway, the Eighth Army commander, was determined to reverse this tide at Chipyong-ni.

The 23rd Infantry Regiment of the 2nd Infantry Division was defending from a tight perimeter inside the eight prominent hills that encircle Chipyong-ni. The 1st Company constituted the regimental reserve. On the night of 11 February 1951, the Chinese launched a massive counteroffensive which left Chipyong-ni as a conspicuous bulge in the X Corps line. The 23rd Regiment was in serious danger of being surrounded and destroyed.

Coordination between the rangers and the rest of the battalion was very weak, and the rangers took friendly fire from several directions. After many of these unnecessary casualties, a handful of rangers reached the top of the objective and, for a short time, the opposing forces each occupied the hill. Fierce fighting ensued in which the ranger platoon leader was killed. In the end, the Chinese regained the hill. The counterattack had failed.

The Chinese were not dislodged until well into the evening by a combined counterattack by the rangers, Company B of the 2nd Battalion, tactical air, tanks, and artillery. Losses were heavy on both sides, but the previously invincible Chinese had been dealt their first defeat of the war.

The rangers' next operation would prove less satisfactory.

By April 1951, Eighth Army troops were grinding forward slowly with the intention of halting along phase line (PL) Kansas, some ten miles north of the 38th parallel. Unfortunately, halting at PL Kansas would leave the Hwachon Dam in the hands of the Chinese. Hwachon Dam is one of the largest in Korea. It holds back the Pukhan River and creates a lake thirteen miles long and about a mile wide. The problem was that the Pukhan River ran through the middle of the IX Corps zone. If the Chinese released the water held by the dam, they would unleash a torrent which could wash away bridges, command posts, and supply points, and split the corps in two.

General Ridgway had opted not to bomb the dam earlier because of its role in supplying water and power to Seoul. However, the IX Corps commander, Major General William Hoge, was now offering him a new alternative. Hoge's plan was to send a small raiding party to blast shut the mechanical hoists which raised and lowered the dam's heavy doors. Once the Army moved past PL Kansas and gained permanent control of the dam, it would be a small matter to repair this damage. Ridgway liked the idea and instructed Hoge to proceed but cautioned him to keep casualties as low as possible.

Military historian Martin Blumenson describes the resultant Hwachon raid as "an operation in frustration." Three Rangers were killed, eleven wounded, and one injured in a fall. Little if anything was accomplished.

Inactivation

In addition to these two major operations, the rangers participated in a host of smaller and less publicized battles. The 2nd and 4th Companies made a combat airborne assault at Munsan-ni, and the 5th Company performed brilliantly during the Chinese "Fifth Phase Offensive." All across the combat zone, rangers were used as "firemen" to maintain contact with the enemy, cover withdrawals, and plug gaps.

In the midst of all this, Colonel Van Houten and his staff continued to urge the Army to form ranger battalions. A draft table of organization was prepared that included four ranger companies, a headquarters company, a service company, and a medical detachment. However, the Army leadership seemed to be moving in exactly the opposite direction. On 14 July 1951, the Eighth Army dispatched a message to the commanders of the 1st Cavalry and the 2nd, 3rd, 7th, 24th, and 25th Infantry Divisions stating that all ranger companies within the command were to be inactivated. By 5 November this action was completed. Many of the individual rangers, however, were transferred to the 187th Regimental Combat Team where their parachutist skills could still be put to good use.

Perhaps because of this early inactivation and the fact that the rangers usually fought at the small unit level, very little of the rangers' exploits during Korea have appeared in the war's written histories. Nonetheless, the Rangers' experience in the war provided a valuable link between their World War II heritage and the role they would soon be called upon to play during Vietnam. In this latter conflict, the rangers would again be organized into individual companies, and the hard lessons they had learned in Korea gave them a solid foundation for the future.

Kevin Dougherty

Bibliography

Blumenson, Martin. "The Rangers at Hwachon Dam," *Army* (December 1967).

———. Far East, U.S. Army Forces Eighth U.S. Army Korea, 4th Historical Detachment, "Action on Hill 628, 8th Ranger Infantry Company (Airborne)" (n.d.).

FM 7–85, *Ranger Unit Operations* (Headquarters, Department of the Army, Washington: 1987).

Gugeler, Russell A. *Combat Actions in Korea* (Office of the Chief of Military History, Washington: 1970).

Red Cross, International (IRC)

Despite noncompliance by North Korea and China, the International Red Cross (IRC) attempted to alleviate the distress of Korean War victims, both military and civilian. Founded by Henri Dunant in 1863, the IRC, based in Geneva, Switzerland, sponsored delegates who agreed to provide aid for war casualties; these neutral volunteers promised not to make political distinctions. The 1949 Geneva Convention iterated that IRC representatives would care for wounded soldiers, prisoners of war (POWs), and civilians in military conflicts.

The Korean War activities of the IRC were limited to inspecting U.N. POW camps and providing for the needs of Chinese and North Korean prisoners. Efforts to cooperate with North Korea met a chilly reception. IRC President Paul Ruegger cabled the North Korean government at Pyongyang to inform them that IRC delegates would inspect North Korean prison camps although that nation had not signed the 1949 Geneva Convention.

Ruegger also contacted Seoul to inform the ROK of wartime humanitarian provisions. IRC representative Frederick Bieri relocated to South Korea in early July, and both the U.S. and South Korea (the Korean Red Cross had been organized after World War II) agreed to cooperate.

Receiving no answer from Pyongyang, Ruegger again cabled the North Koreans, stating that delegate Jacques de Reynier would contact them regarding inspections. Ruegger received no answer to this missive, but Pak Hen Yen, North Korean minister of foreign affairs, informed the U.N. secretary general that North Korea would follow the Geneva Convention codes.

On July 18, Ruegger asked North Korea for a list of prisoners and told Pak Hen Yen that the U.N. forces held several hundred Communist prisoners who were being treated well. When the North Korean government did not reply, Ruegger and Bieri schemed to get delegate Jean Courvoisier into North Korea to inspect the camps.

The U.N. command discouraged Ruegger, stating it could not guarantee Courvoisier's safety. Ruegger next tried to contact the North Korean Red Cross and suggested that Courvoisier enter North Korea through China. But when Courvoisier visited the North Korean embassy in Beijing for a visa, he was rebuffed.

On August 16, Pak Hen Yen transmitted to Geneva a list of fifty prisoners at the Pyongyang prison camp. Ruegger appealed to Jacob Malik, the Soviet Union's representative to the U.N. Security Council, to assist Courvoisier in entering North Korea. When he was again ignored, the frustrated Ruegger scanned Red Cross periodicals, finding a bulletin from the Hungarian Red Cross that stated it would send an ambulance to Pyongyang. Ruegger decided to give one ton of pharmaceuticals and medical instruments to be transported with the ambulance and distributed to U.N. prisoners.

Tchou Nyung-ha, the North Korean ambassador in Moscow, wrote Ruegger and requested that he contact Pyongyang through Moscow. Also, Etienne Florian, undersecretary general of the Hungarian Red Cross, agreed to transport the medicine. Encouraged, Ruegger asked that Courvoisier go to either Pyongyang or Beijing to discuss prisoner treatment.

On September 5, Bieri reported on the condition of Communist prisoners in U.N. camps. Ruegger forwarded this report and several thousand capture cards from Geneva to Pyongyang, and Pak Hen Yen finally issued a list of sixty prisoners. Ruegger wrote additional cables asking permission for delegates to mark civilian safety areas and hospital zones so that enemy aircraft would avoid them. Again the North Koreans did not respond. North Korea also refused to mark prisoner camps or reveal their locations, and U.N. pilots on occasion accidentally attacked them.

Ruegger wrote for lists of prisoners killed and revealed the exact latitude and longitude of camps in South Korea, hoping for cooperation. In the Communist POW camps, U.N. prisoners suffered starvation and the deprivation of sleep, food, and medical care; many endured various levels of torture. Communist guards often retained relief packages and food for themselves.

Atrocity reports caused Ruegger to cable Pak Hen Yen to remind soldiers that noncombatants were to be treated humanely. Likewise, Bieri wrote a fiery letter to Republic of Korea (ROK) President Syngman Rhee protesting the treatment of civilians who were interrogated and often executed as suspected Communist collaborators. The IRC requested Rhee to construct civilian internee camps to keep political prisoners.

In November, Ruegger flew to Moscow, but was prevented from seeing Tchou Nyungha. Ruegger informed his staff of the supplies enroute with the Hungarians and requested lists of newly captured prisoners. After returning to Geneva, Ruegger continued sending telegrams, telling the North Koreans he had 2,000 food parcels for prisoners and that the IRC was giving Communist prisoners cigarettes, games, and candy.

As U.N. troops moved north, Bieri inspected field hospitals and prison camps. He informed Ruegger that the prisoners were given adequate food, clothes, blankets, and shelter. Few prisoners complained, and U.N. camps had sufficient medical supplies. Determined, Ruegger continued to press for North Korean cooperation as well. Although there was no response, IRC delegates monitored radio broadcasts, recording prisoners' names used in propaganda messages.

China initially agreed that the IRC could visit prison camps, but only if accompanied by delegates from the North Korean and Chinese Red Cross. The IRC refused because it did not want to be viewed as aligning with the Communists. The president of the Chinese Red Cross, Madame Li Teh-chuan, refused to transport parcels to prisoners. Ruegger attempted to fly the parcels into Pyongyang in January 1951 but was stopped when he reached Peking.

Delegates continued visiting U.N. POW camps, often unannounced, noting prisoner hygiene, quality of medical care, variety of diet (pickled vegetables and seafood, favorites of Koreans, were ample), and weight gain (each prisoner was weighed monthly). They talked to the prisoners and asked for their comments on conditions, as well as providing them with copies of the Geneva Convention. The IRC delegates dispersed boots, soap, and other requested goods. Reports of these activities were consistently sent to Pak Hen Yen.

In the summer of 1951, Bieri and Reynier noted early problems on Koje-do Island between prisoners and ROK guards. Eastern European Red Cross societies protested germ warfare allegations as a violation of the Geneva Convention, insisting the IRC take action, but Ruegger protested that the IRC had no right to investigate or condemn nations accused of waging germ warfare. U.S. Secretary of State Dean Acheson assured him that the United States had not conducted germ warfare and offered access to sources for an investigation.

Ruegger then asked the North Korean commander in chief for permission to conduct an investigation with specialists chosen by the IRC, but officials at Pyongyang refused. The Communist press suggested that the IRC was not neutral and had intervened to convince prisoners not to return home. As tensions increased

on Koje-do Island, the IRC recommended removing all South Korean guards to avoid political demonstrations. Many prisoners gave reports of torture to IRC delegates, who, although they doubted the complaints, traveled to Tokyo in May to discuss the situation with General Mark Clark; he subsequently banned the IRC from the island.

After the riots on Koje-do Island, the IRC returned in July and protested that the prisoners had been denied food and water and suffered from use of concussion grenades that killed and wounded them. The IRC also continued to solicit cooperation from the Communists. The last acts of the IRC delegates in the Korean War included assisting anti-Communist Chinese repatriates in the neutral zone.

In addition to the IRC, at field, base, and ship hospitals, thousands of national Red Cross volunteers tried to mitigate the wartime conditions. Red Cross medical units from Denmark, India, Italy, Norway, Japan, and Sweden helped military surgeons, and Red Cross groups sent whole blood. Red Cross societies assisted military personnel and their families. A Red Cross field director was affiliated with every major U.S. combat unit to counsel soldiers, and Red Cross clubs and "clubmobiles" offered refreshments and entertainment.

The IRC and national Red Crosses contributed significantly to the humanitarian treatment of Communist prisoners, civilians, and wounded allies. Their efforts to cooperate and coordinate services with the Communists, although persistent, proved futile, resulting in unnecessary casualties behind the lines.

Elizabeth Schafer

Bibliography

Cowdrey, Albert E. *The Medic's War* (1987).

Durand, Andre. *From Sarajevo to Hiroshima: History of the International Committee of the Red Cross* (1984).

International Committee of the Red Cross. *The International Red Cross Committee in Geneva 1863–1943* (1943).

Riley, Nelson J. "Red Cross Clubmobiles Roll in Korea," *Army Information Digest* 9(2)(1954): 11–17.

Smith, John C. "The Red Cross in the Field," *Army Information Digest* 8(2)(1953): 35–41.

White, William L. *The Captives of Korea: An Unofficial White Paper on the Treatment of War Prisoners* (1957).

Republic of (South) Korea Air Force

At the start of the Korean War, the air forces of both North and South Korea were small and outdated. The size and quality of both were drastically improved by their sponsors, but at a price—the air arm of the North became a mere extension of its Chinese and Soviet patrons, while the air service of the South became an adjunct to United States airpower.

Despite half-hearted American support, the Republic of Korea (ROK) established its Air Force on 10 October 1949. During the previous year, official U.S. policy had stressed the creation of a South Korean military that was potent enough to ensure internal order, but not large enough to threaten North Korea. Within this context, American leaders feared that the growth of South Korean airpower would increase the likelihood of war on the Korean peninsula, and that it would confirm the Communist claim that the U.S. actively supported an arms race against Pyongyang. The South Koreans established an air organization under the pretext that they needed an Air Force presence among the ROK Joint Chiefs of Staff. At the time, however, the Air Force actually possessed only ten American T-6 trainers. The ROK subsequently sought an additional thirty-five trainer, reconnaissance, and cargo aircraft from the United States, but without success. By April 1950, the South Korean Air Force thus had 187 officers, thirty-nine of which were trained pilots, and 1,672 enlisted men. It also had a grand total of sixteen aircraft (eight L-4 Grasshoppers and five L-5 Sentinels, both light spotter aircraft, and three T-6 Texan trainers) located at Kimpo and Seoul airfields. The United States did finally provide the ROK Air Force with ten F-51 Mustangs during the dark days of June 1950, but the inexperienced South Korean pilots proved incapable of operating the comparatively heavy aircraft. However, after six months of war the South Korean Air Force did become an integral, albeit limited, part of the United Nations air effort. It later participated, for example, in "Operation Pressure Pump," a massive air assault conducted in July 1952 against thirty separate targets located in Pyongyang, and it flew, along with U.S. Marine and South African aircraft, 1,111 close ground support sorties for frontline U.N. troops in September 1952.

Peter R. Faber

Bibliography

Futrell, Robert F. *The United States Air Force in Korea 1950–1952* (Office of Air Force History, Washington: 1983).

Jackson, Robert. *Air War Over Korea* (Ian Allan Ltd., London: 1973).

Stewart, James T., ed. *Airpower: The Decisive Force in Korea* (Van Nostrand, Princeton, NJ: 1957).

Republic of (South) Korea Army

The South Korean Army performed erratically during the Korean War. Organized on December 15, 1948, from the eight constabulary regiments established in 1946 during the United States military occupation to secure internal peace and protect its borders, the South Korean Army was better known as the Republic of Korea Army (ROKA). During the Korean War, the ROKA underwent modernization and become a more professional fighting force.

Traditional historical accounts, written primarily by American military leaders in the 1950s and 1960s, depicted ROKA's participation in the war as either wholly positive or completely incompetent, with minimal middle ground. Many works even omit mention of ROKA forces. Further, the absence of adequate archival material about the ROKA, as well as English-language histories of Korean forces, enable the perpetuation of outdated interpretations.

Recent works such as ROKA General Paik Sun Yup's *From Pusan to Panmunjom* revealed the strengths as well as the weaknesses of the ROKA during the Korean War. Paik challenged the long-held myth that the ROKA was incompetent, uncommitted, and did not fight its fair share, insisting instead that the troops were merely inexperienced. In the foreword to Paik's book, Generals Matthew B. Ridgway and James A. Van Fleet stated that "we now have the facts to repudiate that cruel, uninformed judgment." (On the other hand, General Paik was hardly a disinterested analyst.)

Before the invasion, the ROKA's prewar troop strength included 98,000 men in eight divisions: the 1st, 2nd, 3rd, 5th, 6th, 7th, 8th, and Capital Divisions. Lacking sufficient and modern weaponry, such as tanks and heavy artillery, the ROKA divided its forces, half along the 38th parallel and half held in reserve. Officers and NCOs were undertrained and leadership positions were often granted as rewards for political favors, resulting in incompetent commanders.

American advisors greatly influenced the ROKA, as the Soviets had the North Korea People's Army (NKPA). After U.S. Army occupation forces withdrew, with the bulk of American troops leaving South Korea by 1949, the Korean Military Advisory Group (KMAG) provided advice and training with the idea that the Republic of Korea could defend South Korea without American protection. Although Brigadier General William L. Roberts, commanding officer of KMAG, publicly championed the ROKA as the "best doggone shooting army outside the United States," he privately had his doubts. But at any rate, U.S. political and military leaders were convinced at the time that the defense of South Korea did not constitute a vital American interest.

Designed as an antiguerrilla constabulary and denied heavy weapons for fear that it might embark on its own "liberation" of the North, the ROKA was unable even to blunt the all-out attack from the North on 25 June 1950. Without heavy weapons, and lacking a strong military tradition and intense training, ROKA forces were no match for invading NKPA troops. Despite an unrealistic contingency defense plan to contain NKPA forces at the 38th parallel, ROKA crumpled in combat, offering limited resistance. Almost half of the soldiers assigned to the 38th parallel were on weekend leave, a development that should give pause to those who question whether North Korea was actually the instigator of the Korean War.

Paik, the twenty-nine-year-old commander of the 1st ROK Division, held his lines along the boundary for several days. The ROK 7th Division defended Uijongbu, and the 1st protected Munsan, sites the NKPA focused on because of their proximity to Seoul. Terrorized by the enemy's T-34 tanks, which they had never seen before, ROKA troops only had antitank guns that could slow, not destroy, this technology. The ROK antitank platoon lacked sufficient training and artillery. Suicide teams climbed on tanks to hand-place grenades.

Major General Kim Hong Il, director of ROKA's strategy supervision team and a senior officer who had been commandant of the Command and General Staff School when the ROKA was founded, wanted ROKA forces to withdraw, but chief of staff Chae Byong Duk (known as "Fat Chae" on the prewar U.S.-ROKA party circuit) had received a message that American intervention was imminent, and ordered officers to hold their positions. The enemy's strength, however, overwhelmed the

ROKA forces, which streamed toward Seoul, with the morale of both officers and men rapidly sinking. Only rumors that General Douglas MacArthur would arrive alleviated total despair.

In Seoul, General Kim tried to reorganize units from the mass of retreating troops, but his efforts were practically destroyed by the catastrophic premature blowing of the main Han River road bridge. Several thousand soldiers and civilians were killed and many more troops and their equipment stranded on the north side of the Han.

In confused delaying actions, the ROKA troops moved south, along with their American allies, on a 200-mile retreat to the Naktong River, where U.N. forces were to make their last-ditch stand at the so-called Pusan perimeter, the ROKA helped U.N. troops hold the important city of Taegu.

Because of manpower shortages in the early months of the war, an experimental program known as KATUSA assigned South Koreans into the U.S. Army. Some critics blamed some battlefield blunders on the U.S. Army for its improperly training these ROKA soldiers.

The invasion necessitated that the ROKA be reconstituted and retrained. The ROKA rebuilt from its low point: the initial eight infantry divisions had been reduced to the size of five. Military police operated a center for stragglers, and in the temporary ROKA headquarters at Suwon, deputy chief of staff for operations Colonel Kim Paik Il created new units from the shattered ones, combining the 5th Division with the list. Men lost in Seoul rejoined their units, now combat experienced and toughened physically and psychologically. The diminished units doubled and were strengthened with weaponry.

Cadets and officers from the South Korea Military Academy experimented with ambush techniques. The rejuvenated ROKA centralized its strength by creating ROK I Corps from the ROK 1st, ROK 2nd, and ROK Capital Divisions. Intermediate units between the divisional and Army headquarters improved the chain of command. A new ROKA chief of staff, Major General Chung Il Kwon, was named. (Chae, dismissed from his post, had fought—and died—bravely in battle during the retreat to the Pusan perimeter.) Shiin Sung Mo now served as minister of defense.

The ROKA defended the central and eastern areas of the Pusan perimeter. Aided by U.N. air and artillery strikes, the ROKA enjoyed some victories, lifting morale. But various problems still hindered ROKA effectiveness, including poor communications technology, influxes of refugees, dissension between units, and most important, persistently poor leadership. The lack of detailed maps necessitated reconnaissance missions, and malaria swept through the ranks.

American-supplied rocket launchers yielded successful antitank warfare, yet hand-to-hand combat still prevailed along the Naktong River line. In the August battle of Tabu-dong, the ROKA 1st Division lost approximately 2,244 men and fifty-six officers in action, although the opposing North Korean People's Army (NKPA) units suffered twice as many casualties. The staggering ROK losses sparked a ROKA investigation of commanders, although little seems to have been done to improve leadership. The best selector was battle; the inept leaders were killed or wounded. But ROKA replacements included volunteers and youths who were not trained for service. They learned, or died, in combat.

By mid-September, the North Korean offensive had been halted and the Pusan perimeter defense line secured. But in the Tabu-dong Valley battles, some U.S. commanders, skeptical of the ROKA's combat ability, hesitated to provide the forces with adequate weapons until troops had proved they would fight. Paik claimed that even with limited weaponry ROKA troops had exhibited a fighting spirit and ingenuity that improved relations with the U.S. forces, building a "foundation of mutual trust that melded us into a team devoted to our cause."

ROKA troops moved north to coordinate with U.N. forces landing at Inchon. After liberating Seoul, ROKA forces trailed American troops north. U.S. troops led the advance because they had river-crossing equipment that the ROKA lacked. Far East command excluded ROKA troops from the attack on Pyongyang because they did not have adequate transportation. Disappointed, Paik convinced General Frank Milburn to permit his troops the chance to lead the attack to Pyongyang.

As the troops moved north, men who had disappeared during the fighting along the Imjin River in June rejoined the ROKA, claiming that they had been unable to cross the Han and had hidden in Seoul. American forces still considered ROKA forces a risk and were reluctant to provide armor support unless it was accompanied by U.S. infantry. Angered, Paik secured enough tanks to advance rapidly on Pyongyang. ROKA forces captured Sibyong, a transporta-

tion and supply center, which boosted the troops' confidence. ROKA soldiers were the first to enter and liberate Pyongyang. After clearing the city of NKPA troops, the ROKA joined the advance to the Yalu.

The ROK I Corps moved forward along the eastern front while the ROK II Corps managed the central area and the ROK 1st Division served on the western front. When they reached the Chongchon River, ROKA officers realized that winter was nearing and that their troops had no appropriate clothes. An uneasiness permeated camp because the roads had emptied of normal activity. Suddenly they were hit and encircled by an enemy force. This ambush of the ROKA by the Communist Chinese Army ushered in an entirely new stage of the Korean War.

Suffering large casualties and great loss of ammunition and supplies, ROKA morale once again sank. Interrogation of Chinese prisoners revealed that the Chinese Communists were specifically aiming at ROKA troops because they considered them weaker than their American counterparts. In fact, the U.N. command did not believe that the Chinese had truly entered the war because they had not attacked U.S. troops. Deputy commander of Chinese Army forces Deng Hua explained his selection of targets: "The Korean Army is deficient in all pertinent aspects. Their training is absolutely insufficient. Three Korean divisions do not equal one American division when it comes to firepower and overall combat strength."

ROKA forces, initially ordered in June to defend territory to their death, were now allowed to withdraw to reconstruct forces. Their removal resulted in large U.N. losses on the front. After a period of recuperation, the ROKA forces returned to the front in November 1950 for the abortive U.N. Christmas offensive to the Yalu.

The Chinese counterattack disintegrated two ROKA divisions. The ROK 1st Division was ordered to withdraw and defend the line from Pyongyang to Wonsan, but in early December it withdrew to the 38th parallel because the division found the line too extended to hold. Suffering heavy losses in the mountainous areas where the Chinese were masters of light infantry warfare, the ROKA remained ill-equipped and fought poorly.

Despairing soldiers chose self-preservation over orders and abandoned the front. Several ROKA division commanders were court-martialed and sentenced to death, then pardoned. ROKA leaders now realized that unification by military force was no longer possible and that retaining territory should be their primary objective. Personnel changes and the creation of a citizens defense force were other temporary solutions to mitigate battlefield failures.

In late February, the ROKA helped restore lines in "Operation Killer," and in March's "Operation Ripper," Seoul was regained. Other notable ROKA participation occurred in "Operation Tomahawk" and "Operation Iron Triangle." But the ROKA withdrew farther from defensive positions in the Chinese third offensive, in the spring of 1951, placing Seoul in danger. ROKA officials emphasized integrity and sacrifice in their exhortations to the troops. Determined to deal with individual soldiers' terror, which they believed was caused by irresponsible commanders, ROKA leaders courtmartialed, and this time actually executed, battalion and company commanders who had fled enemy fire.

Many command mistakes had resulted in the heavy troop losses. Officers such as Brigadier General Choi Duk Shin, commander of the 11th ROKA Division and the first Korean officer to attend the U.S. Infantry School at Fort Benning, Georgia, were relieved of duty because they had relied more on field manuals than tactical sense. Other problems plaguing the ROKA included officials who diverted Army funds from the Citizens Defense Force, and the Kochang Massacre where ROKA slaughtered civilians they vaguely thought were Communist guerrillas.

In the spring counterattack, known as "Operation Thunderbolt," the ROKA advanced, regaining ground. Paik criticized American General Edward M. Almond for placing ROK divisions in the vanguard of attack in the Chinese fourth (counter) offensive instead of supporting them with manpower and equipment. Both the 3rd and 5th ROKA Divisions lost about 3,000 men each, and the 8th ROKA Division suffered no less than 323 officers and 7,142 men killed. Paik bitterly commented that Americans sacrificed Korean soldiers first before American and U.N. troops.

ROKA troops protected Seoul during the April 1951 Chinese fifth offensive (first spring offensive). Responsible for the eastern front, ROKA troops fought well. However, during the sixth Chinese offensive (second spring offensive) on the eastern front, ROKA III Corps collapsed and fled, creating a hole in the line. During this crisis, ROKA I Corps, with U.S. X

Corps, managed to defeat the Chinese in that sector.

In this retreat and confusion, the ROKA headquarters lost operational control over its troops, retaining control only in support tasks such as personnel, administration, logistics, and training. According to Paik, "The debacle of ROK III Corps had dealt a final, mortal blow to the pride of the Republic of Korea Army."

As the battle lines finally stabilized in the summer of 1951, a new relationship between the ROKA and Eighth Army was worked out in which the ROK government provided rations, salary, and uniforms, while the U.S. Army supplied ammunition. ROKA rations, however, were criticized as being poorer than those fed to prisoners, as ROKA purchasing agents sought the cheapest sources of fish and vegetables. Low salaries resulted in men selling even these miserable items on the black market, but ROK President Syngman Rhee considered soldiers to be volunteers (which most were emphatically not) and forbade raises. (There were unsubstantiated rumors that the U.S. Army had indeed supplied its Korean ally with its native dish, Kimchee, but the fiery cabbage mixture had eaten the bottoms out of the cans.) ROKA headquarters also was responsible for disabled veterans but was financially unable to feed and take care of these men.

Army headquarters also housed ROKA recruitment command, which enlisted and arranged for the training of draft-age men, averaging 1,200 recruits daily. Recruit training was vital to replace combat casualties. In the early stages of the war, recruits were literally taken off the street, trained for a week, and sent to the front. Later, ROKA built recruit training centers with a sixteen-week basic training course.

In February 1951, with American assistance, the engineer school for the Korean Army opened to train Korean officers and enlisted men in combat engineering techniques. American soldiers taught ROKA troops how to build bridges, lay mines, and grade roads with bulldozers as well as how to destroy enemy facilities. Several hundred men graduated from this school monthly, greatly enhancing ROKA's engineering capacity.

In May 1951, an immense reorganization sponsored by the U.S. Army attacked every ROKA Division at the front to a U.S. Army unit except for three divisions of ROKA I Corps, the only ROKA corps surviving, which was subordinate to the Eighth Army. Personnel changes included a new Army chief of staff, Major General Lee Chong Chan, a new vice chief of staff, Major General Yu Jae Hung, and a new deputy chief of staff, Brigadier General Lee Jun Sic.

A concentrated training program became ROKA's primary focus. While ROKA forces held their positions on the front in what became static trench warfare along the 38th parallel, President Rhee wanted to double the number of divisions to twenty and to receive more American equipment. American officers refused, stating this was a waste of money based on prior combat performance. Instead they believed American officers should command ROKA units. A concentrated training program, based on Van Fleet's rebuilding of the Greek Army to fight Communist guerrillas, was implemented as a compromise.

At the field training command, Brigadier General Thomas Cross led American officers in the complete nine-week training of every man, except the commander, in a ROKA division. After testing, the ROKA 3rd Division was the first unit to finish the course. It was attached to X Corps. By late 1952, all ten Korean divisions graduated, subsequently losing 50 percent fewer men and equipment at the front than non-trained units, and exhibiting higher confidence. Training modernized and molded the ROKA into a fairly effective fighting force. ROKA troops held 60 percent of the front by 1953, expanding to as much as 75 percent by the end of the war.

Ultimately, eighteen training institutions operated to professionalize the ROKA and increase its combat power. Officers received training at a staff school in Taegu and the Korea Military Academy in Chinhae. Selected ROKA officers attended the U.S. Army Infantry School at Fort Benning, Georgia, and the U.S. Army Artillery School at Fort Sill, Oklahoma.

The newly organized ROKA II Corps, which represented the mature, professional ROKA, was reinforced by U.S. artillery, engineer, and quartermaster groups, with howitzer battalions trained at the ROKA artillery school in Kwangju. Commanded by chief of staff Brigadier General Lee Hyong Sok, ROKA II Corps was attached to IX Corps. The U.S. wanted this new corps to free up American soldiers for European assignments and to emphasize that the ROKA should have primary responsibility for the defense of South Korea. At a ceremony in honor of the new corps, President Rhee truculently stressed that "Our army now has the personnel and the material resources to fight. We must punch through the barbarians

and advance north, unifying the entire country."

During the balance of 1951, the ROKA fought well near the Punchbowl and Heartbreak Ridge. As the front stabilized, the ROKA conducted counterguerrilla warfare in "Operation Ratkiller," killing 5,800 guerrillas and capturing 5,700 in the Chiri Mountains.

During a lull in fighting, the ROKA interrogated prisoners, who indicated a new massing of Chinese. American leaders agreed to provide firepower and supplies to ensure ROKA success. In July 1952, Rhee dismissed the Army chief of staff, Lieutenant Cheneral Lee Chong Chan, because Chan refused to use his military power to insure Rhee's political ambitions to revise the ROK constitution in his favor. Paik replaced Chan.

In September and October 1952, Chinese forces attacked ROKA troops in bitter assaults. At White Horse Hill, the ROKA suffered high casualties (10,000 by the 9th Division), but held onto the hill. Other battles proved, according to Paik, that "The new Korean army fought admirably, revealing to our own people and to the world that we were a different force than we had been. Our combat power could prevail."

Paik noted that one reason ROKA troops had had a poor fighting reputation was due to weak artillery and infantry commanders. At the recommendation of Major General Shin Ung Kyun, Paik devised an artillery command training course to train professional artillery officers. Equipped by the U.S. Army, ROKA artillery units vastly improved. Paik had a legitimate means to promote junior officers, and in honor of his wartime military leadership, Paik was promoted to the rank of full general in January 1953, the first Korean officer to attain that rank.

In the spring of 1953, the United States offered military aid incentives if the ROK would accept the armistice about to be agreed upon with the Communists, and to encourage the maturing ROKA to accept more responsibility at the front so that American troops could withdraw. Rhee threatened to take away the U.N.'s command over the ROKA when he realized that the armistice did not ensure reunification. He enlisted the ROKA's assistance in releasing Communist prisoners to symbolize his opposition to what he considered an appeasing armistice.

As NKPA and U.N. troops battled to maintain and gain artillery territory along the 38th parallel before the armistice froze positions, bitter battles such as the battle of Kumsong, the final enemy offensive, occurred. When the armistice was finally signed, there were 590,911 troops in three corps and sixteen ROKA divisions. The ROKA had provided almost 40 percent of U.N. ground forces.

In addition to the ROKA troops in the field, the Republic of Korea Women's Army Corps, established in 1948, served during the war. ROKA surgeons, nurses, and dentists trained at the ROKA medical field school, and Korean chaplains were specifically selected for Korean troops.

The ROKA strengthened and matured during the Korean War. Paik suggested that the ROKA would have fought better if more realistic prewar training programs and more modern military equipment and competent commanders had been available. He believed coordination between ROKA units was poor and that the ROKA relied too much on U.S. artillery and air support. During the war, immature ROKA troops became trained, equipped, and combat experienced. For the most part, they performed well when reinforced with modern weapons, although they might have been expected to fight better in defense of their home soil. The ROKA, of course, expanded during the war, tripling and creating an infrastructure for training and logistics. It improved its command and developed some sense of esprit de corps. Yet its erratic war performance reflected internal turmoil and political manipulation of the military.

Some American officers, like Lindsey P. Henderson of the 21st Infantry, wrote articles proclaiming "My ROKs Were Good," praising the ROKA forces as good soldiers who trained and fought well. Other military leaders and journalists for major magazines, such as *Life,* focused on negative aspects of the ROKA's combat performance, claiming that they fled positions and abandoned wounded. Some analysts attributed the successes of the Chinese Communist forces to ROKA failures. Paik maintained, to the contrary, that the ROKA retained "organizational integrity, refurbished its ranks, and held where and when it counted most." He depicted the ROKA soldiers as patriotic and sacrificing, embracing discipline as the foundation for making the ROKA an effective fighting force.

After the Korean War, South Korea and the United States signed a mutual defense treaty promising South Korea military security. The ROKA expanded and sent two divisions to Vietnam to help U.S. and South Vietnamese forces.

South Korea's Army and the United States Army continue their defensive alliance, forged in the Korean War, and have made their post-1953 mission primarily one of guarding the 38th parallel from another invasion from the north.

Elizabeth Schafer

Bibliography

Lee, Young Moo. "Birth of the Korean Army, 1945-1950: Evaluation of the Role of United States Occupation Forces," *Korea and World Affairs* 4 (1980).

Republic of Korea Army. Office of Information Headquarters, *Republic of Korea Army* (1954).

Sawyer, Robert K., and W.G. Hermes. *Military Advisors in Korea: KMAG in Peace and War* (1962).

Van Fleet, James A. "Who Says Our Allies Won't Fight?" *Readers' Digest* 62 (1953).

Yup, Paik Sun. *From Pusan to Panmunjom* (1992)

Reserve Forces, U.S.

Reserve forces (which include the Army National Guard, the Air National Guard, the Army reserve, the Naval reserve, the Air Force reserve, and the Marine Corps reserve) played an important part in the Korean War. When the war began, however, they were grossly unprepared. That was not surprising, for the same was true of the active forces. In the period since precipitate demobilization following World War II, all the services, active and reserve, had been neglected, and what forces there were lacked essential equipment, were undermanned, and fell short of high standards in training and readiness. Nevertheless, with war unexpectedly and suddenly in the offing, reserve forces—again like the active forces—did what they could with what they had while striving to overcome their multiple shortcomings.

Existing laws authorized activation of reserve forces either on a declaration of war or the proclamation by the president of a national emergency. Since neither of these conditions pertained early in the Korean War, reliance had to be placed on a one-year extension of the Selective Service Act, which also empowered the president to call reserve components to active duty for up to twenty-one months.

Using this authority, the administration called reserve forces up as units to provide additional force structure and as individuals for fillers for understrength active force units. Combat support and combat service support units were sent to Korea to flesh out the Eighth Army's capabilities, while combat divisions from the National Guard were activated as replacements in the general reserve for units that had been deployed. Eventually these divisions were themselves deployed to Korea and to Europe.

Reserve forces contributed in another way as well, for certain equipment in short supply was withdrawn from reserve component units and issued to the active force. Also, some funds originally allocated for reserve forces were shifted to active force accounts.

As war began the reserve forces were just completing an arduous four-year period of reconstitution after their active service in World War II and subsequent demobilization. One result was a National Guard—now composed of not only the Army National Guard but also a newly constituted Air National Guard—twice its pre–World War II size. Even so, at a high of more than 356,000 men in June 1949, it had still reached only about half its planned strength. More men were willing to serve, but strength limitations had been established in order to stay within budget ceilings.

These personnel deficiencies were matched by severe shortages of equipment. As of 31 March 1949, the National Guard had on hand fewer than 56 percent of the heavy weapons and vehicles it was authorized, and was rather pathetically engaged in screening surplus war stocks left over from World War II in an effort to identify some additional equipment it might be able to use. As the fiscal year ended in June 1950, coinciding with the outbreak of the Korean War, the Air National Guard had some 373 jet fighters in its inventory of 2,655 aircraft overall, but for reasons of economy, annual flying time was restricted to 110 hours per pilot.

The day after hostilities commenced President Harry S. Truman met with his senior military and political advisors to consider the U.S. response. A day later, at another such meeting, it was decided to commit air and naval forces to assist the Republic of Korea (ROK), and at that early stage the president was also advised by senior Army officers that if ground troops were to be committed (a move which they opposed), it would be necessary to mobilize some reserve forces.

Within a week, however, it was clear that, despite the reluctance of senior officers, ground troops would be needed to stop the North Korean onslaught. Army General Omar Bradley, serving as chairman of the Joint Chiefs of Staff, pointed out that the gravity of the situation was forcing a piecemeal commitment of forces, which he correctly called the worst possible way to enter a fight. Just over three weeks after the North Korean invasion of the South began, President Truman announced that he was calling up a number of National Guard units. This decision was driven by necessity, for without at least partial mobilization there would not only be no further replacements available for General Douglas MacArthur's forces in the Far East, but the active contingency forces maintained in the United States for response to any other emergency would be spread dangerously thin.

In rapid succession President Truman approved calling up individuals from the Army Reserve—25,000 at once and what reached a total of another 135,000 over the next eleven months. He also authorized calling up four divisions from the Army National Guard, and nearly ninety other units, including regimental combat teams and antiaircraft, artillery, and engineer battalions, from the Army National Guard and the organized reserve. The entire Marine Corps reserve, some 33,500 men, was also mobilized. By 1 September, barely two months after war had broken out, about 256,000 men from the Army National Guard, the Air National Guard, and the Army, Navy, Air Force, and Marine Corps reserves had been called to active duty.

The principal ground units were the four Army National Guard infantry divisions: the 28th from Pennsylvania; the 40th from California; the 43rd from Connecticut, Vermont, and Rhode Island; and Oklahoma's 45th. Called up in September 1950, they were undergoing post-mobilization training when, in the wake of the Chinese intervention, the Eighth Army found itself being driven relentlessly southward. In mid-December MacArthur cabled an urgent request that the four divisions be sent at once to Japan.

The Joint Chiefs of Staff, fearful that Korea might not be the main threat, that the Communists might be using it as a diversion while their main objective lay in Europe or elsewhere, were unanimously opposed to sending any additional U.S. divisions to the Far East. The mobilized National Guard divisions had served to reconstitute the general reserve, and that was where the joint chiefs wanted to keep them. Nevertheless, again driven by necessity, in April the 40th and 45th Divisions were dispatched to Japan. MacArthur was enjoined not to send them on to the Korean battlefield, but in December 1951 that restriction was also lifted and the two divisions were dispatched to the front.

About a fifth of the Army National Guard, along with a sixth of the Air National Guard, had been called to active duty by the autumn of 1950. Two wings, five groups, and fifteen squadrons of the Air National Guard had also been alerted for call-up.

By 30 June 1951, a year into the Korean War, a third of the Army National Guard and three-fourths of the Air National Guard were on active duty. And during 1951 all twenty-five air reserve wings and twenty-two of the twenty-seven Air National Guard wings, with supporting units, were called up. The Army reserve, or Organized Reserve Corps as it was then called, reached a maximum of 40 percent of its strength on active duty during the war.

The experience of the other services differed substantially. The Navy activated twenty-one naval air squadrons almost at once, but otherwise essentially provided individual replacements drawn from units which did not themselves deploy. By mid-1952 some 6,000 naval pilots and ground officers and about 15,000 enlisted personnel of the naval air reserve had been recalled. Eventually nearly a quarter of the complement of the fleet in the theater of war was composed of reserves. The Marine Corps called its reserve up early and in its entirety, then virtually dissolved it by using the individuals as replacements.

Successive activations meant that by 30 June 1952, two years into the war, more than 150,000 National Guardsmen had been called to active service. Eight infantry divisions had been federalized, and their dispositions reflected the three general roles for activated reserve forces. Two—the 40th and 45th—were serving in Korea, the active combat theater. Two others—the 28th and 43rd—were in Europe, adding to the deterrent force in the theater where senior military and civilian leaders still saw the greatest threat. The other four—the 31st, 37th, 44th and 47th—were in the United States, serving to reconstitute the strategic reserve and to "backfill" for active force units that had deployed. Other units, both combat and service support, were deployed with the European command, the Far East command, in Iceland, and with Army forces in Alaska.

By the same benchmark, 30 June 1952, the Air National Guard had about 80 percent of its assets in active federal service.

The induction strength of the eight divisions called up ranged from 37 to 55 percent of full strength. The shortfalls had to be made up by assignment of individual replacements. Yet the total output of the training centers was being allocated to units already deployed in Korea and Europe, so that mobilized National Guard units were fleshed out with "untrained fillers." The necessity to begin with the basics and bring these men up to required levels of training and proficiency greatly extended the required period of preparation for the mobilized divisions.

As these events unfolded, there was great concern on the part of National Guardsmen over a perennial issue—maintaining the integrity of activated units, rather than seeing them broken up to provide individual replacements for active duty outfits. Already Congress had enacted a provision of law which, overriding existing statutes, authorized the Truman administration for a period of one year to reach into reserve force units and call up individuals rather than the entire outfit.

Another troublesome problem was the perception that the National Guard had become a haven for those who sought to avoid being sent to war. This, too, had to do with maintaining unit integrity—in this case the integrity of units that had not been called to active duty—by protecting their members from the military draft. Since mobilization had been less than total, there were of course units that were not called or deployed. Prudence dictated keeping them intact for possible future activation, but that meant that some drafted individuals would be sent to war while volunteers in the reserve forces stayed behind.

Those reserve forces not mobilized were stripped of equipment for use by the active forces. The Army National Guard gave up motor vehicles, tanks, and other ground weapons, plus light aircraft. Besides 156 M-26 tanks, some 592 M-4 medium tanks were withdrawn from National Guard inventories. The impact is suggested by the fact that, a year into the war, the Army National Guard had on hand only 33 percent of its authorized equipment. Likewise, the Air National Guard was stripped of its F-84 jet fighter aircraft, and even such items as life vests, life rafts, and spare parts for F-51 aircraft were withdrawn for use by the active forces. Thus units not called became progressively less ready. This was a major problem in that military leaders felt, even as they were carrying out a partial mobilization for the Korean conflict, that they needed to maintain the capability for full mobilization should an even larger crisis erupt in Europe or elsewhere.

It is clear, on the basis of number, dispositions, and contributions to the overall campaign, that reserve forces played a major role in this conflict. The numerous deficiencies, often severe, which they had to overcome were largely the product of a half-decade of neglect following World War II demobilization, and were for the most part mirrored in the active forces of the day. To their credit, reserve forces were nevertheless able to make an important contribution to waging the Korean War.

Lewis Sorley

Bibliography

Departments of the Army and the Air Force, *Annual Report of the Chief, National Guard Bureau: Fiscal Year Ending 30 June 1949* (GPO, Washington: 1950 and subsequent years).

Historical Evaluation & Research Organization, *Historical Analysis of Reserve Component Tank Battalion Equipment Problems in the Korean War Mobilization: Final Report* (HERO, Fairfax, VA: 31 January 1985).

Historical Evaluation & Research Organization, *Mobilization in the Korean Conflict: Final Report* (HERO, Dunn Loring, VA: May 1982).

Jacobs, Bruce. "Korea Mobilization: A Backward Glance," *National Guard* (January 1985), p. 40.

National Guard Association of the United States, *Official Proceedings of the 72nd General Conference* (Washington, 23–25 October 1950).

Sorley, Lewis. "Creighton Abrams and Active-Reserve Integration in Wartime," *Parameters* (Summer 1991), pp. 35–50.

Rhee, Syngman (1875–1965)

Only two years after its National Assembly had adopted a constitution, the Republic of (South) Korea (ROK) held its second general election in May 1950. Politically, the unstable situation created by widespread Communist activities, and aggravated by partisan bitterness and violence did not prevent the full and free campaigning that preceded the election, which resulted in an overwhelming victory not for President Syngman Rhee or his political opposition, but for democracy. More than 85 percent of eligible voters went to the polls. The election gave 56 seats in the national assembly to the government party of President Rhee, 26 to members of the Democratic Nationalist party and other opposition parties, and 128 to independents. This clearly was an expression of the people's lack of confidence in the government and the existing political parties. President Rhee's authoritarian hold on Korean politics was being called into serious question.

Rhee, the first president of South Korea, was born in 1875, completed a traditional classical education fitting his noble, if decayed, heritage, and then entered a Methodist school, where he learned English. He became an ardent nationalist and ultimately a Christian; in 1896, he joined with other Korean leaders to form the Independence Club, a group dedicated to Korean independence. When pro-Japanese elements destroyed the club in 1898, Rhee was arrested and imprisoned until 1904. On his release he went to the United States, where in 1910 he received a Ph.D. from Princeton, the first Korean to earn a doctorate. He returned home in 1910, the year in which Korea was annexed outright by Japan. He spent the next thirty years as a spokesman for Korean independence, and in 1919 was elected president of the "Korean Provisional Government" in exile in Washington, D.C. Rhee became the best known Korean leader during World War II and campaigned hard for a policy of immediate independence and unification of the Korean peninsula. He soon built up a mass political organization supported by strong-arm squads. With the assassination of major moderate leaders, Rhee's new party won South Korea's first elections, and he became president in 1948. But political instability and ominous signals from Kim Il Sung's regime in North Korea had made the whole Korean peninsula a tinderbox of the Cold War.

Meanwhile, Secretary of State Dean Acheson and others in the Truman administration were formulating a policy that placed Korea outside the U.S. defense perimeter in East Asia. The North Korean Communists, who had been trying to subvert the ROK by fomenting armed rebellion (as at Yosu and Sunchon in 1948), were led to believe that the time was ripe for an all-out invasion of the South.

In June 1949, Pyongyang Radio, a propaganda station daily pouring out its animosity to the ROK, had announced the formation of the Democratic Front for the Attainment of the Unification of the Fatherland, commonly called the Fatherland Front. The Soviet directors of Pyongyang Radio were constantly devising new propaganda ploys to unsettle the South in a campaign of subversion, arson, terrorism, and guerrilla warfare. The Fatherland Front, composed of twenty to thirty "patriotic political parties," announced a series of elections throughout all Korea during the summer of 1949, whether the ROK approved or not, and predicted that on September 20 the flag of the Democratic People's Republic of Korea (DPRK) would fly over the capitol in Seoul (which it did, for a few months, one year later).

Attempted incursions into the south were closely linked to the propaganda campaign. Communist guerrillas operating in the mountains in the South coordinated their movements with the broadcasts and border skirmishes. The broadcasts insisted that the unification of Korea would be peaceful except for the necessary liquidation of a few "pro-American" and "pro-Japanese" traitors and the big landlords such as "Syngman Rhee and his gang." Obviously, the only way that the Communist flag could be raised over the capitol in Seoul and the only way the president of South Korea, the government, and the national assembly could be liquidated was by military conquest.

On June 25, 1950, North Korea launched an overwhelming and sudden attack across the 38th parallel. The understrength and poorly equipped ROK Army, trained primarily for antiguerrilla operations, was forced to retreat. The United Nations (U.N.) quickly resolved to give military support to the Republic of Korea, and a United Nations command (UNC) was established. Troops from fifteen countries—including the United States, Great Britain, France, Canada, Australia, the Philippines, and Turkey—arrived in Korea to fight side by side with the ROK Army under the flag of the United Nations.

From Taejon, where Rhee's government had fled in the face of Communist infantrymen and tanks, South Koreans were exhorted by their leaders to drive out the invader, but to no avail. Seoul fell on June 28, and South Korean troops straggled in retreat across the Han River bridges. Those members of Rhee's government who had reached Taejon soon moved to Pusan, but after a week they relocated to Taegu to stay closer to the front. Rhee initially had vehemently resisted the advice of his aides and the American ambassador to relocate the government to Pusan, preferring to meet death at the hands of the enemy rather than go abroad to

lead a government in exile. If he was to die, he had declared, it would be on the soil of his native land. Rhee later recanted once he came to realize the grave political implications should he fall into the hands of the North Koreans. One thing was certain: The invasion had brought a respite in Rhee's political wars; politics were put aside, if only for as long as it took to ascertain the South's ability to retain a toehold on the Korean peninsula, along the Pusan perimeter.

Meanwhile, in Tokyo, General Douglas MacArthur decided on a bold stroke: an amphibious landing at Inchon, twenty-five miles west of Seoul, followed by a two-pronged attack against the Communist armies in southern Korea. The success of the Inchon landing on September 15–16 ushered in a new phase of the war. Following the retaking of Seoul by the UNC X Corps on September 28, MacArthur and Rhee made a triumphal entry, driving by motorcade to the gutted capitol building. Rhee sensed victory within his grasp, and he lobbied for an all-out drive to annihilate the North Korean armed forces and liberate the Communist North. On October 7, the U.N. General Assembly approved a resolution permitting punitive action against North Korea and calling for the unification of the peninsula. With shouts of "On to the Yalu," ROK troops poured across the 38th parallel. To the aged Rhee, a lifelong objective appeared in sight.

Rhee moved to capitalize on the U.N. advance across the parallel. As president he believed it fell to him to appoint provisional governors in the Republic of Korea; he now began also to appoint governors to rule in his name over liberated areas of the North. But the United Nations ruled that his government had no authority north of the 38th parallel, and the General Assembly decreed that the government of a united Korea should be determined by U.N.-supervised elections throughout the country. Rhee bitterly opposed this ruling on the grounds that the legitimacy of the Republic of Korea had already been certified by a U.N. commission in 1948. Liberated areas of North Korea were nonetheless kept under military administration in accordance with the U.N. directive.

Early in the war, Rhee effectively gave U.S. President Harry S. Truman an ultimatum. Much as he might wish that Truman would accept his views and make American policy coincide with Korean policy, Rhee intended to pursue what he felt the welfare of his country demanded. Rhee declared: "The government and people of the Republic of Korea consider this is the time to unify Korea, and for anything less than unification to come out of these great sacrifices of Koreans and their powerful allies would be unthinkable. The Korean government would consider as without binding effect any future agreement or understanding made regarding Korea by other states without the consent and approval of the government of the Republic of Korea."

President Rhee also felt that the U.N. command policy of keeping a tight rein on the ROK army was fundamentally wrong. But he also realized that it would be futile for him to criticize the U.N. command, however, either publicly or privately. Neither the Koreans nor the Americans could do anything under stress of the continuing battle to reconcile the differences of language, methods, aims, and perspective on the fighting that widely divided them.

Catastrophe confronted Rhee and his government in November when thousands of Communist Chinese troops eviscerated four South Korean divisions near the Chongchon River, and again in November when Chinese forces repulsed a new U.N. offensive and turned it into a rout. The ominous shadows threatening Seoul on Christmas 1950 finally enveloped the ravaged city as the new year dawned, and on January 4, 1951, Communist forces once again occupied the South Korean capital. As both MacArthur and Rhee noted, it was a new war.

Obscured by the Communist military successes in the winter of 1950–51 was one of the great propaganda defeats for the Communists in the Cold War. In June 1950, a sizable proportion of the South Korean population had elected to take their chances with a Communist occupation. The following January, however, in the face of the Communist advance, an estimated two million Koreans streamed south with the U.N. forces. Seoul became almost a ghost town. At Suwon, south of Seoul, nearly 100,000 Koreans jammed the railroad yards. A people who had endured the Japanese occupation with relative patience was prepared to go to any length to avoid falling under Communist domination. When a U.N. counterattack led by General Matthew B. Ridgway gained ground in late January and early February 1951, the Communists were once again forced to evacuate Seoul. The opposing forces now reached an equilibrium in which the tide could be turned in favor of either side only by enlarging the war in a way neither felt safe doing. It became apparent to most that a resolution of the fighting was more

likely to be found at the conference table than on the battlefield. Like Rhee, however, MacArthur viewed the war in terms of total victory, and he demanded authorization from Washington to bomb Chinese installations in Manchuria. Truman relieved MacArthur of his command in early April, a move that shocked Rhee, who had always supported the general's views on expanding the war. Embittered and contemptuous of the United Nations, he now believed Korea's fate was once again being decided not by Koreans but by statesmen in foreign capitals too timid to risk an all-out war against communism.

As early as January 1951, President Rhee was developing long-range plans for establishment of a Korean–American Society—an idea he hoped would produce major results in building friendship and understanding. Looking beyond the war to measures needed to ensure future security, Rhee noted that Korea's "national existence depends partly on international agreement for common security, and partly on our own military preparations, so that no neighbor can be tempted to make Korea an easy prey." But his political clashes with Truman gradually became more personal in nature, until a wedge had been firmly driven between the two wartime allies. Enmity as much as cooperation would soon characterize the relationship between the Truman and Rhee administrations, and hopes for warmer U.S.–ROK relations remained pinned to Truman's perceptions of U.S. security interests in East Asia.

As a war of stalemate dragged on through the spring and summer of 1951, Syngman Rhee's political wars heated up. With his term as president due to expire soon, Rhee's opponents—who dominated the National Assembly—were determined to overthrow him in the 1952 election, and they found many instances of corruption and malfeasance with which to attack the administration. One such scandal which threatened to undo Rhee involved the National Defense Corps (NDC). The NDC had been an amalgamation of various strong-arm "youth groups" which had been organized as a military unit just before the war. But when the corps actually had to be activated for combat, certain disturbing facts came to light. Those survivors who straggled south in the second evacuation of Seoul were in rags, and many suffered from extreme malnutrition. They brought back stories of nonexistent supplies and leadership. An investigation later revealed that the NDC commander, a son-in-law of

Rhee's defense minister, had embezzled funds allocated for the NDC's food, clothing, and equipment—including rifles and ammunition.

Another scandal which rocked the Rhee administration was the Kochang massacre. In the course of an antiguerrilla campaign in February 1951, a ROK Army detachment lost contact with a group of guerrillas near the village of Kochang. Furious, the South Korean commander accused the villagers of harboring the fugitives. After herding the inhabitants into a schoolyard, he ordered all 200 of the men of the village shot. Attempts by the National Assembly to investigate stories of the massacre were thwarted by Colonel "Tiger" Kim, a favorite of Rhee's whom the president later appointed director of the national police. Kim declared the road leading to Kochang a battle area, and the investigation—if not the stench of murder and military corruption—came to an end. Similar cover-ups obscured massacres and atrocities committed by ROK forces earlier, during the retreat south in the summer of 1950. Although not on the scale of Communist executions of "enemies of the people," many incidents had been witnessed by U.S. troops, to their intense disgust with their ally.

Western diplomats became increasingly critical of Rhee's administration, but the U.S. did not press him for a full accounting of these and other domestic scandals. Unfortunately, Rhee took U.S. noninterference as tacit approval for his excesses, including his contempt for the constitution. The constitution under which Rhee took office in 1948 was one which he had helped to draft, and it incorporated many of the features of a strong executive which he desired—such as emergency police powers. One of these concessions had been that the National Assembly would have the right to elect the president. Knowing that his prospects for reelection by a hostile legislature were next to nil, Rhee reorganized the Liberal party. It would become dominated by leaders of non-Assembly groups which had mass appeal, such as the Korean Federation of Trade Unions, the Korean Women's Association, and the League of Korean Laborers. Although not avowed political organizations, each was, in practice, an action arm of the Liberal party.

In his campaign to secure reelection, Rhee had two basic alternatives. One was to operate within the existing constitutional structure under which the president was elected by the Assembly, but to bring such pressure to bear on the legislature that it would be forced to accept him for a second term. Such a course relied heavily on Rhee's control of the Army and the vulnerability of many opposition legislators to bribes. But it in no way checked the constitutional prerogatives of the Assembly. In the end, Rhee determined on a frontal assault against the Assembly, one which would neutralize it as a rival to the executive. In a series of speeches in the spring of 1952, Rhee equated his enemies in the Assembly with the enemy in the Communist North: both were out to destroy him, and thus to destroy free Korea. Rhee's cronies organized "spontaneous" demonstrations calling for the reelection of Rhee and for the selection of Lee Bum-suk, the new home minister, as his running mate.

On May 25, Rhee and Lee reimposed martial law in Pusan, ostensibly as an antiguerrilla measure. (There were no guerrillas within miles of Pusan.) When the Assembly voted ninety-six to three (with numerous abstentions) to lift martial law, Rhee ordered the arrest of forty-seven assemblymen by ROK Army police and announced that "far-reaching Communist connections have been uncovered, and authorities are taking steps to make a thorough investigation." He continued to wield the powers of his office as though the legislature did not exist. The political war between the president and the Assembly escalated, with more arrests of assemblymen and more charges of a Communist conspiracy to depose Rhee and bring about unification negotiations with Kim Il Sung's North Korean regime. While continuing to insist publicly that he was not a candidate for reelection, he flayed the National Assembly for having "betrayed the will of the people" and began to orchestrate his final maneuver against the Assembly.

With Rhee holding a monopoly of the police and the Army, and now having demonstrated his willingness to override the constitution when pressed, the president was in a position to offer a compromise solution on June 5: In return for the popular election of the president, he was prepared to give the Assembly an increased voice in the selection of Cabinet ministers. Meanwhile, he threatened publicly to dissolve the Assembly if his demands were not met, observing dryly that "the will of the people is more important than the letter of the Constitution." In response to Truman's warning not to take such "irrevocable steps" as dissolving the Assembly, Rhee mollified the U.S. administration—if not the American press—by assuring Truman he would disband the Assembly only as a last resort. Following a new series of "popular demonstrations" instigated by Lee and the home ministry, Rhee announced that while he did not desire another term in office he was prepared to bow to the will of the people. By June 23, 1952, Syngman Rhee had broken his opponents in the Assembly, many of whom remained in hiding to avoid political arrest. By a vote of sixty-one to zero, the National Assembly extended Rhee in office "until the dispute is resolved," which, of course, was past the date of the scheduled election. Rhee's idea of resolving the crisis was to stage an assassination attempt against himself, whip up anti-Communist hysteria, and—making full use of the strong-arm tactics of Lee Bum-suk and martial law commander Won Yong-duk—to browbeat the Assembly. Finally, on July 5, with the entire Assembly under virtual house arrest, by a totalitarian vote of 163 to 0 (with three abstentions), the Assembly amended the constitution to allow for popular election of the president and for an upper house. Once his amendments were passed, Rhee's reelection was a foregone conclusion. When the votes were counted on August 6, 1952, Rhee ran up 5 million votes to 800,000 for Cho Bong-am, his one-time minister of agriculture. With the Assembly's power broken and his own tainted reelection secured, Rhee could now return his attention to the great issue of the Korean War: unification. He continued to devote his energies to opposing any cease-fire without total victory over the Communist North. For Rhee, who turned his oratorical powers against U.N. armistice talks, it was to be "unification or death!"

During the peace negotiations at Kaesong and later at Panmunjom, the Communists at first seemed as much interested in using the conference table as a vehicle for propaganda as in securing a settlement. Yet for all the discouragements, the two sides gradually inched toward agreement. The Communists finally dropped demands for a U.N. withdrawal to the 38th parallel and agreed to the American line-of-contact plan for the demarcation line. Agreement was reached on implementation of the armistice through a Military Armistice Commission aided by joint observer teams. Disagreements over the repatriation of prisoners of war (POWs), however, then stalemated the negotiations for almost two years.

In April 1953, Rhee calculated how best to use his considerable influence to block an armistice which now seemed close. The ROK ambassador in Washington informed the United States that South Korea would withdraw its forces from the U.N. command if the allies agreed to any armistice which permitted Chinese Communist troops to remain on Korean soil. Within a month, the U.S. had countered by offering an attractive package: In return for Rhee's compliance with an armistice, and retention of the ROK Army within the U.N. command, the United States would build up the South Korean Army to twenty divisions and provide the equivalent of a billion dollars for rehabilitating South Korea. Rhee rejected the offer out of hand, saying: "Your threats have no effect upon me. We want to live. We want to survive. We will decide our own fate."

On June 4, the U.N. and the Communist sides reached agreement on all major points concerning POW repatriation. The ROK press denounced the agreement as a sellout. For his part, Rhee attempted to muddy the waters once again, saying he would accept a truce based on simultaneous withdrawal of U.N. and Communist troops in return for a mutual security pact with the U.S., large-scale economic aid, and the retention of U.S. air and naval forces in Korea. Rhee knew that these conditions would never be accepted by the Communists and that insistence on them only meant continuing the war.

Rhee had another trump card to play, and he did, much to the chagrin of the United States and the U.N. command. Since ROK troops manned two-thirds of the front, a sudden decision to remove them from the U.N. command would be a nightmare. Rhee hinted he might even ignore an armistice and continue to fight. But, it turned out, Rhee ordered ROK guards to release 27,000 non-repatriates from their compounds, hoping that his POW release would create such turmoil and recriminations at Panmunjom that the truce talks would be broken off indefinitely. It was impossible to recapture the men, who were formed into labor battalions before being inducted into the ROK Army. The whole incident was an open gesture of defiance which publicly flouted General Mark Clark's authority and demonstrated that Rhee's wishes could be ignored only at the peril of his allies. Since the articles of armistice had already been finalized, Rhee's prisoner release was a bombshell. The Communists raised questions about the U.N. command's ability to control Rhee and the ROK government. Instead of fulfilling Rhee's hopes, however, the results confirmed his fears that the Free World and the Communists alike were determined on a truce at almost any cost. The Communists were so eager to have a truce, even with the division of Korea reaffirmed, that they contented themselves with ritual denunciations of Rhee and the U.N. command. The U.N. was so eager to have a truce that it joined the enemy in denouncing Rhee's action. And both sides agreed that the armistice talks would continue. The most extreme action President Rhee could devise to prevent the continued division of his nation had failed. But neither his own people nor the governments of the world could doubt that he had done his best, short of military adventurism, to avert an armistice. On July 10, 1953, the truce talks resumed. The last act in this tragic drama of war was ready to unfold.

Infuriated by Rhee's "stab in the back," as General Clark called it, Washington dispatched Assistant Secretary of State Walter Robertson to Seoul to persuade Rhee to accept an armistice. For more than two weeks, Rhee and Robertson held bargaining sessions almost daily. Finally, on July 12, Robertson flew to Tokyo with a letter from Rhee to President Dwight D. Eisenhower agreeing not to obstruct an armistice. Rhee's letter to Eisenhower agreeing to a cease-fire was his only substantive concession. In return, Rhee obtained the promise of a ROK-U.S. mutual security treaty, a lump-sum payment of $200 million as the first installment of a long-term economic aid program, and expansion of the ROK Army to twenty divisions.

On July 27, 1953, one of the twentieth century's most vicious and frustrating wars came to a close with the signing of an armistice at Panmunjom. The signing on August 8, 1953, of a mutual security treaty between the ROK and the United States was the culmination of a lifelong ambition, an event which allowed a bitter seventy-eight-year-old man to recall with some satisfaction how, nearly fifty years before, he had traveled to the United States to plead in vain for American protection against the Japanese. Rhee made the signing the occasion for a discourse on Korean history: "Korea has been considered as a weak, minor country, helplessly situated among powerful nations and yet rich in natural resources, thereby attracting many an aggressive power to covet the land. Throughout history Korea has been regarded as a no-man's land whose independence, neighboring powers assumed, is unavoidably dependent on one of the big powers. . . . Following Japan's failure to conquer the whole world, the Allied nations brought up a decision made by themselves which finally caused the tragic division of Korea, north and south. Nevertheless, the united effort of our people, the patriotism of our youth, and the assistance from friendly nations all contributed to developing our armed forces. Now that a defense treaty has been signed between Korea and the United States, our posterity will enjoy the benefits accruing from the treaty for generations to come."

The war had a lasting effect on the South Korean political system. While the war helped solidify President Syngman Rhee's personal political power structure in the short term, it failed to stabilize the political system or to integrate diverse social and political forces. Viewed from a long-range historical perspective, it can be argued that the war exerted a highly dysfunctional impact on South Korean politics. The decline in political stability may be attributed to a variety of specific factors.

First, the extreme rapidity with which North Korea engulfed and ruled nine-tenths of ROK territory resulted in an abrupt discontinuity of the incipient democratic political institutions in the South. Central government agencies were crippled, and the National Assembly, political parties, interest groups, and other political organizations were decimated.

Second, the relative ease of North Korea's initial military victory and South Korea's confused response dealt a serious blow to the Rhee government's legitimacy and competence.

Third, the war disrupted traditional social structures, especially in rural areas, and thus undermined the conservative social and political order. The wartime experiences also challenged the Confucian hierarchy of interpersonal relations within the family and gave impetus to female emancipation.

Finally, the sudden influx of Northern refugees—about two million during the war—complicated South Korea's political processes. Once entrenched in South Korea's political structure, they constituted a powerful, emotional bloc against reconciliation and unification. The lingering suspicions and raw hostility permeating the Korean peninsula still prevail as major obstacles to a final resolution of the Korean War, which American military historian S.L.A. Marshall called the twentieth century's "nastiest little war."

James E. Dillard

Bibliography

Allen, Richard C. *Korea's Syngman Rhee: An Unauthorized Portrait* (1960).

Blair, Clay. *The Forgotten War: America in Korea, 1950–1953* (1987).

Cumings, Bruce. *The Origins of the Korean War: Liberation and the Emergence of Separate Regimes* (1981).

Knox, Donald. *The Korean War: An Oral History* (1985).

Lee Chae-jin, ed. *The Korean War: 30-Year Perspectives* (Claremont, CA: The Keck Center for International and Strategic Studies, 1991).

MacDonald, Callum A. *Korea: The War Before Vietnam* (1986).

Noble, Harold J. *Embassy at War* (1975).

Oliver, Robert T. *Syngman Rhee and American Involvement in Korea: 1942–1960* (1978).

Ridgway, Matthew B. (1895–1993)

The role of General Matthew Bunker Ridgway in the Korean War is a study of incredible military success. After Nathanael Green's retrieval of patriot fortunes in the South during the Revolutionary War, there is no record of any American commander who took a war that was on the threshold of defeat and by personal will and intelligence turned it to success. General Ridgway's command genius in Korea was the culmination of a career that both the United States Army and himself had tracked for success since he graduated from West Point in 1917.

Ridgway was one of that unique cadre of brilliant younger generals who had been blooded as division commanders in World War II, but who were not called to duty in Korea until General Douglas MacArthur was replaced. Only James Gavin of that select group was left out of what became Ridgway's success. James Van Fleet, Mark Clark, and Maxwell Taylor formed a tableau of the best and brightest of the old war-horses who would, with Ridgway's urging, encourage a new cadre of professional battalion and regimental commanders that would turn the Korean War around.

General Ridgway was well established as a lieutenant general and deputy Army chief of staff for plans in Washington in the early winter of 1950. It was a winter of military discontent for the nation as the greatest retreat in the history of the nation was underway as the Chinese pushed U.N. troops southward. The Eighth U.S. Army, under command of General Walton H. Walker, was seriously considering evacuation of all forces from the Korean peninsula. The glory of MacArthur's brilliant invasion behind the enemy at Inchon and his thrust deep into North Korea was soon dissipated as the Chinese intervened. The dimensions of the war became the core of debate among MacArthur, President Harry S. Truman, and the U.N. allies of the United States. The demand for more divisions, the suggestion that Nationalist China be brought into the war, and the prospect for using atomic weaponry all fueled the controversy. However, it was the issue of enlarging the Allied objective to include unification of the two Koreas and possible invasion of China itself that harmed MacArthur.

In Washington, Ridgway was abashed at the propensity of MacArthur for quarreling with orders. To the amazement of his timid peers at Army staff headquarters, Ridgway had commented that removal of an obstreperous commander was not too far-fetched a method of dealing with the matter. Just before Christmas Ridgway was startled to find that he was to replace General Walker, who had been killed in a jeep accident. Following a briefing by MacArthur in Tokyo, Ridgway took physical command of the Eighth Army. He had been assured that the command was his to do with as he wished. MacArthur, of course, was not dissuaded from pursuing the larger agenda for the war that he had established for himself.

Visiting several divisions, the new commander was astonished at the confusion and despair that he found. There was a decided lack of morale and purpose, shoddy discipline, and an atmosphere of defeat. For the dour, almost puritanical, and disciplined hard paratrooper, problems meant opportunity. He quickly spelled out a training regimen that would restore the will of the units. He firmly believed that individual and unit discipline encouraged an esprit that had been lost or unknown. He replaced the retreat mentality with a mindset that made taking the offensive the priority. He was startled at seeing how road-bound the Army was. To Ridgway, ever the infantry soldier, this ran counter to everything basic to effective combat. Showers, changes of clothing, hot meals, mail deliveries, distribution of stationery so that troops could write home, all served to lift spirits. Training between echelons ensured that field soldiers could count on artillery support when and where they needed it. He turned his attention to mobile Army surgical hospital (MASH) units to ensure that the best immediate care of the wounded would be available. He sent word to General J. Lawton Collins that he wanted the best and smartest available battalion and regimental commanders sent to him for assignment. Hidebound unyielding divisional commanders were now confronted with finding a place in their units for these new men. Ridgway quietly ticketed divisional and corps commanders for reassignment out of the theater, always replacing them with new men to match the new will of his army. Old generals were given promotions and commendations and glad-handed out of Korea while Ridgway turned his attention to slashing at the enemy, punishing the adversary and eschewing the old objective of territorial gain. Chief of staff General Collins was encouraged and elated by the transformation despite a dour assessment from the once-euphoric MacArthur. By the end of January 1951, the allies were on the move, hitting both Chinese and North Koreans head-on and winning as they moved relentlessly northward. MacArthur, recognizing that his concept of total victory was fast becoming remote, was not encouraged by the prospect of a stabilized front on the 38th parallel.

Within four months Ridgway had proven good on his word when he arrived in Korea and declared "We're going the other way." The Joint Chiefs of Staff (JCS) in Washington found they could deal directly with Ridgway and thereby circumvent MacArthur, who was becoming increasingly bitter and vocal about being restrained from gaining total victory. This did not prevent the old general from reaping credit for Ridgway's successes in the field, however. His notion of escalating the war was revived as the enemy was pushed north of the 38th parallel, and his statements to the press and to opponents of the administration continued to run counter to national policy on the conduct of the war. The climax of mutual discontent came on April 11, 1951, when President Harry S. Truman peremptorily removed MacArthur from command and thereby from the Army. Ridgway was immediately named to replace him as U.N. commander.

Certain now of gaining his fourth star, Ridgway thought he was in position to name his successor as commander of the Eighth Army. Washington had made the choice for him, however. They selected General James Van Fleet, who had commanded brilliantly both the 82nd Airborne in Europe and against Communist insurgents in Greece after World War II. Like another paratroop general, General James Gavin, Van Fleet was extremely popular with his men and universally regarded as a dynamic, heroic combat commander. He was a particular favorite of President Truman who perhaps saw something of himself in the rugged, no-nonsense openness of the man. Ridgway, a taciturn, almost dour man, abstemious in behavior, had all the qualities of both men as well as their respect; but he did not have the same popularity. Personally he didn't like either man. He didn't want them in Korea, but now that he had Van Fleet he determined to keep tight control of Eighth Army operations even if it meant a constant commute from Tokyo.

The Army was now in good shape and comfortably established on a line running approximately parallel with the 38th demarcation line. These perimeters or "lines" were named after states and cities such as Wyoming, Kansas, and Toledo. The stability encouraged Washington and the U.N. allies to entertain possibilities of an armistice. The expectation was that advantageous territorial positions would be sustained while the enemy would be contained. Van Fleet wanted to launch a new initiative to include a Marine landing from the sea in the northeast. Ridgway was inalterably opposed to the plan but he did give permission to launch bombing raids against Communist airfields in North Korea. Despite an onslaught of MIG-15 fighter planes based in Manchuria, the Air Force prevailed in knocking out the infrastructure of the airfields. The Army was less certain about the result, however, since runways could be restored rapidly and air reconnaissance was limited because of smoke and haze from Chinese brush fires. The frustrated Van Fleet was soon to be in the middle of the greatest single battle of the war. From April 22 to April 30 the Chinese and North Koreans struck in massive force, ostensibly with Seoul as the objective. Eighth Army elements found themselves in desperate straits as South Korean divisions disintegrated under pressure, thereby placing Allied units in jeopardy. The British Brigade was isolated and virtually surrounded before Van Fleet's forces could relieve the pressure. The enemy attack was defeated and lines stabilized despite heavy Allied casualties. A great blow had been delivered to the enemy, and Ridgway noted Van Fleet's leadership.

He also turned his attention to another matter when he cabled Washington of his intention to desegregate the Eighth Army by disbanding all segregated regiments. The men in these units would be transferred to other regiments, thus effectively integrating the Army. This proposal had first been suggested by General William Kean of the 25th Division, one of whose regiments was all black. Ridgway stated that it seemed "un-American and un-Christian for free citizens to be taught to downgrade themselves . . . as if they were unfit to associate with their fellows or to accept leadership themselves." Ridgway developed the procedure and the proportions of numbers of blacks in each unit to be attained. Virtually every general officer favored the plan, as did the joint chiefs; but it was months before total integration became reality. Ridgway's May 14 directive was a large step toward achieving equality in the military.

The Chinese and North Koreans had regrouped by mid-May while Van Fleet was again denied authority to launch an attack using the Marines in a sea invasion near Wonsan to the east. On May 16, the Communists launched a new attack with some 175,000 men, this time east and away from the original Seoul corridor of a month earlier. Again elements of the ROK collapsed as 40,000 men left their positions. Ridgway again made his way to command headquarters. He would not give Van Fleet carte blanche control of all units. He relented in releasing the 187th Regimental Combat Team, an airborne unit being held as a decoy in reserve, and deploying elements of the 3rd Infantry Division to fill gaps and reinforce weakened sectors. By May 30, the attack was repulsed with appalling enemy losses approaching 80,000 casualties. It was the second defeat of the Communists in two months. They were becoming physically and materially exhausted. They had, however, delivered severe blows of their own against a tired Eighth Army.

With Ridgway's permission, Van Fleet on June 3 launched an offensive of his own. The going was very slow. Many units were exhausted, and the new rotation of troops policy had taken effect, causing the loss of veterans. On June 9, Van Fleet and Ridgway agreed to halt the advance. Washington was concerned about discontent developing in the United States. Human losses began to register. In fact, 21,300 Americans had been killed by June 25, 1951. The possibilities of gaining an armistice seemed propitious. Ridgway had also come to realize that a decisive victory was out of the question. Also, U.N. allies became chary about American intentions in the war. On June 30, they got some relief from their worries as Ridgway was authorized to make an overture to negotiate a settlement. He made a radio broadcast to that effect, suggesting a meeting to take place on a Danish hospital ship in Wonsan harbor. Both China and North Korea responded positively but chose to meet instead in Kaesong, which was

very near the 38th parallel. This would compromise Ridgway's territorial position, but pressure to take advantage of the enemy's willingness to negotiate compelled him to accept Kaesong as the site. However, a breakdown occurred almost immediately over the desires of Syngman Rhee for greater territorial advantages north of the 38th parallel, the demarcation of a demilitarized zone, and the non-repatriation of tens of thousands of prisoners of war (POWs), whom Rhee sought to use for political advantage.

The war entered a new phase. Ridgway understood that any renewed offensive would demand huge resources in men and materiel without which there could be no decisive defeat of the enemy. As negotiations dragged on into 1952, the stalemate interrupted only by skirmishes and sporadic artillery and mortar fire, Ridgway's noble work came to an end. In May he was named commander of NATO forces in Europe, succeeding General Dwight D. Eisenhower who would soon become president. General Mark Clark took over the Far East command.

General Ridgway returned to Washington to become Army chief of staff as Eisenhower was being inaugurated. From 1953 until he retired in 1955, Ridgway suffered what he called "the toughest, most frustrating job of my whole career." He had celebrated arguments with Defense Secretary Charles E. Wilson and with Admiral Arthur Radford, chairman of the JCS, over the downgrading of the Army's role in the new defense posture. Years later, he continued to present his views, arguing against the abolition of Selective Service, the admission of women into the military academies, and the concept of an all-volunteer armed force. He was particularly outraged by a 1979 order from the Pentagon which tried to abolish the distinctive red beret worn by the airborne troops. "Our airborne is an elite corps, envied and feared by our foes and admired by our friends, proud of its achievements and its uniform, proud of the airborne image in the public eye and proud of the red beret," he declared in his request for a revocation of the order. Ridgway also became an early and strong critic of U.S. involvement in Vietnam.

In 1986, General Ridgway was awarded the Presidential Medal of Freedom, and in 1991 General Colin Powell, chairman of the joint chiefs, presented him with the Congressional Gold Medal. In 1992 the U.S. Mint struck a bronze medal in his honor, the obverse stating a line he must have liked: "American Soldier."

R

General Ridgway died in retirement at Fox Chapel near Pittsburgh, Pennsylvania, on July 26, 1993, one day shy of the fortieth anniversary of the signing of the armistice ending the Korean War. He was 98. He was buried in Arlington Cemetery on July 30, 1993.

Jack J. Cardoso

Bibliography
Appleman, Roy E. *Ridgway Duels for Korea* (1990).
————. *United States Army in the Korean War* Vol. 2, *South to the Naktong, North to the Yalu* (GPO, Washington: 1981).
Blair, Clay. *The Forgotten War: America in Korea, 1950–1953* (1987).
Cumings, Bruce, ed. *Child of Conflict: The Korean-American Relationship, 1943–1953* (1983).
Goulden, Joseph C. *Korea: The Untold Story of the War* (1982).
Hermes, Walter G. *Truce Tent and Fighting Front*, Vol. 4, *United States Army in the Korean War* (GPO, Washington: 1966).
Kaufman, Burton I. *The Korean War: Challenge in Crisis, Credibility, and Command* (1986).
Rees, David. *Korea: The Limited War* (1964).
Ridgway, Matthew B. *The Korean War* (1967). Also, *Current Biography* (1947), pp. 540–542.
Whelan, Richard. *Drawing the Line: The Korean War, 1950–1953* (1990).

Rotation System
The principle of limited wartime service for American soldiers is as old as the United States Continental line. However, in its wars in the twentieth century, the American Army had switched to service for the duration—most visibly in World War II.

Before the Korean War, the Department of Defense had turned to a limited draft in order to maintain even the skeleton of a regular Army. Although most Army leaders preferred universal military training, Congress was not sympathetic. With national security supposedly assured by a monopoly (later only supremacy) in nuclear weapons, the force structure of the Army was a political compromise based on a small regular Army, National Guard units, and reserves.

In July 1950, shortly after the first American forces were sent to fight in the Korean War, the Army announced that draftees would not be sent to Korea. This initial optimism was short-lived, although the services did try to meet growing demands for manpower by first calling up National Guard units and the reserves. In the first year of the Korean War, the services inducted 585,000 draftees and called up 806,000 guardsmen and reservists. At the same time soldiers were being sent to Korea, others were being sent to beef up the NATO alliance, and still more were detailed to restore the strategic reserve in the United States.

The performance of guardsmen and reservists in combat often was not particularly good. Many of these soldiers had not seen active duty during World War II. At the same time, there were numerous complaints of severe personal hardships and questions about justice from inactive reservists called to duty and fighting their second war in a decade. In early 1951, to mute public criticism of the war, appease the civilian soldiers, and restore military morale, the Department of Defense introduced a rotation policy.

The system was based on "points." Soldiers received four points a month for serving in a line unit, a battalion, or lower echelon. This included infantry and support units, but not artillery. Artillery duty was three points a month. Regimental and division people whose duties kept them shuttling back and forth to the front got three points a month, whereas those who remained in the rear received two points a month. Service in Japan garnered one point a month, except for soldiers wounded in combat who received four points until reassigned. When a man reached thirty-six points he was rotated out and discharged, unless he wished otherwise. Few wished otherwise.

In retrospect, rotation was a bad idea. First, it made great demands on manpower, only solved by drafting another 1.2 million men. It also increased demands on transportation; by 1952, 35,000 men were being rotated each month. The effect of rotation on military efficiency was, paradoxically, almost completely counterproductive. As a serviceman's time to rotate came ever closer, he became increasingly focused on leaving the peninsula alive and less interested in doing his assigned duties. Survival depended not on beating the enemy, but on beating the clock. By disassociating a soldier's primary duty (waging war) from his primary personal objective (living to tell about it), the services diminished the individual's commitment to fighting on to victory. At the same time, rotation played havoc with the development of cohesive and effective units; it removed soldiers who had learned the bitter lessons of modern warfare and replaced them with new men who were inexperienced. A new man in the service was a "recruit" for the first six months, then moved to the rank of private. When the public noticed a large number of "Rct" listings on the killed in action (KIA) reports, the Army quietly dropped the rank. The rotation system reflected the dilemmas of a liberal democracy waging a limited war in peacetime—but it did nothing to resolve those dilemmas.

David M. Esposito

Bibliography

Cohen, Eliot. *Citizens and Soldiers* (1985).

Millett, Allan, and Peter Maslowski. *For the Common Defense* (1984).

Schnabel, James. *U.S. Army in the Korean War: Policy and Direction—The First Year* (United States Army, Washington: 1972).

Royal Navy

The British Admiralty quickly responded following the United Nations (U.N.) Security Council vote authorizing military assistance to the Republic of Korea by placing Royal Navy components in Japanese waters at the disposal of Vice Admiral C. Turner Joy, the commander of U.S. naval forces, Far East. Within days, an array of British vessels, including the light carrier HMS *Triumph*, all under the command of Rear Admiral William G. Andrewes, flag officer second in command, Far Eastern station, were actively operating in Korean waters. The Royal Navy was prohibited, however, from supporting United States naval operations in the Formosa Strait for fear that Communist China would act aggressively against the British possession of Hong Kong. Such a ban remained in effect for the duration of fighting in Korea. On 2 July 1950, the cruiser *Jamaica* and frigate *Black Swan* participated in the destruction of five North Korean torpedo and motor gunboats in the first and, for all practical purposes, only hostile naval engagement of the conflict. The following day aircraft from *Triumph*, stationed off the west coast of Korea, began striking inland targets as well as flying combat air and antisubmarine patrols over Anglo-American Task Force 77. As the situation on land continued to deteriorate, the decision was made to institute a maritime blockade of the peninsula.

Admiral Andrewes was charged with command of the west coast support group, later the west coast support element of Task Group 96.5. He was also given supervisory control of Commonwealth naval forces from Australia, Canada, and New Zealand, whose similar training and tactics made operational integration with the Royal Navy a simple task. However, Andrewes was also given administrative authority over all non-American United Nations warships—a more challenging proposition. Through summer typhoons and frigid winter weather, the ships of the west coast support element maintained an effective blockade as far north as 39°30' throughout the conflict. British ships, however, also continued to see duty along the east coast as situations, such as the seige of Wonsan, warranted. Other Royal Navy duties in the frenzied opening weeks of hostilities included coastal fire support, which was hampered by communication problems with friendly ground forces; escort duty between Japan and Korea, and carrier-based aviation strikes. Of special note was the duty performed by the crew of His Majesty Hospital Ship HMHS *Maine*, the first U.N. hospital ship in the theater, in the evacuation and treatment of wounded Allied soldiers. The British commander established Royal Navy theater headquarters at the U.S. naval facilities at Sasebo (Japan) to improve liaison with U.S. naval forces, Far East, the other Commonwealth naval commanders, his superior in Singapore, and U.N. Army and Air Force headquarters. Due to its presence in western waters, the Royal Navy became heavily involved in support of Operation Chromite as part of Joint Task Force Seven, providing reconnaissance, interdiction, cover, and screening missions for the U.N. amphibious invasion of Inchon. At the same time, British naval contingents assisted in diversionary measures along the opposite coast.

Following the success at Inchon, U.N. naval forces were realigned under Task Force 95. The British remained in control of the west coast support group, which contained the carrier, surface blockade and patrol, and west coast island defense elements. Now that U.N. forces were on the offensive above the 38th parallel, the Royal Navy was forced to deal with a different danger. Unable to match United Nations naval efforts, the North Koreans sought to redress the imbalance with an intense use of moored and drifting mines along the shallow Yellow Sea coast. It was fortunate that efforts at reducing this threat in the fall of 1950 proved successful, because Communist Chinese intervention soon forced the Royal Navy to assist in evacuating the overwhelmed U.N. ground forces. One of the most successful, and hazardous, withdrawals occurred at Chinnampo on 5 December 1950 when a Commonwealth-led force of destroyers penetrated the mine-swept Taedong-gang estuary in hazardous weather to evacuate personnel from the Pyongyang region. For his leadership during the crucial opening months of the conflict, Andrewes was promoted and transferred in April 1951; he was replaced in the theater by Rear Admiral A. K. Scott-Montcrieff.

Once the ground war stagnated and armistice negotiations opened, Royal Navy surface operations settled into basically routine blockade, patrol, and coastal bombardment missions. One noteworthy effort, which lasted from summer until late November 1951, was the penetration of the muddy Han River estuary to collect vital hydrographic information. Commonwealth ships were under constant threat from Communist-held positions on the northern bank while performing channel survey soundings and bouy placement duties in the shallow, tide-swept estuary. As negotiations continued at Kaesong, and later Panmunjom, a battle developed for control of strategic west coast islands north of the 38th parallel; they provided bargaining chips for negotiators burdened with an indecisive ground campaign.

Unfortunately, the Royal Navy was unable to halt a hostile invasion of Taehwa-do, the only U.N.-held island of strategic value near the mouth of the Yalu, in late November 1951. The British then increased efforts to provide material and counter-battery support to other friendly-occupied islands for the remainder of the conflict. Rear Admiral E.G.A. Clifford became the final senior British naval officer in the Korean theater when he took command of Commonwealth forces in September 1952. By this time the duties of the Royal Navy were well defined, understood, and remained basically routine. With the signing of the armistice on 27 July 1953, Royal Navy vessels began the evacuation of west coast island garrisons above the demarcation line. The efforts of the Royal Navy in the Korean conflict were far from token, with from roughly 3,500 to 5,500 personnel serving at any one time on board a total of thirty-four ships rotated during the fighting. Other Commonwealth naval forces further increased the number of sailors and ships off Korea. The British and Australians maintained a continuous light carrier presence in the theater, and flew approximately 25,000 sorties in support of the west coast support group and U.N. ground forces. Surface vessels maintained a successful blockade of the west coast, supported amphibious invasions and evacuations, and provided fire support against hostile coastal batteries and lines of supply and communication. An important partner of the Commonwealth ships of the line was the Royal Fleet Auxiliaries Service, which sent eighteen ships into the theater to provide logistical support for naval combat operations. Hence, the Royal Navy and its Commonwealth adjuncts made important contributions in the U.N. effort to maintain an independent Republic of Korea.

William E. Fischer, Jr.

Bibliography

"British Commonwealth Naval Operations During the Korean War," *Royal United Services Institute Journal*, 96 (1951): 250–255, 609–616; 97 (1952): 241–248.

British Commonwealth Naval Operations, Korea, 1950–53 (Ministry of Defense, London: 1967).

Farrar-Hockley, Anthony. *A Distant Obligation. The British Part in the Korean War*, Vol. 1 (HMSO, London: 1990).

Field, James A., Jr. *History of United States Naval Operations: Korea* (GPO, Washington: 1962).

The History of the United Nations Forces in the Korean War, 7 vols. (Ministry of Defense, Seoul: 1972–77).

See also BRITISH CONTRIBUTION; GREAT BRITAIN AND THE KOREAN WAR; UNITED KINGDOM

Rusk, Dean (1909–1994)

Born in rural northern Georgia in 1909, David Dean Rusk was educated in Davidson College in North Carolina, did graduate work at Oxford on a Rhodes Scholarship, and taught government and international relations at Mills College from 1934 to 1940. During World War II, Rusk served as chief of war plans to General Joseph Stilwell in Asia, and accepted a position with the Pentagon's operations division in 1945. In this later capacity, Rusk and a fellow colonel were responsible for recommending the 38th parallel as the preferred demarcation line between Soviet and U.S. liberating and occupying forces in Korea to the State/War/Navy Coordinating Committee.

In the postwar period, Rusk moved to the State Department, becoming director of special political affairs in 1947, and deputy undersecretary of state in 1949. A great admirer of General George C. Marshall, Rusk considered Secretary of State Dean Acheson to be too focused on Europe to the neglect of Asia. In 1950, following attacks on the State Department by Senator Joseph McCarthy and the resignation of the assistant secretary of state for Far Eastern affairs, Rusk offered himself as replacement. In that position, he privately doubted the wisdom of the U.S. withdrawal from South Korea, but claimed just before the North Korean invasion that the Republic of (South) Korea could hold off an "unlikely" North Korean attack. It would not be Rusk's last miscall.

Rusk was deeply involved in plans to counter the North Korean attack of 25 June 1950, counseling both American resistance and an appeal to the United Nations. Following the successful U.S. landings at Inchon, Rusk further supported military operations to liberate all of Korea, although he remained firmly against a war with China. Disturbed by what he regarded as the insubordination of U.N. commander in chief General Douglas MacArthur, and suspecting that the general planned to resign amid hysterical outbursts, Rusk advised President Harry S. Truman that he could not delay plans to fire him. Truman agreed, firing MacArthur in April 1951.

One month later, Rusk, in a major speech, unwisely termed the People's Republic of China a "puppet" of the Soviets, thereby inhibiting a future realistic assessment of the growing strains between the two Communist giants.

Rusk also held primary responsibility for drafting the peace treaty with Japan. Having recommended the appointment of his friend John Foster Dulles as chief negotiator, Rusk and Dulles arranged the San Francisco peace conference of the fall of 1951 to preclude any Soviet objections to a draft treaty already completed. Recalling the Soviet refusal to sign the treaty, Rusk admitted in his memoirs that "I don't blame them [the Soviets]; those rules of procedure were outrageous, and I blush to think of my own role in those parliamentary maneuvers."

In 1952, Rusk left government to become president of the Rockefeller Foundation. In 1961, he returned to Washington as secretary of state, serving in this capacity until the coming of the Nixon administration in January 1969. He became much better known to the public during the Vietnam War for his stolid defense of the policies of the Johnson administration. His perception of that conflict was deeply shaped by his experiences during the Korean War. Rusk accepted a professorship at the University of Georgia in 1970, retiring in 1984. Rusk died at his home in Athens, Georgia on December 20, 1994.

Stanley Sandler

Bibliography

Acheson, Dean. *Present at the Creation: My Years in the State Department* (1969).
Cohen, Warren I. *Dean Rusk* (1980).
Rusk, Dean. *As I Saw It* (1990).
Schoenbaum, Thomas J. *Waging Peace and War: Dean Rusk in the Truman, Kennedy and Johnson Years* (1988).

See also STATE DEPARTMENT, U.S.

R

S

Seoul

As the capital of the Republic of Korea (ROK), Seoul was occupied four times during the Korean War (1950–1953). The largest city in Korea, Seoul had served as a capital of the Korean peninsula since ancient times. Chosen by General Yi Song-gye as his capital in 1392 when he moved the Yi Dynasty to the city, Seoul (which means capital) has been the main target of revolutionary groups throughout Korean history.

At World War II diplomatic conferences, plans to divide Korea into two zones, with the north under Soviet control and the south under U.S. occupation, were drawn up to accept the surrender of the Japanese-occupied nation. American forces under Major General John R. Hodge occupied the southern half of Korea in September 1945.

In May 1948, South Koreans elected a National Assembly that established the Republic of Korea with Seoul as its capital. The veteran conservative nationalist Syngman Rhee had returned to Seoul after a forty-year exile in the United States.

A large city resting on the north bank of the Han River and surrounded by mountains, Seoul, the nucleus of communications, industry, and military and political leadership, was the primary target of the North Korean People's Army (NKPA) when it crossed the 38th parallel in the pre-dawn hours of 25 June 1950. Only fifty miles from the border, Seoul was quickly occupied by the NKPA, which encountered only confused resistance from the ROK Army, which was demoralized by its enemies' tanks and air strikes. A catastrophe occurred when the road bridge over the Han River, jammed with retreating troops and civilians, was prematurely blown up by ROK Army engineers, killing hundreds and stranding much of the ROK Army and its equipment on the wrong side. The city fell on 27 June.

North Korean troops confiscated property and purged former ROK officials and "bourgeois" citizens. "People's courts" were held in the streets with the crowd—often children—determining if the accused would live or die. NKPA soldiers pasted posters of Stalin and North Korean premier Kim Il Sung on seemingly any free surface. They impressed many citizens to replace Army losses, and many, half-trained, would lose their lives facing ferocious U.N. firepower at the Pusan perimeter.

Yet even at this disastrous stage of the war, General Douglas MacArthur, U.N. commander in chief, envisioned an amphibious landing at Inchon, the port of Seoul, and a move on to the ROK capital. This was indeed the operation that, beginning on 15 September, projected X Corps, consisting of Marine and Army forces, ashore at Inchon. The X Corps then linked with Eighth Army, which had broken out of the Pusan perimeter, and both moved on Seoul.

Very much conscious of international attention, MacArthur pushed his troops to liberate Seoul by 25 September, three months to the day of the outbreak of war. But U.S. forces encountered stubborn resistance, the city was badly damaged in the house-to-house and barricade-to-barricade fighting, where tanks proved vital in clearing the enemy. Although the city was, prematurely, officially declared secure on 26 September, it was not until 28 September that MacArthur could turn the capital over to President Rhee.

Seoul's two million residents were traumatized by the battle, but many rushed into the streets, greeting their liberators, waving the ROK flag, and sometimes hindering the fighting.

As U.N. troops pushed north to liberate North Korea, ROK authorities conducted purges of those they believed had aided the Communists. Some executions were at least temporarily blocked by U.S. troops. But there had been no one to moderate the Communists' vengeance toward "enemies of the people," as mass graves showed.

Unfortunately, the liberators engaged in some looting, taking books, medals, costumes, and other national treasures, as well as commandering what few pitiful consumer goods survived the occupation and battle.

In the late autumn of 1950, Chinese Communist troops entered the war, and U.N. forces were pushed back, abandoning liberated Pyongyang. Seoul itself was ordered evacuated on 3 January 1951; bridges were once again blasted, and the U.N. Army and the inevitable civilian refugees crossed the slushy Han River on pontoon bridges in much worse weather but in far better order than during the evacuation of June 1950. The Communists occupied Seoul for the second and last time on 4 January. The Chinese, seemingly at the end of their supply lines and under constant U.N. air attack, made little progress south of the Han.

In February, U.N. forces began their methodical move northward in operations Killer and Ripper, and Seoul was liberated again on 15 March without a fight. Both the Communist occupation and the U.N. liberation had been without drama. The second Communist occupation found few enough "reactionaries"; most had presumably been eliminated in the previous summer or had fled, and the Communists seemed to have little heart for defending the ruined city to the death this time.

Now a shattered shell and home to a mere 200,000, Seoul had only symbolic significance. In the words of *Time* magazine, "The fourth fall of Seoul was a sad business, something like the capture of a tomb." The city's citizens suffered from rampant disease, thousands of children were orphaned; food, water, and power were nonexistent. Seoul was threatened with capture yet again, in April 1951, as Communist forces launched another offensive southward. The U.S. Army I Corps defended the city, emplacing artillery in the capitol grounds, beating back this final enemy threat to the city.

Four decades after the end of the Korean War, Seoul is a city still intensely security-conscious; the distance between the ROK capital and the border with an aggressive North Korea is still less than fifty miles. Air traffic is strictly regulated above the city and bridges conceal guard booths and roadblock material. But contemporary Seoul has recovered so well from its war wounds that signs of battle damage have been long obliterated under new construction. South Korea is a charter member of the "Asian Tigers" club, economic powerhouses that challenge Japan itself for economic advantage. In 1988 Seoul, to North Korea's intense disgust, hosted the Summer Olympics. With its skyscrapers and superhighways, and that Third World symbol of economic power, an underground metro; as well as its carefully nurtured folk villages, Seoul remains the heart of the Republic of Korea.

Elizabeth Schafer

Bibliography

Appleman, Roy E. *Disaster in Korea: The Chinese Confront MacArthur*. U.S. Army in the Korean War (1989).

Blair, Clay. *The Forgotten War: America in Korea, 1950–1953* (1988).

Heinl, R., Jr. *Victory at High Tide: The Inchon-Seoul Campaign* (1979).

Riley, John W., Jr., and W. Schramm. *The Reds Take a City* (1951).

Signal Corps, U.S. Army

General Douglas MacArthur's Far East command was caught unprepared when the Korean War began, and his Signal Corps was no exception. There was a serious shortage of trained personnel, in particular cryptographic specialists, and some of the Eighth Army's signal equipment was old or in bad repair. In general, the shortages were a result of post–World War II budget cutting, but the Eighth Army's problems can also be blamed in part on lack of proper maintenance after a training exercise in the period just before the North Korean attack. Poor maintenance was itself symptomatic of lax discipline and inadequate training among the troops occupying Japan in 1950. Shortages of signal equipment would have been far worse, however, had it not been for Operation Roundup, a pre–Korean War campaign to reclaim American equipment abandoned in the Pacific theater after World War II.

The emergency buildup of United States forces in Korea during the summer of 1950 imposed a great strain upon the Signal Corps. The problem was compounded by the paucity of native communications facilities in Korea. The fall of Seoul in the earliest days of the war caused a drastic shrinkage of what few communications assets there were in South Korea. Fortunately, the famous Mukden cable, a pre–World War II, Japanese-built system that ran the length of the peninsula, was still more or less in working order when MacArthur's signalmen began to arrive in Korea. According to one signal officer, the Mukden cable saved the American communications situation in the early phase of the Korean War.

The Mukden cable, however, was for the most part a strategic communications system, and the Signal Corps was also responsible for the Eighth Army's tactical signaling. Some of the problems involved in performing the latter task—apart from poorly maintained equipment—resulted from the hasty retreats that the Eighth Army's various elements carried out from the Han River to Taejon and then to Taegu and the Pusan perimeter. During these withdrawals, Korean refugees, and sometimes even American soldiers, cut American signal wire in order to tie up their bundles. Radio communications personnel were hard pressed because division frontages were greater than in World War II, that is, greater than the frontages for which their radios had been designed. Moreover, the Eighth Army had no subordinate army corps headquarters—another result of budget cutting—forcing the Eighth Army commander, Lieutenant General Walton H. Walker, to manage all of his divisions himself; yet the table of organization and equipment (TO&E) of his field army headquarters did not provide enough signal terminals for such management because the TO&E had been designed on the assumption that a field army would possess two or more corps.

These were some of the problems faced by the U.S. Army's chief signal officer, Major General Spencer B. Akin—who had been MacArthur's signal officer during World War II—and by Major General George I. Back, Far East command's signal officer as of 1950. To meet the emergency, they began to feed Signal Corps units into Korea, ready or not. The 304th Signal Operations Battalion, for example, reached Korea (from Japan) during July 1950 and immediately brought about an improvement in the signal position. Then the Department of the Army ordered the creation of two army corps headquarters in the late summer of 1950 in order to assist Walker's headquarters; yet there was only one signal battalion in the entire U.S. Army available for service with a corps headquarters. Therefore, a scratch team was assigned to I Corps, and

the 101st Signal Battalion was activated in August for service with IX Corps, although it was only at cadre strength. X Corps, MacArthur's reserve, received the 4th Signal Battalion at 60 percent strength.

Expedients could be and were found to fill the gap during the emergency. In July 1950, for example, personnel from the 24th Division's Signal Company, a tactical organization, were detached to perform an essentially strategic function, maintaining the Mukden cable. In August and September, the Eighth Army's acting signal officer, a full colonel, physically helped to install wire communications because of the shortage of qualified enlisted men. Radios were made to achieve miracles of range by "bouncing" radio waves off mountainsides and valley walls. In a grimmer kind of expedient, signal personnel found themselves fighting as infantry as a result of guerrilla attacks on signal installations and the fluid nature, at the time, of the Korean battlefield. Signalmen were more often in combat during the Korean War than during World War II; the 4th Signal Battalion, for example, helped to fight off Communist infiltrators during the Chinese offensive of November 1950.

Complaints about inadequate communications became fewer in number after the first month or two of the war. Even after MacArthur's victory at Inchon and the Eighth Army's subsequent race northward, the Signal Corps was able to cope—although sometimes just barely—with the fast-moving situation and the expanding territory to be covered. The Chinese intervention then forced a new United Nations retreat and an eventual stalemate, but never again would the signal situation be as desperate as it had been in July and August of 1950. Field wire and VHF relay and terminal equipment were still listed as critically short even as of mid-1951, but that shortage was probably to be attributed more to the desire of Americans for lavish logistical support than to any truly desperate need. At any rate, these signal "shortages" did not cause any serious deficiencies in the Eighth Army's overall performance in 1951, or thereafter.

Karl M. Larew

Bibliography

Appleman, Roy E. *South to the Naktong, North to the Yalu* (Office of the Chief of Military History, Washington: 1961).

Gugeler, R.A. *Combat Actions in Korea* (1954).

Marshall, Max L. *The Story of the U.S. Army Signal Corps* (1965).

Schnabel, James F. *United States Army in the Korean War: Policy and Direction: The First Year* (Office of the Chief of Military History, Washington: 1972).

Westover, J.G. *Combat Support in Korea* (1965).

See also COMMUNICATIONS

Smith, Oliver P. (1893–1977)

Born in Menard, Texas, on 26 October 1893 and raised in California, Oliver Prince Smith graduated from the University of California at Berkeley in 1916. Shortly after the United States entered World War I in April 1917, he was commissioned as a second lieutenant in the United States Marine Corps reserve. The next year, while stationed on Guam, he transferred to the regular Marine Corps. Between the world wars, Smith held a variety of troop and staff assignments, was attached for four years to the *Garde d'Haiti* (a combined Army and police force in Haiti), completed the field officers' course at the Army Infantry School, took the full two-year course at the *École Supérieure* in Paris, France, and taught amphibious operations at the Marine schools at Quantico, Virginia. Tall and slim, soft-spoken, unfailingly courteous, and nicknamed "the professor," Smith gained a reputation as an intellectual during these years and was recognized as an expert on amphibious warfare.

After America's entry into World War II, Smith served for almost two years as executive officer of the division of plans and policies at Marine Corps headquarters. In March 1944, he assumed command of the 5th Marine Regiment and took part in operations on New Britain in the South Pacific. Promoted to the rank of brigadier general soon afterward, Smith was named assistant commander of the 1st Marine Division; and in September 1944, he participated in the Peleliu campaign, commanding the operations on the beach during the first day of the landing. Later that year, Smith was appointed Marine deputy chief of staff to United States Army Lieutenant General Simon B. Bucker, commander of the American Tenth Army, a post Smith held throughout the Okinawa campaign. Following the war, Smith commanded the schools at Quantico, was assistant commander of the Marine Corps and chief of staff, and was a member of Marine Corps boards that examined the influence of atomic weapons on the future of amphibious warfare and the steps the Marines should take to ensure their leadership in amphibious warfare.

When President Harry S. Truman committed American forces to the defense of the Republic of Korea (ROK) in the summer of 1950, Smith, now commanding the 1st Marine Division with the rank of major general, was given the job of carrying out an amphibious landing deep behind the North Korean lines at Inchon, South Korea. The operation entailed a complicated assault in a narrow harbor with extremely high tides, and Smith initially doubted its feasibility. Nevertheless, after working out the details with naval commanders, he successfully landed his division at Inchon on 15 September 1950, catching the North Koreans completely by surprise. From Inchon the Marines pushed inland to Seoul, the capital of South Korea; and after heavy fighting, secured the city by the end of the month. These successes were marred, however, by Smith's strained relations with his immediate superior, U.S. Army Major General Edward M. Almond, commander of the X Corps. A forceful, energetic individual, Almond treated Smith in a rude, high-handed manner and complained that Smith, a cautious commander who favored careful tactical maneuvers, was too sluggish in advancing on Seoul. Smith, meanwhile, believed that Almond was reckless and too concerned with personal and headline-grabbing triumphs.

In October 1950, Smith's division landed on the east coast of North Korea and headed north toward the Chosin Reservoir with the ultimate goal of driving to the Yalu River to complete the United Nations conquest of North Korea. Again Smith and Almond were at odds. Pursuant to the instructions of U.N. commander General Douglas MacArthur, Almond advocated a rapid advance to the Yalu, while Smith thought this movement would lead to disaster. In his opinion it would leave his men widely dispersed far inland in the mountains in the dead of winter, without adequate flank protection, and dependent upon a single, winding, narrow road for supplies. Having no confidence in his mission, Smith moved slowly north from Hungnam, a port city along the coast, through Koto-ri to Hagaru-ri and Yudam-ni in the vicinity of the Changjin (Chosin) Reservoir, insisting that at every stage reserves of ammunition and supplies be stockpiled, that the road from Hungnam be improved, and that an airstrip be built near the reservoir to ferry in supplies and take out casualties. These precautions may well have saved his command in the weeks of retreat to follow.

On 27 November 1950, the Chinese Communists launched a massive counterattack against the X Corps and cut the road stretching eighty miles back to Hungnam in several places, trapping the Marines. After conferring with Almond, Smith decided to withdraw his division to Hungnam. Almond told Smith to leave his heavy equipment and artillery. But Smith, never doubting the ability of the Marines to fight their way out of the Chinese entrapment, was determined to conduct "an orderly and honorable withdrawal" and bring out his equipment, wounded, and even as many of his dead as possible. Regrouping his forward units and attached Army units at Hagaru-ri, he withdrew from the Changjin area, all the time making sure that he controlled the hills overlooking the road. Opposed by no less than eight Chinese divisions, fighting through numerous enemy roadblocks as they made their way south, and forced to endure subzero temperatures, the Marines suffered thousands of battle casualties and cases of frostbite. Yet Smith's dogged leadership and crucial air support enabled them to maintain their tactical integrity and inflict 25,000 casualties on the Chinese. Asked by a journalist on 6 December if the Marines were retreating, Smith, in a widely circulated quotation that earned him great acclaim at home, defiantly replied: "We are not retreating, we are just advancing in a different direction." By 11 December, after thirteen harrowing days, Smith's force finally arrived at Hungnam, where his division was evacuated by sea. In a brilliant feat of military management, Smith had saved his division and given American morale a desperately needed boost at a critical time in the Korean War.

Following a period of recuperation, Smith's 1st Marine Division was attached to the IX Corps and took part in the American Eighth Army's counteroffensive in South Korea in February 1951. When the corps commander suddenly died, Smith temporarily commanded the corps until an Army general arrived to take his place, one of the few times that a Marine commanded a combined Army-Marine division or corps. On 24 April 1951, Smith relinquished command of the 1st Marine Division and returned to the United States to command Camp Pendleton, California. In 1953, he was promoted to lieutenant general and given command of the fleet Marine force, Atlantic. Two years later he retired with the rank of general. Smith died in Los Altos, California, on 25 December 1977.

John Kennedy Ohl

Bibliography
Appleman, Roy E. *Escaping the Trap: The U.S. Army X Corps in Northeast Korea, 1950* (Texas A & M University Press, College Station: 1990).
Blair, Clay. *The Forgotten War: America in Korea, 1950–1953* (Times Books, New York: 1987).
Goulden, Joseph C. *Korea: The Untold Story of the War* (McGraw-Hill, New York: 1981).
Montross, Lynn, and Nicholas A. Canzona. *The Inchon-Seoul Operation* (Historical Branch, U.S. Marine Corps, Washington: 1954).
———. *The Chosin Campaign* (Historical Branch, U.S. Marine Corps, Washington: 1957).
Montross, Lynn, Hubbard D. Kuokka, and Norman W. Hicks. *The East-Central Front* (Historical Branch, U.S. Marine Corps, Washington: 1962).

See also MARINES, U.S.

Smith, Task Force
See TASK FORCE SMITH

South African Forces
Despite their fervent anticommunism, the reluctance of South Africa's Boer population to send military forces outside the African continent forestalled the Union of South Africa from contributing ground forces to the U.N. coalition in Korea. Instead, the nation dispatched a fighter squadron composed of veterans of World War II flying piston-engine P-51 Mustangs, also of World War II vintage. The pilots had fought notably in Italy during that conflict. All South African armed forces for World War II and Korea were volunteers, as the government appreciated the dissention that conscription would ignite between Boer and Briton.

A charter member of the United Nations, South Africa had become controversial because of its racial policies. But its decision, on 4 August 1950 to dispatch a fighter squadron to aid U.N. forces then embattled along the Pusan perimeter, was well-received in the West. The

South African Nationalist government explained that any additional contribution would prove too much of a strain on the nation's resources.

The motives for South Africa's small but symbolic contribution were varied. Although traditionally suspicious of foreign alliances and the deployment of its forces outside southern Africa, the Nationalists wished to develop ties with western nations in order to acquire security from the Communist threat. Fearful of communism's apparently growing international strength, South Africa sought membership in the Western coalition. It had, in fact, already participated in the Berlin Airlift just two years previous. The Nationalists believed that South Africa would be rewarded for its assistance in the war, and that it would be in a better position to regain the Simonstown naval base, then controlled by the Royal Navy.

Upon its arrival, South African Air Force No. 2 Squadron initially joined U.N. air assets at the K-9 Airfield outside Pusan. Too small to be independent, the SAAF squadron was attached to the 5th U.S. Air Force. As fighter pilots, the South Africans escorted USAF aircraft and strafed transportation routes, railroads and bridges, and napalmed crucial targets. Because their Mustangs were slower than American models, SAAF pilots concentrated on strafing missions, blowing klaxon horns as they dived into the attack. The squadron helped maintain U.N. air superiority, but its achievements were often lost to the records due to its operating within the USAF.

In April 1951, the SAAF squadron joined Australian and Canadian pilots because its base at Masan Airfield was undergoing repairs after heavy use. Viewing themselves modestly as the second tier of Commonwealth defenses, the South Africans permitted British officers to direct their bombing and to select targets. Although the U.S. Far East Air Force wanted to establish a Commonwealth wing, which would, of course, have included SAAF No. 2 Squadron, South Africa refused and instead joined the Americans at liberated Pyongyang East, North Korea, in late November.

Americans considered the South African pilots as professional and likeable. One Marine pilot characterized them as "half of them square-headed blond Dutchmen with heavy accents and funny first names, the rest proper English types named Nigel or Geoff. Good soldiers." (Needless to say, all SAAF pilots and ground crew were white.)

During 1952–1953 the South Africans' elderly Mustangs were replaced with F-86 Sabres. From July to August 1952, No. 2 Squadron unleashed their ordnance during Operation Pressure Pump, a twenty-four-hour blitz of Pyongyang. By October 1953, South Africa had withdrawn her squadron from Korea. Of the 826 SAAF pilots operating from No. 2 Squadron in the Korean War, thirty-four had died. Nine South African POWs were repatriated. South Africa withdrew its force before the unified withdrawal of the remaining Commonwealth forces; already the Commonwealth ties were fraying for South Africa. Indeed, the Nationalist government had removed itself from wartime conferences, refusing to sign the warning statement to China in March 1952 or the resolutions stressing the freedom of repatriation choice, as well as the postwar conferences at Geneva in 1954.

Elizabeth Schafer

Bibliography

Barber, James, and John Barratt. *South Africa's Foreign Policy: The Search for Status and Security 1945–1988* (1990).

McGregor, P.M.J. "History of No. 2 Squadron, SAAF, in the Korean War," *Military History Journal* (June 1978).

Moore, D.M. "SAAF in Korea," *Mioitaria* (1980).

Tucker, E.N., and P.M.J. McGregor. *Per Noctem Per Diem: The Story of 24 Squadron, South African Air Force* (1961).

South Korea

See REPUBLIC OF (SOUTH) KOREA

Soviet Union: Responsibility for the Korean War

Although the behavior of the Soviet Union during the Korean War is fairly clear, its possible complicity in starting the conflict remains in dispute.

Soviet–American tensions over Korea began with the division of the peninsula on August 16, 1945. To the United States, the 38th parallel was only a temporary military boundary designed to expedite the surrender of Japanese troops. To the Soviet Union, however, it immediately became a political border. The Soviets wanted to communize Korea for several reasons: to safeguard their recent gains in Manchuria, to check an American presence in Japan and the Korean peninsula, and to delimit the Communist revolution in China. In order to realize these objectives, the Soviet Union had to ensure the political survival of Kim Il Sung, a professional revolutionary trained by Moscow. From 1945–50, it did so through deft diplomacy.

The Soviets also promoted North Korean military interests. Beginning in 1947, they repeatedly called for the immediate and simultaneous withdrawal of Soviet and American forces from the Korean peninsula. Such a step would not only prevent the United States from organizing and training an effective South Korean Army, it would leave the Republic of Korea (ROK) vulnerable to invasion. When the Americans procrastinated over withdrawal, the Russians blandly announced in December 1948 that they had unilaterally recalled their forces. The unverified Soviet examples, along with military requirements in Europe, did pressure the U.S. to withdraw its forces seven months later, with no promise of military assistance to fill the void. From this point on, lightly armed South Korea was at a distinct military disadvantage. The Soviets sought to sustain this disadvantage by avoiding a formal military treaty with Kim Il Sung. Such a treaty would have aroused Western suspicions and inspired South Korea to seek a similar pact with the United States. As a result, it is possible that the North Koreans entered into a mutual defense treaty with China instead. (Despite *glasnost* and the opening of some files, the existence of such a treaty and its relationship to the Soviet Union remains a mystery.)

Few scholars deny that the Soviets took the above steps. What they do debate is the Soviet Union's immediate complicity in the Korean War. To the Cold Warriors who opposed monolithic communism and its quest for world domination, it was Joseph Stalin who was responsible for the conflict. The evidence was circumstantial but seemingly damning. In 1949, for example, Kim Il Sung received $40 million in credits to buy Soviet arms. (That these arms included outdated 122mm artillery pieces and aging T-34 tanks went unstated.) Also, Mao Tse-Tung's December 1949–January 1950 visit to Moscow seemed suspicious. Did the lengthy visit indicate Sino-Soviet cooperation was at an impasse, or was it necessary to coordinate a well-supported attack by Kim Il Sung against the Republic of Korea? The latter interpretation dominated Western think-

ing until Nikita Khrushchev wrote in his memoirs that Kim Il Sung was responsible for the Korean War.

After Khrushchev's disclosure, and because of recent revisionist critiques of the Cold War, the historiography of the Korean War began to change. The focus shifted from the containment of monolithic communism to the role of domestic Korean politics. Seen from a local perspective, the Korean War was an example of internecine strife. It was part of a civil war that had already claimed 100,000 lives prior to 1950, and it was a conflict Kim Il Sung and Syngman Rhee, the autocratic president of the ROK, had expected and probably even welcomed. Under these circumstances, the revisionists argued, only limited cooperation existed between Kim Il Sung and Joseph Stalin. The North Korean leader not only agitated for national unity, he also sought political independence from the Soviet Union and China. Stalin, in contrast, had to be circumspect. He did not want to further militarize America's containment policy nor provide an excuse for an arms race; he feared the presence of foreign troops near Vladivostok; and he hoped to preserve, although in vain, Red China's limited influence in Asia. As a result, the revisionists claim, Stalin acquiesced unenthusiastically to Kim Il Sung's aggression, or was not consulted at all.

Recently released Soviet documents, however, seem to undercut the above interpretation. They confirm that Kim Il Sung was not Stalin's puppet, but they do suggest that the Soviet Union actively promoted rather than merely supported North Korean aggression. From the beginning Russian advisors and pilots controlled particular military operations and participated in combat, while Soviet leaders provided a steady stream of mixed-quality arms. And the muted Russian response to early North Korean aggression did not necessarily reflect confusion or noncommittal concern, but hinted at a probing strategy designed to bloody the United States at limited cost. If the cost grew prohibitive, the Soviets could then withdraw their support without embarrassment or accountability. This interpretation of events makes the Soviet Union more culpable than revisionists allow, but it does not make it solely accountable for a local dispute.

In 1990, for example, Li San-cho, North Korea's ambassador to the Soviet Union in the 1950s, conceded that Premier Stalin had indeed approved Kim Il Sung's invasion plans and had provided the necessary military sup-

S

port. It is a matter of record that Sir Girja Bajpai, secretary-general of the Indian Foreign Office, advised the British high commissioner to India that China's leaders were under enormous pressure from Stalin to take military action in Korea. Sir Girja added that the Chinese were resisting such pressure, fearing that a resulting war with the United States would prove devastating. And it should be noted that a small but high-level Soviet military mission arrived in Pyongyang in December of 1948, consisting of five generals and two colonels; four of the generals were armor specialists. The Korean People's Army was indeed to be built around an armor core for its southward invasion. Tank specialists from Mongolia were required to have five years' armor experience, a secondary education, fluency in Russian, and, of course, political reliability. About ten Soviet advisors were attached to each North Korean division. In addition, the Soviets built two refineries for the distillation of armor fuel. Finally, the bulk of North Korean military equipment captured in the first year of the war was of 1948–1949 vintage.

However, although Soviet responsibility for actually starting the Korean War remains uncertain, there is a consensus that after the failed Chinese offensive of April 1951, the Soviet Union sought to return to the status quo ante. Stalin had hoped to reap the benefits of a short, victorious war, but he now faced a prolonged conflict whose outcome was uncertain, that put foreign troops on his doorstep, encouraged the growth of "American militarism," and legitimized China as the major regional power. As a result of these considerations, and beginning with a 23 June 1951 radio address by Stalin's delegate to the U.N., Jakob Malik, the Soviet Union signaled its interest in a diplomatic settlement. But the U.N. and Communist sides proved pertinacious bargainers through the following two years of truce negotiations. It took the death of Stalin, and possibly an American threat of nuclear war, to break the interminable deadlock. With the death of the Soviet leader, the USSR turned its interests inward; North Korea and China could no longer rely on generous materiel and diplomatic aid from the Soviet Union.

Peter R. Faber

Bibliography

Cumings, Bruce, ed. *Child of Conflict: The Korean-American Relationship, 1943–1953* (1983).

Goncharov, S., J. W. Lewis, Xue Litai, *Uncertain Partners: Stalin, Mao and the Korean War.* (1993).

Heller, Francis, ed. *The Korean War: A 25-Year Perspective* (1977).

Kim Chum-kon, *The Korean War, 1950–53* (1980).

Lowe, Peter. *The Origins of the Korean War* (1986).

Rees, David. *Korea: The Limited War* (1964).

Weathersby, K. "The Soviet Role in the Early Phase of the Korean War: New Documentary Evidence," *The Journal of American-East Asian Relations* (Winter 1993).

———, translator and commentator. "New Findings on the Korean War." *International History Project Bulletin* (Fall 1993).

State Department, U.S.

The United States State Department was as unprepared for the North Korean attack on South Korea in June 1950 as any other part of the U.S. government. The department was concerned about the survival of the Republic of Korea (ROK), but feared subversion, not invasion. State did not have a favorable opinion of President Syngman Rhee and his government, and economic aid for Korea had trouble passing Congress.

The most famous expression of the State Department's attitude toward Korea was Secretary of State Dean Acheson's speech in January 1950 which left Korea outside the U.S. defensive perimeter in the Pacific. Often overlooked was his comment in that speech that the ROK could depend on the support of the United Nations (U.N.).

The major concern of the State Department's Far Eastern section in early 1950 was the new Communist government in China. Acheson planned to allow the Communists to overrun Taiwan as they had Hainan early in 1950 and then attempt to woo China away from its Russian connection. The phrase "Mao Tze Tito" (linking Mao Tse-Tung with Yugoslavia's Marshal Tito) expressed Acheson's hopes.

In the early discussions between the State Department and members of the Defense Department gathered in emergency sessions to discuss the invasion, all agreed on several general ideas that governed U.S. actions in Korea. First, there would be no repetition of the appeasement they all believed contributed to early Axis successes in World War II; second, that the U.N. must be called in lest it go the way of the League of Nations, which showed itself powerless in the face of aggression; and finally that the Soviet Union was behind the attack.

Concern about the intentions of the Soviet Union remained paramount in State Department thinking throughout the Korean War. While the department did not believe Korea was the beginning of World War III, it considered a larger war a distinct possibility, particularly if the U.S. overcommitted its existing military resources in Korea. It also feared that if the attack were not resisted Stalin would be encouraged to repeat the technique elsewhere. State felt that U.S. actions in Korea would show Stalin that direct military attack did not work and reassure America's friends in the rest of the world that the U.S. would come to their aid if the Communists attacked.

The State Department was concerned about the possible reactions of both friends and enemies when the U.S. intervened militarily in the fighting in Korea. The Soviet reply to inquiries by the department led State's officials to believe that the Soviets would not respond hastily or violently to U.S. military actions. On the other hand, most of America's friends in the world offered support, sometimes military. State considered these offers of combat support of great importance and worked hard to get as many members of the U.N. as possible to send units to Korea.

It is almost always easier to start a war than to stop one and the State Department began, early on, to consider how to bring the fighting to an end. Most members of the department believed that simply returning to the prewar boundary (the 38th parallel) and stopping was not a satisfactory way to conclude the fighting. For one thing, the enemy might not stop firing on U.N. troops. Another consideration was that without a formal agreement to end the war the U.N. might need to keep significant forces in place in case fighting continued around the 38th parallel or broke out again after the North Koreans had a chance to reorganize. State was also concerned about how to properly punish aggression, and about the recovery of U.N. troops captured by North Korea.

When General Douglas MacArthur landed at Inchon in September 1950, the question of bringing the war to a satisfactory conclusion became urgent. An immediate answer was required regarding the question of crossing the 38th parallel. Could or should the U.S. attempt to prevent the South Koreans from crossing? Should U.S. forces cross, and if so for what object? Almost for the first time, State had difficulty in framing a recommendation. There were numerous problems concerning the crossing and differing opinions among the responsible Department officials who were also under pressure from the Defense Department to authorize MacArthur to move north. Some advisors wanted to stop at the 38th and begin negotiations. However, as the U.S. did not recognize the government of North Korea—insisting with the U.N. that the U.N.-sponsored ROK government in the South was the only legitimate government—whom did the U.N. talk to and how did one open the discussions? To negotiate with the North Korean regime was to afford them de facto recognition. In the end, in the euphoria of military success, State decided not to seek discussions but to sponsor a U.N. resolution calling (in effect) for the unification of Korea under the ROK government. While State supported crossing the 38th, it showed increasing concern about the reactions of China and the Soviet Union. The Chinese intervention late in 1950 rendered the question temporarily mute.

Moot General Matthew B. Ridgway restored the situation in the spring of 1951 by retaking Seoul, State remained committed to getting out of Korea. The department was furious when MacArthur upstaged their efforts to open negotiations. But with China in the war the State Department dominated Korean policy making, and State's policy was to negotiate a settlement based on the 38th parallel and to oppose any actions that might hinder bargaining. In line with this position, State insisted that the military be restrained and not allowed to do anything (like advancing beyond the 38th) that might hinder State's efforts to settle on the basis of the prewar situation.

Various diplomatic initiatives by State paid off in June 1951 when the Soviet representative to the U.N. indicated that the Communists might be receptive to a U.S./U.N. cease-fire proposal. Still troubled by the lack of direct diplomatic links to the Communist countries concerned, the department favored a strictly military cease-fire for bringing the fighting to an end. Under instructions from the State Department, General Ridgway proposed a meeting with the opposing commanders, and they accepted.

State kept tight control of the discussions that began at Kaesong in early July 1951. It accepted a military demand for a more defensible frontier than the 38th, one along the current line of contact between the contending armies. The two years of talks that followed were marked by repeated disagreements between State and the military over the proper positions to be taken in the negotiations and about what military actions by the U.S./U.N. might encourage the Communists to stop the fighting.

After bitter bargaining sessions (and renewed U.S. military pressure) the two sides agreed that the existing battle line would divide the Korean peninsula at the conclusion of the fighting. The contestants then spent a great deal of time and rhetoric arguing points that seem faintly ridiculous after the passage of forty years. These disagreements included such items as repairs to airfields in North Korea and the introduction of fresh personnel and equipment to Korea. The major disagreement was over the disposition of POWs.

The State Department also had to deal with the dissatisfaction of America's ally, the ROK. Syngman Rhee was understandably upset by State's determination to end the war without the reunification of Korea. The department was so deeply attached to its position that it considered removing Rhee.

Perhaps the most lasting memorial to State's efforts in Korea is the still remaining division of Korea roughly along the 38th parallel, an end so determinedly sought by the department after China's entry into the war.

Jack Gifford

Bibliography

Acheson, Dean. *The Korean War* (1971).
Foot, Rosemary. *The Wrong War: American Policy and the Dimensions of the Korean Conflict 1950–1953* (1985).
Paioe, Glenn. *The Korean Decision* (1968).
Schnable, James F. *Policy and Direction: The First Year* (Office of the Chief of Military History, United States Army, Washington: 1972).

See also ACHESON, DEAN; DULLES, JOHN FOSTER; MUCCIO, JOHN J.; RUSK, DEAN

Stone, I.F. (1907–1989)

Gadfly, journalist, columnist, author, critic of President Harry S. Truman and America's involvement in the Korean War, Isadore Feinstein "Izzy" Stone wrote for numerous news journals throughout his life. He began his career with the *Philadelphia Inquirer* in 1927. He worked as an editor for the liberal magazine *The Nation* between 1938 and 1946, serving as the magazine's general editor between 1940 and 1946. He was a reporter and columnist for the liberal daily *PM* and its successor papers through much of the 1940s; he was also a frequent contributor to *The New York Review of Books* and other publications. From 1953 to 1971, he wrote and published *I.F. Stone's Weekly* (later *I.F. Stone's Bi-Weekly*), which set high journalistic standards in America.

Stone often supported political and social causes long before they became popular with mainstream American liberals. He was an outspoken opponent of America's early Cold War policies, of the antisubversive actions taken by the Truman administration in the late 1940s, and was an early supporter of civil rights for black Americans. He was also an early and outspoken critic of America's involvement in the Vietnam War, and in his later life Stone was revered by antiwar liberals who saw his early opposition to the war as a courageous and insightful stance. However, many of his opinions caused him to be often cast as a pariah by journalists and more moderate liberals.

Stone wrote a number of books, including *Business as Usual: The First Year of Defense* (1941), which was a scathing indictment of America's military unpreparedness prior to World War II. In 1946, he wrote *Underground to Palestine*, which recounted his own involvement in the Jewish struggle to obtain a homeland. In his *The Hidden Story of the Korean War*, published in 1952, Stone improbably argued that the Korean War began when South Korea initiated hostilities by attacking North Korea in hopes of receiving Western military assistance to reconquer all of Korea. This conspiracy theory has not been borne out by history, but the work remains an important study of America's involvement in the Korean War. In 1988, Stone published his last book, the bestseller, *The Trial of Socrates*.

Gary A. Donaldson

Bibliography

Bain, George. "The World According to I.F. Stone," *MacClean's,* 35 (July 24, 1989).
"I.F. Stone, 1907–1989," *The Nation*, 37 (July 10, 1989).
Stone, I.F. *A Time of Torment* (1967).
———. *The Haunted Fifties* (1963).
———. *The Hidden Story of the Korean War* (1952).

T

Taegu

Although never captured by the Communists, Taegu was probably the most embattled city of the Korean War. A critical rail and road center in southeastern South Korea, the city of Taegu in the months immediately after the North Korean invasion of South Korea in June 1950 was the temporary seat of the Republic of Korea (ROK) government and the location of the headquarters of the South Korean Army and the American Eighth Army. Situated about sixty miles north of Pusan, the key port for supplying United Nations (U.N.) forces in Korea, it normally had a population of 300,000, but by August 1950 it had been swollen by no less than 400,000 refugees. During the last weeks of July, the North Koreans pushed down the road from Taejon toward Taegu, and by early August they were poised to seize the city. Five North Korean divisions, the 1st, 3rd, 10th, 13th, and 15th, with a total of 35,000 men, were spread fanwise across a forty-mile arc west and north of Taegu. Facing them were the American 1st Cavalry Division and the ROK 1st and 6th Divisions, also totaling 35,000 men. If the North Koreans seized Taegu, the U.N. forces would lose a major anchor around which a perimeter defense for Pusan might be maintained.

The North Koreans began their assault against Taegu on August 4, 1950. Along the Naktong River and in the surrounding hills west of Taegu, the 1st Cavalry Division battled with the North Korean 3rd and 10th Divisions in more than a week of fierce fighting. Despite steady American air and artillery bombardment, the North Koreans crossed the Naktong and overran some of the 1st Cavalry Division's forward posts. But eventually the North Koreans were repulsed after heavy casualties on both sides. North of Taegu the enemy enjoyed greater success. Holding a two-to-one numerical advantage over the South Koreans opposing them, the North Korean 1st, 13th, and 15th Divisions broke through the South Korean defenses, and by August 15 they were within fifteen miles of the city. Simultaneously, a breakthrough along the east coast enabled the North Koreans to capture Pohang and threaten Taegu from the "back door."

As the North Koreans approached, panic spread through Taegu, especially after North Korean shells fell on the city three times between August 18 and August 20. President Syngman Rhee of South Korea moved his government to Pusan, and fear-stricken refugees clogged the roads to the south, forcing police and troops to stop their flight so that military convoys could bring supplies up from Pusan. To help save the city, the United States Far East Air Forces carried out a "carpet-bombing" operation on August 16 against supposed North Korean concentrations in an area along the west side of the Naktong River opposite the ROK 1st Division, using no less than ninety-eight B-29 bombers. The bombing achieved little, however, for the North Korean "concentrations" had already been dissipated by moves of various divisions up and down the front. More important, Lieutenant General Walton H. Walker, commander of the Eighth Army, rushed the American 27th and 23rd Infantry Regiments to backstop the ROK 1st Division as well as a ROK task force to reinforce the beleaguered ROKs in the vicinity of Pohang. Beginning on the night of August 18 the 27th Infantry battled the North Korean 13th Division in the area of the "Bowling Alley," a narrow valley north of Taegu with high mountains on each side and a road running straight north–south for several miles. Night after night the North Koreans sent armored vehicles and troops down the Bowling Alley. But the 27th Infantry held firm; and by August 27, American firepower had completely stopped the North Koreans, about the first good news for the U.N. to come out of Korea. At the same time, the 23rd Infantry fought the North Korean 1st Division to a standstill when the enemy attempted a flanking maneuver to the east.

At the end of August, Walker withdrew the 27th and 23rd Regiments from the Taegu front so that they could be used elsewhere along the Pusan perimeter and had the 1st Cavalry Division, beefed up by additional battalions, extend its front further north and east. On September 2 the North Korean 1st, 3rd, and 13th Divisions, totalling 22,000 men, renewed the assault on Taegu. They hit hard north of Taegu, and the 1st Cavalry Division "reeled in disarray." Several days later the division withdrew to defensive positions in an arc about eight miles above Taegu, where the battle seesawed for days. Taegu was again on the verge of capture by the North Koreans, and Walker decided to transfer his own main headquarters and the ROK headquarters to Pusan. The decisive struggle took place on Hill 314, a 1,000-foot peak just seven miles north of Taegu. The North Koreans captured it on September 11, and from there they could ob-serve all 1st Cavalry Division movements and mortar Taegu. The next day the Americans recovered the hill at a frightful cost, finally relieving the North Korean pressure north of Taegu. During the following days the Americans and ROK troops pushed back the three North Korean divisions, and by September 15 the North Koreans were beginning to withdraw.

The victory in the Taegu sector coincided with other Eighth Army victories along the Pusan perimeter, and on September 15 the Korean War entered a new phase when the American X Corps struck deep behind the North Korean lines at the port of Inchon on the west coast of South Korea. On September 16 the Eighth Army went on the offensive. In the Taegu sector the American 24th and 1st Cavalry Divisions began crossing the Naktong River on September 20 and attacked northward toward Taejon. Six days later the 1st Cavalry Division linked up with X Corps, and by the end of September 1950, South Korea was liberated.

John Kennedy Ohl

Bibliography

Alexander, Bevin. *Korea: The First War We Lost* (1986).

Appleman, Roy E. *South to the Naktong, North to the Yalu* (Office of the Chief of Military History, Washington: 1961).

Blair, Clay. *The Forgotten War: America in Korea, 1950–1953* (1987).

Fehrenbach, T.R. *This Kind of War* (1963).

Hoyt, Edwin P. *The Pusan Perimeter* (1988).

Taejon

Taejon was the scene of the worst American defeat of the Korean War. Following the North Korean invasion of South Korea on June 25, 1950, the U.S. 24th Infantry Division was rushed from Japan to Korea in a desperate effort to delay the North Korean advance south from Seoul. Hastily brought up to wartime strength, ill-trained, mentally and physically unprepared for combat, and lacking adequate firepower, the division's three infantry regiments were shattered by the North Korean 3rd and 4th Divisions in several engagements between Seoul and Taejon, a city of 130,000 people and an important road center in southwestern Korea, approximately 100 miles south of Seoul.

After the North Koreans breached the Kum River line on July 16, Major General William F. Dean, commander of the 24th Division, determined that Taejon could not be held, and in the morning of July 18, he ordered that the city be completely evacuated the next day. However, at noon on July 18 Lieutenant General Walton H. Walker, commander of the American Eighth Army, visited Dean in Taejon and asked him to hold the city two more days so that the 1st Cavalry Division, presently arriving from Japan, could deploy south and east of Taejon to help stabilize the battlefield. Dean agreed, although his surviving men were in his words "weakened, dispirited, and exhausted" and desperately in need of rest and reorganization. Possibly he believed that the new 3.5-inch bazookas that were just reaching Korea would enable his men at last to neutralize the terrifying T-34 tanks that had spearheaded the North Korean advance. He may also have believed that the 34th Infantry Regiment, which had yet to make a strong fight because of a lack of aggressive leadership and unit cohesiveness, would perform better under the new commander he had just installed.

Since neither the 19th nor the 21st Infantry Regiments of the 24th Division could muster more than a battalion of troops, the primary defense of Taejon fell on the 34th Infantry, the bulk of which Dean placed in the northwestern and western outskirts of Taejon. Lighter units were placed in the southwestern and southern outskirts. Dean placed the 21st Infantry east of the city along the Taejon–Taegu road to keep open the exit through which his men would withdraw and kept the 19th Infantry in reserve. The North Koreans, as Dean anticipated, planned to launch their main attack down the Seoul–Pusan highway from the northwest. But contrary to his expectations, they also planned to attack from the west with a sophisticated encircling movement from the southwest, where American defenses were the weakest.

The battle for Taejon began early on July 19 with air strikes by both sides (the last time the already decimated North Korean Air Force would make any serious moves), followed by the North Korean assault. The North Korean 3rd Division hit the northwestern sector hard with artillery and tanks, while the North Korean 4th Division attacked from the west. To bolster the beleaguered defenders, Dean sent the 19th Infantry into the line as a backup for the 34th Infantry and even went to the front himself to direct tank fire. Plagued by poor communications and exposed flanks, the Americans were under "severe and relentless pressure" all day, and by nightfall they had contracted some of their positions back toward Taejon and were threatened by a massive envelopment from the southwest and the south.

In the predawn hours of July 20 the North Koreans renewed their assault, and before long they cracked the main defensive line. The 34th Infantry and the accompanying units from the 19th Infantry virtually disintegrated as fighting bodies and retreated to the south, eliminating the last organized resistance before Taejon. By daybreak, small groups of North Korean troops and tanks were making their way into Taejon itself. During the ensuing confused fighting in the center of the city, American bazooka teams (including Dean in one instance) and artillery destroyed ten North Korean tanks. However, the fate of the city was already decided, as other North Korean forces were passing to the American rear in an attempt to cut off the 24th Division's line of retreat. Concluding early in the afternoon of July 20 that he had given Walker his two days, Dean decided to begin the American retreat from Taejon immediately rather than wait for nightfall as he had originally intended.

During the next hectic hours disaster befell the Americans. Trying to get clear of the burning city, American convoys encountered roadblocks on the roads east and south of Taejon and suffered heavy losses in men and equipment. Other troops endured "hair-raising" experiences as they attempted to escape the North Korean trap by walking east and south through the mountains. Dean, who barely escaped Taejon, was cut off from most of his scattered division when his jeep driver took a wrong turn and headed south on the road to Kumsan. Forced by a North Korean roadblock to abandon their vehicles, Dean and his party took to the hills. Shortly after midnight Dean was injured and separated from his companions, and for thirty-six days he worked his way south before he was finally captured by the North Koreans.

American casualties in the battle for Taejon were frightful. Of the 3,933 men of the 24th Division engaged in the battle, nearly 30 percent (1,150) were dead, wounded, or missing. Of these about fifty were known dead, and an appalling 900 were missing in action (most of these were killed, many of them after they had been captured). Yet Dean had fulfilled his commitment to Walker, and thereafter the Korean War entered a new phase. Other American divisions were taking up positions, south and east of Taejon, and no longer would the 24th Division and the South Korean Army have to stand alone.

John Kennedy Ohl

Bibliography

Appleman, Roy E. *South to the Naktong, North to the Yalu, June–November 1950* (Office of the Chief of Military History, Washington: 1961).

Blair, Clay. *The Forgotten War: America in Korea, 1950–1953* (1987).

Blumenson, M. *Withdrawal from Taejon 20 July 1950.* Far East, United States Army Forces, Eighth United States Army Korea, Military History Section, 4th Historical Detachment. n.d.

Dean, William F., and William L. Worden, *General Dean's Story* (1954).

Task Force Smith

Task Force Smith was the first U.S. Army ground maneuver unit to enter combat in Korea. On June 30, 1950, President Harry S. Truman authorized General Douglas Mac-

Arthur to commit ground forces under his command to Korea, and MacArthur in turn instructed General Walton H. Walker, commander of the Eighth Army, to order the 24th Division there. Early on July 1 the Eighth Army provided for a makeshift infantry battalion of the 24th Division to be flown to Korea in the six C-54 transport aircraft available. The remainder of the division followed by water. The initial force was to make contact with the enemy and fight a delaying action. This was Task Force Smith, "that arrogant display of strength" that MacArthur hoped would fool the North Koreans into thinking a larger force was at hand. Some officers assumed that even this small force would give the North Koreans pause once they realized whom they were fighting.

Task Force Smith was named for Lieutenant Colonel Charles B. Smith, commanding officer, 1st Battalion, 21st Regiment, 24th Infantry Division. It comprised 406 officers and men: half of the battalion headquarters company, two understrength rifle companies (B and C), a communications section, a recoilless rifle platoon and two mortar platoons. In addition to its rifles, the task force had two 75mm recoilless rifles, two 4.2-inch mortars, six 2.36-inch "bazooka" rocket launchers, and four 60mm mortars. Each man was issued 120 rounds of ammunition and two days' C-rations. Most of the men were twenty years old or less; only one-sixth had seen combat.

The men of Task Force Smith left Japan on the morning of July 1. General William Dean, 24th Division commander, ordered Smith to block the main road to Pusan as far north as possible.

The men landed at an airfield near Pusan and moved north to Taejon by train, arriving there on the morning of July 2. Smith ordered his men to rest while he and his staff officers drove north to reconnoiter. About three miles north of Osan, Smith found an ideal blocking position, a line of low rolling hills about 300 feet above the level ground. This position also commanded the main railroad line to the east, and afforded a clear view to Suwon, about eight miles north.

On July 4 the task force was joined at Pyongtaek by part of the 52nd Field Artillery Battalion: half each of headquarters and service batteries, and all of A Battery with six 105mm howitzers, seventy-three vehicles, and 108 men under the command of Lieutenant Colonel Miller O. Perry. In the late afternoon of July 4, Smith, Perry, and some others made a final re-

connaissance of the position that Smith had selected. The combined infantry and artillery moved out of Pyongtaek by truck, arriving at the position about 0300. In cold, rainy weather they dug foxholes. The American position extended about a mile on both sides of the Suwon–Osan road. The troops laid telephone lines to four of the howitzers, placed in a concealed position some 2000 meters to the south. One 105mm howitzer was positioned halfway between the battery and the infantry position in order to enfilade the road and serve as an anti-tank gun. Volunteers from the artillery made up four .50 caliber machine gun and four 2.36-inch bazooka teams and joined the infantry position to the north. The infantry vehicles were located just to the south of their position; the artillerymen had concealed their trucks just north of Osan. The Americans were vulnerable to enemy flanking attacks, lacked the means to stop enemy tanks, and were without reserves.

At dawn on the 5th Smith ordered his artillery, mortars, and machine guns to conduct registration fire. Steady rain precluded air support. Further, because of earlier, disastrous cases of U.N. aircraft hitting friendly ground forces, all air support that day was confined to north of Suwon. Shortly after 0700, movement was detected to the north. Within half an hour, a column of eight North Korean T-34 tanks, part of the 107th Tank Regiment of the 105th Armored Division, approached across the open plain from Suwon. At 0800 the artillery received a request for a fire mission and at 0816 the first American ground fire of the Korean War was opened against the tanks, about 2,000 yards in front of the infantry position. The high explosive (HE) rounds had no effect on the tanks, which had their hatches closed. The battery had only six armor-piercing high explosive antitank HEAT rounds available (one-third of the total on hand when the 52nd was loading at Sasebo, Japan), all of which were given to the single howitzer forward. Antitank mines would have stopped the enemy advance, but there were none in Korea. Smith ordered 75mm recoilless rifle fire withheld until the column of tanks reached the 700-yard range. The recoilless rifle crews scored direct hits, again without apparent effect. The tanks stopped and opened fire with their 85mm main guns and 7.62mm machine guns. Second Lieutenant Ollie Connor fired twenty-two 2.36-inch bazooka rounds at the enemy armor, all from close range, including a number at the more vulnerable rear ends of the T-34s, but there was no apparent damage. The 2.36-inch rounds could not penetrate the armor of the T-34. Smith later said he believed that the rounds had deteriorated with age. The 3.5-inch bazooka round would have been effective, but again, there were none in Korea.

As they approached the lone 105mm gun forward, the two lead tanks were hit and damaged, probably by HEAT rounds. One caught fire and two of its crew members came out of the turret with their hands up; a third came out with a burp gun and fired it against an American machine gun position beside the road, killing an assistant gunner, undoubtedly the first American fatality of the Korean War. The third tank through the pass, however, knocked out the forward 105mm howitzer with its cannon fire. The other tanks swept on south past the artillery battery, which fired HE rounds against them. One tank was disabled and ultimately abandoned.

Additional enemy tanks soon swept past the American position, causing some of the battery crewmen to run from their guns. Officers and NCOs continued to service the guns, and the men returned. One other tank was disabled by a hit in the track. By 1015 the last of thirty-three North Korean tanks had driven through the American position, killing or wounding some twenty Americans by machine gun and shell fire. Most of the vehicles parked immediately behind the infantry position were destroyed. The wire communications link with Battery A had been chewed up by the tanks as they passed. Fortunately there were no accompanying infantrymen; the tankers were unable to locate the artillery battery firing on them and the T-34s rumbled on toward Osan. A lull of about an hour followed. The steady rain continued and the defenders used the time to improve their position. At about 1100, three more tanks were sighted advancing from the north. Behind them was a column of trucks, followed by miles of infantry on foot. These were men of the 16th and 18th regiments of the North Korean 4th Division. The column was apparently not in communication with the tanks that had preceded it.

It took about an hour for the head of the column to reach a point about 1,000 yards from the American position, when Smith ordered fire opened. American mortars and machine guns swept the enemy column, causing heavy casualties, but did not stop the three tanks. These advanced to within 300 yards and raked the ridge with shell and machine gun fire. Smith had no communication with the artillery battery, which he believed had been destroyed.

Smith held his position as long as he dared, but casualties mounted rapidly. His men were down to less than twenty rounds of ammunition apiece and the enemy threatened to cut off the position. The enemy tanks were to the rear of the American position, and Smith consolidated his force in a circular perimeter on the highest ground east of the road. The enemy was now using mortar and artillery fire. About 1630, Smith ordered a withdrawal, remarking, "This is a decision I'll probably regret the rest of my days." The plan was for an orderly leap-frogging withdrawal, with one platoon covering another. Under heavy enemy fire, the poorly trained American troops abandoned weapons and equipment in sometimes precipitous flight. Not all of them had received word of the withdrawal and it was at this point that the Americans suffered most of their casualties. When they reached the battery position Smith was surprised to find it intact with only Perry and one other man wounded. The artillerymen disabled the five remaining howitzers by removing their sights and breechblocks. Then all walked to the outskirts of Osan where they recovered most of their trucks that had been hidden earlier. South of Osan the Americans were forced to detour, and some stragglers were picked up. Fortunately there was no enemy pursuit. At Chonan, only 185 men of the task force could be accounted for. Subsequently, C Company commander Captain Richard Dashmer came in with 65 more, bringing the total to 250. More trickled back to American positions during the following week. One survivor even made it from the west coast by sampan to Pusan. In the battle approximately 150 American infantrymen were killed, wounded, or missing. All five officers and ten enlisted men of the forward observer liaison, machine gun, and bazooka group were lost. North Korean casualties in the battle before Osan were approximately 42 dead and 85 wounded; four tanks had been destroyed or immobilized. The enemy advance was delayed perhaps seven hours.

The North Koreans continued their offensive south against more and more units of the 24th Division. On July 6 they forced an American withdrawal from the next blocking position at Pyongtaek, held by the 34th Regiment. The 21st Regiment imposed another slight delay on the enemy in front of Chochiwon, but both regiments suffered heavily in these actions. However, these and other battles over the period to July 21 did purchase some time for the 1st Cavalry and 25th Infantry divisions to be rushed from Japan.

Task Force Smith is also noteworthy in that an anonymous American machine gunner of the unit became the first battle death of the Korean War. (Soon after Task Force Smith was annihilated, a mistaken report claimed that the first American battle death of the war was a Private Kenneth Shadrick. But Task Force Smith was engaged between 0800 and 1100 hours, and twenty Americans were killed in the engagement; Shadrick was killed at about 1600 hours the same day.) Task Force Smith's action is noteworthy almost entirely because it was the first ground clash between invading North Korean and defending U.S. forces. It was hardly a major clash of arms, and only momentarily delayed the enemy. But this "arrogant display of strength" (and not much strength at that) may have accomplished more than the battle-weary, dispirited American troops could have realized at the time. The diary of a killed North Korean soldier recorded that "Near Osan there was a great battle."

Spencer Tucker

Bibliography

Appleman, Roy E. *South to the Naktong, North to the Yalu (June–November 1950)* (Office of the Chief of Military History, Washington: 1961).

Cannon, M.C. "'Task Force Smith': A Study in (Un)Preparedness and (Ir)Responsibility," *Military Review* (February 1988).

Collins, J. Lawton. *War in Peacetime: The History and Lessons of the Korean War* (1969).

Gugeler, Russell A. *Combat Actions in Korea* (Office of the Chief of Military History, Washington: 1954).

Ludvigsen, E.C. "The Failed Bluff of Task Force Smith: An 'Arrogant Display of Strength,'" *Army* (February 1992).

Taylor, Maxwell D. (1901–1987)

Lieutenant General Maxwell Davenport Taylor, who had served with distinction as the commander of the 101st Airborne Division during World War II, assumed command of the Eighth Army in Korea on 11 February 1953. During his tenure he helped orchestrate the armistice negotiations to include applying subtle pressure to South Korean President Syngman Rhee, transitioning the Eighth Army effort to a largely defensive posture, and assisting in the postwar recovery of South Korea. Additionally, Taylor stressed the need for thorough patrolling, a complete eight-week training program for reserve divisions before they entered the line, a plan to get the maximum effect from the artillery, and the requirement for better concealment for troops skylined on Korea's many pieces of high ground.

By the time Taylor assumed command of the Eighth Army, the war had settled down to a situation analogous to World War I, in which the U.N. could not justify a major frontal attack against its well-protected foe and the Communists lacked the resources. The war was obviously going to be concluded by negotiation, and Taylor's mission was to defend the Eighth Army's lines "with minimum losses consistent with maintaining the integrity of the position." The Chinese, however, were eager to end the war on a winning note, and near the end of March 1953, they began their final offensive which continued almost to the signing of the armistice. On the evening of 23 March, the Chinese launched a double-barrelled attack on both Old Baldy and Pork Chop Hills in the 7th Infantry Division's sector. In the first two days of fighting for the hills, the 7th Infantry suffered more than 300 dead, wounded, and missing in action as the enemy committed its troops freely without regard for human life. The corps and division commanders began making preparations for counterattacks to regain Old Baldy, but after considering all factors, Taylor demonstrated remarkable self-discipline. The hilltop was of limited tactical value, and Taylor and others recognized that the loss of life was simply not worthwhile.

Nonetheless, Taylor found defensive warfare frustrating. His restrictions went so far as to require him to get permission from Washington before conducting attacks of greater than two battalion strength. The actions at Old Baldy and Pork Chop Hills caused Taylor to prepare for similar situations in the future. He ordered a study of all Eighth Army outposts to determine which were worth fighting for and which would have little impact on the U.N. defensive line if lost.

One of Taylor's characteristics as a combat commander, both during World War II and in Korea, was his insistence on active patrolling. He felt that the patrol offered two fundamental benefits. The first was obviously the tactical intelligence to be gained through reconnaissance. Secondly, and perhaps equally important, was the fact that patrolling provided officers with valuable experience they could not gain elsewhere.

Patrolling was especially critical in Korea as the Chinese were masters at locating gaps in U.N. defenses and infiltrating to the rear. Taylor felt that the Eighth Army's patrolling was inadequate, and he took great pains to improve this condition. One of the measures he initiated was the practice of bringing leaders of selected patrols to his headquarters for debriefing. Many patrol leaders found this to be a greater ordeal than the patrol itself, but Taylor continued the procedure right up to the armistice.

Taylor had spent his earlier years in the Army as an artillery officer, and his interest in the branch did not wane. Prior to reporting to Korea, he had served as deputy chief of staff to General Joseph Collins. One of Taylor's assignments in this capacity was to respond to claims by then Eighth Army commander Lieutenant General James Van Fleet that artillery ammunition in Korea was in short supply. Taylor tracked the flow of the ammunition from manufacture to expenditure and concluded that although the flow was sometimes irregular, there was always enough ammunition to meet the needs of the tactical situation. On assuming command of the Eighth Army himself, Taylor was able to make an even closer inspection. On 12 March, he issued a press release which noted that he had all the artillery ammunition he required.

Once the ammunition issue was settled, Taylor set out to find ways to improve the effects of artillery. One program he instituted was the practice of moving artillery units frequently in order to maintain their basic mobility. However, the Chinese often attacked at night and in such a rapid fashion that the effects of artillery were limited. To restore the usefulness of this powerful arm, Taylor's men began fortifying their outposts to the extent that they could stay inside their positions and call friendly fire on top of themselves. The United Nations command's extensive use of artillery helped negate the enemy's manpower advantage and keep U.N. casualty tolls low.

Taylor, however, was destined to spend far more time worrying about irresponsible actions by the South Koreans than about military initiatives by the enemy. South Korean President Syngman Rhee was at best a difficult ally. Rhee had spent most of his adult life fighting for Korean independence, and the idea of accepting an armistice which did not include the unification of his country under his rule was anathema. Rhee was also adamantly opposed to turning over any North Korean prisoners of war who did not desire repatriation, and the use of an Indian custodial force to supervise the exchange.

Rhee's obstinance taxed Taylor's patience, diplomacy, and self-discipline much as did the requirement to adopt a defensive stance. To prepare for all contingencies, Taylor had his staff draft "Plan Everready," which addressed three possibilities: a refusal of ROK forces to respond to United Nations directives, an attempt by ROK forces to initiate unilateral action, and a situation in which the ROK forces or the civilian population became openly hostile toward United Nations forces.

On 4 June, the United Nations and Communist negotiators reached agreement on all major points of the prisoner of war exchange. Three days later, Rhee did in fact take unilateral action by promulgating special security measures throughout Korea, recalling his officers from United States training schools, and stepping up his "march North" propaganda in radio broadcasts. On 17 June, Rhee denounced any armistice in Taylor's presence and repeated his determination to act on his own. The next day he ordered the release of 27,000 North Korean non-repatriates, whose fate had been a key factor in the armistice negotiations, provoking the fury of the Communists and the frustration of his allies.

In the midst of these developments, Taylor kept a cool head and took measures to control the damage and maintain a working relationship with Rhee. After listening to Rhee's iteration of his intention of continuing the fight alone, Taylor proceeded to remind him of the deficiencies of the ROK Army. This force would need time to convert itself into a balanced structure capable of even defending South Korea, and the truce would provide this time. Apparently this reality had previously escaped Rhee's attention, and he began to speak in more temperate tones.

Rhee did, however, continue to be a thorn in the side of the United Nations throughout the negotiations, but the patience, tact, and resolution of Taylor and men like him would allow the armistice talks to be concluded. Before then, however, the Communists launched their final offensive.

One of the targets was again the highly contested Pork Chop Hill area. The 7th Infantry withstood a series of assaults, but the Chinese were able to gain control of a portion of the crest. It was obvious that the enemy intended to secure the objective without regard to casualties. Again Taylor showed remarkable control in saving American lives in the final days of the war. Pork Chop Hill was of limited tactical value and, after consulting with the corps and division commanders, he authorized a withdrawal. This maneuver deceived the enemy, and nearly two days would pass before they realized that they owned the hill. When the Chinese finally took possession of the prize, they were hit with all the artillery the 7th Infantry had at its disposal.

On 27 July the armistice was finally signed at Panmunjom, and the process of rebuilding began. Taylor was especially sympathetic to the South Koreans who, unlike the Germans in World War II, had not brought destruction upon themselves. The result was the Armed Forces Aid to Korea (AFAK) program. Under this program, the Eighth Army provided equipment and expertise to supplement Korean labor and materiel in the massive task of reconstruction. In addition to the AFAK program, Taylor initiated other measures to rebuild Korea. He encouraged programs for U.S. units to "adopt" Korean children who had been bombed out of their orphanages and helped displaced farmers return to their lands.

In 1954, Taylor earned his fourth star and left Korea for Tokyo to become the head of all Army forces in the Far East. Before then, however, he had completed a five-section report which outlined lessons learned from the war. Two key themes were the infantry's paramount role in the war and the importance of logistics on a battlefield far from home. Taylor further argued that the character of the war had nullified the United States' powerful weapons such as the Navy's big ships, the Air Force's bombers, and the Army's tanks. This condition, combined with the decision not to use nuclear weapons, placed a premium on conventional forces, specifically the infantry. Taylor also addressed the cost of the war. United States soldiers wanted to live while at war in accordance with American standards at home, and ice cream parlors, post exchanges, and snack bars were commonplace. This mentality also manifested itself in the tremendous expenditures of ammunition in relatively insignificant actions. The war had indeed been very expensive. Seizing this point, Taylor recommended that the weapons of all three services be studied to determine their cost effectiveness. Taylor cautioned that "Expensive and complicated gadgets of infrequent use should not be allowed to absorb resources needed to support the most flexible weapon in our arsenal, the infantry soldier."

As Eighth Army commander, Taylor had headed a force of nearly a million men under arms. He had followed strict orders from Washington to maintain a defensive posture while at the same time thwarting some of the fiercest enemy attacks of the war. In the process he had increased the combat effectiveness of his command. Perhaps more important, Taylor had avoided the potential pitfall of becoming preoccupied with Rhee and had remained sensitive to the political realities of Washington.

Kevin Dougherty

Bibliography

Clay, Blair. *The Forgotten War* (1987).

Hermes, Walter. *Truce Tent and Fighting Front* (Office of the Chief of Military History, Washington: 1966).

Ridgway, Matthew. *The Korean War* (1967).

Taylor, John. *General Maxwell Taylor: The Sword and the Pen* (1989).

Taylor, Maxwell. *Swords and Plowshares* (1972).

38th Parallel

This line of latitude constituted the *ad hoc* border between the Republic of Korea (ROK) in the south and the Democratic People's Republic of Korea (DPRK) in the north of the peninsula at the time the Korean War began. It became a boundary line as a result of hasty preparations for accepting Japan's surrender during the last days of World War II. On August 15, 1945, President Harry S. Truman proposed to Joseph Stalin, and received his approval for, General Order Number One, which included a provision for the temporary division of Korea at the 38th parallel into two zones of military occupation, with the Soviet Union accepting the surrender of Japanese troops in the north and the United States in the south. This last-minute arrangement was necessary because the president had discarded the four-power trusteeship plan for the postwar reconstruction of Korea proposed by President Franklin D. Roosevelt during World War II. The 38th parallel division resulted in the emergence of two Koreas and the determination of each government to achieve reunification of the peninsula on its own terms, and would lead to the outbreak of the Korean War.

In his memoirs, Truman claimed that the decision to divide Korea at the 38th was the product of military expediency and convenience. In reality, political and strategic considerations were also responsible for Korea's partition. When Truman became president in April 1945, Moscow's establishment of Communist governments in Eastern Europe persuaded him that Stalin would pursue the same objective in Korea. If the Soviet Union dominated Korea, it could undermine Chiang Kai-shek's position in China and place the security of Japan in jeopardy. Therefore Truman began to search for a way to occupy Korea unilaterally. His decision to use the atomic bomb against Japan was in part aimed at forcing Tokyo to surrender quickly, thereby preempting Soviet entry into the Pacific war.

Truman's gamble failed. On August 8, Stalin acted to ensure that he would play a role in reconstructing Asia after World War II, declaring war on Japan and sending the Red Army into Manchuria and Korea. Two days later, the State-War-Navy Coordinating Committee (SWNCC) ordered Colonels C. H. Bonesteel and Dean Rusk (later secretary of state) to find a line in Korea that would harmonize the political desire to have U.S. forces receive the surrender as far north as possible with the inability of the closest U.S. troops on Okinawa to reach the area before the Soviets occupied the entire Korean peninsula. Bonesteel and Rusk quickly decided on the 38th parallel and the SWNCC incorporated the line in General Order Number One. The Joint Chiefs of Staff endorsed this decision, satisfied that the 38th parallel provided for U.S. control over both the capital at Seoul and sufficient land to apportion zones of occupation to China and Britain. (Ironically, in 1896, Japan had rejected Russia's proposal for a division of Korea along the same line into spheres of influence.) Many American officials doubted that the Soviets would accept the same proposal now, but Stalin approved it, probably in hopes of receiving a voice in the reconstruction of Japan. Truman's refusal to grant the Soviet leader an equal role in determining Japan's future meant that Korea's reunification was unlikely from the start.

Scholars have criticized the decision to divide Korea into zones of military occupation. Certainly the line was ill advised as a permanent boundary since it cut across natural areas of geographic, cultural, topographic, and climatic continuity. On the west coast, for example, the Ongjin peninsula was part of the American zone, yet the U.S. had no land connection to that area. But Truman did not think that the partition would become permanent. With the deterioration of relations in Europe, however, Korea became a captive of the Cold War, as neither the Soviets nor the Americans would permit the removal of the 38th parallel division, each fearing that this move might allow its rival to dominate a reunited Korea. Given the alternative of total Soviet control, Truman thought he had achieved a major success. The Red Army could have occupied the entire peninsula, only Stalin's acceptance of the surrender agreement prevented Communist domination throughout Korea. However, most Koreans refused to accept this argument and denounced the U.S. for dividing Korea in 1945 and failing to reunite the peninsula during the Korean War. This explains in part the refusal of the Truman administration to accept the 38th parallel as the basis for a demilitarized zone during the armistice negotiations. Today, the boundary between the two Koreas follows exactly the front line as it was on the day the cease-fire was signed, except for the Ongjin peninsula and the area around Kaesong. Both Koreas ended the war with roughly the same amount of territory they possessed on the day the war began.

James I. Matray

Bibliography

Grey, A.L., Jr. "The Thirty-Eighth Parallel," *Foreign Affairs* (April 1951).

Matray, J.I. *The Reluctant Crusade* (1985).

McCune, S. "The Thirty-Eighth Parallel in Korea," *World Politics* 1 (1949).

Paul, M. "Diplomacy Delayed: The Atomic Bomb and the Division of Korea, 1945," in B. Cumings, ed., *Child of Conflict* (1983).

Sandusky, M. *America's Parallel* (1983).

Topography and Terrain

The Korean peninsula extends approximately 500 miles (835 km) from the Asian mainland. With a variable width of 90–220 miles (150–365 km), Korea constitutes 85,000 square miles (200,847 sq km). Bounded to the east by the Sea of Japan (East Sea), to the west by the Yellow Sea and Korea Bay, and to the south by the Korea (Tsushima) Strait, the peninsula stretches to the south-southeast from its northern border with the Chinese province of Manchuria. China's Shandong Peninsula lies 115 miles (190 km) to the west, and Japan is 125 miles (206 km) to the southeast. Divided arbitrarily along the 38th parallel in 1945, the peninsula contains both the Democratic People's Republic of Korea (North Korea) and the Republic of Korea (South Korea). The armistice agreement of July 27, 1953, modified this international border by establishing a demilitarized zone (DMZ) 2.4 miles (4 km) wide and 145 miles (241 km) long. This division allotted 55 percent of the peninsula to the North, with the remainder claimed by the South.

Mountains cover 70 to 80 percent of the Korean peninsula. Mount Paektu, rising to 9,000 feet (2,744 meters) along the North Korean–Chinese border, is the highest peak. Mount Halla, at 6,400 feet (1,950 meters) on the island of Cheju-do, marks South Korea's highest elevation. From Mount Paektu in the north, the Mach'ol range extends to the southeast. From the Mach'ol range, the Pujollyong range runs to the southwest. In addition, the Hamgyong range occupies the northeastern part of the peninsula. In the north central portion, the Nangnim range runs generally north and south, with the Chogyu range extending westward from the Nangnim. The Myohyang range constitutes a southwest extension of the Nangnim range, and the Ahomi range runs southwestward from the east coast north of the DMZ. Surrounded by the Mach'ol, Nangnim, and Pujollyong ranges, the Kaena plateau incorporates 3,600 square miles (10,000 sq km) and represents the largest upland plateau on the peninsula. To the south, the Taebaek range runs north and south along the entire east coast. The Charyong range orients southwest to northeast below Seoul, and the Sobaek range extends north and south to the central portion of South Korea. Mount Chiri and the Chiri Massif occupy much of the south central peninsula.

Drainage from these mountain ranges determines river patterns throughout Korea. The Yalu and Tumen Rivers trace North Korea's northern border with China (615 miles/1,041 km) and with Russia (10 miles/16 km). The Yalu flows east to west for 475 miles (790 km) and is navigable for 405 miles (678 km). The Tumen flows west to east for 312 miles (520 km). The Taedong River flows east to west for 238 miles (397 km) in the vicinity of the North Korean capital of Pyongyang. The Imjin River crosses the DMZ, flowing north to south before turning westward. The Han River extends 308 miles (514 km), and serves the South Korean capital of Seoul. Its tributary, the Pukhan, feeds the Han from the north. The Kum River flows

east to west for 240 miles (401 km), serving the city of Taejon. In the southwest, the Somjin River flows north to south. Finally, in the southeast, the Naktong River flows generally north to south and serves the city of Taegu.

Korea's arable land constitutes 20 to 30 percent of the peninsula and lies generally along the west coast and the major rivers. In the north, the Chaeryong plain and the Pyongyang peneplain serve the Pyongyang vicinity. In addition, the Yonbaek, Anju, and Unjon plains rest along the west coast, while the Hamhung and Kilchu plains mark the east. To the south, the Han River plain serves the Seoul vicinity, and the Pyongtaek coastal plain lies south of the capital. The Kum and Naktong Rivers form extensive basins, and the Yongsan and Homan plains serve the southwest.

With a few natural harbors along the east coast, most Korean ports are situated to the south and west. Nevertheless, the Wonsan-Hungnam-Hamhung area provides relatively ice-free ports. Moreover, Yongil Bay and Ulsan Bay provide adequate harbors for the ports of Pohang and Ulsan, respectively. Amid numerous ports along the south and west coasts, Pusan and Inchon constitute the largest. Tidal variations affect port traffic, and Inchon's thirty-three-foot differential is the second highest in the world.

Dotted with 3,579 islands, Korea's indented coastline traces 5,400 miles (8,640 km). Cheju-do, Korea's largest island, lies to the southwest of the peninsula. Ullung sits in the Sea of Japan, and Kanghwa rests north of Inchon. Two other islands—Koje-do and Paengyong-do—gained some notoriety during the Korean War. The former contained the United Nations prison camps where Communist inmates rioted in May–June 1952. The latter, lying just south of the 38th parallel off the west coast, housed a regimental-size headquarters for North Korean partisans. Other west coast islands provided haven for anti-Communist forces and downed pilots.

Korea's major population centers lie along the coasts or astride the major transportation route from Pusan through Seoul to Pyongyang. Road and rail networks also connect Pyongyang and Seoul with Wonsan on the east coast. Pyongyang, the capital of North Korea, lies in the western part of the Democratic People's Republic, approximately 100 miles north of the 38th parallel. Wonsan, the principal port on North Korea's east coast, lies 110 miles (184 km) north of the 38th parallel. A road and rail communications center, Wonsan stretches for two miles along the narrow east coast. The ancient capital of Kaesong lies two miles (3.3 km) south of the 38th parallel and north of the Imjin River. Under Communist control during much of the Korean War, Kaesong remained a North Korean city.

In the south, Seoul lies close to the west coast and is served by the port of Inchon. Built on an estuary of the Yom-ha River, Inchon enjoys a protected ice-free port with a tidal basin. There are no beaches, but a sixteen-foot seawall protects the city at high tide. Two channels lead into the harbor: Flying Fish Channel is fifty miles long and thirty-six to sixty feet deep. The tidal basin is 1,700 feet long, 750 feet wide, and forty feet deep (fourteen feet at low tide). A breakwater and Wolmi and Sowolmi Islands separate the inner and outer harbors. The inner harbor becomes a mud flat at low tide with a narrow, shallow channel. A causeway connects Wolmi-do, or Moon Tip Island, with Sowolmi-do (Island). Rising 335 feet above sea level, Wolmi-do's rocky, circular hill measures 1,000 yards in diameter.

To the south along the Seoul-Pusan transportation line, Taejon and Taegu constitute road and rail hubs for southern Korea. The Kum River forms a veritable moat around Taejon at the western base of the Sobaek Mountains. Taegu lies astride the Naktong River as it flows southward toward the port of Pusan.

Some terrain features and geographical areas are noteworthy for historical significance or military importance. The Changjin (Chosin) Reservoir, situated fifty-six miles (93 km) north of Hamhung, extends forty miles (67 km) northward from Koto-ri. The Chongchon River valley, three to twenty miles wide, stretches southwestward sixty-five miles (110 km) south of the Yalu River and forty-five miles (74 km) north of Pyongyang. Two road and rail routes run northward to the Yalu, one through Sinanju to Kanggye and the other through Unsan. The Iron Triangle—formed by Chorwon (west base), Kumhwa (east base), and Pyongyang (north apex)—constitutes an area of relatively flat terrain surrounded by the mountains of east central North Korea. Twenty to thirty miles (33–50 km) north of the 38th parallel and fifty miles (85 km) northeast of Seoul, this area represents a rail and road communications hub connecting east and west. Finally, in the southeast, the "Naktong Bulge" describes a semicircular area outlined by a westward turn of the Naktong River seven miles (12 km) north of the confluence of the Naktong and Nam Rivers.

Characterized by mountainous terrain, river obstacles, an underdeveloped transportation network, limited port facilities, and few population centers, the Korean peninsula provided a formidable challenge to the armed forces of both sides during the Korean War.

For the U.S. soldier in Korea, the peninsula's topography and terrain could be simply summarized as "one damn hill after another." GIs of a more humorous bent liked to claim that Korea was actually the largest country in the world: If its terrain could be hammered flat, it would cover the earth.

James Sanders Day

Bibliography

U.S. Army Far East Command, Military Intelligence Section, General Staff, Theater Division, Geographical Branch. *Northern Korea* (1950).
———. *Southern Korea* (1951).

Truman, Harry S. (1884–1972)

Vice president Harry S. Truman succeeded to the office of president of the United States on the death of Franklin Roosevelt on April 12, 1945. Sorely unprepared, uninformed, and inexperienced, Truman was thrust into the position of the leader of the Free World in a crisis time.

The two atomic bombs dropped on Japan brought a sudden end to World War II on August 14, 1945. Americans immediately faced a postwar period filled with economic uncertainties at home and the growing threat of military conflict with the Soviets on a number of fronts overseas. President Truman was forced to deal with both of these dilemmas during his presidency.

In response to Soviet pressures around the world, Truman adopted a policy of "toughness" in his dealings with Moscow. That policy was stated firmly in the Truman Doctrine (which promised aid to countries threatened by Communist expansion) and its economic counterpart, the Marshall Plan. By 1947, Truman's hard-line stand against Soviet aggression had brought on an equally hard-line response from the Soviets. What had been an effective prewar U.S.-Soviet alliance had deteriorated into a Cold War that would distract much of the world for the next forty years.

On the domestic front in the immediate postwar period, Truman hoped to expand and extend the New Deal, but he was uncomfortable with New Dealers. That led him to replace most of Roosevelt's appointees with his own loyal men. On September 6, 1945, the president sent to Congress a peacetime program that was a continuation and enlargement of the New Deal. It included expansion of unemployment insurance, extension of the Employment Service, an increased minimum wage, a permanent Fair Employment Practices Commission, a plan for slum clearance and low-rent housing, and a public works program. The entire program was later dubbed the Fair Deal.

The paramount postwar American economic problem faced by Truman was inflation, not depression as many had projected. The tasks of restraining consumer spending while convincing labor to hold off on wage demands and businesses to hold down price increases became insurmountable for the new and inexperienced president. A series of strikes in 1946 threatened to push the American economy into an inflationary spiral. Truman forced settlements between labor and management in the mining and railroad industries, and allowed substantial wage increases in the auto and steel industries. In 1945 and 1946, the Truman administration, through its Office of Price Administration, tried to control the economy through price freezes. But by late 1946, after pressure from nearly all sides of the economy, controls were finally lifted except for those on rents, sugar, and rice.

In 1946, Truman signed the Employment Act, which was designed to achieve full employment in America. Also in that year, the president created the Atomic Energy Commission, a civilian agency to regulate the use and deployment of atomic energy. In 1947, Truman signed the National Security Act which established the National Security Council and the Central Intelligence Agency (CIA), and made permanent the Joint Chiefs of Staff. In 1949, the Housing Act was passed with Truman's leadership, and the president is credited with making a number of advances in the cause of civil rights for American blacks, including the desegregation of the armed forces.

In November 1946, the Democrats suffered a severe defeat in the congressional elections. The result was the 80th Congress, the first Republican-controlled Congress in sixteen years. Bent on dismantling the New Deal, the 80th Congress moved to limit the power of labor, lower taxes, and ride their successes on to victory in the 1948 presidential election. Not surprisingly, Truman clashed with the 80th Congress over a number of issues, but the most important was Congress's attempt to regulate and restrict organized labor. Truman vetoed the controversial 1947 Taft-Hartley Act, which banned the closed shop and restricted the power of organized labor in a number of other ways. The bill was passed over Truman's veto, but his actions increased his standing with organized labor. Twice in 1947, the 80th Congress passed tax cuts only to watch Truman veto them with the claim that they favored the wealthy. In 1948 a third tax cut bill was passed over Truman's veto.

In September 1946 Truman fired Henry Wallace, his secretary of commerce. Wallace was the darling of the Democratic left, and the president's actions alienated that wing of the party. Wallace ran for president on the Progressive party ticket in 1948; however, support for his candidacy from the Communist party worked against Wallace in the campaign and destroyed any possibility of a victory.

Having lost the support of liberals by firing Wallace and alienating southerners by supporting civil rights, Truman appeared to be headed for certain defeat in 1948 at the head of a deeply divided party. However, Truman held together the disparate factions of his party in a surprising upset of the Republican candidate, Thomas Dewey. Truman's tough stand against communism (at home and abroad), his vetoes of the Taft-Hartley Act and proposed tax cuts, his berating of the Republican-dominated 80th "do nothing" Congress, and the president's celebrated "whistle-stop" tours are considered the important factors in turning the 1948 election in his favor.

In Europe, the Berlin Airlift straddled Truman's two terms, from April 1948 to May 1949. In April of 1949, the North Atlantic Treaty Organization (NATO) was formed as a mutual defense pact against possible Soviet aggression in Europe.

Domestically, America's second "Red Scare" began during Truman's administration, and may in fact have been precipitated by the president to forestall attacks from the increasingly volatile right wing of both political parties. In March of 1947, Truman had inaugurated a loyalty program that subjected all federal workers to investigation as to their beliefs. The program was designed to enhance Truman's respectability among the growing number of American anti-Communists, but it set off an anti-Communist hysteria that led to a number of notorious espionage trials and accelerated the rise to national prominence of Senator Joseph McCarthy.

In addition, Congress in 1950 passed the McCarran Act over the president's veto. The bill required Communist and Communist-front organizations to register with the federal government. It also empowered the federal government to arrest persons suspected of subversive activities. Without excessive hyperbole, Truman in his veto message denounced the act as "the greatest danger to freedom of the press, speech, and assembly since the Sedition Acts of 1798." Truman's veto of this popular bill was little short of heroic. But his stance caused his popularity to slump between 1950 and 1952, and enabled the Republicans to affix the unfair label of "soft on communism" on Truman's Democrats to the end of his administration.

Thus, the anti-Communist fervor of the 1950s well predated the Korean War. Although there were indeed Communists unearthed during the period, the damage done to the nation through the abrogations of personal liberty, false accusations, and the exercise of power by untrammeled regional fanatics undoubtedly outweighed any damage to national security inflicted by a few genuine Communists.

Truman's second term was dominated by the rise of Communist power in Asia, and the Korean War. In late 1949, Communist forces under Mao Tse-tung defeated the U.S.-supported Nationalist armies of Chiang Kai-shek, and mainland China became the focus of communism in Asia.

In April 1950, Truman recorded his views on the Communist threat in National Security Council Paper No. 68 (NSC-68), which contended that communism was a monolithic, aggressive threat directed from Moscow, and recommended rather drastic U.S. peacetime mobilization to face the threat. Before Truman could attempt to put NSC-68's rather overwrought recommendations into effect, the Korean War erupted, and America, more or less, went to war. The Korean War would dominate Truman's foreign and even his domestic policy to the end of his second term in 1953.

The Republicans politically exploited the Korean War stalemate. Although at first applauding Truman's decision to intervene, they later began to claim that not only had the Democrats "lost" China to the Communists in 1949, now they could not, or would not, defeat the Communists in Korea.

For one supposedly soft on communism, Truman presided over a huge escalation of defense spending caused by the war. Between 1950 and 1953, the United States increased its defense budget from $14 billion to $44 billion. By the latter year, fully 60 percent of the federal budget was earmarked for defense, and defense expenditures reached a percentage of GNP never approached since. The result was an economic boom that kept incomes rising and unemployment low until 1954. But with the boom came a problem that had haunted Truman since he came to office in 1945: inflation. Through the Office of Price Stabilization, the Truman administration tried to hold down inflation's worst ravages. But Truman's economic policies were severely shaken in the aftermath of an attempted price hike by steel manufacturers and a subsequent strike by steelworkers. Truman seized the mills as a wartime necessity, but his action was reversed by the Supreme Court. But for the most part, the war, unpopular as it was, generally diverted attention from the U.S. domestic scene.

By 1952, the president had lost most of the popularity he had gained by his triumph against the "experts'" odds in November of 1948. The Republicans were gathering strength through a number of issues that included the perceived problem of communism at home, corruption, inflation, and the war. Truman's seeming impotence in the face of the war played into the hands of his political enemies, who demanded total victory in Korea.

The corruption issue came to the forefront with the news that the administration had to fire no less than 250 employees of the Internal Revenue Service. Eventually, nine senior Democrats were jailed for malfeasance. The press began to recall Truman's onetime association with the notorious Pendergast machine in Missouri. The IRS, "Mink coat," "five percenter," and other egregious scandals, plus the Truman administration's seeming lackadaisical response, were subsumed by gleeful Republicans under the generic term "The Mess in Washington." It did not help matters that the president's military aide, the bumbling, flabby, Brigadier General Harry Vaughan, was widely believed to have used his office to personal gain.

Perhaps the nadir of Truman's presidency took place in early 1952, when Truman's outside investigator, probing IRS malfeasance, was fired by the U.S. attorney general, whereupon that public servant was, in turn, fired by Truman.

By 1952, Truman was exceptionally unpopular among the American people and even with the Democratic leadership. With an emaciated 23 percent approval rating (a record low), his chances in the 1952 election seemed minuscule. In addition, the Republicans were beginning to focus their attentions on the extremely popular General Dwight D. "Ike" Eisenhower. But there was always the "miracle" of 1948 to recall. Nonetheless, and not surprisingly, Truman announced in March 1952 that he had decided to forego a third term. (Truman was exempt from the provisions of the XXII Amendment, the Republicans' posthumous revenge against the uniquely four-term Franklin Roosevelt. Truman had merely filled Roosevelt's fourth term, and was at any rate specifically excepted from the amendment's provisions.)

Harry Truman, although about as "typical" an American as could ever be found, was not a popular president in his final years in office, if the polls were any indication. His decisive, even courageous, action against Communist aggression in June 1950 was offset by the stalemate with which the Korean War concluded. His reputation, at least among historians, remains high for his principled stand in opposition to the worst excesses of domestic anti-Communist hysteria, despite his misguided loyalty program. Many also revere his memory for his mostly abortive "Fair Deal" social program. For most Americans with longer memories, Truman will be best remembered for his nose-thumbing upset victory in 1948 and his decision to take America into the Korean War. Historians note his decision to drop the atomic bomb over Japan, but he should also be remembered for the fact that, despite pressures to the contrary, he did not drop the bomb over Korea.

Gary A. Donaldson

Bibliography

Donovan, Robert. *Tumultuous Years: The Presidency of Harry S. Truman, 1949–1953* (1982).

Ferrell, Robert. *Harry Truman and the Modern American Presidency* (1983).

Gosnell, Harold. *Truman's Crises: A Political Biography of Harry S. Truman* (1980).

Hamby, Alonzo. *Beyond the New Deal: Harry S. Truman and American Liberalism* (1973).

Jenkins, Roy. *Truman* (1980).

Reichard, Gary. *Politics As Usual* (1988).

Turkish Brigade

Harassed by Communist-instigated unrest throughout the 1940s, Turkey received Allied military and economic support. Turkish President Bayar sought continued security in a Western alliance and agreed on July 25, 1950, to send troops to Korea in order to emphasize cooperation with the West.

The Turkish military advance party arrived in Pusan on October 12, with the 5,190-member Turkish Infantry Brigade disembarking five days later. The Turkish Brigade peaked with 5,455 men and was commanded by Brigadier General Tahsin Yazici, who had been a division commander at Gallipoli in World War I.

The Turks bivouacked at Taegu to train and receive supplies. They were first attached to the U.S. IX Corps and then to the 25th Infantry Division. The Turkish armed forces command consisted of a regimental combat team with three infantry battalions and engineers and artillery to support them in addition to a brigade staff consisting of Yazici, his assistant commander Colonel Celal Dora, and Major Faik Turun and Major Recai Baturalp.

The Turks easily acclimatized to Korea because it was geographically similar to Turkey. The Turks experienced problems obtaining adequate bread supplies, a basic component of their diet; the allies secured bakers and portable ranges especially to bake loaves for the Turks. As Moslems, the Turks naturally refused pork; other Turkish culinary requests included strong coffee, spices, and butter. The Turk also had wider feet than most Allied soldiers, causing problems in securing sizeable shoes.

The U.N. commanders worried about possible conflicts between the Turks and their World War I foes, Australia and New Zealand, but few, if any, problems surfaced between them. The relationship between the Turks and the Americans was more tenuous. The Turks were often upset that American troops did not notify them of withdrawals or give them fire support.

On November 20, the Turkish Brigade was detached from the 25th and transferred to IX Corps reserve. Their first time in combat was at Tokchon on November 26. As part of the IX Corps, General John B. Coulter sent the Turkish Brigade to Tokchon to guard the flank of the 2nd Infantry Division. Unfortunately, the Turks were not informed of the current battle status or how to coordinate with other troops. Yazici misinterpreted the instructions, believing he was supposed to return, and abandoned the Allied flank.

Without an intelligence report, the Turks assumed they would meet the enemy. Unable to distinguish between South Koreans and the Chinese, the Turks were unaware that ROK soldiers were retreating and fired at the ROKs, believing they were the enemy. Originally lauded as an overwhelming victory, a Nisei (Japanese-American) interpreter uncovered what really happened and subsequently the debacle was concealed, but South Korean resentment smouldered.

The Turks neared Wawon where they engaged in true battle on the 26th. The Allied commanders tried to stop the Turks from advancing on Wawon because the enemy was in the area in strength. A message was relayed to the IX Corps liaison officer to the Turkish command. However, the information was not forwarded. Another example of failed communications was on November 27 when Allied commanders tried to move the Turks to hills near Kunu-ri to check the Chinese. The Turks were ambushed on November 29 and decimated. Later, a Turkish motor convoy, ignoring the shot-up vehicles by the road from the first ambush, was also attacked. The Turks were quickly defeated, as unexpected machine gun fire sprayed them, losing all their vehicles in one battalion and suffering heavy casualties.

After the ambush, the Turkish Brigade withdrew from positions near the Chongchon River as the Chinese pushed back the U.N. forces. Commanders, unsure of what was going on, tried to determine the Turks' position. They estimated that one-half of the Turkish forces remained and that their ammunition, artillery, and tank support were decreasing but sufficient. These reports did not account for the heavy casualties inflicted on the Turks, and the many who had retreated to Pyongyang by driving ambulances and trucks.

The Turks reached Pyongyang by the first of December, upset at the allies' failed support. Captain Ismail Catalogy, aide to Yazici, said: "Many men are bitter." Afterward, Allied commanders realized the Turks had lost 20 percent of their men, 90 percent of their communications equipment and vehicles, and only had six working artillery pieces. On December 13, General Walton H. Walker presented Yazici and fifteen Turkish officers and men Silver Star and Bronze Star medals for their gallantry. The Turkish Army itself did not issue any medals for military valor.

Some Turks left Pyongyang December 13 to support the 25th Infantry Division on Kanghwa-do Island to patrol and watch for enemy crossing the mouth of the Han River. Again confused about who was the enemy, the Turks fired at refugees, killing many. This action upset the island's governor, necessitating a diplomatic visit from Brigadier General Vennard Wilson, assistant commander of the U.S. 25th Infantry Division.

The Turks were evacuated to Kaesong to recuperate and reorganize. At Kaesong they were attached to the 2nd Infantry Division. Eighth Army sent a liaison officer to report on the status of the Turks. He noted the extreme loss of men, jeeps (112 destroyed of 125), and 1.5- and 2.5-ton trucks (143 of 216). Yazici complained that the Turks had, from the beginning, 60 percent fewer vehicles than American forces. The discussions were held in Turkish, which the liaison officer could not understand, and he complained that it was difficult to control the Turks because of the language barrier and argued that the Turks needed to be moved from Kaesong because they were unruly. After fifteen days to reorganize and reequip, the Turks were moved to Sosa-ri.

In January 1951, the Turkish Brigade substituted for the 24th Infantry Regiment in the battle to regain Seoul. After artillery pounded a hill northeast of Suwon, the Turks, using fixed bayonets, boldly overran the Chinese, building morale for both the Turks and the allies. As a result of the Turks' bayonet charges, Ridgway decided to have all infantry units fix bayonets to rifles.

While in Seoul, the Turks dug in near the Han River and were also ordered to guard Kimpo Airfield. In February they advanced to Hill 431, where they repeatedly attacked the enemy in what was chronicled as a great bayonet attack. Although offensively able, they suffered reverses in April 1951 while defending Seoul. Yazici, on leave in Tokyo, was not there to command his soldiers when they were surrounded and shattered by Chinese troops. Although the Turkish artillery managed to escape, the 24th Regiment's flank was exposed.

After being regrouped, the Turks were used in campaigns moving north to the Iron Triangle positions. The Turks continued their bayonet charges while the allies sought to gain a strong line of contact in case truce talks were finalized.

On May 5, 1953, Major General Samuel T. Williams named Brigadier General Sirri Acar in charge of the Turkish armed forces command

and detailed him to defend outposts known as Nevada, Berlin, and East Berlin, ten miles northeast of Panmunjom. On May 25 the enemy, trying to obtain a better line for the demilitarized zone, attacked, and the Turks counterattacked, using their bayonets. They held the line until the end of May. On May 29 they were ordered to withdraw.

Opinions of Turkish contributions in the Korean War are mixed. Some contemporaries and historians considered them valiant and heroic while others felt they caused problems and setbacks. The Turks were criticized for language difficulties, including inability to respond to orders. The lack of translators caused communication channels to be closed; yet some Turks learned basic English terms for equipment and maneuvers, and American advisors were able to translate basic vocabulary. The average American GI almost invariably lauded the fighting ability of the "terrible Turk." One, possibly apocryphal, story has a Turkish patrol coming upon a group of sleeping Chinese around a campfire. The heads of all but one are silently severed and placed between the legs of the unfortunates. The terror upon awakening of the surviving enemy soldier could only be imagined. Many GIs swore this, or something like it, was a true story.

In the field the Turks were resourceful and improvised well, especially when lacking supplies: in one instance they secured planks with wooden pegs when they lacked nails to build a bridge. Many Turks were heavily infested with parasites, causing problems for surgeons who had to cope with roundworms that crawled through sutures and incisions, spreading infection. Desiring privacy and seeking religious purity, the Turks often bathed wearing their clothes. Morally strict, the Turks were upset at open discussion of venereal diseases in camps.

As prisoners, the Turks were lauded for their tenacity and refusal to collaborate. No Turkish prisoners died or embraced communism during the war. This survival can be attributed to their familiarity with hardship and ability to collect and eat nutritious weeds, such as dandelions, and bark and bulbs.

A total of 14,936 Turks served in the Korean War. Of these, 741 died, 2,068 were wounded, 234 were captured, and 173 were listed as missing in action. The Turkish veterans of the Korean War were awarded the honorary title of "Ghazi."

Elizabeth Schafer

Bibliography
Ahmad, Feroz. *The Turkish Experiment in Democracy 1950–1975* (1977).
Far East U.S. Army Forces, Eighth U.S. Army Korea, *Turkish UN Brigade Advisory Group, 20 November–13 December 1950* (n.d.).
Gordon, Harry. "The Turks Were There," in Norman Bartlett, *With the Australians in Korea* (1954).
Ozselcuk, Musret. "The Turkish Brigade in the Korean War," *International Review of Military History* (1980): 253–272.
Tamkoç, Metin. *The Warrior Diplomats: Guardians of the National Security and Modernization of Turkey* (1976).

U

United Nations Partisan Infantry (UNPIK)
Reaching a peak strength of 22,000 in 1953, this force was largely composed of North Koreans who conducted raids behind Chinese and North Korean lines under the direction of the U.S. Army. Based on off-shore islands, mainly along the west coast of North Korea, the partisans claimed some 69,000 enemy casualties from January 1951 until the conclusion of the armistice agreement in the summer of 1953.

Most of the partisans were from Hwanghae province, North Korea, an agricultural and fishing region whose inhabitants had close social, family, and commercial ties with Seoul. Kim Il Sung's Draft Act of 1947 had alienated many citizens of Hwanghae, causing them either to flee to South Korea or engage in some forms of resistance to the regime in Pyongyang. After the Inchon invasion and the subsequent advance of U.N. forces into North Korea, these elements offered their assistance (using captured Russian weapons) in protecting U.N. lines of communication. An estimated 6,000 to 10,000 partisans made their way south after the debacle near the Yalu, seized fishing smacks along the coast, and established themselves on islands off North Korea.

The U.S. Eighth Army provided food, clothing, and shelter for the partisans and began a training program on the island bases. Active operations were begun in early 1951. Partisan missions included raids against Chinese and North Korean lines of communications and headquarters, intelligence-gathering tasks, and on-shore adjustment of naval gun fire. Additionally, the partisans attempted to establish guerrilla bases in North Korea. This latter activity was not successful. However, the partisans were able to recruit citizens from the north, adding to their ranks on the islands. During the war, the partisans engaged in twenty-two parachute operations, most of which failed to achieve their purposes. On the whole, the partisans were employed against Chinese and North Korean manpower, a futile task in view of the near inexhaustable supply of Chinese soldiers.

An average of about 200 American soldiers directed and supported the partisans on the islands. Some Americans and a limited number of British soldiers and officers accompanied the partisans on their raids. The raids were primarily accomplished using a fleet of disguised fishing vessels, a fleet that grew to well over 200 vessels by the end of the war.

A number of command and control arrangements were tried throughout the nearly two and a half years of partisan employment: control by the Eighth Army, control by the theater command, the Far East command, and control by Army Forces Far East. None of these arrangements proved particularly satisfactory.

The UNPIK forces saw the first combat employment of U.S. Army Special Forces ("Green Berets") personnel, a contingent of these officers and enlisted men arriving on the islands toward the end of the war.

Controversies associated with the partisans included frequently voiced suspicions that they inflated their claims, and committed violations of the Geneva Convention. Approximately 12,000 of the partisans joined the ROK Army at war's end, the others disappeared into the back streets of Seoul, but some made their way back to their homeland. U.S. military authorities were never committed to unconventional warfare in Korea, which may go far to explain the mixed record of the UNPIK.

Rod Paschall

Bibliography

Anderson, E. *Banner Over Pusan* (London: 1960).

Cleaver, Frederick, et al. *Partisan Warfare in Korea, 1951–1954* (Operations Research Office, Johns Hopkins University, Baltimore: 1956).

Darragh, S. "Hwanghae-do: The War of the Donkeys," *Army* (November 1984).

Day, J.S. "Partisan Operations in the Korean War," thesis, University of Georgia, 1989.

Fondataro, S.A. "A Strategic Analysis of U.S. Special Operations during the Korean Conflict, 1950–1953," thesis, Command and General Staff College, Fort Leavenworth, KS, 1988.

Paschall, R. "Special Operations in Korea," *Conflict*, 7, no. 2 (1987).

U.S. Air Force
See AIR FORCE, U.S.

U.S. Air Force Combat Cargo Command
See COMBAT CARGO COMMAND, U.S. AIR FORCE

U.S. Army Cavalry Units
See CAVALRY UNITS, U.S. ARMY

U.S. Army Civil Affairs and Military Government
See CIVIL AFFAIRS AND MILITARY GOVERNMENT, U.S. ARMY

U.S. Army Corps of Engineers
See ENGINEERS IN THE KOREAN WAR

U.S. Army Rangers
See RANGERS, U.S. ARMY

U.S. Army Signal Corps
See SIGNAL CORPS, U.S. ARMY

U.S. Home Front
See HOME FRONT, U.S.

U.S. Logistics
See LOGISTICS, U.S.

U.S. Marine Corps
See MARINE CORPS, U.S.

U.S. Naval Air Operations in the Korean War
See NAVAL AIR OPERATIONS IN THE KOREAN WAR

U.S. Navy
See NAVY, U.S.

U.S. Reserve Forces
See RESERVE FORCES, U.S.

USSR
See SOVIET UNION

U.S. State Department
See STATE DEPARTMENT, U.S.

Vandenberg, Hoyt S. (1899–1954)

Hoyt Sanford Vandenberg, air force officer, chief of staff, U.S. Air Force, 1948–1953, and nephew of prominent U.S. Senator Arthur H. Vandenberg (R-Michigan) was born in Milwaukee, Wisconsin, on January 24, 1899. He graduated near the bottom of his class at the United States Military Academy in 1923 and was commissioned a second lieutenant in the U.S. Army Air Service. In the 1920s and early 30s, he was assigned to various flight schools, both as student and instructor, and as a flight commander. In 1936, he attended the Command and General Staff School, and in 1938, the Army War College. During World War II, he earned an outstanding reputation as a top planner and organizer. In 1942 he was instrumental in forming the 12th Air Force. The following year as chief of staff, Northwest African Strategic Air Force, he played a major role in directing airpower in the North African, Sicilian, and Italian campaigns. The year 1944 found the skilled P-51 and B-17 pilot involved in planning and providing Allied airsupport for the Normandy invasion. He then commanded the 9th Air Force, whose success paved the way for the Allied advance through Europe.

Following the end of the war, he became director of military intelligence (G-2) of the Army general staff, and in 1946, President Harry S. Truman appointed him director of the newly created Central Intelligence Agency (CIA). The next year he became vice-chief of staff of the recently independent Air Force, and in 1948, Truman appointed him chief of staff, U.S. Air Force, thereby making him the nation's highest ranking Air Force officer.

No sooner had he assumed his new post than he was faced with the challenge of airlifting the means to sustain the city of Berlin and its citizens against the Soviet blockade. In ten months, the Berlin Airlift flew the nearly 300,000 missions needed to convince the Soviets to abandon their efforts to cut off the city. Even more taxing was the ongoing battle among the Army, Navy, and Air Force for the limited dollars available in the very austere pre-1951 Truman defense budgets. Even though the Air Force was a favorite of the administration and the Congress, a total defense budget of only $13 million made for extremely limited spending. Although a believer in a balanced force, he was forced by fiscal considerations to make his top priority strategic rather than tactical air power. His position was in line with public and political opinion that all the U.S. had to do to win the next war was to have the long-distance bombers needed to drop atomic bombs on the enemy.

When war came to Korea in the summer of 1950, Vandenberg was a supportive but less than enthusiastic advocate of U.S. involvement. His caution rested primarily on a conviction that the Soviet Union was using the Korean theater as a diversionary operation for an ultimate attack on Europe. That belief played a major role during his first year of the war, because he did not want to do anything that would widen the war by bringing the Soviet Union into the hostilities. Initially he believed that U.S. air and sea power would halt the aggression, but following a trip to the theater of operations, he backed General Douglas MacArthur's call for land forces. He supported advancing into North Korea to destroy enemy forces but did not want to proceed too close to the Chinese or Russian borders lest such action precipitate their entry into the war.

From the early fighting until the end of the war, Vandenberg was under heavy pressure from Army commanders to shift the control of tactical air support from the Air Force to the Army. He withstood such pressure by stating his conviction that the World War II experience demonstrated the soundness of his position. He reduced the pressure somewhat in the fall of 1950 when he reestablished the tactical air command (which he had previously eliminated), but he never really quieted his Army critics on the matter.

While the Inchon invasion was a high point in the career of General MacArthur, it marked the beginning of Vandenberg's concern about MacArthur's ability properly to use the considerable military power that he had received. Like the other members of the Joint Chiefs of Staff (JCS), Vandenberg was resentful that MacArthur had delayed informing them of his invasion plans to a point where they had no alternative but to go along with it. Although an admirer of MacArthur, Vandenberg felt the U.N. commander's growing advocacy of military actions that would widen the war were ill advised. Consequently, he supported Truman's April 1951 decision to remove MacArthur.

In late 1950, following Chinese entrance into the war, and again in late 1951, Vandenberg seriously considered the advisability of U.S. withdrawal from the conflict. Such thinking and his concern with avoiding expansion of the war led to some criticism that he failed to give proper attention to the conduct of the war. Like many other commanders of the time, he never fully learned to deal with the new situations brought on by limited war. For example, Vandenberg and his staff never came up with new nighttime tactics to meet the Communists' ability to move supplies under cover of darkness. Sometimes he just moved slowly. Such was the case when he held a number of the new, badly needed, F-86 Sabre jets in the U.S. and Europe rather than commit them to Korea.

In spite of his shortcomings he was a popular and highly regarded chief of staff. His high standing among the administration, his peers, politicians, and the public rested upon unquestioned integrity, an ability to articulate the Air Force position, and interpersonal skills in dealing with subordinates and superiors. It was such factors, along with a desire to maintain continuity of leadership in wartime, that led the president to extend Vandenberg's appointment for two years, until 1953.

Early in 1952, as the stalemate continued and U.N. casualties mounted, Vandenberg became increasingly committed to intensifying the military pressure on the enemy in hopes of increasing their willingness to more seriously negotiate an end to the war. Prior to this time, he had been a strong advocate of interdiction, but he began urging action that would destroy the enemy's resources. Thus, in April, he convinced the JCS to bomb heretofore off-limits targets such as hydroelectric plants, oil refineries, and dams. It was therefore not surprising that in March of 1953, Vandenberg joined with the JCS to recommend to President Dwight D. Eisenhower the extensive use of strategic and tactical nuclear weapons to end the war. His new more belligerent tone was brought about in part by the frustration of a protracted war and a desire to end the war before he retired or before his cancer-ridden body gave out. On June 30, 1953, just four weeks before the cease-fire was signed, Vandenberg retired, and nine months later, April 4, 1954, he died in Washington, D.C.

Keith D. McFarland

Bibliography

Bradley, Omar, with Clay Blair. *A General's Life* (1983).

Condit, Doris M. *History of the Office of the Secretary of Defense, 2, The Test of War, 1950–53* (1988).

Meilinger, Phillip S. *Hoyt S. Vandenberg: The Life of a General* (1989).

Schnabel, James F., and Robert J. Watson. *The History of the Joint Chiefs of Staff: The Joint Chiefs of Staff and National Policy, 3, The Korean War* (1979).

Van Fleet, James A. (1892–1992)

James Alward Van Fleet was born in Coytesville, New Jersey, on March 19, 1892, and raised in Florida. He graduated from the United States Military Academy at West Point in 1915 and was commissioned as a second lieutenant of infantry. The following year he participated in the Mexican border campaign of 1916–1917. During World War I he commanded a machine gun battalion in the 6th Division and saw action in the Gerardmer sector and in the Meuse-Argonne offensive. In the interwar period, Van Fleet endured the round of peacetime assignments: teaching military science at Kansas State Agricultural College, South Dakota State College, and the University of Florida; he was a student and an instructor at the Infantry School, a unit instructor of the organized reserve at San Diego, California; commanded a battalion in the 42nd Infantry Regiment in Panama, served with the 5th Infantry Regiment at Fort Williams, Maine, commanded a battalion in the 29th Infantry Regiment; and, beginning in February 1941 with the rank of colonel, commanded the 8th Infantry Regiment.

Unlike his contemporaries, America's entry into World War II did not bring Van Fleet rapid promotion to general rank or high command. When Van Fleet had been at the Infantry School, George C. Marshall, then assistant commandant in charge of the academic department, had confused him with someone else who had a similar name and was a well-known alcoholic. Consequently, as Marshall's importance in the Army grew in the 1930s, culminating in his appointment as chief of staff in 1939, Van Fleet's career progression suffered. He was not selected either for the Command and General Staff College or the Army War College. The pattern continued after Pearl Harbor, so that in 1944 Van Fleet was still commanding the 8th Infantry with the rank of colonel. On D-Day he led the 8th Infantry, part of the 4th Division, ashore at Utah beach, Normandy, and several weeks later in the capture of Cherbourg, France. In these actions Van Fleet displayed courage under fire and demonstrated that he was a driving leader who got things done. Thereafter, with the confusion about his identity finally "cleared up" to Marshall's satisfaction, Van Fleet's rise was spectacular.

Promoted to the rank of brigadier general, Van Fleet was assistant commander of the 2nd Division during the St. Lo breakout and the capture of Brest, France, and commanded the 4th Division during the Siegfried Line campaign and the 90th Division during the operation to capture Metz, France, and the Battle of the Bulge. In March 1945, Van Fleet, now holding the rank of major general, assumed command of the III Corps, leading it through the American First Army's encirclement of the Ruhr pocket in Germany and the American Third Army's drive into Austria. By the end of the war, General Dwight D. Eisenhower, supreme commander of the Allied Expeditionary Force, regarded Van Fleet as one of the "greatest fighting" soldiers in his command.

Immediately following the war Van Fleet held several commands in the United States, and in 1947 he was transferred to the European command in Frankfurt, Germany. In February 1948, he was appointed director of the Joint U.S. Military Advisory and Planning Group in Athens, Greece, with the responsibility for advising the Greek government in its struggle against Communist insurgents. Soon after, he was promoted to the rank of lieutenant general and named a member of the Greek National Defense Council. During the next two years Van Fleet struggled to turn the Greek Army into an effective fighting force, overseeing its training, organization, and operations. On his recommendation incompetent officers were sacked, more maneuver battalions created, and aggressive offensive actions undertaken. Backed by massive American aid and assisted by the faulty tactics of the insurgents and the decision of Marshal Josip Tito of Yugoslavia to close the Yugoslav-Greek border through which the insurgents were supplied, the Greek Army, in a personal triumph for Van Fleet, had completely routed the Communists by the end of 1949.

After duty as commander of the Second Army in the United States, Van Fleet was sent to Korea in April 1951 to command the American Eighth Army as the replacement for General Matthew B. Ridgway, who had succeeded General Douglas MacArthur as Far East commander. The Eighth Army was more or less straddling the 38th parallel. Van Fleet arrived just as the Chinese Communists and the North Koreans were preparing to launch their single greatest military effort of the Korean War. In a fierce battle that lasted from April 22 to April 29 he skillfully withdrew the Eighth Army's front line, shifted the IX and X Corps to prevent an enemy breakthrough to Seoul, and inflicted 70,000 casualties on the enemy. Following the rebuff of another Communist attack in May, Van Fleet took the offensive and inflicted 200,000 casualties on the Communists in a drive north of the 38th parallel to the Iron Triangle area of North Korea. There General Ridgway concluded that a deeper advance into North Korea would be too costly, and had Van Fleet construct fortifications on the "Kansas" and "Wyoming" lines while the U.N. command pursued cease-fire talks. Van Fleet later complained that he had the Communists on the run in June 1951 and that he could have won the war by advancing to the Yalu River if he had not been halted. In this complaint he was expressing the frustration of a blunt soldier who saw victory and defeat in absolute terms. In fact, the Eighth Army probably did not possess the strength to advance even as far as Pyongyang, North Korea; and if it did, the price in casualties would have been too high considering the likely results. Notwithstanding his later statement, Van Fleet in June 1951 recognized that further advances were neither desirable nor feasible and agreed with Ridgway's decision to stand on the Kansas and Wyoming lines.

In August 1951 Van Fleet, recently promoted to full general, launched a limited offensive in eastern Korea after truce talks had stalled; and after two months of bitter fighting, he seized Heartbreak Ridge and Bloody Ridge. He followed up this offensive with another limited offensive in central Korea in October. Van Fleet's offensives inflicted heavy casualties on the Communists but at a high cost in U.N. casualties as well. When truce talks resumed, Ridgway in November 1951 ordered Van Fleet to cease offensive action and emphasize an active defense of the existing front line.

During 1952, Van Fleet chafed under the restrictions placed on him by the Truman administration's commitment to a limited war strategy in Korea. Seeing no point in fighting battles for the same hills and concerned about the combat readiness of his army, he produced plans for a major offensive. But Ridgway and his successor, General Mark Clark, saw little profit in such an operation. As a result, except for costly limited attacks in the Iron Triangle area in the summer and fall, Van Fleet engaged only in small-scale actions and artillery duels. Relying heavily on firepower to minimize his own casualties, he demanded greatly increased ammunition allowances. However, inadequate domestic production and resupply problems forced him to ration ammunition, and later he complained that he had been handicapped by shortages. Despite his differences with his superiors, Van Fleet was an able army commander. By constantly working to keep the Eighth Army at peak fighting efficiency, he maintained it as an effective and reliable force capable of delivering devastating blows against the Communists.

Van Fleet likewise worked to revitalize the South Korean Army. He started new training programs and pressed for its expansion to prepare it for offensive action. In the process he made it into a formidable fighting force and was recognized by the South Koreans as the "father" of their army. To the chagrin of many of his colleagues, Van Fleet also strongly identified with the authoritarian government of South Korean President Syngman Rhee and its opposition to the truce talks and the repatriation of prisoners and its desire to unify Korea militarily.

Grieving over the loss of his son, an Air Force pilot who was shot down while on a mission over North Korea in 1952, and embittered by the strategy of limited war in Korea followed by the Truman administration and then by President Eisenhower's administration, Van Fleet relinquished his command of the Eighth Army in February 1953, and two months later retired from the Army. On his return to the United States he sparked controversy by charging that he had been denied the opportunity to achieve total victory in Korea by political decisions in Washington, D.C., and by the failure of Washington to provide him with adequate quantities of ammunition. These charges aroused the interest of politicians who believed that Communists must be firmly defeated everywhere, but they were strongly challenged by Ridgway, Army chief of staff General Joseph L. Collins, and Lieutenant General Maxwell Taylor, Van Fleet's replacement with the Eighth Army. In 1954, Van Fleet served as Eisen-hower's special ambassador to the Far East, and in 1961–1962 he was a consultant on guerrilla warfare for the office of the secretary of the Army. Quiet, self-assured, Van Fleet stands out for his record as a combat commander and for his achievements in Greece and Korea.

John Kennedy Ohl

Bibliography

Blair, Clay. *The Forgotten War: America in Korea, 1950–1953* (1987).

Hermes, Walter G. *Truce Tent and Fighting Front, United States Army in the Korean War* (Office of the Chief of Military History, Washington: 1966).

Mossman, Billy. *Ebb and Flow: November 1950–July 1951*, United States Army in the Korean War (Center of Military History, Washington: 1990).

Schnable, James P. *Policy and Direction: The First Year* (Office of the Chief of Military History, Washington: 1972).

Veterans of the Korean War

Like all veterans of foreign wars, those returning home to the U.S. from Korea faced the usual problems of postwar readjustment: finding a job, getting reacquainted with family and friends after a long absence, trying to make the often difficult transition from soldier to civilian. However, the 6.8 million Korean-era veterans also confronted new challenges that differentiated them from those who had been demobilized to near-unanimous acclaim after World

Wars I and II. Concluding not with decisive victory but with inconclusive armistice, the Korean War elicited disturbing accusations that U.S. servicemen, particularly those who had been held as prisoners of war (POWs), had somehow failed to uphold the highest standards of moral and military resolve. As a result, the attitude of the American public was often skeptical, and even occasionally antagonistic, casting the returning Korean veteran as the war's unfortunate scapegoat.

When large numbers of Korean veterans first started to arrive home in the spring of 1953, there were few indications that they would be treated any differently from their predecessors. The docking in New York on April 3 of the first Korean War troopship, for instance, produced a homecoming unmistakably reminiscent of 1945: khaki-clad soldiers crowding the ship's rails, thousands thronging the docks below, and a confetti-strewn parade up Broadway to city hall. However, in the same issue of the *New York Times* that headlined these events, a short five-paragraph story expressed fears that American soldiers captured in Korea had been converted by Communist "brain-washers" to espouse the cause of the enemy. Not long afterward, when some 4,000 American POWs were repatriated in mid-1953, the accusations of brainwashing were compounded by charges that these U.S. fighting men were fundamentally different from the celebrated heroes of World War II who had licked the Germans and Japanese. The popular press suggested that the new veterans lacked courage, pride, esprit de corps, discipline, assertiveness, individualism, and traditional American toughness. Even the non-POWs were characterized as robot-like conformists, unusually docile and indifferent to their surroundings, seemingly unfazed by their wartime experiences. Not surprisingly, the public responded with apathy at best and hostility at worst.

Perhaps the most damaging allegation was that no other veterans in American history had ever been so weak-willed and dishonorable. As articulated by journalist Eugene Kinkhead and psychiatrist William E. Mayer, the moral breakdown of American troops in Korea was "something new in history," an odious stain that had never before tarnished the United States. They pointed to the fact that twenty-one American soldiers had defected to the People's Republic of China at the time of the prisoner exchange; and they maintained that the failure of a single POW to escape from captivity was an unprec-

edented disgrace on the American national character. Although later studies were able to moderate considerably the conclusions of Kinkhead and Mayer, they did not receive nearly as much attention in the popular press. The public image of the Korean veteran as a vacillating turncoat was difficult to dislodge.

This negative image in the public mind was reinforced by relatively unflattering depictions of Korean veterans in popular film and literature. For instance, in the film *Niagara* (1953), George Loomis is a psychoneurotic Korean veteran recently released from a military mental hospital. Although battle-fatigued veterans like Loomis had been a cinematic staple since the 1920s, they had always been cured of their afflictions by the end of the film. In *Niagara*, however, the veteran is not only never rehabilitated, he descends even further into insanity, murdering his wife before being swept away by the titular falls. Other Korean veterans who similarly fail to live happily ever after include: the drug-addicted Johnny Pope in Michael V. Gazzo's *A Hatful of Rain* (1955), also a 1957 motion picture; Brick, suffering from severe emotional wounds, in *Five Against the House* (1955); Raymond Shaw, the programmed assassin, in Richard Condon's *The Manchurian Candidate* (1959), later a 1962 motion picture; the brainwashed Stuart, confined to a mental institution, in *Shock Corridor* (1963); and the alienated Vincent Bruce in *Lilith* (1964).

Not surprisingly, this negative popular image of Korean veterans was translated also into legislative and economic terms. For instance, when a new G.I. Bill of Rights for Korean veterans was passed by Congress in 1952, it provided for only three-fourths of the benefits awarded the veterans of World War II. Korean veterans, for example, did not qualify for any of the supplemental funds (up to $500 per year in the case of World War II veterans) for college tuition and books. Similarly, the long-standing failure to erect a Korean War veterans memorial in Washington seemed indicative of the relatively low regard in which Korean veterans have been held.

Although Vietnam veterans were accorded their own national memorial in 1982, it is interesting to note that the G.I. Bill for Vietnam veterans likewise excluded many of the supplemental benefits that a grateful nation in 1944 had awarded World War II veterans. Indeed, in many respects, the attitude of the public toward Korean veterans prefigured the treatment initially accorded servicemen returning from Viet-

V

nam. Yet, while the latter group was conspicu-
ously rehabilitated during the Reagan presidency as part of a general reassessment of the
war in Vietnam, most Korean veterans still
await their public redemption.

James I. Deutsch

Bibliography

Barrett, George. "Portrait of the Korean Vet-
eran," *New York Times Magazine*, 9
(August 1953).
Kinkhead, Eugene. *In Every War But One*
(1959).
Mattila, J. Peter. "G.I. Bill Benefits and En-
rollments: How Did Vietnam Veterans
Fare?" *Social Science Quarterly*, 59
(1978).
Severo, Richard, and Lewis Milford. *The
Wages of War: When America's Soldiers
Came Home—From Valley Forge to
Vietnam* (1989).
Wubben, H.H. "American Prisoners of War
in Korea: A Second Look at the 'Some-
thing New in History' Theme," *Ameri-
can Quarterly*, 22 (1970).

WAC

See WOMEN'S ARMY CORPS

Wake Island Conference (October 15, 1950)

This meeting between President Harry S. Truman and General Douglas MacArthur took place as U.N. forces, confident that complete victory was near, were advancing into North Korea. Writers have debated the reasons for the conference, advancing a number of explanations. First, Truman, who liked to travel, had never met MacArthur and may have wanted to gain a better understanding of the general. Second, MacArthur, in his VFW message, appeared to threaten the People's Republic of China. Concerned about the possibility of Chinese military intervention in Korea, Truman may have wanted to make clear to MacArthur that it was important to avoid further belligerent pronouncements. Third, Truman possibly was reacting to a recent U.S. air attack on a Soviet airfield sixty-two miles from the Korean border, and might have been anxious to prevent a repetition of the incident. Finally, Truman almost certainly had domestic politics in mind, specifically the upcoming congressional electoral campaign, when he traveled 18,000 miles to confer with MacArthur, who he had privately scorned as "God's righthand man." In fact, the idea for the meeting originated with the president's staff as a public relations move to offset the declining popularity of the president and the Democratic party that resulted from charges of treasonous behavior and the early battlefield reverses in Korea. At Wake, Truman could move into the spotlight shining on MacArthur as U.N. forces pushed on to the Yalu River and victory.

On October 14, 1950, Truman flew to California where he was joined by a few key advisors, including W. Averell Harriman, Philip C. Jessup, Dean Rusk, and General Omar N. Bradley. After a stopover in Hawaii, the presidential party flew on to Wake Island, but Truman refused to leave the plane until MacArthur, who had arrived the night before, appeared at the foot of the landing ramp. "General MacArthur," the president recalled sourly, "was at the airport with a shirt unbuttoned, wearing a greasy ham and eggs cap that evidently had been in use for twenty years." Although MacArthur resented being called away from Tokyo to provide Truman a political boost, he greeted the president warmly, but did not salute the commander in chief. Before the formal session, the two men drove to a quonset hut for a private meeting lasting about forty minutes. Later accounts from both men characterized the conversation as rambling and amicable, but the president later claimed that MacArthur "spent some time apologizing" for his VFW message. During the conference, MacArthur did not dissent when the president said that there was "no need to cover" the issue of Taiwan because the "General and I are in complete agreement."

At 7:36 A.M., the conferees gathered in a concrete and frame building where for just ninety-six minutes, in an informal and convivial atmosphere, they swiftly and superficially touched on an array of topics. There was no agenda and no one sought to probe deeply into any complicated questions. MacArthur stated that Korea's rehabilitation would require a three-year program costing $450 million, which was half the amount of the administration's projections. John J. Muccio, the U.S. ambassador to the Republic of Korea who had accompanied MacArthur to Wake, concurred, also stating that reunification would present no problems because "Koreans are Koreans." Truman agreed with MacArthur and Muccio that the U.S. should support the legitimacy of the Republic of Korea and a direct role for President Syngman Rhee's government in the reconstruction of North Korea. In reply to the president's question about the chances of Chinese or Soviet intervention, MacArthur exuded confidence: "Very little. Had they interfered in the first or second months it would have been decisive. . . . We no longer stand hat in hand." Because the U.N. had command of the air, he said, "if the Chinese tried to get down to Pyongyang, there would be the greatest slaughter." By Thanksgiving, all resistance in North Korea would end before the Soviets had time to move troops into a position to intervene.

Before the meeting ended at 9:12 A.M., MacArthur told Bradley that since the Eighth Army would be in Japan by Christmas, the Joint Chiefs of Staff could redeploy one division in Europe during January 1951. After voicing opposition to war crimes trials, MacArthur spoke in favor of an early peace treaty for the Japanese and stronger measures to defeat the Communists in Indochina. Truman suggested that everyone should leave after lunch, but agreed to an earlier departure after the general said that he was anxious to return to Tokyo. In closing the meeting, Truman declared: "This has been a most satisfactory conference." The president's staff people then prepared a wordy and vacuous communique and, after pinning a fourth oak leaf cluster on MacArthur's Distinguished Service Medal and a Medal of Merit on Muccio, Truman took off at 11:35 A.M. for Hawaii and the United States. Clearly, the Wake Island Conference did not constitute a serious attempt to deal with major questions of policy. When Rusk slipped Truman a note during the meeting questioning the rapid and shallow nature of the discussions, the president responded that the quicker the session was over the better. Later, MacArthur's assurances that China would not enter the war made Wake Island infamous. However, the general had merely confirmed prevailing opinion in Washington that victory in the Korean War was at hand.

James I. Matray

Bibliography

Donovan, R.J. *Tumultuous Years: The Presidency of Harry S. Truman, 1949–1953* (1982).

Foreign Relations of the United States, 1950, VII: *Korea* (1976).

Kaufman, B.I. *The Korean War: Challenges in Crisis, Credibility and Command* (1986).

Spanier, J.W. *The Truman-MacArthur Controversy and the Korean War* (1959).

Wilz, J.E. "Truman and MacArthur: The Wake Island Meeting," *Military Affairs,* 4 (1978).

Walker, Walton H. (1889–1950)

General Walton Harris Walker was the commander of the Eighth Army in the early part of the Korean War conflict and successfully conducted the defense of the Pusan perimeter. A native of Belton, Texas, Walker entered Victoria Military Institute (VMI) in 1907 and later transferred to the U.S. Military Academy at West Point, graduating in 1912. He was awarded the Silver Star medal for bravery in action during World War I.

During the interim war years Walker held a variety of assignments. In 1924, he married Caroline Victoria Emerson of Baltimore and they had a son, Sam Sims, who graduated from West Point in 1946. Walton Walker excelled in the training of troops and held a number of progressive training positions prior to World War II. He also had picked up the nickname of "Johnnie Walker," derived from a brand of scotch whiskey he favored. He assumed command of the 3rd Armored Division in early 1942. During World War II he was a protégé of General George S. Patton and rose to the rank of lieutenant general (brevet). Walker was also awarded the Distinguished Service Cross, the Army's second highest award for valor. He was well respected by Patton and he developed a reputation as a tough leader and fighter.

After World War II he filled several assignments before taking command of the Eighth Army, which was performing occupation duty in Japan. There he obtained his permanent promotion to major general. The Eighth Army was composed of four divisions, the 1st Cavalry, 7th, 24th, and 25th Infantry Divisions. The combat readiness of the Eighth Army had declined due to congressionally imposed postwar budget and personnel cuts. The troops were largely undertrained, lacked sufficient equipment, and had grown soft with the relaxed pace of their occupation duty. Only 10 percent of the soldiers had combat experience. Despite the cuts, which were largely beyond his control,

Walker instituted a massive training program toward the latter part of 1949 to upgrade the combat readiness of the Eighth Army. Unfortunately, the training exercises and programs were too late to adequately prepare the occupation forces with the combat skills they would desperately need in the coming months.

The Korean War broke out on June 25, 1950, with a massive multi-front attack by the North Korean Army across the 38th parallel, an artificial border which divided North and South Korea. On June 30, General Walker received his battle orders formally committing his forces to the Korean conflict. On July 13, Walker was placed in charge of all U.S. Army forces in Korea, and four days later was also put in charge of all South Korean forces. General Walker's initial orders were to engage the North Korean Army as far north as possible and defeat them. It was commonly thought that the North Koreans would turn and run once they ran into American soldiers. Walker, on the contrary, was under no illusions about the capabilities of the Eighth Army. However, he had already run afoul of his superior, General Douglas MacArthur, and was in no position to question the orders he had received.

By July, with the fall of Taejon, it was apparent to General Walker that the Eighth Army would be forced to pull back even further. He feared for the safety of his own command post in Taegu, the nerve center of the perimeter defense. By late July his forces equaled in numbers the invading North Korean Army, although many of his troops were engaged in supply and support roles. However, the quality of the Allied forces remained deficient and the North Koreans held the initiative. Walker had the unenviable task of conducting a delaying action with his Eighth Army until sufficient forces could be built up to launch a counteroffensive into the North Korean Army's rear area. By now his perimeter had shrunk to an area roughly fifty miles wide by one hundred miles in length from north to south. This became known as the "Pusan perimeter."

One critical advantage General Walker possessed was that his military intelligence assets had broken the North Korean radio codes. Thus Walker knew every major North Korean movement prior to its occurrence. He had his major units deployed on the front lines, yet kept a mobile reserve that could be rushed in to plug any local breakthrough. His ability to read the enemy's radio traffic enabled Walker to rush reinforcements to where they were needed on short notice. Often Walker could be found at the front line personally appraising the battle situation and issuing orders to local commanders. He told one commander that he only wanted to see him behind the lines in his coffin!

After numerous battle debacles and more than a hundred miles of retreating, the Eighth Army's morale was low. During a conference in Taegu with General MacArthur, it was determined that there could no longer be any retreating by the Eighth Army. Shortly after the meeting, on July 29, General Walker issued his famed "Stand or Die" order to the beleaguered defenders of the Pusan perimeter. This command was timely, for an all-out North Korean offensive was launched against the perimeter in five different spots on September 1. General Walker's use of Marines and U.S. Army troops as a fire brigade to contain any North Korean breakthrough proved to be a sound strategy, and forestalled a forced withdrawal from the Korean peninsula.

General Walker's holding mission was part of the overall strategy of General MacArthur. MacArthur's plan was to launch a flanking attack deep behind enemy lines at the port of Inchon. The Inchon landing took place on September 15. General Walker planned his own breakout attack from the perimeter for September 16. By that time Walker felt that the North Korean forces would be demoralized with the knowledge that the landings had effectively cut off their lines of supply and retreat. Unfortunately for Walker, the North Korean soldiers had not heard of the Inchon landing and instead launched their own attack, which stalled the American breakout attempt in the Waegwan area. To top it off, the weather was overcast, preventing the use of close air support. Ultimately, the North Korean resistance began to crumble and the weather cleared, which allowed the employment of air assets. General Walker's forces gained the initiative on the northern, northwestern, and western fronts with successive assaults against the crumbling North Korean Army. While the South Korean Army led the attack up the eastern seaboard, the 1st Cavalry Division and others attacked up the main highway leading roughly northwest toward Taejon and recaptured the city. On September 27 the linkup with the 7th Division which had landed at Inchon was completed just north of Osan, approximately twenty miles south of Seoul. Of the approximately 100,000 North Korean soldiers surrounding the Pusan perimeter only 25,000 to 30,000 are believed to have ever made it back to North Korea.

General Walker continued leading the Eighth Army in its attack across the 38th parallel into North Korea. The capture of the North Korean capital of Pyongyang was completed on October 20. On October 24, General Walker established his advance headquarters in North Korean Premier Kim Il Sung's abandoned headquarters building. As the Eighth Army moved north there arose a dispute between political and military forces in Washington, which wanted to limit the war, and General MacArthur, who wanted to carry the attack to complete victory.

In October 1950, Chinese soldiers were encountered for the first time north of Unsan in North Korea. Despite mounting evidence of increasing resistance, General MacArthur hinted that American troops would begin returning home by Christmas, much to the consternation of General Walker. This belief of an early victory was so widespread that several United Nations members held back some of the troops they had earmarked for the Korean campaign.

This optimistic view would change quickly as the situation on the northern front lines rapidly deteriorated. In a series of vicious firefights the Eighth Army was stalled in its tracks and put on the defensive. MacArthur optimistically (or perhaps naively) ordered General Walker to press on with the attack toward the Yalu River despite the increasingly hostile weather, numerous supply shortages, and evidence of massive Chinese intervention.

General Walker was reluctant to blindly press on with the attack at this point of the war, notwithstanding his past association with George S. Patton. He increasingly feared Chinese intervention and he had no illusions of a quick victory. Walker prudently delayed resuming the offensive while he tried to replace his personnel losses and build up his logistical supplies. He expressed fear of being forced to conduct a general retreat. His prudent delaying of the offensive gained him enemies in MacArthur's Tokyo headquarters. Compounding Walker's problems was the separation of his command from the X Corps, which was on the eastern flank of the Korean peninsula and commanded by the impetuous Major General Edward M. Almond. The Taebek mountain range effectively split the Eighth Army under Walker from General Almond's X Corps which consisted of U.S. Marines, the 7th Army Division

and South Korean Army forces. Walker's right flank was exposed to the inhospitable Taebaek mountain range. This same mountain terrain was simultaneously being used by the Chinese to infiltrate thousands of troops to the flanks of the Eighth Army.

General Walker finally launched the offensive that was designed to take the Eighth Army from beyond the narrow waist of the Korean peninsula all the way to the Chinese border on the Yalu River. Initially there was little resistance but then the hidden, massed Chinese forces struck. On November 25, 1950, the Chinese launched a massive attack on the right flank, which was held by the South Korean Army. In a matter of hours three entire South Korean Army divisions were routed and Walker's right flank ceased to exist. By November 26 the battle situation verged on disaster, with the survival of Walker's entire Eighth Army threatened.

Shortly thereafter, Walker attended a conference in Tokyo with MacArthur. The conclusion of the meeting was that Walker's Eighth Army would withdraw to the south to avoid being totally outflanked by the Chinese. The withdrawal of the Eighth Army was a mixed story of success and disaster. The 24th and 25th Divisions withdrew in relatively intact condition. The 2nd Division suffered severe losses in personnel and equipment.

General Walker withdrew from Pyongyang and moved his Eighth Army steadily southward toward the 38th parallel. He conducted a series of delaying actions in the face of the numerically superior Chinese. By this time Walker had fallen out of favor with his superiors, including Douglas MacArthur, and was being considered for replacement. There had already been suggestions at higher levels as early as the previous August during the Pusan perimeter battles that Walker be replaced.

By early December, Walker had moved his Eighth Army south of the 38th parallel and prepared for the expected Chinese invasion. He continued his habit of speeding from unit to unit, meeting with commanders and troops to assess the overall situation. On December 22, 1950, Walker was killed in an accident while trying to pass a stalled column of South Korean Army vehicles near Seoul. He had been on his way to an awards ceremony to decorate soldiers of his Eighth Army. General Walton H. Walker was buried in Arlington National Cemetery.

David Kangas

Bibliography

Appleman, R.E. *South to the Naktong, North to the Yalu* (GPO, Washington: 1961).

Blair, Clay. *The Forgotten War: America in Korea 1950–1953* (1987).

Goulden, J.C. *Korea: The Untold Story of the War* (1982).

Haynes, R.S. "Walton Harris Walker," in *Dictionary of American Military Biography*, R.J. Spiller and J.G. Dawson III, eds. (1984), pp. 1153–1156.

Robertson, W.G. *Counterattack on the Naktong* (Combat Studies Institute, Fort Leavenworth, KS: 1950).

Rothe, A.R. "Walton H. Walker," *Current Biography, Who's News and Why* (1950).

Whitney, Courtney (1897–1969)

The son of a United States Department of Agriculture official, Courtney Whitney was born in Takoma Park, Maryland, on May 20, 1897. In 1917 he enlisted as a private in the aviation section of the Army Signal Corps reserve, and the following year was commissioned a second lieutenant. Commissioned in the regular Army in 1920, Whitney served with the Army Air Corps at airfields in Louisiana, Mississippi, the District of Columbia, and the Philippines, and earned a law degree from National University in Washington, D.C., before resigning his commission in 1927 to practice law in Manila. By 1940, he had developed a very profitable corporate practice, forged ties with many influential Filipinos, and become friends with General Douglas MacArthur, commander of the United States Army Philippines Division from 1928 to 1930 and military adviser to the Philippine Commonwealth government from 1935 to 1941.

In 1940, Whitney was commissioned a major in the Officers Reserve Corps and appointed assistant chief of the legal division of the Army Air Forces. Still assigned to that branch after the United States entered World War II in December 1941 he became a member of MacArthur's "Bataan Gang." He was later named assistant judge advocate of the Army Air Forces in February 1943. Later that year, MacArthur had Whitney transferred to his Southwest Pacific area headquarters to lead the Philippine regional section, which was responsible for promoting guerrilla activities in the Philippines. After American forces returned to the Philippines in the fall of 1944, Whitney became chief of the civil affairs section and as-

sisted Filipino officials in restoring government to the liberated islands. Capable, hard working, and above all loyal, Whitney impressed MacArthur with his intellect and achievements in these posts, and by the end of the war, Whitney, now a brigadier general, had emerged as MacArthur's closest advisor and confidant. Others were not as impressed with Whitney, and many colleagues were jealous of his special relationship with MacArthur. MacArthur's enemies in the press regarded him as abrasive, aloof, opportunistic, lickspittle, and pompous, not to mention stupid.

Following the war Whitney was at MacArthur's side during the reconstruction of Japan, heading the powerful government section of MacArthur's headquarters (SCAP, or Supreme Commander Allied Powers) in Tokyo, Japan. Putting together an able staff of civilian and military experts, he purged militarists and ultranationalists from Japanese public life, advised the Japanese on the revision of their statutes, and implemented a host of administrative, civil service, electoral, fiscal, and police reforms. At the same time, he became absolutely essential to MacArthur, representing him to the press, advising him, listening to him, anticipating his every need, and reading and reacting to situations as he would himself. In effect, Whitney was MacArthur's alter ego.

After the outbreak of the Korean War in June 1950, Whitney was appointed military secretary of MacArthur's United Nations command. He went with MacArthur on all of his trips to Korea and in October 1950 accompanied MacArthur to Wake Island for the general's famous meeting with President Harry S. Truman. When Truman fired MacArthur in April 1951, Whitney returned to the United States with the general and sat with him as his counsel and advisor during the Senate's inquiry into MacArthur's relief and Truman's Far Eastern policy.

At the end of May 1951 Whitney retired from the Army with the permanent rank of major general to serve as MacArthur's personal secretary. Following MacArthur even into civilian life, the next year he joined Remington Rand as MacArthur's assistant after the general was named chairman of the board. The two men remained inseparable until MacArthur's death in 1964. During these years Whitney was MacArthur's most outspoken defender whenever controversy enveloped the general. In 1956, he published *MacArthur: His Rendezvous With History*, a hagiography which covered MacArthur's career from 1941 to 1951 and earned him a considerable sum of money, but which was not well received by reviewers. Whitney died in Washington on May 21, 1969.

John Kennedy Ohl

Bibliography

James, D. Clayton. *The Years of MacArthur, 3, Triumph and Disaster, 1945–1964* (1985).

Manchester, William. *American Caesar: Douglas MacArthur, 1880–1964* (1978).

Whitney, Courtney. *MacArthur: His Rendezvous with History* (1956).

Wildes, Harry E. *Typhoon in Tokyo* (1956).

Willoughby, Charles A. (1882–1972)

The man destined to serve as MacArthur's G-2 (intelligence) from 1941 throughout the Korean War was born in Heidelberg, Germany, in 1882, the son of an American mother and a German aristocrat named Tscheppe-Weidenbach. Willoughby was, however, a "man of deliberately vague origins" who variously claimed to be the son of a German baron or a refugee from some sort of unspecified persecution. (Only in 1951 did a *Reporter* magazine staffer discover that Willoughby was in fact the illegitimate son of a ropemaker.) In 1910, Willoughby came to the U.S. and entered the U.S. Army as Private Adolph Charles Weidenbach. Shortly thereafter he won a commission and changed his name to Charles A. Willoughby. When he and MacArthur first met in the mid-1930s, Willoughby was a captain teaching military history at the command of General Staff School, Ft. Leavenworth, Kansas. Shortly before Pearl Harbor, MacArthur summoned Willoughby to the Philippines, and made the Spanish and Japanese-speaking officer, known as "Sir Charles" for his pomposity, his intelligence chief.

MacArthur would have searched in vain for a more loyal staff officer than Willoughby. MacArthur had the greatest confidence in his G-2, a member of the so-called Bataan Gang, described as "a loyal inner circle of admirers . . . whose unquestioning adulation might serve to shield him [MacArthur] from unpleasant realities." This so-called MacArthur factor was to play a major role in the type of intelligence Willoughby produced for MacArthur. One authority has noted, "Willoughby was the ideal man to be MacArthur's G-2. He knew exactly what MacArthur wanted to hear, and he told him exactly that, and no more." A man of strong opinions seldom sidetracked by the facts, Willoughby excelled at writing the "baroque communiques" favored by MacArthur. Drawn by Willoughby's research skills and experience, MacArthur had already commissioned him to write a four-volume history of the Pacific war; thus, as colleagues noted, Willoughby often spent as much time ghostwriting as he did doing intelligence work. Besides a love for history, Willoughby and MacArthur also shared a distrust of nontraditional means of intelligence collection, i.e., the CIA's penchant for the use of covert agents to provide intelligence. They instead preferred the more traditional intelligence provided by attaches, prisoners of war (POWs), and captured enemy documents. As Clay Blair has concluded concerning this curious relationship between MacArthur and Willoughby, "Willoughby basked in the reflected glory and genius of his commander. Willoughby's views thus powerfully influenced those of the entire intelligence community in the Far East Command. A challenge to Willoughby's views was tantamount to a challenge to MacArthur; no one in the intelligence community was willing to undertake that challenge."

Willoughby has often been charged with bungling his G-2 duties during the Korean War, especially concerning Chinese intervention. However, scholars have pointed to Willoughby's limited sources of intelligence information as a partial explanation for the flawed intelligence provided. One source of information was the Korean Liaison Office, a surveillance detachment Willoughby had created on his own initiative before the Korean War. As early as 30 December 1949, Willoughby, now a brigadier general, sent several reports to Washington indicating the possibility of a North Korean invasion of South Korea in March or April 1950; however, Willoughby's personal opinion was that such was unlikely. On 19 February 1950, Willoughby passed on two agent reports, also discounted, one predicting a North Korean invasion in March, another in June. On 10 March the Korean Liaison Office sent Willoughby an agent's report stating that the North Korean timetable had been delayed, and it would be June before the invasion occurred. However, later that month, Willoughby predicted that there would be no civil war in Korea; a more likely scenario, he claimed, would involve continued psychological and guerrilla warfare directed against the Seoul government. It should be noted that in drawing such a conclusion, Willoughby was hardly alone—State Department and CIA analysts in Tokyo had also concluded that any type of North Korean military action in the summer of 1950 was unlikely. The formal means used by Willoughby to disseminate whatever intelligence information he uncovered was the Daily Intelligence Summary (DIS), issued from Far East command, Tokyo, to the Pentagon, to Allied liaison officers in Tokyo, and to the United Nations General Assembly. Though described by one authority as "a conglomeration of rumor, speculation, and unevaluated bits and pieces of information," a careful reading of the DIS still pointed strongly toward a North Korean attack.

When North Korean forces did invade the South on Sunday, 25 June 1950, Willoughby allayed the fears of U.S. Army Chief of Staff General J. Lawton Collins and Deputy Chief of Staff Lieutenant General Matthew B. Ridgway in an optimistic report which admitted that a major invasion of the South was underway, but pointed out that the Republic of Korea army was withdrawing in good order, that morale was still relatively high, and that the Rhee government was stable. Willoughby did add in his report, however, that as a precaution, American women and children in South Korea were being evacuated from Inchon by ship, with naval and air protection. The fact that at the time two North Korean divisions were threatening an important road junction at Uijongbu, and that there were forty tanks reported within five km of the city was either unknown or unmentioned. Collected and promptly dismissed was another classic attack indicator which noted that since early 1950 there had been a mass exodus of all families living within two miles north of the 38th parallel. As the G-2, however, Willoughby was able to explain it away. He believed the presence and danger of North Korean mines planted along the border, the need for troop billets, the inability to farm under the circumstances, and the fear of armed conflict had prompted this hasty exodus. Willoughby admitted that he had heard of invasion threats and that the North Koreans were certainly capable of attacking, yet still believed none of these factors were strong enough to justify an invasion threat warning.

The earliest mention of possible Chinese intervention in the Korean conflict came with the publication of the 31 August 1950 issue of the DIS, which suggested that Chinese Communist troop movements into Manchuria over a period of time might be "preliminary to entering the Korean theater." A U.S. I Corps attack on 9 October 1950 as U.N. forces rolled toward North Korea prompted saber rattling from the Chinese, but was largely ignored by Willoughby and others. By early October Willoughby estimated that there were thirty-eight regular Chinese Communist divisions, approximately 300,000 troops, in Manchuria, twenty-four divisions of which were massed at crossing points along the Yalu River. Yet Willoughby once again hedged his bets by describing these troop movements as "probably in the category of diplomatic blackmail." He further closed the door on an expansion of the conflict when he added that the Chinese and Soviets "have decided against further expensive investment in support of a lost cause . . . The Chinese Communists, if called upon, would furnish replacements through discreet integration with Korean units." While Willoughby argued that the Kremlin's unwillingness to go to war was the key factor in keeping Soviet and Chinese ground forces out of the conflict, U.S. naval intelligence analysts, with access to the same data, had come to the exact opposite conclusion—namely that Chinese ground forces had *already* been committed in North Korea.

Willoughby's principal source of information here was the Nationalist Chinese on Formosa (Taiwan). While one author has described their information as "relatively accurate," Willoughby had no network of native agents to confirm or deny any Yalu River crossing. Furthermore, aerial reconnaissance was useless since Chinese Communist forces hid during the day, moving primarily at night. Even had the Communists been more cooperative, the Air Force had not one photo interpreter to evaluate the data.

Willoughby's DIS of 28 October 1950 implied that the most auspicious time for Chinese intervention had passed, and then commented that Chinese Communist forces (CCF) had had no combat experience against a major power, and that their training was hampered by a diversity of equipment and an intermittent ammunition supply. However, Willoughby's low opinion of CCF may well have been influenced more by racial prejudice than by military intelligence information. As U.S. ambassador to South Korea John J. Muccio noted, Willoughby was "full of disdain for the capabilities of the Chinese, of all classes." Even as evidence of Chinese intervention continued to pile up, Willoughby persisted in viewing the conflict through rose-colored glasses. In late October Willoughby stated that while a North Korean surrender was unlikely, "Organized resistance on any large scale has ceased to be an enemy capability."

The very next day Willoughby's daydream was rudely interrupted when an entire ROK corps was routed by three full Chinese field armies. Willoughby's only response was that "an unknown number of Chinese . . . were incorporated into North Korean units to assist in the defense of border areas." Because of few POWs and conflicting information, no other conclusions could be drawn. Yet the disquieting voices continued. A U.S. Eighth Army report dated 27 October announced the capture of two CCF soldiers who claimed a massive Chinese intervention in Korea was underway. Yet Willoughby primly concluded that their stories were "unconfirmed and therefore unaccepted." Two days later Willoughby had the opportunity to personally interrogate sixteen other CCF POWs. While he admitted that they were indeed Chinese, he dismissed them as possible stragglers or volunteers, of no real significance. Thus Willoughby could conclude in his report covering 16–31 October to the U.N. Security Council, "There is no positive evidence that Chinese Communist units, *as such* (emphasis added), have entered Korea." Even as late as 31 October the most Willoughby would admit was that "greater credence must be given" to reports of Chinese intervention.

Willoughby's Pollyanna pronouncements failed to convince MacArthur's field commanders, however. There had been serious questions in their minds ever since the first CCF prisoner had been taken on 25 October, and the number of Chinese prisoners continued to grow, to fifty-five by 2 November. To calm the fears of his skittish colleagues, Willoughby flew to South Korea in early November. He promptly dismissed the Chinese presence as "no more than a battalion of troops from each of the (Chinese) units identified." On 2 November Chinese authorities acknowledged the presence of their troops in Korea, but described them as volunteers. Puzzled, Willoughby warned Washington, already uneasy, that if the Chinese opted for full intervention, they could quickly commit twenty-nine of their forty-four divisions currently along the Yalu. The prospect of approximately 232,000 CCF troops with 150 aircraft in support commanded Washington's undivided attention.

Ironically, as Willoughby's sense of disquiet grew, MacArthur's optimism expanded, especially as Chinese attacks stalled. Yet even as MacArthur planned a new offensive in the first half of November, Willoughby, grudgingly admitting Chinese intervention and its dangers, now believed that the Chinese were intent upon full prosecution of the war. He correctly reasoned that with the war at the frontier, Chinese supply lines would be much shorter than previously, and on 15 November warned that there were still nearly 300,000 seasoned Chinese troops north of the Yalu who, given their abilities to move at night using back roads, could suddenly appear on the battlefield. In short, Chinese forces in early November exhibited all the classic attack indicators, which Willoughby and his staff now belatedly recognized, but which continued to be ignored by MacArthur.

If the reality of Chinese intervention in the war came only slowly to Willoughby, the numbers of those troops he believed were actually involved came equally slowly. For example, on 3 November, in the face of ever-increasing CCF attacks, Willoughby upgraded his estimate of Chinese intervention from 16,000 to 34,000, a figure which, as one authority notes, was "wildly off the mark"; a more accurate figure was 300,000 or more. Not until 24 November was Willoughby inclined to raise his estimate to "at least 41,000," with a figure of 71,000 added as insurance. On that same day, by means unknown to and understood by virtually no one, Willoughby confidently proclaimed that U.N. forces were facing exactly 82,799 North Korean soldiers. Even worse, Willoughby passed his bizarre figures on to field commanders, who at least partially based their tactical decisions on these figures. Thus, based on Willoughby's (and other) estimates, U.S. Eighth Army commander General Walton H. Walker believed he was facing an enemy force of about 50,000, about evenly divided between CCF and NKPA (North Korean People's Army) forces. Had this estimate been accurate, Walker would have had a numerical superiority of about 2:1. The truth, however, was almost exactly the reverse—the enemy facing Walker may well have numbered about 203,000, nearly twice the Eighth Army's strength. Willoughby got closest to the truth when on 31 December, still somehow able to estimate enemy forces to the last man, he estimated that U.N. forces were faced by a total Communist force of 443,406 men, broken down into 276,173 Chinese and 167,233 North Koreans, with 650,000 Chinese reinforcements believed to be in Manchuria, and 250,000 more believed to be en route.

Ever since the war, Willoughby has been blamed for steadfastly underestimating the presence, number, and danger of enemy forces facing U.N. forces in Korea. Yet, as noted, Willoughby suffered from a lack of extensive intelligence sources. Also, he was certainly not alone within the intelligence community in his threat assessments. Even after the first CCF POWs were taken, there were many doubters, Willoughby chief among them, who denied that the tiger by the tail was the CCF. Willoughby argued, not illogically, that if the CCF were going to intervene, they would have done so before the NKPA forces had been routed and before the Eighth Army had gone on full offensive with its naval and air support. Or, as Willoughby put it on another occasion, "Was Communist China prepared to take the stunning gamble of throwing its ground forces into war against a country possessing the atom bomb and complete air control of the campaign area?"

Yet, in the final analysis, it is difficult to exonerate Willoughby of responsibilities for the intelligence failures of the Korean War. As one authority has concluded, part of the problem with intelligence collection in Korea was "a lack of competent leadership." While Willoughby only reflected the attitude of his mentor, MacArthur, in the words of X Corps G-3 Colonel Jack Chiles—"MacArthur did not *want* the Chinese to enter the war in Korea. Anything MacArthur wanted, Willoughby produced intelligence for . . . In this case, Willoughby falsified the intelligence reports . . . He should have gone to jail." Ambassador Muccio described Willoughby as one of two key men vying for MacArthur's favors, and a man who prevented MacArthur from getting the intelligence he had to have in order to make the right decisions. Finally, General J. Lawton Collins, Army chief of staff, concluded, "Willoughby was wishy-wishy—back and forth as to whether he thought that the Chinese were going to come in or not come in. There's no question about it: he gave MacArthur, in my judgment, poor G-2 intelligence." Thus, Willoughby, a man eager to a fault to please his superior, came to a realization of the truth grudgingly, and failed in the most critical of skills required of an intelligence expert—to advise a commander accurately and in a timely manner of the size and scope of the enemy force facing him."

David A. Foy

Bibliography

Blair, Clay. *The Forgotten War: America in Korea, 1950–1953* (1987).

Goulden, Joseph C. *Korea: The Untold Story of the War* (1982).

McGovern, William. *To the Yalu: From the Chinese Invasion of Korea to MacArthur's Dismissal* (1972).

Wilson, Charles E. (1886–1972)

Born in New York City on November 18, 1886, and reared by his widowed mother, Charles Edward Wilson quit school in 1889 at the age of twelve to work with the Sprague Electrical Works, which later was acquired by General Electric. Highly ambitious and hard-working, he rose from stock boy with Sprague Electrical to president of General Electric in 1939. During World War II, Wilson was a key figure in the War Production Board, holding a number of important positions relating to production matters and eventually, as executive vice chairman, taking charge of the board's day-to-day operations. A large, driving man with a fiery temper and self-confidence to the point of arrogance, Wilson was credited with significant achievements in increasing the production of war goods. His tenure was also marked by bitter jurisdictional and policy battles with the military and with fellow board members that ultimately led him to resign in the summer of 1944 and return to General Electric.

In the postwar years General Electric prospered under Wilson's direction, in part because of the far-reaching restructuring program he instituted. He also launched an aggressive anti-union campaign that had a profound impact on General Electric and on American industry and earned him the enmity of organized labor. No Neanderthal, Wilson at the same time carried out important public functions, including chairing in 1946–47 the President's Committee on Civil Rights. Its report, *To Secure these Rights*, was a major departure point for race relations in the United States.

At the request of President Harry S. Truman, Wilson left General Electric in December 1950 to head the newly created Office of Defense Mobilization, which was charged with overseeing all mobilization and stabilization activities and agencies growing out of the Korean conflict. From the outset Wilson was embroiled in controversy. He angered labor and farm groups by initially excluding them from the decision-making hierarchy in the mobilization and stabilization program, blasted striking railroad switchmen for "aiding the Soviet Union" by delaying rearmament, and vigorously advocated a schedule of wage and price controls that labor charged favored big business.

Wilson's service as director of defense mobilization culminated in March 1952 in a nasty dispute with the president. Faced with the likelihood of a steel strike unless workers received substantial wage increases, the Wage Stabilization Board, an agency under Wilson's wing, recommended a major wage increase that it said industry could afford with at most a modest price increase. Shocked by the liberality of the proposed settlement and sympathetic to steel executives, Wilson argued that the steel companies were entitled to price increases sufficient to offset the higher wages and apparently came away from a meeting with the president on March 24 with the impression that he had White House support. On March 28, however, Truman, under pressure from labor and the board, made it clear to Wilson in a tense meeting that he supported the board's recommendations as a basis of collective bargaining. Believing that he had been betrayed by Truman, Wilson later that day submitted his resignation, promptly accepted by Truman, in an intemperate letter castigating the administration for capitulating to organized labor and for reneging on a promise of compensatory price increases.

After a brief return to General Electric, Wilson joined W.R. Grace and Company, becoming chairman of the board before retiring in 1956. Often referred to as "Electric Charlie" to distinguish him from "Engine Charlie," Charles Erwin Wilson of General Motors and secretary of defense in the Eisenhower administration; Wilson died in Bronxville, New York, on January 3, 1972.

John Kennedy Ohl

Bibliography

"Charles E. Wilson's Own Story of Break with Truman," *U.S. News and World Report* (2 May 1952).
Donovan, Robert J. *Tumultuous Years: The Presidency of Harry S. Truman, 1949–1953* (1982).
Hamby, Alonzo. *Beyond the New Deal: Harry S. Truman and American Liberalism* (1973).
Marcus, Maeva. *Truman and the Steel Seizure Case: The Limits of Presidential Power* (1977).

Women's Army Corps

When the North Koreans invaded South Korea on 25 June 1950, the Women's Army Corps (WAC) had just integrated eligible members of the corps into the regular Army. Also, during the previous two years, many former WAC enlisted women with prior service and former WAC officers had entered the Organized Reserve Corps (later called the Army reserve). The WACs had proved their value to the Army during World War II but it had taken almost three years for Congress to pass the law in 1948 that gave them a permanent place in the Army by granting them regular Army and reserve status.

With the onset of the Korean War, the need for WAC officers and enlisted women increased dramatically. Beginning in July 1950, commanders in the Far East command and other overseas commands placed many requisitions for WAC officers and enlisted women to fill noncombat positions (typists, stenographers, finance clerks, personnel specialists, supply clerks, medical technicians and corpsmen, etc.) vacated by men who were sent to Korea and other overseas locations.

In the United States, draft calls doubled, reservists were recalled on active duty voluntarily and involuntarily, and entire reserve units were ordered on active duty for assignment to Korea, other overseas locations, and to critical vacancies at home. At the new WAC training center at Fort Lee, Virginia, 250 women enlistees and reenlistees arrived every Monday morning to begin basic or refresher training. More than 1,200 WAC inactive duty reserve officers and enlisted women voluntarily returned on active duty. Approximately fifty WAC reservists were involuntarily recalled on active duty. The Army suspended discharge of WAC personnel based on marriage in August 1950. Congress suspended (for male and WAC personnel) nondisability retirements and extended enlisted and officer obligations for one year.

The director of the corps throughout the WAC expansion for the Korean War was Colonel Mary A. Hallaren of Lowell, Massachusetts. Serving as WAC director from 1947 to 1953, she had led and won the fight for regular and reserve status for the WACs and other servicewomen.

To most women in the service, an overseas posting was the most desirable assignment. And during the Korean War, almost every WAC who was eligible and wanted to serve overseas was able to go. The number of WAC units in Japan alone increased from two in 1950 to nine by 1953. Most were hospital units. A WAC unit was opened in Okinawa in 1951 containing both administrative and medical personnel. The number of women assigned to the Far East command increased from 629 in 1950 to 2,600 a year later. WAC strength in the European command increased by 300 between 1950 and 1951. During the first year of the war, the WACs momentarily expected that a unit would be formed at Fort Lee to go to Korea—Pusan or Seoul—where it would be attached to the Eighth Army, Forward. But Army commanders in Korea believed the combat then was too unpredictable, moving up and down the peninsula as it did, to bring in a WAC unit. Late in 1951, when the lines were fairly stalemated, the Eighth Army commander asked for a WAC unit, but by this time, WAC recruiting had declined so much that Colonel Hallaren had to admit that corps strength was too low to maintain a WAC unit there. She did assign about a dozen enlisted women and one officer to the major headquarters in Korea during 1951 and 1953 as stenographers, translators, and administrative aides.

During the war, the shortage of male soldiers in some overseas commands increased opportunities for women to serve in supervisory positions and to increase their numbers in some military occupational specialties where there had been little room for them before the war. For example, in the U.S. military hospitals in Japan to which came many of the combat soldiers wounded in Korea, WAC sergeants became ward masters—jobs previously held only by men. In other locations women held the senior NCO jobs in motor pools, mess halls, post offices, and other post functions. The women performed well in these positions, supervising both men and women, and their success paved the way for WACs to serve again in these positions as they had during World War II.

Although the number of WACs increased from 7,259 on 30 June 1950 to 11,932 on 30 June 1951, from then on enlistments declined. Truce talks began and fierce combat abated. Women who had been inspired by patriotism and the country's manpower requirements no longer felt needed. This was noted in the other women's services as well.

For help on this problem and for advice regarding military women, in October 1951 the secretary of defense created the Defense Advisory Committee on Women in the Services (DACOWITS). He charged this committee of influential civilian women leaders to spearhead a unified recruiting drive that would increase the women's services by 72,000 during 1952—the WACs share was 20,000. A massive recruiting effort was launched, the WAC band at Fort Lee went on a country-wide tour, colleges and

schools opened their doors to recruiters, and actresses like Helen Hayes and Irene Dunne assisted in the campaign. It proved of little avail—at the end of 1952 the Women's Army Corps had almost 500 less members than it had in 1951! The other women's services did not achieve their goals either but had fared better, increasing their strength by several thousand Navy and Air Force women. The Women Marines, traditionally the smallest of the women's services, had increased their strength by almost 400 women.

The poor WAC showing helped bring about some long-needed changes for Army women. Congress appropriated funds for the construction of a training center specifically for the WACs at Fort McClellan, Alabama; the Army authorized new summer and winter uniforms for women; it added some new military occupational specialties to the WAC assignment list along with training courses for them, and the recruiting command improved the training of recruiters for WAC officers and enlisted women.

When the armistice was signed at Panmunjom in July 1953, WAC strength was much higher (9,925) than it had been at the start of the war; the Corps now had eleven years' experience as part of the Army and its women had served in two major wars. The members of the Women's Army Corps could look to the past with pride and to the future with hope for peace and continued good service.

Bettie J. Morden

Bibliography

Morden, Bettie J. *The Women's Army Corps 1945–1978* (U.S. Army Center of Military History, Washington: 1990).

Rosenberg, Anna M. "Women in the Armed Services Program" (Department of Defense, Office of Information), November 1951.

Schnabel, James F. *Policy and Direction, The First Year*, United States Army in the Korean War (1972).

Stremlow, Mary V. *A History of the Women Marines, 1946–1977* (History and Museums Division, HQ, U.S. Marine Corps, Washington: 1986).

Strength of the Army Reports (STM-30), 1950 through 1953.

Strength of the Army Reports (STM-30), 1953 through 1958.

Treadwell, Mattie E. *The Women's Army Corps, United States Army in World War II* (U.S. Army Center of Military History, Washington: 1954).

X Corps
Inchon to the Yalu

X Corps was an unusual, one-of-a-kind organization. All corps are, of course, uniquely configured for their missions and thus tend to break many organizational rules, but X Corps was unusual even by "normal" corps standards. It was hurriedly organized to plan for and conduct an amphibious assault at Inchon which would dramatically reverse the tide of war in Korea in September 1950. It was then shifted to the opposite coast of Korea and operated in the northeast of the peninsula as a virtually independent striking force of MacArthur's in a plan to liberate all of Korea by Christmas. Then, under massive and unexpected Chinese assaults, X Corps managed to regroup, retreat, and then withdraw from the coast in one of the greatest amphibious evacuations in history. Despite that ordeal, corps units entered the fray in South Korea alongside the rest of the Eighth Army within weeks.

The X Corps was activated on 26 August, barely in time for the Inchon landings it was supposedly responsible for planning. According to one contemporary observer, X Corps was a "hasty throwing together of a provisional Corps headquarters" and was "at best only a half-baked affair." The staff of the 1st Marine Division necessarily did much of the planning for and execution of the Inchon landings since X Corps was neither fully formed nor experienced enough in amphibious operations to operate as a functional headquarters. However, there was no question as to who would be in overall command of the operation.

The newly appointed commanding general of this new corps was Major General Edward M. (Ned) Almond, who retained his position as MacArthur's chief of staff of Far Eastern command. This did not sit well with many senior leaders in Korea, notably Lieutenant General Walton Walker, Eighth Army commander, with whom Almond had a major personality clash. In addition, upon assumption of his new command, Almond almost instantly quarreled with Major General Oliver P. Smith, the commander of the 1st Marine Division which, along with the anemic 7th Infantry Division, comprised his corps. Despite the obvious professionalism of these senior leaders, personality continued to have a major impact on military operations.

The commander in World War II of the black 92nd Infantry Division in Italy, Almond was hot-tempered, prickly, hard-charging, and aggressive to a fault. Aside from MacArthur himself, there are few other commanders in the Korean War so controversial. Almond liked bold and flashy maneuvers with scant regard for caution or flanks, and venerated General MacArthur. He liked to create special task forces and had a tendency to tell regiments and even battalions directly how to fight their battles without going through command channels. He often showed up in person near the point of an attack to spur the "lagging" unit commanders to greater speed, regardless of the situation. This style spoke well of Almond's personal bravery, but bypassing normal command channels while conducting fast and fragmented attacks set dangerous precedents; precedents which helped cause the heavy loss of life in the "race to the Yalu" campaign of November 1950.

The confusion and coordination problems within X Corps began during the Inchon landings on 15 September. The landing of the 1st Marine Division and the 7th Infantry Division went off virtually without a problem against the overwhelmed North Korean defenders. However, the capture of Seoul proceeded slowly according to Almond's and MacArthur's timetable. Almond did not endear himself to his units (specially Smith's Marines) with his excessive prodding to move faster and his meddling down to regimental and battalion level. Only the overwhelming power of the U.N. forces prevented serious consequences of these first problems of coordination and personality at the corps level.

After the capture of Seoul and the link-up with Eighth Army forces, rather than coming under Eighth Army and moving directly north, X Corps was withdrawn back over the Inchon beachhead (causing massive confusion and supply bottlenecks) and landed on the east coast of Korea at Wonsan and Iwon. The landings on 25 and 29 October established the U.S. and Republic of Korea (ROK) forces in northeast Korea, but the Corps was virtually isolated from the remainder of the U.N. forces. General Almond began drawing supplies directly from Japan, bypassing Eighth Army supply channels, and rapidly built up his forces. The corps, now including the newly arrived 3rd Infantry Division, was set for a "race to the Yalu" against crumbling North Korean opposition. It seemed as if the war was winding down to a successful close.

The heady optimism of October and November 1950 soon disappeared as massive Chinese intervention crippled and threw back X Corps units from the Yalu and isolated several major Marine and Army formations near the Chosin Reservoir. General Almond and his staff had blindly followed the guidance of MacArthur's supremely optimistic Far Eastern command which seemed to ignore or discount sign after sign of massive Chinese intervention. Based on guidance from MacArthur, Almond directed his units to race to the Yalu without regard to flanks or enemy forces.

Almond pushed his units hard, especially the more conservative 1st Marine Division. General Smith, leery of an operation in such mountainous terrain far from the sea, tried his best to move cautiously, at the cost of numerous prodding visits from Almond. Any of the other division staffs who attempted to plan careful, conservative troop concentrations discovered their subordinate units taken away from them by X Corps orders in the headlong rush to be the first to reach the Yalu.

This helter-skelter dispersion of forces occurred across the entire front, so sure were Almond and his staff of enemy weakness. The intelligence prejudices of MacArthur's Far Eastern command, in particular the intelligence estimates of General Charles A. Willoughby, insisted that Chinese intervention was not possible and would result in massive Chinese casualties by U.N. airpower if it did occur. This optimism colored the plans and ideas of all subordinate commands. Almond himself, shortly after the start of the Chinese offensive, visited the site of an isolated regimental combat team (Task Force MacLean) which only a few days later was to be overwhelmed and destroyed during its attempt to break the encirclement of a Chinese division. He told the officers of the task force:

> The enemy who is delaying you for the moment is nothing more than remnants of Chinese divisions fleeing north . . . We're still attacking and we're going all the way to the Yalu. Don't let a bunch of Chinese laundrymen stop you.

At the start of massive Chinese intervention, the corps staff at first tried to ignore it or downplay its effect on corps offensive plans. Almond himself, seeking guidance from MacArthur, flew to Tokyo and conferred with him on 28 November. Even while corps units were being attacked and cut off by thousands of Chinese, Almond waited until MacArthur made a decision to "readjust his front by withdrawing from the contact with the enemy until it was clearer to all concerned the extent of the invasion." Almond returned to Korea on the morning of 29 November, and only then proceeded to direct the G-3 and the other staff officers to begin planning for halting the X Corps attack to the northwest and the withdrawal of the corps. In response to Almond's guidance, and in an attempt to react to the rapidly changing situation to which none of their contingency plans applied, the X Corps staff prepared a series of orders, each outlining vastly different types of operations. They then proceeded to publish these orders in rapid succession, changing the plans each time before the subordinate divisions could do more than begin to react to them. As at Inchon, the corps specified missions for regiments and even battalions without even coordinating the changes with their respective divisions. The result was chaos, as some units were given three completely conflicting sets of orders for large-scale movements in different directions within seventy-two hours. Only the determination and courage of the American soldier kept disaster at bay while the corps staff grappled with the new situation.

Withdrawal from Hungnam

Granted a breathing space by stubborn American units, the X Corps planners managed to arrange, supervise, and execute a series of complex operations beginning in early December. These operations included finishing the successful withdrawal (a "breakout to the coast") of the 1st Marine Division from the Chosin Reservoir, consolidating the corps in the Hungnam port area, and then executing the deliberate, progressive withdrawal of men and supplies out of Hungnam by 23 December.

The withdrawal of X Corps units was in the following order: 1st Marine Division, I ROK Corps (3rd Division and Capital Division), 7th Infantry Division and 3rd Infantry Division. The Marines were loaded from 9–14 December, the I ROK from 15–17 December, 7th Infantry Division from 18–21 December and 3rd Infantry Division 21–24 December. The Marines, who had just finished a highly publicized and almost disastrous withdrawal from the Chosin Reservoir, were loaded onto ships first. The ROK troops, whose condition, even though most of their withdrawal was unopposed, was quite poor, came next. Since the 3rd Infantry Division was the freshest unit of all—only a few of their battalions had seen combat up to this point—they were the logical choice to stay behind as the rearguard until the last. They covered the withdrawal of the mangled 7th Infantry Division. (The 7th, after the destruction of Task Force Faith at Chosin, was virtually a two-regiment division.)

During the final stages of the withdrawal, conventional artillery, naval gunfire, and close air support effectively prevented any major enemy concentrations from proving a danger to the beachhead. The Hungnam perimeter contracted gradually, according to the corps plan. Chinese and North Korean forces were kept off balance and thus were not able to exploit the opportunity. What few attacks there were occurred on 16, 18, and 19 December, but nowhere did the enemy units penetrate the main line of resistance (MLR). These probing attacks did generate intelligence for the Chinese Communist forces (CCF), but before that intelligence could be exploited, the U.S. forces would conduct a deliberate withdrawal to new defensive positions. The CCF would thus have to start all over again in the face of withering air and naval gunfire.

Finally, on 24 December, the last three battalions (one from each regiment) of the 3rd Infantry Division which had been covering the removal of their regiments from the perimeter, abandoned their final strongpoints and loaded onto landing craft. Planned demolitions of bridges and rail lines were carried out as these units retreated under close air and naval gunfire support. The few military supplies left (mostly unserviceable or, in the case of some frozen dynamite, too dangerous to move) were detonated as the final convoy sailed for Pusan. While not a flawless operation, the withdrawal under enemy pressure of 105,000 men, 17,500 vehicles, and 350,000 tons of supplies over the space of three weeks was a truly outstanding operation. The evacuation from Hungnam was no Dunkirk, but it was still a retreat and a demoralizing defeat after the high hopes of November.

Into the Line with the Eighth Army

Even while planning and conducting the withdrawal of the Marines from Chosin and the evacuation of the corps from Hungnam, X Corps planners had worked on unloading men and supplies at the ports of Pusan and Pohang and preparing them for insertion into the defensive line. The hard-pressed Eighth Army, still reeling from its own clashes with the Chinese, had only these forces to operate as any reserve. By now under the command of Lieutenant General Matthew B. Ridgway, the Eighth Army had reached a crisis and there was no longer any discussion of maintaining X Corps as a separate corps. Rapidly assembling the 1st Marine, 7th, and 3rd Divisions, Almond began moving his forces north from Pusan on 28 December. By the start of the New Year, the corps was in its assembly areas. However, the 1st Marine and 3rd Infantry Divisions were withdrawn into Army reserve. Ridgway reorganized his units and by 7 January, X Corps consisted of the 2nd Infantry Division (still not recovered from its near destruction by the Chinese along the Chongchon River), 7th Infantry Division, and the ROK 2nd, 5th and 8th Divisions. It was placed along a twenty-two-mile front with the mission of defending Wonju, a key road junction.

The Defense of Wonju

Almost immediately, X Corps faced a series of attacks from 7–22 January by the North Korean II and V Corps. Smashing into the vulnerable 2nd Division, the North Koreans drove the

Americans out of the town. The division commander, Major General Robert B. McClure, obtained Almond's permission for a limited withdrawal but did not establish a defensive line until his units had retreated more than four miles from Wonju. Almond, furious at this move, ordered McClure to counterattack and retake the town. Despite a furious battle at Hill 247 with heavy casualties inflicted on the North Koreans, Wonju remained in enemy hands. Almond, unsatisfied with Major General McClure's leadership, asked General Ridgway's permission to relieve McClure on 13 January and Ridgway somewhat reluctantly agreed. Almond replaced McClure with Major General Clark L. "Nick" Ruffner, Almond's chief of staff. This was just the first of many replacements of commanders by members of Almond's "nursery" in what looked like a conscious policy.

Thunderbolt and the Battles for Hoengsong
Beginning on 25 January, X Corps participated in the Eighth Army's Operation Thunderbolt, quickly retaking Wonju. This operation was followed by Operation Roundup on 4 February which involved an ambitious X Corps attack on Hongchon with the 5th and 8th ROK Divisions supported by armored and artillery support teams from the 2nd and 7th Divisions and the 187th Airborne Regimental Combat Team. The attack kicked off almost on schedule but the combined units quickly found that the terrain was a greater enemy than the North Koreans. Narrow roads, sharp ridges and broken ground slowed the attack. Then, on 11 February, the CCF, organized into four armies (66th, 40th, 39th, and 42nd), smashed into the corps along the entire front. The 8th Division (ROK) was virtually destroyed, U.S. support units (roadbound with their armor and artillery) were cut off and decimated, losing dozens of artillery pieces. The battle soon developed into a frantic defense of Hoengsong. Despite heroic exertions, the corps was forced to retreat south of Hoengsong by 13 February at a cost of 11,800 casualties (1,900 of them Americans), thirty-four howitzers (twenty by the Americans), and hundreds of crew-served weapons, vehicles, and other equipment.

Wonju Again and Operations Killer and Ripper
The Chinese forces did not closely follow the retreating X Corps, and General Almond and his division commanders were able to reestab-lish defensive lines north of Wonju. However, the 23rd Regimental Combat Team of the 2nd Infantry Division was cut off and surrounded at Chipyong-ni and conducted an epic three-day defense against four Chinese regiments. Despite heavy losses and the failure at Chipyong-ni, the Chinese continued to attack the corps through 18 February. Then turning the tables, General Ridgway ordered a counterattack (Operation Killer) with X Corps moving north on the attack on the 21st. The 7th Division spearheaded the advance on the corps right followed by a planned link-up operation with the 2nd Infantry Division on the 22nd. Unfortunately, an unexpected change in the weather led to heavy rain, melting snow, and muddy roads. The plodding attack ran into little enemy opposition as the Chinese and North Koreans slowly withdrew to the north. By the end of the first week in March, most of the objectives of the corps were reached, roughly along a line known as Arizona, but the enemy was as elusive as ever. The X Corps portion of Ridgway's next offensive, Operation Ripper, was to advance north approximately twenty miles, in sector, to a line called Idaho and clear all enemy units in the way. A further advance to line Cairo was anticipated. The corps quickly achieved most of its territorial objectives in the face of minor enemy opposition. Phase I of the operation lasted from 6–15 March and Phase II continued until 31 March. Further advances to the north were made by X Corps as part of Operations Rugged and Dauntless from 1–22 April. By the middle of April, X Corps was positioned firmly along line Kansas, just in time to defend against the CCF spring offensive.

The Battle of the Soyang River
The Chinese and North Korean attacks on 22 April did not catch the X Corps of General Almond unprepared. Elements of the North Korean 45th Division attacked two regiments of the 7th and 2nd Infantry Division on the 24th of April but ran into massive artillery fire. Almond was forced to withdraw part of the 2nd Infantry Division, but only in order to maintain contact with the 1st Marine Division of the IX Corps on the left as it withdrew slightly under enemy pressure. However, by the end of April, the X Corps was forced to pull back, along with the rest of Eighth Army, to the No Name line. Renewed enemy attacks against No Name line occurred from 16–20 May with the main enemy attack centered on X Corps, by then consisting of the 1st Marine Division, the 2nd Infantry

Division, and the 5th and 7th ROK Infantry Divisions. CCF attacks on the ROK III Corps on the X Corps right flank quickly crumbled the ROKs, exposing the 2nd Infantry's flank. Some six Chinese divisions poured down on Major General Ruffner's division. Using a flexible defensive, Almond allowed tactical withdrawals to improve defensive positions and authorized increased levels of ammunition expenditure. He asked for, and received, two regiments of the 3rd Infantry Division from General James A. Van Fleet (who had replaced Ridgway after Ridgway replaced MacArthur). Despite substantial enemy penetration, the line held and X Corps was able to go on the offensive on 23 May as part of the Eighth Army counterattack. Almond had been given the 187th Regimental Combat Team and immediately launched it north to take the high ground near Hangye and, with the 2nd Infantry Division, move on Inje. Meanwhile, the 1st Marine Division was to drive a spearhead toward Yanggu and trap the enemy between them and the 2nd Infantry Division. The 187th established a shaky bridgehead over the Soyang River on the 24th of May as the 38th Infantry attacked toward Inje on their right. The 23rd Infantry moved into the bridgehead slowly and many enemy units were able to avoid Almond's trap. Almond ordered the 187th over the Soyang toward Inje on the 27th. They took that town despite heavy enemy rearguard action. At this point, Almond met with Van Fleet on a proposed amphibious landing at Tongchon, north of the 38th parallel, to outflank the enemy units. Much to Almond's and Van Fleet's dismay, Ridgway vetoed the plan because of its political consequences, and X Corps reverted to the defensive. While Almond's later claims of inflicting more than 90,000 casualties on the Chinese in the battle of Soyang River were probably overstated, it is certain that the operation was very costly to the Chinese.

After the major victory at Soyang, X Corps role in the I and IX Corps offensive, Piledriver, was as a secondary attack. The Marines (sup-ported by the ROK Marines) drove north to the Punchbowl on 4 June, achieving a breakthrough on 11 June. New defensive lines were established along an extension of line Kansas. Those lines would change very little over the ensuing months of small unit combat.

Stalemate

The battle of the Soyang River and the advance to line Kansas were the last actions of General Almond as Commander of X Corps. He returned to the United States to become commandant of the Army War College in its new quarters at Carlisle Barracks, Pennsylvania. He was replaced by Major General Clovis E. Byers, whose tenure lacked most of the dramatic fighting and intense controversy which characterized Almond's command of X Corps. In essence, the corps settled down to positional warfare in many ways similar to that of World War I. Small unit actions, patrolling, trenches, and fortified hilltops were the order of the day rather than grand amphibious landings, sweeping maneuvers, or offensives characterized by multiple axes of advance. Stories of the operations of X Corps from June 1951 to the signing of the armistice belong to the platoons, companies, and battalions of infantry, armor, and artillery that fought them rather than to the commander and staff of X Corps.

Richard W. Stewart

Bibliography

Appleman, Roy. *Escaping the Trap: The U.S. Army X Corps in Northeast Korea, 1950* (1990).

Blair, Clay. *The Forgotten War: America in Korea 1950–1953* (1987).

Heinl, Robert. *Victory at High Tide* (1979).

Mossman, Billy C. *Ebb and Flow: November 1950–July 1951* (Center of Military History, Washington: 1990).

Stanton, Shelby L. *America's Tenth Legion: X Corps in Korea, 1950* (1989).

Stewart, Richard W. *Staff Operations: The X Corps in Korea, December 1950* (1991).

Bibliography

This is a compilation of English-language writings dealing exclusively, or at least primarily, with the Korean conflict. No attempt was made to include or exclude writings on any basis of scholarship or persuasiveness. Some of these works are more or less obviously polemical, political, propagandistic, tendentious, or combinations of all four. Others are of lasting historical validity. The less historically valuable works nonetheless may give the "flavor" of strongly held opinions with an immediacy often lost in works of more detached scholarship. Excluded, however, are ephemeral popular magazine articles, as well as those that deal with the war only in part, and self-generated unit histories.

Bibliographies

Association of Asian Studies. *Cumulative Bibliography of Asian Studies 1941–1965; 1966–1970* (1970–72).

Blanchard, Carroll Henry. *Korean War Bibliography and Maps of Korea* (1964).

Cowart, Glenn C. *Miracle in Korea: The Evacuation of X Corps from the Hungnam Beachead* (Columbia, South Carolina: 1992).

Cumings, Bruce. "Korean–American Relations: A Century of Conflict and Thirty-Five Years of Intimacy," in *New Frontiers in American–East Asian Relations: Essays Presented to Dorothy Borg*, ed. Warren I. Cohen (1983).

Dornbusch, C.E. *Histories of American Army Units, World Wars I and II and Korean Conflict with Some Earlier Histories* (Department of the Army, Washington: 1956).

———. *Histories, Personal Narratives, United States Army: A Checklist* (1967).

Edwards, Paul M. *The Pusan Perimeter: An Annotated Bibliography* (Westport: 1993).

Georgetown University Medical Center. *An Annotated Bibliography of Literature Relevant to the Interrogation Process* (December 1957).

Goncharov, S. , J.W. Lewis, and Xue Litai. *Uncertain Partners: Stalin, Mao, and the Korean War* (1993).

Hyatt, Joan, comp. *Korean War, 1950–1953: Selected References* (Air University Library, Maxwell AFB: 1990).

Kim, Han-kyo, and Hong Kyoo Park, eds. *Studies on Korea, a Scholar's Guide* (1980).

Koh, Hesung Chun, and Joan Steffens, eds. *Korea: An Analytical Guide to Bibliographies* (1971).

Lee, Chong-Sik, and Pyoung Hoon Kim. "Korea and the Korean War," *Soviet Foreign Relations and World Communism: A Selected Annotated Bibliography of 7,000 Books in 30 Languages*, comp. and ed. Thomas T. Hammond (1965).

Leopold, Richard W. "The Historian's Task," *The Korean War: A 25-Year Perspective*, ed. Francis H. Heller (1977).

Lord, John M., et al. *A Study of Rear Area Security Measures . . . Korea (1950–1953)* (Counterinsurgency Information Analysis Center, Special Operations Research Organization, American University, Washington: July 1965).

McFarland, Keith D. *The Korean War: An Annotated Bibliography* (1986).

O'Quinlivan, Michael, comp. *An Annotated Bibliography of the United States Marines in the Korean War* (Historical

Branch, HQ, U.S. Marine Corps, Washington: 1962).

Rhodes, Edward J.M. *The Chinese Red Army, 1927–1963: An Annotated Bibliography* (1964).

Robinson, Mary Ann, comp. *The Home Front and War in the Twentieth Century* (1982).

Silberson, Bernard S. *Japan and Korea: A Critical Bibliography* (1962).

———. *Communist North Korea: A Bibliographic Survey* (GPO, Washington: 1971).

———. *Korean Conflict: A Collection of Historical Manuscripts on the Korean Campaign Held by the U.S. Army Center of Military History* (Library of Congress Photoduplication Service, Washington: 1975).

Periodical Articles

Foot, Rosemary. "Making Known the Unknown War: Policy Analysis of the Korean Conflict in the Last Decade," *Diplomatic History*, 15 (Summer 1991).

McMahon, Robert J. "The Cold War in Asia: Toward a New Synthesis?" *Diplomatic History*, 12 (Summer 1988).

Paige, Glenn D. "A Survey of Soviet Publications on Korea, 1950–56," *Journal of Asian Studies*, 17 (August 1958).

Park, Hong-Kyu. "American Involvement in the Korean War," *History Teacher*, 16 (February 1983).

Shapiro, Seymour. *Brainwashing: A Partial Bibliography* (SORO, American University, Washington: 28 October 1958).

West, Philip. "Interpreting the Korean War," *American Historical Review* (February 1988).

Weathersby, K. "The Soviet Role in the Early Phase of the Korean War: New Documentary Evidence," *The Journal of American–East Asian Relations* (Winter 1993).

———, translator and commentator. New Findings on the Korean War," *Cold War International History Project Bulletin* (Fall 1993).

Atlases, Compilations

Atlas of the Arab–Israeli Wars, the Chinese Civil War, and the Korean War (1986).

Declassified Documents Quarterly Catalog (1975–).

Esposito, Vincent J., ed. *The West Point Atlas of American Wars*, 2 Vols. (1959).

Hartman, Tom, and John Mitchell. *A World Atlas of Military History 1945–1984* (1984).

Matray, James, ed. *Historical Dictionary of the Korean War* (1991).

Summers, Harry G. *Korean War Almanac* (1990).

General, Political, Military

Alexander, Bevin. *Korea: The First War We Lost* (1986).

Beech, Keyes. *Tokyo and Points East* (1954).

Berger, Carl. *The Korea Knot: A Military-Political History* (1965).

Blair, Clay. *The Forgotten War: Americans in Korea, 1950–1953* (1987).

Brady, James. *The Coldest War: A Memoir of Korea* (1990).

Cai Chengwen and Zhao Yongtian. *A Factual Record of the Korean War* (1990).

Collins, J. Lawton. *War in Peacetime: The History and Lessons of Korea* (1969).

Cowart, Glenn. *Miracle in Korea: The Evacuation of X Corps from the Hungnam Beachhead* (1993).

DeWeerd, Harvey A. *The Triumph of the Limiters: Korea* (1968).

Donnelly, Charles H. *United States Defense Policies Since World War II* (GPO, 85th Congress, 1st Session, House Document No. 100, Washington: 1957).

Donovan, Robert J. *Nemesis: Truman and Johnson in the Coils of War in Asia* (1984).

Fehrenback, T.R. *This Kind of War: A Study in Unpreparedness* (1963).

Flint, Roy K., Peter W. Kozumplik, and Thomas J. Waraksa. *The Arab–Israeli Wars, The Chinese Civil War, and the Korean War* (1987).

Foot, Rosemary. *The Wrong War: American Policy and the Dimensions of the Korean Conflict* (1985).

Goulden, Joseph C. *Korea: The Untold Story of the War* (1982).

Guttman, Allen, comp. *Korea and the Theory of Limited War* (1976).

Halliday, John, and Bruce Cumings. *Korea: The Unknown War* (1988).

Hastings, Max. *The Korean War* (1987).

Haynes, Richard F. *The Awesome Power: Harry S. Truman as Commander in Chief* (1973).

Heller, Francis Howard. *The Korean War: A 25-Year Perspective* (1977).

Jackson, Robert. *Air War Over Korea* (1973).

James, D. Clayton. *Refighting the Last War: Command and Crisis in Korea, 1950–1953* (1992).

Kalickie, J.H. *The Pattern of Sino-American Crises: Political-Military Interactions in the 1950* (1975).

Kaufman, Burton Ira. *The Korean War: Challenges in Crisis, Credibility, and Command* (1986).

Kim Chum-Kon. *The Korean War, 1950–53* (1980).

Kim Chullbaum, ed. *The Truth About the Korean War* (1991).

Knox, Donald, and Alfred Coppel. *The Korean War: Uncertain Victory: The Concluding Volume of an Oral History* (1988).

Kolko, Joyce, and Gabriel Kolko. *The Limits of Power: The World and United States Foreign Policy, 1945–1954* (1972).

Kriebel, P. Wesley. "Unfinished Business—Intervention Under the U.N. Umbrella: America's Participation in the Korean War, 1950–1953," in *Intervention or Abstention: The Dilemma of American Foreign Policy*, ed. Robin Higham (1975).

LaFeber, Walter. *America, Russia, and the Cold War, 1945–1984: A Quarter Century of American Foreign Policy* (1974).

Leckie, Robert. *Conflict: The History of the Korean War, 1950–53* (1962).

MacDonald, Callum A. *Korea: The War Before Vietnam* (1987).

McGovern, James. *To the Yalu: From the Chinese Invasion of Korea to MacArthur's Dismissal* (1972).

———. *The Military History of the Korean War* (1963).

Martin, H.G. "Korea—Some Tactical Lessons," *Brassey's Annual: The Armed Forces Yearbook* (1951).

Middleton, Harry Joseph. *The Compact History of the Korean War* (1965).

O'Ballance, Edgar. *Korea: 1950–1953* (1969).

O'Shaughnessy, John F., Jr. "The Chinese Intervention in Korea: An Analysis of Warning," thesis, Defense Intelligence College, 1985.

Oliver, Robert Tarbell. *Syngman Rhee and American Involvement in Korea, 1942–1960* (1978).

———. *Verdict in Korea* (State College, PA: 1952).

Paige, Glenn D. *The Korean Decision* (1968).

Rees, David. *Korea: The Limited War* (1964).

Rose, Lisle Abbott. *Roots of Tragedy: The United States and the Struggle for Asia, 1945–1953* (1976).

Rush, Eugene J. *Military Strategic Lessons Learned from the Korean Conflict as They Related to Limited Warfare* (U.S. Army War College: 1974).

Scalapino, Robert A., and Chong-Sik Lee. *Communism in Korea*, 2 vols. (1972).

Schnabel, James F. *U.S. Army in the Korean War, Policy and Direction: The First Year* (U.S. Army Center of Military History: 1972).

———, and Robert J. Watson. *The Korean War* (Joint Chiefs of Staff, Historical Division: 1979), vol. 3 of *The History of the Joint Chiefs of Staff: The Joint Chiefs of Staff and National Policy*, 5 Vols. (1978–86).

Simmons, Robert R. "The Communist Side: An Exploratory Sketch," *The Korean War: A 25-Year Perspective*, ed. Francis H. Heller (1977).

———. "The Korean Civil War," *Without Parallel: The American-Korean Relationship Since 1945*, ed. Frank Baldwin (1974).

———. *The Strained Alliance: Peking, Pyongyang, Moscow, and the Politics of the Korean Civil War* (1975).

Spurr, Russell. *Enter the Dragon: China's Undeclared War Against the U.S. in Korea, 1950–1951* (1988).

Srivastava, M.P. *The Korean Conflict: Search for Unification* (1982).

Stokesbury, James L. *A Short History of the Korean War* (1988).

Stone, I.F. *The Hidden History of the Korean War* (1952, 1969).

Stueck, William W. *The Road to Confrontation* (1981).

Thompson, Reginald William. *Cry Korea* (1951).

U.S. Armed Forces in Korea. *U.S. Army Military Government in Korea, September 45–June 50.* (n.d.).

U.S. Army Korean Civil Affairs Command. *Reference Handbook of the Government of the Republic of Korea* (n.d.).

U.S. Army Military Government in Korea. *Ordnances, 24 September 1945–24 October 1946.*

United States Congress Senate Committee on Government Operations, Subcommittee on Korean War Atrocities. *Korean War Atrocities Hearing* (1954).

——, Congress Senate Committee on the Judiciary. *The Korean War and Related Matters* (1955).

——, Department of State. *A Historical Summary of United States–Korea Relations with a Chronology of Important Developments 1834–1962* (1962).

Utley, Freda. *The China Story* (1951).

Weaver, William Gaulbert. *Some Aspects of the Korean War, As Viewed from the Early 1950's* (1966).

Whelan, Richard. *Drawing the Line: The Korean War, 1950–1953* (1990).

Williams, W.J. *A Revolutionary War: Korea and the Transformation of the Postwar World.* Military History Symposium of the United States Air Force Academy (1993).

Wint, Guy. *What Happened in Korea? A Study of Collective Security* (1954).

General, Periodical Articles

Air University Quarterly Staff. "The Korean War Speaks to the Indo-Chinese War," *Air University Quarterly Review*, 7 (Spring 1954).

Austin, W.R. "Lessons of Korea," *Academy of Political Science Proceedings*, 24 (January 1951).

Barclay, C.N. "Lessons of the Korean Campaign," *Brassey's Annual: The Armed Forces Yearbook*, ed. H.G. Thursfield (1954).

Blum, Stanley D. "Sharing the Burden," *Journal of International Affairs*, 6 (Spring 1952).

Calingaert, Daniel. "Nuclear Weapons and the Korean War," *The Journal of Strategic Studies*, 2 (June 1988).

Cheek, Leon B., Jr. "Korea: Decisive Battle of the World," *Military Review*, 32 (March 1953).

"Chinese Communism, Korea, and the United Nations," *World Today* (January 1951).

Cottrell, Alvin J., and James E. Dougherty. "The Lessons of Korea: War and the Power of Man," *Orbis*, 2 (Spring 1958).

DeWeerd, Harvey A. "Lessons of the Korean War," *Yale Review*, 40 (Summer 1951).

Drummond, Stuart. "Korea and Viet Nam: Some Speculations About the Possible Influences of the Korean War on American Policy in Viet Nam, *Army Quarterly and Defence Journal*, 97 (October 1968).

Endicott, Stephen L. "Germ Warfare and 'Plausible Denial': The Korean War 1952–53," *Modern China*, 5 (January 1979).

Fleming, D.F. "What Is Our Role in East Asia," *Western Political Quarterly*, 18 (March 1965).

Foot, Rosemary. "Nuclear Coercion and the Ending of the Korean Conflict," *International Security*, 13 (Winter 1988–89).

Friedman, Edward. "Problems in Dealing with an Irrational Power: America Declares War on China," *America's Asia: Dissenting Essays on Asian-American Relations* (1971).

Gittings, John. "Talks, Bombs and Germs: Another Look at the Korean War," *Journal of Contemporary Asia*, 2 (November 1975).

Graebner, Norman "A Global Commitment: The Truman Years," *Current History*, 57 (August 1969).

Hartmann, Frederick H. "The Issues in Korea," *Yale Review*, 42 (September 1952).

Jervis, Robert. "The Impact of the Korean War on the Cold War," *Journal of Conflict Resolution*, 24 (December 1980).

"The Korean War Speaks to the Indo-Chinese War . . . as We Move to Save Southeast Asia, What Can We Apply from Our Experience in Korea?" *Air University Quarterly Review* (Spring 1954).

Mahony, Thomas H.O. "Lessons from Korea," *American Academy of Political and Social Science Annals*, 276 (July 1951).

Mitchell, C. Clyde. "Political and Economic Significance of the Korean War," *International Journal*, 5 (Autumn 1950).

Paige, Glenn D. "On Values and Science: The Korean Decision Reconsidered," *American Political Science Review*, 71 (December 1977).

Pike, Douglas, and Benjamin Ward. "Losing and Winning: Korea and Vietnam as Success Stories," *Washington Quarterly*, 10 (Summer 1987).

Price, Thomas J. "Constraints on Foreign Policy Decision Making: Stability and Flexibility in Three Crises," *International Studies Quarterly*, 22 (September 1978).

Smith, Gaddis. "After 25 Years—The Parallel," *New York Times Magazine*, 124 (22 June 1975).

Soustelle, Jacques. "Indo-China and Korea: One Front," *Foreign Affairs*, 29 (October 1950).

Stevenson, Adlai E. "Korea in Perspective," *Foreign Affairs*, 30 (April 1952).

Stueck, William. "The Korean War as International History," *Diplomatic History*, 10 (Fall 1986).

Tarpey, John F. "Korea: 25 Years Later," *U.S. Naval Institute Proceedings*, 104 (August 1978).

Van Ginneken, Jaap. "Bacteriological Warfare," *Journal of Contemporary Asia*, 7 (1977).

Warner, Geoffrey. "The Korean War," *International Affairs*, 56 (January 1980).

Wolfers, Arnold. "Collective Security and the War in Korea," *Yale Review*, 43 (June 1954).

Wright, Quincy. "Collective Security in the Light of the Korean Experience," *American Society of International Law Proceedings*, 45 (April 26–28 1951).

Origins of the War

Acheson, Dean. *Present at the Creation: My Years in the State Department* (1969).

Ambrose, Stephen E. *Rise to Globalism: American Foreign Policy Since 1938* (1983).

Blum, Robert M. *Drawing the Line: The Origins of the American Containment Policy in East Asia* (1982).

Buhite, Russell D. *Soviet-American Relations in Asia. 1945–1954* (1981).

Cho Soon Sung. *Korea in World Politics, 1940–1950* (1967).

Cumings, Bruce. *The Origins of the Korean War*, 2 vols. (1981–1990).

Dobbs, Charles M. *The Unwanted Symbol: American Foreign Policy, the Cold War, and Korea, 1945–1950* (1981).

Gaddis, John Lewis. "Korea in American Politics, Strategy, and Diplomacy, 1945–1950," in *The Origins of the Cold War in Asia*, eds. Yonosuke Nagai and Akira Iriye (1977).

————. *Strategies of Containment: A Critical Appraisal of Postwar American National Security Policy* (1982).

Gordenker, Leon. *The United Nations and the Peaceful Unification of Korea: The Politics of Field Operations, 1947–1950* (1959).

Gunther, John. *The Riddle of MacArthur: Japan, Korea, and the Far East* (1950).

Hammond, Paul Y. "NSC-68: Prologue to Rearmament," in *Strategy, Politics, and Defense Budgets*, eds. Warner R. Schilling and Paul Y. Hammond (1962).

Hitchcock, Wilbur W. "North Korea Jumps the Gun," in *Nationalism and Communism in Asia: The American Response*, Norman A. Graebner, ed. (1977).

Iriye, Akira. *The Cold War in Asia: A Historical Introduction* (1974).

King, O.H.P. *Tail of the Paper Tiger* (1961).

Lowe, Peter. *The Origins of the Korean War* (1986).

Masao, Okonogi. "The Domestic Roots of the Korean War," in *The Origins of the Cold War in Asia*, eds. Yonosuke Nagai and Akira Iriye (1977).

Matray, James I. *The Reluctant Crusade: America's Foreign Policy in Korea, 1941–1950* (1985).

McCune, George McAfee. *Korea Today* (1950).

Merrill, John. *Korea: The Peninsular Origins of the War* (1989).

Oliver, Robert T. *Why War Came in Korea* (1950).

Paige, Glenn D. *The Korean Decision: June 24–30, 1950* (1968).

————. *1950: Truman's Decision. The United States Enters the Korean War* (1970).

Pollack, Jonathan. "The Korean War and Sino-American Relations," in *Sino-American Relations, 1945–1955: A Joint Reassessment of a Critical Decade*, eds. Yuan Ming and Harry Harding (1989).

Ryan, Mark A. *Chinese Attitudes Toward Nuclear Weapons: China and the United States During the Korean War* (1989).

Schaller, Michael. *The American Occupation of Japan: The Origins of the Cold War in Asia* (1985).

Seoul YONHAP, translation by the Foreign Broadcast Information Service. "Former North Korean General Comments on War," *FBIS Daily Report—East Asia*, 1–2 (November 1990).

Slusser, Robert M. "Soviet Far Eastern Policy, 1945–50: Stalin's Goals in Korea," in *The Origins of the Cold War in Asia*, eds. Yonosuke Nagai and Akira Iriye (1977).

Stueck, William Whitney. *The Road to Confrontation: American Policy Toward China and Korea, 1947–1950* (1977).

Tsou, Tang. *America's Failure in China, 1941–1950* (1963).

U.S. Department of State. *North Korea: A Case Study in the Techniques of Takeover* (1961).

———. *The Record on Korean Unification 1943–1960: Narrative Summary with Principal Documents* (1960).

Origins of the War, Periodical Articles

Acheson, Dean. "Crisis in Asia—An Examination of U.S. Policy," *United States Department of State Bulletin*, 22 (January 23, 1950).

Buhite, Russell D. "Major Interests: American Policy Toward China, Taiwan, and Korea, 1945–1950," *Pacific Historical Review*, 4 (August 1978).

Chaffee, Wilbur. "Two Hypotheses of Sino-Soviet Relations as Concerns the Instigation of the Korean War," *Journal of Korean Affairs*, 6 (October 1976, January 1977).

Cohen, Warren I. "Conversations with Chinese Friends: Zhou Enlai's Associates Reflect on Chinese-American Relations in the 1940s and the Korean War," *Diplomatic History*, 11 (Summer 1987).

Crofts, Alfred. "The Start of the Korean War Reconsidered," *Rocky Mountain Social Science Journal*, 7 (April 1970).

Downey, Betsy. "In Which 'Mr. X' Goes to Asia: George Frost Kennan and Containment in China and Korea: 1947–1950," *Mid-America* (January 1990).

Gaddis, John Lewis. "Was the Truman Doctrine a Real Turning Point?" *Foreign Affairs*, 52 (January 1974).

Gittlesohn, John. "War and Remembrance: Forty Years on the Origins of the Korean War Inspire Debate and Reassessment," *Far Eastern Economic Review* (July 19, 1990).

Gordenker, Leon. "The United Nations, the United States Occupation, and the 1948 Election in Korea," *Political Science Quarterly*, 73 (September 1958).

Grey, Arthur L., Jr. "The Thirty-Eighth Parallel," *Foreign Affairs*, 29 (April 1951).

Gupta, Karunakar. "How Did the Korean War Begin?" *China Quarterly*, 52 (October-December 1972).

Hitchcock, Wilbur W. "North Korea Jumps the Gun: Did Kim Il Sung, or Stalin Plan the Korean War?" *Current History*, 20 (March 1951).

Hwang, Byong-Moo. "Misperception and the Causes of the Korean War," *Revue Internationale d'Histoire Militarie*, 70 (1988).

Judd, Walter H. "The Mistakes That Led to Korea," *Reader's Digest*, 57 (November 1950), condensed from *Congressional Record*, 96, part 8.

Leffler, Melvin. "The American Conception of National Security and the Beginnings of the Cold War, 1945–48," *The American Historical Review*, 89 (April 1984).

Matray, James I. "America's Reluctant Crusade: Truman's Commitment of Combat Troops in the Korean War," *Historian*, 42 (May 1980).

———. "Captive of the Cold War: The Decision to Divide Korea at the 38th Parallel," *Pacific Historical Review*, 50 (May 1981).

McGlothan, Ronald. "Acheson, Economics, and the American Commitment in Korea, 1947–50," *Pacific Historical Review*, 58 (February 1989).

Oliver, Robert T. "The Impasse in Korea," *American Mercury* (April 1947).

———. "Why War Came to Korea," *Current History*, 19 (September 1950).

Simmons, Robert R. "Some Myths About June 1950," *China Quarterly*, 54 (April-June 1973).

Snyder, Richard C., and Glenn D. Paige. "The United States Decision to Resist Aggression in Korea: The Application of an Analytical Scheme," *Administrative Science Quarterly* (December 1958).

Soh, Jin Chull. "The Role of the Soviet Union in Preparation for the Korean War," *Journal of Korean Affairs*, 3 (January 1974).

Spanier, John. "The Korean War as a Civil War," *Orbis*, 19 (Winter 1976).

Stueck, William. "Cold War Revisionism and the Origins of the Korean Conflict: The Kolko Thesis," *Pacific Historical Review*, 42 (November 1973).

———. "The Soviet Union and the Origins of the Korean War," *World Politics*, 28 (July 1976).

Toner, James H. "The Making of a Morass," *Military Review*, 57 (October 1977).

Warner, Albert L. "Why the Korean Decision Was Made," *Harper's* (June 1951).

Wells, Samuel F., Jr. "Sounding the Tocsin: NSC 68 and the Soviet Threat," *International Security*, 4 (Fall 1979).

U.S. Military (includes Air Force, Navy, Marines, support, etc., but not unit histories)

Almond, Edward M. *Conference on United States Military Operations in Korea, 29 June 1950–31 December 1951* (U.S. Army War College: n.d.).

Anderson, Ellery. *Banner Over Pusan* (1960).

Appleman, Roy E. *Disaster in Korea: The Chinese Confront MacArthur* (1989).

———. *East of Chosin: Entrapment and Breakout in Korea, 1950* (1987).

———. *Ridgway Duels for Korea* (1990).

———. *Escaping the Trap: The U.S. Army X Corps in Northeast Korea, 1950* (1990).

———. *South to the Naktong, North to the Yalu, United States Army in the Korean War* (U.S. Army Center of Military History: 1961).

Bailey, C., et al. *Battle Anaylsis, Wonsan, Rear Area Operations, Rear Area Security, 3rd Infantry Division, Korea, November 1950* (U.S. Army Command and General Staff College: 1984).

Barker, A.J. *Fortune Favours the Brave: The Battle of the Hook* (1974).

Barclay, C.N. "Lessons of the Korean Campaign," *Brassey's Annual: The Armed Forces Yearbook*, ed. H.G. Thursfield (1954).

Bauer, K. Jack. "Dan Kimball, 31 July 1951–20 January 1953," in *American Secretaries of the Navy, 1913–1972*, ed. Paolo Coletta (1980).

Beech, Keyes. *Tokyo and Points East* (1954).

Berger, Carl. *An Introduction to Wartime Leaflets* (Special Operations Research Office, Washington: 1959).

Berger, F.M., et al. *Chosin Reservoir: Defensive Retrograde Winter, 1st Marine Division, 27 November–11 December, 1950* (U.S. Army Command and General Staff College, Combat Studies Institute: 1983).

Berry, Henry. *Hey, Mac, Where Ya Been? Living Memories of the U.S. Marines in the Korean War* (1988).

Blakeley, H.W. *U.S. Marine Corps Operations in Korea, 1950–1953*, 5 vols. (U.S. Marine Corps, Historical Branch, Washington: 1954–1972).

Blunk, Chester L. *"Every Man a Tiger": The 731st USAF Night Intruders Over Korea* (1987).

Bogart, Leo, et al. *Social Research and the Desegregation of the U.S. Army: Two Original 1951 Field Reports* (1969).

Bok, Lee Suk. *The Impact of U.S. Forces in Korea.* (National Defense University, Washington: 1987).

Brady, James. *The Coldest War: A Memoir of Korea* (1990).

Brainard, Morgan. *Then They Called for the Marines* (formerly *Men in Low Cut Shoes*): *A Marine Rifle Company in Korea, 1950–1951* (1989).

Brown, David. *The United States Air Force in Korea, 1950–1953* (Office of Air Force History, Washington: 1983).

Bussey, Charles M. *Firefight at Yechon: Courage and Racism in the Korean War* (1991).

Cagle, Malcom W., and Frank Albert Manson. *The Sea War in Korea* (U.S. Naval Institute, Annapolis: 1957).

Carter, Gregory A. *Some Historical Notes on Air Interdiction in Korea* (1966).

Center for Naval Anaylsis. *Study of Land/Air Trade-Offs*, 9 vols. (1970).

CINCPACFLT: *Korea Interim Evaluation Reports, 1950–1953*, 6 reels (1987).

Clark, Mark. *From the Danube to the Yalu* (1954).

Clever, Frederick W., et al. *U.N. Partisan Warfare in Korea, 1951–1954* (1956).

Coletta, Paolo. "Francis P. Matthews, 25 May 1949–31 July 1951," in *American Secretaries of the Navy, 1913–1972* (1980).

Condit, Doris M. *History of the Office of the Secretary of Defense*, 2, *The Test of War, 1950–1952* (1988).

Cowart, G.C. *Miracle in Korea: The Evacuation of X Corps from the Hungnam Beachhead* (1992).

Cowdrey, Albert E. *The Medics' War, United States Army in the Korean War* (Center of Military History, 1987).

———. *Development of Aeromedical Evacuation in the USAF, 1909–1960*, Vol. 2, (USAF Historical Division, Research Studies Institute, Air University, Maxwell AFB, Alabama: May 1960).

Davis, Larry. *Air War Over Korea: A Pictorial Record* (1982).

———. *Mig Alley* (1978).

Day, James S. "Partisan Operations in the Korean War," thesis, University of Georgia, 1989.

Detzer, David. *Thunder of the Captains: The Short Summer in 1950* (1977).

DeWeerd, Harvey A. *Strategic Surprise in the Korean War* (1962).

Dews, Edmund, and Felix Kozacka. *Air Interdiction: Lessons from Past Campaigns* (1981).

Dixon, Joe C., ed. *The American Military and the Far East: Proceedings of the Ninth Military History Symposium, United States Air Force Academy* (Office of Air Force History: 1980).

Drucker, Arthur J., and Kenneth H. Bradt. *A Survey of Opinions of Officers and Senior NCO's in Korea: III, Factors Contributing to Maintenance of Morale Under Combat Conditions* (Department of the Army, Personnel Research Section: 1952).

DuBravac, Stephen E., et al. *Battle Analysis. Rear Area Operations, Rear Area Security, 1st Marine Division, Kojo, Korea, 21 October–13 November 1950* (Marine Historical Office: n.d.).

Evaluation of the USAF in Korea (Air University: 1951).

Evans, Douglas K. *Sabre Jets Over Korea: A Firsthand Account* (1984).

Fanton, Jonathan Foster. "Robert A. Lovett: The War Years," Ph.D. dissertation, Yale University, 1978.

Farmer, James A., and M.J. Strumwasser. *The Evolution of the Airborne Forward Air Controller: An Anaylsis of Mosquito Operations in Korea* (1967).

Fehrenbach, T.R. *The Fight for Korea: From the War of 1950 to the Pueblo Incident* (1969).

Field, James A. *History of United States Naval Operations: Korea* (Office of Naval History: 1962).

Flint, Roy K. "The Tragic Flaw: MacArthur, the Joint Chiefs, and the Korean War," Ph.D. dissertation, Duke University, 1975.

———. "Task Force Smith and the 24th Division: Delay and Withdrawal 5–19 July 1950," *America's First Battles 1776–1965*, eds. Charles E. Heller and William A. Stofft (1986).

Fondataro, S.A. "A Strategic Analysis of U.S Special Operations during the Korean Conflict, 1950–1953," thesis, U.S. Army Command and General Staff College, 1988.

Forney, James I. *Logistics of Aircraft Maintenance During the Korean War,* thesis, Air Force Institute of Technology, 1988.

Frank, Pat. *The Long Way Round* (1953).

[Futrell, Robert Frank]. *United States Air Force Operations in the Korean Conflict, 25 June-1 November 1950,* SAF Historical Study No. 71 (Department of the Air Force: 1952).

———. *United States Air Force Operations in the Korean Conflict, 1 November 1950–30 June 1952,* USAF Historical Study No. 72 (Department of the Air Force: 1955–1956).

———. *United States Air Force Operations in the Korean Conflict, 1 July 1952–27 July 1953,* USAF Historical Study No. 127 (Department of the Air Force: 1956).

———. "The Korean War," in Alfred Goldberg, *A History of the United States Air Force, 1907–1957* (1957).

———. *The United States Air Force in Korea 1950–1953* (1961).

Gardner, Lloyd C. *The Korean War* (1972).

Geer, Andrew. *The New Breed: The Story of the U.S. Marines in Korea* (1952).

Gerdner, Gordon. *Gordon Gammack, Columns from Three Wars* (1979).

Giangreco, D.M. *War in Korea* (1990).

Giusti, Ernest H. *Mobilization of the Marine Corps Reserve in the Korean Conflict, 1950–1951* (Historical Section, HQ, U.S. Marine Corps: 1951).

Grodecki, Thomas S. "From Powder River to Soyang; the 300th Armored Field Artillery in Korea. A Case Study of the Integration of the Reserve Component into the Active Force" (Center of Military History, Washington: n.d.).

Gugeler, Russell A. *Combat Actions in Korea* (Office of the Chief of Military History: 1970).

———. *Combat Actions in Korea: Infantry, Artillery, Armor* (1954).

Gurney, Gene. *Five Down and Glory: A History of the American Air Ace* (1972).

Hackworth, David H., and Julie Sherman. *About Face* (1989).

Hallion, Richard. *The Naval Air War in Korea* (1986).

Hamel, Eric M. *Chosin: Heroic Ordeal of the Korean War* (1981).

Hansen, K.K. "Psywar in Korea," typescript (Office of the Joint Chiefs of Staff: 1960).

Harris, Charles, et al. *The First Battle of the Naktong Bulge* (U.S. Army Command and General Staff College, Combat Studies Institute: 1984).

Harriss, Elliot, "Operation Strike," in *The UnAmerican Weapon* (1967).

Harriss, W. W. *Puerto Rico's Fighting 65th U.S. Infantry: From San Juan to Chorwan* (1980).

Herbert, Anthony B. *Herbert—the Making of a Soldier* (1982).

Higgins, Marguerite. *War in Korea: The Report of a Woman Combat Correspondent* (1951).

Hinshaw, Arned L. *Heartbreak Ridge: Korea, 1951* (1989).

Hoare, Wilber W. "Truman," in *The Ultimate Decision: The President as Commander in Chief*, ed. Earnest R. May (1960).

Hoyt, Edwin Palmer. *The Pusan Perimeter: Korea, 1950* (1984).

Hopkins, William B, and S.L.A. Marshall. *One Bugle, No Drums: The Marines at Chosin Reservoir* (1986).

Huston, James A. *Guns and Butter, Powder and Rice: U.S. Army Logistics in the Korean War* (1989).

Jackson, Robert. *Air War Over Korea* (1973).

Jacobs, Bruce. *Korea's Heroes: The Medal of Honor Story* (1961).

Jones, Charles, and Eugene Jones. *The Face of War* (1951).

Joseph, Robert Gregory. "Commitments and Capabilities: United States Foreign and Defense Policy Coordination, 1945 to the Korean War," thesis, Columbia University, 1978.

Kahn, E.J. *The Peculiar War: Impressions of a Reporter in Korea* (1952).

Kahn, Lessing A., and Julius Segal. *Psychological Warfare and Other Factors Affecting the Surrender of North Korean and Chinese Forces* (1953).

Karig, Walter, Malcom W. Cagle, and Frank A. Mason. *The War in Korea* (1952), Vol. 6 of *Battle Report*, 6 vols., 1944–52. (USN).

Kemp, Robert F. *Combined Operations in the Korean War* (U.S. Army War College: 1989).

Kendall, John M. "The Inflexible Response: United States Army Mobilization Doctrine 1945–1954," thesis, Duke University, 1979.

Knox, Donald. *The Korean War: Pusan to Chosin: An Oral History* (1987).

———. *Uncertain Victory* (1988).

Korea, 1950. (Office of the Chief of Military History: 1952).

Langley, Michael. *Inchon Landing: MacArthur's Last Triumph* (1979).

Lee, Suk Bok. *The Impact of U.S. Forces in Korea* (National Defense University: 1987).

Lichterman, Martin. "To the Yalu and Back," *American Civil-Military Decisions: A Book of Case Studies*, ed. Harold Stein (1963).

Leckie, Robert. *The March to Glory* (1960).

Lord, John M., et al. *A Study of Rear Area Security Measures . . . Korea (1950–1953)* (Counterinsurgency Information Analysis Center, Special Operations Research Office, American University: July 1965).

Lott, Arnold S. *Most Dangerous Sea: A History of Mine Warfare and an Account of U.S. Navy Mine Warfare Operations in World War II and Korea* (U.S. Naval Institute: 1959).

Macho, Dean C. *The Day I Went Regular* (Air War College, Air University: 1970).

MacDonald, Charles B. *The Last Offensive* (Office of the Chief of Military History: 1973).

Markiewicz, Thomas R. "An Examination of the Factors Involved in the Mobilization of Strategic Sealift Assets," thesis, Naval Postgraduate School, 1983.

Marshall, S.L.A. *Commentary on Infantry Operations and Weapon Usage in Korea, Winter of 1950–51* (ORO 1952).

———. *The River and the Gauntlet: Defeat of the Eighth Army by the Chinese Communist Forces, November, 1950, in the Battle of the Chongchon River, Korea* (1953).

———. *Pork Chop Hill: The American Fighting Man in Action, Korea, Spring, 1953* (1956).

Marshall, Thomas Lee. "The Strategy of Conflict in the Korean War," thesis, University of Virginia, 1959.

Martin, H.G. "Korea—Some Tactical Lessons," *Brassey's Annual: The Armed Forces Yearbook*, ed. H.G. Thursfield (1951).

McAleer, John, and Billy Mossman. *Unit Pride* (1981).

McGovern, James. *To the Yalu: From the Chinese Invasion of Korea to MacArthur's Dismissal* (1972).

Meade, E. Grant. *American Military Government in Korea* (1951).

Mesko, Jim. *Armor in Korea: A Pictorial History* (1984).

Miller, Francis Trevelyan. *War in Korea and the Complete History of World War II* (1955, Armed Services Memorial edition).

Miller, John, Jr., Owen J. Carrol, and Margaret E. Tackley. *Korea 1951–1953* (Office of the Chief of Military History: 1956).

Millett, Allan R. *Semper Fidelis: The History of the United States Marine Corps*, rev. ed. (1991).

Montross, Lynn. *Cavalry of the Sky: The Story of U.S. Marine Combat Helicopters* (1954).

———, and Nicholas Canzona. *The Inchon-Seoul Operation* (Historical Branch, U.S. Marine Corps: 1954).

———. *The Chosin Reservoir Campaign*, Vol. 3 of *U.S. Marine Operations in Korea, 1950–1953* (1987).

———, H.D. Kuoka, and Norman W. Hicks. *The East-Central Front* (Historical Branch, U.S. Marine Corps: 1962).

Moskin, J. Robert. *The U.S. Marine Corps Story* (1982).

Mossman, Billy C. *Ebb and Flow: November 1950–July 1951, 5, United States Army in the Korean War*, 5 vols, 1961–1990 (Department of the Army, Center of Military History, Washington: 1990).

Muller, John H. *Wearing the Cross in Korea* (1954).

Murphy, E. Lloyd. *The U.S./U.N. Decision to Cross the 38th Parallel, October 1950: A Case Study of Changing Objectives in Limited War* (Air War College, Air University: 1968).

Ney, V. "The United States Soldier in a Nonviolent Role," *Combat Operations Research Group for U.S. Army Combat Developments Command* (n.p.: July 1967).

Nicholls, Jack C., and Warren E. Thompson. *Korea: The Air War 1950–1953* (1991).

Noble, H.J., and Frank Baldwin, Jr., eds. *Embassy at War* (1975).

Operations Research Office. *Utilization of Negro Manpower in the Army* (1955).

Pal, Krishnan, et al. *Battle Analysis, Yongsan, Rear Area Operations (24th Infantry Division 11–13 August 1950)* (Army Command and General Staff College, Combat Studies Institute: 1984).

Peifer, William H. *Supply by Sky: The Quartermaster Airborne Development, 1950–1953* (Office of the Quartermaster General, Historical Branch: 1958).

Pease, Stephen E. *Psywar: Psychological Warfare in Korea, 1950–1953* (1992).

Pittman, Phill, et al. *The Battle of Sukchon-Sunchon: Defensive Encircled Forces: Allied Forces: 187th Airborne, RCT, Enemy Forces: North Korean, 239th RGT, 20–25 October 1950* (Army Command and General Staff College, Combat Studies Institute: 1984).

Poats, Rutherford M. *Decision in Korea* (1954).

Poole, Walter S. *The History of the Joint Chiefs of Staff: The Joint Chiefs of Staff and National Policy*, Vol. 4, *1950–1952* (1979).

Preston, H.O., et al. *A Study of Ineffective Soldier Performance Under Fire in Korea, 1951* (ORO, October 1954).

Pugh, H. Lamont, et al. *The History of the Medical Department of the United States Navy, 1945–1955* (NAVMED P-5057, Washington: 1958).

Radio Operations Division, 1st Radio Broadcasting and Leaflet Group, "Report on Psywar Radio Operations with the KOREAN BROADCASTING SYSTEM, August 1951–March, 1952 (n.p., n.d.), typescript, copy in U.S. Army Special Operations Command Historical Archives, Fort Bragg, NC.

Rawlins, Eugene W. *Marines and Helicopters 1946–1962* (Marine Corps, Histories and Museums Division, Washington: 1976).

Reed, John C. *An Analysis of Chinese Communist Aggression in Korea in 1950 and the Possibility of Recurrence in Vietnam* (Air War College, Air University: 1968).

Reister, Frank A. *Battle Casualties and Medical Statistics: U.S. Army Experience in the Korean War* (Department of the Army, Surgeon General: 1973).

Ridgway, Matthew B. *Soldier: The Memoirs of Matthew B. Ridgway*, as told to Harold H. Martin (1956).

———. *The Korean War . . .* (1967).

———. *Pictorial History of the Korean War, 1950–1953 . . .* (n.p.: 1954, Veterans of Foreign Wars Memorial edition).

Robertson, William Glenn. *Counterattack on the Naktong, 1950* (Army General Command and General Staff College, Combat Studies Institute: 1985).

Romrell, Calvin J. "The Logistics Planning Process of the Far East Air Materiel Command During the Korean War," thesis, Air Force Institute of Technology, 1962.

Rosenthal, Carl. "Korea (1950–1953)," in J.M. Lord, et al., *Study of Rear Area Security Measures* (Special Operations Research Office, American University: July 1965).

Rush, Eugene J. *Military Strategic Lessons Learned from the Korean Conflict as They Related to Limited Warfare* (U.S. Army War College: 1974).

Sawyer, Robert K. "United States Military Advisory Group to the Republic of Korea," 3 parts, typescript (Office of the Chief of Military History: n.d.).

———. *Military Advisors in Korea: KMAG in Peace and War* (Office of the Chief of Military History: 1962).

Schnable, James. *Policy and Direction: The First Year, United States Army in the Korean War* (Office of the Chief of Military History: 1972).

———, and Robert J. Watson. *The History of the Joint Chiefs of Staff: The Joint Chiefs of Staff and National Policy*, Vol. 3, *The Korean War* (1979).

Schratz, Paul R. *Submarine Commander: A Story of World War II and Korea* (1988).

Simpson, Albert F. Historical Research Center. *USAF Credits for the Destruction of Enemy Aircraft, Korean War* (Air University, Aerospace Studies Institute, USAF Historical Division: 1963).

Snyder, Don J. *A Soldier's Disgrace* (1987).

Stanton, Shelby L. *Hell or High Water: MacArthur's Landing at Inchon* (1989).

———. *U.S. Army Uniforms of the Korean War* (1992).

———. *America's Tenth Legion: X Corps in Korea, 1950* (1989).

Stewart, James T., ed. *Airpower: The Decisive Force in Korea* (1957).

Stewart, Richard W. *Staff Operations: The X Corps in Korea, December 1950* (Combat Studies Institute: 1991).

Strawbridge, Dennis, and Nannette Kahn. *Fighter Pilot Performance in Korea* (1955).

Suchetta, Lawrence V. "Guerilla Warfare and Airpower in Korea, 1950–1953," typescript photocopy (Aerospace Studies Institute: January 1964).

Taylor, Roger C. *Mig Operations in Korea* (Air University, Maxwell AFB, Alabama: 1986).

Thomas, R.C.W. "The Campaign in Korea," *Brassey's Annual: The Armed Forces Yearbook*, ed. H.G. Thursfield (1953).

———. *The War in Korea, 1950–1953: A Military Study of the War in Korea* (1954).

Thompson, Annis G. *The Greatest Airlift: The Story of Combat Cargo*.

Thompson, Reginald William. *An Echo of Trumpets* (1964).

Toland, John. *In Mortal Combat: Korea, 1950–1953* (1991).

Tomedi, Rudy. *No Bugles, No Drums: An Oral History of the Korean War* (1993).

Ulanoff, Stanley W., ed. *Fighter Pilot* (1962).

United States, Department of the Air Force. Air Division (Combat Cargo), 315th. *Flexible Air Transport* (1951).

———. Historical Division. *United States Air Force Operations in the Korean Conflict, 1 November 1950–30 June 1952* (Department of the Air Force, Washington: 1953).

———. *USAF Tactical Operations: World War II and Korean War, with Statistical Tables* (USAF Historical Division, Liaison Office: 1962).

———. Aerospace Studies Institute, Concepts Division. *Guerilla Warfare and Airpower in Korea, 1950–53* (Air University, Aerospace Studies Institute: 1964).

———. Department of the Army, Armed Forces in Korea, *U. S. Military Government in Korea, September 45–June 50* (n.d.).

———. "Ordinances," 24 September 1945–24 October 1946. (n.d.).

———. Eighth Army, Staff Historian's Office. *Key Korean War Battles Fought in the Republic of Korea* (Eighth Army Headquarters: 1972).

———. *Korean Conflict: A Collection of Historical Manuscripts on the Korean Campaign Held by the U.S. Army Center of Military History* (1975), 9 reels.

————. Korean Civil Affairs Command. *Reference Handbook of the Government of the Republic of Korea* (n.d.).

————. Department of Defense. *Report from the Secretary of Defense to the President of the United States on Operations in Korea during the Period 25 June 1950 to 8 July 1951* (Office of the Chief of Military History: n.d.).

————. "Pertinent Papers on the Korean Situation," 8 vols. (Office of the Joint Chiefs of Staff: 1953).

————. *Korean Battle Honors: Consolidated List of Units Cited* (Office of the Chief of Military History: 1957).

————. Joint Chiefs of Staff. *Records of the Joint Chiefs of Staff, Part 2, 1946–1953*, Microform: *The Far East*, 13 reels with guide (1979–1983).

————. Department of the Navy. *The History of the Chaplain Corps, United States Navy*, Vol. 6, *During the Korean War, 17 June 1950–27 June 1954* (Department of the Navy: 1960).

Verdi, John M. *First Hundred: A Memoir of the Korean War* (privately printed: n.d. [c. 1988]).

Westover, John Glendower. *Combat Support in Korea: The United States Army in the Korean Conflict* (Office of the Chief of Military History: 1955).

Zimmerman, Leroy. *Korean War Logistics, Eighth United States Army*. (U.S. Army War College: 1986).

U.S. Military Forces, Articles

"Air Power in Korea: Ground Support," *U.S. Naval Institute Proceedings*, 78 (February 1952).

Air University Quarterly Staff. "Korea—An Opportunity Lost," *Air University Quarterly Review*, 9 (Spring 1957).

"Air War in Korea," *Air University Quarterly Review*, 4 (Fall 1950).

"The Air-Ground Operation in Korea," *Air Force*, 34 (March 1951).

Albert, Joseph, and Billy C. Wylie. "Problems of Airfield Construction in Korea," *Air University Quarterly Review*, 5 (Winter 1951–52).

Amody, Francis J. "Skyknights, Nightmares, and MIGs," *American Aviation Historical Society Journal*, 34 (Winter 1989).

"The Attack on Electric Power in North Korea: A Target System is Studied, Analyzed, and Destroyed," *Air University Quarterly Review*, 6 (Summer 1953).

Avedon, Herbert. "War for Men's Minds," *Military Review*, 33 (March 1954).

Barrett, George. "Portrait of the Korean Veteran," *New York Times Magazine* (9 August 1953).

Barth, George B. "The First Days in Korea," *United States Army Combat Forces Journal*, 1 (March 1952).

Bhagat, B.S. "Military Lessons of the Korean Conflict," *Military Review*, 32 (December 1952).

Blakeley, Michael E. "Disaster Along the Ch'ongch'on: Intelligence Breakdown in Korea, *Military Intelligence*, 34 (July-September 1992).

Blakeley, H.W. "Esprit de What? Our Army and Morale," *Quartermaster* (July 1986).

Blumenson, Martin. "MacArthur's Divided Command: An Assessment in the Light of Army Doctrine," *Army*, 7 (November 1956).

Boatner, Mark M, III. "Countering Communist Artillery," *Combat Forces Journal* (September 1953).

Burns, Charles V. "Air Traffic Control in the Far East," *Air University Quarterly Review*, 7 (Summer 1954).

Cagle, Malcolm W. "Errors of the Korean War," *U.S. Naval Institute Proceedings*, 84 (March 1958).

Cannon, Michael. "Task Force Smith: A Study in (Un)preparedness and (Ir)responsibility," *Military Review*, 68 (February 1988).

Canzona, Nicholas A. "Reflections on Korea," *The Marine Corps Gazette*, 35 (November 1951).

Cline, Tim. "Forward Air Control in the Korean War," *American Aviation Historical Society Journal*, 21 (Fall 1976).

Collins, J. Lawton. "A Dismantled Army Goes to War," *Army*, 19 (December 1969).

Colon, William. "Task Force Smith," *Infantry*, 70 (January-February 1980).

Connor, Arthur W., Jr. "The Army Debacle in Korea, 1950, Implications for Today," *Parameters*, 22 (Summer 1992).

————. "Breakout and Pursuit: The Drive from the Pusan Perimeter by the 1st Cavalry Division and Task Force Lynch," *Armor*, 17 (July-August 1993).

———. "Jousting with their Main Guns: A Bizarre Tank Battle of the Korean War," *Armor*, 17 (January-February 1993).

Cowdrey, Albert E. "'Germ Warfare' and Public Health in the Korean Conflict," *Journal of the History of Medicine and Allied Sciences*, 39 (April 1984).

———. "Development of Aeromedical Evacuation in the USAF, 1909–1960"; "Air War in Korea," *Aeronautical Engineering Review*, 11 (June 1952).

Daly, Robert W. "Did We Lose the Korean War?" *U.S. Naval Institute Proceedings*, 87 (June 1961).

Darragh, Shaun. "Hwanghae-do: The War of the Donkeys," *Army* (November 1984).

Davis, Lou. "Jet Fighter-Bombers—How Good Were They?" *Aviation Age*, 20 (November 1953).

Eagleston, Glenn T., and Bruce H. Hinton. "Eyes, Speed, and Altitude," *Air University Quarterly Review*, 4 (Summer 1951).

Edwards, Harry W. "A Naval Lesson of the Korean Conflict," *U.S. Naval Institute Proceedings*, 80 (December 1954).

Hoyt, Edwin C. "United States Reaction to the Korean Attack: A Story of the Principles of the United Nations Charter as a Factor in American Policy Making," *American Journal of International Law*, 55 (January 1961).

Hudson, G.F. "Korea and Asia," *International Affairs*, 27 (January 1951).

Flanagan, William J. "Korean War Logistics: The First Hundred Days," *Army Logistician*, 18 (March-April 1986).

Greenhough, Robert B. "Communist Lessons from the Korean Air War," *Air University Quarterly Review*, 5 (Winter 1952–53).

Gulley, Lee R. "Psychological Warfare in Korea," *Boeing Magazine*, 23 (May 1953).

Heasly, Morgan B. "Mountain Operations in Winter," *Military Review*, 32 (June 1952).

Heilbrun, Otto. "The Future of Deep Penetration," *Army Quarterly and Defense Journal*, 98 (July 1969).

Heinl, Robert D., Jr. "The Inchon Landing (September 1950): A Case Study in Amphibious Planning," *Naval War College Review*, 19 (May 1967).

Herz, Martin F. "Psychological Warfare Against Surrounded Troop Units," *Military Review*, 30 (August 1950).

HQ FEAF Bomber Command. "Heavyweights Over Korea," *Air University Quarterly Review*, 7 (Spring 1954).

Jensen, Ann. "To the Yalu," *U.S. Naval Institute Proceedings*, 116 (February 1990).

Key, William G. "Combat Cargo: Korea, 1950–51," *Pegasus*, 17 (November 1951).

Kintner, William R. "Pork Chop: Battle for a Korean Outpost," *Combat Forces Journal*, 5 (March 1955).

Kitchens, John W. "Cargo Helicopters in the Korean Conflict," *United States Army Aviation Digest* (November–December 1992, January–February 1993).

Kmiecik, Robert J. "Task Force Smith: A Revised Perspective," *Armor*, 99 (March-April 1990).

Kropf, Roger F. "U.S. Air Force In Korea: Problems That Hindered the Effectiveness of Air Power," *Airpower Journal*, 4 (Spring 1990).

Larew, Karl G. "Inchon Invasion not a Stroke of Genius or Even Necessary," *Army*, 38 (December 1988).

Ludvigsen, E.C. "An Arrogant Display of Strength": The Failed Bluff of Task Force Smith," *Army* (May 1992).

Malkin, Lawrence. "Murderers of Koje-do!" *MHQ: The Quarterly Journal of Military History*, 5 (Summer 1993).

Marion, Forrest L. "The Grand Experiment: Detachment F's Helicopter Combat Operations in Korea, 1950–1953, *Air Power History*, 40 (Summer 1993).

Marshall, S.L.A. "Our Mistakes In Korea," *Atlantic* (September 1953).

———. "Operations Mishandled on Pork Chop Hill?" *Army-Navy-Air Force Register*, 80 (20 June 1959).

———. "Pork Chop Hill Five Years After," *Army*, 9 (July 1959).

Marshall, Thurgood. "Summary Justice—The Negro in Korea," *Crisis*, 58 (1951).

Martin, M.T. "Medical Aspects of Helicopter Air Evacuation," *Journal of Aviation Medicine* (1952).

Matray, James I. "Truman's Plan for Victory: National Self-Determination and the Thirty-Eighth Parallel Decision in Korea," *Journal of American History*, 66 (September 1979).

Mattia, Hugh J. "Air Force Procurement in Japan," *Air University Quarterly Review*, 6 (Fall 1953).

Mentzer, R.A., Jr. "Research from the Battle-field: Military History Detachments in Wartime Korea," *Army History*, 19 (Summer 1991).

Millberry, R.J. "Engineer Aviation Forces In Korea," *Air University Quarterly Review* (Fall 1953).

Minifie, James M. "Caught Short on Korea," *Nation*, 171 (22 July 1950).

Mrazek, J.E. "Civil Assistance in Action," *Military Review* 35 (October 1955).

Nelson, Carl G. "REMCO, A Korean War Development," *Air University Quarterly Review* (Spring 1953).

"Newspaper Report on Morale of U.S. Soldiers in Korea," *U.S. Army Attache, Great Britain* (R-226–53) (29 January 1953).

Norman, John. "MacArthur's Blockade Proposals Against Red China," *Pacific Historical Review*, 26 (May 1957).

Nowell, Robert B. "The Air Terminal Group," *Air University Quarterly Review*, 7 (Summer 1954).

"Paper Bombs in Korea," *New York Times Magazine* (25 February 1951).

Parker, Roy H. "Religion at Work," *Chaplain*, 9 (1952).

Paschall, Rod. "Special Operations in Korea," *Conflict*, 7, no. 2 (1987).

Phillips, D.W. "Air Force Psychological Warfare in Korea," *Air University Quarterly Review* (Summer 1951).

Pirnie, Bruce R. "The Inchon Landing: How Great Was the Risk?" *Joint Perspectives*, 3 (Summer 1982).

Pogue, L. Welch. "The Significance of the Helicopter," *Technical Review* (1952).

"Psychological Warfare in Korea: An Interim Report," *Public Opinion Quarterly*, 15 (Spring 1951).

Purkiser, H.L. "What's New in Signals," *Military Review*, 31 (1952).

"The Qualities of an Air Force Ace," *American Aviation*, 18 (28 March 1955).

Ridgway, Matthew B. "Troop Leadership at the Operational Level: The Eight Army in Korea," *Military Review* (April 1990).

Roberts, Chris. "Tactical Air Power Lessons from Korea," *Interavia*, 9 (1954).

Rougeron, Camille. "Some Lessons of the War in Korea," *U.S. Naval Institute Proceedings*, 79 (June 1953).

Schaad, Carl W. "Fire Support Coordination," *Combat Forces Journal* (September 1952).

Schnabel, James F. "The Inchon Landing: Perilous Gamble or Exemplary Boldness?" *Army*, 9 (May 1959).

Skaggs, D.C. "The KATUSA Experiment: The Integration of Korean Nationals into the U.S. Army, 1950–1965," *Military Affairs* (April 1974).

Taylor, L.G. "Flying Training in Fifth Air Force," *Air University Quarterly Review*, 6 (Winter 1953–54).

Tomlinson, H. Pat. "Inchon: The General's Decision," *Military Review*, 47 (April 1967).

United States Department of State. "Leaflets Warn Korean Refugees of Destruction of Native Towns," *United States Department of State Bulletin*, 23 (11 December 1950).

Vale, Charles F. "Combat Through the Camera's Eye," *Army Information Digest* (March 1953).

Voigtlander, Karl A. Von. "The War for Words," *Army Information Digest* (1953).

Walker, Stanley L. "Logistics of the Inchon Landing," *Army Logistician*, 13 (July-August 1981).

West, Philip. "Interpreting the Korean War," *American Historical Review*, 94 (1989).

Weyland, Otto P. "The Air Campaign in Korea," *Air University Quarterly Review* (Fall 1953).

Wiley, Noble J., Jr. "The Pen Supports the Sword," *Army Information Digest* (1953).

Zahl, Harold A. "Toward Lighter Signal Equipment," *Army Information Digest* (June 1953).

Zimmerman, Don Z. "FEAF: Mission and Command Relationships," *Air University Quarterly Review*, 4 (Summer 1951).

U.N. Forces

Ayers, Charles. "The U.S. Army and the Development of the ROK Army: 1945–1950," report by Army–Air Force Center for Low Intensity Conflict (Langley Air Force Base: n.d.).

Barclay, C.N. *The First Commonwealth Division: The Story of British Commonwealth Land Forces in Korea, 1950–1953* (1954).

Bartlett, Norman, ed. *With the Australians in Korea* (Australian War Memorial, Canberra: 1954).

Canada, Army General Staff, Historical Section. *Canada's Army in Korea: The United Nations Operations, 1950–1953, and Their Aftermath* (1956).

Carew, Tim. *Korea: The Commonwealth at War* (1967).

Clemov, C.W.A. "New Zealand, the Commonwealth, and the Korean War: A Study in Government Policy and Unofficial Opinion," thesis, University of Aukland, 1967.

Dayal, Shiv. *India's Role in the Korean Question* (1959).

Farrar-Hockley, Anthony. *The British Part in the Korean War*, Vol. 1, *A Distant Obligation* (1990).

———. *The Edge of the Sword* (1954).

Fox, W.J. "History of the Korean War: Inter-Allied Co-Operation During Combat Operations," United States Army, Far East Command (n.d.).

Gordon, Harry. "The Turks Were There," in Norman Bartlett, *With the Australians in Korea* (1954).

Grey, Jeffrey. *The Commonwealth Armies and the Korean War: An Alliance Study* (1989).

Korea (Republic of). *The History of the United Nations Forces in the Korean War*, 6 vols. (Ministry of National Defense, [Seoul], 1972–1977).

Kwak, Tae-Hwan. "United States–Korean Relations: A Core Interest Analysis Prior to United States Intervention in the Korean War," thesis, Claremont Graduate School, 1969.

MacDonald, Callum A. *Britain and the Korean War* (1990).

McCormack, Gavan. *Cold War, Hot War: An Australian Perspective on the Korean War* (1983).

Montyn, Jan, and Dirk A. Kooiman. *A Lamb to the Slaughter* (1985).

Odgers, George. *Across the Parallel: The Australian 77th Squadron in the United States Air Force in the Korean War* (1954).

O'Neill, Robert. *Australia in the Korean War, 1950–53*, 2 vols. *Strategy and Diplomacy* (Australian Government Publishing Service, Canberra: 1981); *Combat Operations* (Australian Government Publishing Service, Canberra: 1985).

Paik Sun Yup. *From Pusan to Panmunjom* (1992).

Skordiles, Komon. *Kagnew, the Story of the Ethiopian Fighters in Korea* (1954).

Stairs, Denis W. "The Role of Canada in the Korean War," thesis, University of Toronto, 1969.

Thorgrimsson, Thor, and E.C. Russell. *Canadian Naval Operations in Korean Waters, 1950–1955* (Department of National Defence, Canadian Forces HQ, Naval Historical Section, Ottawa: 1965).

Tucker, E.N., and P.M.J. McGregor. *Per Noctem Per Diem: The Story of 24 Squadron, South African Air Force* (1961).

United Kingdom, Ministry of Defence. *British Commonwealth Naval Operations, Korea, 1950–53* (1967).

Wood, Herbert Fairlie. *Strange Battleground: The Operations in Korea and Their Effects on Canada* (1966).

U.N. Military Forces, Articles

Boatner, Mark M. "The French Battalion at Arrowhead (Korea—October 1952)," *Revue Historique de l'Armee* (1954).

Cameron, Robert C. "The Lost Corps," *Military Review*, 33 (May 1953).

"Canada's Army in Korea," *Canadian Army Journal*, 9, parts 2–5 (January 1955–January 1956).

Cooling, Benjamin F. "Allied Interoperability in the Korean War," *Military Review*, 63 (June 1983).

Goodrich, Leland M. "The United Nations and the Korean War: A Case Study," *Academy of Political Science Proceedings*, 25 (January 1953).

Hall, Thomas A. "KMAG and the 7th ROK Division," *Infantry*, 79 (November–December 1989).

Holly, David C. "The ROK Navy," *U.S. Naval Institute Proceedings*, 78 (November 1952).

Kim Sang Mo. "The Implications of the Sea War in Korea (From the Standpoint of the Korean Navy)," *Naval War College Review*, 20 (Summer 1967).

McGregor, P.M.J. "History of No. 2 Squadron, SAAF, in the Korean War," *Military History Journal* (June 1978).

Moore, D.M. "SAAF in Korea," *Militaria* (1980).

O'Ballance, Edgar. "The Turkish Contribution," *Military Review*, 35 (August 1955).

Ozselcuk, Nusret. "The Turkish Brigade in the Korean War (25th June 1950–27th July 1953)," *Review Internationale d'Histoire Militaire*, 46 (1980).

Ramsey, R.W. "Columbian Battalion in Korea and Suez," *Journal of Inter-American Studies*, 9 (October 1967).

Sheehan, Vincent. "The Case for India," *Foreign Affairs*, 30 (1976).

Soward, F.H. "The Korean Crisis and the Commonwealth," *Pacific Affairs*, 24 (June 1951).

Taubenfeld, H.J. "International Armed Forces and the Rules of War," *American Journal of International Law*, 45 (October 1951).

Communist Military Forces

Atkins, E.L., H.P. Griggs, and Roy T. Sessums. *North Korean Logistics and Methods of Accomplishment* (1951).

Bradbury, William Chapman. *Mass Behavior in Battle and Captivity: The Communist Soldier in the Korean War*, eds. Samuel M. Meyers and Albert D. Biderman (1968).

Bueschel, Richard M. *Communist Chinese Air Power* (1968).

Burchett, Wilfred G. *This Monstrous War* (1953).

Burchett, Wilfred, and Alan Winnington. *Koje Unscreened* (1953).

———. *Again Korea* (1968).

Byfield, R.S. *Logocide, the Fifth Weapon*, privately printed (1953).

Chen, T.H.E. "The Resist-America Aid-Korea Campaign in Communist China," University of Southern California, Department of Asiatic Studies, Studies in Chinese Communism, typescript, series 1, no. 4 (15 February 1951).

———. *The Communists' New Weapon: Germ Warfare* (1953).

———. *Communist Propaganda Techniques* (1964).

Ching-wen Chou. *Ten Years of Storm* (1960).

Corr, Gerard H. *The Chinese Red Army: Campaigns and Politics Since 1949* (1974).

Cunningham, O. *Communist Indoctrination and Interrogation Techniques in Korea* ([British] Air Ministry, Science, no. 4, London: 1 March 1954).

Dispositions of Nineteen Captured U.S. Airmen on Their Participation in Germ Warfare in Korea (Department of Cultural Relations with Foreign Countries, Ministry of Culture and Propaganda, DPRK: 1954).

George, Alexander L. *The Chinese Communist Army in Action: The Korean War and Its Aftermath* (1967).

Griffith, Samuel B., II. *The Chinese People's Liberation Army* (1967).

Halpern, A.M. "Bacteriological Warfare Accusations in Two Asian Propaganda Campaigns," Research Memorandum (RM)-76, April 25, 1952 (1952).

Harris, Richard. "Chinese Armed Forces," *Brassey's Annual: The Armed Forces Yearbook*, ed. H.G. Thursfield (1951).

Harris, William R. "The Adaptation of Communist Strategy to Nuclear and Thermonuclear Weapons, 1945–1953," typescript (1966)

I-Shan Chiang. "The Military Affairs of Communist China," *Communist China 1949–1959* (1961).

Jencks, Harlan W. *From Muskets to Missiles: Politics and Professionalism in the Chinese Army, 1945–1981* (1982).

Kahn, Lessing A., et al. *A Study of North Korean and Chinese Soldiers' Attitudes Toward the Korean War* (1952).

Kim Il-Sung. *Unity Based on Revolutionary Comradeship Is the Source of the Invincibility of the People's Army: Speech at a Banquet Given in Honour of the 25th Anniversary of the Foundation of the Heroic Korean People's Army, February 8, 1973* (Pyongyang: 1973).

McMichael, S.R. *An Historical Perspective on Light Infantry* (U.S. Army Command and General Staff College, Combat Studies Center: 1987).

Meyers, Samuel M., and Albert D. Biderman. *Mass Behavior in Battle and Captivity: The Communist Soldier in the Korean War* (1968).

"New Facts on U.S. Germ Warfare in Korea and China" (Supplement to *Peoples China*, 15 March 1953).

O'Ballance, Edgar. *The Red Army of China* (1962).

Peng Dehuai. *Memoirs of a Chinese Marshal: The Autobiographical Notes of Peng Dehuai (1898–1974)* (1984).

Preston, H.O., et al. *Study of Ineffective Soldier Performance Under Fire in Korea, 1951* (1954).

Rigg, Robert B. *Red China's Fighting Hordes* (1952).

Riley, John W., and Wilbur Schramm. *The Reds Take a City: The Communist Occupation of Seoul, with Eyewitness Accounts* (1951).

Ryan, Mark A. *Chinese Attitudes Toward Nuclear Weapons: China and the United States During the Korean War* (1989).

Ryan, William L., and Sam Summerlin. *The China Cloud: America's Tragic Blunder and China's Rise to Nuclear Power* (1967).

[Anon.] *Shall Brothers Be . . .* (1952).

Spurr, Russell. *Enter the Dragon: China's Undeclared War against the U.S. in Korea, 1950–1951* (1988).

Statements by Two Captured U.S. Officers on Their Participation in Germ Warfare in Korea (1952).

Tunstall, Julian. *I Fought in Korea* (1953).

United States, Department of the Army. ATIS Research Supplement, no. 3, Far East Command, GS, 15, (November 1950).

———. #104 (1951).

———. *Handbook on the Chinese Communist Army* (Washington: 1952).

———. Far East Command. *History of the North Korean Army* (1952).

———. *Order of Battle Handbook: Chinese Communist Forces, Korea and the North Korean Army* (HQ, Far East Command, G-2 Tokyo: 1 October 1955).

———. *Tables of Organization and Equipment of the North Korean Army* (HQ Far East Command, G-2 Tokyo: 1 July 1957).

———. *North Korean Armed Forces*, pamphlet 30–52 (Washington: 11 July 1962).

———. Department of State. *North Korea: A Case Study in the Techniques of Takeover* (January 1961).

Way, A.E. "Study of a Random Sample of 'American POW Messages' Directed at Target USA by Radio Peking" typescript copy in U.S. Army Special Operations Command, Fort Bragg, NC (U.S. Army Psychological Division, n.d.)

Whiting, Allen S. *China Crosses the Yalu: The Decision to Enter the Korean War* (1960).

Whitson, William W. *The Chinese High Command: A History of Communist Military Politics, 1927–1971* (1973).

Zelman, Walter A. *Chinese Intervention in the Korean War: A Bilateral Failure of Deterrence* (1967).

Communist Military Forces, Periodical Articles

Albright, Joseph G. "Two Years of MIG Activity," *Air University Quarterly Review*, 6 (Spring 1953).

Baldwin, Hanson W. "China as a Military Power," *Foreign Affairs*, 30 (October 1951).

Brayson, Benson Lee. "The Organization of the Chinese Communist Army," *Armor*, 64 (March-April 1955).

Cheng, J. Chester. "The Dynamics of the Chinese People's Liberation Army: Regularization and Revolutionization, 1949–1959," *Military Review*, 54 (May 1974).

"Chinese Communist 'Germ Warfare' Propaganda," U.S. Army, Liaison Office, Hong Kong (R-74–52) (10 April 1952).

Clark, M.W. "Communist Charges Re Release of American Prisoners; Text of Letter Sent on 29 June 1953," *United States Department of State Bulletin*, 29 (13 July 1953).

"Communist Camouflage and Deception," *Air University Quarterly Review*, 6 (Spring 1953).

"Commission of International Association of Democratic Lawyers Report on War Crimes in Korea" (10 April 1952).

"Communist Bacteriological Warfare Camp," Foreign Service Department, Brazil (10 April 1952).

"Entry into the Korean War Remembered," *Beijing Review*, 33 (9 November 1990).

Farrar-Hockley, Anthony. "A Reminiscence of the Chinese People's Volunteers in the Korean War," *China Quarterly*, 98 (June 1984).

———. *Collection of Critical Reviews of Some Recent Experimental Literature Pertinent to the Interrogation Process* (Washington: December 1957).

———. *Power and Resistance in Interrogation* (Washington: December 1957).

Hanrahan, Gene Z. "The People's Revolutionary Military Council in Communist China," *Far Eastern Survey*, 23 (May 1954).

Hao Yufan and Zhai Zhihai. "China's Decision to Enter the Korean War: History Revisited," *China Quarterly*, 121 (March 1990).

Harris, William R. "Chinese Nuclear Doctrine: The Decade Prior to Weapons Development (1945–1955)," *China Quarterly*, 21 (January-March 1965).

Hunt, Michael H. "Beijing and the Korean Crisis, June 1950–June 1951," *Political Science Quarterly*, 107 (Fall 1992).

Kozaczka, Felix. "Enemy Bridging Techniques in Korea," *Air University Quarterly Review*, 5 (Winter 1952–53).

Meyers, Gilbert L. "Intervention by Chinese Communists," *Air University Quarterly Review*, 4 (Summer 1951).

"Mig Maneuvers," *Air University Quarterly Review*, 6 (Winter 1953–54).

Niessel, A. "The Army of Communist China," *Military Review*, 35 (June 1955).

Sterne, Paul J. "The Build-Up of Enemy Air Potential," *Air University Quarterly Review*, 4 (Summer 1951).

Thach, Joseph E., Jr. "Modernization and Conflict: Soviet Military Assistance to the PRC, 1950–60," *Military Review* (January 1978).

Thomas, R.C.W. "The Chinese Communist Forces in Korea," *Military Review*, 32 (February 1953).

Weller, Jac. "CHICOM-Small Arms and Tactics," *Marine Corps Gazette*, 46 (December 1962).

Whiting, Allen S. "New Chinese Communist," *World Politics*, 7 (July 1955).

Wilson, Paul E. "What Makes LUKE Run," *Military Review*, 34 (August 1954).

American Home Front

Caridi, Ronald J. *The Korean War and American Politics: The Republican Party as a Case Study* (1969).

Condit, Doris M. *The Test of War 1950–1953*, Vol. 2 of 2 vols., *History of the Office of the Secretary of Defense*, 1984–1988 (Office of the Secretary of Defense: 1988).

Connally, Thomas Terry. *My Name is Tom Connally* (1954).

Dewey, Thomas E. *Journey to the Far Pacific* (1952).

Donovan, Robert J. *Tumultuous Years: The Presidency of Harry S. Truman, 1949–1953* (1982).

Gosnell, Harold Foote. *Truman's Crises: A Political Biography of Harry S. Truman* (1980).

Gietschier, Steven P. "Limited War and the Home Front: Ohio During the Korean War," thesis, Ohio State University, 1977.

Harris, Louis. *Is There a Republican Majority? Political Trends, 1952–1956* (1954).

Horne, Gerald. *Communist Front? The Civil Rights Congress, 1946–1956* (1988).

Mantell, Edwin Matthew. "Opposition to the Korean War: A Study in American Dissent," thesis, New York University, 1973.

Morgan, Anne Hodges. *Robert S. Kerr: The Senate Years* (1977).

Mueller, John E. *War, Presidents, and Public Opinion* (1973).

Osmer, Harold H. *U.S. Religious Journalism and the Korean War* (1980).

Ponturo, Emma J. "Korea," in R. W. Coakley, et al., *Antiwar and Antimilitary Activities in the United States, 1846–1956* (Office of the Chief of Military History: 11 March 1970).

Riggs, James Richard. "Congress and the Conduct of the Korean War," thesis, Purdue University, 1972.

Smith, Robert B. "Disaffection, Delegitimation, and Consequences: Aggregate Trends for World War II, Korea, and Vietnam," *Public Opinion and the Military Establishment*, ed. Charles C. Moskos, Jr. (1971).

Stevenson, Adlai E. "Korea," *Major Speeches of Adlai E. Stevenson 1952* (1953).

Stein, Bruno. "Labor Participation in Stabilization Agencies: The Korean War Period as a Case Study," thesis, New York University, 1959.

Titus, James, ed. *The Home Front and War in the Twentieth Century: The American Experience in Comparative Perspective. Proceedings of the Tenth Military History Symposium, 20–22 October, 1982* (U.S. Air Force Academy: 1984).

Truman, Harry S. *Memoirs* (1955–56).

Wells, S.F., Jr. "Sounding the Tocsin: NSC-68 and the Soviet Threat," *International Security* (1979).

Wilz, John Edward. "The Korean War and American Society," *The Korean War: A 25–Year Perspective*, ed. Francis H. Heller (1977).

Home Front, Periodical Articles

Anderson, David L. "China Policy and Presidential Politics, 1952," *Presidential Studies Quarterly*, 10 (Winter 1980).

Armstrong, John P. "The Enigma of Senator Taft and American Foreign Policy," *Review of Politics*, 17 (April 1955).

Banks, Samuel. "The Korean Conflict," *Negro History Bulletin*, 36, no. 6 (1973).

Caine, Philip D. "The United States in Korea and Vietnam: A Study in Public Opinion," *Air University Quarterly Review*, 20 (November–December 1968).

Caridi, Ronald J. "The G.O.P and the Korean War," *Pacific Historical Review*, 37 (1968).

Cuff, R. "From the Controlled Materiels Plan to the Defense Materiels System, 1942–1953," *Military Affairs*, 51 (January 1987).

"Defense Production Act of 1950: Terms and Early Action," *Monthly Labor Review*, 71 (October 1950).

Elowitz, Larry, and John W. Spanier. "Korea and Vietnam: Limited War and the American Political System," *Orbis*, 18 (Summer 1974).

Fleischmann, Manny. "Policies and Procedures for Limited Mobilization," *Annals of the American Academy of Political and Social Science*, 278 (November 1951).

Flynn, George Q. "The Draft and College Deferments During the Korean War," *Historian*, 50 (May 1988).

Griffith, Robert. "The Chilling Effect," *Wilson Quarterly*, 2, no. 3 (Spring 1978).

Hamby, Alonzo L. "Public Opinion: Korea and Vietnam," *Wilson Quarterly*, no. 2 (Summer 1978).

Hamilton, Richard F. "A Research Note on the Mass Support for 'Tough' Military Initiatives," *American Sociological Review*, 33 (June 1968).

Herzon, Federick D., John Kincaid, and Verne Dalton. "Personality & Public Opinion: The Case of Authoritarianism, Prejudice, & Support for the Korean and Vietnam Wars," *Polity*, 11 (Fall 1978).

Janeway, Eliot. "The International Imperative and Mobilization," *Yale Review*, 40 (Spring 1951).

Lofgren, Charles A. "'Mr. Truman's War': A Debate and Its Aftermath," *Review of Politics*, 31 (April 1969).

Mack, Louise J. "Price Movements During a Year of Korean Hostilities," *Monthly Labor Review*, 73 (August 1951).

Marwell, Gerald. "Party, Region, and the Dimensions of Conflict in the House of Representatives, 1949–1954," *American Political Science Review*, 61 (June 1967).

McLellan, David S. "Dean Acheson and the Korean War," *Political Science Quarterly*, 83 (March 1968).

Mitchell, Donald W. "Mobilization Progress: A Summary of Our Industrial Mobilization," *Current History*, 23 (September 1952).

Muller, John E. "Presidential Popularity from Truman to Johnson," *American Political Science Review*, 65 (March 1971).

Pasternak, Robert. "A Review of Prices in a Year of Price Stabilization," *Monthly Labor Review*, 74 (April 1952).

Perkins, Dexter. "Dissent in Time of War," *Virginia Quarterly Review*, 47 (Spring 1974).

Reday, Joseph. "Industrial Mobilization in the U.S.," *U.S. Naval Institute Proceedings*, 79 (October 1953).

Rings, E. Eleanor. "The Effects of Mobilization on Automobile Employment," *Monthly Labor Review*, 74 (January 1952).

Rossiter, Clinton. "Impact of Mobilization on the Constitutional System," *Academy of Political Science Proceedings*, 30 (May 1971).

Ruddick, P.T. "Stopping the War: The Eisenhower Administration and the Search for an Armistice in Korea," *Paradigms*, 6 (Spring 1992).

Suchman, Edward A., Rose K. Goldsen, and Robin M. Williams, Jr. "Attitudes Toward the Korean War," *Public Opinion Quarterly*, 17 (Summer 1953).

———. "Student Reaction to Impending Military Service," *American Sociological Review*, 18 (June 1953).

Thomas, James A. "Collapse of the Defensive War Argument," *Military Review*, 53 (May 1973).

Toner, James H. "American Society and the American Way of War: Korean and Beyond," *Parameters*, 11 (May 1981).

Whitney, Richard W. "Mobilizing Public Opinion," *Military Review*, 30 (March 1951).

Wood, Helen. "Effect of Mobilization Programs on Employment Opportunities," *Monthly Labor Review*, 71 (December 1950).

Yin-Hsieh, Clarence. "The Truman Administration's Military Budgets During the Korean War," thesis, University of California, Berkeley, 1978.

Film, Literary, and Media Coverage of the War

Axelsson, Arne. *Restrained Response: American Novels of the Cold War and Korea, 1945–1962* (1990).

Daniels, Dwight C. *The Military and the Media: Historical Perspectives and Perspective Study of the Relationship,* thesis, Air Force Institute of Technology, 1985.

DiCola, Louis F. *The Korean War as Seen by the* CHICAGO TRIBUNE, *the* NEW YORK TIMES, *and* THE TIMES *of London,* thesis, Kent State University, 1981.

Myrick, Howard A. "Critical Analysis of Thematic Content of United States Army Orientation Films of the Korean War, with Implications for Formulating Limited War Orientation," thesis, University of Southern California, 1968.

Notopoulos, Joseph J. "The Influence of the Principles of the Containment Policy upon the Military Strategy of the Korean War," thesis, American University, 1964.

Media Coverage of the War, Periodical Articles

Cleary, Thomas J., Jr. "Aid and Comfort to the Enemy," *Military Review,* 48 (August 1968).

Mee, Charles L., Jr. "Are You Telling Them that It Is an Utterly Useless War?" *Horizon,* 18 (Winter 1976).

Namenwirth, J. Zvi, and Richard Bibbee. "Speech Codes in the Press," *Journal of Communication,* 25 (Spring 1975).

Sherer, Michael. "Comparing Magazine Photos of Vietnam and Korea," *Journalism Quarterly,* 65 (Fall 1988).

Diplomacy of The War

Acheson, Dean. *The Korean War* (1971).

Bohlen, Charles. *Witness to History* (1973).

Bowles, Chester. *Ambassador's Report* (1954).

Farley, Miriam S. "The Korean Crisis and the United Nations," in *The State of Asia: A Contemporary Survey* (1953).

Goodrich, Leland Matthew. *Korea, A Study of U.S Policy in the United Nations* (1979).

Heimsath, Charles H. "India's Role in the Korean War," thesis, Yale University, 1957.

Johnson, U. Alexis, and J. Olivarus McAllister. *The Right Hand of Power* (1984).

Kaplan, Lawrence S. "The Korean War and U.S. Foreign Relations: The Case of NATO," in *The Korean War: A 25-Year Perspective,* ed. Francis H. Heller (1977).

Lyons, Gene Martin. *Military Policy and Economic Aid: The Korean Case, 1950–1953* (1961).

Major Problems of United States Foreign Policy 1951–52 (1951).

Mayers, David Allan. *Cracking the Monolith: U.S. Policy Against the Sino-Soviet Alliance, 1949–1955* (1986).

Ovendale, Ritchie. *The English-Speaking Alliance: Britain, the United States, the Dominions, and the Cold War, 1945–1951* (1985).

Pollack, Jonathan. "The Korean War and Sino-American Relations." *Sino-American Relations, 1945–1955: A Joint Reassessment of a Critical Decade,* eds. Yuan Ming and Harry Harding (1989).

Simmons, Robert R. *The Strained Alliance: Peking, P'yongyang, Moscow, and the Politics of the Korean Civil War* (1975).

Smith, Gaddis. *Dean Acheson* (New York: 1972), Vol. 16 of *The American Secretaries of State and Their Diplomacy,* 20 vols., 1927–85.

Spanier, John W. *American Foreign Policy Since World War II* (Congressional Quarterly, Washington: 1988).

Stairs, Denis. *The Diplomacy of Constraint: Canada, the Korean War, and the United States* (1974).

United States Department of State. *United States Policy in the Korean Crisis,* Far Eastern Series, 34 (July 1950).

———. *The Conflict in Korea: Events Prior to the Attack on June 25, 1950,* 45, Far Eastern Series (1951).

———. *Korea* (August 1951).

———. *Bulletin(s).* 1945–1953.

———. *The Korean Problem at the Geneva Conference, April 26–June 15 1954* (1954).

———. *A Historical Summary of United States–Korean Relations, 1934–1962,* Far Eastern Series, 11 (November 1962).

———. *Foreign Relations of the United States, 1950* Vol. 7, *Korea* (1976).

———. *1951*, Vol. 7, *Korea and China* (1983).

———. *1952–54*, Vol. 15, *Korea* (1984).

———. *American Foreign Policy 1950–1955: Basic Documents*, 2 vols. (GPO, Washington: 1957).

———. *United States Policy in the Korean Conflict July 1950–February 1951*.

Vyshinsky, A.Y. *Korea: Speeches at the Seventh Session of the U.N. General Assembly* (1952).

———. *The Korean Question* (1952).

Yi Ki-Tong. Seoul SINMUN. Translation by the Foreign Broadcast Information Service. "It Took Mao Zedong Three Agonizing, Sleepless Nights to Decide to Dispatch Troops to the Korean War," *FBIS Daily Report—East Asia* (29 March 1991).

Zimmerman, William. "The Korean and Vietnam Wars," in *Diplomacy of Power: Soviet Armed Forces As a Political Instrument* (1981).

Diplomacy of the War, Periodical Articles

Acheson, Dean G. "Our Far Eastern Policy: Debate, Decision, and Action," *United States Department of State Bulletin*, 24 (30 April 1951).

"The Acheson Testimony," *Current History*, 21 (August 1951).

Altstedter, Norman. "Problems of Coalition Diplomacy: The Korean Experience," *International Journal*, 8 (Autumn 1953).

Bernstein, Barton J. "The Atomic Bomb and American Foreign Policy, 1941–1945: An Historiographical Controversy," *Peace and Change*, 2 (Spring 1974).

———. "New Light on the Korean War," *International History Review*, 3 (April 1981).

———. "Truman's Secret Thoughts on Ending the Korean War," *Foreign Service Journal*, 57 (November 1980).

Boyle, Peter G. "Britain, America, and the Transition from Economic to Military Assistance, 1948–1951," *Journal of Contemporary History*, 22 (July 1987).

Brands, H.W. "The Dwight D. Eisenhower Administration, Syngman Rhee, and the 'Other' Geneva Conference of 1954," *Pacific Historical Review* (February 1987).

Dayal, Rajeshwar. "The Power of Wisdom," *International Journal*, 29 (Winter 1973–74).

Dingman, Roger, "Atomic Diplomacy During the Korean War," *International Security*, 13 (Winter 1988–89).

Dockrill, M.L. "The Foreign Office, Anglo-American Relations and the Korean War, June 1950–June 1951," *International Affairs*, 62 (Summer 1986).

"Exchange of Notes Between the U.S. Ambassador in Moscow and the Deputy Foreign Minister of the Soviet Union Concerning the Korean Situation," *International Organization*, 4 (August 1950).

Farrar, Peter N. "Britain's Proposal for a Buffer Zone South of the Yalu in November 1950," *Journal of Contemporary History*, 18 (1983).

Foot, Rosemary. "Anglo-American Relations in the Korean Crisis: The British Effort to Avert an Expanded War, December 1950–January 1951," *Diplomatic History*, 10 (Winter 1986).

George, Alexander L. "American Policy-Making and the North Korean Aggression," *World Politics*, 7 (January 1955).

Graebner, Norman A. "Dean G. Acheson (1949–1953)," in *An Uncertain Tradition: American Secretaries of State in the Twentieth Century*, ed. Norman A. Graebner (1961).

Heimsath, C.H. "Indo-American Relations; Effects of the Korean Conflict," *Journal of International Relations*, 6 (October 1953).

Jong-Yil, Ra. "Special Relationship at War: The Anglo-American Relationship During the Korean War," *Journal of Strategic Studies*, 7 (September 1984).

LeFeber, Walter. "NATO and the Korean War: A Context (NATO Over Forty Years)" *Diplomatic History*, 13 (Fall 1989).

Keefer, Edward C. "President Dwight D. Eisenhower and the End of the Korean War," *Diplomatic History*, 10 (Summer 1986).

Kim, Gye-Dong. "Who Initiated the Korean War?" in James Cotton and Ian Neary, eds., *The Korean War in History* (1989).

Kim, Hok-Joon. "China's Non-Involvment in the Origins of the Korean War: A Critical Reassessment of the Traditionalist and Revisionist Literature," in James Cotton and Ian Neary, eds., *The Korean War in History* (1989).

"Korea: Proving Ground for Collective Action Against Aggression," *United Nations Bulletin*, 15 (1 August 1953).

Mazuzan, George T. "America's U.N. Commitment, 1945–1953," *Historian*, 40 (February 1978).

McLellan, David S. "Dean Acheson and the Korean War," *Political Science Quarterly*, 83 (March 1968).

Mosely, Philip E. "Soviet Policy and the War," *Journal of International Affairs*, 6 (Spring 1952).

Nakajima, Mineo. "Foreign Relations from the Korean War to the Bandung Line," in *The Cambridge History of China*, 14: *The People's Republic*, Part I, *The Emergence of Revolutionary China 1949–1965*, eds. Denis Twitchett and John K. Fairbank.

———. "The Sino-Soviet Confrontation: Its Roots in the International Background of the Korean War," *Australian Journal of Chinese Affairs*, 1 (January 1979).

O'Neill, Robert. "Constraint with Honor," *International Journal*, 29 (Summer 1974).

Oliver, Robert T. "Syngman Rhee and the United Nations," *Pacific Spectator*, 7 (Autumn 1953).

Paddleford, Norman J. "The United Nations and Korea: A Political Resume," *International Organization*, 5 (November 1951).

Park, Chang Jin. "American Foreign Policy in Korea and Vietnam: Comparative Influence of Small States upon the Superpowers: United States–South Korean Relations as a Case Study 1950–53," *World Politics*, 28 (October 1975).

Stairs, Denis. "The United Nations and the Politics of the Korean War," *International Journal*, 25 (Spring 1970).

Steinberg, Blema S. "The Korean War: A Case Study in Indian Neutralism; India's Attitude Toward North Korean Aggression and Chinese Intervention; The Neutral Nations Repatriation Commission," *Orbis*, 8 (Winter 1965).

Truman-MacArthur Controversy

Flint, Roy K. "The Tragic Flaw: MacArthur, the Joint Chiefs, and the Korean War," thesis, Duke University, 1975.

Higgins, Trumbull. *Korea and the Fall of MacArthur: A Précis in Limited War* (1960).

Hunt, Frazier. *The Untold Story of Douglas MacArthur* (1954).

James, D. Clayton. *Triumph and Disaster, 1945–1964*, Vol. 3 of *The Years of MacArthur* (1970).

Kenney, George C. *The MacArthur I Know* (1951).

Lee, Clark G., and Richard Henschel. *Douglas MacArthur* (1952).

Long, Gavin M. *MacArthur as Military Commander* (1969).

Lowitt, Richard, comp. *The Truman-MacArthur Controversy* (1967).

MacArthur, Douglas. "Mr. Truman Yielded to Counsel of Fear," *U.S. News and World Report* (17 February 1956).

———. *Reminiscences* (1964).

———. *A Soldier Speaks: Public Papers and Speeches of General of the Army Douglas MacArthur* (1965).

Manchester, William R. *American Caesar: Douglas MacArthur (1880–1964)* (1978).

Potter, Allen R. "The Truman-MacArthur Controversy: A Study in Political-Military Relations," thesis, U.S. Army Command and General Staff College, 1972.

Rovere, Richard H., and Arthur M. Schlesinger, Jr. *The General and the President and the Future of American Foreign Policy* (1951).

———. *The MacArthur Controversy and American Foreign Policy* (1965).

Schaller, Robert. *Douglas MacArthur: The Far Eastern General* (1989).

Smith, Robert. *MacArthur in Korea: The Naked Emperor* (1982).

Spanier, John W. *The Truman-MacArthur Controversy and the Korean War* (1959).

Truman, Harry S. "MacArthur Was Ready to Risk General War. I Was Not," *U.S. News and World Report* (17 February 1956).

United States Congress Senate, Committee on Armed Services and Committee on Foreign Relations. *Hearings . . . to Conduct an Inquiry into the Military Situation in the Far East and the Facts Surrounding the Relief of General of the Army Douglas MacArthur from His Assignments in that Area* (1951).

———. *The Military Situation in the Far East and the Relief of General MacArthur*, 8 reels with guide (1977).

Whitney, Courtney. *MacArthur: His Rendezvous with History* (1956).

Wildes, Harry Emerson. *Typhoon in Tokyo* (1956).

Willoughby, Charles A., and John Chamberlain. *MacArthur, 1941–1951: Victory in the Pacific* (1956).

Wiltz, John Edward. "The MacArthur Inquiry, 1951," *Congress Investigates, 1972–1974,* eds. Arthur M. Schlesinger, Jr. and Roger Bruns (1975).

Truman-MacArthur Controversy, Periodical Articles

James, D. Clayton. "Command Crisis: MacArthur and the Korean War," in *The Harmon Memorial Lectures in Military History,* 240 (USAF Academy, 1982).

Lofgren, C.A. "Mr. Truman's War: A Debate and Its Aftermath," *Review of Politics,* 31 (April 1969).

Lowe, Peter. "An Ally and a Recalcitrant General: Great Britain, Douglas MacArthur, and the Korean War 1950–51," *English Historical Review,* 105 (July 1990).

O'Ballance, Edgar. "The MacArthur Plan," *Royal United Services Institution Journal,* 110 (August 1965).

Roper, Elmo, and Louis Harris. "Press and the Great Debate: Survey of Correspondence in the Truman-MacArthur Controversy," *Saturday Review of Literature,* 34 (14 July 1951).

Wiltz, John Edward. "The MacArthur Hearings of 1951: The Secret Testimony," *Military Affairs,* 39 (December 1975).

Prisoners of War

"American Prisoners of War," USAF Attache, Belgium (IR-63–52) (27 June 1952).

Biderman, Albert D. *March to Calumny: The Story of American POW's in the Korean War* (1963).

Blair, Clay. *Beyond Courage: Escape Tales of Airmen in the Korean War* (1957).

Bradbury, William C. *Mass Behavior in Battle and Captivity: The Communist Soldier in the Korean War* (1968).

Brown, Wallace L. *The Endless Hours: My Two and a Half Years as a Prisoner of the Chinese Communists* (1961).

Bureau of Social Science Research, Inc. "Further Analysis of POW Follow-up Study Data," Report (1 February 1965).

"Chinese Communist 'Report of Interrogation of U.S. Prisoners of War,'" U.S.

Army Liaison Office, Hong Kong (R-98–52) (27 May 1952).

Chinese People's Committee for World Peace. *Statements by Two Captured U.S. Air Force Officers on Their Participation in Germ Warfare in Korea* (1952).

"Communist Methods of Interrogation of POWs in Korea," U.S. Army Attache, Sweden (R-211–54) (30 July 1954).

"Communist Propaganda Re Korea POWs," U.S. Army Attache, Norway (R-251–53) (17 November 1953).

"Communist Retention of U.S. POWs," *United States Department of State Bulletin,* 29 (20 July 1953).

"Communist War in POW Camps," *United States Department of State Bulletin,* 28 (16 February 1953).

Crosbie, Philip. *March 'til They Die* (1956).

Dean, Philip (pseudonym). *I Was a Captive in Korea* (1953).

Dean, William L. *General Dean's Story* (1954).

Democratic People's Republic of Korea, Department of Cultural Relations with Foreign Countries, Ministry of Culture and Propaganda, *Depositions of Nineteen Captured U.S. Airmen on Their Participation in Germ Warfare in Korea* (1954).

Great Britain, Foreign Office. *Korea: A Summary of Further Developments in the Military Situation, Armistice Negotiations and Prisoner of War Camps up to January 1953* (1953).

———. *Korea: The Indian Proposal for Resolving the Prisoners of War Problem* (1952).

———. Ministry of Defence. *Treatment of British Prisoners of War in Korea* (1955).

Gruenzer, Norman. *Postal History of American POWs: World War II, Korea, Vietnam* (1979).

Hansen, Kenneth K. *Heroes Behind Barbed Wire* (1957).

Hunter, Edward. *Brainwashing in Red China* (1951).

———. *Brainwashing: The Story of Men Who Defied It* (1956, 1960).

Jones, Francis S. *No Rice for Rebels: A Story of the Korean War* (1956).

Kim, Myong Whai. "Prisoners of War as a Major Problem of the Korean Armistice, 1953," thesis, New York University, 1960.

Kinkhead, Eugene. *In Every War But One* (1959).
———. *Why They Collaborated*, 2nd ed. (1960).
MacDonald, James Angus. *The Problems of U.S. Marine Corps Prisoners of War in Korea* (History and Museums Division, HQ, U.S. Marine Corps, Washington: 1988).
Mahurin, Walker M. *Honest John: The Autobiography of Walker M. Mahurin* (1962).
Mayer, W.E. "Brainwashing," in *Symposium of the Neuropsychiatric Conference, Far East Command, U.S. Army Hospital, 8167th Army Unit, Tokyo, Japan, May 3 and 4, 1954.*
Mayo, C.W. "Role of Forced Confessions in the Communist Germ Warfare Propaganda Campaign; Statement 26 October 1953," *United States Department of State Bulletin*, 49 (9 November 1953).
Meerloo, J.A.M. "Thought Control and Confession Compulsion," in *Explorations in Psychoanalysis* (1953).
Meyers, Samuel M., and William C. Bradbury. *The Political Behavior of Korean and Chinese Prisoners of War in the Korean Conflict: An Historical Analysis* (August 1958).
Millar, Ward M. *Valley of the Shadow* (1955).
Moakley, Geoffrey S. "U.S. Army Code of Conduct Training: Let the POW's Tell Their Stories," thesis, U.S. Army Command and General Staff College, 1976.
The Neutral Nations' Report Commission Korea (1954).
Nierman, Florence. *A Study of Chinese and North Korean Surrenders* (5 September 1952).
Pasley, Virginia. *21 Stayed: The Story of the American GIs Who Chose Communist China: Who They Were and Why They Stayed* (1955).
Pate, Lloyd. *Reactionary!* (1956).
People's Committee for World Peace. *United Nations POWs in Korea* (1953).
Sander, H.J. *Analysis of the Korean War Prisoner of War Experience* (1960).
Santucci, Peter S., and George Winokur. "Brainwashing as a Factor in Psychiatric Illness: A Heuristic Approach," *A.M.A. Archives of Neurology and Psychiatry*, 74 (1955).
Sargent, William. *Battle for the Mind* (1957).

Schein, Edgar M. "Some Observations on the Chinese Indoctrination Program for Prisoners of War," *Report, Army Medical Service Graduate School*, 37 (October 1955).
———, et al. *Coercive Persuasion: A Socio-Psychological Analysis of the "Brainwashing" of American Civilian Prisoners by the Chinese Communists* (1961).
———. *Development, Training Applications, and Assessment of the Code of Conduct for U.S. POWs* (HQ, USAF Analysis Program, SE Asia Prisoner of War Experience, Washington: 1974).
Segal, Julius. *Factors Related to the Collaboration and Resistance Behavior of US Army POWs in Korea* (December 1956).
Snyder, Don J. *A Soldier's Disgrace* (1987).
Sommers, Stan, comp. *The Korea Story* (American ex-Prisoners of War [n.p., n.d.]).
"Spanish Press Reaction to Treatment of American POWs," U.S. Army Attaché, Spain (R-754–53) (13 November 1953).
"Spanish Press Reaction to Treatment of UN POWs," U.S. Army Attaché, Spain (R-790–53) (2 December 1953).
Strassman, H.D., et al. "A Prisoner of War Syndrome: Apathy as a Reaction to Severe Stress," paper read at American Psychiatric Association, 9–13 May 1955.
"3 Years in North Korean Prisons," U.S. Army Attaché, France (R-633–53) (21 May 1953).
Thompson, Elizabeth M. *War Prisoner Repatriation* (3 December 1952).
Thompson, James. *True Colors: 1004 Days as a Prisoner of War* (1989).
Thornton, John W., and John W. Thornton, Jr. *Believed to Be Alive* (1981).
Tucker, Gwynn. "Effects of Organizational Structure on American Enemy Prisoner of War Operations, " thesis, U.S. Army Command and General Staff College, 1990.
United Nations. General Assembly. *Reports of the Neutral Nations Repatriation Commission Covering the Period Ending 9 September 1954* (1954).
———. *Bulletin*. "Prison Breaks Threaten Armistice," 15 (1 July 1953).
———. Command. *Operations Instructions Reference Enemy Prisoners of War*, pamphlet (UNC Headquarters: 7 October 1950).

————. Military Armistice Commission, "Meetings of the Committee for the Repatriation of Prisoners of War. . . . ," mimeographed minutes (8 June-18 September 1953).

————. Joint Red Cross Activities. Daily journals and files, 6 August-6 September 1953.

————. Prisoner of War Camp No. 1. Daily journal and log of Special Headquarters established for Neutral Nations Inspection Team, 25 August-5 September 1953, typescript and enclosures (1953).

————, and Far East Command. General Staff, Military Intelligence Section. "The Communist War in POW Camps: The Background of Incidents Among Communist Prisoners in Korea," mimeographed report (28 January 1953).

————. Report of the United Nations Command on the Operation of the Neutral Nations Repatriation Commission (1954).

United States Air Force Personnel and Training Research Center. "Some Operational Implications of the 'Michigan Attitude Change Project' for POW Survival Training," by E. Paul Terrance, memorandum (Homestead AFB, NV: 20 October 1954).

United States, Department of the Army. *Handling Prisoners of War*: Field Manual 19–40 (November 1952).

————. G-2. "Treatment of POWs in North Korea," Translation Section, G-2010–A, n.d. (Translated from Swedish periodical *Henvarnet*, November 1953).

————. Army Forces, Far East. *Logistical Support to Prisoners of War, July 1951–July 1953*, 1 reel (Library of Congress: 1977).

————. Army Pacific Military History Office. *The Handling of Prisoners of War during the Korean War*, 1 reel (1960).

————. Korean Communications Zone. *Extract of Interim Historical Report, Korean War Crimes Division, Cumulative to 30 June 1953* (n.d.).

————. *The U.S. Fighting Man's Code*, DA Pamphlet 21-71 (November 1955).

————. *Communist Interrogation, Indoctrination, and Exploitation of Prisoners of War* (Department of the Army: 1956).

————. *Some Observations on the Chinese Indoctrination Program for Prisoners of War* (Army Medical Services Graduate School, Office of the Surgeon General: October 1955).

————. *Communist Interrogation, Indoctrination, and Exploitation of Prisoners of War*, DA Pamphlet 30-101 (15 May 1956).

————. Central Intelligence Agency, Foreign Documents Division. "How the Chinese Communists Treat Prisoners of War," translation of No. 470 (14 October 1955).

————. Congress, House Committee on Appropriations. *The Prisoner of War Situation in Korea*: Hearings . . . 82nd Cong., 2nd Sess. (1952).

————. Foreign Affairs, Subcommittee on the Far East and the Pacific. *Return of American Prisoners of War Who Have Not Been Accounted for by the Communists Hearing . . . 27 May 1987* (1957).

————. *POW/MIA's in Indochina and Korea. Hearing* (1991).

————. Senate, Committee on Government Operations. *Communist Interrogation, Indoctrination and Exploitation of American Military and Civilian Prisoners: Hearings* (1956).

U.S. Congress, Committee on Government Operations. Permanent Subcommittee on Investigations. *Communist Interrogation, and Exploitation of American Military and Civilian Prisoners. Report of the Committee on Government Operations: Made by Its Permanent Subcommittee on Investigations*, 84th Congress, 2nd Session, Senate, Report No. 2832 (1957).

————. Subcommittee on Investigation. *Communist Interrogation, Indoctrination, and Exploitation of American Military and Civilian Prisoners*, Hearings . . . June 19, 20, 26, and 27, 1956. 84th Congress, 2nd Session (1956).

————. House, Committee on Un-American Activities. *Investigation of Communist Propaganda Among Prisoners of War in Korea (Save Our Sons Committee). Hearing* (1956).

————. Department of State. "Legal Considerations Underlying the Position of the United Nations Command Regarding the Issue of Forced Repatriation of Prisoners of War," mimeographed copy (24 October 1952).

————. "Release of Anti-Communist Prisoners from UN Camps and Correspondence," *United States Department of State Bulletin*, 28 (29 June 1953).

Vetter, Harold J. *Mutiny on Koje Island* (1965).

Voelkel, Harold. *Behind Barbed Wire in Korea* (1953).

Wang, Tsun-Ming. *Anti-Communist: An Autobiographical Account of Chinese Communist Thought Reform* (Psychological Warfare Division, Human Resources Research Office, George Washington University, Washington: November 1954).

Way, A.E. "Study of a Random Sample of 'American POW Messages' Directed at Target USA by Radio Peking," typescript copy in U.S. Army Special Operations Command, Fort Bragg, NC (U.S. Army Psychological Division, n.d.).

Weintraub, Stanley. *War in the Wards: Korea's Unknown Battle in a Prisoner-of-War Hospital Camp*, 2nd ed. (1976).

White, William Lindsay. *The Captives of Korea: An Unofficial White Paper on the Treatment of War Prisoners: Our Treatment of Theirs, Their Treatment of Ours* (1957).

Wills, Morris B., and J. Robert Moskin. *Turncoat: An American's 12 Years in Communist China: The Story of Morris R. Wills as Told to Robert J. Moskin* (1968).

Witherspoon, John A. "International Law and Practice Concerning Prisoners of War During the Korean Conflict (1950–1954)," thesis, Duke University, 1968.

Zellers, Larry. *In Enemy Hands: A Prisoner in North Korea* (1991).

Prisoners of War, Periodical Articles

"Allegations on POWs Denied," *Beijing Review*, 36 (4 January 1993).

Ball, Harry F. "Prisoner of War Negotiations: The Korean Experience and Lesson," *Naval War College Review*, 21 (September 1968).

Bauer, Raymond E., "Brainwashing: Psychology or Demonology?" *Journal of Social Issues*, 13, no. 3 (1957).

Boatner, Haydon L. "The Lessons of Koje-Do," *Army*, 22 (March 1972).

"Communist Indoctrination of American Prisoners," *Army Information Digest*, 8 (July 1953).

"Complaint of the Mass Murder of Korean and Chinese Prisoners of War by the United States Armed Forces on the Island of Pongan," *International Organization*, 7 (February 1953).

"Disposition of POWs: Complete Text," *Current History*, 25 (September 1953).

Djang, H. "What Do They Confess?" *Christian Century*, 69 (20 August 1952).

Douglas, P.H. "Korean POW Issue," *Vital Speeches*, 19 (1 July 1953).

Dulles, Allen W. "How the Communists Wash Brains," *Combat Forces*, 3 (July 1953).

Dulles, John Foster. "Report of POWs: Witnessing the Return of U.S. POWs in Korea," *Department of State Bulletin*, 29 (24 August 1953).

Edwards, Norman B. "Prisoners of War," letter and study (15 October 1952).

"Forced Confessions: Menticide," *Science Newsletter*, 60 (21 July 1951).

Foreman, K.J. "What is Brainwashing?" *Christian Century*, 70 (6 May 1953).

Grey, Jeffrey. "Commonwealth Prisoners of War and British Policy During the Korean War," *Royal United Services Institute Journal*, 133 (Spring 1988).

Gutteridge, J.A.C. "The Repatriation of Prisoners of War," *International and Comparative Law Quarterly*, 2 (April 1953).

Hill, G. "Brainwashing: Time for a Policy," *Atlantic Monthly* (1955).

Hinkle, L.E., and H.G. Wolff. "Communist Interrogation and Indoctrination of 'Enemies of the State,'" *Archives of Neurology and Psychiatry*, 76 (1956).

Hook, Sidney. "Heresy, Yes; Conspiracy, No," *Commonwealth*, 58 (15 May 1953).

————. "Why They Switch Loyalties," *The New York Times Magazine* (26 November 1950).

"India Learns About Reds, Neutral Nations Repatriation Commission," *America*, 90 (14 November 1953).

"Indian Village; Prisoner Exchange," *Commonwealth*, 59 (30 October 1953).

"InterCamp Olympics, Pyoktong," U.S. Army Attaché, Great Britain (R-2278–53).

Kaempffert, W. "Prescription for Our POWs," *Science Digest*, 34 (December 1953).

Kinkhead, E. "The Study of Something New in History," *New Yorker*, 33, no. 36 (1957).

Leviero, Anthony. "For the Brainwashed: Pity or Punishment?" *New York Times Magazine* (14 August 1955).

Levin, Bernard. "Great Wash," *Spectator* (26 August 1960).

Lifton, R.J. "Home by Ship: Reaction Patterns of American Prisoners of War Repatriated from North Korea," *American Journal of Psychiatry*, 110 (1954).

Lyons, Willian P. "Prisoners of War and the Code of Conduct," *Naval War College Review*, 20 (December 1967).

Manes, Donald L. "Barbed Wire Command," *Military Review*, 43 (September 1963).

Mann, George. "Bunk About Brainwashing," *Science Digest* (April 1957).

Merloo, J.A.M. "Pavlov's Dog and Communist Brainwashers," *New York Times Magazine* (30 May 1954).

———. "The Crime of Menticide," *American Journal of Psychiatry*, 107 (1952).

———. "Morale," *Military Review* (1954).

———. "Pavlovian Strategy as a Weapon of Menticide," *American Journal of Psychotherapy*, 8 (1954).

———. "The Psychology of Treason and Loyalty," *American Journal of Psychotherapy*, 8 (1954).

Miller, James G. "Brainwashing: Present and Future," *Journal of Social Issues*, 13, no. 3 (1957).

Montgomery, Fred M. "Survival of the Mind," *United States Army Aviation Digest* (January 1960).

Palmer, C.B. "War for the POWs Mind," *New York Times Magazine* (13 September 1953).

Potter, Pitman B. "Repatriation of Prisoners of War," *American Journal of International Law*, 46 (July 1952).

"POW Types Who Gave In," *Science Newsletter*, 64 (10 October 1953).

"Question of Atrocities Committed by the North Korean and Chinese Communist Forces Against United Nations Prisoners of War in Korea," *International Organization*, 8 (February 1954).

"Reaction to Brainwashing," *Science Newsletter*, 70 (15 September 1956).

Richardson, Walton K. "Prisoners of War as Instruments of Foreign Policy," *Naval War College Review*, 23 (September 1970).

Schein, E.M. "The Chinese Indoctrination Program for Prisoners of War: A Study of Attempted Brainwashing," *Psychiatry*, 19 (1956).

———. "Epilogue: Something New In History," *Journal of Social Issues*, 13, no. 3 (1957).

———. "Reaction Patterns to Severe, Chronic Stress in American Army Prisoners of War of the Chinese," *Journal of Social Issues*, no. 3 (1957).

———, W.F. Hill, H.L. Williams, and A. Lubin. "Distinguishing Characteristics of Collaborators and Resistors Among American Prisoners of War," *Journal of Abnormal and Social Psychology*, 55 (1957).

Sondern, Frederick, Jr. "Brainwashing to John Hayes," *Reader's Digest*, 67 (July 1955).

Segal, H.A. "Initial Psychiatric Findings of Recently Repatriated Prisoners of War," *American Journal of Psychiatry*, 3 (1954).

———. "Correlates of Collaboration and Resistance Behavior Among U.S. Army POWs in Korea," *Journal of Social Issues*, 13, no. 3 (1957).

Starr, Anthony. "Torture without Violence," *New Statesman*, 59 (12 March 1960).

Staton, Thomas F. "The Battle for Men's Minds," *Air Power Historian*, Part 1, Part 2 (April, July 1960).

Stockwell, F. O. "What is Brainwashing?" *Christian Century* 70 (28 January 1953).

Sutker, P.B., et al. "Cognitive Deficits and Psychopathology Among Former Prisoners of War and Combat Veterans of the Korean War," *American Journal of Psychiatry*, 148 (January 1991).

"What Happened in the POW Camps" (From the Official Report of the Advisory Committee on Prisoners of War), *Combat Forces*, 6 (October 1955).

Williamson, Carl E. "Name, Rank, and Service Number," *Military Review*, 37 (August 1957).

Winokur, George. "The Germ Warfare Statements: A Synthesis of a Method of and the Extortion of False Confessions," *Journal of Nervous and Mental Diseases*, 122 (July 1955).

———. "Brainwashing, A Social Phenomenon of Our Time," *Human Organization*, 13 (1955).

———. "The Germ Warfare Statements," *Journal of Nervous and Mental Diseases*, 122 (1955).

Wubben, H.A. "American Prisoners of War in Korea: A Second Look at the 'Something New in History' Theme," *American Quarterly*, 22 (Spring 1970).

Armistice Negotiations and the Armistice

U.S. Armed Forces Far East, Psywar Section. "The Armistice Negotiations, Korean Conflict, 1951, 1952, and 1953," 1, 2 [n.d.], typescript.

Bernstein, Barton J. "The Struggle Over the Korean Armistice: Prisoners of Repatriation?" in *Child of Conflict: The Korean-American Relationship*, ed. Bruce Cumings (1983).

Dalferes, George L.J. *A Study of the Geneva Conference of Far Eastern Affairs of 1954* (Air War College, Air University: 1967).

Dille, John. *Substitute for Victory* (1954).

"Documents and Materials on the Korean Armistice Negotiations" (1953).

Foot, Rosemary. *A Substitute for Victory: The Politics of Peacemaking at the Korean Armistice Talks* (1990).

Goodman, Allan E., ed. *Negotiating While Fighting: The Diary of Admiral C. Turner Joy at the Korean Armistice Conference* (1978).

The 1954 Geneva Conference: Indo-China and Korea (1969).

Joy, C. Turner. *How Communists Negotiate* (1955).

————. *Negotiating While Fighting: The Diary of Admiral C. Turner Joy at the Korean Armistice Conference* (1978).

Kinney, A.J. *Korean Armistice Negotiations* (195?).

"The Korean Armistice: Summaries and Excerpts from the Armistice Signed by Representatives of the United Nations Command and of the Korean People's Army and Chinese People's Volunteers, Panmunjom, July 27, 1953," *Documents on American Foreign Relations 1953*, ed. Peter V. Curl (1954).

Lewane, Leonard Lamarr. "Fighting and Negotiating Against the Communists," thesis, George Washington University, 1969.

United States. "Military Armistice in Korea and Temporary Supplementary Agreement Signed at Panmunjom, Korea, July 27, 1953; Entered into Force July 27, 1953," *United States Treaties and Other International Agreements*, 4 (1955).

————, State Department. *Foreign Relations of the United States, 1952–54*, Vol. 16, *The Geneva Conference* (1981).

Vatcher, William Henry. *Panmunjom: The Story of the Korean Military Armistice Negotiations* (1958).

[Winnacker, Rudolph A.] "Notes on the Korean Armistice," typescript (Historical Office, Office of the Secretary of Defense, August 1956).

Armistice Negotiations, Periodical Articles

Acheson, Dean. "The Truce Talks in Korea: A Full Report to the United Nations," *Harper's Magazine*, (January 1953).

"The Attack on the Irrigation Dams in North Korea," *Air University Quarterly Review*, 6 (Winter 1953–54).

Bacchus, Wilfred A. "The Relationship Between Combat and Peace Negotiations: Fighting While Talking in Korea, 1951–1953," *Orbis*, 17 (Summer 1973).

Blechman, Barry M., and Robert Powell. "What in the Name of God is Strategic Superiority?" *Political Science Quarterly*, 97 (Winter 1982–83).

Blumenson, Martin. "Neutrality and Armistice in Korea," *Military Review*, 47 (June 1967).

Brands, Henry W., Jr. "Dwight D. Eisenhower, Syngman Rhee, and the 'Other' Geneva Conference of 1954," *Pacific Historical Review*, 56 (February 1987).

Burke, Arleigh A. "The Hazards of Negotiating with the Communists," *Reader's Digest*, 93 (October 1968).

Carroll, E.J., Jr. "Limited War-Limited Peace?" *Military Review*, 48 (June 1968).

Clarke, Bruce C. "Negotiations: Korean Lessons," *Military Review*, 48 (June 1968).

"Documents Relating to the Armistice Negotiations in Korea," *U.S. Department of State Bulletin*, 41 (November 1961).

Guelzo, Carl M. "The Korean Balance Sheet: After Eight Years of Arbitration," *Military Review*, 41 (November 1961).

————. "Exceptional War, Exceptional Peace: The 1953 Cease-Fire in Korea," *Military Review*, 56 (July 1976).

Hermes, Walter G. "The Military Role in the Korean Truce Negotiations," *Military Review*, 44 (November 1954).

Jom, Pan Mun. (pseud.) "Armistice Talk," *Army*, 10 (June 1960).

Keefer, Edward C. "President Dwight D. Eisenhower and the End of the Korean War," *Diplomatic History*, 21 (Summer 1986).

Martin, David L., and Anthony D. Nastri. "The Foot of a Duck," *U.S. Naval Institute Proceedings*, 103 (April 1977).

Rongguang, Shang. "Panmunjom Negotiations: Veteran Soldier and His Book," *Beijing Review*, 33 (16 July 1990).

Scheidig, Robert E. "A Comparison of Communist Negotiating Methods," *Military Review*, 54 (December 1974).

Simon, Ernest A. "The Operation of the Korean Armistice," *Military Law Review*, 52 (October 1972).

Toner, James H. "The 1953 Cease-Fire in Korea," *Military Review*, 56 (July 1976).

Wilz, J.E. "Truman and MacArthur: The Wake Island Meeting," *Military Affairs*, 42 (December 1978).

Contributors

Steven Agoratus
Carnegie-Mellon University

Steven M. Avella
Marquette University

D. Randall Beirne
University of Baltimore

Joseph S. Bermudez, Jr.
Merrick, New York

Laura M. Calkins
Oglethorpe University

Jack J. Cardoso
Buffalo State College,
Buffalo, New York

Thomas A. Cardwell
Colonel, Commander, USAF Studies
  and Analyses Agency

R. W. Coakley
U.S. Army Center of Military History

Albert E. Cowdrey
U.S. Army Center of Military History

John Cranston
U.S. Army Armor Center and Fort Knox

James Sanders Day
U.S. Military Academy
West Point, NY

D. Colt Denfield
2nd Infantry Museum
Republic of Korea

James I. Deutsch
George Washington University

Michael J. Devine
Illinois State Historical Society

James E. Dillard
U.S. Air Force Academy

Gary A. Donaldson
Xavier University

Kevin Dougherty
Captain, U.S. Army

Carl Eigabrodt
Port Orchard, Washington

David M. Esposito
Bucknell University

Peter R. Faber
USAF, Yale University

Anthony Farrar-Hockley, General Sir, GBE,
  KCB, DSO, MC
UK Cabinet Office, Historical Section

William E. Fischer, Jr.
U.S. Air Force Academy

Mike Fisher
University of Arizona

David A. Foy
U.S. Army

Jack Gifford
Combat Studies Institute
U.S. Army Command and General Staff
  College

Thomas E. Graham
Northern Illinois University

Jeffrey Grey
University of New South Wales
Australian Defence Force Academy

Richard P. Hallion
Chief, Office of Air Force History

Walter Hermes
U.S. Army Center of Military History

John S. Hill
Ohio State University

G. Horne
University of California
Santa Barbara

Ian A. Horwood
University of Missouri-Columbia

James A. Huston
Lynchburg College

T.A. Kaminski
University of Illinois

David Kangas
Captain, USAR

Hubert L. Koker
Editor, *Air Defense Artillery*

Karl M. Larew
Towson State University

William Leary
University of Georgia

Donald D. Leopard
State Unviersity College at Buffalo

Jing Li
Rice University

Edward J. Marolda
U.S. Naval Historical Center

James I. Matray
University of Southern California

Donald McBride
Wilson College
Chambersberg, Pennsylvania

William I. McCorkle
Baylor University

Keith D. McFarland
East Texas State University

Raymond A. Mentzer
Montana State University

Bettie J. Morden
U.S. Army Center of Military History

John Kennedy Ohl
Mesa Community College
Mesa, Arizona

Rod Paschall
U.S. Army Military History Institute

W.D. Pederson
Louisiana State University at Shreveport

Barbara Peterson
University of Hawaii

Stanley Sandler
Directorate of History and Museums
U.S. Army Special Operations Command
Fort Bragg, North Carolina

Elizabeth Schafer
Loachapoka, Alabama

P.J. Scheips
U.S. Army Center of Military History

John William Schiffeler
University of California
Berkeley

James F. Schnable
Joint Chiefs of Staff, Historical Division

Lewis Sorley
Potomac, Maryland

Richard W. Stewart
Director, U.S. Army Special Operations Command Directorate of History and Museums

Spencer Tucker
Chairman, Department of History,
Texas Christian University

Richard Voeltz
Cameron University
Lawton, Oklahoma

John Edward Wilz
Indiana Univeristy

E.J. Wright
U.S. Army Center of Military History

David T. Zabecki
Freiburg, Germany

Index

Page references to encyclopedia entries appear in boldface.

and Operation Ripper, 212–213
and the outpost wars, 213–214
reserves, 207, 298, 299, 300
Seoul captured by 34, 144, 208, 362
troop strength in Korea, 199, 206
at Wolmi-do, 143–144, 208
at Wonsan, 34, 209, 211, 243
at Yudam-ni, 34, 89, 210–211
See also United States: military units of
Marshall, George C., 45, 139, 151, 155, 173, **215–217**
Marshall, S.L.A., **217–220**
Marshall Plan, 1, 174, 230, 335
Martin, Joseph W., 155
Masan, 33, 213
MASH (Mobile Army Surgical Hospital), 129, 197, 198, 220–223, 307
*M*A*S*H* (film), 112
"M*A*S*H" (television series), 112
Masses and Mainstream, 20
MATS. *See* Military Air Transport Service
Matthews, Francis, 254
May, Alan Nunn, 124
McCarran Internal Security Act, 137, 337
McCarthy, Joseph R., 2, 22, 76, 137, 139, 216, 276, 313, 337
McCarthyism, 2, 97, 116, 139–140
McClure, Robert B., 280, 364
McDonnell aircraft. *See under* aircraft
McKee, Frederick, 75–76
Medical Field Service School, 223
medical service, **220–224.** *See also* hospitals
The Medics' War, 133
Menzies, R.G., 43
Midway, 238
MIG aircraft. *See under* aircraft
MIG Alley, 13, 237, 266, 269
Milburn, Frank W., 93, 120, **224–225,** 284, 295
Military Advisors in Korea: KMAG in Peace and War, 132–133
Military Air Transport Command, 9
Military Air Transport Service, 15, 16, 164, 221
Military Armistice Commission, 100, 305
military government. *See* Army, U.S.: civil affairs and military government
Military Sea Transportation Service, 150, 196, 241–242
mine warfare, 34, 105, 188–189, 209, 243, 311–312, 328, 355
missionaries, 68, 69, 169, 171
Missouri, 241, 243
Mobile Army Surgical Hospitals. *See* MASH
Molotov, V.M., 121, 122
Monclar, Ralph, 115, 128
Mossman, Billy C., 132
MSTS. *See* Military Sea Transportation Service
Muccio, John J., 1, 177, 178, 179, **225–226,** 349, 357
Mu-Jong, 250, 251
Mukden, 91
Mukden cable, 91–92, 317
Munsan, 26, 83, 185, 290, 294

Murrow, Edward R., 56, 140
Musan, 4, 5
Muste, A.J., 21

N

Naktong Bulge, 79, 207, 208
Naktong River, 33, 54, 105, 334, 335
and Pusan perimeter, 106, 185, 282, 284, 285–286, 294–295
and Taegu, 33, 63, 325–326
Nam Il, 25, 26, 98–99, 121, 122
napalm, 17, 128, **227–228,** 232, 283, 285, 287, 288
National Defense Corps, 303
National Extraordinary Anti-Epidemic Committee, 46
National Guard, 22, 86, 151, 299, 300, 310
Nationalist China. *See* China, Nationalist
National Press Club, 1, 50, 176
National Security Act of 1947, 66, 149, 336
National Security Council, 51, 66, 174, 177, 216, 228, 254, 264, 336
National Security Council papers:
NSC-8, 174
NSC-8/2, 174
NSC-48/2, 176
NSC-68, 176, 228–229, 337
NSC-147, 254, 255
NATO, 1, 2, 103, 123, 138–139, 150, **228–230,** 336
naval air operations, 12, **230–240,** 241, 269, 300
Navarre, Henre-Eugene, 147
NAVFE, 240, 244
Navy, Korean People's. *See* Korean People's Navy
Navy, U.S., **240–244**
aircraft of, 7–9, 130, 132, 269
air support provided by, 16, 17. *See also* naval air operations
and Louis A. Johnson, 149–150
reserves, 298, 299
See also United States: military units of
Navy Hospital Corps, 223
Nehru, Jawaharlal, 2, 145–146
Netherlands forces, 121, 127, 241, **244–246**
Neutral Nations Repatriation Commission, 30–31, 97, 100
Newcastle, 241
New Jersey, 241
New Zealand forces, 42, 55, 58, 121, 143, 241, **246–247,** 311, 338
Nitze, Paul, 176
Nixon, Richard M., 137, 139
NKPA. *See* Korean People's Army
NNRC. *See* Neutral Nations Repatriation Commission
No Name line, 207, 364
North American aircraft. *See under* aircraft
North Atlantic Treaty Organization. *See* NATO
North Korea. See Korea, Democratic People's Republic of
North Korean People's Air Force. *See* Korean